"Well written and excellently organized . . . the most comprehensive basic text in the marketing field."

"Represents the clearest and strongest statement on the marketing concept ever to appear in a marketing textbook . . . it is superb."

"Far superior to any other basic marketing text."

—from pre-publication reviews

The new material and extensive changes provided in this second edition of **Basic Marketing: Concepts, Decisions, and Strategies** include twelve entirely new chapters. The remaining chapters have been completely rewritten and incorporate the most current practices and recent trends. New products, new techniques and concepts, new illustrations, and new census figures make this the most up-to-date and comprehensive book on basic marketing available.

This well written, interesting material permits the reader to grasp the complexities of marketing and understand its important role in business. The material explains the influence of market research, especially on new products, and management's use of marketing for pricing strategies and other selling decisions. The discus-

(continued on back flap)

Basic Marketing

Prentice-Hall, Inc., *Englewood Cliffs, New Jersey*

BASIC

EDWARD W. CUNDIFF

Chairman, Department of Marketing Administration
Graduate School of Business
University of Texas at Austin

RICHARD R. STILL

Professor of Marketing and Business Policy
College of Business Administration
University of Georgia

SECOND EDITION

MARKETING

Concepts, Decisions, and Strategies

TO KATY STILL AND PEGGY CUNDIFF

SECOND EDITION

Basic Marketing

Concepts, Decisions, and Strategies

Edward W. Cundiff and Richard R. Still

13-062638-4

Library of Congress Catalog Card Number: 79-138478

Printed in the United States of America

Current printing (last digit):
10   9   8   7   6   5

PRENTICE-HALL INTERNATIONAL, INC., *London*
PRENTICE-HALL OF AUSTRALIA, PTY. LTD., *Sydney*
PRENTICE-HALL OF CANADA, LTD., *Toronto*
PRENTICE-HALL OF INDIA PRIVATE LIMITED, *New Delhi*
PRENTICE-HALL OF JAPAN, INC., *Tokyo*

PREFACE

This is a basic marketing book, stressing decisions on the marketing mix and on strategy formulation. As a comprehensive introductory text, it is designed to meet the needs not only of students specializing in marketing but of those taking only the basic course. Our first hope is that this book will provide both groups with a clear grasp of marketing's place in business and society. In addition, we are convinced that marketing is a most interesting field, and we hope those using this book will come to share this belief.

The dominant theme is that marketing is an important "subsystem" of the business organization. Marketing is mainly concerned with the matching of markets and products and the effecting of ownership transfers. Through its marketing activities, the business organization relates to its environment and, through these relationships, advances toward its objectives. Thus, the philosophy inherent in "the marketing concept"—market orientation, subordination of departmental goals to company goals, and unification of company operations both to meet market requirements and to achieve operating results in accord with company goals—permeates the entire book.

This philosophy of marketing—and business—is reflected in the content of the book's seven parts. Part One is the general introduction and features a chapter on the marketing concept, analyzing social, technological, and organizational changes that make the concept highly relevant to today's business firm. A chapter on the marketing organization explores organizational implications of both the marketing concept and modern organization theory. Discussion in this Part's final chapter concentrates on the decision-making process in marketing management.

Part Two focuses on markets. A market segmentation chapter emphasizes the importance of this concept in analyzing both consumer and industrial markets. Two chapters on buyer behavior relate economic and behavorial theory to marketing behavior and provide an overview of psychological and socio-cultural concepts as they pertain to buyer behavior.

Parts Three through Six are devoted to the four chief components of marketing strategy—products, distribution, promotion, and price. Part Three includes one chapter on product innovation and the product life cycle and two chapters on the formulation of product-market strategies. Part Four's subject matter is the distribution structure and the determination of marketing channel and physical distribution objectives and policies. Part Five covers the promotional program, including the roles of personal selling and advertising. Part Six surveys pricing decisions, objectives, policies, strategies, and procedures.

Marketing planning and controlling are discussed in Part Seven. Marketing research's role in decision-making and strategy formulation is stressed throughout the book. A separate chapter here provides added emphasis, analyzing marketing research's relationship to marketing information systems. A legal environment chapter relates legal restraints to marketing decision-making and strategy formulation. The final chapter, Chapter 24, is concerned with determination of overall marketing strategy—developing a combination of inputs to achieve the desired outputs—and with evaluating overall marketing strategy through marketing audits.

Marketing arithmetic, sales analysis, and marketing expense analysis are covered in the appendix.

Those familiar with this book's earlier edition will recognize the substantial changes made in this edition. Not only has there been extensive reorganization of the subject matter; twelve of the twenty-four chapters are entirely new, and the rest have been thoroughly revised. Three-quarters of the questions and problems at the ends of chapters are new, and numerous illustrations and figures have been added. All census and other statistics have been updated. Throughout the entire book we have made a special effort to present and interpret the subject matter in ways that students will find clear, meaningful, and interesting.

Many people made important contributions to this book. Among our past and present colleagues, those who were especially helpful include: W. T. Tucker of the University of Texas, Hiram C. Barksdale of the University of Georgia, G. B. Saunders and M. J. Thomas of Syracuse University, J. M. Rathmell of Cornell University, A. D. Shocker of the University of Pittsburgh, and J. G. Hauk of the University of Puerto Rico. These colleagues not only articulated specific suggestions and criticisms but stimulated our thinking on what should and should *not* be included in a basic marketing book.

Considerable assistance and advice were received also on either the first or this edition from the following marketing professors: Leon G. Schiffman of The City University of New York; Perry Bliss of the State University of New York at Buffalo; Robert J. Holloway of the University of Minnesota; Jon G. Udell of the University of Wisconsin; Donald L. Shawver of the University of Missouri; Thomas L. Berg of New York University; and E. A. Weisser, Jr., of Robert Morris College.

Many present and past Prentice-Hall personnel provided tireless help, encouragement, and criticism. Deserving of special mention are: Chester C. Lucido, Jr., Marketing Editor; Martin Greene, formerly Project Planning Editor; John F. Pritchard, formerly Business Books Editor, and Shirley Covington, of College Book Editorial-Production Department.

We also owe, of course, a very special debt to our wives for providing sympathetic understanding and encouragement, without which this book could not have been completed.

For all the assistance we have received—both that acknowledged above and throughout the book, as well as that from other colleagues, businessmen, and our past and present students—we express our sincere gratitude.

Richard R. Still
Edward W. Cundiff

CONTENTS

PART 4   DISTRIBUTION

PART 7   MARKETING PLANNING AND CONTROLLING

PART 1

INTRODUCTION

INTRODUCTION

1

THE MARKETING FIELD

Except for occasional hermits, few people are completely self-sufficient. Most people have to satisfy all their material wants through outside sources and, in satisfying these wants, find that they must take part in various activities incidental to obtaining needed goods and services from outside sources of supply. As consumers, people perform some of these activities themselves. For example, they shop for the goods and services they need. They read and listen to advertisements (and talk with sales persons, look around stores, and do window shopping) to find out what is available in which qualities at what prices. And they are continually deciding among stores, products, brands, and models. Again as consumers, people are the "targets" of many activities performed by others: those who devote their time and efforts to getting information to consumers (e.g., advertisements), researching them to obtain information (e.g., on the likely marketability of some new product), getting the goods and services to them, and, ultimately, "selling" them. The result of these consumer-performed and business-performed activities is a flow of goods and services from producers to consumers.

DEFINITION OF MARKETING

Marketing, according to the American Marketing Association, consists of the performance of business activities that direct the flow of goods and services from producer to consumer or user.[1] In other words, marketing is the term used to describe collectively those business functions most directly concerned with the demand-stimulating and demand-fulfilling activities of the business enterprise. These activities interlock and interact with one another as components of the total system—by which an enterprise develops and makes its products available, distributes them through marketing channels, prices them, and promotes them. Specifically, then, in our view, marketing is the business process by which products are matched with markets and through which transfers of ownership are effected.

Product-Market Interrelationship

The interrelatedness of *product* and *market* is an essential idea, so our definition states, in part, that "marketing is the business process by which products are matched with markets." The notion we want to convey here is that marketing and production activities are interlocked—that these two major business functions (namely marketing and production) certainly depend on each other, since we can only market products which can be produced, and we should only produce those that can be marketed. Thus, it is logical to think of marketing as the business process by which specific products are matched up with specific markets, while thinking of production as the business process concerned with manufacturing these products.

We must, however, recognize that most companies do not manufacture products which fit markets exactly. This exact fit happens only in the comparatively rare instances where products are made to order for individual customers. For most companies, precise fitting of products to markets is extremely difficult, if not wholly impossible. One important reason is that although markets are usually made up of large numbers of present and prospective customers who have some needs in common, each customer may have rather individual ideas about the characteristics a product should possess. Furthermore, a company must standardize certain product characteristics if it is to take economic advantage of mass produc-

[1] Committee on Definitions, *Marketing Definitions* (Chicago: American Marketing Association, 1960), p. 15.

tion methods. However, the products manufactured should still be attractive enough to ultimate buyers so that sales will be large enough to
return adequate profits. Accordingly, management usually decides on products with characteristics falling somewhere between what individual consumers most generally prefer and what can be produced at the lowest unit
cost. In other words, the problem is both one of marketing and of production: it is to select, manufacture, and market products which possess as
many as possible of those characteristics considered desirable by large numbers of customers and prospects (i.e., by those who make up the "markets"),
and to do this with as little sacrifice of manufacturing economies as possible.

Top management bears the ultimate responsibility for solving
this problem, but marketing management plays a large role in the solution.
Marketing research uncovers the product characteristics wanted by final
buyers in various markets, and top management (working with both marketing and production executives) translates these wants into product specifications. Where products have been developed through technical research
carried on within the company, marketing research is used to find and
measure potential markets. Thus, ideas for products may come either from
the markets or from inside the company itself, and marketing research is
useful in both instances. Through skillful application and combination of
what we will call the marketing "controllables" (e.g., pricing, advertising,
and personal selling), marketing management may stimulate and expand
markets for old as well as new products. Ordinarily, these different strategies

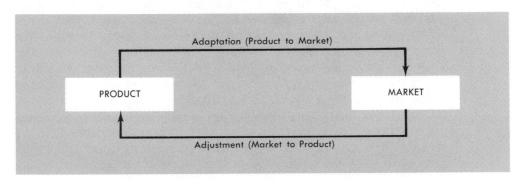

for bringing products and markets together are combined: some products
are designed according to specifications set by marketing research on the
basis of its studies of what the market wants and expects (i.e., the product
is "adapted" to the market); a search is carried on for markets for new
products with features derived from technical research; and certain marketing controllables (price, personal selling, advertising, other promotion,
and distribution policy) are manipulated toward the end of gaining and

holding market favor for both old and new products (i.e., the market is "adjusted" to the product). The success of the entire enterprise, measured in terms of profit and growth, depends not only on the efficiency with which marketing and production activities are performed, but, as we have just seen, on the skill and effectiveness with which these two sets of important business activities are blended. So it is no accident that modern management regards marketing and production as interdependent subsystems. It considers marketing the subsystem by which specific products are matched up with specific markets and considers production as the subsystem charged with manufacturing these products. The two subsystems are inseparable, and management can ill afford to think of them otherwise.

Ownership Transfers

Ownership transfers occur repeatedly as products flow from producers to final buyers. For instance, a manufacturer may sell his output to wholesalers who, in turn, resell it to retailers who, again in turn, resell it to consumers. In this instance, every unit of the manufacturer's product that is finally purchased by a consumer has had its ownership transferred three times (manufacturer to wholesaler, wholesaler to retailer, retailer to consumer). Notice that for a transfer of ownership to take place, buying as well as selling is necessary. Consumers, as we noted before, are the "targets" of marketing activities—the whole flow of goods and services from producers to consumers anticipates this final buying action by consumers. All the selling and buying transactions that occur up to the time that the product is made available for consumer purchase are preliminaries. Only when that last buying transaction by a consumer, in the sequence of selling-buying transactions, takes place can the last selling transaction (by a retailer) occur. Even companies, such as IBM and Xerox, that lease certain products rather than selling them outright actually are engaged in effecting ownership transfers: While the product itself, such as a computer in IBM's case, may not be sold, the lease transaction carries with it the right to use and benefit from the services the product is capable of providing during the period of the lease. The lessor "sells" the services his product can provide, and the lessee "buys" them. In all cases, then, the effecting of ownership transfers is an essential ingredient of marketing; consequently, we include this point explicitly in our definition.

Summing Up

We believe, then, that marketing may best be described in terms of product-market interrelationships and of ownership transfers. Marketing management seeks to match up goods and services with markets and to effect transfers in the ownership of these goods and services. Consequently, in our view, *marketing is the business process by which products are matched with markets and through which transfers of ownership are effected.* The business process of marketing, then, includes all those business activities involved in moving goods and services from manufacturers and other producers to final consumers and users, plus those activities involved in evaluating these markets and adjusting product characteristics to market needs.

MARKETING AND SOCIETY

In any society, patterns of consumption are directly affected by and dependent on the structure and the efficiency of the marketing system. By a "pattern of consumption," we mean not only how much of what kind of goods and services are made available for consumption but also how much of these goods and services are actually consumed and in what manner. By "structure of the marketing system," we mean the whole network of marketing institutions that serves society's needs. At one end of this network, producers initiate the flow of goods and services and various intermediaries (e.g., wholesalers and retailers) maintain this flow, finally discharging the goods and services for consumption and use. "Efficiency" here refers to the value added to goods and services through the performance of marketing activities. Generally speaking, marketing adds value to goods by changing their ownership and by changing their time and place of consumption. For example, Idaho potatoes at harvest time are of less value to the grower than they are three months later (change of time) after they have been shipped and received in Pittsburgh (change of place), and when they are finally bought by a restaurant owner (change of ownership).[2] Marketing adds value to services (e.g., business, medical, entertainment, and educational services) by performing the services involved. A retail store, for example, that provides credit facilities for its customers (making it possible for customers to take possession of their purchases now and to pay for them later) adds value to the extent that customers take advantage of their credit privileges. Patterns of consumption, then, are determined both by the structure of the marketing system which is set up to carry the flow of goods and services from producers to consumers and users, and

---

[2] To be sure, non-marketing operations also add value to Idaho potatoes. Certainly the mature tubers which are dug out of the ground are worth more than the seed potatoes put into the ground (value added through planting, growing, and harvesting); and the restaurant workers, as they scrub, bake, and otherwise prepare this food item for diners' eating pleasure also add value. These, however, are instances where value is added to a product by changing its *form*—in other words, adding value by operations more akin to manufacturing than to marketing.

by the value added to these goods and services through performance of marketing activities. Undoubtedly, this is what Paul M. Mazur, a New York investment banker, had in mind when he referred to marketing as "the delivery of a standard of living." [3]

The Standard of Living

The standard of living refers both to the actual pattern of consumption of goods and services and to the *manner* of living. The structure and efficiency of the marketing system strongly influence the pattern of consumption but have only a limited influence on the manner of living (i.e., on the manner in which goods and services are consumed). Differences in the manner of living are caused by such factors as family and class traditions, educational and cultural influences, and social pressures of membership in different groups. Different combinations of such causes result in different manners of living, even though the particular goods and services consumed may be the same. Under one standard of living, for instance, food may be prepared expertly and served elegantly (with linen, fine china, silver, by candlelight), while under a second standard of living, the same food may be poorly prepared and served in a most unattractive manner (perhaps on a bare table top and dished up in tin plates).[4] Even though the marketing system has only a limited influence over the manner of living, marketers must, in making decisions, take into account those sociological and other variables that cause different people to have different standards of living. If they are to shape the actual pattern of consumption, marketers must take these variables into consideration as they manipulate marketing controllables, such as price, advertising, and personal selling. The end results of such manipulations are reflected in changes in consumption patterns, and, in this way, marketers participate in the delivery of a standard of living.

Economic Determinants of the Standard of Living

Marketing, of course, is not the sole determinant of the standard of living. It is one of the triumvirate of important economic determinants —production, purchasing power, and marketing—affecting the standard

[3] P. M. Mazur, "Does Distribution Cost Enough?" *Fortune*, November 1947, p. 138.

[4] This illustration adapted from: P. H. Nystrom, *Economic Principles of Consumption* (New York: Ronald Press, 1929), p. 245.

of living. Too often, businessmen and other economic observers have contended that some one of these three is the key to all problems concerning the standard of living. The fact is that any standard of living is economically determined by an interaction of production, purchasing power, and marketing. Consumption, of course, is limited by production, since goods must first be produced before they can be consumed. Similarly, consumer purchasing power (combined with the propensity to consume) is necessary if production is to be converted into consumption.

In the past, the conventional way of looking at marketing was to consider it merely as the means through which production and purchasing power were converted into consumption. Thus, production and its derivative, purchasing power, were considered the really important economic forces, and marketing was thought of as playing the necessary but secondary role of allocating the outputs of the nation's factories, mines, farms, forests, and fisheries to those who consumed these outputs. This view was a great deal more valid in the distant past than it is now; to understand why, it is helpful if we review the relative impact of production, purchasing power, and marketing in various stages of economic development.

ECONOMIC DEVELOPMENT AND THE STANDARD OF LIVING   Both the combined and the relative impact of the three main economic determinants—production, purchasing power, and marketing—vary with the stage of a country's economic development. Take the United States as an example. During the early phases of its history, production was cast in the key role. In the period of initial colonization, however, production was directed mainly to the exploiting of the country's vast natural resources—fertile land, abundant forests, rich mineral deposits, readily accessible water power, and the like. Little in the way of manufacturing facilities existed, except for occasional water-wheel powered grain mills, back-country whisky stills, and other primitive operations. This situation continued without much change up to the eve of the American Revolution, when the need to supply the revolutionary forces and to compensate partially for lost imports gave impetus to the building of manufacturing facilities—e.g., gunpowder plants, musket factories, textile mills, and ship-building yards. Both before and after the Revolution, and especially with the great westward push of the pioneers, there were severe manpower shortages and these accounted not only for the introduction and prolonged use of slaves, but for the development of production methods capable of turning out more goods with less human labor than had ever before been thought possible. Though quantities of most goods were usually smaller than the quantities that were needed, wages and profits were relatively high, and consumer purchasing power rose continually. For these reasons, disposing of the country's output was not very difficult, and marketing presented no great problems.

During most of the nineteenth century and well into the twentieth, market demand for most goods was usually far in excess of what the country could produce. Successive waves of immigrants arrived and added to this strength of market demand, even before they were absorbed into the nation's labor force. The imbalance of demand with supply was added to by the economy's need to pay off debts to European creditors, debts incurred in connection with both the financing of new production facilities and the westward frontier expansion. As is still typical in today's developing economies (e.g., Colombia, Indonesia, and Ghana), limited domestic investment capital was available, and it was necessary to attract foreign capital to finance many, if not most, of the nation's railroads and early manufacturing enterprises. Through the mechanisms of international trade, the economy paid its installments on these debts, at first in the form of raw materials (e.g., cotton, tobacco, and lumber) and later in the form of exports of manufactured goods. Because the country's productive capacity was used not only to supply a fast-growing domestic market but to satisfy claims of foreign creditors, there was almost continuous pressure to expand production further.

Throughout the nineteenth century and into the twentieth, the U.S. population grew rapidly but still remained small, relative to industry's needs for labor. This put, as we said earlier, a premium on devising ways to economize on the use of manpower in production. At the same time, even though the manpower shortage persisted, the domestic market was growing, too, and there were increasing numbers of people with high *real* incomes (i.e., high in terms of actual purchasing power). Since their dollar incomes rose faster than prices, most consumers were able to buy more and more goods—in other words, consumer purchasing power was still rising. Though there was still pressure on the country's productive capacity, American production ingenuity was not to be denied. New ways were found to step up factory outputs, thus hurrying the day when some parts of this productive capacity would eventually exceed market demand. But the important point to note here is that real incomes (i.e., actual purchasing power) rose faster than money incomes, thus making possible a continued strong upward thrust in the American standard of living.

After the Civil War, the rise of trade unions and the growth of social legislation brought about a reduction in the average work week, from as much as sixty or seventy hours to forty hours or even less. Working conditions, at the same time, were constantly improving and the general level of education was rising. These trends left the worker with an increasing amount of leisure time and a far less exhausted body and mind with which to enjoy it.[5] Since workers, along with most everyone else, possessed in-

[5] Mazur, "Does Distribution Cost Enough?" p. 197.

creasing amounts of purchasing power, they also had the financial means with which to buy what we know today as "leisure time" goods and services (e.g., hunting and fishing equipment, sporting goods, and movie and theater tickets). These trends served, then, to add further strength to market demand, but they called for the development and production of new products as much as they did for continued expansion in the output of established products. Large segments of the American consuming public were looking for goods and services with which they could occupy their increasing leisure time. They were, in effect, developing new "wants."

EVOLUTION OF MARKETING   Nineteenth-century marketing systems developed almost as by-products of the systems used for production. Producers considered marketing a relatively unimportant side-line activity, since much of what they made was made to order and, in effect, was sold before it was manufactured. What they did produce in anticipation of receiving orders, they disposed of by selling directly from their workshops or by displaying their goods in public marketplaces. Because these producers were in close contact with their markets, they were almost instinctively aware of consumer preferences. Their day-to-day contacts with their customers made it easy for them to anticipate the demand for their products. Furthermore, their skills were manufacturing skills; since manufactured goods of any kind were generally in short supply, there were few problems in selling and little selling skill was necessary.

As manufacturers began to increase their output, and as they switched from producing to order to producing in anticipation of orders, markets in and near the industrial towns could no longer absorb their particular factories' output. "Drummers" (i.e., traveling salesmen) were put on the road to obtain orders from more distant markets and itinerant peddlers in their horse-drawn buggies moved from town to town (buying their stocks in one place and selling them in the next). Wholesale institutions, active in towns along the Atlantic Seaboard since Colonial times, also began appearing in inland population centers and, by the end of the Civil War, were well established in larger towns and cities everywhere. In retailing, frontier trading posts gave way first to country general stores and later, with the growth of population centers, to more specialized grocery, hardware, feed and grain, and other retail stores. In the cities, especially after the Civil War, department stores opened, and the first chain-store systems were organized. To serve the far-spread farming and ranching population, the first mail-order houses began operations.

Selling problems were beginning to be important, but most manufacturers still preferred to concentrate on making products rather than on selling them. Many felt that their products were in certain ways unique and could "sell themselves." However, most manufacturers did realize that their products had to be made available for sale in non-local markets. Some handed the entire selling task to exclusive sales agents, who specialized in distributing products to wholesale and retail middlemen scattered in many markets. Most dealt with limited numbers of wholesalers, who assumed the responsibility for selling the products to retailers in their selling areas. But even where the products were sold to wholesalers, manufacturers considered marketing far less important than manufacturing. Wholesalers and retailers did nearly all of the marketing work and, for the most part, manufacturers were happy to leave it that way.

During this period, which lasted until early in the twentieth century in the United States and until very recently in most other countries, economic conditions permitted manufacturers to devote little attention to marketing. The economy, although growing rapidly, was still primarily agrarian, and supplies of manufactured goods rarely were large enough to meet the demand. Consumers were effectively forced to accept whatever goods were made available. Under these conditions, manufacturers could afford to concentrate on manufacturing and leave marketing primarily to the middlemen.

By the early twentieth century, however, it was increasingly clear that the nation's network of marketing institutions served as an important mechanism by which the products of different industries located in different places were exchanged among different market areas. This mechanism made possible area specialization of production (e.g., textiles in New England, meat-packing in Chicago, citrus growing in Florida and California, lumbering in the Pacific Northwest and later, automobile manufacture in Detroit, flour-milling in Minneapolis, and shoe manufacture in St. Louis) and helped, because of mass production economies, to achieve lower costs of production. The same marketing network performed the function of making the geographical dispersal of consumption possible. New Englanders could now enjoy citrus fruit grown in Florida and California, and Californians and Floridians could readily buy textiles produced in New England. Thus, with the passing of every year, more goods were being made available to more people, and the "self-contained, self-sufficient" community passed out of existence. With the development of both production facilities and marketing outlets from one end of the country to the other, with each area tending to specialize in producing what it could produce best, and with marketing outlets everywhere selling the products of all areas, the world was witnessing the birth and growth of the first great modern "common market"—i.e., the American common market.[6]

[6] The Roman Empire, of course, provides a well-known example of an ancient "common market." Very close commercial relations existed among all the Roman territories bordering on the Mediterranean Sea. Professor Henri Pirenne, for instance, in referring to the late third century, notes that "both manufactured and natural products

The manner in which American marketing evolved was strongly influenced by what has been called the greatest sales promotion (as well as political) instrument ever forged—the revolutionary doctrine that "all men are created equal." [7] Unlike much of Europe and most other parts of the world, where elaborate systems of social stratification kept people rigidly in their places, the United States early adopted an almost universal democracy of the marketplace. Americans, regardless of their social class, have never been restricted as to the goods and services they have a "right" to consume. What the richest and most aristocratic members of society consume, members of lower classes also have the right to consume—or at least to want to consume. Not everyone has the money to buy an ocean-going pleasure craft, but all have the *right* to want one. What a wealthy woman wears on New York's Fifth Avenue on Easter Sunday, every working girl has the right to want and to buy, if not the designer's "original," then at least an imitator's copy. This doctrine that everyone is equal, or at least starts out equal, has been a prime factor in making mass markets for many products possible. And these mass markets, in turn, have made mass production possible. Such democracy in the marketplace has, for example, turned the making of golf clubs from a handicraft operation into a mass production industry—once the sport of only the "upper crust," golfers today are numbered in the millions.

Mass markets for most products did not, of course, develop spontaneously, even though, during the first three decades of the twentieth century, industry after industry adopted mass production techniques—sometimes with spectacular increases in production and sales. By the early 1930's, the supply of many manufactured goods was exceeding the demand. It was common for manufacturers to find themselves faced both with excess production capacity and increasing competition for customers. It was during this period that the vitally important roles that could be played by personal selling, advertising, and other marketing "controllables" first came to be recognized. Personal selling's main role has been to effect ownership transfers (through multiple levels of middlemen) and to assure that final sales to consumers are consummated; advertising's main role has been to inform the buying public of what is available and to motivate them to buy. Thus, in moving goods through marketing channels (i.e., from producers to consumers) personal selling's function has been to "push" and advertising's function has been to "pull." These basic push and pull marketing strategies, which are usually used together rather than singly, have been backed up

---

were . . . extensively dealt in: textiles from Constantinople, Edessa, Antioch, and Alexandria; wines, oils and spices from Syria; papyrus from Egypt; wheat from Egypt, Africa, and Spain; and wines from Gaul and Italy." See: H. Pirenne, *Medieval Cities* (Princeton: Princeton University Press, 1925), Doubleday Anchor Edition, p. 2.

[7] Mazur, "Does Distribution Cost Enough?" p. 197.

by marketing research, product development and improvement, pricing, dealer organization and cooperation, and physical distribution of the goods themselves. And the basic push and pull strategies have been supplemented through the evolution and imaginative use of such devices as installment credit. When limited consumer purchasing power seemed to block market expansion for such "big ticket" items as automobiles, furniture, and large appliances, installment credit came to the rescue and provided consumers with a way to augment their purchasing power by pledging future income. For many people, the size of the "monthly payment" has become as important a buying consideration as the total price. Thus, in the installment credit device, marketing found a way around apparently limited purchasing power in the marketplace. The "capacity to consume" was there, and marketing used installment credit to free it. It is possible, then, to develop a mass market for a product, but only if there is the necessary capacity to consume that product and only if marketing effort succeeds in unlocking that capacity.

Some people contend that business emphasis may shift from the present concern with marketing to finding new ways for expanding the capacity to consume. Traditional economic thinking has been that human wants are insatiable (i.e., that no matter how much people consume, they will always want more of something), but recently this thinking has been challenged. Professor Galbraith, for one, argues, in effect, that most wants of U.S. consumers would have long since been satisfied had it not been for the "manufacturing of demand" for each succeeding new product introduced to the marketplace, and he argues further that "the fact that wants can be synthesized by advertising, catalyzed by salesmanship, and shaped by the discreet manipulations of the persuaders shows that they [that is, the wants] are not very urgent." [8] In the past the main problem was to produce enough to meet the needs of the market. In the present it is to market all that can be produced, and in the future it may be to find new ways for expanding the capacity to consume. There is no denying the fact that in a gradually growing list of industries, the capacity to produce has become larger than what the market will readily absorb, and more and more manufacturers are coming to consider marketing not only a problem for middlemen but for themselves as well. But this still leaves the interesting question of whether in an increasingly opulent society there might be some sort of natural limit on the capacity to consume. [9]

POWER OF THE CONSUMER   As a society advances to successively higher stages of economic development, the consumer's function in

[8] J. K. Galbraith, *The Affluent Society* (Boston: Houghton Mifflin, 1958), pp. 156, 158.

[9] Professor Reavis Cox has highlighted the nature of this possible business dilemma of the future in a very novel way. See his "The Outlook for Costs Imposed and Values Added by Distribution," in *Report of the Twenty-Eighth Boston Conference on Distribution* (Boston: Retail Trade Board, 1956), p. 50ff.

the economic process becomes increasingly important. In the early stages, when production is still the main problem, marketing focuses chiefly on the physical distribution of goods; consumers, as such, do not present much of a problem. But as production capacity catches up with and, in some cases, gets to be larger than market demand, increasing attention is paid to the power of the consumer. Thus, as an economy of scarcity evolves into one of plenty, business shifts its emphasis from production problems to marketing problems and, in firm after firm, marketing receives recognition as the mechanism responsible both for initiating and maintaining the flow of income into the business. The flow of business income is, of course, the result of the outward flow of goods and services from producers to consumers— a flow which marketing also initiates and maintains. The consumer becomes a force to be reckoned with—a fact obvious to retailers (they deal directly with consumers and obtain all of their income from sales made to consumers), less obvious to wholesalers (they deal with retailers, not with consumers, but their income depends indirectly, though importantly, on consumers' purchases), and probably least obvious to manufacturers, raw materials suppliers, and other primary producers (who, typically, are furthest removed from direct dealing with consumers). Sooner or later, however, all levels of distribution are forced to acknowledge that the consumer not only stands at the end of the marketing channel, but provides the spark (i.e., by buying) which starts the chain reaction of sales and income all along the marketing channel. Marketing industry's products is no longer just a matter of selling to the next distribution level but is, in addition, one of persuading ultimate consumers and final users to buy.

In the economy of plenty, then, the basic business (and marketing) problem is one of activating consumers, as individuals and as members of groups, into buyers. Society as a whole becomes more consumption-oriented and less production-oriented.[10] Traditional attitudes about the virtues of production and the natural sinfulness of consumption, rooted in an economic philosophy inherited from the age of scarcity, are modified although not completely eliminated. Society and businessmen are literally forced to recognize that consumer behavior dominates the whole economic process (unless consumers buy, goods may back up in the marketing channel, and ultimately the wheels of production may stop turning) and, thus, at least in the eyes of businessmen, production becomes a little less virtuous and consumption a great deal less sinful.

An economy of plenty can become one of surplus. This has already occurred in some economic sectors of the United States. Greatly improved agricultural techniques, for instance, although requiring both less labor and less land, have resulted in almost terrifying farm surpluses. Even now we are at the place where, as a result of technological progress (evidenced, in some cases, not only by automated production lines but by

[10] On this point, see: Galbraith, *Affluent Society*, Ch. 21.

almost fully-automated factories), more and more people are being released from industrial production. A slow transition is going on, in converting workers' abilities for use in providing the vast quantity of services that are needed for society's further advancement.[11] More manpower, in other words, is being switched from the production of goods to the providing of services, which include education, government, recreation, travel, and the health services—which must usually be rendered by human beings rather than by machine.[12] Expansion of such services characterizes the society which is beginning to turn from conditions of plenty to conditions of surpluses. We are not, however, apt to see the day when production capacity exceeds the capacity to consume in every line of goods. New products will continue to appear, present products will continue to be improved, and marketing ingenuity will go on uncovering and developing new markets. But, as Professor Seibert warns, "the progress of industrial automation is destined to be delayed unless we can develop the mass markets to absorb this contemplated mass production." [13] Undoubtedly, we will be hard-pressed to find ways to increase consumption of the outputs of the new automated factories, just as we have been in marketing agricultural surpluses in the past. Hence, businessmen very likely will give increasing emphasis to finding better solutions to their firms' marketing problems. And they are likely to accord consumer behavior (i.e., buying and consuming behavior) ever-increasing recognition as the crucial determinant of economic progress and business success.

MARKETING AS A FIELD OF STUDY

Business, although not yet fully convinced of the value of scientific marketing, has devoted a great deal of time and money to the search for universal laws and principles. In an ideal economic society (i.e., in a Utopia), it would be possible to "engineer" consumption just as we have been largely able to engineer production—to the point of day-in, day-out predictability. This has not happened. Every one of our so-called marketing principles seems to have its exceptions, which, in their turn, often seem to be new-found principles. And few, if any, of these so-called principles can be applied to all firms, at all times. One wry marketer has suggested that we do away

[11] See: M. Kestnbaum, "Redressing the Balance," *The Saturday Review*, January 17, 1959, p. 26.

[12] We doubt, for instance, that marketing professors will ever be fully supplanted by teaching machines. So far, not even the original teaching machine, the book, has kept their number from growing!

[13] J. C. Seibert, "Marketing's Role in Scientific Management" in R. L. Clewett (ed.), *Marketing's Role in Scientific Management* (Chicago: American Marketing Association, 1957), p. 2.

with the factor that has been frustrating us all along. If we are naive enough to bite, he answers "the human factor." The inescapable fact is that the consumer is a human being, capricious by nature, and anything but a machine designed to consume the output of our factories. While he will permit us to make some generalizations about him, it is doubtful whether he will ever allow us any "universal truths." The alert marketer recognizes this.

QUESTIONS AND PROBLEMS

1. Explain and contrast the terms in each of the following pairs:
   a. marketing and production
   b. standard of living and manner of living
   c. purchasing power and real income
   d. "push" marketing strategy and "pull" marketing strategy

2. Henry Ford, pioneer automobile manufacturer, once said "the consumer can choose any color he wants, so long as it's black." Contrast this statement with the modern philosophy of marketing and production.

3. "He who builds a better mousetrap will find the world beating a path to his door." How much truth is there in this age-old saying? Has it ever been true?

4. Economists often define production as "the creation of any good or service that people are willing to pay for." Compare this definition with the concept of production held by businessmen (and by most business students). According to this definition, can marketing be considered a form of production or not? Why?

5. It is a fact that every year total sales in this country exceed the total purchases of goods and services by consumers. What reasons might you advance to explain this?

6. Someone has said that "marketing both begins and ends with the consumer." Explain.

7. How does marketing add value to goods? Give a few examples.

8. Suppose that the government of one of the developing nations (e.g., Peru or Ecuador) employed you as a marketing consultant and gave you the assignment of "making recommendations conducive to raising the standard of living of the inhabitants." How might you go about carrying out this assignment?

9. Explain how consumption is affected by production, purchasing power, and marketing.

10.   Why has the "self-contained, self-sufficient" community passed out of existence in this country?

11.   Comment on the extent to which "democracy in the marketplace" has been a factor in developing mass markets for each of the following products: sports cars, television receivers, air travel, extension telephones.

12.   What does leisure time have to do with marketing?

13.   "If advertising, salesmen, and other forms of marketing effort had just not been so persistent, American consumers would have long ago been satisfied with their lots." Do you agree? Why or why not?

14.   One recent visitor to the U.S.S.R. reported that "there are really no salesmen in Russia, and the closest thing to a Madison Avenue type is a *tolkach* (pusher), a charmer whose persuasive skills are applied to buying, not selling." Assuming that this report is true, how might you explain it?

15.   What part, if any, has installment credit played in raising the American standard of living?

16.   Employment figures show that the number of people employed in marketing has been increasing more rapidly than the number working in production. What are the main reasons for this?

17.   Many marketers contend that "the solution to every marketing problem lies with the consumer." Is this contention valid? Why or why not?

18.   "There is a natural limit on the capacity to consume and that is why we have agricultural surpluses in this country." Do you agree or disagree? Why?

19.   "In a developing economy, it is patently more blessed to produce than to consume." Discuss.

20.   What reasons are there for believing that marketing will be of increasing importance in the future?

2

THE MARKETING
CONCEPT

As company after company has achieved the capability of producing in excess of existing demand, more and more executives have become aware of the need for reappraising marketing's role in business operations. There has been growing recognition of significant changes in markets, in technology, and in the ways of reaching and communicating with markets. Coupled with the growth in size and complexity of business organizations, these changes have made it important to reevaluate not only marketing's role but company goals themselves. Out of this setting has evolved the "marketing concept" which, in essence, is a philosophy of management.

The diagram below portrays the essential features of the marketing concept. A company operating under this concept takes its principal direction from the marketplace—i.e., from its knowledge and understanding of its customers' wants and desires. This understanding becomes, then, the main basis for organizing operations: all aspects of company operations (not only marketing, but production, financial, and other aspects) are geared toward satisfying customers' wants and desires. But the organiza-

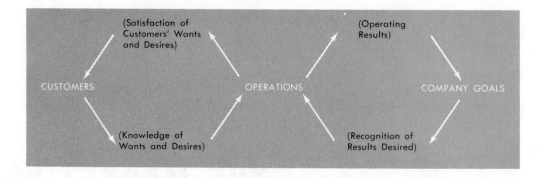

tion of operations is also influenced importantly by the company's over-all goals; operating managers (i.e., heads of departments) must recognize the results top management wants if they are to manage their operations in ways that not only satisfy customers' wants and desires but facilitate achievement of company goals. The marketing concept, then, has three main features: (1) a market or customer orientation, (2) subordination of departmental goals to company-wide goals, and (3) a unification of company operations both to satisfy customers' wants and desires and to achieve operating results in accord with over-all company goals.

ENVIRONMENTAL FACTORS INFLUENCING ADOPTION OF THE MARKETING CONCEPT

Certain key environmental factors provide the setting within which companies following policies consistent with the marketing concept can reasonably expect satisfactory results. Consider the consumer goods field: population and income trends have caused large potential markets to exist for the continual parade of product improvements and new products which, in turn, has been made possible through advances in science and technology. These particular "market" and "product" factors have produced a rising crescendo of competitive activity as more and more marketers seek shares of consumers' buying power. Competitive activity has been further heightened by the development and growth of successive new waves of mass communications media and by evolution and changes in marketing channels, making it possible to adjust the marketing controllables in new ways. These factors have influenced consumer goods marketers in their philosophy and organization; they have become less "product-oriented" and more "market- or customer-oriented," gearing their operations primarily to customers' wants and desires and only secondarily to particular products. Promotional emphasis, at the same time, has shifted from selling the product *per se* to selling the *function* that the product will perform for customers

—e.g., rather than promoting the technical features of a self-cleaning electric oven, one marketer of this product now advertises "this oven will clean itself, permitting the user to avoid a dirty and time-consuming job."

These environmental factors have most directly affected the consumer market; consequently, industrial goods companies have been slower to adopt the marketing concept. Nevertheless, developments in the consumer goods market have a "spillover" effect on the industrial market, and industrial marketers also are adjusting their operations according to the marketing concept. For example, the marketing vice-president of International Minerals and Chemicals Corporation, a producer of phosphates and potash sold to fertilizer manufacturers, has written:

> We have become a truly customer-oriented company, and our marketing concept is successfully translated into daily work activity. This spirit has permeated our customer groups, and our image among them is one of productiveness and assistance—the company with a constructive program to help the customer through trying times.[1]

Each of the key environmental factors influencing adoption of the marketing concept, first among consumer goods marketers and then as a "spillover" among industrial goods marketers, is examined more closely in the following discussion. The reader should keep in mind this analogue: Changes in marketing are similar to the changes that take place when a series of stones are tossed into a pond. Each stone causes a ripple which results in a whole series of ripples, each succeeding ripple further removed from the initial point of impact. In marketing, the uncontrollable factors, like the stones, cause the initial ripples and the consumer market begins to change. These changes result in changes among retailers, then among wholesalers, and finally among consumer goods manufacturers. Then, "spillovers" take place as changes in the consumer market cause changes in the industrial market. In other words, marketing changes usually start in consumer goods markets and at the consumers' end of marketing channels and work back to the manufacturers' end, and eventually the repercussions of these changes are felt and adjusted to by industrial goods marketers.

Mass Markets and Mass Affluence

POPULATION GROWTH   Consumer goods markets are made up of people with money, and the American market has been growing both in population and in income. Total U.S. population, as shown in Exhibit 2-1, has grown from fewer than 100-million people in 1910 to around

---

[1] A. E. Cascino, "A Case Study in Marketing Management," *Business Horizons*, Fall 1959, p. 60.

205-million in 1970. The population projection for 1980 is from 228 to 250-million (depending upon the assumption regarding the fertility rate), and by the year 2010 population will exceed 300-million. In terms of total population, then, the U.S. consumer market more than doubled in size

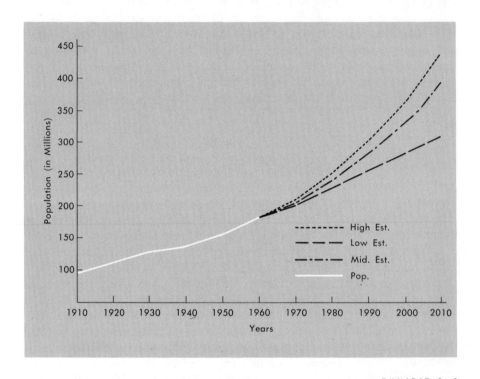

EXHIBIT 2–1

Population of the United States: 1910–1960 with Projections to 2010
(in Millions of Persons)

from 1910 to 1970, and there will be a further increase of nearly 50 percent in the next forty years. Growth in total population means more consumers and a larger market, and the American population is growing at a net rate of between two and three-million persons a year. Thus, large and growing potential markets exist for the widening stream of new consumer products being introduced to the market.

GROWING NUMBER OF HOUSEHOLDS   For some products market growth is more closely related to the total number of households and the formation of new households than it is to the total population and its growth. This is particularly true of certain durable consumer goods, such as household appliances and automobiles.[2] The number of households in 1970 was roughly 60-million, and in recent years an average of over 850,000 new households has been added annually. But the rate of new household formation is expected to accelerate, so the predictions are that there will be approximately 75-million households by 1980 and nearly 85-million by 1985. Since the number of households is increasing at a faster pace than the total population, marketers of many durable consumer goods can look forward to potential markets growing more rapidly than the consumer market as a whole.

GROWTH IN DISPOSABLE PERSONAL INCOME   Purchasing power is essential for the conversion of consumer wants and desires into market demand, and income is the chief source of purchasing power for most people. Total disposable personal income (what people have left over to spend or save after paying their taxes) grew from a little more than $83-billion in 1929 to more than $589-billion in 1968 and was running at an annual rate of nearly $609-billion in early 1969 (in terms of current dollars).[3] In terms of purchasing power (i.e., real income), the growth has not been as great, but it is still striking: Stated in constant (1958) dollars, the increase was from $150.6-billion in 1929 to $497.5-billion in 1968, a net gain in purchasing power of about 230 percent. It is estimated that by 1975, $282-billion of additional disposable personal income will be available for a total of $870-billion; by 1980, there will be a further gain of $245-billion, bringing total disposable personal income in that year to over a trillion dollars. Thus, in 1980 disposable personal income will be approximately double the 1968 showing.[4]

In terms of current dollars, annual per capita disposable income rose from $705 in 1929 to $3,431 in 1968, and is predicted to reach $5,760 in 1980. Compared to 1968, then, per capita disposable income will see an increase of 67 percent in 1980. In the period 1929-1968, the increase was nearly 400 percent. The American market has been growing increasingly affluent, and the trend is still in that direction.

[2] There is a difference between a "household" and a "family." The U.S. Bureau of the Census defines a household as consisting of "all persons who occupy a housing unit" and a family as "a group of two persons or more related by blood, marriage, or adoption and residing together." Thus, every family is a household but not every household is a family. There are more households than families and, generally speaking, there has been a more rapid increase in households (especially those consisting of individuals) than in households composed of families. See: Bureau of the Census, *Current Population Reports*, Series P-20, No. 166, August 24, 1967.

[3] National Industrial Conference Board, *Business Outlook Chartbook—Summer 1969.*

[4] F. H. Graf, *Marketing Changes in the 70's* (Chicago: A. C. Nielsen Company, 1969).

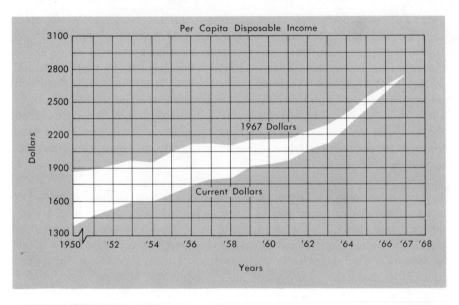

Per Capita Disposable Income

EXHIBIT 2—2

Source: National Industrial Conference Board, Inc., *A Graphic Guide to Consumer Markets: 1968–1969*, p. 26.

Exhibit 2-2 shows the rise in per capita disposable income from 1950 to 1967 and helps illustrate the impact of rises in the price level in purchasing power during this period. Per capita disposable income is stated both in 1967 dollars and in dollars reflecting the price level of each year during the period. Thus, in terms of constant (1967) dollars, per capita disposable income rose from under $1900 in 1950 to roughly $2700 in 1967, an increase of about 42 percent. In spite of increases in prices, then, the American consumer has enjoyed continuing increases in the amount of purchasing power at his disposal.

INCREASES IN DISCRETIONARY INCOME   Not only is the trend toward larger disposable incomes, but households have increasing amounts of *discretionary income*. A household has discretionary income when it has money left over after buying essential food, clothing, shelter, transportation, and other items it regards as "necessities." A family with such income may spend it, save it, or use it for both spending on "non-necessities" and saving. Past experience shows, however, that a rise in discretionary income usually results in more spending for non-necessities (so-called *discretionary spending*).

Both discretionary income and discretionary spending are difficult to measure, since families differ with respect to what they regard as necessities and non-necessities, and even the same family changes over time. Realistically, too, some so-called discretionary spending may not be out of current income at all, but rather on credit or from past savings, gifts, or inheritances.[5] In spite of the elusiveness of these concepts, they are important. There is little doubt that as a family's income goes up, it buys more items previously regarded as luxuries. Conversely, as a family's income goes down, it discontinues buying not only luxuries but even some items previously considered necessities.

Discretionary spending grew, as Exhibit 2-3 shows, from roughly $90-billion in 1946 to around $195-billion in 1967. Continuing increases in the amounts of consumer discretionary purchasing power have resulted in great expansions in the market potentials for such products as automatic dishwashers, color television sets, and home swimming pools. Furthermore, with the average consumer becoming more affluent with each passing year, he also is becoming more particular in what he buys and more choosy in what he will accept. This increasing consumer sophistication has led more and more manufacturers to research consumers' wants and desires more thoroughly and to develop and market products more closely in line with findings. At the same time, growth in market potential for non-necessities has stimulated additional firms to enter such markets, thus adding to the incentive all competitors have for adjusting their products more closely to what consumers demand.

MORE MULTI-EARNER FAMILIES   One reason for the rise in the number of families with discretionary income is that over one-third have more than one person employed. In most multi-earner families, the wife is the second person employed. Prior to World War II, during which war work was considered a patriotic duty, the wife's "rightful" place generally was considered to be in the home. Moreover, during the depression of the 1930's, the scarcity of jobs and the large number of unemployed created pressures against employed men's wives taking jobs. With the disappearance of both the social stigma and the economic barrier, the number of working wives rose rapidly.

[5] Probably the best data on discretionary spending are compiled by the National Industrial Conference Board, Inc. This organization constructs a statistical series on *discretionary purchasing power*, which provides a measure of the current resources available to households after they have purchased essentials (such as necessary food, clothing, etc.) and taken care of fixed outlays (mortgage payments, repayments of debt obligations, property tax payments, and the like). This series also takes into account purchasing power over and above that derived from current disposable personal income—for example, consumer credit and bank loans. From these calculations, NICB arrives at estimates of total discretionary spending, total discretionary saving, and estimates on a per capita basis of discretionary purchasing power, discretionary saving, and discretionary spending. See: National Industrial Conference Board, Inc., *A Graphic Guide to Consumer Markets: 1968–1969*, pp. 30-31.

More than 60 percent of the 28-million women in the work force today are married. Of these working wives, one third contribute from 10 to 30 percent of their families' total income, a second third contribute from 30 to 50 percent, and the remaining third 50 percent or more.[6] It is interesting to note also that 60 percent of the families in the $10,000-to-$15,000 income class have reached this bracket because of a working wife.[7]

Since it is rare for a wife's income to be set apart from that of her husband, the spending behavior of a multi-earner family tends to

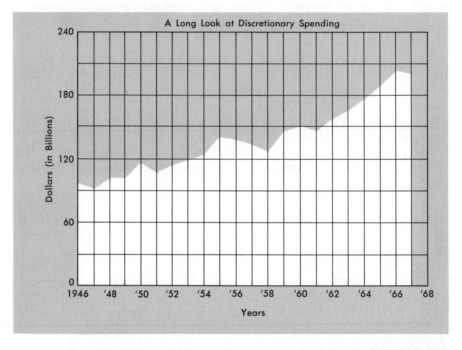

EXHIBIT 2–3

Source: National Industrial Conference Board, Inc., A Graphic Guide to Consumer Markets: 1968–1969, p. 30.

resemble that of a family with the same size income from a single source. The multi-earner family, in other words, has more money left over for

[6] National Industrial Conference Board, In., A Graphic Guide to Consumer Markets: 1968–1969, p. 21.
[7] Editors of Fortune, Markets of the Seventies (New York: The Viking Press, 1967), p. 106.

discretionary spending than it would have if it had only one person working. In 1967, the median income of families with working wives was $9,956, while the median income of families without working wives was $7,611.[8]

EVENING-OUT OF INCOME DISTRIBUTION PATTERN   Closely related to the trend toward increased discretionary income is the trend involving an evening-out of the income level among consumers. This trend is contributing importantly to the growth of mass markets for many items, such as motorboats—"luxuries" which, in the recent past, only a few could afford. A few generations back, income distribution was like a pyramid with the vast bulk of the incomes (i.e., the low incomes) at the pyramid base. Today, the pattern of income distribution is being reshaped into the form of a diamond, with a large middle-income group positioned between a "rich" minority above them and a "poor" minority below them.[9]

Mean average family income reached $9,019 in 1967,[10] with 63 percent of all U.S. families in the middle income group (incomes between $5,000 and $15,000), 12 percent in the "rich" minority (incomes over $15,000), and 25 per cent still in the "poor" minority (incomes under $5,000).[11] Thus, a growing proportion of U.S. families receive incomes at levels allowing for increasing amounts of discretionary spending.

The continuing tendency for more people to have more income has caused, and is causing, new mass markets to develop. This has happened as more and more products once regarded as "luxuries" become "necessities." Washing machines, radios, television sets, telephones, and automobiles all have—for ever-increasing segments of the population—moved from the luxury class to the necessity class.[12]

"NEW" ATTITUDE TOWARD DEBT   Increases in discretionary spending also can be traced to the growing willingness of American consumers to use credit. Ever since the great depression of the 1930's, less and less stigma has been attached to credit buying, and fewer people accumulate savings in order to pay cash for such products as automobiles, television sets, furniture, and major household appliances. Each year, for instance, more than six of ten new car buyers and five of ten used car

---

[8] *Statistical Abstract of the U.S.—1969*, p. 326.

[9] *Sales Management*, November 10, 1968, p. 94.

[10] U.S. Bureau of the Census, *Current Population Reports*, Consumer Income Series P-60, No. 59, April 18, 1969, p. 2.

[11] U.S. Bureau of the Census, *Current Population Reports*, Series P-60, No. 55, August 5, 1968, p. 4.

[12] For a stimulating discussion of this and other effects of income flow diffusion, see: W. Gross, "Income Flow Diffusion and Marketing Strategies," *Business Topics*, Autumn 1966, pp. 70-77.

buyers buy on credit.[13] Many "cash" buyers borrow from banks, finance companies, and other lenders, so, in effect, they also buy on credit by making their payments to lenders rather than directly to sellers. Buying on credit has become a way of life for millions, including many who could pay cash but prefer credit buying.

The volume of consumer credit outstanding (not including home mortgages) in April 1969 came to more than $113-billion. Around four-fifths of that amount was installment credit used to finance purchases of automobiles and other major consumer durables, while one-fifth was non-installment credit (single-payment loans, retail charge accounts, and other short-term debts). As recently as 1960, total consumer credit outstanding stood at only $56-billion. In less than ten years, the amount of credit has more than doubled, rising on a per capita basis from about $310 to $540 per year.

By buying now and paying later, a consumer can command more purchasing power than that represented by his current income. But, of course, purchases made today on credit must eventually be paid for. In this connection, repayments of installment credit obligations took 15 percent of consumers' disposable personal income in 1968, while the ratio of new installment credit to disposable personal income was 16.8 percent.[14] Thus, consumers have been assuming new debts at a slightly faster rate than they have been paying off old obligations. Probably this is because the incomes consumers expect to receive in the future have a relationship to present spending patterns. Presumably, consumers' spending, particularly for automobiles, furniture, major appliances, and other durables, is influenced by their optimism or pessimism about future income.[15] As might be expected, personal debt is most common among younger families, a group that includes heavy purchasers of major appliances and furniture and a group, too, that generally has rather low incomes but is optimistic about future prospects for higher incomes.

The amount of credit a consumer can obtain is directly related to the size of his present income, so lower income groups generally have smaller credit amounts than higher income groups. But, as noted earlier, the long-range trend is for incomes to rise, so we can expect still further expansions in credit buying in the future. Marketers of such products as

---

[13] In 1968, 69 percent of the new cars and 50 percent of the used cars were bought on installment credit or other borrowing. See *Statistical Abstract of the U.S.—1969*, p. 552.

[14] "Consumption and Saving Patterns Since Mid-1968," *Federal Reserve Bulletin*, June 1969, p. 469.

[15] Although the results are not entirely conclusive, this hypothesis appears to have been borne out by the *Annual Survey of Consumer Finances* made by the Survey Research Center of the University of Michigan since 1948.

mobile homes, boats, and camping trailers have adopted credit plans to accelerate expansion of their markets; and "go now—pay later" travel plans have made international air travel possible for the average man. In addition, the spreading use of bank-sponsored credit card plans has made it progressively easier for consumers to buy on credit, even from those retailers who formerly sold for cash only. The changing attitude toward debt, along with this increasing ability of consumers to obtain credit, then, has added to the intensity of the competition for the consumer's dollar.

Technological Change

The accelerating pace of technological change is a second major environmental factor strongly influencing adoption of the marketing concept. Technological change has time and again brought overnight obsolescense to products, whole product lines, and even entire industries while, at the same time, it suddenly creates vast new markets for other products and industries.[16] Thus, technological change is a key element in the competitive struggle among companies. Consider, for example, the effect of American Cyanamid's market introduction of Achromycin tetracycline in 1953 on sales of Aureomycin chlortetracycline, which had been marketed since 1948. Aureomycin sales, after an almost continuous upward trend in 1950–1953, plummeted by nearly 40 percent during the first full year of the sale of Achromycin—thus illustrating the devastating effect a new product can have on an existing market.[17]

In an environment of mass affluence and accelerating technology, no company has a guarantee that its product will not be made obsolete by some technological advance. Recognizing this, total expenditures for research and development (R & D) soared from under $2-billion in 1945 to nearly $24-billion in 1967.[18] A large portion of these funds for R & D were supplied by the federal government to support research in defense and defense-oriented industries, as well as in connection with the space exploration program; however, there were also great increases in R & D expenditures by private companies. Therefore, in a growing number of companies, and especially in those with substantial R & D efforts, product life cycles have become shorter as new products are accounting for an increasing proportion of sales. Armstrong Cork Company, for instance,

[16] D. N. Judelson, "The Conglomerate—Corporate Form of the Future," *Michigan Business Review*, July 1969, p. 10.

[17] E. Mansfield, *The Economics of Technological Change* (New York: W. W. Norton and Co., Inc., 1968), p. 7.

[18] *Statistical Abstract of the U.S.—1968*, p. 525.

could trace almost half of its 1968 sales volume to products of its own development introduced during the previous ten years.[19]

Technological developments in one industry have often resulted in products' being sold to markets traditionally supplied by companies in a different industry. Both consumer and industrial markets have been affected, as noted by one keen observer:

> . . . the high-research industries increasingly invade the territory of the technologically backward. The invasion of the textile industries by the chemically-derived synthetics is one example. . . . Another is the introduction of new materials into building—such as plastics, pre-stressed concrete, aluminum—leading to the adoption of new techniques of prefabrication and flow-line production. Similarly, the development of numerically-controlled machine tools (largely as a result of research work done in the Air Force and M.I.T. into ways of machining complex parts) has brought aerospace and electronics companies into traditional machine-tool markets on a growing scale.[20]

There is every reason to expect that the pace of technological change will continue to accelerate in the years ahead. In this regard, two research executives of TRW, Inc., a billion-dollar company operating in diverse industries, predict that 80 percent of all the major scientific discoveries and inventions that will be well-known 45 years from now will have occurred during the professional career of this year's college graduate.[21]

Numerous predictions have been made about the nature and direction of future technological change. Kahn and Wiener have listed 100 areas in which it is probable that technological innovation will occur by the year 2000. Among the areas on their list are the following: [22]

1. New sources of power for ground transportation (storage battery, fuel cell, propulsion (or support) by electro-magnetic fields, jet engine, turbine, and the like).

2. Three-dimensional photography, illustrations, movies, and television.

3. Practical use of direct electronic communication with and stimulation of the brain.

4. Generally acceptable and competitve synthetic foods and beverages (e.g., carbohydrates, fats, proteins, enzymes, vitamins, coffee, tea, cocoa, and alcoholic liquor.)

---

[19] *1968 Annual Report*, Armstrong Cork Company.

[20] M. Shanks, *The Innovators* (Baltimore: Penguin Books, 1967), p. 79.

[21] H. Q. North and D. L. Pike, "'Probes' of the Technological Future," *Harvard Business Review*, May–June 1969, p. 69.

[22] See H. Kahn and A. J. Wiener, *The Year 2000* (New York: The Macmillan Co., 1967), pp. 51-55.

5. New and improved materials and equipment for buildings and interiors (e.g., variable transmission glass, heating and cooling by thermoelectric effect, and electroluminescent and phosphorescent lighting.)
6. Personal "papers" (perhaps even two-way pocket phones) and other personal electronic equipment for communication, computing, and data processing programs.
7. Inexpensive (less than $20.00) long lasting, very small battery operated TV receivers.
8. Home computers to "run" the household and communicate with the outside world.
9. Home education via video and computerized and programmed learning.
10. Artificial moons and other methods for lighting large areas at night.

Fantastic progress, then, is being made in science and technology. An ever-growing number of new products is being introduced to the market each year, some of them causing the growth of whole new industries and some sounding the death knell for others. Each year, too, the list of products from which consumers may more nearly satisfy their wants and desires grows longer.

Growth of Mass Communications Media

The great growth of mass communications media has been a third environmental factor helping bring about adoption of the marketing concept. Even the newspaper, at least as a mass medium, did not come into being until the turn of the twentieth century; certain technological advances made in the late nineteenth century (e.g., the telegraph, the linotype, and the rotary press) made possible both mass circulation and rapid delivery.[23] Similarly, magazines as mass media grew rather slowly until the 1921 founding of *Reader's Digest* (which carried no advertising for many years) and the 1923 appearance of *Time*, which were followed by *Newsweek* in 1933, *Life* in 1936, and *Look* in 1937.

The later development of audio and audio-visual media brought the most profound change in mass communications. These media shifted the initiative, partly at least, from receiver to sender—"Once the receiver had made his basic choice, the sender was in charge. The machine, or the force behind it, controlled the pace, the repetitions, the emphasis, the

[23] R. C. O'Hara, *Media for the Millions* (New York: Random House, 1961), p. 88.

timing." [24] Station KDKA, Pittsburgh, went on the air in 1920, heralding the advent of radio, coast-to-coast network broadcasting began in 1927, and the medium achieved great growth during the 1930s, and early 1940s. Black-and-white television was introduced commercially in 1945 and became a truly national mass medium with the first coast-to-coast live transmission on September 1, 1951. Color television was inauguarated in 1960. By the late 1960s, sixteen out of every seventeen U.S. homes, representing 96 percent of the population, had television. Each new medium grew more rapidly than its predecessors, and each made it possible to "spread the word" about new product developments faster and more widely and—for the most part—more effectively, than before.

The development and growth of mass communications media of different kinds also made it possible for advertising to play a larger role in marketing. The ever-accelerating rate of technological change coupled with businessmen's desires to secure the economic advantages of large-scale production has resulted in increasing pressures for rapid development of mass markets. Professor Backman comments on advertising's expanding role as follows:

> Advertising plays a major role in our economy because new products are offered in ever greater numbers, and existing products must be called to the attention of new consumers who are added to the market as a result of expansion in incomes, the population explosion, and changes in tastes. Potential markets also expand as incomes rise and as consumers are able to purchase products they could not afford previously. Continuous large-scale advertising is necessary to provide reminders to old customers and to provide information to new customers.[25]

A reflection of marketers' increasing use of advertising is shown in the trend of advertising expenditures in the United States: from total expenditures of about $2-billion annually prior to World War II to nearly $18-billion in 1968.[26]

Existence of diverse types of mass communications media is a highly important feature of the modern marketing environment. Thus, in a developed country, such as in the United States, the person wanting additional details or desiring to check on some piece of information can easily turn to another medium. If he hears a radio commercial advertising a new product, for instance, he can look for additional details in newspaper or magazine advertisements or watch for television commercials promoting

[24] W. Schramm, "Its Development," in C. S. Steinberg (ed.) *Mass Media and Communication* (New York: Hastings House, Publishers, 1966), p. 46.
[25] J. Backman, *Advertising and Competition* (New York: New York University Press, 1967), p. 23.
[26] *Statistical Abstract of the U.S.—1969*, p. 775.

the same product. Unlike the majority of people in developing countries (such as in India, Peru, or Ghana), most Americans have numerous secondary sources of information (i.e., other mass media) besides the always-present source of "other people." From the marketer's standpoint, then, the development and growth of different kinds of mass communications media has made it possible to deliver advertising messages in more ways, each medium reinforcing messages delivered by other media and each boosting the combined impact on potential customers.

Changes in Marketing Channels

Changes in marketing channels are the fourth major environmental factor influencing adoption of the marketing concept. Such changes have occurred at a more rapid rate, generally speaking, than changes in either markets or technology. At one time, a manufacturer could expect his marketing channels to remain stable and appropriate over a long period. But appearance of new types of distributive institutions, shifts in operating methods of older institutions, and development and change in physical distribution systems have created new "distribution problems" and new "distribution opportunities" for the manufacturer.

This dynamic situation is described by Peter Drucker who writes: "I have never seen a decision with respect to distributive channels that was not obsolescent five years later and badly in need of new thinking and fundamental change." [27]

In order to solve distribution problems and capitalize on the opportunities present, the manufacturer must continuously reevaluate his distribution policies and methods and make appropriate adjustments. Yet, there appears to be a particularly strong inclination for manufacturers to resist changes in the area of distribution policies and methods; typically, they not only do not solve the problems but they fail to take advantage of new ways for reaching and/or serving the market or new segments of it.

Since the 1930s, many new types of distributive institutions have appeared. The supermarket, a retailing innovation of the 1930s, made tremendous inroads in food marketing, combining low-price, self-service, and cash-only policies to secure high sales volume. Independents were the first supermarket operators, but large grocery chains soon followed. Planned shopping centers, most of them situated in fast-growing and high-income suburban areas, were a development of the 1940s. Starting about the same time, new institutions appeared emphasizing the price appeal in retailing traditionally high-margin lines—the discount house selling nationally-

[27] P. F. Drucker, *Managing for Results* (New York: Harper & Row, 1964), pp. 23-24.

advertised appliances and other "hard goods," and the discount department store handling most of the merchandise lines traditionally stocked by long-established department stores. In these and similar cases, the stimulus for developing a new form of institution resulted from a search for opportunities to adjust retailing methods more closely to the changed needs and expectations of consumers. Unfortunately, some older retail institutions viewed these same opportunities as "problems" and failed to make needed adjustments until increasingly severe competition either forced competitive changes or caused them to close their doors.

Nevertheless, the forward-looking managements of many other long-established retail institutions not only made counteradjustments in their operating methods but came up with a few innovations of their own. Many "downtown" department stores, for example, set up full-scale department stores in larger shopping centers, and the variety store chains met discount house competition by setting up their own discount operations. Thus, there has been one round of change after another in the ways retailers (and other distributors) do business, each intensifying the manufacturer's need to keep his distribution policies dynamic and in line with changing market situations.

In the face of rising competition for the consumers' dollar, retail institutions, particularly the larger companies, have made changes in operating methods of great significance to consumer goods producers. One of the first such changes involved the successful attempt by large retailers to circumvent wholesale middlemen and to buy directly from manufacturers, thus capturing part or all of the margin previously obtained by wholesalers and allowing the retailer greater flexibility in setting prices. A second was retailers' adoption of private brands, thus providing a way to shift consumers' loyalty away from producers and to increase retailers' bargaining power with the source of supply. In cases where manufacturers refused to supply private-brand merchandise on the desired terms, many large retailers began producing items for themselves, thereby adding to the competition faced by the "bypassed" manufacturers.[28] In numerous instances, too, large retailers set up *buying committees*—groups that make buying decisions—leaving individual "buyers," with whom manufacturers' salesmen typically deal, only limited decision-making power. These are but a sampling of the many changes in retailers' operating methods that have complicated and intensified the competition faced by manufacturers in distributing their products to ultimate consumer markets.

The consumer market for some merchandise lines also has been invaded by marketers who previously operated in other fields. At the retail level, traditional drugstore items, such as aspirin and mouthwashes, are

---

[28] On this point, see: G. G. Fisch, *Organization for Profit* (New York: McGraw-Hill Book Co., 1954), p. 232.

being stocked by grocery outlets, while druggists retaliate by adding certain food items. Petroleum marketing companies now sell such items as coffee pots, golf clubs, miniature TV sets, cameras, and short-wave radios to their credit-card holders by mail. The chains of redemption centers operated by trading stamp companies represent large outlets for many kinds of products previously sold only through conventional retailers, such as department stores, sporting goods stores, and appliance dealers. Numerous similar examples exist. This multiplication of potential outlets make it ever more critical for the manufacturer to continually check the appropriateness of existing channel arrangements. The range of distribution options open to the manufacturer has broadened considerably, making it easier for potential buyers to locate and buy his product. This lessens the chance that potential buyers influenced by advertising will be unable to find his product within a reasonable searching time.

Noteworthy improvements in transportation also have been occurring, making it possible to distribute products faster, more economically, and more widely than ever before. Among these are jet air freight, containerized shipping (rail, ocean, and air), piggyback (combining highway and rail carriers), fishy-back (combining highway and water carriers), and the unitized train. Whole new transportation "systems" also have been developing—the Canadian Pacific, for example, now emphasizes its role in moving shipments between the Orient and Europe through a combination of air, ocean, rail, and highway transport media. Similarly, the Burlington Northern (formerly the Great Northern) promotes its "land bridge" concept by which it connects the Far East with Europe. Technological gains in the design, manufacture, and utilization of transport equipment have taken us, for instance, from the slower propeller-type plane, to the supersonic jet. Doubtless these, and technological advances still to come, will make still further gains possible in the ease with which manufacturers may distribute their products not only nation-wide but throughout the entire world. Manufacturers who choose to restrict their distribution to certain areas will find themselves confronting an increasing number of new competitors from elsewhere.

Summary of Environmental Factors
Influencing Adoption of the Marketing Concept

The four main environmental factors helping bring about adoption of the marketing concept can be summed up as follows:

1. More people have more money.
2. More things are being produced—more types of products, more

versions of individual products, and closer adaptations of individual product characteristics to the wants and desires of particular market segments.

3. People can be informed about these products through more mass communications media.

4. There are more ways to move products to markets, institutionally as well as physically.

As these trends continue, and every reason exists for thinking they will, we can expect further rises in the tempo of competitive activity. Consumers have an increasing number of ways to spend the higher incomes they receive. At the same time, more and more companies participate in the contest to make these additional sales. Under these environmental circumstances, the company following policies consistent with the marketing concept is helping to insure its own survival and is in a good position to capitalize on marketing opportunities as they unfold.

ORGANIZATIONAL CONDITIONS PRECEDING ADOPTION OF THE MARKETING CONCEPT

Three conditions internal to the business organization, all representing maladjustments to the environmental changes and trends previously discussed, generally precede management's recognition of the necessity for adopting the marketing concept. These are: (1) a product orientation, (2) communications difficulties and uncoordinated proliferation of specialists, and (3) conflicts among departmental goals. Each of these conditions is analyzed in the following discussion.

Product Orientation

The traditional orientation of top management in many companies, particularly those emphasizing mass production, focuses mainly on the product. Simply described, product orientation involves falling in love with the company's own products, making them better (technically, mechanically, and aesthetically), improving the production process, bringing down product costs, and the like, while at the same time neglecting changes in the market and the competitive situation. It should not be too surprising that production specialists, engineers, and other technical "experts" often dominate the product-oriented company, marketing's role being visualized as that of "moving the product." Often this means "selling" the product rather than "marketing" it.

Top management in the product-oriented company expects marketing operations to serve the seller's interests alone and not those of buyers. Management becomes entranced with the beauty and miracles of mass production, its main efforts are directed toward achieving ever-more-efficient manufacturing, and it assigns marketing the task of selling increased outputs—literally, if necessary, of "forcing it down customers' throats." If the fact that the company has produced a "better mousetrap" doesn't cause the "world to beat a path to the company's door," the marketing department is expected to go out and sell the output any way it can.

The great danger in the product-oriented company is that top management will not know what business the company really is in. "Knowing what business a company is in" means recognizing that it is in business to serve a market and not simply to dispose of a product.[29] Companies in the motion picture industry after World War II, for instance, considered themselves in the business of "making movies," rather than in the market-oriented business of "providing entertainment." This caused them to view the introduction of television as a "threat" when they should have welcomed it as an "opportunity" to expand their entertainment business.

Other examples of industries made up mainly of product-oriented companies are easy to find. Local transport companies in large cities still are inclined to think of themselves as "bus companies, subway systems, and the like" rather than as being in the business of "providing transportation." This has led large numbers of their former passengers to find other ways to meet their transportation needs. Commercial banks, too, traditionally have thought of themselves as being in the "banking" business, not in the business of "providing financial services" for their depositors and borrowers —such as the safekeeping of funds, investment of funds, making money available when needed, keeping records, and giving expert advice. Hotels and resorts, as another example, are not really in the business of "renting rooms and selling meals" but in the business of "providing places to relax and sleep and preparing food and drink which customers cannot only endure but enjoy."

The company with a product orientation, then, takes a selfish view. It conceives its main purpose as one of making its product available to the market, not of servicing a market with changing wants and preferences. It, therefore, runs the risk that the market now buying the product will find some more satisfactory way of meeting its needs. Eventually the owners of horse-drawn buggies nearly all bought automobiles! Where did that leave the manufacturers of buggies? As a pure matter of survival, then,

[29] In his widely-quoted article "Marketing Myopia," Theodore Levitt cites numerous examples of product-oriented companies in product-oriented industries not knowing what business they are (or were) in. See: *Harvard Business Review*, July-Aug. 1960, pp. 45-56. The example of the motion picture industry is paraphrased from Levitt's article.

companies with product orientations have had to change them in order to stay in business at all.[30]

Communications Difficulties and Uncoordinated Proliferation of Specialists

Manufacturing enterprises, small and large, perform basically the same major activities: (1) they make a product, (2) market it, and (3) determine whether the combination of (1) and (2) was profitable or not. These activities—production, marketing, and finance—are common to every manufacturing company.[31] As a company grows, these activities are split down into smaller and smaller parts, each a charge of a specialist. Complexities of administering the growing number of people in an organization also helps bring a wide range of bureaucratic positions and careers into existence. Furthermore, as an organization grows, there is a tendency for departmental walls to rise ever higher, causing some tasks to be duplicated in different departments, as department heads and others holding bureaucratic positions seek to build their "own little empires."

As the number of specialists multiplies, personnel tend to lose the ability to communicate effectively with others not sharing their particular specialties. One reason for this is certainly defensible—it traces directly to the economies involved in having technical or specialist languages, ones that save communication time for persons sharing the same specialties. Engineers speak "engineeringese" to each other, accountants use accounting language, salesmen have their own special terminology, and so do the numerous other specialists found in large companies. However, communications difficulties arise because the existence of specialist languages also causes the same things and events to have a large variety of "special meanings" for different specialists.[32]

Another reason for the tendency of communications to lose effectiveness can be traced to the need certain specialists feel for justifying their own positions, i.e., for legitimization of their status. One way specialists seek to legitimatize their positions is to *invent* languages others cannot fully understand; thus they are spurred into transforming everyday speech into technical jargon and, in some cases, even into mathematical formulae.

---

[30] Admittedly, however, some companies with product orientations have been "lucky" enough to survive for extended periods. Levitt cited the petroleum industry as an outstanding example. See Levitt, *ibid*.

[31] Distributing enterprises (i.e., wholesalers and retailers) also perform three major activities but, since they generally buy rather than make what they market, the activities are procurement, marketing, and finance.

[32] On this matter, see: T. Burns and G. M. Stalker, *The Management of Innovation* (London: Tavistock Publications Ltd., 1961), p. 155.

Worse yet, in a company where this is happening, there also is a tendency for the proliferation of specialists to be uncoordinated. So they are inclined to work at cross purposes, and frictions and inefficiencies, as well as communications problems, permeate the entire organization.

Existence of frictions, inefficiencies, and communications difficulties often causes top management to become preoccupied with internal operations. Painfully aware that hoped-for economies of large-scale operations are not being realized, management tends to devote its main efforts to improving the technical aspects of operations and, likely as not, moves in the process toward product orientation. Thus, management exhibits a growing inability and unwillingness to see opportunities on the outside caused by market shifts, technological changes, and the like. Theodore Levitt cites several examples:

> . . . General Electric turned down the opportunity to get exclusive American rights to manufacture and distribute neon lights, saying there was no market for them. A new small company had to be organized by Europeans in the United States to pioneer this big, profitable market. Frozen orange juice had to be started by a company not in the food business. The big hotel chains fought the motel idea for years, in spite of its greater customer-satisfying benefits. The big vacuum-tube manufacturers (with the exception of Philco) vigorously resisted the transistor idea.[33]

Conflicts Among Departmental Goals

Also stemming from the strong drives within each department for different specialists to justify their own positions is the conflict among departmental goals. In the production department, costs are uppermost in importance—thus, the natural emphasis is on reducing costs in every possible way—minimizing the number of product lines, standardizing product variety, lengthening the interval between model changes, and maximizing the length of production runs. Within the marketing department, in contrast, everything tends to revolve around sales volume—hence, sales are pushed by any means available—pressures are exerted to offer the widest variety of products, to change models at short intervals, to get the products into every conceivable outlet, to promote them continuously and heavily, and to price them at or below competitive levels.

One might expect in these circumstances that the finance department would mediate the differences between these opposing pressures

[33] *Innovation in Marketing* (New York: McGraw-Hill Book Co., Inc., 1962), p. 15.

by the production and marketing departments—i.e., to assume top-management's responsibility—but finance specialists also are caught up in the effort to justify their own positions. Often this takes the direction of maximizing short-run returns to stockholders, neglecting not only to take into account customers' wants and desires but also opposing the undertaking of research and development work needed to keep the firm competitive, frustrating the efforts of both production and marketing to install innovations that cost money in the short-run but pay off in the long-run, and generally trying to minimize costs and maximize revenues at one and the same time.

As each department emphasizes attainment of its own "natural" goals, then, the potential of the total enterprise for serving its markets profitably over the long-run is reduced. With each department striving to optimize its own performance, the company's over-all performance is less than optimal.

CONCLUSION—THE MARKETING CONCEPT

Three main features distinguish the company managed according to the philosophy symbolized by the marketing concept: (1) adoption by management of a predominantly market, or customer, orientation (2) subordination of departmental goals to a set of goals for the company as a whole, and (3) unification of company operations so as both to serve markets effectively and to meet company goals.

Market Orientation

In adopting a market, or customer, orientation, management focuses on the market (i.e., on the customers, and their wants and desires) primarily and on the product only incidentally. Thus, in the company operating under the marketing concept, a good deal of emphasis is put on using marketing research to keep abreast of market trends and developments and on doing research and development work (even if it results in making present products obsolete). Specifically, management exerts every effort to keep up-to-date on the changing answers to five important questions:

1. What business are we really in?
2. Who are our customers?
3. What do they want and desire?
4. How can we communicate most effectively with them?
5. How can we best distribute our products to them?

Formulation of Company Goals

Top management takes the lead in formulating a set of company goals to which goals of individual departments are subordinated. Thus, tangible recognition is given to the fact that the company exists to achieve something as a company rather than as a collection of uncoordinated individual departments. Such "total company goals" as achieving a given profit level or a certain return on the investment become of prime importance. Therefore, in working toward achievement of a given profit level, for instance, the production department is made aware that obtaining low manufacturing costs is not enough. Similarly, the marketing department is guided towards placing less emphasis on high sales volume and more on making profitable sales. Likewise, the financial department is alerted to top management's desire not only to provide a satisfactory short-run return for the stockholders but to serve the company's markets profitably over the long-run. In other words, every effort is bent toward optimizing the company's performance over the long-run, recognizing that this undoubtedly means less than optimal performance of individual departments.

Unification of Company Operations

In seeking to achieve company goals through effectively serving chosen markets, management works continuously to unify company operations—i.e., to weld the different parts of the organization into an efficient operating system. Such an orchestration of effort is required in order to correct organizational deficiencies, such as the communications difficulties arising among the increasing number of specialists employed and the parallel tendency for their proliferation to go uncoordinated. Management strives, in other words, to secure a "synergistic" effect—to achieve greater total results than could be obtained by the individual departments working separately and not coordinated with each other. Therefore, a company managed under the marketing concept must plan, organize, coordinate, and control its entire operation as *one system directed toward achieving a single set of objectives applicable to the total organization.*

QUESTIONS AND PROBLEMS

1. Why do marketing changes generally seem to appear first in consumer goods markets rather than in industrial goods markets?

2. List five products with markets more closely related to the total number of households than to the total population.

3. Distinguish between disposable income and discretionary income. How closely is discretionary income related to discretionary spending?

4. Analyze the trends existing in the income distribution pattern of the U.S. What direction do you expect future trends will take? Why? What will be the significance for marketing?

5. Explain how technological change contributes to the rising tempo of competition.

6. What is "technological forecasting?"

7. Discuss how the growth of different mass media has affected the role of advertising in marketing.

8. What new types of distributive institutions have appeared recently? What "niches" have they filled?

9. Outline the main environmental factors that have helped bring about adoption of the marketing concept. Do you anticipate that these factors will continue to play an influential role in shaping the nature of marketing in the future? Why or why not?

10. Explain the differences between a company with a "product" orientation and one with a "market" orientation.

11. As an enterprise grows, there is a tendency for communications to lose effectiveness. Why? What can be done to improve this condition?

12. How can less than optimal over-all performance result in a company when each of its departments emphasizes attainment of its own goals?

13. What *businesses* are the following concerns really in?
    a. A commercial bank
    b. A city bus system
    c. An electric utility
    d. A hotel
    e. An outdoor movie

14. Explain fully what the marketing concept is all about. How would you convince a skeptical businessman of its value?

3

THE MARKETING ORGANIZATION

The organization is the mechanism through which management translates its business philosophy into action. As this philosophy changes, management not only shifts its orientation and sets new company objectives but also makes changes in the organization. In a company making the transition to the marketing concept, top management: (1) emphasizes a market, or customer, orientation, (2) adopts a set of company goals consistent with that orientation and to which departmental goals are subordinated, and (3) unifies operations organizationally, both to satisfy the market's wants and desires and to achieve company goals.

In moving toward the marketing concept, especially significant changes occur in the marketing organization. It serves as the company's main link with the market and, in adapting company operations to fit the market environment more appropriately, decisions are made and implemented on such marketing controllables as products, brands, prices, marketing channels, physical distribution, advertising, and personal selling. The marketing organization provides the vehicle not only for making these decisions but for implementing them. It includes both a network of executives responsible mainly for making decisions (the executive organization) and subordinate groups concerned primarily with carrying out these decisions (the working organization).

Discussion in this chapter focuses mainly on the organizational problems and decisions involved in making the transition to the marketing concept. However, we must first review some aspects of modern organization theory and analyze the relationship of basic company goals to the marketing organization. This sets the stage for our analysis of the organizational implications of the marketing concept. After this analysis, discussion shifts to certain important issues involved in structuring the internal organization of the marketing department.

MODERN ORGANIZATION THEORY—SOME PERTINENT ASPECTS

Modern organization theory unites what is valuable in traditional organization theory with findings and principles from the social and natural sciences, resulting in a systematic and integrated view of human organization. Modern organization theory, in other words, is not a completely new development; it consists of traditional theories of organization incorporated with newer theories and concepts. However, in this section, our main concern is with certain concepts associated more closely with the "newer" organizational theory. Concepts and notions drawn from traditional organization theory are introduced into the discussion in succeeding sections.[1]

The Organization as a System

Perhaps the most noteworthy characteristic of modern organization theory is that it is mainly based upon a "micro" point of view—the study of the organization as an integrated whole. This study has an analytical foundation and relies heavily upon empirical data and the relationships of many factors.[2] This leads modern organization theory to look upon an

---

[1] For an overview of modern organization theory, see: J. A. Litterer, *Organizations: Structure and Behavior* (New York: John Wiley & Sons, 1963). For an interesting collection of articles, see: W. A. Hill and D. M. Egan, *Readings in Organization Theory* (Boston: Allyn and Bacon, Inc., 1966).

[2] For supporting data, modern organization theory relies heavily on "microcosmic" research studies, generally drawn from scholarly journals of the previous twenty years or so.

organization as a "system," and, because of this orientation, analysis emphasizes consideration of the following questions:

1. What are the strategic parts of the system?
2. What is the nature of their mutual dependency?
3. What are the main processes in the system linking its parts together and facilitating their adjustment to each other?
4. What are the system's goals?

In studying a particular organization, the modern organization theorist considers the surrounding environment as well as the organization itself. Frequently, in fact, it is meaningful to think of a particular company as being a part (i.e., a "subsystem") of its environment (i.e., a larger system). Similarly, the internal workings of the organization may be regarded as being comprised of numerous smaller "subsystems" (i.e., of individuals and groups). This point of view provides frameworks for analyzing the possible effects of decentralization and delegation of authority, enlargement of job responsibility at different organizational levels, participation at all levels in making decisions, and participation by individuals in appraising their own performances. Considerable attention is paid, too, to each individual's expectations concerning his job, the demands that the job makes on the individual, and conflicts that result; relations between formal and informal groups provide a framework for this type of analysis.[3]

Communication As a Linking Process

Considered as a system, the parts of an organization are not only interrelated but are meshed together by certain processes, one of the most important being communication. Communication is defined as "the process of passing information and understanding from one person to another." Thus, an organization may be thought of as a number of intertwined communication networks. Communications involves more than techniques, more than the passing of information through formal media, more than the manipulation of such techniques as non-directive interviewing and merit rating. For optimum efficiency in communications, there must be not only a desire to communicate but *esprit de corps* in the organization. Communication and the organization, then, are inseparable, and the manage-

---

[3] In fact, a substantial part of modern organization theory rests on research findings in social psychology relative to reciprocal patterns of behavior stemming from role demands generated by both formal and informal groups, and "whole" perceptions (i.e., of the nature of the total organization) peculiar to the individual.

ment of an organization largely involves the solution of problems in communication.

System "Balance"

"Balance" among the various parts of the system is also important to the modern organizational theorist. Balance relates to the maintenance of harmonious relationships within the organization, particularly under conditions of change, which will permit achievement of over-all system (i.e., company) goals with as much efficiency as possible. Therefore, subordination of the goals of subsystems to those of the system itself is a critical aspect of the problem of maintaining balance. Another involves effective coordination of the several subsystems with respect both to day-to-day operations and to the implementation of longer-range plans. "Perfect" balance is rarely, if ever, attainable, but represents instead an "ideal" state toward which the managers of an organization work. Things could hardly be otherwise in the highly dynamic environments within which modern organizations exist.

COMPANY GOALS AND THE MARKETING ORGANIZATION

Any organization is more than just a group of people.[4] In order to exist at all, an organization must have goals or objectives. Therefore, an organization consists of a group of people brought together to participate in a common effort directed toward accomplishing certain goals. The basic objectives of a company, then, indicate, to a large extent, what the company wants to be, since they tend to override and to permeate the rest of its administration. Seven such objectives having important implications for marketing organizations are discussed below.

1. DESIRED FINANCIAL RESULTS   Traditionally, business enterprises are intended to be economic institutions. It is reasonable to assume, therefore, that the desire for profit lies behind the establishment of most companies. The organizers, in other words, generally anticipate that a company's operations will generate profits. Furthermore, once a company's operations are under way, profits must be forthcoming on a sufficiently regular basis to permit its continued survival.

---

[4] Much of the content of this section was suggested by Michael J. Thomas of Syracuse University.

How much profit is desired and how it is measured varies with the enterprise. Some companies set profit objectives in terms of a given number of dollars to be received within a specified period, others in terms of a certain percentage of profit on sales volume, others in terms of a given rate of return on the stockholders' investment or total assets employed. Many other variations of profit objectives exist.

The company's profit objective is important for the marketing organization. It has implications both for the amount of sales volume that should be obtained and for the bounds within which costs should be held. Also significant is the time span within which a target profit objective is to be reached, inasmuch as this span influences trade-off relationships between investments for current profit and those for future payoff.[5]

2. DESIRED PLACE IN THE INDUSTRY   In each industry in which it participates, a company defines its desired place in terms of such variables as: size of operation, major function (manufacturing, wholesaling, retailing, etc.), quality and price levels for its products, and specialization or diversification of its activities. Different decisions on these variables result in different types of marketing organization. For instance, a company that strives to be the largest in its industry (in terms of sales volume) requires a different type of marketing organization than one seeking to build the reputation of being the first to introduce product innovations to the market or one that wants to have the reputation for the highest quality.

3. DISPOSITION TOWARD CHANGE   Does the company emphasize stability or dynamics? Whichever emphasis the company chooses has a profound influence on both its character and administration. The company emphasizing stability, for example, is unwilling to take any but the smallest risks, stays with established operating patterns as long as possible, and resists making changes until others have proven the value beyond all doubt. By contrast, the firm emphasizing dynamics, maintains a continuous search for better ways of doing things, is aggressive in implementing changes, and is willing to assume substantial risk in pioneering and adopting innovations.

By and large, a company's attitude toward change determines the type of people who are attracted to its employ and also the scheme by which they are welded into an organizational framework. Clearly, firms operating under the marketing concept have opted in favor of emphasizing dynamics. They recognize the necessity for making continual adjustments in the company's operations and organizational structure to adapt to changing market requirements and competitive conditions.

[5] On this matter, see: H. I. Ansoff, *Corporate Strategy* (New York: McGraw-Hill Book Co., 1965), pp. 32-33.

4. SOCIAL PHILOSOPHY   What kind of business citizen does the company want to be? In setting this objective, top management takes into account:

(a) Community relations—Will the firm be a "good neighbor?" Will it encourage its executives and other employees to contribute to, and participate in, community functions? Or will it be content just paying local taxes and obeying local laws?

(b) Governmental responsibility—Both local and national governmental regulations and activities infringe upon the company's operations in numerous ways: markets, prices, taxes, competition, and the like.

The basic objectives controlling a company's relationships with the community and governmental units permeate and affect the operations of all company departments and, most certainly, operations of the marketing department.

5. POSTURE WITH RESPECT TO COMPETITION   Closely related to a company's desire to be a particular kind of business citizen is its desired posture toward its competitors. If a company desires a "lone wolf" type of image, it has little or no contact with competitors, and does not participate in any cooperative efforts (such as industry-financed research or advertising). Most companies, however, cooperate to some extent with their competitors. In nearly all industries, for instance, companies affiliate with industry trade associations for some purposes. Industry cooperation, nevertheless, must be within certain legal bounds; legislation and court decisions dictate the extent to which competitors can enter into price agreements, allocate customers or territories, and the like. Therefore, in deciding how far to go with industry cooperation, a company also must consider the possibility of legal complications. A company's posture with respect to its competition, then, has direct implications for the marketing organization such as, for example, whether or not it will incorporate features permitting aggressive selling and advertising.

6. DESIRED CUSTOMER SERVICE IMAGE   There is a world of difference between a company seeking long-run customer benefit and satisfaction and one emphasizing quick and "one-time" sales. This facet of the company image is important not only to customers, but to all company departments producing, selling, and servicing the product line. Thus, marketing organization is influenced significantly by the nature of this desired image.

7. Relationships with Suppliers   Some companies attempt to derive profit by playing one competing supplier against another. Others try to develop lost-lasting relationships with suppliers, believing that in the long run this results in the most economical and dependable sources of supply. Numerous variations exist between these two extreme positions. The nature of a company's desired relationships with suppliers has indirect but important implications for marketing organization, since such relationships affect product quality, repair and replacement parts, pricing practices, and the like.

In some situations, too, a company deliberately seeks to establish reciprocal relationships with its suppliers, whereby they agree to buy from it part or all of their requirements of the types of products produced by the company. In other cases, a company's suppliers take the initiative in setting up such relationships. Wherever reciprocal relationships of this sort exist, provisions must be incorporated in the organization for close coordination of marketing and purchasing policies and activities.

MARKETING ORGANIZATION
AND THE TRANSITION TO THE MARKETING CONCEPT

How far a company moves toward adoption of the marketing concept is, of course, a decision for top management. Numerous factors, including such things as executives' personalities and backgrounds of experience, influence this decision, but perhaps the most critical is top-management's appraisal of the current state and probable future intensity of competition. As brought out in the previous chapter, the competitive tempo rises with: the development of mass markets composed of affluent masses, acceleration in the pace of technological change, appearance and growth of multiple mass communications media, and development of new marketing channels and changes in established channels. The more directly these environmental trends impinge upon a company's operations, the more severe is its competition, and the more crucial is the marketing concept to its survival.

Because the marketing organization is positioned between the rest of the company and the market and is highly sensitive to competitive moves, its management must bear major responsibility for bringing the need for the adoption of the marketing concept to top management's attention. However, when top management has not yet adopted this concept, marketing management must accept company objectives (as derived from the then-current business philosophy) as constraints within which marketing decisions must be made and carried out, until the philosophy is modified.[6] As top management's business philosophy shifts, the design and structure of the marketing organization also changes.

Historical Shifts in Top Management's Business Philosophy

PRODUCTION EMPHASIS   During the era when production problems were regarded as of prime importance, top management generally recognized the need only for a highly skeletal marketing organization. A slow rate of technological change made product changes infrequent, marketing channels were well-defined and adhered closely to traditional patterns, little personal selling or advertising was required due to the absence of strong competition, and pricing was mainly on the basis of what the market would bear. Under these conditions, then, the marketing organization was little more than an adjunct to the factory, charged with physically distributing its output.

PERSONAL SELLING EMPHASIS   Later, as introduction and refinement of mass production techniques caused greatly increased factory outputs, top management gradually shifted its main concern from production problems to personal selling problems. Typically the key problem became one of selling at as high a price as possible what the factory could turn out. Advertising and other marketing activities were given definitely a supporting role, being viewed mainly as means for making personal selling more effective. The products and the quantities of each to be manufactured were determined according to what the factory was capable of producing, and the sales force was charged with selling that output. Thus, for most companies, the sales organization either constituted the entire marketing organization or else was placed in a position dominating other marketing activities such as advertising.

MARKET EMPHASIS   More recently, growing numbers of top managements have recognized that rather than focusing solely on what the factory can produce, it makes far more sense to determine what consumers want and then design and manufacture products capable of satisfying those wants. There has been, consequently, a gradual change from an orientation concerned with, or fixation on, selling products to one of serving target markets.

With this change in orientation, far-sweeping organizational changes have occurred. Marketing research has become an important

---

[6] For a thoughtful discussion of this situation, see: J. M. Rathmell, *Managing the Marketing Function* (New York: John Wiley & Sons, Inc., 1969), pp. 311-15.

component of marketing organizations, as it has seen increasing use in improving management's knowledge and understanding of the market. Product research and development has gained greatly in organizational stature since, as the last chapter brought out, income and other changes have made consumers steadily more sophisticated in what they will accept and buy, while at the same time technological advances have made it possible to tailor product characteristics more closely to what consumers want. Advertising's stature in the marketing organization has been elevated, as development and expansion of mass communications media have helped make advertising a more powerful element in marketing strategy—even though personal selling, and the sales department, continue as the "backbone" of most marketing organizations. Similarly, changes in marketing channels, in operating methods of distributive institutions, and in physical distribution facilities, have made channel and distribution decisions more important and have earned a place in a growing number of marketing organizations for specialized units to make and implement distribution decisions. Finally, in industry after industry, the competitive tempo has risen, making pricing decisions of greater importance and sometimes causing reallocations of decision-making authority in this area. Summing up, then, all types of marketing decisions have been rising in importance, and this is being reflected in changed organizational structures. More and more companies have moved toward adoption of the marketing concept.[7]

Company Organization and the Marketing Concept

A company that adopts the marketing concept should restructure its organization accordingly. Fairly often, however, the necessity for restructuring goes unrecognized. As one writer comments, "Companies may have the will and the desire to serve the customer, but all too often they are inadequately organized to do so. Proper organization must result in a total integration and coordination of all of the factors that can influence the final sale."[8] There must be, in other words, total integration and coordination of all corporate functions (marketing, research and development, manufacturing, financial, etc.) into a single operating system directed toward achieving company goals and, at the same time, effectively serving the market and its changing wants and desires. This does not mean that

---

[7] For an interesting account of the emerging importance of marketing in one company (Pillsbury), see: R. J. Keith, "The Marketing Revolution," *Journal of Marketing*, January, 1960, pp. 35-39.

[8] A. E. Cascino, "Organizational Implications of the Marketing Concept," in W. Lazer and E. J. Kelley (eds.), *Managerial Marketing; Perspectives and Viewpoints*, rev. ed. (Homewood, Ill.: Richard D. Irwin, Inc., 1962), p. 371.

marketing or any other function should dominate the organization. It means that all functions should be welded into an operating system whose components are so orchestrated that the market is served effectively while company goals are being reached.

The organizational structure of a company operating under the marketing concept is subject to frequent, sometimes drastic, modifications. Changes in environmental factors, such as technological breakthroughs by competitors or changes in distributive institutions, require reappraisals of the appropriateness of the present organization and possible modifications. The organization must not be so rigid that it is difficult to adapt to changing conditions as they unfold. Ideally, the organization should have a built-in flexibility that causes it naturally to adapt to unstable conditions, when problems and requirements for action come up which cannot be broken down and allocated to particular specialists within a clearly-defined hierarchy. In other words, the hierarchy itself should change with changing conditions, each of its members performing his specialty according to his understanding of the company's objectives. In this type of organization system:

> Jobs lose much of their formal definition in terms of methods, duties, and powers, which have to be redefined continually by interaction with others participating in a task. Interaction runs laterally as much as vertically. Communication between people of different ranks tends to resemble lateral consultation rather than vertical command.[9]

The need for built-in flexibility is especially evident in the top-management structure. There must be a capability for adjusting smoothly and rapidly not only to continuing business expansion but to significant changes in products and markets, to mergers and acquisitions, to sudden shifts in competitors' strategies, and the like. That is why more and more companies are setting up "offices of the president," where important policy decisions are taken not by the chief executive alone but by a small group of executives working closely with him.[10] Among others, General Electric, Boise Cascade, General Mills, Mead, Borden, and Pet have all set up such presidential offices from which the president and his deputies oversee the company's most vital operations, and in which each contributes not only his special expertness but his general decision-making skills to the joint solution of company problems. Besides providing built-in flexibility at the top-management level, proponents say the "office of the president" scheme brings a broader sweep of company operations under continual surveillance

---

[9] T. Burns and G. M. Stalker, *The Management of Innovation* (London: Tavistock Publications Ltd., 1961), p. 5.

[10] A. R. Forest, "Marketing Information Center," *Sales/Marketing Today*, August-Sept. 1969, p. 10.

from the top, provides a back-up system should a key executive die or leave, and constitutes a high-level training ground for succession.[11]

Communications, Decisions, and the Organization

Communications, decisions, and the organization are so interrelated as to be inseparable in practice. A decision occurs, according to Dorsey, on "the receipt of some kind of communication; it consists of a complicated process of combining communications from various sources and it results in the transmission of further communication(s)."[12] Communications, being required for decisions, constitute the life blood of the functioning organization. So communication is one of the main processes linking the parts of the organizational system together and facilitating their adjustment to each other. March and Simon describe the communication networks, or channels, as follows:

> Associated with each program is a set of information flows that communicate the stimuli and data required to evoke and execute the program. Generally this communication traverses definite channels, either by formal plan or by the gradual development of informal programs. Information and stimuli move from sources to points of action; instructions move from points of decision to points of action; information of results moves from points of action to points of decision and control.[13]

Some communiction networks are planned, others develop through usage. The planned networks follow the hierarchical lines of authority as set up by the formal organization; unplanned networks develop among individuals with common backgrounds or interests who establish informal groups and who find communication easy or necessary. New technologies, such as the installation of a data processing system in a company, cut across superior-subordinate work relationships, affecting the jobs of people in different departments and work groups. Superimposing a vertical organization on such lateral relationships as this results in unplanned, or informal, communications networks. Thus, a marketing researcher, in setting up a plan for processing information obtained from a consumer survey, may seek directly the help of a computer programmer,

---

[11] See "The 'New Management' Finally Takes Over," *Business Week*, August 23, 1969, p. 60.

[12] J. T. Dorsey, Jr., "A Communication Model for Administration," *Administrative Science Quarterly*, December 1957, p. 309.

[13] J. G. March and H. A. Simon, *Organizations* (New York: John Wiley & Sons, 1958), pp. 166-67.

who works in a different department, instead of going through his and the other man's "bosses." In such cases, information feedback is most likely to come through informal, rather than formal, communications channels.

For efficiency's sake, then, marketing management must recognize the existence of informal as well as formal organizational structures. Informal structures develop either because of failures to provide for all communication and decision-making needs within the formal structure, or because other channels of communication are easier or more natural for the communicators. For example, there are two types of functional marketing activities: those that are solely the concern of marketing and those that are the joint concern of marketing and one or more other parts of the organization. The first type includes personal selling, while the second type embraces such activities as product research and development, production planning and scheduling, and (fairly often) physical distribution. The first type can be clearly and easily defined in the organizational structure, but the second type involves cooperative effort among different parts of the organization and does not usually show up on formal organization charts. In many instances, in fact, the second type receives no formal recognition anywhere and simply exists and operates on an informal basis.

Organizational Responsibility for Marketing Policy Formulation

As a company reorganizes in line with the philosophy of the marketing concept, it should take a hard look at the ways in which responsibility is assigned for formulating marketing policies. Traditionally, sales force management, advertising, marketing research, and the building and maintaining of relationships with marketing channels, have been recognized as marketing activities. Traditionally, too, responsibility for formulating policies in these areas has been assigned to marketing executives. But certainly other departments, such as production and finance, have strong interests in how salesmen are trained and operate, in the messages conveyed through advertising, and in the type of information gathered through marketing research. Thus, in the modern organization, good reasons exist for encouraging non-marketing executives to participate in making policies for these areas of marketing.

By the same token, marketing executives should share the responsibility for making policies elsewhere in the organization when there are important marketing implications. One such area is pricing, which very often is the responsibility of the treasurer, controller, or production manager, or some combination of these executives. Another is the product line, which historically has been the province of production, or research and development, or both. Still another is physical distribution, involving control over inventories, transportation, and storage, which often has either been under the direction of the production department or else segregated into a separate department. Still another involves financial controls over marketing operations, traditionally a responsibility of the accounting department or controller.

There is little question that policies with respect to pricing, products, physical distribution, and financial controls over marketing have important implications for marketing. By their very natures, these are interfunctional activities and, as such, marketing executives should share the responsibility for formulating policies on them. Especially when a company is trying to adjust its operations to conform with the marketing concept, every effort must be made to "reduce the height of walls between departments." The main way to do this is to discard traditional authority and job-task relationships whenever they prevent or act as deterrents to achieving effective coordination of the organization as an operating system.

Integration of Marketing Activities

As executives have come to recognize marketing as a major business function, one requiring coordination of numerous subactivities, they have been led to reexamine the ways in which marketing activities are incorporated in the formal organizational structure. Sales force management, advertising, and marketing research, for example, traditionally all have been organized as separate departments reporting directly to top management. Integration, or centralization, of these activities under a single high-ranking marketing executive, by improving coordination, should increase marketing effectiveness. There has been a strong trend in this direction in American companies.

INTERNAL ORGANIZATION OF THE MARKETING DEPARTMENT

If a marketing department is very small, its executives necessarily must handle all types of problems. But in a large marketing department, the fact that there are numerous executives and a multiplicity of responsibilities makes dividing the work not only desirable but important. Therefore, in a large marketing organization, a great many executives are specialists, with technical knowledge of activities such as advertising, marketing research, or physical distribution. Responsibility for dividing the work among these specialists and others' rests squarely on the chief marketing executive's shoulders.

The Chief Marketing Executive

Increasing centralization of marketing responsibilities and growing complexity of the marketing function in large companies has led top management into recognizing the need for a new kind of chief marketing executive. All chief marketing executives, of course, must be extremely versatile and possess a high degree of administrative skill. The new chief marketing executive in the larger organization no longer is directly in charge of the sales organization. He delegates authority for sales force management to a subordinate, the general sales manager. This new type of chief marketing executive has been further described as being:

> . . . more thoughtful, sometimes skilled more in handling ideas than in handling men. He is more objective, analytical, less emotionally involved in his assignment. He has begun demanding research—searching for ideas, thinking of both strategy and tactics.[14]

Because the new type of chief marketing executive is not directly involved in managing the sales force, he has more time to plan other marketing activities and to coordinate the work of the various staff divisions, which have grown both in numbers and influence. Established staff divisions, such as advertising, marketing research, and credit management, now brought together under his direction, exert a greater total impact on marketing strategy and tactics. New staff divisions, such as product management and physical distribution, are occupying increasingly important niches in the marketing organization.

Dividing Marketing Line Authority

Line authority carries with it the *general power to require* execution of orders by those lower in the organizational hierarchy. Nearly all executives, at least those with people reporting to them, have some line authority. But, by definition, line executives are those in the direct chain of command whose jobs consist mainly of managing subordinates who directly accomplish the company's objectives. In a marketing organization, then, the chief marketing executive is also its top line executive, and the

[14] D. R. Longman, "The Role of the Marketing Staff," *Journal of Marketing,* July, 1962, pp. 31-32.

direct chain of command runs from him down through the sales organization (since it is the salesmen who ultimately and directly perform the work leading to company objectives). However, since the chief marketing executive usually assigns the over-all responsibility for managing the sales organization to a subordinate, the sales vice president or the general sales manager then is regarded as the marketing organization's principal line executive.

The principal line executive manages the sales force directly when it is small. But as the sales force becomes larger, a point is reached where line authority must be divided. Normally this is done by splitting the sales force into sub-groups. Each sub-group is then placed in charge of a line assistant who reports to the top sales executive.

The underlying reason for dividing line authority geographically is to improve the sales force's effectiveness, accomplished by increasing the frequency of executive contacts with salesmen and by simplifying and strengthening their supervision. Each subordinate sales manager devotes his major efforts toward improving the performances of the salesmen under him. Whether he is permanently based in his assigned area or not makes little difference—increases in the availability and speed of public transportation have all but eliminated the need for this requirement, which once was nearly universal. The Underwood-Olivetti Company, for example, houses all of its regional sales executives in the New York home office in order to maximize communication and coordination at the management level; however, these executives are frequent commuters to their assigned regions.

GEOGRAPHIC DIVISION   When a sales force is deployed over a wide geographical expanse, line authority is often divided on a geographical basis. The total marketing area is split into smaller units, often called "regions" or "divisions," and regional or division sales managers are placed in charge. Large national organizations covering the market intensively sometimes further subdivide the line authority under each regional or division sales manager among district managers. Division of authority along geographical lines is especially appropriate when the nature of the market or the characteristics of consumers or both vary significantly from region to region. In such instances, each sales region or division can adapt its selling methods more closely to the needs and customs of local markets.

PRODUCT DIVISION   Sometimes a company's products dictate the organization of its sales force. When variations among products require considerably different selling methods and different technical knowledge on the salesmen's parts, line authority may be divided on a product basis and separate sales forces set up for each product or group of products. General Electric requires different kinds of salesmen to sell large electrical generators and small household appliances. Generator salesmen need considerable technical training and must be prepared to wait years sometimes for their first order from a utility company; small appliance salesmen need very little technical training and perform rather routine selling work. It would be wasteful to use the more technically-trained men to sell both types of products, so separate groups of salesmen are maintained, each qualified to sell its particular product line and each reporting to its own sales executive.

Maintaining separate sales forces for different products is expensive, because it frequently results in several salesmen covering the same geographical areas. For this reason, the benefits should clearly outweigh the extra cost. Benefits are greatest for companies selling broadly diversified lines of products, for those reaching different markets with different products, and for those with unique selling problems for individual products.

CUSTOMER OR MARKETING CHANNEL DIVISION   When customers or marketing channels for a product or group of products vary substantially, it may be appropriate to divide line authority and set up separate sales forces on that basis. A power-saw manufacturer may sell the identical product to two very different markets—the lumber industry and the construction industry. These two markets have different geographical characteristics (lumbering is heavily concentrated in the Northwest and Southeast; whereas construction is broadly distributed relative to population and industrial concentration) and different buying practices. Under these circumstances, separate sales forces probably should be used.

Many consumer goods producers sell the same products through multiple marketing channels. Part of the factory's output may reach the consumer through wholesale distributor and independent retailer channels, while another part may go through chain stores buying directly from the factory. Still another part may be sold through export middlemen to foreign markets. The type of selling required in each case may be quite different, and the number and kinds of buyers will vary. (It takes, for example, only a very few salesmen to reach all chain store buying offices in the United States, but it takes dozens or hundreds to reach all wholesalers.) Producers with such varied marketing channels often find it advantageous to split line authority by channels and to organize separate sales forces for each channel.

DIVIDING LINE AUTHORITY ON MORE THAN ONE BASIS   A great many companies use more than one basis for dividing line authority over the sales force. Large sales forces require several levels of management, and different methods of division may be used at different levels. When product differences dictate a division of line authority according to products, the sales force may be divided accordingly; but if further division is required, it may be done geographically. The resulting organization would provide sales specialization both in terms of different products and geographical differences in the market.

Division of Marketing Staff Authority

Staff people theoretically have purely advisory roles with no place in the command structure and without the right to give orders, but this clear distinction does not exist in practice. The nature of the staff executive's work gives him an intimate and broad view of line executives' problems that almost inevitably bestows on him *informal* authority. Added to this is the fact that staff work is intellectual in character. As Pfiffner and Sherwood express it: "Line administrators tend to be conservative, pragmatic, and inclined to make decisions on the basis of their experience and accumulated value systems. The staff person has his time free to gather data, study, reflect, and come up with solutions arrived at through intellectual processes. He is the thinking and planning arm of the organization. He must inevitably wield power." [15] Furthermore, with higher management relying more and more heavily on processed information, the staff authority to advise becomes an authority to *screen* and, thus, to make decisions.

The division and allocation of staff authority is an important organizational decision for marketing management. It involves, in large measure, fact-finding, analysis and planning, and coordinating activities.[16] Generally, division and allocation of staff authority is on the basis of areas of special competence, as will be illustrated in our discussion of Exhibit 3-1.

In the marketing organization, as elsewhere in a company, the informal authority of staff people often extends downward in the management hierarchy. As the chief marketing executive recognizes a staff executive as an expert rather than just an advisor in his area of competence, lower levels of management become aware of this recognition. Thus, they tend to accept staff recommendations as being backed by top management. The development of such a dual chain of command creates a more complicated organizational structure than that implied by the usual organization chart showing formal line and staff relationships.[17]

[15] J. M. Pfiffner and F. P. Sherwood, *Administrative Organization* (Englewood Cliffs, N. J.: Prentice-Hall, Inc., 1960), p. 173.

[16] Pfiffner and Sherwood suggest that three basic elements are involved in staff work: fact-finding, planning, and organizing. They use the term "organizing" in a sense closely akin to coordinating. *Ibid.*, p. 176.

[17] R. Carzo, Jr., "Organizational Realities," *Business Horizons*, Spring, 1961, p. 99.

The Product Manager

One type of marketing executive who does not fit neatly into either the line or staff categories is the product manager. Especially in large multi-product companies, product managers are becoming increasingly common and more important. The main reason is that in many cases, a simple two-way (line and staff) division of marketing authority may cause individual products to receive inadequate attention. As mentioned before, many companies divide line authority in the sales organization geographically or by markets rather than by products. But even where the field sales force is organized according to products, central office staff activities (e.g., advertising) in behalf of all the products normally are headed up by the same individuals. The result, then, too often is that no one executive is specifically responsible for the success or failure of particular products. It is entirely possible that some products will receive too little or too much promotion, that advertising programs for particular products will not be coordinated properly with sales activities, and that changes in customer wants and competitors' actions with respect to individual products will go unheeded. The product manager's position was created in an attempt to fill such vacuums. A product manager serves, in effect, as a deputy marketing director for a particular product or group of products. The nature and scope of his responsibility and authority varies considerably in different companies, but he normally concerns himself with all phases of the planning, execution, and control of marketing activities for his group of products. Thus, the broad scope of his duties tends to make him both a line and staff executive with respect to the products for which he is held responsible.

Organization Under the Marketing Concept

Exhibit 3-1 shows a fairly typical formal marketing organizational structure for a large company operating under the marketing concept. Marketing operations are divided into three principal categories: marketing services (mainly staff responsibilities), management of personal selling (including the line organization and staff activities closely related to sales force operations), and product management (which, as pointed out above, involves both line and staff activities). The subdivisions on the marketing services side illustrate the broad range of staff type responsibilities. Those under the general sales manager, who is the principal line executive in this organization, are: field sales (made up of line executives managing the sales force); sales training (a staff activity directed toward increasing selling efficiency); sales service (a staff activity involving installation, maintenance, and repair services); and physical distribution (concerned with inventory

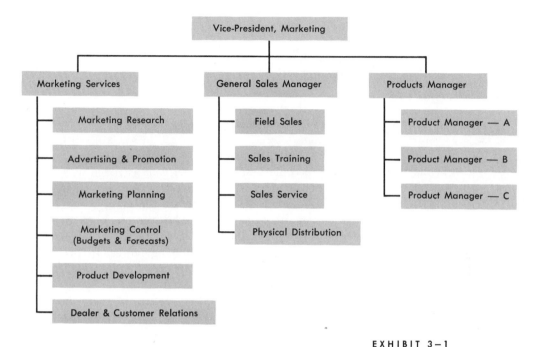

EXHIBIT 3–1

Formal Organization Under the Marketing Concept

management and movement of customers' sales orders). Those under the products manager are in charge of product groups A, B, and C. As brought out earlier, each product manager serves as a deputy marketing director and is responsible for coordinating all marketing activities (staff as well as line) exerted in behalf of his products.

Staff executives generally are concentrated at the central marketing headquarters, because most of their activities tend to be similar for all products, marketing channels, and geographic regions. Centralization allows coordination of their efforts and a pooling of financial resources so that the best available personnel and facilities can be brought together. Without good staff liaison at headquarters, some parts of the organization might make decisions in their own best interest, rather than in the best interests of the company as a whole: e.g., long-range marketing research or R & D projects might be omitted because of their immediate adverse effects on a particular division's profits. A strong central staff keeps division executives aware of the need for giving first consideration to broad company objectives and policies.

In very large marketing organizations, it still may be necessary to provide staff assistance in field sales offices. In such instances, it must be decided whether (organizationally) to place these staff field executives under the authority of central office staff executives or under local line executives. As in other organizational decisions, the solution rests in compromise among the authority, communication, coordination, and human relations needs of the individuals and groups involved.

Delegation of Decision-Making Authority

With the increasing demands on the time of the modern marketing manager, it has become desirable to delegate as much authority as possible to subordinates. Yet, this is something management is particularly reluctant to do. As Koch expresses it, "There are too many managers who simply will not trust their subordinates, and who want to keep the fun of the game to themselves." [18] Increasingly, however, lower-ranking marketing executives are being granted more decision-making power. In overhauling its marketing organization, Mobil Oil Company, for instance, granted regional marketing managers authority to make decisions on service station sites without higher approval.[19] Nevertheless, because so many marketing problem situations are non-routine, the natural tendency is for many chief marketing executives to retain the bulk of decision-making power.

Span of Control

The number of people an individual marketing executive can effectively control varies widely under different circumstances. The span of control, i.e., degree of centralization or decentralization of decision-making authority, is determined by the top marketing executive. His decision may be influenced by such factors as his evaluation of traditional views, his desire for self-reliance among his subordinates, and the importance he attaches to having good communications.

THE TRADITIONAL VIEWPOINT   The notion that a narrow span of control is desirable is basic to traditional organization theory. The argument is that there is some optimum number of men that can be effectively controlled by a supervisor, that optimum number being below the maximum. And, in general, any reduction in span of control is considered an improvement by the traditional organization theorist.

[18] Edward G. Koch, "Three Approaches to Organization," *Harvard Business Review*, March-April 1961, p. 162.

[19] *Business Week*, August 15, 1959, p. 70.

CRITICISM OF TRADITIONAL VIEWPOINT   Herbert Simon has been among the most effective critics of the traditional view. He points out that no two people seem to agree on an ideal span of control—since the executive's personality, the geographic dispersion of those being supervised, and the nature of the work all affect the ideal number of subordinates.[20] Not much research has been done to support either the traditional view or Simon's criticism. Critics of the narrow-span-of-control concept base their arguments on observed inconsistencies and personal observation of effective administrative situations with very broad spans of control.

The main criticism of the narrow span of control is that it results in a proliferation of administrators. In a sales force of 300 salesmen, for example, reducing the span of control from 30 to 15 increases the number of supervisors from 10 to 20 and, since 20 supervisors would be too many for one sales manager to control, it would also be necessary to add a layer of two to four district sales managers between the sales manager and the sales supervisors. Despite such criticisms, however, the traditional concept still has strong advocates.[21]

Willingness to accept the concept of a broad span of control is correlated with an executive's confidence that operations can run smoothly without his constant personal supervision. Lack of such confidence implies ineffective control by the executive. This point is well-illustrated by W. T. Jerome, III:

> Where there is an effective system of executive control, the span of control can be, and should be, greatly extended. The span can be extended because the process of planning, programming, and appraisal if properly conducted serves as a self-policing, self-motivating, sort of control. In other words, the direction of operations is done more by goals, rather than by an ever-present superior.[22]

RELATION TO DELEGATION OF AUTHORITY   If an executive is willing to delegate considerable authority to subordinates, his span of control can be broadened markedly. In fact, for those who consider maximum delegation desirable, a broader span of control is effective in insuring its achievement. An example is the Sears, Roebuck and Company organization:

---

[20] H. A. Simon, "The Proverbs of Administration," *Public Administration Review*, Winter 1946, pp. 53-67.

[21] For a carefully documented defense of the narrow span of control, see: L. F. Urwick, "The Span of Control—Some Facts about the Fables," *Advanced Management*, November 1956, pp. 5-18.

[22] W. T. Jerome, III, *Executive Control—The Catalyst* (New York: John Wiley & Sons, 1961), pp. 129-30.

In an organization with as few supervisory levels as Sears, it is obvious that most key executives have so many subordinates reporting to them that they simply cannot exercise too close supervision over their activities. By this means, substantial decentralization of administrative processes is practically guaranteed.[23]

COMMUNICATION AND SPAN OF CONTROL   The need for constant communication between a superior and his subordinates is often put forth as an argument for a narrow span of control. If this argument is valid, then improvements in communication should make possible broader spans of control. Improvements in management information systems (through electronic data processing and other means) should provide the executive with more complete and accurate information than he could ever obtain through personal communications with his subordinates. In effect, such improvements widen his "reach." [24] As management information systems become increasingly more sophisticated, the need for middle levels of executives to receive, interpret, and transmit information should be greatly reduced.

Committees and the Marketing Organization

A committee is a group of people who meet by plan to discuss and/or make decisions on particular subjects. It is a formal organization set up by management, and contrasts with the informal groups that develop spontaneously or informally.[25] Committees found in marketing organizations are used most frequently for analyzing particular subjects (i.e., for bringing different points of view together) rather than for making decisions.

Whether or not committees, as such, should be allowed to make decisions is debatable. One writer says decision making by committees is acceptable only on a temporary basis to "shore up deteriorating middle-management quality." His argument is that in the long run management by committee makes it difficult for junior executives to make decisions on their own and for top management to appaise their decision-making ability; it removes the risk of poor decisions from the executives' shoulders; it may lose its effectiveness because of domination by a few strong executives; and it slows down the decision-making process.[26]

[23] J. C. Worthy, "Factors Influencing Employee Morale," *Harvard Business Review*, January–February 1950, pp. 61-73.

[24] S. Edmunds, "The Reach of an Executive," *Harvard Business Review*, January–February 1959, pp. 87-96.

[25] H. G. Hicks, *The Management of Organizations* (New York: McGraw-Hill Book Co., 1967), p. 351.

[26] A. Patton, "Old-Fashioned Initiative for Modern Enterprise," *Successful Patterns for Executive Action*, Excerpts edited from the *Harvard Business Review*, 1962, pp. 57-64.

Nevertheless, the strong need for effective coordination in marketing management makes committee management seem promising for certain types of marketing decisions. Examples include the formulation of marketing strategies, the drafting of promotional plans, and planning of the market introductions for new products. Dale has laid down three requirements for effective decision-making by committee: "homogeneity of outlook (toward the goals of their firm), egalitarian status, and heterogeneity of ability.[27] These requirements normally would be met in a committee of top marketing executives.

Some of the criticism leveled against committee management has been generated by its misuse—that is, its use in decision areas where it is not appropriate. James R. Adams points out that creativity is one such area:

> I have never had any objection to group thinking and planning. The more information and the more viewpoints that can be brought to bear on a problem, the better for everyone who is to have a hand in the solution. But it is my honest opinion that a committee can't create an advertisement or intelligently criticize one. Creativity is an individual business.[28]

CONCLUSION

Marketing organization increasingly reflects a fine sense of appreciation for the importance of the market. As a company makes the transition to the marketing concept, it becomes more and more clear that not only should management look to the market for guidance but that the entire company should be geared toward serving that market. Thus, the concept of total company organization, as well as marketing organization, should be dynamic: development of an ideal organizational structure is a task never finished. An organization that is satisfactory today may prove inadequate tomorrow because of changes in the marketing situation. Markets themselves change because of changes in income, shifts of population, changes in tastes and life styles, and the like. These changing characteristics of the market, coupled with technological changes, result in a flow of new products and continual modifications in old products. Furthermore, important developments in mass communications media and in marketing channels have been occurring, and more such changes should be anticipated. A significant change in any market factor, in other words, can reduce the effectiveness of an organizational structure not only for serving the market's needs but as a vehicle for achieving the company's objectives. Since market factors

[27] E. Dale, *Planning and Developing the Organization Structure*, Research Report No. 20 (New York: American Management Association, 1952), p. 28.
[28] *Sparks Off My Anvil* (New York: Harper & Brothers, 1963), pp. 45-46.

are forever in a state of change, continual monitoring and regular reappraisal of organizational effectiveness is imperative.

Additionally, the organizational structure may require modification because of changes in personnel. One basic purpose of formalizing the organizational structure is to strive for optimum use of the talents of a company's personnel, both through identifying and defining responsibilities and through making the best possible assignment for each member of the organization. An organization plan must be tailored, in large part, to the individuals involved. Therefore, important personnel changes require re-evaluations of the organization structure and possibly realignments of responsibilities.

QUESTIONS AND PROBLEMS

1. "Management of an organization largely involves the solution of problems in communication." How does this generalization apply to the management of a marketing organization? Give some examples.

2. What are the implications of the company's profit objective for the marketing organization?

3. Company A wants to have the largest sales volume in its industry. Company B wants to be the first to introduce product innovations in the industry. Assuming that both A and B compete in the same industry, how would these differences in goals likely result in rather different types of marketing organizations?

4. Comment on the various company objectives that have direct implications for a company's marketing organization.

5. Who is responsible for bringing the need for adopting the marketing concept to top-management's attention? Why?

6. As more and more "market emphasis" has permeated top-management's business philosophy, what changes have come about in marketing organization?

7. Should the marketing function dominate the organization in a company operating under the marketing concept? Why or why not?

8. "Good reasons exist for encouraging non-marketing executives to participate in making policies for some areas in marketing." To what extent do you agree (disagree) with this statement? Should the marketing executive also be encouraged to participate in making policies in certain areas outside of marketing?

9. What reasons lie behind the trend in U.S. companies toward centralizing such activities as sales force management, advertising, and

marketing research under a single high-ranking marketing executive? Is this trend likely to continue?

10. Which type of responsibility, staff (e.g., marketing research manager) or line (e.g., sales manager), is likely to give the best preparation for the new job of chief marketing executive?

11. "Staff executives represent the thinking arm of the organization and line executives tend to react more automatically on the basis of experience." Evaluate.

12. Would it be proper to say that line marketing responsibilities and authority are described in the formal organization and that staff responsibilities are described in the formal organization, but staff authority is a part of the informal organization? Which kind of authority is more important?

13. Under what circumstances should a marketing organization divide line authority geographically? By products? By marketing channels? On more than one basis?

14. Why are product managers becoming increasingly common and more important? What does the product manager's job consist of?

15. It has been said that the use of product managers results in conflicting demands on the time of salesmen and excessive intra-company product competition. Comment.

16. "Improved communication between a company's home office and its field salesmen should eliminate the need for district sales managers and supervisors." Comment.

17. When an executive's span of control is widened, his subordinates have more independence and authority. What is the effect on coordination and cooperation? What relationship does span of control have to communication?

18. What are the arguments for and against allowing committees to make certain types of marketing decisions?

19. The almost continuous change in the structure of many marketing organizations has been explained as resulting from the dynamic character of marketing. Do you agree? Why or why not?

20. Does it make much sense to establish separate sales forces to sell the same product to two different markets since a salesman who knows his product should be able to sell it to anyone? Explain.

21. "A man with ten bosses has no boss. Similarly, when decisions are made by a committee, there is no one individual responsible, so decisions tend to be made irresponsibly." Comment.

4

MARKETING MANAGEMENT —DECISION-MAKING

Marketing management is concerned with the direction of purposeful activities toward the attainment of marketing goals. Marketing management *directs*, makes things happen—it does not merely drift with the tide. It *directs purposeful activities*, consciously planned, organized, coordinated, and controlled. Further, managerial effort in marketing is *goal-directed*—marketing, if it is worthy of the name, "knows where it is going."

Marketing management's chief concern is with activities. While management must also be concerned with people, it must be most concerned with what people *do*. People are used to perform the activities required in the effort to reach marketing goals. Similar reasoning applies to the management of money—marketing and other management executives are not so much interested in money *per se* as they are in what money can do. Nor does management manage physical facilities, capital equipment, or anything else *as such*. Management directs the activities that the so-called "factors of production" are capable of performing.

The term "marketing management" is used more often in referring to the marketing operations of manufacturers than to those of middlemen. The main reason is that marketing managers in manufacturing firms manage and make decisions on a wider variety of marketing-type activities. These marketing managers are concerned with the marketing organization, products, brands, marketing channels, physical distribution, pricing, advertising, and personal selling, matters about which marketing managers in all "make and sell" businesses make decisions. Managers in wholesale and retail firms (those in "buy and sell" businesses) make some decisions parallelling those of the manufacturer's marketing manager. In retailing, for example, decisions are made on store organization, merchandise handled, brand policy, pricing, advertising, and personal selling. But retailers make no decisions comparable to those of manufacturers on marketing channels and many phases of physical distribution. Furthermore, whereas middlemen make decisions on such essentially non-marketing problems as financial structure, organization of non-selling personnel, store design, and store equipment, the marketing manager in a manufacturing firm devotes himself primarily to purely marketing-type activities. Regardless of the differences found on different distribution levels, marketing management everywhere is concerned with directing purposeful activities to reach marketing goals.

Sales volume, net profits, and growth in sales volume and in profits are the three main "financial-type" marketing goals and, certainly, these are also the main goals of the company. Top management holds marketing management accountable for initiating and maintaining sales income, for adjusting sales volume and expenses so that profits result, and for seeing to it that the business grows. Even without management, there would still be marketing in the sense that products would somehow find their ways to markets. But such a passive approach likely would result in small sales volumes, few profits, and little growth. Despite the excellence of a product, its chances of ever being sold in volume at a satisfactory profit are restricted if its maker lacks essential management skills. Modern marketing managers do not wait passively for marketing to "just happen." They make it happen!

THE MANAGERIAL FUNCTIONS IN MARKETING

Marketing executives, like other managers, accomplish their work through planning, organizing, coordinating, and controlling functions. These functions are performed by both high-level and low-level marketing executives, by both the marketing vice president and the district sales manager, for example. Differences among the positions are largely in the relative emphasis given to each of the management functions. While the marketing vice president usually emphasizes planning a good deal more than the district sales managers, the district people spend considerably more time on organizing than he does.

Planning

A marketing manager must be a skilled planner. In a manufacturing firm, for example, he cooperates with other executives in setting company-wide goals. Many of these are marketing goals and are expressed in such terms as *planned sales volume* and *expected net profit*. Not only does he help decide how much sales volume and net profit the firm should anticipate, he assumes major responsibility for "making these figures come true." He plans "how the company is to get from where it is to where it wants to go." Furthermore, he decides whether and how each goal, e.g., planned sales volume, should be divided into sub-goals for individual products, specific marketing areas, definite time intervals, or segments of the marketing organization. Considering the company's capabilities and each of his subordinates' strengths and limitations, he parcels out the responsibilities for reaching these sub-goals.

Organizing

A marketing manager must design an appropriate organization for achieving the assigned goals. He must make certain that organizational policies and practices are compatible with marketing plans and that the organization has the necessary capabilities for achieving the marketing goals. Under his direction and guidance, the organization drafts promotional programs and campaigns, sets up marketing methods and procedures, and makes other decisions and takes other actions for executing the policies and implementing the marketing plans. For effective discharge of these responsibilities, a marketing manager needs to be an effective organizer.

Coordinating

A marketing manager in a manufacturing company not only coordinates the work of his different subordinates, he coordinates his own efforts with those of executives in other departments—manufacturing, personnel, finance, and others. He coordinates advertising plans with selling plans and both of these with manufacturing schedules and plans for physical distribution of the goods for sale. Furthermore, he coordinates the manufacturer's promotional efforts with those of the middlemen handling the product.

A marketing manager's need for skill in coordination is further emphasized by his place in the organizational structure. In retailing and wholesaling, marketing managers, whatever their formal titles, are *the* top-management people—they are the chief executives. Marketing managers in manufacturing firms are ordinarily not located at the very top of the organizational structure. Generally they report to the president and executive vice-president and are considered associates of the top-management team, rather than top-management itself. The marketing manager's subordinates are specialists—the sales manager, advertising manager, sales promotion manager, director of marketing research, and sometimes others such as a new products manager, distribution and warehousing manager, and credit manager. He is responsible for coordinating the efforts and activities of all these subordinates. In large companies manufacturing many different products, there are often several marketing managers, each directing marketing activities for some product or line of products. In these situations, the efforts of the different marketing managers are coordinated on an over-all company-wide basis by a marketing vice-president.

Controlling

Marketing managers also need skill in controlling. There are four phases of the controlling function: (1) establishment of performance standards, (2) measurement and "feedback" of performance results, (3) evaluation of actual performance against the standards, and (4) action as indicated by the evaluation. When, for example, a marketing manager assigns sales and profit goals to subordinates, he is establishing standards against which he can later appraise their performances. If a subordinate's performance does not measure up to standard, the marketing manager determines the extent to which the variation was caused by factors within the subordinate's control. Depending on the outcome of this evaluation, he decides on appropriate actions. The primary purpose, then, of any system of controls is to set the stage for decision and action.[1] Effective control keeps the organization "on course" as marketing management steers toward the company's set goals.

[1] On this point and for an intriguing analysis of managerial control, see: W. T. Jerome, III, *Executive Control—The Catalyst* (New York and London: John Wiley & Sons, 1961), p. 70.

BASIC PROBLEM OF MARKETING MANAGEMENT

Marketing management's basic problem is illustrated in Exhibit 4-1. This problem is to adjust the forces under marketing management's control within an environment composed of diverse and ever-changing forces outside its control. These forces are known, respectively, as the *controllables* and the *uncontrollables*. Controllables can be directly influenced by decisions and actions of the individual firm and include such factors as the organization, products, brands, prices, marketing channels, physical distribution, advertising, and personal selling. The uncontrollables consist

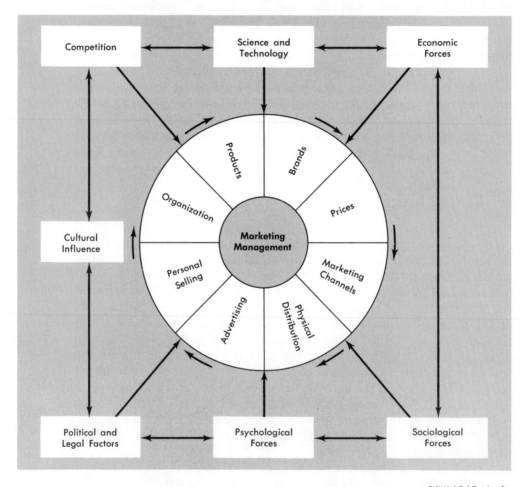

EXHIBIT 4—1

Diagram Illustrating the Basic Problem of Marketing Management mainly of those competitive, scientific and technological, economic, sociological, psychological, and political and legal phenomena which the individual firm can influence only indirectly if at all. Marketing management seeks to manipulate the controllables in terms of the uncontrollables, in ways that result in sales volume, profit, and business growth. As management plans, organizes, coordinates and controls the application and the adjustment of the controllables, it must ever keep the uncontrollables in mind. Collectively, the uncontrollables make up the environment in which the firm must operate, while the controllables are the means by which it adapts to that environment.

For the marketing manager, the uncontrollables include such factors as the amount of consumers' disposable incomes, the distribution of those incomes and the propensity of consumers to spend it, the trend of fashion, the psychological peculiarities and behavior patterns of present and prospective buyers, and the substance and judicial interpretation of the law. But there are still other factors which the marketing manager must take into account in his decision-making that are largely beyond his control. While he has some freedom in selecting marketing channels, for example, he has little control over the structure of the distribution complex—i.e., the types of middlemen, their numbers and locations, their operating characteristics, and their relationships with each other and with various markets. His decision on marketing channels, therefore, is limited by the different combinations of existing types of middlemen that can be (and are willing to be) joined together for that purpose. Furthermore, there are certain situations within the firm itself not under the marketing manager's direct control. He can, for example, exert only indirect influences over production costs and general administrative expenses, yet both are highly relevant in making decisions on prices. This last example emphasizes the marketing manager's need for skill in coordinating marketing decisions with those made elsewhere in the company.

Although the marketing manager can exercise little, if any, influence over the uncontrollables, this in no way lessens their importance to him. As he makes decisions on such controllables as prices, products, the sales force, and advertising, the uncontrollables limit the range of possible and appropriate decisions. At the same time, the interactions of uncontrollable forces often provide an alert marketing manager with opportunities for making profitable readjustments of the controllables. A shift in the distribution of consumer income resulting in increased leisure time for more people, for example, may suggest the need for a new product, or for a change in advertising or distribution policy. Dynamic marketing management is characterized by continual adjustment and readjustment of controllables in relation to the uncontrollables, which make up the environment.

These adjustments must be so made that opportunities inherent in the environment are capitalized upon as fully as possible. Marketing management's responsibility is to make these adjustments; i.e., to direct purposeful activities in such ways as to facilitate the achievement of marketing goals. Working within an environment of uncontrollables, marketing management directs the application of controllables, and it does this through planning, organizing, coordinating, and controlling.

MARKETING DECISION-MAKING

To achieve marketing goals, marketing management must make decisions and carry them out. A marketing manager must be able to recognize problem situations, determine possible alternative solutions, appraise alternatives, and select the most appropriate ones. Finally, he must be capable of taking action. Thus, decision-making results in the choice of a course of action with respect to what should or should not be done in a given problem situation. A decision, therefore, can be defined as the particular course of action chosen by a decision-maker as the most effective means at his disposal for achieving the goal or goals he is currently emphasizing, or for solving the problem that is bothering him.[2]

Decisions may be made either with minimal forethought, or after considerable analysis and deliberation. The first class of decisions, those made quickly, are known as intuitive decisions. The second class, those made only after a great deal of analysis and deliberation, are called rational decisions.

Intuitive Decision-Making

Not every problem is important enough to justify the rigorous analysis and lengthy deliberation needed for rational decision-making. A supermarket manager, for example, cannot spend much time deciding whether to stock one or two dozen crates of tomatoes for his weekend trade. And then there are situations so serious that decisions must be made at once —before the problems get worse. A swimsuit manufacturer, for example, caught with an unexpectedly large inventory near the season's end, cannot delay his decision—the longer he waits, the worse the problem gets. And, even if a marketing executive could consider *all* problems before they became serious, the sheer number of decisions required would force him to make most of them intuitively. In short, most decisions are made intuitively—in marketing and elsewhere in business.

[2] M. H. Jones, *Executive Decision Making*, rev. ed. (Homewood, Ill.: Richard D. Irwin, 1962), p. 5.

In making an intuitive decision, an executive does not draw solely on his "intuition." As far as possible, he draws on his previous experience and his knowledge of similar problem situations, combining common sense and judgment. Certainly, many of his and others' experiences with similar situations may have had their own peculiarities, but an intuitive decision is rarely a pure guess. Only when there is no information whatever is an intuitive decision based wholly on "hunches," and "feelings as to what is best."

Considerations of time and expense may force the marketing manager to make many decisions intuitively, but he should try, as far as possible, to confine his intuitive decision-making to relatively unimportant matters. Minor decisions such as "should we hold our regular weekly sales meetings on Mondays or Fridays" can certainly be made without a great deal of analysis or deliberation. If the decision is in favor of Mondays and it later turns out that Fridays would have been a better choice, the decision can easily be changed. Similarly, the decision-maker can deal with many routine questions as they arise, as he can, for example, in determining whether or not to renew the office's subscription to *Business Week*—not much money "rides on" this decision and, regardless of the decision he makes, he can always reverse it later. All minor decisions are alike in that their consequences, financial and otherwise, are not particularly important, and it is relatively easy to change them if that becomes necessary. Clearly, the implication here is that a marketing manager must be able to discriminate between major and minor problem situations requiring decisions. Such discrimination involves assessments of possible consequences and estimates of the ease with which decisions can be changed—mental processes calling for considerable judgment and keen insight.

Rational Decision-Making

Rational decision-making should be used in all major marketing problem situations. Major marketing problems have two characteristics: (1) Because they arise at irregular intervals, decisions on them should not have to be made very often; and (2) They have important consequences which must be lived with for a long time as it is extremely difficult and "awkward" to change such a decision once it is made. Major marketing problems may involve the introduction of new products, opening up new markets, changing the basic structure of sales organizations, choosing marketing channels, or determining the types and amounts of personal selling and advertising and other elements in "promotional mixes." The consequences of decisions on major marketing problems commonly also affect not only marketing operations but those of other departments. For instance, the decision to introduce a new product not only has consequences for the marketing department but directly affects the production department and may significantly influence such departments as personnel, finance, purchasing, engineering, and accounting. Therefore, another earmark of many major marketing problems is that decisions on them have important consequences across departmental lines. Decisions on major marketing problems are highly critical ones, then, and should be reached only after thorough analyses and serious deliberations. Their possible consequences are of such high and far-reaching importance that a marketing executive cannot risk making them intuitively.

How does a marketing executive make a rational decision? What sort of analysis and deliberation does he use? To start off with, we can say that rational decision-making requires rather formal patterns of thinking and logical approaches to problem-solving. To shed further light on rational decision-making, we must first review some economic theory. Afterwards, we will address ourselves directly to the question of how a marketing executive goes about making rational decisions.

DECISION-MAKING BY "ECONOMIC MAN"   The concept of "economic man," borrowed from traditional economic theory, furnishes the basis for the "theory of decision-making under certainty." The assumptions made about economic man are that: he is fully informed about all problem situations he encounters; he knows all the alternative solutions that are open to him; he absolutely knows the consequences (or outcome) of each alternative; he makes wholly "rational" decisions. Economic man has more than just complete information about all the problems he meets; an important side-assumption makes him even more fortunate—each alternative solution has only *one outcome*, or set of consequences, and it is *certain*. Thus, economic man is also blessed with perfect foresight—he can predict the consequences of his decisions with absolute accuracy.

Armed with complete information and perfect foresight, economic man proceeds to make fully rational decisions. These fully rational decisions are possible because of two other assumptions made about economic man's behavior. The first is that he can *weakly order* alternative solutions according to the desirability of their outcomes. By "weak ordering," we mean that presented with any two sets of consequences, or outcomes, call them A and B, economic man can tell whether he prefers A to B, B to A, or is indifferent to them. Implicit in the notion of "weak ordering" is the idea that economic man can state his preferences but may not necessarily be able to determine *how much more* he prefers his first choice to his second choice, his second to his third, and so on. However, economic man is consistent in all of his preferences—if he prefers A to B and B to C, then he also prefers A to C. The second assumption that makes economic man's rational decision-making possible is that he always chooses that alternative which will maximize something he considers desirable. Writers have differed on the "something" that economic man maximizes in his decision-making. Bentham (1784-1832) believed that economic man made decisions in order either to maximize pleasure or minimize pain. Bentham's successors, including such great economists as Gossen, Walras, Jevons, Menger, and Alfred Marshall, variously assumed that economic man made decisions "to maximize satisfaction," "to maximize utility," or to "maximize net gains."

Although actual marketing decisions are never made under conditions of certainty, the theory provides some helpful hints for the "real world" decision-maker. For one thing, it points up the importance of having information about the problem situation. For another, it suggests that the ability to predict the consequences of alternative courses of action is a definite help. There is the notion, too, that the decision-maker should state his preferences—i.e., weakly order the consequences of different alternatives—and make his choice in line with his goal—i.e., in order to maximize something. The theory implies, then, that the marketing decision-maker should evaluate alternative solutions to a problem in terms of what they will contribute to the goal he is currently emphasizing, then make his choice accordingly.

REQUIREMENTS FOR RATIONAL DECISION-MAKING   What must a decision-maker have in order to make rational decisions? First, he must be able to clearly conceptualize specific problem situations. He cannot reach an intelligent decision unless he has the problem "sized-up" accurately—he has to know what the problem is in order to solve it. Second, he needs pertinent, factual information about the problem and must be capable of using it in his analysis. Both rational and intuitive decisions are more likely to turn out right the more they are based on "facts." Third, he must be able to predict the possible consequences of each alternative solution (course of action). Therefore, conceptualization, information, and prediction are three main keys to rational decision-making. Later we will discuss these keys more fully but, for now, notice what happens when we turn these key requirements around—we have the excuses executives come up with when they attempt to defend an intuitive decision made in a major problem situation. (1) "It's difficult to conceptualize this problem" and "this problem is hard to describe." (2) "We don't have enough pertinent and reliable information about this question" or "we don't have the facts we need," and (3) "It's hard to tell what to predict" and "nobody knows what will happen."

UNCERTAINTY AND RISK   Decisions on major marketing problems are made in the face of uncertainty. Such decisions are, of course, made for the future, and executives—unlike "economic man"—have yet to find a way of predicting the future with absolute certainty. The environment in marketing is one of diverse and ever-changing uncontrollable forces interacting in complex ways, and this makes prediction difficult. The consequences of alternative courses of action are rarely so clear-cut that the best ones can be selected with no risk of being wrong. There are almost always some variables in marketing problems about which the decision-maker has little or no information, and rarely does he have enough time to investigate them all exhaustively. Even if there were sufficient time to gather complete information, the great expense involved would likely outweigh any benefits that might come from such maximum reduction of uncertainty. We must realize that having *all* the facts does *not* mean the elimination of uncertainty but only that the chances of accurate prediction are better than with less complete information. What an executive needs is information that is complete enough for him to be able to conceptualize the problem clearly and to make reasonably accurate predictions of the likely consequences of alternative solutions. Lack of *this* much information often leads to faulty conceptualizations of problems and to compounding errors in predictions.

Progress is being made in supplying today's marketing executive with many facts and figures which were once considered impossible or too expensive to obtain. This results not only from advances in computer technology and the increasing sophistication of management information systems but from the application of new marketing research methodologies. In spite of the growing abundance of information available, marketing decisions are still made in the face of uncertainty and probably always will be. The marketing decision-maker needs not only to recognize the existence of uncertainties but also the ever-present risk that his decisions will be in error.

The "trick" seems to be in estimating just how much risk there is in each alternative solution to a given problem. Decisions are made more readily and with more confidence when an executive thinks of them as *calculated risks*, rather than as "blind stabs in the dark." Since in marketing decision-making there is no such thing as capitalizing on absolute certainties, an executive should strive to make his decisions calculated risks. Ideally, he should have a quantitative expression of the uncertainties present in a problem; as, for example, the chances that some event will or will not occur.[3]

Problem Identification and Conceptualization

Marketing executives almost all agree that most problems are harder to identify than to solve. They say "problems hardly ever come clearly labeled as such—the executive must be perceptive enough to smell them

[3] For an explanation and illustration of a method used for deriving and quantifying probability figures of this sort, see: C. W. Churchman, R. L. Ackoff, and E. L. Arnoff, *Introduction to Operations Research* (New York: John Wiley & Sons, 1957), pp. 559-73.

out." In fact, it is so rare in business for everything to go smoothly that, when this happens, executives worry that something has gone wrong without their knowing it. Clearly, executives cannot deal with problems, i.e., make decisions on them, until they become aware of them and are able to conceptualize their nature.

How does an executive go about recognizing and identifying problem situations? Probably the most promising approach is to search for situations where performance is capable of being improved. If there is some way of measuring performance and of appraising it against some standard, this should be an effective method for identifying problem situations. But standards can be wrong; the setting of standards for appraising marketing performance is still far from being an exact science. Standards that are wrong, set either too high or too low, may be worse than *no* standards at all. Still, if a company has a good system of control—where performance standards are well-defined, where there are efficient methods of recording and reporting actual performance, and where executives make intelligent use of these standards in evaluating performance—the search for situations requiring decision and action is greatly facilitated.

Unfortunately, even the best control system does not call attention to every problem. Quite often, an executive must know about problems that are still germinating and which have not yet become serious enough to be picked up by the control system. This suggests that marketing decision-makers need something similar to the diagnostic skill of a medical doctor. Because a patient doesn't feel well and suspects that something may be wrong, he visits a doctor. Through skillful examination, questioning, and interpretation of the symptoms, the doctor tries to uncover the trouble. When specific symptoms are present in given combinations, the doctor's education and experience enable him to calculate the chances that the patient has certain ailments, and he makes his identification accordingly. A marketing decision-maker also has to be something of a diagnostician. He must be skilled not only in recognizing the symptoms of existing problems, but also in heading off problems-to-be. In this latter respect, marketing decision-makers are in a sense practicing "preventive medicine"—in attempting to anticipate problems and in making and implementing appropriate decisions before problems arise or at least before they become serious.

Like a medical doctor, a marketing decision-maker needs to have access to information about the problem situation. If he is correctly to conceptualize the problem, he must ask the right questions of those who have pertinent information to give. He must also be a keen analyst of the information he already has and of that which is especially gathered to shed light on the problem. In other words, a decision-maker requires skills both in examining what he suspects is a problem situation and in analyzing the available facts pertaining to it.

Thus, for both the medical doctor and the business decision-maker, problems exist only in the context that something "is not functioning properly" or "is about to malfunction." Therefore, there must be some concept of what constitutes proper functioning. When a decision-maker meets a problem, he knows it is a problem either because of warnings flashed by the management control system or, more frequently, because of his skill as a diagnostician. In perceiving problem situations requiring decisions, an executive must constantly rely on his understanding of and "feel for" the norms, standards, or goals relative to which a situation can be identified as a problem.

Logical Analysis of Problem Situations

Earlier we summed up three key requirements of rational decision-making in the words *conceptualization, information,* and *prediction.* The preceding section was mainly concerned with problem identification and was a preliminary explanation of the part played by conceptualization in rational decision-making. The important role of conceptualization will become increasingly clear as we examine the details of different marketing problem situations. For now, however, it is sufficient to think of conceptualization as being the way an executive visualizes or "sees" a particular problem requiring decision. But we should not forget the points that an executive needs *information* in order to identify and conceptualize problems accurately and that an executive also needs information complete enough for him to be able to *predict* the likely consequences of alternative solutions with reasonable accuracy. Information, in other words, is needed for both problem conceptualization and prediction.

The rational decision-making process involves logical analysis of the problem situation. According to two well-known management consultants, there are four steps in any logical analysis of a business problem: [4]

1. Recognize, define, and list all available alternatives. (There is no problem, if there aren't at least two alternatives.)
2. Select a means of measuring each alternative in terms of desired results. (We call this the "decision criterion.")
3. Forecast the results of each alternative in terms of the decision criterion.
4. Construct a "decision rule," by which the most attractive results can be identified and thus the most desirable alternative selected.

Notice how closely these steps resemble economic man's decision-making procedure. Economic man knows all the alternatives; step one tells the real life decision-maker to strive for the same knowledge. Economic

[4] R. E. Ball and A. A. Gilbert, "How to Quantify Decision-Making," *Business Horizons,* Winter 1958, pp. 73-79.

man weakly orders alternatives according to the desirability of their outcomes and predicts (forecasts) these outcomes; steps two and three ask the real life decision-maker to do the same thing. Finally, economic man always chooses an alternative according to a decision rule that seeks to maximize the desirability of the outcome, and the business decision-maker is advised in step four to provide himself with such a decision rule.

Logical analysis of a problem situation starts with the development of alternative solutions or courses of action. The quality of the decision that will result from application of the four-step procedure depends largely on the executive's success in recognizing all the feasible alternatives. Little advice, unfortunately, can be offered as to "a best way" of formulating solutions to marketing problems. But we can say that they are found mainly through the application of "ingenuity" in analyzing a problem. Some alternatives are obvious, but others are much less so. Experience with similar and related problem situations helps, and so does knowledge of marketing in general and of how others have dealt with similar problems. But ingenuity consists of much more than just relying on past experience and imitating other decision-makers. One source suggests another extremely important ingredient of ingenuity:

> We need fresh, original, distinctive, and independent thinking to develop alternatives that are neither copied from the past nor from our neighbor but are original and peculiarly adapted to the circumstances at hand.[5]

So, applying ingenuity in the search for alternative solutions requires that an executive be creative. Past experience, although helpful, is not enough, since what were appropriate solutions to yesterday's problems may not be appropriate to today's. Nor can a decision-maker safely imitate the solutions to similar problems adopted by others, for every company is to some extent unique. Thus, two companies with "similar" problems often arrive at quite different solutions, if each chooses the most appropriate solution for its particular set of circumstances. In developing alternatives, an executive must try very hard to be creative in his thinking and outlook— he should be critical of stereotyped solutions and look for ones that are uniquely suited to the problem at hand.

Marketing Goals, Decision Criteria, and Decision Rules

Management consists of goal-directed effort and, in many respects, this fact clears away much of the mystery in marketing decision-making. The

[5] W. H. Newman and C. E. Summer, Jr., *The Process of Management* (Englewood Cliffs, N.J.: Prentice-Hall, 1961), p. 278.

goals management strives to reach or those implicit in given problem situations are the sources of the criteria according to which alternative courses of action can be determined and appraised. Marketing decision criteria are, in short, derived from marketing goals. Applying these criteria to alternative solutions is management's method of weighing the relative appropriateness of each proposed solution. Suppose, for example, that a marketing executive must choose between two possible prices for a product. How should he decide which to use? He needs both a *decision criterion* and a *decision rule*. Probably his decision criterion in this instance would be that of profit, and the executive would *predict* the effects on profit of selling the product at each of the proposed prices. His decision rule would probably be to select the price which he predicts will contribute the most to profit. Notice that the profit decision criterion and rule derive directly from the profit goal of marketing management.

PROFIT   The use of profit as a criterion and a rule for marketing decision-making merits further consideration. Which profit do we mean? Short-run, long-run, or what? The answer is "optimum dollar profit." This is defined as the dollar profit which provides maximum returns over the long-run. Hence, long-run dollar profit is the decision criterion and maximum long-run profit is the decision rule which marketing management should apply in the logical analysis of most major marketing decisions.

Using long-run dollar profit as the main decision criterion and maximum long-run dollar profit as the main decision rule tends to put the analysis of major marketing problems into proper perspective. If a marketing manager views problem situations in this light, he is far more likely to consider them rationally and to avoid making rash or unwise decisions. He is more apt to consider the relevant factors bearing on such problems. He avoids looking at the probable effect on sales volume or on costs separate from their effects on long-run dollar profit. He avoids, too, the common pitfall of thinking of present profits apart from future profits. By focusing on long-run dollar profit, he forces himself to think in terms of relationships. He considers the relationship of sales volume to costs and the relationship of both of these to short-run dollar profits and to long-run dollar profits. This is the proper perspective for rational decision-making in marketing.

SALES VOLUME   The sales volume goal of marketing management provides another decision criterion and rule, but the modern marketing manager looks upon sales volume more as a necessary preliminary to the earning of dollar profit than as a marketing goal of overriding importance. The old-style "sales manager" emphasized sales volume for its own sake. The modern marketing manager still wants sales volume but, in contrast, he wants it to be made up of those sales which eventually will result in maximum long-run dollar profit. Note carefully we are *not* saying that the sales volume goal is unimportant. Dollar profits are impossible unless there are also dollar sales, and a certain minimum level of sales volume is needed in any company for it to reach efficient and profitable levels of production and marketing activity. Maximum long-run dollar profit may be at the very top of the hierarchy of marketing goals, but the sales volume goal is only one step below.

GROWTH   The growth goal is the source of another decision criterion and rule but, like the sales volume goal, it is below long-run dollar profit in the hierarchy of marketing goals. When growth is used as a decision criterion and rule, marketing management generally has in mind "long-run growth in dollar profit." The reader will recognize that this is *almost* equivalent to using maximum long-run dollar profit as the criterion and rule. A moment's reflection, however, reveals that it is possible for a firm to maximize long-run dollar profit and not have any long-run growth in dollar profit at all. If the general trend of business is unfavorable, therefore, growth is a questionable criterion and rule for decision-making. Similarly, it is inappropriate to use the growth criterion and rule when a company operates in a declining industry unless, of course, growth is used in the sense of minimizing shrinkage in long-run profits. Growth is most appropriately used as a decision criterion and rule in companies that are parts of true "growth industries"—ones whose sales and profits are growing far more rapidly than the economy as a whole. Even in these cases, though, the use of long-run dollar profit should put the situation requiring decision into a more proper perspective.

SHARE-OF-THE-MARKET   Companies often set marketing goals other than those of profit, sales volume, and growth. These give rise to additional decision criteria and rules. Some top-managements, for example, strive first and foremost for a specified share of the total industry's sales. In such companies, the decision criterion would be the probable effect of each alternative course of action on the company's share of the market; the decision rule would be to select the alternative which will contribute the most to capturing the maximum share. Although share-of-the-market may be a defensible decision criterion in some cases, it is usually inferior to that of profit. If, for example, a company is fighting to gain a foothold in a market where competitors are already well-established, it makes some sense to set some specific percentage of the total market as the primary marketing goal. In the long run, however, it does little good to capture this share, if sales are not made in such ways that long-run company profits tend toward the maximum. When share-of-the-market is established as the main marketing goal, thus resulting in a share-of-the-market decision criterion and rule, management usually is thinking (or should be) of this as an intermediate check point on the longer road to maximum long-run dollar profit.

The Profit Decision Criterion and the Operating Statement

Because long-run dollar profit is so important as a decision criterion, it is essential that today's marketing manager be familiar with the nature of the relationships of profit to other items on the company operating statement—also called profit and loss statement. Our purpose in this section is to show how the operating statement can be used in analyzing marketing problems and in making decisions on them.

The operating statement of any firm (retail, wholesale, or manufacturing) is based on two basic accounting formulas:

1. Sales — Cost of Goods Sold = Gross Margin (or Gross Profit)
2. Gross Margin — Expenses = Net Profit

With the numbers filled in, combined, and arranged in conventional accounting style, the operating statement (in skelton form) might appear as follows:

Sales	$1,000,000
Less: Cost of Goods Sold	650,000
Equals: Gross Margin (Gross Profit)	$ 350,000
Less: Expenses	250,000
Equals: Net Profits	$ 100,000

This is a highly simplified operating statement, but it can be a valuable tool for the marketing executive to use in analyzing problems and in making decisions.[6] To illustrate, suppose a marketing manager wants to decide whether to divide his sales force into two parts, each specializing in selling part of the product line. Let us assume that he has decided to use profit as the decision criterion and maximum long-run profit as the decision rule. Assume further that he either has available all the necessary facts and figures, or is able to arrive at usable estimates for those that are missing. Here are some of the items this marketing decision-maker would have to consider:

What will be the effect on sales volume of splitting the sales force on the basis of products?

[6] More detailed operating statements are explained and discussed with regard to their use in marketing decision-making in the Appendix.

To what extent will the two groups of salesmen be calling on different or the same lists of customers and prospects? What effect will this have on total sales? On total expenses?

Will the change in sales volume affect costs of goods sold? How?

If expenses are increased by the change, will there be a more than offsetting increase in gross margin? If so, how much?

What will be the effects on sales volume, cost of goods sold, gross margin, and expenses if the sales force is not split as proposed?

Are there other alternatives besides those proposed? (For the sake of keeping this illustration simple, assume there are not.)

As a starter, the marketing manager would want to obtain figures on the present breakdown of last year's operating statement according to the two groups of products. Let's assume he asks the accounting department for this breakdown and receives the following:

	Operating Results—Last Year		
	Product Group I	*Product Group II*	*Total*
Sales	$600,000	$400,000	$1,000,000
Cost of Goods Sold	350,000	300,000	650,000
Gross Margin	$250,000	$100,000	$ 350,000
Expenses *	180,000	70,000	250,000
Net Profits	$ 70,000	$ 30,000	$ 100,000

* Since many expenses, such as the sales manager's salary, are shared by both groups, they can only be apportioned to the product groups on a somewhat arbitrary basis. If, as in this case, an allocation is needed to facilitate analysis, the best available basis of allocation, such as apportioning total expenses according to the relative number of order lines (i.e., lines on customers' order sheets) accounted for by orders for products in each group, should be selected. In the hypothetical company considered here, we are assuming that accounting records were kept in such a manner that sales, cost of goods sold, and hence gross margin figures could all be readily broken down according to product groups. In many real-life companies, the record-keeping is such that a breakdown of this kind could be made only after a great deal of resifting and rearranging of original accounting records. But enlightened marketing managers today are insisting that accounting records be so organized that they lend themselves readily to the analysis of marketing problems. A whole branch of subject matter—marketing cost accounting and analysis—has developed to expedite analyses of this sort.

Having received the operating statement in the form requested, the marketing manager proceeds to use it as a source of information for making his predictions of the consequences of each of the two alternatives.

Regardless of the alternative finally decided upon, it will be in effect for an indefinite future period. So the marketing manager goes ahead and makes his predictions, or projections, in terms of average annual operating results.[7] He makes separate projections of operating results under each of the two alternatives: continued use of a single sales force, and use of two "product group" sales forces. These two *pro forma* (i.e., "projected") statements appear below:

Alternative 1: Continuation of Single Sales Force— Projection of Average Annual Operating Results

	Product Group I	Product Group II	Total
Sales	$650,000	$420,000	$1,070,000
Cost of Goods Sold	375,000	315,000	690,000
Gross Margin	$275,000	$105,000	$ 380,000
Expenses	200,000	75,000	275,000
Net Profit	$ 75,000	$ 30,000	$ 105,000

Alternative 2: Two "Product Group" Sales Forces— Projection of Average Annual Operating Results

	Product Group I	Product Group II	Total
Sales	$750,000	$600,000	$1,350,000
Cost of Goods Sold	410,000	440,000	850,000
Gross Margin	$340,000	$160,000	$ 500,000
Expenses	280,000	90,000	370,000
Net Profit	$ 60,000	$ 70,000	$ 130,000

By working through the several estimates needed to complete the two *pro forma* operating statements, the marketing manager forces himself to consider all the factors bearing on the decision which conceivably might affect net profit. After analyzing demand and competitive factors, he con-

---

[7] Because we want to keep this example simple, we are using projections of average annual operating results. This is appropriate procedure whenever management is unable or unwilling to state a specific number of years during which the decision is to be in effect. Whenever management is able to state a finite period over which the decision is to be in effect, projections are made for each of the successive operating periods which are then "discounted" in terms of the present value of future dollars and totaled to provide a statement of the long-run operating results.

cludes that no change in prices will be needed. His investigation also shows that there will be some variation in the percentage relationship of cost of goods sold to sales volume, but not important variation. But significant variations are likely to occur in expenses. By organizing his analysis this way, he has had to quantify his estimates of each of these factors under both alternatives and this has served to check any tendency toward loose thinking.

Comparing these projections with last year's operating results, the marketing manager now has some basis for thinking that, regardless of the alternative selected, total sales and net profits are likely to be higher than they have been. Under Alternative 2, as might be expected, concentrated effort by specialized salesmen should result not only in higher total sales, but in higher sales of each Product group, especially of Product Group II. In this particular case, the percentage relationship of cost-of-goods-sold to sales for both product groups under both alternatives does not vary significantly; although, with higher sales volumes, there is a slight percentage decline in this relationship. The greatest variation is in the expenses category: for Product Group I, under Alternative 1, increasing sales from $600,000 to $650,000, a bit more than 8 percent, causes expenses to rise by about 11 percent; but under Alternative 2, adding 25 percent to sales, from $600,000 to $750,000, requires more than a 60 percent rise in expenses. In the case of Product Group I, the net effort of this change in the expenses-to-sales relationship is to increase net profit at the $650,000 sales level and to decrease it at the $750,000 level. Contrast this with what happens to Product Group II— increased expenses and cost-of-goods-sold effectively cancel out any profit gain when sales rise from $400,000 to $420,000; but, as sales increase to the $600,000 level, expenses increase less than proportionately and net profit more than doubles.

Since maximum long-run net profit was the decision rule, the marketing manager decides on Alternative 2. Having decided in favor of this alternative, one of his next moves might well be to consider what might be done to reduce the expenses for Product Group I. From the estimates in the *pro forma* statements, it appears offhand that these expenses could be reduced and net profit increased if sales were kept below the $750,000 level. This might or might not be true, but the matter at least merits further investigation. Our example, thus, has uncovered another benefit which results from using the profit decision criterion: other important situations affecting net profit are called to management's attention.

Incremental Analysis and Decision-Making

Incremental analysis, i.e., comparing alternatives by the *changes* they effect in operating data rather than by their total impact on operating results, helps to bring differences among alternative solutions into clearer focus. Remember that, in the previous illustration, estimates showed that changes in expenses would account for most of the variation in net profit. The analysis could have been sharpened had the marketing manager considered only *incremental changes*. After all, the only sales dollars relevant to the decision are those that vary with it, and the only part of cost-of-goods-sold bearing on the decision is the part which changes with sales volume. Similar reasoning holds with regard to expenses—only the incremental changes in expense are pertinent to the decision. After determining incremental changes in sales, cost of goods sold, and expenses, the incremental gross margin and incremental net profit can be calculated. Using the data from our earlier illustration and calculating the incremental figures for each of the two alternatives, the incremental projections are as shown below:

Projections of Average Annual Incremental Changes in Operating Statement

Incremental Change in	Under Alternative 1			Under Alternative 2		
	Product Group I	Product Group II	Total	Product Group I	Product Group II	Total
Sales	+$50,000	+$20,000	+$70,000	+$150,000	+$200,000	+$350,000
Cost of Goods Sold	+ 25,000	+ 15,000	+ 40,000	+ 60,000	+ 140,000	+ 200,000
Gross Margin	+ 25,000	+ 5,000	+ 30,000	+ 90,000	+ 60,000	+ 150,000
Expenses	+ 20,000	+ 5,000	+ 25,000	+ 100,000	+ 20,000	+ 120,000
Net Profit	+ 5,000	—0—	+ 5,000	− 10,000	+ 40,000	+ 30,000

Thus, we have introduced the concept of *incremental net profit*. This is defined as the change (increase) in average annual net profit resulting from the implementation of a managerial decision with respect to any one of a number of possible aspects of a firm's operations.[8] Incremental net profit, in other words, is the difference between the projected net profit and the previous net profit. Incremental net profit under Alternative 1 in the illustration is $5,000, while under Alternative 2 it is $30,000. This means that adopting Alternative 2 should mean $25,000 more added to net profit than if Alternative 1 were adopted. Notice, however, that the incremental

[8] These aspects may include, among others, such matters as diversification into different product lines, differentiation of existing products, changing marketing channels or the intensity of distribution, increasing sales effort through salesmen or advertising or both, and the improvement of warehousing and shipping efficiency. See: M. H. Spencer and L. Siegelman, *Managerial Economics* (Homewood, Ill.: Richard D. Irwin, 1959), pp. 123-24.

net profit in Alternative 2 accrues entirely from Product Group II and that Product Group I actually shows an incremental net loss. This incremental net loss results from the fact that the $90,000 incremental gross margin for Product Group I under Alternative 2 is lower than the $100,000 in incremental expenses. If Alternative 2 is adopted, therefore, the marketing manager should look into the possibilities of reducing expenses for Product Group I.

When using incremental analysis to decide among alternative courses of action, an executive needs an appropriate decision criterion and rule. We stated previously that long-run dollar profit should be the main decision criterion and maximum long-term dollar profit the main decision rule. If we are to use incremental analysis, this criterion and rule require modification. The decision criterion becomes incremental long-run dollar profit, and the decision rule is to select that alternative resulting in the largest incremental long-run dollar profit. These modifications are necessary because incremental analysis involves considering only figures relevant to the decision. In practical decision-making, this decision criterion and decision rule often undergo further change and become "average annual" instead of "long-run" incremental dollar net profits.

Whether a decision-maker uses average annual incremental profit or long-run incremental profit as his decision criterion and rule, he still has to determine how long a period of time to use as a basis for making the calculations. In decision theory, this is called the "payoff" period. Generally, the payoff period should be long enough to capitalize fully on the opportunities, and short enough to avoid undue risk. This may be a valid generalization, but it isn't a great deal of help to the decision-maker. Somewhat more helpful is the fact that a reciprocal relationship exists between the length of the payoff period and the desired rate of return on investment. For instance, and greatly simplifying, if management wants to recover at least 10 percent of the funds invested in a program each year, the maximum length of the payoff period would be 100 percent ÷ 10 percent or 10 years.[9] In other words, management would want its investment returned within ten years. There would, of course, be no profit if something in addition to the investment were not returned during that time. Thus, in our example, if the investment is to return a profit, it is necessary for the life of the investment to be longer than the payoff period, i.e., it has to be longer than ten years. Even though calculating the length of the payoff period and the life of the investment may seem confusing and unduly complicated, a

---

[9] Actually we would have to *discount* the expected incremental profit at some desired rate of return on investment. The inward flow of profit, which appears over many periods projected in the future, would have to be separated and converted into dollars of the same time period via the discount rate. Many complications are encountered in making these calculations. For a good discussion of these complications and suggestions for making the needed computations, see: Spencer and Siegelman, *op. cit.*, pp. 120-24, 381-96.

marketing decision-maker cannot afford to neglect this task. Only if he makes these calculations, is it possible for him to think fully in terms of the "average annual" or the "long-run" net profit, whether incremental or not.

Handling Uncertainties in Marketing Decision-Making

Evaluation or comparison of decision alternatives, whether according to the incremental dollar net profit criterion or other criteria, requires the quantification of future operating experience. This means that the decision-maker needs estimates for such basic factors as selling prices, unit sales volumes, cost of goods sold per unit of product, and expenses per unit of product sold. When any sort of profit criterion is used, these factors are set into three equations:

1. Selling Price per unit $\times$ Sales Volume in units $=$ Sales Volume in dollars

2. Cost of Goods Sold per unit $\times$ Sales Volume in units $=$ Cost of Goods Sold in dollars

3. Expenses per unit $\times$ Sales Volume in units $=$ Expenses in dollars

Notice that we have to use these three equations in order to get the figures needed for completing the two basic accounting equations, which we used in our earlier example. These accounting equations are:

4. Sales Volume − Cost of Goods Sold = Gross Margin
5. Gross Margin − Expenses = Net Profit

For each course of action being evaluated, therefore, the decision maker needs a set of four estimates—estimates for selling price per unit, cost of goods sold per unit, expenses per unit, and sales volume in units. These estimates are predictions, and predictions, especially in the marketing area, are hazardous. Regardless of the excellence of the predicting techniques and procedures and the predictor's competence, there is always some chance that these estimates will be in error. Competitors' actions, for instance, may upset the most careful forecast of future operating results, even though an attempt has been made to anticipate them. Moreover, changes in a multitude of complex economic, psychological, social, and legal forces (the "uncontrollables"), are always exerting influences on a company's cost and expense structure and on its sales situation; these changes may upset the most carefully prepared forecasts. Thus, the marketing decision-maker definitely needs some way to handle these uncertainties.

The main technique used for dealing with uncertainties involves the use of probability distributions. Put briefly, a probability distribution gives the "odds" for and against the occurrence of a certain outcome: i.e., it shows the proportion of the time that one can expect a certain outcome. Assume, for example, that a marketing manager asks his marketing research department to prepare a *probability forecast* of the average annual sales for a new product that the company is planning to introduce. He instructs the researchers to consider two different selling prices in making the forecasts— $1.15 per unit and $1.25 per unit. Notice that the marketing manager in this illustration made his own estimates of selling price. Because this decision concerns the selling price to be placed on a new product, the decision is to be made from among different selling prices, the decision alternatives.

Also notice that the decision criterion here cannot be incremental net profit inasmuch as the company does not have any operating experience with the new product. Because of this, the marketing manager will use the *contribution (to net profit and fixed expenses)* decision criterion, which is defined as total gross margin less total variable expenses. These variable expenses are of the "out-of-pocket" type that will be incurred when the new product is added and include such items as advertising expenses for the new product and salaries of special salesmen hired to promote it. Because he is using the contribution decision criterion here, the marketing manager plans to evaluate the two alternative prices according to the total number of dollars each will contribute to net profit and fixed expenses.

In due time, the requested forecasts come to the marketing manager in the following form:

If unit selling price is $1.15	The probability is	That sales will be
	5%	0—50,000 units
	80	50,000—100,000
	15	100,000—150,000

If unit selling price is $1.25	The probability is	That sales will be
	30%	0—50,000 units
	65	50,000—100,000
	5	100,000—150,000

In other words, if unit selling price is set at $1.15 there are 80 chances out of 100 that sales volume will be between 50,000 and 100,000 units. Notice, however, that there are 20 chances out of 100 that sales will be either above or below that range. Similarly, if unit selling price is set at $1.25, there are 65 chances out of 100 that sales volume will be in the 50,000—100,000 range and 35 chances out of 100 that it will not. Thus, the risk of having sales fall outside this particular range is greater with the $1.25 price than with the $1.15.

Before he can evaluate the two selling prices according to the contribution criterion, the marketing manager needs some more estimates. He needs estimates for the cost of goods sold per unit and for variable expenses per unit at various levels of sales volume. So he asks the controller to provide these estimates for sales volumes of 25,000 units, 75,000 units, and 125,000 units. Notice that these volumes are the midpoints for each of the sales volume ranges for which he has received probability forecasts. In order to simplify this illustration, assume that the controller is able to provide these estimates with absolute certainty.[10] He estimates that variable expenses per unit will amount to 20¢ at all three sales volume levels. He further estimates that cost of goods sold per unit will amount to 70¢ at a volume of 25,000, 60¢ at 75,000, and 50¢ at 125,000.

With the data received from the marketing researchers and the controller, the marketing manager is ready to go on with his calculations. His first step is to compute the contributions for each selling price at each sales level. These calculations are shown below:

(Units × Price) — (Units × Unit Cost of Goods Sold) — (Units × Unit Variable Expenses) = Contribution before Uncertainty Taken into Account

$$(\ 25{,}000 \times \$1.15) - (\ 25{,}000 \times \$0.70) - (\ 25{,}000 \times \$0.20) = \$ \ 6{,}250$$
$$(\ 75{,}000 \times \ 1.15) - (\ 75{,}000 \times \ 0.60) - (\ 75{,}000 \times \ 0.20) = \ 26{,}250$$
$$(125{,}000 \times \ 1.15) - (125{,}000 \times \ 0.50) - (125{,}000 \times \ 0.20) = \ 56{,}250$$

$$(\ 25{,}000 \times \$1.25) - (\ 25{,}000 \times \$0.70) - (\ 25{,}000 \times \$0.20) = \$ \ 8{,}750$$
$$(\ 75{,}000 \times \ 1.25) - (\ 75{,}000 \times \ 0.60) - (\ 75{,}000 \times \ 0.20) = \ 33{,}750$$
$$(125{,}000 \times \ 1.25) - (125{,}000 \times \ 0.50) - (125{,}000 \times \ 0.20) = \ 68{,}750$$

His next step is to take into account the uncertainties as to sales volume. He has got probability figures on these uncertainties from marketing research, and it is time now to work them into the calculations. For this purpose, it is convenient to use a decision matrix (see Exhibit 4.2). On the first and fourth lines of this matrix, the marketing manager writes in the probability percentages representing the chances of each sales level occurring at each of the two proposed prices. On the second and fifth lines, he inserts the figures for estimated contribution. Then, he multiplies each contribution figure on line two by the probability percentage directly above it on line one; he repeats this process for the figures on line five and the percentages on line four. The resulting computations are inserted on lines three and six respectively. Next, the marketing manager adds lines three and six hori-

[10] Had the controller not been able to furnish these estimates with absolute certainty, he would provide sets of estimates together with a statement of the probability of each estimate occurring. The technique for handling probability estimates of unit costs and expenses is essentially the same as that used with probability forecasts of sales volume.

zontally and puts these totals in the boxes on the right-hand side of the matrix. The decision criterion is contribution, and the decision rule, in our example, is to select the selling price with the highest *expected* contribution.

EXHIBIT 4–2

Decision Matrix—Contribution
Incorporating Probabilities

Forecasted Sales	25,000 (0—50,000)	75,000 (50,000— 100,000)	125,000 (100,000— 150,000)	Expectation
1. Probability of Sales Level if $1.15 price used	.05	.80	.15	
2. Contribution at $1.15 price	$6,250	$26,250	$56,250	
3. 1.×2.	$312.50	$21,000	$8,437.50	$29,750
4. Probability of Sales Level if $1.25 price used	.30	.65	.05	
5. Contribution at $1.25 price	$8,750	$33,750	$68,750	
6. 4. × 5.	$2,625	$21,937.50	$3,437.50	$28,000

Comparing the totals in the two boxes, the expectation for the highest contribution is greater at the $1.15 price than at the $1.25 price. Thus, the decision is to use the $1.15 price.

This approach, with appropriate modifications made according to the type of problem under study, can be used for a wide variety of marketing decisions. The chief requirements for using it are that: (1) the required numerical data are or can be made available, and (2) given outcomes can be expressed in terms of the probabilities of their occurrence. The form, or design, of the decision matrix, of course, can readily be altered in any way which facilitates the making of computations and comparisons.

This illustration, though long and seemingly involved, is actually a highly simplified one and, to keep it simple, we have made a number of assumptions. Even though we have simplified this illustration greatly, the important thing to grasp is the general nature of this approach. It provides a technique for taking uncertainties into account in decision-making and it is extremely versatile—it can be modified and adapted in many ingenious ways to facilitate the analysis and deciding of many classes of marketing problems. The decision-maker, however, should avoid using this approach rigidly—it is not a rigid mold but a flexible pattern requiring modifications appropriate to the particular decision being made and to the decision criterion and rule being used.

CONCLUSION

Marketing men must have management and decision-making skills—analysis and discussion in this chapter have focused on these skills. Competent managers must be well grounded in the practice of management. In marketing, this means that executives must know how to apply planning, organizing, coordinating, and controlling skills to the management of marketing activities. It means, too, that they need skill in making decisions and in carrying through the analyses leading up to decisions. Many of the decisions marketing executives make are intuitive in nature. Others, especially highly important ones made rather infrequently, require more formal approaches. Some of these approaches have been illustrated in this chapter. In making either intuitive or rational decisions, the modern marketing manager needs considerable ingenuity, uncommon imagination, and a great deal of common sense.

QUESTIONS AND PROBLEMS

1. What does management *manage?* What does marketing management manage? What functions are performed by managers? By marketing managers? How does the job of the marketing executive differ from the jobs of other executives?

2. "It is the first duty of a business to survive," writes Peter Drucker in *The Practice of Management* (New York: Harper & Bros., 1954), p. 46. Explain how this statement is consistent with the main marketing (and company) goals discussed in this chapter.

3. "Even without management, there would still be marketing." If this statement is true, how can management's role in marketing be justified?

4. Explain the meaning of the following terms:
   a. planning
   b. organizing
   c. coordinating
   d. controlling
   e. controllable
   f. uncontrollable
   g. economic man
   h. weak ordering
   i. decision
   j. decision-making

5. "Marketing management's basic problem is to adjust the forces under its control within an environment composed of diverse and ever-changing forces outside its control." Give some examples of how

changes in certain uncontrollables may call for changes in the ways in which a company applies its controllables.

6.   Show how the three main marketing goals (sales volume, net profits, and growth) are related and interdependent.

7.   "The establishment and definition of marketing goals are necessary prerequisites to marketing decision-making." Discuss.

8.   Compare intuitive decision-making and rational decision-making. Under what sets of circumstances should marketing managers make intuitive decisions? Rational decisions?

9.   Contrast the decision-making procedure of economic man with the four steps in the logical analysis of a business problem (as given in this chapter).

10.   Discuss the relationship of information, problem conceptualization, and prediction in marketing decision-making.

11.   Appraise the importance of a company's system of controls from the standpoint of the marketing decision-maker.

12.   Explain how marketing decision-makers might use probability distributions in dealing with uncertainties.

13.   What marketing goals, decision criteria, and decision rules might be appropriate in each of the following situations? Explain your reasoning in each instance.

a. Company A is planning to introduce its product in a market area where local competitors are very strong.

b. Company B has operated its plant at only 50 percent of capacity for several years. Consequently, unit manufacturing costs are higher than the industry average. If Company B could utilize the full capacity of its plant, unit manufacturing costs would be comparable to those of its chief competitors.

c. For a long period of years, Company C's product has been the largest seller in the industry. Recently, one of C's main competitors has been making a strong bid for industry leadership and, in the process, has been cutting prices.

d. Company D's main product has experienced declining sales for a number of years, due mainly to the introduction of substitutes by companies in competing industries.

14.   Explain how the contribution decision criterion differs from the incremental-net-profit decision criterion. In what sets of circumstances might it be appropriate to use each of these criteria?

15.   The marketing manager of the Rogers-Dunn Company, a men's hosiery manufacturer, is considering the advisability of changing his firm's pricing and promotional policies. Currently, one-million pairs

are sold annually to retailers at a price of $1.20 per pair, and total promotional expenditures amount to $100,000. At the current rate of production, cost of goods sold per unit (i.e., per pair of hosiery) is 60¢. The marketing manager has outlined various possible alternatives, secured necessary estimates for each, and has summarized them as follows:

a. If the price to retailers is left at $1.20 per pair and total promotional expenditures remain at $100,000, the sales forecast for next year is 1,200,000 pairs. At that sales rate, unit cost of goods will be 55¢.

b. If the price to retailers is reduced to 90¢ per pair and total promotional expenditures remain at $100,000, the sales forecast for next year is 1,500,000 pairs, and unit cost of goods sold will be 50¢.

c. If the price to retailers is left at $1.20 per pair and total promotional expenditures are increased to $200,000, the sales forecast for next year is 1,300,000 pairs and cost of goods sold per unit will be 54¢.

d. If the price to retailers is reduced to 90c per pair and total promotional expenditures are increased to $200,000, the sales forecast for next year is 1,700,000 pairs and cost of goods sold per unit will be 45¢.

Assuming that the marketing manager has ruled out all other alternatives but these four, which alternative should he select, and why?

16. The marketing manager of Conant Products Company is faced with the problem of deciding which of two prices should be placed on a new product. The two prices under consideration are $10 and $12. The marketing research department has prepared probability forecasts of average annual sales of the new product for each of the two prices as follows:

If unit selling price is $10	The probability is	That sales will be
	10%	0— 5,000 units
	40	5,000—10,000
	40	10,000—15,000
	10	15,000—20,000

If unit selling price is $12	The probability is	That sales will be
	15%	0— 5,000 units
	55	5,000—10,000
	25	10,000—15,000
	5	15,000—20,000

The controller has estimated cost of goods sold per unit at $6 at a volume of 2,500, $5 at 7,500, $4.50 at 12,500 and $4 at 17,500. The controller states that variable expenses per unit will amount to $2 per unit at all four sales volume levels.

What price should be placed on the new product, and why?

PART 2

MARKETS

5

MARKET SEGMENTATION

Marketing, as defined earlier, is the business process by which products are matched with markets and through which ownership transfers are effected. A marketer's success depends importantly on his knowledge of both his markets and his products and on his skills in effecting ownership transfers. Thus, it is no accident that markets and products are the twin foundations on which all marketing study is based. In Part Two we analyze market concepts in detail and in Part Three related product concepts. Equipped with an adequate understanding of these concepts, later analysis focuses directly on formulation of marketing strategy, whose fundamental purpose is to effect ownership transfers through such means as promotion, pricing, and making the product available for sale to final buyers through appropriate marketing channels. In the present chapter, we first examine the concepts of "market" and market segmentation. Analysis then turns to various bases for segmenting consumer and industrial markets. The chapter closes with a discussion of segmentation and marketing strategy.

MARKETS AND MARKET SEGMENTATION

Definition of "Market"

Depending on the way it is used, the term "market" has several different meanings. The American Marketing Association, through its definitions committee, suggests two:

1. The aggregate of forces or conditions within which buyers and sellers make decisions that result in the transfer of goods and services.
2. The aggregate demand of the potential buyers of a commodity or service.[1]

In an earlier report, this committee suggested two additional meanings:

3. The place or area in which buyers and sellers function.
4. (As a verb) To perform business activities which direct the flow of goods and services from producer to consumer or user.[2]

According to the first definition, markets are made up of people who buy and sell. The second definition highlights the notion that the market for a product also represents the demand for that product. The third carries the sense that a market is a place where products change hands, the fourth defines market as an activity.

In this chapter, we will, for the most part, use the term "market" in the sense of the second definition—i.e., as it consists of the aggregate demand of the potential buyers of a product. We must, however, amplify this definition a bit to fit the needs of our discussion. An aggregate demand is a composite of the individual demands of all the potential buyers of a product. But an aggregate demand, or total market, also consists of the sum of the demands of different *segments* of the market, each made up of a group of buyers, or buying units, who share qualities that render the segment distinct and make it of significance to marketing. Thus, in the second definition, a market is not only an aggregate demand for a product but the sum of the demands of different market segments. According to the original definition, aggregate demand represents the total of the demands of all

---

[1] Committee on Definitions, *Marketing Definitions* (Chicago: American Marketing Association, 1960), p. 15.
[2] "Report of the Definitions Committee of the American Marketing Association," *The Journal of Marketing* (October 1948), pp. 202ff.

potential buyers. This definition is now modified so that certain subtotals of demand, each representing the demand sum of a given market segment, are added together and then considered collectively as *the market*.

Concept of Market Segmentation

The concept of market segmentation is based on the fact that markets, rather than being homogeneous, are really heterogeneous. No two buyers or potential buyers of a product are ever identical in all respects. However, large groups of potential buyers share certain characteristics of distinctive significance to marketing, and each such group constitutes a market segment. By grouping individuals into market segments, a degree of homogeneity is attained, making it possible to tailor optimal marketing strategies to each segment. The sum of all such market segments is known as *the market*. Businessmen often say "market" when they really mean "market segment." In our discussion *a* market means a market segment; *the* market means the total or whole market.

The market for every product is segmented to some extent. However, in some instances, market segmentation may exist only in the sense that some buyers buy and use more of a product than others. In fact, heavy user vs. light user market segmentation is widely recognized as significant. Different marketing programs are commonly needed to stimulate demand among the heavy users and the light users, and still a different program to convert non-users (another market segment) into either light or heavy users.

Knowing the market, then, is prerequisite to a marketer's success. Knowing the market, however, means knowing the different market segments which make up the total market. Alternatively put, it is essential that the marketer know not only "who buys the product" but to recognize that not all buy for the same reasons. Only if he has this knowledge will the marketer be in position to design optimal marketing strategies.

Existence of a group of individuals with common characteristics does not in itself constitute a market segment. Only when they have common characteristics as *buyers* are they a market segment. Teenagers, for example, have always been part of the general population, but only recently have they taken on the characteristics of a distinct market segment. There was a time when the typical teenager received little or no spending allowance and had very little influence on the spending done on his behalf. As most teenagers can testify, a different set of circumstances exists today. The teenager now has much more spending money, not only from a more generous allowance but often supplemented by other income, and he exerts a strong influence over the pattern of spending done by others on his behalf.

To the extent that teenagers as consumers act differently than do other age groups, there is a teenage market segment.

The distinctive marketing characteristics of each market segment make it profitable for the marketer to adapt his product and marketing program to meet the needs of each. Thus, it is important for the marketer to distinguish the different market segments making up the total market for his product.

The broadest market division is that which separates the consumer market from the industrial market. This division, so broad that each part is too extensive to be properly considered as a market segment, separates potential buyers into two categories—ultimate consumers and industrial users. An ultimate consumer buys either for his own or for his family's personal consumption. An industrial user buys to further the production of other goods and services.

There are important differences between ultimate consumers and industrial users, their ways and means of purchasing differing considerably. Ultimate consumers buy in much smaller quantities and generally for consumption over much shorter time periods than do industrial buyers. More importantly, ultimate consumers are not usually as systematic in their buying as are industrial users. Some industrial users are business enterprises which exist to make profits, this encouraging them to adopt systematic purchasing procedures. Other industrial users are non-profit institutions (e.g., governmental agencies, schools, and hospitals) whose operations are audited and reviewed by outside authorities, which condition also is conducive to the adoption of systematic purchasing procedures. Similarly, ultimate consumers spend only part of their time buying, whereas the industrial user, an organization of some size, employs professionals who devote all of their time and effort to purchasing. Furthermore, the ultimate consumer spreads all his buying skill over a wide range of goods and services, whereas the professional tends to specialize and, therefore, has more opportunity to perfect his purchasing skills. These are only a few of the many differences between ultimate consumers and industrial users. They should, however, illustrate the point that marketers must use significantly different approaches in marketing products to each of the two broad classifications of markets.

ULTIMATE CONSUMERS

Every individual may be classified as an ultimate consumer, and there were approximately 205-million people in the United States in 1970. The population will grow to at least 260-million by 1990 at the most conservative estimate. Under these conditions of population growth, even the marketer who just manages to maintain his share of the market can expect an increasing sales volume assuming, of course, that he adapts his product and marketing techniques to the changing requirements of the consumer market.

In analyzing the consumer market, the household is often a more significant analytical unit than the individual. Although it is true that individuals do the consuming, most of their purchases are not made for their own personal consumption, but for the households of which they are members. Other purchases are jointly made by two or more persons who make up a household. Still other purchases are of products which are consumed by all members of the household—such as household appliances. More than one member of a household may have an income, but usually all or part of these incomes are pooled for spending purposes. In addition, household members who do not have incomes still assist in spending the household income. In 1970, there were some 60-million households in the United States, each with an income averaging over $9,000, most of which was spent for consumer goods and services.[3]

BASES FOR DIVIDING CONSUMER MARKETS

Market segments are groupings of consumers according to such characteristics as income, age, degree of urbanization, race or ethnic classification, geographic location, or education. These represent some but not all the possible ways in which markets can be segmented. In addition, market segments can be broken down into sub-segments by cross-classifying a grouping of market segments in terms of a different grouping system. The following table, for instance, shows how an analyst might break down income market segments into sub-segments according to the ages of income recipients, each box representing a sub-segment. The box marked "X," then, would represent those persons with incomes of $10,000 and over who are in the 18–24 age group.

TABLE 5–1

	Income Group			
Age Group	Under $5,000	$5,000– $7,499	$7,500– $9,999	$10,000 & Over
18–24				X
25–34				
35–44				
45–54				
55 & Over				

[3] Estimates from U.S. Department of Commerce, Bureau of the Census.

Income Market Segments

Because income is the main source of consumer purchasing power, market segmentation based on income is entirely logical. An individual's income, in most cases, limits not only how much he can buy but what specific products he buys. The person with a low income, for example, is often so hard-pressed to pay for such necessities as food, clothing, and shelter that he cannot afford to buy tickets for the opera and contents himself instead with attendance at the neighborhood theater. Similarly, persons with relatively low incomes who buy new homes are much more likely, because of financial pressures, to plant their own trees and shrubs than they are to employ the services of landscape gardeners. Whereas low incomes result in highly restricted consumption, the only limit to consumption at the upper end of the scale is the availability of products. For incomes between the two extremes, patterns of buying and consumption vary considerably from one income step to the next.

In delineating income market segments, we must arbitrarily set dividing lines between different income levels. If we set a $5,000-$6,999 income market segment, a person with a $4,999 income will fall into the next lower market segment, even though he may share certain consumer characteristics with the person who has a $5,000 income. In spite of this limitation, there is considerable advantage in segmenting consumers according to their income, for in no other way can we derive a usable measure of buying power. Table 5.2 shows the distribution of income among United States households in 1960 and 1970. In 1960, more households were earning between $5,000 and $6,999 than any other range of income, but by 1970,

TABLE 5-2
Annual Income per American Household in 1960 and 1970

Annual Income (Before taxes)	Percentage of Total Households 1960	1970
Under $3,000	21.8%	7.8%
$ 3,000–$ 4,999	20.4%	9.4%
$ 5,000–$ 6,999	23.4%	11.0%
$ 7,000–$ 9,999	20.1%	23.5%
$10,000–$14,999	10.8%	28.5%
$15,000 and Over	3.6%	19.8%

Source: United States Department of Commerce, Bureau of the Census and 1970 projections by U.S. News & World Report Economic Unit.

more were earning in the $10,000 to $14,999 range than any other. This was a sizable increase in the number of families with large amounts of disposable income. At the same time the number earning below the "poverty" level [4] decreased markedly during the ten years. Relatively speaking, then, the $10,000 to $14,999 income segment of the market became over two and one-half times as important in numbers during the ten-year period. Thus, the market for luxury items purchased by this market segment has increased much more rapidly than has total population. At the same time, the lower income market segment has been shrinking.

Recognition of the existence of different income market segments leads to the question, "Do members of each segment spend their money in the same ways?" An exhaustive survey of consumer spending made by Life Magazine provides an answer. Although this study is no longer current, it supports earlier evidence on consumer expenditures and essentially the same situation probably still exists.

Table 5.3, based on the Life study, divides America's households

[4] According to the U.S. Census Bureau, officially designated "poverty" levels were $3,060 in 1960 and an estimated $3,358 in 1968.

TABLE 5–3

Percentage Division of Total Spending Among U.S. Households of Various Incomes, 1956

	Household Income Before Taxes		
	Under $3,000	$3,000 to $5,000	$5,000 or more
Per Cent of U.S. Households	32%	34%	34%
Total Expenditures	19	34	47
Food, Beverages, Tobacco	22	35	43
Food	22	35	43
Alcoholic Beverages	20	30	50
Tobacco	22	36	42
Clothing, Accessories	17	35	48
Home Operation, Improvement	18	35	47
Home Furnishings, Equipment, Appliances	17	32	51
Medical, Personal Care	21	33	46
Automotive	16	34	50
Recreation	17	34	49
Other *	16	33	51

* Includes life insurance premiums and non-medical professional services.
Source: Derived from data contained in *Life Study of Consumer Expenditures*, Vol. 1, 1957. Also see R. H. Ostheimer, "Who Buys What? Life's Study of Consumer Expenditures," *The Journal of Marketing* (January 1958), p. 266.

into three income segments, each with approximately the same number of households, and shows that the top segment (incomes of $5,000 and over) accounted for nearly half of all spending. The middle segment (incomes of $3,000 to $5,000) accounted for 34 percent of all spending, the lower segment (incomes under $3,000) for a little less than one-fifth. Upper income households account for disproportionately large shares of total spending relative to their numbers, and this is especially apparent with respect to the following product categories: home furnishings, equipment, and appliances; alcoholic beverages; automotive; recreation; and clothing. By contrast, such disproportionality, while still present, is not nearly so marked in the food and tobacco categories.[5]

Although households have different amounts of money available for spending, there is remarkable conformity in spending patterns among households in different income groups. By spending pattern, we mean the *percentage* division of a household's total expenditures into spending for each major category of goods and services. The *Life Study of Consumer Expenditures* showed that, with the exception of spending on food, households in different income groups spend about the same percentage for each product category. Households with under $4,000 in annual income spend around one-third of the total for food, while those with over $7,000 in income spend only one-fourth of the total for food. But in buying products in other major categories, all households, regardless of their income class, allocate nearly the same proportions of their total budgets.[6]

However, similarity in spending patterns as measured by the shares of the budget allotted to major categories does not mean that all households are equally good market prospects. Table 5.4 shows how American consumers divided their expenditures among different product categories between the years 1955 and 1967. Analysis of the table shows that consumer expenditures for recreation increased from 5.5 percent to 6.2 percent during the period. If we assume that different income groups spend about the same percentage of income on recreation, households with incomes of $3,000 spend only $186 per year but those with incomes of $15,000 spend $930 per year. Higher-income households represent much the better market prospects for recreation and recreation equipment.

Current data on the incomes of different market segments is very helpful to the marketer in estimating the number of potential customers who can afford to buy his products. When these data are related to spending patterns, such as those uncovered by the *Life* study, the marketer is able to differentiate more clearly among income market segments. If he is

[5] R. H. Ostheimer, "Who Buys What? Life's Study of Consumer Expenditures," *The Journal of Marketing*, January 1958, p. 266.
[6] *Ibid.*

TABLE 5-4

Personal Consumption Expenditures, By Type of Product: 1955 to 1967

TYPE OF PRODUCT	1955	1960	1964	1965	1966	1967
Percentage	100.0	100.0	100.0	100.0	100.0	100.0
Food, Beverages,[a] and Tobacco	28.4	26.9	25.1	24.8	24.7	24.1
Clothing, Accessories, and Jewelry	11.0	10.2	10.1	10.0	10.3	10.3
Personal Care	1.4	1.6	1.8	1.8	1.7	1.7
Housing	13.3	14.2	14.8	14.7	14.5	14.4
Household Operations	14.7	14.4	14.5	14.3	14.3	14.2
Medical Care Expenses	5.0	5.9	6.4	6.5	6.6	6.9
Personal Business	4.0	4.6	5.0	5.1	5.2	5.4
Transportation	14.0	13.3	12.8	13.4	13.0	12.9
Recreation	5.5	5.6	6.1	6.1	6.1	6.2
Private Education and Research	0.9	1.1	1.3	1.4	1.4	1.6
Religious and Welfare Activities	1.3	1.5	1.4	1.4	1.4	1.4
Foreign Travel and Other, Net	0.6	0.7	0.7	0.7	0.7	0.8

[a] Includes alcoholic beverages.
Source: Dept. of Commerce, Office of Business Economics; *The National Income and Product Accounts of the United States, 1929-1965, Survey of Current Business,* July 1968, and unpublished data.

planning marketing strategy for a line of golfing equipment, for instance, he very definitely would promote higher-priced clubs more intensively to the $10,000–$14,999 income segment than to the $3,000–$4,999 income segment.

Sex as a Basis for Market Segmentation

The roles of men and women in American society have undergone considerable change. A continuing movement towards full equality of legal rights and social privileges has broadened women's opportunity for participating in economic and political activities. Approximately one-third of adult American women are employed in the work force and have incomes of their own to spend; labor-saving appliances are providing the remaining two-thirds with more time free from domestic responsibilities, and, consequently, more time for family shopping. In general, too, they are better educated and better informed than were their mothers and grandmothers. The result is that American women have either sole or major responsibility for buying many kinds of goods and are exerting an increasing amount of influence on buying decisions of all kinds.

The information in Table 5-5 provides some insights on the relative influence exerted on purchase decisions by husband and wife. These data were compiled from a two-and-one-half year study of a cross-section of families in all parts of the United States. Interviews were obtained from both husbands and wives. Notice that among the decision areas studied, one—car purchases—is attributed to husbands primarily, while another—purchases of household goods and furniture—was thought to be controlled by wives more often than by husbands. It is possible that there are other "husband-dominated" areas which were not studied, such as home repairs and gardening equipment, and there may be other "wife-dominated" areas such as interior decorating, rugs, and draperies.[7] Both husbands and wives were asked the same questions, and their answers were tallied separately under columns "A" and "B" in Table 5.5. It is interesting to note that, with only one important exception, husbands and wives were in very close agreement about who makes family decisions. In decisions on money and bills, six percent more women than men believed that this was entirely or predominantly the wife's decision, while five percent more men than women believed that this responsibility was shared equally.

With women playing an increasingly important role in buying

[7] E. H. Wolgast, "Do Husbands or Wives Make the Purchasing Decisions?" *The Journal of Marketing*, October 1958, p. 153.

TABLE 5—5
Husbands' and Wives' Report Regarding Decision-Making Patterns

Who in Your Family Decides?

	When it's time to buy a car		About savings		Money and bills (from a nonpanel study)		When it's time to buy household goods, appliances, furniture, etc.	
	Husbands A	Wives B	Husbands A	Wives B	Husbands A	Wives B	Husbands A	Wives B
Wife Only	3%	3%	27%	26%	39%	43%	24%	25%
Wife Predominantly	1	1	2	6	b	2	12	10
Both Equally	31	23	47	49	31	26	53	51
Husband Predominantly	5	9	3	4	2	2	4	5
Husband Only	51	54	18	13	27	27	4	6
Don't Buy (don't save)	7	9	3	2	b	b	2	2
Not Ascertained	2	1	a	a	1	—	1	1
Number of Cases	354	297	343	301	454	505	354	307

a "Not ascertained's" were excluded here.
b Less than 0.5%.
Source: E. H. Wolgast, "Do Husbands or Wives Make the Purchasing Decisions?," *Journal of Marketing*, October 1958, p. 153.

decisions and consumption in America, it is important to recognize the shifts in the sexual composition of the population. In 1960, there were 1,915,000 more females than males in the United States: in 1970 there were 4,000,000 more.[8] This is an increase by females of almost .5 percent of the population, from 50.5 percent to 51 percent.

Market segmentation along sexual lines exists for some but not all products. For example, men and women do not differ significantly as buyers of toothpaste. Yet, for a wide variety of cosmetics and grooming aids and for clothing, men and women are in different market segments. The two segments often require entirely different marketing strategies, with different methods of distribution, packaging, promotion, and pricing.

Even with sexually neutral products, it is possible to appeal to only male or female buyers. The introduction in 1969 of *Virginia Slims* cigarettes as a product designed only for women was an attempt to gain a unique advantage in the female market segment. More difficult is the task of changing the image of a product that has formerly served only the male or female segment of the market so as to make it acceptable to both. With the advent of longer hair styles for men in the late 1960s, the need arose for improved methods of keeping men's hair looking well groomed. Hair spray, a product originally introduced for women, was the natural answer, but it was necessary to change the image by introducing new brands with masculine names and packaging to persuade men to accept this product as a grooming aid.

Age Market Segments

Table 5.6 shows United States population divided by age groupings and sex from 1960 projected to 1990. When market segments are set up in terms of chronological age, the total population may be separated into such groups as children, teenagers, adults, and the aged.

The children's and infants' market segment has long been recognized as a distinct grouping of consumers. Many products are designed specifically for this market segment, including not only clothing and toys but such items as scaled-down furniture and specially-prepared foods and beverages. The marketing problems presented by this segment are unique because the child, who actually uses or consumes the product, is seldom the one who does the buying. Marketers, however, realize that children can influence buying decisions, this influence increasing with the age of the child, and advertisers have demonstrated that appeals directed even to very young children cause them to bring strong buying pressure to bear on their parents. Witness the television programs for children on which the com-

[8] U.S. Bureau of the Census, Department of Commerce.

TABLE 5–6

Current and Projected Population, by Age and Sex: 1960 to 1990

Year, Series, and Sex	Total, all ages	Under 5 years	5-9 years	10-14 years	15-19 years	20-24 years	25-34 years	35-44 years	45-54 years	55-64 years	65 and over	14 and over	18 and over	21 and over
TOTAL														
1960	180,684	20,364	18,825	16,910	13,467	11,116	22,911	24,223	20,581	15,627	16,659	127,335	116,123	108,836
1965	194,592	20,404	20,515	18,959	17,051	13,679	22,369	24,438	22,047	16,968	18,162	138,299	124,186	114,858
1970—A	208,615	21,317	20,591	20,668	19,100	17,261	25,315	22,961	23,326	18,491	19,585	150,075	134,267	123,413
B	207,326	20,027												
C	206,039	18,740												
D	204,923	17,625												
1975—A	227,929	27,210	21,468	20,741	20,807	19,299	31,423	22,459	23,532	19,831	21,159	162,836	145,940	133,657
B	223,785	24,350	20,184											
C	219,366	21,211	18,903											
D	215,367	18,323	17,793											
1980—A	250,489	31,040	27,341	21,616	20,879	20,997	36,997	25,376	22,147	21,032	23,063	174,234	158,229	145,388
B	243,291	27,972	24,492	20,334										
C	235,212	24,298	21,366	19,056										
D	227,665	20,736	18,489	17,948										
1985—A	274,748	33,288	31,160	27,478	21,753	21,068	40,699	31,384	21,705	21,236	24,978	187,963	168,956	157,096
B	264,607	30,325	28,103	24,635	20,475							186,166	168,759	
C	252,871	26,645	24,443	21,514	19,200							184,351	168,576	
D	241,731	23,030	20,894	18,643	18,095							182,768	168,424	
1990—A	300,131	35,015	33,403	31,290	27,596	21,939	42,449	36,864	24,542	20,028	27,005	206,427	183,346	167,916
B	286,501	31,493	30,451	28,239	24,762	20,668						201,710	181,010	167,084
C	270,770	27,462	26,784	24,586	21,651	19,400						196,619	178,616	166,267
D	255,967	23,765	23,182	21,044	18,788	18,300						191,977	176,509	165,566
MALE														
1960	89,352	10,352	9,572	8,595	6,815	5,560	11,324	11,873	10,142	7,561	7,537	62,208	56,529	52,853
1965	95,884	10,416	10,424	9,636	8,656	6,884	11,096	11,961	10,741	8,133	7,936	67,250	60,056	55,333
1970—A	102,541	10,887	10,507	10,500	9,694	8,711	12,609	11,289	11,263	8,746	8,336	72,699	64,672	59,167
B	101,882	10,228												
C	101,225	9,571												
D	100,656	9,002												
1975—A	111,994	13,898	10,958	10,580	10,555	9,741	15,729	11,082	11,347	9,267	8,836	78,764	70,179	63,953
B	109,879	12,437	10,303											
C	107,622	10,835	9,649											
D	105,581	9,360	9,083											

TABLE 5–6 (Cont'd)

Year, Series, and Sex	Total, all ages	Under 5 years	5-9 years	10-14 years	15-19 years	20-24 years	25-34 years	35-44 years	45-54 years	55-64 years	65 and over	14 and over	18 and over	21 and over
TOTAL														
1980—A	123,185	15,857	13,958	11,030	10,634	10,596	18,557	12,576	12,726	9,745	9,507	84,249	76,089	69,567
B	119,510	14,290	12,504	10,376										
C	115,386	12,413	10,908	9,724										
D	111,533	10,594	9,440	9,159										
1985—A	135,305	17,008	15,910	14,024	11,084	10,674	20,418	15,630	10,554	9,828	10,175	90,986	81,294	75,260
B	130,129	15,494	14,350	12,573	10,433							90,070	81,193	
C	124,137	13,614	12,481	10,980	9,783							89,144	81,100	
D	118,450	11,768	10,669	9,515	9,220							88,337	81,022	
1990—A	148,056	17,893	17,059	15,972	14,065	11,122	21,338	18,398	11,994	9,312	10,904	100,195	88,423	80,570
B	141,100	16,094	15,551	14,415	12,620	10,475						97,792	87,234	80,147
C	133,073	14,034	13,679	12,550	11,034	9,830						95,198	86,015	79,731
D	125,518	12,146	11,840	10,742	9,575	9,271						92,833	84,943	79,375
FEMALE														
1960	91,352	10,013	9,254	8,314	6,652	5,556	11,587	12,350	10,437	8,066	9,121	65,127	59,594	55,983
1965	98,708	9,988	9,091	9,323	8,395	6,794	11,273	12,477	11,306	8,835	10,226	71,069	64,130	59,525
1970—A	106,075	10,430	10,085	10,169	9,407	8,551	12,706	11,672	12,063	9,744	11,249	77,376	69,595	64,246
B	105,444	9,799												
C	104,814	9,169												
D	104,268	8,623												
1975—A	115,935	13,312	10,510	10,161	10,252	9,558	15,695	11,376	12,185	10,564	12,323	84,072	75,761	69,703
B	113,907	11,912	9,881											
C	111,743	10,376	9,254											
D	109,787	8,963	8,710											
1980—A	127,304	15,183	13,383	10,586	10,245	10,401	18,440	12,801	11,422	11,287	13,556	89,985	82,139	75,821
B	123,781	13,682	11,988	9,958										
C	119,826	11,885	10,458	9,332										
D	116,133	10,142	9,049	8,789										
1985—A	139,443	16,280	15,249	13,454	10,669	10,394	20,282	15,754	11,151	11,408	14,802	96,977	87,663	81,836
B	134,479	14,831	13,753	12,062	10,042							96,096	87,566	
C	128,734	13,031	11,962	10,554	9,417							95,207	87,476	
D	123,280	11,262	10,225	9,128	8,876							94,431	87,402	
1990—A	152,075	17,122	16,344	15,318	13,532	10,817	21,112	18,465	12,548	10,715	16,102	106,231	94,923	87,346
B	145,400	15,399	14,899	13,824	12,142	10,193						103,918	93,776	86,937
C	137,697	13,428	13,105	12,055	10,617	9,570						101,421	92,601	86,535
D	130,449	11,620	11,342	10,301	9,214	9,030						99,145	91,566	86,191

[In thousands. Estimates as of July 1. Includes Armed Forces abroad. Projections based on current estimates and projections of the population by age and sex for July 1, 1966, and imply an annual net immigration of 400,000. The underlying projections of fertility were computed by the "cohort" method and imply that completed fertility of all women (i.e., the average number of children per 1,000 women at end of childbearing) moves gradually toward the following levels: Series A, 3,350; Series B, 3,100; Series C, 2,775; and Series D, 2,450. Series A results do not differ substantially from those obtained by assuming that the average annual level of fertility in the 1962–66 period will persist throughout the projection period]

Source: Dept. of Commerce, Bureau of the Census; Current Population Reports, Series P-25, No. 381.

mercials are directed specifically to children. The continued use of such programs and commercials by advertisers is some evidence of their effectiveness. This market which comprises some 60-million children today will increase to around 100-million by 1990.

Recognition that teenagers constitute a separate market segment has come only fairly recently. For many years, marketers classified teenagers either as children or as adults, using some age, such as 15 to 16, as the dividing line. Today, however, it is a rare marketer who does not realize that teenagers are a distinct market segment. Being neither children nor adults, teenagers are a distinct social as well as age grouping. They have their own social rules and, what is most significant to marketers, their own patterns of buying behavior and product and brand preferences. Furthermore, teenage social groups exert strong influences on individual buying decisions. Addressing themselves to the special qualities of this segment, marketers, for example, design typewriters especially for high school and college use and compound beauty preparations specifically for adolescent complexions. Marketers also advertise directly to teenagers, using copy and commercials phrased in the teenagers' own language. Among the companies which approach the teenage market segment in this way are Coca-Cola, Remington Arms, Eastman Kodak, and John H. Breck (Shampoos).[9] Table 5.6 indicates that teenagers number from 21 to nearly 40-million consumers today, depending on the ages included.

Marketers still do not fully recognize the existence of a "senior citizen" or "oldster" market segment. As the average life span has increased, the size of this segment has expanded greatly. There has also been significant growth in the importance of this market segment relative to others. Population statistics show that persons in the over-65 age group in 1940 were only 6.9 percent of the total; in 1960 they were nearly 8.7 percent; and in 1970 they were roughly 9.0 percent. By 1990, about 27-million people, or about 10 percent of the population, will be in the over-65 group. With the almost complete disappearance of large multi-generation families and with the greater degrees of financial independence, made possible by social security and company retirement plans, more and more older people are maintaining their own households. Although there is little doubt that these households make up a separate market segment, many aging people do not want to be identified as "old and apart." While some housing developers have been very successful in developing and selling "retirement communities," they have discovered that many aging people prefer to live in "mixed-age communities." Clothing designers also are learning that there is only a small demand for separately identifiable old people's styles. But marketing

---

[9] For an interesting description and analysis of the teenage market segment, see: E. Gilbert, *Advertising and Marketing to Young People* (Pleasantville, N.Y.: Printers' Ink Books, 1957).

men should recognize that aging people, although they will reject anything that is clearly "old and apart," do, in the very nature of their needs, constitute a distinct market segment. In housing, for example, not only are their space requirements minimal, but the prices they can pay are often limited by the size of their retirement incomes. Recognizing this, home builders have begun to include some smaller retirement homes, although not labeled as such, in housing developments built primarily for younger families.

Market segmentation by stage in the life cycle, a concept developed by the Survey Research Center of the University of Michigan, classifies households according to the age of the household head, marital status, and the presence or absence of children. Households in the first stage are those in which there are no children and the household head is under the age of 40, married or unmarried. Second stage households include young children with or without older children. Third stage households include older children but no young children, and fourth stage households are ones with heads aged 40 or older who are married but who have no children under the age of 20 residing in the household. In households of the fifth and final stage, there are no children and the household head is single and aged 40 years or older.

Consumers have different needs at varying stages in the life cycle. Newly married couples, for example, are especially large buyers of furniture and household goods. Families with young children are very good customers for labor-saving appliances. Families with teenage daughters spend sizable sums on girls' and women's clothing. Table 5.7 shows how expenditures on selected items vary with the stage in the life cycle.

| | | No Children | Children | | No Children | |
	All House-holds	Single or Married Head under 40	Under 10	10–19 only	Married Head 40 or over	Single Head 40 or over
Total Expenditures	$4,110	$4,332	$4,607	$4,881	$3,639	$2,350
Prepared mixes	5	3	6	5	4	2
Major Appliances	84	87	107	89	68	33
Household waxes, Polishes, Cleaners	5	4	7	5	5	2
Women's and Girls' Clothing	210	236	196	298	195	158

TABLE 5–7
Average Annual Expenditures per Household
on Selected Items by Stage in the Life Cycle

Source: Data assembled from *Life Study of Consumer Expenditures*, Vol. 1, 1957.

Market Segments According to Degree of Urbanization

For many products, suburban households represent not only a richer but a larger market segment than do either urban or rural households. Suburban households are located in metropolitan areas outside the incorporated limits of large central cities. Rural households include both farm households and those in towns and villages of under 2,500 population. The *Life Study of Consumer Expenditures* showed that suburbanites, who only made 31 percent of total purchases, accounted for nearly half of the total spending on removable floor coverings and about 45 percent of the dollar purchases of sporting goods—phenomena tracing directly to suburban households' characteristically higher incomes,[10] and probably also to the tendency for suburban living to be more oriented towards "keeping up with the Joneses." Not only do suburban households spend more proportionately on many product categories but, as Table 5.8 indicates, people in suburbia now constitute the largest population group. By contrast, the population of central cities has remained relatively stable, while farm population has declined significantly.

TABLE 5–8
U.S. Population by Location of Residence—1960 and 1970

	1960	1970
Central cities	58,600,000	58,900,000
Suburbs	58,600,000	78,800,000
Small towns and nonfarm areas	47,100,000	54,500,000
Farms	13,310,000	8,900,000
Total U.S.	177,610,000	201,100,000

Source: 1960 U.S. Census Bureau; 1970, projections by *U.S. News and World Report* Economic Unit based on Census projections.

Market Segmentation by Ethnic and Racial Groups

The United States has been described as a melting pot of cultures and national groups, but this blending of peoples and cultures has not been complete. And, although an identifiable American national culture *has* emerged, it has not equally permeated all portions of society or all geographic regions. In parts of the American Southwest, for example, a Spanish

[10] Ostheimer, *op. cit.*, pp. 268-69.

or Mexican influence is still noticeable; in Minnesota, in the states surrounding it, and in the Puget Sound area, a Scandinavian flavor is still apparent. These areas of foreign ethnic flavor are found in various parts of the country and in clearly definable neighborhoods in cities. Although ethnic differences tend to decrease with each succeeding generation, their continuing existence helps to explain certain differences in consumer motivation and behavior that would not exist in a nation of people with a common cultural heritage. There has also been a tendency for the United States to evolve as a multiracial society with different patterns of social behavior in each racial group. These ethnic and racial factors contribute to the segmentation of the American market.

The continued existence of separate racial groups within the American society requires careful evaluation of racial groups as market segments. In many instances, different racial groups do not differ as consumers do across the entire spectrum of purchases. Thus, members of the Chinese community in San Francisco resemble the Caucasian residents of that city in most of their purchases, but with respect to food, many of them have unique wants and preferences. The same is true of American Indian communities.

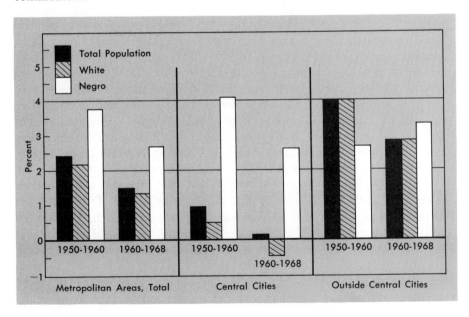

EXHIBIT 5–1

Metropolitan Areas—Average Annual Percentage Change in
Population by Race: 1950 to 1960 and 1960 to 1968
Source: Department of Commerce, Bureau of the Census.

Blacks, by far the largest racial minority group in the United States also represent a unique market segment for certain products. Many manufacturers produce products specifically targeted for the black market and design their distribution and promotional programs so as to most effectively reach this market segment. However, many factors that set the black market apart as a distinct segment are not really racial factors.[11] Many black buying patterns are better explained by the fact that a larger-than-average proportion of blacks are at the poverty income level. Important also is the geographical distribution of black population and trends in its mobility. Exhibit 5-1 shows that blacks are increasing their share of the population most rapidly in metropolitan areas, but they are increasing more rapidly than whites in all areas.

Geographical Market Segments

Within different parts of the United States, there are sufficient variations in consumption patterns to justify geographical market segmentation. These variations are the result of differing cultural heritages, topography, and climates and have significant implications for the marketers of some products. Furniture manufacturers, for example, find that consumer style preferences vary considerably among different geographic sections. The Southern consumer shows a much stronger preference for traditionally styled furniture than does the Mid-westerner. Similarly, many a Far Western consumer has a noticeably strong preference for furniture styles which show certain oriental influences. Other examples of distinctive regional preference are to be found in food, clothing, floor coverings, paint, and housing. Differences in climate also make for geographic market segmentation. For instance, areas with very hot summers are much better markets for home and automobile air conditioners. Similarly, those areas which have considerable winter snow are the most fertile sales areas for winter sports equipment.

Even more important to the marketer than regional variations in culture and climate are the regional variations in income. Table 5.9 shows the changes in total per capita income, by states and regions for selected years, 1929 through 1967. Despite the substantial gains made by the Far West, Southeast, and Southwest in per capita income during the period, the Mideast and Great Lakes regions are still far richer markets. To the soap manufacturer, these income differentials are of small importance, but to the automatic dishwasher manufacturer, the higher income regions are much riper selling areas. In analyzing the per capita incomes of different regions, however, we must remember that inter-regional variations in income are

[11] For an interesting analysis of the Negro market and of other low income consumers see, F. D. Sturdivant, *The Ghetto Marketplace* (New York: The Free Press, 1969).

TABLE 5—9
Changes in Total Per Capita Personal Income,
by State and Regions, Selected Years, 1929-67

State and Region	Total per capita Personal Income Percent of continental United States					Percent increase	
	1929	1940	1950	1957	1967	1929 to 1967	1957 to 1967
Continental United States	100.00	100.00	100.00	100.00	100.00	630	79
New England	8.32	8.15	6.73	6.57	6.34	456	77
Maine	.56	.57	.48	.45	.41	439	63
New Hampshire	.38	.36	.31	.31	.34	550	90
Vermont	.26	.23	.20	.18	.19	423	90
Massachusetts	4.51	4.32	3.45	3.29	3.06	397	73
Rhode Island	.69	.68	.57	.50	.48	402	76
Connecticut	1.92	1.99	1.72	1.84	1.86	608	81
Mideast	32.06	20.50	26.36	25.46	23.91	445	69
New York	16.47	14.92	12.43	11.86	11.02	389	68
New Jersey	4.33	4.37	3.86	4.07	4.12	591	77
Pennsylvania	8.79	8.17	7.30	6.76	5.93	392	59
Delaware	.28	.34	.31	.35	.30	693	69
Maryland	1.47	1.67	1.67	1.81	2.01	900	99
District of Columbia	.72	1.03	.79	.61	.53	442	61
Great Lakes	23.61	22.69	22.51	22.46	21.25	557	69
Michigan	4.44	4.60	4.79	4.84	4.66	666	72
Ohio	6.04	5.86	5.72	6.01	5.38	548	61
Indiana	2.30	2.42	2.66	2.64	2.56	709	74
Illinois	8.50	7.59	7.10	6.82	6.53	462	69
Wisconsin	2.33	2.22	2.24	2.15	2.12	560	75
Plains	8.87	8.30	8.80	8.08	7.71	536	73
Minnesota	1.80	1.87	1.86	1.78	1.78	625	82
Iowa	1.66	1.62	1.68	1.46	1.38	503	68
Missouri	2.66	2.52	2.53	2.39	2.20	505	71
North Dakota	.30	.29	.35	.27	.25	528	76
South Dakota	.34	.29	.35	.31	.28	505	63
Nebraska	.95	.74	.86	.76	.71	445	69
Kansas	1.16	.97	1.17	1.11	1.11	597	73
Southeast	11.67	13.23	15.17	15.38	16.92	959	95
Virginia	1.23	1.62	1.78	1.82	2.03	1107	100
West Virginia	.93	.99	.98	.89	.68	428	42
Kentucky	1.19	1.16	1.26	1.21	1.24	659	80
Tennessee	1.15	1.27	1.46	1.39	1.49	849	91
North Carolina	1.22	1.49	1.82	1.72	1.96	1073	106
South Carolina	.55	.74	.83	.81	.92	1123	104
Georgia	1.18	1.35	1.56	1.57	1.83	1029	98
Florida	.88	1.25	1.61	2.17	1.73	2171	121
Alabama	1.00	1.02	1.18	1.21	1.22	794	79
Mississippi	.67	.60	.71	.61	.72	681	105
Louisiana	1.01	1.10	1.30	1.39	1.44	939	78

TABLE 5−9 (Cont'd)

State and Region	Total per capita Personal Income Percent of continental United States					Percent increase	
	1929	1940	1950	1957	1967	1929 to 1967	1957 to 1967
Arkansas	.66	.64	.68	.59	.66	632	97
Southwest	4.97	5.21	6.50	6.79	6.94	918	82
Oklahoma	1.26	1.10	1.11	1.07	1.05	512	76
Texas	3.21	3.54	4.61	4.73	4.77	985	81
New Mexico	.20	.25	.35	.41	.40	1352	72
Arizona	.30	.32	.43	.58	.72	1649	119
Rocky Mountain	1.88	2.03	2.23	2.24	2.17	738	71
Montana	.36	.40	.42	.37	.31	521	50
Idaho	.26	.31	.34	.30	.29	700	63
Wyoming	.18	.19	.21	.19	.15	527	46
Colorado	.75	.79	.86	.96	.99	864	83
Utah	.33	.34	.40	.42	.43	839	79
Far West	8.62	9.89	11.70	13.02	14.21	1101	96
Washington	1.36	1.47	1.77	1.68	1.75	832	84
Oregon	.75	.86	1.09	.98	.98	846	80
Nevada	.09	.13	.14	.19	.25	1914	136
California	6.42	7.43	8.70	10.17	11.23	1176	97
Outside Continental U.S.					.55		107
Alaska					.16		89
Hawaii					.39		117

Source: "Personal Income, 1968 and Disposable Income, 1929-68 by States and Regions," *Survey of Current Business*, April, 1969, pp. 16-32.

not usually as great as the difference between urban and rural incomes within a single region. Hence, because Birmingham, Alabama and Cincinnati, Ohio are both large cities, the income of a person who lives in Birmingham is closer to that of the resident of Cincinnati than it is of an Alabama farmer.

Educational Attainment and Market Segmentation

Variations in education have a pronounced effect on the buying habits and patterns of individual consumers. But there is also a close relationship between education and income, so that it is difficult to say whether a college graduate buys an item because of his education or because of his high income. Sometimes, of course, a person has much education but a low income, causing him to scrimp on other things to buy such items as books and high-class magazines. For the most part, though, it is probably true that educational and income factors jointly influence the consumer to have a better-than-average library and to subscribe to magazines such as *Fortune*. Yet, many persons who have achieved high income status with less education may buy the same books and subscribe to the same publications in order to conform. If the income variable could be held constant, it undoubtedly would be very clear that variations in education result in unique market segments for many kinds of products and services. We might, then, know for sure whether educational or income factors or both are responsible for such phenomena as the following: the majority of encyclopedia buyers have had no formal education beyond high school; most buyers of classical records have had some instruction in music; Scotch whisky and other hard liquors are more preferred by persons with college educations than by persons with less, while beer and ale are the most popular drinks of persons without college educations.

The *Life Study* showed that households headed by persons with "some college or beyond" (one-fifth of all households) accounted for 26 percent of total spending, but they made 31 percent of the expenditures for frozen foods, 30 percent of the housing expenditures, and 32 percent of the photographic equipment expenditures. By contrast, households headed by persons who did not finish grade school (also about one-fifth of all households) did only 13 percent of the total spending, and made only 11 percent of the frozen foods expenditures, 11 percent of housing expenditures, and 8 percent of photographic equipment expenditures. This indicates that households headed by persons with college educations not only have more money but spend proportionally more on items where buying decisions are strongly influenced by the sophisticated and discriminating tastes that college educated individuals are likely to possess. Expenditures on frozen food, housing, and photographic equipment are directly related to the consumer's education, but there are some products for which the consumer's demand is inversely related to the amount of his education. Spending on cooking, baking, and salad ingredients, for example, tends to be higher in the lower educational levels. Households headed by persons who did not finish grade school make 32 percent of the expenditures in this category, and households headed by persons with "some college or beyond" make only 19 percent.[12] Probably differences in dietary preferences and eating habits, both of which are doubtless influenced by education, explain this inverse relationship.

Table 5.10 shows the shifting relative importance of various segments of the market by level of education. In the period from 1947 to 1968, the percentage of the population with less than five years of elementary school dropped from 10.6 percent to 5.9 percent of the total in the group 25 years of age and older. In the 25 to 29 years of age category, the drop was from 4.3 percent to 1.1 percent. During these same years the proportion of the total group over 25 years of age having completed four

---

[12] All percentage figures in this paragraph are taken from the *Life Study of Consumer Expenditures*, Vol. 1, 1957.

years of college increased from 5.4 percent to 10.5 percent. These increases in the level of education of the U.S. population have important implications for marketers serving these market segments.

TABLE 5–10
Level of School Completed—Total Population:
1947 to 1968 [1]

	Total			
	Years completed (percent distribution)			
Age and Year	Less than 5 years of elementary school	4 years of high school or more	4 years of college or more	Median school years completed
Persons 25 years old and over				
1947 [2]	10.6	33.1	5.4	9.0
1957	9.1	41.6	7.6	10.6
1960	8.3	41.1	7.7	10.5
1965	6.8	49.0	9.4	11.8
1967	6.1	51.1	10.1	12.0
1968	5.9	52.6	10.5	12.1
Persons 25–29 years old				
1947 [2]	4.3	51.4	5.6	12.0
1957	2.7	60.2	10.4	12.3
1960	2.8	60.7	11.1	12.3
1965	2.0	70.3	12.4	12.4
1967	1.1	72.5	12.4	12.5
1968	1.1	73.2	14.7	12.5

[1] Persons 25 years old and over as of March of year indicated, except as noted. Based on Current Population Survey; includes inmates of institutions and members of the Armed Forces living off post or with their families on post, but excludes all other members of the Armed Forces.
[2] As of April.
Source: *Statistical Abstract*, 1969, p. 107.

Religion and Market Segmentation

American society has a basically Judaeo-Christian religious heritage, and this has shaped its cultural development. Whereas some religions stress passive acceptance of life and man's role, the Christian and Jewish religions emphasize the perfectability of man and his environment and, hence, encourage him to improve himself and his way of life. Therefore, the production and consumption of goods are acceptable activities because they contribute to the welfare of society. Within the American Judaeo-Christian religious pattern, there are many individual sects and creeds, and, although they share similar feelings about the over-all roles of production and consumption in society, the patterns of consumption of selected foods, beverages, and apparel vary among these religious groups. Consequently, marketers of a few products, such as Kosher foods and ministerial and religious garments, design their products for and target their marketing efforts specifically for such market segments as the Jewish religious groups, the Catholic religious hierarchy, and various Protestant sects.

INDUSTRIAL USERS

Industrial users make purchases to further the production of other goods and services. The goods and services so produced may be destined either for the ultimate consumer market or for other parts of the industrial market, which includes both private enterprises and government agencies. Any organization, private or public, that makes purchases in order to facilitate the performance of manufacturing, marketing, or institutional activities is an industrial user. Thus, the different types of industrial users engaged in producing and marketing products range all the way from the individual farmer to the large manufacturer. Those engaged in marketing services are as diverse as the independent insurance agent and free-lance writer at one extreme to the large hospitals, theaters, and hotels at the other. Also included are transportation and public utility companies, schools, military installations, prisons, and all other types of governmental units. In short, any organization is classed as an industrial user if it purchases some goods and services *not for resale in the same form* but in order to use them in connection with its operation. Therefore, to the extent that they buy products for resale in the same form, retailers, wholesalers, and other middlemen are not considered industrial users. But when retailers, wholesalers and other middlemen buy products (e.g., display equipment and cash registers) and services (e.g., accounting service and the advice of business consultants) for use in furthering their operations, they are considered industrial users.

The industrial market is a large one [13] and, like the consumer market, is made up of many market segments. Therefore, market segmenta-

---

[13] It has been estimated that nearly one half of all goods marketed are industrial goods. See: R. S. Alexander, J. S. Cross, and R. M. Cunningham, *Industrial Marketing*, rev. ed. (Homewood, Ill.: Richard D. Irwin, 1961), pp. 5-6.

tion is as important for industrial as for consumer goods. Separating industrial users into groups facilitates analysis of the industrial market. There are many bases which can be used in segmenting the industrial market, the four most important and most used bases being kind of business or activity, geographical location of the user, usual purchasing procedure, and size of user.

Kind of Business or Activity

One of the most useful ways of segmenting the industrial market, and the one used by practically all government agencies, is known as the S.I.C., or Standard Industrial Classification System. Under this system, all places of business are classified into one of ten divisions covering the entire field of economic activities:

1. Agriculture, forestry, and fisheries.
2. Mining.
3. Construction.
4. Manufacturing.
5. Transportation, communication, electric, gas, and sanitary services.
6. Wholesale and retail trade.
7. Finance, insurance, and real estate.
8. Services.
9. Government.
10. "All others" or "nonclassifiable establishments."

Each of these ten divisions is broken down into several "major groups" representing specific kinds of business. The manufacturing division, for example, is broken down into such major groups as textile mill products, printing and publishing, and chemicals and allied products, each major group having assigned to it a two digit S.I.C. number. Manufacturers of furniture and fixtures would be classified under S.I.C. #25. Still further classification is effected through three and four digit numbers with manufacturers of household furniture coming under S.I.C. #251, and manufacturers of metal household furniture coming under S.I.C. #2514. Thus, by using the S.I.C. system, the industrial market can be divided into relatively small, medium, or large market segments. A knowledge of this system is essential to the market analyst who uses reports published by governmental agencies.[14]

[14] For a description of the Standard Industrial Classification System and a full listing of S.I.C. numbers and classifications, see Technical Committee on Industrial Classification, *Standard Industrial Classification Manual* (Washington, D.C.: U.S. Government Printing Office, 1957).

Geographical Market Segments in the Industrial Market

Segmentation of the industrial market, like the consumer market, may also be done on a geographical basis. Such factors as variations in topography, climate, and historical tradition cause considerable variation in the way industrial marketing is conducted in different areas. The topography of an area, for example, affects the types and costs of transportation available for shipping industrial goods. Thus, a firm marketing a heavy and relatively cheap industrial item, such as cement or coal, often can cultivate a distant industrial user only if transportation rates are low enough to permit successful competition with similar suppliers nearer the particular user. Similarly, variations in climate affect the needs of industrial users for building materials and heating and cooling equipment, just as the same variations cause differences in the demand for certain consumer products. Differing regional traditions may, for example, show up in a greater demand for labor saving devices in areas where wage rates are relatively high. Regional differences, based partly on tradition and partly on management philosophy, also affect whether or not manufacturers provide in-plant feeding, recreation, and health-care facilities for their employees, these facilities being much more common in the Northeast and Midwest than elsewhere throughout the country.

In addition, different geographical segments of the industrial market exist because some kinds of business and service organizations seem to settle in certain areas. Some types of industrial users form geographical clusters because their locations have been dictated by the source of raw materials: the lumber industry in the Pacific Northwest and the copper mining industry in Arizona, Montana, and Utah. Others locate at points enjoying relatively easy access both to raw materials and to large markets; for example, the major concentrations of the steel and automobile industries in the Great Lakes region. The pressing need for reservoirs of highly-talented scientific personnel is the major reason why numerous companies in the electronic component industry are located in and around Boston, San Francisco, and on Long Island. A combination of historical accident, the momentum of an early start, and tradition appears to account for the presence of numerous insurance company home offices in Hartford, much of the shoe industry in New England, New York, Pennsylvania, and Missouri, and the bulk of the entertainment industry in Southern California and New York City.

Because of this tendency for some kinds of industrial users to locate in a small number of areas, marketers selling to such users have to adjust their marketing procedures accordingly. Even though most companies in an industry may be located in a few areas, there almost always are a few situated elsewhere. This leads many marketers of industrial products, such as those selling shoe findings, to maintain their own full-time salesmen in areas where most customers are concentrated and either to call less frequently on outlying accounts or to reach them through middlemen. Similarly, such marketers often operate their own warehouses in areas of customer concentration and rely on shipments from the factory for supplying customers situated elsewhere. Marketers generally find that it costs more to sell to outlying customers than to those concentrated geographically. Under these conditions, then, different marketing approaches and programs are usually needed.

Not all of the industrial market is characterized by geographical clustering. Some types of users, such as schools and small retailers, are simply located wherever there are people. Others—such as military installations, some kinds of wholesalers, and agencies of state and local governments—while not to be found everywhere are still rather widely dispersed. Nevertheless, in formulating distribution policies and deciding upon selling procedures, the concentration or lack of concentration of the industrial users of the product is a highly important consideration. In either case, the industrial marketer can benefit by separating his potential users into market segments on the basis of geography.

Industrial Market Segmentation on the Basis of Usual Purchasing Procedures

Industrial users are generally more systematic buyers than are ultimate consumers. But even among industrial users, there is much variation in the amount of consideration given to buying different items. The purchase of a major installation, such as a blast furnace or cement kiln, requires extensive market and other technical investigations plus the approval of several high executives in the industrial user's organization. In the same firm, however, the purchase of supplies such as office stationery or pencils is a routine procedure of concern only to the purchasing agent. The industrial marketer must apply different selling tactics and stagies to each of these buying situations.

Purchasing procedures may vary even for the same industrial product. An industrial user who is buying an item as original equipment will usually follow a more complex purchasing procedure than if he were buying the same item as a replacement. Because of relative unfamiliarity and lack of experience with the product, the industrial user buying an item as original equipment demands fuller and more technical information about it, often conducts an exhaustive study of potential suppliers and their products, and more of the user firm's executives participate in the buying decision. When the item is being bought as replacement equipment, experience, and familiarity with the product make it possible for the buying decision to be made in a more routine fashion. Recognizing this, some industrial marketers have further separated their markets into original equipment and replacement equipment segments.

Industrial Market Segmentation by Size of User

In the industrial market there is a much wider range in the size of customers than there is in the consumer market. Industrial users may vary in size from those with very few employees to those with many thousands of employees. They vary all the way from the small machine shop in an old garage to industrial giants such as Lockheed Aircraft and RCA. Consequently, the size of an industrial purchase may vary greatly. Because it normally is more economical to sell in large lots than small, the industrial marketer often sets lower prices for purchasers placing large orders than for those buying in small quantities. More important, this characteristic is often the main reason why marketers frequently use different methods for reaching industrial users who vary greatly in size. Ample reason exists for market segmentation based on the size of industrial users.

CONCLUSION—SEGMENTATION AND MARKETING STRATEGY

A few products, such as salt and sugar, are purchased and consumed in relatively equal amounts by all elements of the consumer market. Similarly, stationery and office supplies are purchased and used by nearly all industrial users. Yet, it is difficult to think of any product which appeals in like form to both industrial and consumer markets. The producer needs to offer different products or at least variations in similar products to satisfy these two kinds of markets. Although both ultimate consumers and industrial users use stationery, they are not satisfied with the identical stationery.

Market segmentation exists even for products which are consumed essentially by the entire market. Thus, although all consumers require salt, they do not need exactly the same product. The informed producer recognizes that some geographic regions require iodized salt because of the absence of iodine or other elements in the environment. He also packages his product so as to serve different consumer needs. He provides bulk packages for normal household use but throw-away-shakers for picnics and vacation and holiday use. The alert marketer recognizes that even the same customer may buy a product to serve different needs at different times, and he optimizes his sales by serving each need with a different product.

Recent new product introductions by the Ford Motor Company illustrate the importance of identifying and serving market segments. The automobile industry has for many years segmented its market by offering product variations to serve different needs. Various models and price ranges within models have been offered to serve different income segments. Different body styles have been offered from sporty convertibles to sedate sedans to serve different age and geographic segments. The Ford Mustang was designed to meet the needs of a market segment not previously considered large enough to justify separate treatment. Demographers pointed out that by the middle to late 1960s the proportion of the American population in the 20-to-30 year age group would be considerably greater than before, be better-educated, and have a higher average income. No automobile had been specifically designed for this age group up to that time, primarily because their numbers were relatively small and many young people could not afford new cars. Ford designed the Mustang specifically to serve this market segment. Body styling and performance characteristics were in line with the preferences of young people. The price was kept moderate enough to be acceptable to this age group but with variations possible through optional features. Promotion was planned to appeal to the 20-to-30 year age group. The result of this carefully planned marketing strategy was a highly successful product, which was acceptable to the target market segment.

Recognition of the existence of market segmentation is necessary to successful marketing strategy. Effective marketing plans are based upon careful evaluations of the target markets. In most instances this means selecting and serving certain segments of the total market. Few products are potentially satisfying to all people; instead, each product must be modified and marketed to meet the unique preferences of each target market segment.

QUESTIONS AND PROBLEMS

1. "With products being differentiated more and more, markets are certain to become increasingly segmented." Agree or disagree? Why or why not?

2. Of what value is a breakdown of markets by industrial users and ultimate consumers, since the same individual, when buying a typewriter for his office is an industrial user, and when buying a typewriter for his home is an ultimate consumer? Is he really likely to act differently in these two situations?

3. Is market segmentation a concept equally valuable to marketers of all

kinds of products? Would it be of much help to a soap producer? An automobile manufacturer? A life insurance company? An airline?

4. If a family's income doubles (increases from $10,000 to $20,000), what would you expect to happen to its relative expenditures for food? Clothing? Housing?

5. In American society, the housewife has become the primary purchasing agent for the family. Is it probably true that with this greater responsibility for buying has gone an increased authority to make buying decisions?

6. Under what conditions should a manufacturer consider segmenting his market along sexual lines? With such segmentation, what differences would probably be necessary in the two marketing programs?

7. Analyze the figures and projections concerning the age and sex of the U.S. population given in Table 5-6 from the standpoint of their significance for each of the following:
   a. A manufacturer of dolls and doll apparel
   b. A producer of school furniture
   c. A manufacturer of sterling silver and stainless steel flatware
   d. A pharmaceutical maker.

8. A retired elderly couple with an income of $10,000 a year from retirement benefits and social security may have as much buying power as a couple in their twenties with an income of $15,000 a year. Explain how this might be true. In what different ways would they be likely to spend their income?

9. Explain the marketing significance of market segmentation by stage in the life cycle.

10. Would you expect the U.S. rural market to be much different from the urban and suburban markets in terms of preferences for clothing, food, and leisure time activities? Are these differences likely to be larger or smaller than regional or geographic differences within like groups, e.g., urban dwellers?

11. To what extent do ethnic and racial market segments exist in the United States? Would you anticipate that such segments as now exist will become more pronounced or disappear? Why?

12. Would it be accurate to assume that regional differences in consumer preferences are rapidly disappearing with improved communication and transportation? Explain.

13. Why do lower-education-level families spend considerably more money on cooking, baking, and salad ingredients than college-level families? Do eating habits and income differences provide a complete explanation? Explain.

14. Would the Standard Industrial Classification System provide an equally satisfactory basis for segmenting the market for drill presses as for typewriting paper? Why or why not?

15. Why should San Diego, California, prove to be a more promising market for the products of a Seattle, Washington, lumber mill than Denver, Colorado?

16. If it makes sense to identify different segments of the industrial market as potential purchasers of original equipment and replacements, does it make equally good sense to differentiate these products and use separate salesmen? Explain.

6

BUYER BEHAVIOR: ITS ECONOMIC AND PSYCHOLOGICAL ASPECTS

The behavior of buyers, both businessmen and individual consumers, is influenced by numerous uncontrollables. If management is to use the controllables (i.e., product, price, promotion, and distribution) effectively, clear understanding of these uncontrollables is essential. Of particular interest to marketing management are economic, psychological, and socio-cultural uncontrollables. all of which exert significant influences on buyer behavior. These uncontrollables are analyzed in this and the next chapter.

Analysis in this chapter focuses upon the economic and psychological uncontrollables. We will first consider various contributions by economists to the theory of buyer behavior, including the model of economic man, sorting theory, and the income-expenditures model. Then, we will examine certain aspects of buyer behavior explainable only in terms of psychological theories and concepts. In the course of this examination, we shall explore various ideas from each of the three major approaches to the development of a psychological theory of buyer behavior: the laboratory or experimental, the clinical, and the Gestalt. Equipped with an understanding of the economic and psychological uncontrollables, the groundwork will have been laid for our analysis of the socio-cultural uncontrollables, which are discussed in Chapter 7.

ECONOMIC FACTORS AFFECTING BUYER BEHAVIOR

Economic theorists were the first to advance formal explanations of buyer behavior. Economists generally visualize a market as made up of homogeneous buyers who act in a predictably similar fashion and the economic process as the matching of homogeneous segments of supply with homogeneous segments of demand. Economic theory describes man as a rational buyer who has perfect information about the market and uses it to obtain optimum value for his buying effort and money. Price is regarded as his strongest motivation. He compares all alternative sellers' offerings, and, since all competing products are homogeneous in every respect, he buys the offering with the lowest price. Above all, economic man's behavior is rational. Under these circumstances his buying choices are predictable and yield maximum value.

In many situations the model of economic man helps us understand and even predict consumer buying behavior. It explains why many a housewife selects the food store with the most or best "week-end specials" for her Friday shopping trip. It explains why a special price on Brand X may attract the patronage of a customer who normally purchases Brand Y. It also explains why a consumer, having decided to buy a new Ford station wagon, will visit several Ford dealerships to get the best trade-in and net price.

However, for the most part, decision-making by individuals is far too complex and too involved to reduce to the simplistic model of economic man. For example, while it may explain why a buyer chooses one Ford dealer over another, it does not explain why he decided to buy a Ford instead of a Chevrolet, a station wagon instead of a sedan, a V–8 instead of a six. To understand buyer behavior, we must consider numerous and diverse factors. Nevertheless, economists have contributed importantly in other ways to our understanding of buyer behavior. In addition to the economic man model, as we shall shortly see, several other economic concepts are highly useful in explaining buyer behavior.

The Sorting Model

In striving for a realistic explanation of buyer behavior, we must discard one assumption that pervades the concept of economic man—that markets are homogeneous. Heterogeneity, not homogeneity, characterizes markets. The entire notion of market segmentation (described in Chapter 5) is based on the realization that buyers are not all alike, that they differ in numerous and diverse ways. Furthermore, this heterogeneity is evident on both the supply and demand sides of every market. Marketing, considered as an economic process, has the goal of matching heterogeneous segments of supply with heterogeneous segments of demand. This goal is achieved through the marketing mechanism know as "sorting."

The whole economic process starts with conglomerations and ends with assortments.[1] A conglomeration contains two or more types of goods, but they have not been brought together for the purpose of serving the needs of a particular individual or group. An assortment is also a collection of two or more types of goods, but unlike a conglomeration, the goods in an assortment either complement each other directly or are jointly capable of serving the needs of a particular individual or group.[2] The intermediate phases in moving goods from a heterogeneous supply segment to a heterogeneous demand segment consist of the four types of sorting with which much of marketing is concerned. Alderson describes these types of sorting as follows:

> Starting with a conglomeration, we can perform the operation of *sorting out*, which breaks the collection into various types of goods. Sorting out results in a set of separate supplies which may be regarded as homogeneous in terms of the classification being used by the sorter. Given small homogeneous supplies, it is possible to create larger supplies by adding one to another. This building-up of a larger supply may represent the *accumulation* over a period of time from a single sorting operation, or it may represent the bringing together in a single place products which meet standard specifications but are drawn from different localities . . . Once a large homogeneous supply has been accumulated, it may . . . be broken down by a process of apportionment or *allocation*. Division of the total supply is made in terms of the requirements of various operating units whose claims are to be met. Allocation may take place within a single organization in terms of planning and control, or it may take place through the market and be determined by such a consideration as price. Finally, there is the step of using supplies to build up assortments. This process may be designated as *assorting*, or the putting together of unlike supplies in accordance with some pattern determined by demand.[3]

---

[1] The ideas which form the basic substance of this section are contained in the writings of the late Wroe Alderson, a distinguished management consultant, who was a major contributor to the development of marketing theory. See: W. Alderson, *Marketing Behavior and Executive Action* (Homewood, Ill.: Richard D. Irwin, 1957), especially Chapter VII. Also see: W. Alderson, "The Analytical Framework for Marketing," in D. J. Duncan (ed.), *Proceedings of the Conference of Marketing Teachers from Far Western States* (Berkeley: University of California, 1958), pp. 15-28.

[2] Alderson, *Marketing Behavior and Executive Action*, op. cit., pp. 199-200.

[3] *Ibid.*, p. 201.

During the process of marketing, all these types of sorting are used in matching supply with demand. Whereas economic theory has emphasized scarcity rather than the unique character of consumer's needs and has paid most attention to the allocation phase of sorting, marketing theory places the emphasis on assorting, the final sorting step required in meeting the needs of consumers. In other words, marketing theory attempts to explain consumer buying behavior in terms of what consumers are trying to do. Essentially, consumers are engaged in building assortments, in replenishing or extending inventories of goods for use by themselves and their families. This, according to Alderson, means that the consumer buyer enters the market as a problem-solver. Solving a problem, either on behalf of a household or on behalf of a marketing organization, means reaching a decision in the face of uncertainty. In the double search which pervades marketing, the consumer buyer and the marketing executive are opposite numbers. The consumer buyer looks for goods in order to complete an assortment, while the marketing executive looks for buyers who need his goods.[4]

This viewpoint is consistent with those economic theories that explain competition among sellers by emphasizing innovative competition, product differentiation and differential advantage. The position occupied by every firm engaged in marketing is in some respects unique. Each firm is differentiated from all others by the characteristics of its products, its services, its geographic location, or its particular combination of these features. Therefore, the survival of each firm requires that it present, to some group of buyers, a differential advantage over all other suppliers. A marketing organization sells to a core market, composed of buyers who prefer this source, and to a fringe market, made up of buyers who find the source acceptable, at least for occasional purchases.[5]

The "Income-Expenditures" Model

Of the many factors affecting the strength of buyer demand, income is by far the most powerful. Purchasing power in the hands of consumers and other spending units, most of it current income, is a basic ingredient of the economic process. Products may be produced and consumers may "want" to buy them, but no exchange takes place unless there is purchasing power in the form of money (or some money substitute such as credit) with which to complete purchase-sale transactions. It is appropriate, then, for us to consider the way in which purchasing power is generated. Economists have developed various "models" in their attempts to explain this process.

[4] Alderson, "The Analytical Framework of Marketing," *op. cit.*, pp. 17-18.
[5] *Ibid.*, p. 18.

For some years, economists have held that total spending depends on the "circular" flow of income. Consumers spend their incomes to buy products from businesses, and businesses pay their employees (who are also consumers) for providing services. Furthermore, businesses buy from and sell to each other, and every such transaction involves the exchange of products and/or services by one side in return for money from the other side. In every purchase-sale transaction, the buyer looks upon the transaction as requiring spending, while the seller looks upon it as providing income. Thus, the flow of income is from businesses to employee consumers, from consumers to businesses, and from businesses to businesses. If such intermediaries as wholesalers and retailers are disregarded, it is easy to see that John Jones gets the money to buy a room air conditioner by working at a steel mill. The steel mill gets the money to pay John Jones by selling steel to the manufacturer of room air conditioners. The manufacturer of room air conditioners gets the money to pay for the steel by selling room air conditioners to John Jones and other consumers.

Economic Factors Affecting Personal Consumption Spending

DISPOSABLE PERSONAL INCOME   Goods and services are produced for purposes of consumption; purchasing power is used to convert production into consumption; and disposable personal income represents potential purchasing power in the hand of consumers. Therefore, there is a relationship between total disposable personal income and total personal consumption spending. Economists have made many studies of this relationship, which they call the "consumption function." [6]

Occasionally, personal consumption spending equals or actually exceeds disposable personal income, as happened during the depression of the 1930s. In such instances, consumers spend purchasing power from sources other than current income—for example, from savings or grants of credit.

In most years, however, people spend only part of their income. Normally, disposable personal income exceeds personal consumption spending. Disposable personal income is used both for personal consumption spending and for saving, and there is usually a fairly stable relationship between the amount of income, the proportion spent, and the proportion saved. Only when spending or income is drastically curtailed does this relationship change markedly. During World War II, for example, shortages

[6] For example, see: M. Friedman, *A Theory of the Consumption Function* (Princeton, N.J.: Princeton University Press, 1957). For some comments on the theory expounded by Professor Friedman, see those of J. Tobin, T. Morgan, I. Friend, and G. H. Orcutt in: L. H. Clark (ed.), *Consumer Behavior* (New York: Harper & Brothers, 1958), pp. 447-62.

of many consumer goods forced people to divert more of their incomes into savings. Immediately after the war the relationship shifted in the opposite direction, as people spent higher proportions of their incomes and dipped into their savings in order to buy items that had long been on their shopping lists.

PROPENSITIES TO CONSUME AND TO SAVE   The relationship which we have called the "consumption function," is also known as the *average propensity to consume*. If disposable personal income in some year comes to $600-billion and personal consumption spending is $550-billion, the average propensity to consume is 550 ÷ 600 or roughly 92 percent. Therefore, in this year, on the average, people would spend about $92 out of every $100 received. They would save, on the average, the remaining $8. The *average propensity to save* would be 8 percent. The average propensities to consume and to save indicate the divisions which consumers normally make of their total disposable incomes. They do not indicate, unless average propensities remain unchanged, what changes in spending and saving to expect if total incomes should rise or fall. Sometimes average propensities do not change with changes in income, but they usually do.

In order to facilitate analysis of the way people allocate changes in their total incomes between spending and saving, economists have developed two additional concepts—the *marginal propensity to consume* and the *marginal propensity to save*. If disposable personal income should rise from $600-billion to $610-billion, businessmen would be interested in learning what proportion of the additional $10-billion consumers might decide to spend and what proportion they might decide to save. Suppose that out of the $10-billion of "marginal" income, consumers spend $9-billion and save $1-billion. The proportion spent (9 ÷ 10, or 90 percent, is called the *marginal propensity to consume*. The proportion saved (1 ÷ 10), or 10 percent, is known as the *marginal propensity to save*. Occassionally the average and marginal propensities to consume and save are identical, but usually they are not.

Business analysts, including marketing analysts, are usually more interested in examining the effect of changes in income on spending and saving than they are in the average relationships. This interest is understandable. Consider what happens to personal consumption spending with a change in income. The percentage of disposable personal income used for personal consumption spending rose from 90 percent in 1967 to 91 percent in 1968, an increase of only one per cent. In other words, the average propensities to consume and save changed very little.

But what happened to the marginal propensity to consume? From 1967 to 1968, disposable personal income rose from $546.5-billion to $590-billion, while personal consumption spending went up from $492.3-

billion, to $536.6-billion. There was, then, a $43.5-billion increase in income and a $44.3-billion increase in consumer spending. Dividing the change in spending by the change in income (44.3 ÷ 43.5), the marginal propensity to consume was actually about 102 per cent—that is, people were spending all of the extra $43.5-billion in income and then some! This result to some extent reflects the inflationary prices characteristic of the late 1960s; ten years earlier, the marginal propensity to consume hovered around 70 percent. *Personal consumption spending tends both to rise and fall at a slower rate than does disposable personal income,* but in inflationary periods, spending sometimes rises faster than income. Generally, however, in years of higher income, a lower proportion of income is spent and a higher proportion is saved. In years of lower income, the proportion spent tends to increase and that saved declines. The *marginal* propensity to consume and to save concepts take into account the rates of change. The *average* propensity to consume and to save concepts do not. That explains why analysts consider the two marginal concepts so valuable.

SIZE OF FAMILY, SIZE OF FAMILY INCOME, AND CHANGES IN FAMILY INCOME   Size of family income and size of family obviously affect patterns of spending and saving but, unfortunately, little research has been reported on these relationships. One study made several years ago disclosed that in urban families with low incomes, average personal consumption spending exceeded income. It also showed that the average propensity to consume tended to decline rather rapidly as income rose above the poverty level.[7]

A second study, made a few years later, provided some insights on spending behavior relative to household gross income (i.e., income before taxes). It confirmed what businessmen had long assumed—average annual household spending rises with increases in gross income per household. Households with above-average incomes are above-average spenders, those with below-average incomes are below-average spenders. But contrary to what is commonly assumed, this study reported that the number of people in a household appears directly related to the size of annual household income. As the number of people in a household increases, annual household income rises—perhaps because more household members have incomes and/or because people with larger incomes can afford larger families. This study also revealed that high-income households accounted for a disproportionately high share of total spending—53 percent of the households with above-average incomes accounted for 67 percent of total spending.[8]

Findings such as these imply that significant changes occur in the

[7] See: *Study of Consumer Expenditures, Incomes, and Savings* (Philadelphia: Wharton School of Finance and Commerce, University of Pennsylvania, 1956), Vol. 18.
[8] *The Life Study of Consumer Expenditures,* 1957, Vol. 1, pp. 18-21.

spending and saving patterns of a family as it moves from one income
bracket to another. Thus, changes in the distribution of U.S. families relative
to income brackets may bring about important changes in propensities to
consume and to save.

CONSUMERS' INCOME EXPECTATIONS   The incomes which consumers expect to receive in the future have some bearing on their present
spending patterns. In particular, spending for automobiles, furniture, major
appliances, and other durables, tends to be influenced by consumers' optimism or pessimism about future income. The existence of this tendency
was evident in the results of the several annual surveys made for the
Federal Reserve Board by the Survey Research Center of the University
of Michigan. Consumers' expectations of higher or lower income have a
direct effect on spending plans.

The Federal Reserve Board in 1959 initiated a *Quarterly Survey
of Consumer Buying Intentions.* FRB officials believed that the previous
annual surveys did not provide adequate information on buying plans
since shifts in plans during a year went undetected. The survey now
emphasizes a six-month consumer planning period, which the FRB considers more realistic as a planning horizon than a one-year period. The
quarterly surveys provide information on buying plans broken down by
family income groups and by age of heads of households. In addition to
presenting data on the timing of planned purchases, information on buying
plans is reported in three ways—"definitely," "probably," and "maybe." Thus,
this study takes into account the varying degrees of certainty of consumer
buying plans.

Another source of information on consumers' income expectations and related data is the *Survey of Consumer Attitudes and Buying
Plans* conducted on a "continuous" basis for the National Industrial
Conference Board. The stated purposes of the NICB survey are to identify
the expectational determinants of consumer spending and saving and to
improve methods of analysis of consumer behavior. Among other items included in this survey are "current household income compared with six
months before and six months hence" and "opinions about current and
anticipated economic conditions (business, employment, and household
income)" broken down by income groups. Respondents' opinions are
categorized as "good," "normal," "bad" or "other" (i.e., "no opinion" or
"not determined"). Information is also reported on consumers' "plans to
buy automobiles, homes, home improvements and accessories, and appliances within six months."

CONSUMERS' LIQUID ASSETS   Consumers' buying plans are influenced, especially in regard to such "big ticket" items as automobiles and

major appliances, by the size of their holdings of liquid assets, i.e., cash and other assets readily convertible into cash (e.g., balances in checking and savings accounts, shares in savings and loan associations, deposits in credit unions, U.S. savings and other government bonds, and readily marketable stocks and bonds). Even though a consumer may actually buy with current income, the freedom with which he spends is influenced by his accumulation of liquid assets. Retired and unemployed individuals may use liquid assets to buy everyday necessities. Other consumers may use liquid assets to meet major medical bills and other emergencies.

CONSUMER CREDIT   Availability of consumer credit has greatly influenced the pattern of consumer spending. For example, credit has been a powerful factor in making possible the rapid growth of the markets for mobile homes, boats, camping trailers, and the like.[9]

Personal debt includes all short- and intermediate-term consumer debt other than charge accounts and excludes mortgage and business debt. Personal debt, thus defined, is equivalent to installment credit—i.e., the consumer pays his debt in a number of installments. Generally speaking, more than half of all spending units have such debts. The size of income is directly related to the amount of credit a consumer can obtain. Lower income groups tend to have either no debt or smaller amounts of debt than higher income groups. Since 1964, the volume of installment consumer credit has been approximately four times the volume of noninstallment credit.[10]

DISCRETIONARY INCOME   A family with money left after buying such necessities as food, clothing, shelter, and transportation, has discretionary income. During the 1960s, families with disposable personal incomes of less than $5,000 generally had little or no discretionary income. But, as families moved above $5,000, they had extra income with which they could exercise a number of options. They could buy better food and drink or better furniture, or they could take a small flyer in the stock market, or they could spend it all on one big fling, like a trip to Europe.

By the time families move above the $10,000 income level, about half of their income is discretionary, and the decisions are not between purchasing certain items or others but rather of choosing an entire life style. The skilled laborer with a $12,000 income could choose to live in a working class neighborhood and style and save a large portion of his income, or he could choose to live like a junior executive. It is estimated that in 1970 more than half of all disposable income was discretionary.

A growth in discretionary income usually results in increased

[9] *Federal Reserve Bulletin*, June 1969, p. 471.
[10] *Federal Reserve Bulletin*, December, 1969, pp. 54-57.

spending. After deciding to spend some or all of the increased income, a family must decide how to spend it. Discretionary income may be used to buy nondurables, durables, services (e.g., household operation, housing, and transportation), or some combination of these broad categories.

Even small fluctuations in income cause sharp repercussions in consumers' purchases of durables. Part of this situation traces to the fact that consumers can postpone or speed up their purchases of such durables as automobiles, furniture, and major appliances. If a family is temporarily short of income, it can always use the old refrigerator for another year or so. Or if the family finds itself suddenly with more discretionary income, it may replace the refrigerator this year instead of next. The quick response of durable goods' expenditures to income changes arises also from the wide use of installment credit in financing such purchases. Consumers are more willing to increase installment debt when income is rising and are more reluctant to incur additional indebtedness when income is declining. Lenders are also more agreeable to the process of debt creation in prosperous times.

Factors Affecting Business Spending

"Gross private domestic investment" includes the business counterpart of personal consumption spending. Marketers selling products to the industrial and the residential construction market are especially interested in the factors that affect this component of the gross national product. Usually, about three-quarters of gross private domestic investment is accounted for by business spending (on plant, machinery and equipment, and on inventories). The remaining one-quarter consists of investments in housing made by individuals.

Business spending—i.e., business investment—depends largely on businessmen's appraisals of opportunities for profits. Economists use a special concept, the *marginal efficiency of investment,* to describe the anticipated net return on a given investment. Marginal efficiency of investment depends on such matters as the sales and profit outlook for the products manufactured and/or marketed by the entreprise, the chances that investment will improve manufacturing or marketing efficiency or both and thus bring down the costs of doing business, the corporate income tax rate (businessmen tend to compute rates of return on investment *after taxes*), and the general business outlook. Businessmen compare the marginal efficiency of investment with the costs of obtaining money to invest in order to determine whether a given investment will "pay out" a sum sufficient to cover the risks involved. Money for business investment is obtained from the personal savings made by individuals, from what business itself "saves" in the form of retained earnings, and from funds set aside to cover the depreciation of business assets.

THE "MULTIPLIER" EFFECT   Changes in business investment cause rather exaggerated changes in consumer income. If business investment is increased, the investment eventually is paid out in the form of income to people who are also consumers. Consumers save part of their increased incomes but spend the larger portion. This spending, in turn, becomes additional income to other consumers who also save but re-spend most of the extra money. Again and again this re-spending and income-generating process is repeated. The *multiplier* is the name given the number of times the final increase in income exceeds the new investment. If the marginal propensity to consume is known, it is possible to compute the multiplier. For example, if the marginal propensity to consume is .90, the multiplier is computed as follows:

$$\text{Multiplier} = \frac{1}{1 - \text{m.p.c.}} = \frac{1}{1 - .90} = \frac{1}{.10} = 10$$

In this illustration, then, $1 of new business investment results ultimately in an addition to income of $10 ($1×10). The multiplier effect explains how a change in business investment can cause consumer income to fluctuate widely. As indicated earlier, however, there are many factors that affect income, and business investment is only one.

THE "ACCELERATION" PRINCIPLE   Just as business investment affects consumer income and consumer spending, so does consumer spending have a reverse effect on business investment and spending. This effect is called the "acceleration" principle. The principle itself traces to the fact that the demand for industrial goods derives from the demand for the final products which find their way to consumers. Quantitative changes in the sales of a final product tend to cause greatly magnified changes in the production and sale of the industrial goods used to make that final product. Operation of the acceleration principle is illustrated in Table 6.1. Note the assumptions listed at the bottom of this table. In base year plus one, there is a 10 percent increase in the demand for product X, and this causes a 100 percent increase in the demand for the machines used to manufacture product X. Demand for product X increases again in base year plus two, and machine demand rises by 50 percent over the year before. In base year plus three, demand for product X declines by 3,000 units (a drop of less than five percent), but machine demand falls by 80 percent. In base year plus four, product X demand declines another 5,000 units (a little over 8 percent), and machine demand is non-existent. The acceleration principle also tends to operate in both the accumulation and the liquidation of inventories by manufacturers, wholesalers, and retailers in response to changes in consumer spending resulting from changes in consumer incomes. However, the principle is mainly used as an analytical framework in which

TABLE 6–1

The "Acceleration" Principle Illustrated [a]

Year	Unit Demand for Product X (Final Product)	Machines for Making Product X in Use	Demand for Replace- ment Machines	Demand for Additional New Machines	Total Demand for Machines
Base	50,000 units	50	5	0	5
Base plus 1	55,000 "	55	5	5	10
Base plus 2	65,000 "	65	5	10	15
Base plus 3	62,000 "	62	3	0	3
Base plus 4	57,000 "	57	0	0	0

[a] Assumptions:
 1. This firm is the sole maker of the machines used to produce product X, and these machines can be used for no other purpose.
 2. The 50 machines in use during the base year are evenly spaced as to age, and average machine life is 10 years. In the base year, 10 percent of the machines are in the tenth year of use, 10 percent are in the ninth year, etc.
 3. Each machine is used to full capacity and produces 1,000 units of product X per year.
 4. There is no unused production capacity in the base year, and each year everything that is produced is also sold.

to study the often drastic fluctuations in demand occurring in industries producing capital goods and equipment.

The Effect of Government Spending

Neither the income-expenditures model nor any other model of the economy can ignore the roles of government as a spender and tax collector. Government purchases of goods and services normally amount to more than one-fifth of the gross national product. In fact, government spending is second in size only to personal consumption spending and far exceeds the third largest component, namely gross private domestic investment.

In the income-expenditures model, government exercises significant controls over the flow of national income. In siphoning off part of national income as it collects taxes, it shrinks the amounts individuals and businesses have for consumption and investment spending purposes. It adds to the flow of national income when it buys goods and services—providing individuals and businesses with more funds for consumption and investment expenditures. If the amount of income drained off as taxes equals the amount of government spending, government's influence is neutralized. But, if government spending exceeds total taxation, there is a net addition to national income. The reverse situation also holds: if total taxation is larger than government spending, there is a net reduction in national income. This, then, is how government fits into the income-expenditures model: it exerts a stimulating or repressing influence on market demand. The government also exerts other influences on market demand through its power to control the quantity of money in circulation. Government controls the quantity of money mainly by making loans and granting loan guarantees and by influencing the reserve needs of banks through regulation by the Federal Reserve System.

PSYCHOLOGICAL FACTORS AFFECTING BUYER BEHAVIOR

Although economic theories and concepts are useful in analyzing many aspects of buyer behavior, there are other aspects explainable only in terms of psychological theories and concepts. Why do consumers act the way they do? Why do individual consumers exhibit certain attitudes? Psychology, focusing mainly on the "internal" forces directing the activities of individuals, attempts to provide answers to such questions. Where the economist makes assumptions about the motivations of buyers, the psychologist attempts not only to describe but to explain these motivations. Thus, in explaining buyer behavior, psychology takes up the task where economics drops it. It is not surprising, then, that in its treatment of the practical problems of moving goods, marketing has often seemed more to resemble applied psychology than economics.[11]

There have been three major approaches to the development of a psychological theory of human behavior: the laboratory or experimental, the clinical, and the Gestalt. Laboratory psychology has concentrated on physiological tensions or body needs as motivational forces and has experimented both with human beings and animals. In clinical psychology, the basic physiological drives are examined, as they are modified by social forces. Frequent conflicts between the needs of the individual and social restrictions may result in repression of motives, which, nevertheless, may still exert strong driving forces on human actions. Clinical psychologists attempt to uncover these repressed and unconscious motives through the use of psychoanalytical techniques such as depth interviewing. Depth interviews are conducted as informal, lengthy, and unstructured conversations, in which the interviewer attempts to uncover unexpressed, and frequently unrecognized, reasons for the actions of the person interviewed. Gestalt psychology, often called social psychology, regards the individual and his environment as an indivisible whole. It holds that the individual always re-

[11] "The Motivation of Consumer Buying," *Cost and Profit Outlook*, January 1954, p. 1.

acts in an environment, and actions must be viewed both in terms of the individual and the environment. Furthermore, in Gestalt psychology, individual behavior is considered to be directed toward a goal or goals and to be the resultant of both the motives of the individual and his reaction to the environment. Each approach adds to our understanding of human behavior. Thus far, no single psychological theory of consumer behavior is completely adequate or satisfactory for all purposes and, consequently, marketing has borrowed theoretical concepts which seem most applicable and fruitful in particular instances.[12] Some of the theories and concepts borrowed by marketing from psychology are examined below.

Learning Theory

Studies of learning, and the related areas of recognition and recall and habitual response, have furnished marketers with a number of keys to understanding consumer behavior and with concepts especially useful in planning and implementing programs designed to stimulate consumer demand. Concepts borrowed from learning theory help in answering such questions as these: How do consumers learn about products offered for sale? How do they learn to recognize and recall these products? By what processes do they develop habits of purchase and consumption?

THE ASSOCIATIVE BOND CONCEPT   In studying the learning process, psychologists have been greatly influenced by the associative bond concept, also known as connectionism, which found its chief exponent in Thorndike.[13] In considering any unit of activity of the individual, Thorndike saw three aspects: first, a *stimulus* or situation affecting the individual; second, a *response* by the individual; and third, a *connection* between the stimulus and response, enabling the former to produce the latter. This connection is called the S-R bond. Thorndike and his followers came to regard learning as a process involving the building of new bonds and organizing these into systems of bonds.

The newer trend in psychological thinking is to regard the S-R bond concept as an oversimplification, to look instead at the total experience of the individual, and to consider learning a process in which total functions are altered and rearranged to make them more useful to the individual. Particular stimuli will not always activate predictable responses, because motives and other factors internal to the individual also affect responses

---

[12] E. L. Grubb, and H. L. Grathwohl, "Consumer Self Concept, Symbolism, and Market Behavior," *Journal of Marketing*, October 1967, pp. 22-27.
[13] See: E. L. Thorndike, *Human Learning* (New York: Appleton-Century, 1931), pp. 117-22.

to external stimuli. What does this mean for the marketer? Simply that the consumer is influenced not only by external stimuli—e.g., the marketer's advertising and promotional efforts—but also by internal factors.

What are the basic factors influencing learning? One writer states that repetition, motivation, conditioning, and relationship and organization are all important.[14] However, as we shall see, these have different degrees of relevance for marketing.

REPETITION   Repetition, necessary for the progressive modification of psychological functions, must be accompanied by attention, meaning, interest, and a goal if it is to be effective. Mere repetition of situations or stimuli does not promote learning, and advertisers who depend on it alone are wasting both their efforts and their advertising dollars.

MOTIVATION   The motives of an individual are the most important factors involved in initiating and governing his activities. Activity in harmony with one's motives is satisfying and pleasing, but activity not in harmony with one's motives is annoying at best and frustrating at worst. When, in a given situation, an individual has several motives, they may either reinforce each other, which promotes learning, or be in conflict, which hinders learning. The motivation of individuals is a topic of considerable interest to marketing professionals, especially those responsible for preparing advertising and sales presentations. Neither they, nor psychologists, have thus far been able to reach more than partial agreement as to what constitutes even the most common or basic motives. Members of each group have identified numerous motives, but there is much opportunity for further research. One such list is presented and analyzed in a later section of this chapter.

CONDITIONING   Conditioning is a way of learning by which a new response to a particular stimulus is developed. For example, the sight of just any glass bottle does not evoke any standard response, but the sight of one particular type of bottle makes most Americans think of Coca-Cola. Through a long-range advertising effort and continued exposure of this symbol, the Coca-Cola Company has conditioned the American public to recognize its bottle. The conditioned response establishes a temporary rather than a permanent behavior pattern and, if it is not frequently reinforced by the original stimulus, the conditioned response soon disappears. Thus, only by frequent and massive advertising and continued exposure of the bottle symbol has the Coca-Cola Company retained the conditioned response. Marketing men must remember, however, that all individuals do

[14] O. Mowrer, *Learning Theory and the Symbolic Processes* (New York: John Wiley & Sons, Inc., 1963), p. 225.

not respond equally well to conditioning, nor are their reactions generally predictable.

RELATIONSHIP AND ORGANIZATION   Meaningful relationships and organization are also factors which facilitate learning. To put it another way, learning effectiveness is enhanced if the thing to be learned is presented in a familiar environmental setting. Thus, a salseman more effectively demonstrates a vacuum cleaner by using it on the customer's carpet and showing her the dirt it has picked up than by describing its capacity and cleaning power. The housewife is interested in the performance specifications of the machine only as they are directly related to the job of cleaning her carpets. There are obvious implications in this for the advertiser and salesman. Sales messages should relate the products to the consumer's needs and interests if they are to succeed in attracting his attention and laying the groundwork for purchase.

IMPLICATIONS FOR MARKETING   Marketing men have too often relied entirely on repetition and conditioning to achieve consumer "learning" about their products. Learning can take place in the absence of motivation and relation and organization, but it is a slow expensive process, and retention is poor. When an individual is strongly motivated, he may learn with only one or two repetitions. A person who has been troubled with excessive tooth decay may hear just once about a promising new dentifrice that helps prevent decay, and he will remember the name and buy it; yet, another person who has never had a cavity in his life might only learn the name of the same dentifrice after countless repetition. Meaningful relation and organization also speed up the learning process. It is easier to remember the name Band-Aid than a name such as Acme Plastic Strips, because Band-Aid is a combination of syllables from bandage and first aid —words that describe the product—whereas Acme describes anything, and plastic strips is too general to connote bandages. Ignorance of the existence of and interrelationship between other factors in learning has led many marketing men to rely almost solely on repetition and conditioning. Learning can be achieved with repetition alone, but, when product or market knowledge is meaningful and important to a consumer, he learns it more quickly.

Particularly for the advertiser, but also for the planner of long-range promotional programs, there is significance in the psychological explanation of retention and forgetting. Retention can be explained in terms of impressions left in the nervous system as a result of learning. Forgetting, or "negative retention," develops with the deterioration of these impressions. The more meaningful the material learned—i.e., the more the learner completely understands it—the greater the rate of retention and the lower the rate of forgetting.[15] Retention curves for both meaningful and un-meaningful materials, plotted as functions of time, drop most rapidly im-mediately after learning and then gradually decline until the material is almost or entirely forgotten. This phenomenon is particularly important with respect to long-run campaigns of promotion or advertising. Messages should be spaced closely enough so that they fortify the learning process. If they are too far apart, information learned from earlier messages will have been forgotten and must be entirely relearned.

Some Concepts From Clinical Psychology

The principle research techniques employed in the relatively new field of motivation research are based primarily on concepts originally developed by clinical psychologists. Among the most important of these concepts are those of the unconscious, rationalization, projection, and free association.[16]

THE UNCONSCIOUS   The concept of the unconscious originated with Sigmund Freud, the founder of psychoanalysis. Freud believed that consciousness was only a small part of the total mind, that, like an iceberg, its larger part existed below the surface of awarness.[17] According to Freud, the mind contains ideas and urges, some conscious and some beneath the threshold of consciousness, all, however, influencing behavior. The fact that people are not usually consciously aware of their motives explains why consumers are often unable to explain their real reasons for buying or not buying. Recognizing the existence of the unconscious mind, motivation researchers have resorted to indirect research approaches such as depth interviewing.[18] More conventional research approaches, such as direct ques-tioning, have been unable to provide data sufficiently reliable to justify predictions of consumer behavior. One mail-order house, for instance, took advance proofs of catalog pages to a number of women, asked them which style of dress and which colors they preferred, and then tabulated the most popular and least popular styles and colors. Actual sales, however, showed

[15] B. Berelson, and G. Steiner, *Human Behavior; An Inventory of Scientific Findings* (New York: Harcourt, Brace and World, 1964), p. 102.

[16] F. Kerlinger, *Foundations of Behavioral Research* (New York: Holt, Rine-hart and Winston, 1965), pp. 64-65.

[17] C. S. Hall, *A Primer of Freudian Psychology* (New York: Mentor edition published by arrangement with the World Publishing Company, 1954), p. 54.

[18] For a highly entertaining account of the controversy stirred up by the increasing use of depth interviewing in consumer studies, see: P. Stryker, "Motivation Research," *Fortune*, June 1956, pp. 144-47 and 222-32.

no correlation with the preferences recorded in the survey.[19] Practical marketers, of course, have long known that there are often wide discrepancies between what people say they will buy and what they actually do buy.[20]

RATIONALIZATION   Rationalization, a psychiatric concept, has long been put to practical use by advertisers but has only recently been reflected in consumer research techniques. Rationalization is the mental process of finding reasons to justify an act or opinion that is actually based on other motives or grounds, although this may or may not be apparent to the rationalizer.[21] In advertising, rationalization often takes the form of providing a reader or listener with a plausible, acceptable reason for buying in situations where the prospect may be unwilling, consciously or unconsciously, to admit the real buying reason. For instance, the manufacturer of an expensive, showy automobile provides an "acceptable reason for buying" by stressing such features as economy in operation and high trade-in value. In some situations, rationalization is provided by the purchaser personally. Take the case of the woman who buys a mink coat to impress her friends. She explains the purchase to them by saying it is warmer and will wear longer than a less expensive coat. Thus, the most common kind of rationalizing is the attempt to justify decisions or actions by finding "good" reasons for them.[22] The prevalence or rationalization in our society explains why such direct questions as "why did you buy this?" or "what were your reasons for buying?" so often fail to uncover the real buying motives. Thus, where it is suspected that rationalizing is a factor in consumer decision-making, indirect research approaches, such as depth interviewing, are used.

PROJECTION   Projection is another concept from clinical psychology. It is the name given to the type of reaction that occurs when a person, seeing someone facing a certain problem or situation, interprets the other person's reactions in terms of his own. In other words, he ascribes his own motives to that other person. Putting the projection concept to practical use, motivation researchers have designed projective techniques which provide a means for uncovering consumers' hidden or unconscious motives and attitudes. For example, the *stimulus picture* is a type of projec-

[19] E. Dichter, "Strategy of Human Motivation," *Public Relations Journal,* October, 1967, pp. 59-60.

[20] However, for a timely and well-worded warning to management not to rely blindly on motivation research, see: T. Levitt, "M-R Snake Dance," *Harvard Business Review,* November-December 1960, pp. 76-84.

[21] E. K. Strong, Jr., *Psychological Aspects of Business* (New York: McGraw-Hill, 1938), p. 129.

[22] N. L. Munn, *Psychology,* 3rd ed. (Boston: Houghton Mifflin, 1956), p. 149.

tive technique. Such pictures were used in one study designed to secure information from farmers and their wives as to which "reference groups" influenced their decisions to buy new products.[23] Virtually all projective techniques have two things in common: First, they are designed to elicit a range of responses rather than a single stereotyped and predictable reaction. And second, they are constructed so as "to entice the subject into revealing himself without his being aware of the fact that he is doing so." [24]

PRINCIPLE OF FREE ASSOCIATION   The principle of free association, which traces to Freud and is used extensively in psychoanalysis, has also been put to use by motivation researchers in developing indirect research techniques. As Newman says, "the basic idea is that if a person gives up the usual logical controls he exercises over his thoughts and says whatever comes into his mind at the moment in the presence of a skilled listener, unconscious feelings and thoughts can be discovered." [25] Thus, the techniques of depth interviewing represent an application of the principle of free association. Many depth interviewing techniques take the form of word association tests in which respondents are asked to give the first word that comes to mind for each of a list of unrelated words. Given the word *snow*, for example, the respondent might reply *shovel*. Among the many applications of the word association tests are those of screening possible names for new products, measuring the penetration of advertising appeals, and approximating the market shares of different competitors.

Basic Needs and Buyer Behavior

Psychological studies indicate that human activity, including buying behavior, is directed toward satisfying certain basic needs. Not every individual acts in the same way in his effort to fullfill these needs; the actions of each depend upon the nature of the needs themselves but are modified by his particular environmental and social background. The motivation for any specific action derives from the tensions built up to satisfy basic needs, and frequently some of these needs are beneath the threshold of consciousness. Whatever action is taken is directed toward reducing these tensions.

Although clinical psychologists have not agreed on a single list of basic needs, the different lists available show more agreement than dis-

[23] Reference groups are those groups with which particular individuals would prefer to be associated. Each individual accepts the behavior norms of his reference group as he makes decisions and takes action.

[24] OSS Assessment Staff, *The Assessment of Men* (New York: Rinehart, 1948), p. 71.

[25] J. W. Newman, *Motivation Research and Marketing Management* (Boston: Harvard Graduate School of Business Administration, Division of Research, 1957), p. 65.

agreement in the basic needs they suggest. In one list, Maslow enumerates basic needs in their order of importance for most people. According to him, an individual normally tries to satisfy the most basic needs first and, satisfying these, he is then free to devote his attention to the next one shown in the list. The Maslow list is presented below:[26]

1. *The Physiological Needs.* This group includes needs for satisfying hunger, thirst, sleep, and so forth. These are the most basic needs, and until they are satisfied, other needs are of no importance.
2. *The Safety Needs.* In modern society these needs are more often for economic and social security rather then for physical safety.
3. *The Belongingness and Love Needs.* The need for affectionate relations with individuals and a place in society is so important that its lack is a common cause of maladjustment.
4. *The Esteem Needs.* People need both self-esteem, a high evaluation of self, and the esteem of others in our society. Fulfillment of these needs provides a feeling of self-confidence and usefulness to the world; failure to fulfill these needs produces feelings of inferiority and helplessness.
5. *The Need for Self-Actualization.* This is the desire to achieve to the maximum of one's capabilities and, although it may be present in everyone, its fulfillment depends upon the prior fulfillment of the more basic needs.
6. *The Desire to Know and Understand.* These needs refer to the process of searching for meaning in the things around us.
7. *The Aesthetic Needs.* These needs may not appear to be present among many individuals because of their failure to satisfy more basic needs, but among some individuals the need for beauty is important.

Very often, the marketing success of a product depends on its ability to satisfy several needs at once. Now that motivation research techniques are available with which to identify the strength or weakness of a product in terms of the need it fulfills, the concept of basic needs and the theory that individuals normally try to satisfy them in some order are especially significant to marketing.

Imagery and Buyer Behavior

Images are the formalized impressions residing, consciously or unconsciously, in the minds of individuals with regard to given subjects. Images can be thought of as pictures which arise somehow before the "inner

[26] A. H. Maslow, *Motivation and Personality* (New York: Harper and Brothers, 1944), pp. 80-85.

eye," or sounds which are heard by the "inner ear." [27] Patterns of buying behavior are influenced by the images consumers have of different products, particular brands, companies, retail outlets, and of themselves. It follows that differences between individuals, products, or brands result in different images, but differences in images are not necessarily based on real or measurable differences.

The functional characteristics of two brands may be essentially identical, but purely subjective factors are likely to conjure up quite different images of the two brands. All brands of aspirin are identical in composition, since aspirin is a chemical compound; yet they do not all have identical brand images. A single factor, an old and established reputation, increases consumer confidence and makes it possible for Bayer Aspirin to sell at premium prices. Because such images definitely affect consumer buying behavior, marketers and advertisers are increasingly taking them into account in drafting promotional plans and programs. Motivation research is being used not only to identify the nature of images but to detect the implications for marketing action.

SELF-IMAGE   The self-image is the picture a person has of himself—the kind of person he considers himself and the kind of person he imagines others consider him. What lies behind this image and what causes it to be the type of image it is? No one seems to have a complete or clear explanation of the self-image. But it is apparent that the complex of impressions which result in the self-image is affected both by physiological and psychological needs, some conscious and some unconscious. Among those at the level of consciousness, to complicate matters further, are some which the individual willingly discusses and others which he is unwilling to admit. Certain of these needs are partially shaped, or at least influenced, by socioeconomic factors such as education, sex, occupation, age, cultural background, amount and source of income, memberships in and relationships to different social groups, and regional and local customs and mores. But behind the self-image also lie those internal psychological factors that determine the individual's personality, his stage of intellectual development, and the extent of his emotional maturity.

Different people have different kinds of self-images and, from the standpoint of marketing, this gives rise to market segmentation along psychological lines. For instance, the woman who sees herself primarily as a good housewife and mother exhibits a different total pattern of buying behavior than does the woman who sees herself as a social leader or professional careerwoman. One of the basic tenets of motivational research is that in many buying situations an individual prefers to buy those products

[27] A. E. Birdwell, "Study of the Influence of Image Congruence on Consumer Choice," *Journal of Business*, January 1968, p. 76.

and brands whose images appear consistent with his self-image.[28] However, the power of the self-image as a buying influence varies from individual to individual, and even within the same individual, as he makes different buying decisions at different times.

PRODUCT IMAGE   A product image is a stereotype which is conjured up by an individual when he thinks of the product. Most products have not one but several images. For example, some consumers may consider a motor boat a means of conveyance over water with a specified load capacity and the power and speed necessary to perform its function. Other consumers, probably the majority, think of the same boat as a means of exciting the interest, admiration, and even the envy of people they wish to impress. They may be more interested in the "status symbol effect"— e.g., the visual impact and styling—than in seaworthiness and maneuverability. Individual consumers may select an outboard motor with far more horsepower than they actually need, for the prestige such a motor may bring. Indeed, some individuals apparently receive more satisfaction from owning such a boat (and having others aware of the fact) than they do from operating it.

Psychologists use the term ego-involvement to describe the sort of situation in which the consumer seeks to identify his self-image with the product image. Some products have a high capacity for ego-involvement, others have less, and some have none at all. This has led one psychologist to classify consumer products according to their demands on the consumer:

A. Demands of ego-involvement in the external symbols which the product conveys
   1. *Prestige products*. Products in this group not only represent some image or personality attribute, but become that attribute. Includes automobiles, homes, clothing, furniture, art objects, newspapers, and magazines. These products extend or identify the ego of the consumer in a direction consistent with his self-image, in such a way as to give him individuality.

[28] There is conflicting evidence on the importance of the self-image in some buying situations. For instance, H. G. Baker, an executive of the now-defunct Edsel Division, Ford Motor Company, is on record as saying "A make thus becomes a very real extension of the owner's DESIRED personality, and something he derives gratification from, if the personality fits." See: H. G. Baker, "Sales and Marketing Planning of the Edsel," in R. L. Clewett, *Marketing's Role in Scientific Management* (Chicago: American Marketing Association, 1957), p. 130.

But the findings of one empirical study challenge this notion that the buyers of one make of automobile possess different personalities than the buyers of a competing make. See: F. B. Evans, "Psychological and Objective Factors in the Prediction of Brand Choice: Ford Versus Chevrolet," *The Journal of Business*, October 1959, pp. 340-69.

2. *Maturity products.* These products are typically withheld from younger people. Initial use symbolizes maturity of the consumer. Intrinsic product merit is not a factor, at least in the initial stages of use. Includes cigarettes, cosmetics, coffee, beer, and liquor.

3. *Status products.* These products impute class membership to their users. The intrinsic merit of products in this class is an important factor in continued usage. However, consumers tend to select "big-name" brands because they believe such brands impute "success," "substance," "quality," or similar attributes. Packaged foods and gasoline are often in this class. Where prestige products connote leadership, status products connote membership.

4. *Anxiety products.* Those products alleviate some presumed personal or social *threat.* This class includes soaps, dentifrices, "health" foods, perfumes, and razors. This class involves ego-defense, whereas the three previous classes are concerned with ego-enhancement.

B. Hedonic demand

5. *Hedonic products.* These products depend on their sensory character for their appeal. Moreover, their appeal is immediate and highly situational. This category includes snack items, many types of clothing, and pre-sweetened cereals. Visual (style) features of any product fall within this area: automobile design and color are examples.

C. Functional demands

6. *Functional products.* These are products to which little cultural or social meaning has, as yet, been imputed. Included in this class are the staple food items, fruits, vegetables, and most building products.[29]

Marketers have long known that different consumers attach different meanings to the same product. The psychological character of a product is a true character which has been imputed to it by society as a whole through long periods of time; it is independent of the psychological character (or personality) of particular individuals. Psychological research is often necessary to uncover and identify the different images people associate with a product. Sometimes, users and non-users have quite different images of a product. Although simple marketing research techniques of the question-and-answer variety can separate the users from the non-users, more sophisticated techniques, such as the projective ones, are required to explain the reasons for non-use.

[29] W. A. Woods, "Psychological Dimensions of Consumer Decision," *Journal of Marketing,* January 1960, pp. 17-18.

A famous pioneering study, utilizing projective techniques, was conducted to determine the reasons for non-use of instant coffee. Blind taste-tests had shown that most consumers could not detect a flavor difference between instant and regular coffee, but direct questioning continued to show "different flavor" as the primary reason for non-use. The researcher made up two shopping lists, identical in all respects except that one included a brand of regular coffee and the other included Nescafé. Making alternate use of each shopping list, and with no respondent being aware of the other list, the researcher asked one hundred housewives to "Read the shopping list. Try to project yourself into the situation as far as possible until you can more or less characterize the woman who bought the groceries. Then write a brief description of her personality and character." A significant number of the respondents described the purchaser of Nescafé as lazy and a poor planner.[30] Since this study, instant coffee manufacturers have de-emphasized the convenience and speed of preparation of their product and have promoted its superior flavor. As a result, the proportion of non-users has steadily declined. Evidently, then, the product image of instant coffee has been modified for most consumers.

That different classes of users of a product or service see it quite differently has also been verified. In a study of air travel, for instance, several categories of passengers were identified and their images of air travel determined. For the inexperienced air traveler, the flight was a glamorous adventure. For the businessman traveling frequently, air travel meant good schedules, dependability, and excellent service. For the vacationer, air travel was a source of fun. The same study revealed that different airlines varied in their attractiveness for each group and that no one line was equally attractive to all groups.[31]

BRAND IMAGE   The brand image, another stereotype, results from all the impressions consumers receive, from whatever sources, about a particular manufacturer's brand of product. These impressions may derive from actual experience with the brand; hearsay about it; reputation of the company manufacturing it; the packaging; the brand name; the tone, format, and content of the advertising presentation; and the specific media in which its advertising has appeared. In the minds of consumers who are familiar with a particular brand, there tends to be considerable consistency in the brand image or, as it is sometimes called, the brand personality. But for competing brands of a product, there are usually, in the minds of consumers,

---

[30] M. Haire, "Projective Techniques in Marketing Research," *Journal of Marketing*, April 1950, pp. 649-56.

[31] P. Martineau, "The Public Image—Motivational Analysis for Long-Range Merchandising Strategy," *The Frontiers of Marketing Thought and Science* (Chicago: American Marketing Association, 1957), pp. 11-21.

distinctive images for each brand. The same holds for companies and institutions: retail stores exhibit quite distinct images or personalities; corporations have different corporate images.[32] Even airlines possess their own images—the public mind may characterize one as friendly and folksy, another as glamorous and adventurous, and still another as business-like and dependable.

Every brand image derives partially from a product image. The product image relates to the fundamental aims and satisfactions, both practical and symbolic, which individuals seek or find in a particular area of consumption. The brand image relates to the configuration of ideas, feelings and meanings consumers attach to specific versions of the product image.

Consumers' appraisal of the distinctiveness of a brand's physical attributes not only affects the brand image but has important implications for marketing strategy. When consumers believe the brand to be physically different from competing brands, the brand image centers on the brand as a specific version of the product. In this instance, depending on whether the manufacturer considers the image favorable or unfavorable, physical attributes of the product may be retained or changed, and marketing strategy may be directed toward reinforcing or altering the image.

But when consumers believe that a brand does not have differentiating physical attributes, the brand image may be associated with the personalities of the people who are thought to buy it. One writer suggests that the manufacturer of such a product, who seeks growth through an increasing market share, can follow one of three alternative marketing paths: (1) Try to associate his brand with the public image that is desired or will be desired by most people, (2) Try to give his brand several different images so that he can reach several market segments or (3) Adopt multiple brands, each of which is strongly identified with the image desired by a significant market segment.[33] The role of brand images in marketing, then, reaches its height when competing brands are very much alike, for in these instances the marketer, through advertising, merchandising, and packaging, seeks to build a brand image that fits the psychological needs of the target market segments.

Through the long-continued use of particular advertising and selling appeals, many brands have acquired definite images. In numerous cases, a particular brand image was shaped deliberately and management is well-advised to identify its nature. Otherwise, ignorance of the brand image may result in inappropriate promotional programs. For example, if the image is a favorable one, the use of inconsistent sales and advertising appeals is

[32] Birdwell, *op. cit.*, p. 77.
[33] G. H. Brown, "Brand Images Among Low Priced Cars," in R. M. Hill (ed.), *Marketing Concepts in Changing Times* (Chicago: American Marketing Association, 1960), p. 61.

not only likely to be ineffective but may even confuse or alienate existing customers.

Similarly, before introducing a new brand to the market or an established brand to a different market, management should determine the sort of image it wishes to build. Take the case of Marlboro cigarettes. When the market for filter cigarettes began growing rapidly, as a side-effect of the "cancer scare," Marlboro was already an established brand of filter cigarettes. However, up to that time the filter market had been composed primarily of women, and Marlboro definitely had a strong feminine image. Philip Morris, Inc., owner of the Marlboro brand, undertook a long-range program designed to provide the brand with a masculine image. Such devices as "the rugged male with a tattoo" were used in Marlboro advertisements in the effort to tap the huge new market segment of male filter smokers. Such campaigns to alter a brand image must be carefully planned and executed. If they are not, the present market for the brand may be lost without making so much as a dent in the intended market.

Festinger's Theory of Cognitive Dissonance

According to Festinger's theory of cognitive dissonance, when a person chooses between two or more alternatives, dissonance or discomfort will almost always occur because the person knows that the decision made had certain disadvantages as well as advantages. After making his decision, the person therefore tends to expose himself to information that he perceives as likely to support his choice and to avoid information that is likely to favor the rejected alternatives.[34] Although Festinger evidently intended his theory to apply only to situations involving postdecision anxiety, it seems reasonable that it should also hold for situations involving predecision anxiety—a buyer may panic as he reaches the time of decision, and either rush into buying as an escape from the problem or delay it because of the difficulty of deciding among alternatives. Thus, a buyer may experience predecision or postdecision discomfort or dissonance, or both.

In marketing, an important function both of advertising and of the salesman is to reduce both predecision and postdecision anxiety or dissonance. According to Zaltman, there are at least two ways to accomplish this: (1) by repeating and reemphasizing the advantages of the product involved and stressing the relative disadvantages of the other alternatives; and (2) in cases of dissonance traceable to the buyer's feeling that he is buying or has purchased an item not sanctioned by the relevant reference group, by trying to show that many characteristics of the chosen item are similar to products the buyer has foregone but which are approved by his

[34] L. Festinger, A *Theory of Cognitive Dissonance* (Evanston, Ill.: Row Peterson and Company, 1957).

particular reference group.[35] In other words, the buyer experiencing cognitive dissonance should be reassured that his decision is or was a wise one. This can be done by providing information that will permit the buyer to rationalize his decision.

Motivations of Ultimate Consumers Versus Industrial Users

Much has been written concerning differences in the buying motivations of ultimate consumers and industrial users. Generally, it is concluded that ultimate consumers are emotional buyers, and that they are motivated more strongly by emotional than by rational considerations. On the other hand, industrial users are portrayed as essentially rational buyers.

The concept of need gratification renders meaningless the dual classification of motives as rational or emotional. Under this classification system, an individual attempting only to fulfill the most basic needs is influenced solely by motives classed as rational. A person at the level of bare subsistence wants the most for his money in terms of quantity, quality, and dependability. But most Americans live far above the subsistence level, and the majority of their purchases are directed toward fulfilling other of the basic needs. Distinctiveness, emulation, and pride in personal appearance (allegedly emotional buying motives) may be perfectly rational means of fulfilling belongingness or esteem needs. In this sense, it might be claimed that all consumer buying motives are rational. However, certain motives are generally agreed to be more rational than others and, since man thinks of himself as a rational creature, people tend to express their motives in the most rational way possible. Earlier we referred to this tendency as rationalization, and another example now may assist in clarifying that concept. The buyer of an expensive automobile may explain that the high price is justified in terms of greater durability and better trade-in-value, but he may have actually made the purchase to fulfill esteem needs. Often, these esteem needs may be totally beneath the threshold of consciousness, and the buyer of the high-priced auto may honestly believe that his buying motives were "rational."

Industrial users tend to be more "rational" in their buying than ultimate consumers. They buy to fill the needs of their organizations, and these needs normally are of a very practical nature. But it should not be forgotten that organizations are composed of individuals, that one or more individuals in these organizations do the buying, and that these individuals have personal needs which sometimes become enmeshed with their roles as buyers. Thus, even industrial purchases may be made on irrational, or

[35] G. Zaltman, *Marketing: Contributions from the Behavioral Sciences* (New York: Harcourt, Brace & World, Inc., 1965), p. 63.

emotional, bases, as in the case of the purchasing agent who buys from a certain supplier because the salesman is his good friend.

CONCLUSION

In this chapter, analysis has focused upon two groups of the major uncontrollable determinants of buyer behavior—those of an economic and psychological nature. The marketing man can exert only indirect influences over these behavioral determinants. Nevertheless, he must take them into account as he plans and directs such controllables as the product, distribution, promotion, and price.

Sorting theory, in which consumers are visualized as building highly individualized assortments of goods, provides a conceptual economic framework that helps to explain consumer buying behavior. The income-expenditures model, a much more complex conceptual framework, helps the marketing man to understand the other major uncontrollable economic determinants of market demand. Disposable income is the chief, but by no means the only, determinant of personal consumption spending. Significant changes occur in the spending and saving patterns of families as they increase in size or shift from one income bracket to another. Credit serves as purchasing power by exchanging claims to future income for present spending. Rises in discretionary income and changes in its distribution among families are likely to have effects on spending patterns for durables, nondurables, and services. Business spending and investment enters into the income-expenditures model both in the way it generates income and the way income accelerates it. Government also plays a dual role in the model. No part of the model operates independently. Each part (consumers, businesses, and government) influences and is influenced by all the others. Interactions among the parts, such as those evident in the multiplier effect and the acceleration principle, show how strongly the sectors of our economy are bound together.

In using the fruits of psychological research, the marketing man must start with the thesis that buyer behavior is but a special case of human behavior in general. The psychological factors influencing individual action are also operative when that individual is acting as a buyer. In order to understand the psychological aspects of consumer behavior, the marketer needs to be acquainted with the underlying psychological theory. Learning theory provides insights on how buyers learn about and forget products. Clinical psychology deals with some of the unconscious reasons for human (and buyer) behavior and also provides a description of the basic needs that motivate human activity. The psychological concept of imagery provides an analytical framework for studying how consumer and other buyers see products, brands, and themselves.

QUESTIONS AND PROBLEMS

1. Show how sorting theory can be used to explain the economic process whereby conglomerations are converted into assortments.

2. In terms of the four types of sorting, demonstrate how marketing theory differs from economic theory.

3. Demonstrate how sorting theory might be applied in explaining the buying behavior of consumers.

4. "The survival of a firm requires that it present, to some group of buyers, a differential advantage over all other suppliers." List some forms of differential advantage, and give examples of companies presenting each form.

5. Of the many factors affecting the strength of market demand, why is income considered the most powerful?

6. Discuss the relationships which exist among the following: production, consumption, purchasing power, disposable personal income.

7. Why are marketing analysts usually more interested in the marginal propensity to consume than they are in the average propensity to consume? Would this be as true of the analyst of the market for sports cars as of the analyst of the market for breakfast cereals? Why?

8. What possibilities are there for influencing the propensity to consume through such marketing activities as advertising, personal selling, trading stamp plans, liberal credit terms, and so on?

9. "Marketing men have a vested interest in shifting the peak of the income distribution curve as far to the right as possible." Explain and evaluate this statement.

10. Of what significance, if any, would studies of consumers' income expectations be for: (a) a manufacturer of tape recorders; (b) a mail-order house specializing in "do-it-yourself" electronic kits; (c) a manufacturer of tires for passenger cars; (d) a manufacturer of photographic equipment and supplies?

11. One young married man recently used the installment plan to buy a new automobile and to furnish his newly-purchased house (which was financed through a 30-year mortgage). When the young man told his father about this, the older man was horrified and said, "Your mother and I got where we are today because we saved our money, paid cash for all major purchases, and never paid a dime of interest to an installment seller." The son replied, "If I waited to pay cash for these things, I would have a long grey beard before I could enjoy them!" Which side of this argument would you take and why?

12. Of what significance would a forecast of the magnitude and distribu-

tion of discretionary income be for: (a) a chain of grocery super-markets; (b) a manufacturer of patio and outdoor furniture; (c) a major domestic airline; (d) an importer of Scotch and Canadian whiskies; (e) a local transit company?

13. Why do you think a company selling tire-making machines might carry on an advertising program directed not to potential buyers of tire-making machines but to potential buyers of tires? Does this sort of strategy make sense for any company whose product has a derived demand? Why?

14. Explain the various influences exerted by government spending and taxation on market demand.

15. "Automation and other technological changes have greatly increased the efficiency with which capital can be used, so it now is taking fewer dollars of new investment to produce a dollar's worth of out-put. This drop means new investment projects now require less cash —hence, they create fewer jobs and less purchasing power." Comment on this statement and interpret its significance for marketing.

16. Why do you suppose many advertisers have relied primarily on repetition to achieve customer recognition of their products, when learning is more easily achieved with proper motivation?

17. Would you say that many consumers have become conditioned to "shut out" (not see or hear) all advertising to which they are ex-posed? What are the implications for advertisers?

18. Would it be fair to say that when a conscious and an unconscious motive conflict, the conscious motive will dominate? Through ration-alization, the consumer finds a "sensible" or "reasonable" excuse for actions motivated by "frivolous" reasons. What is the implication for marketing?

19. Does the concept of projection help in motivating the consumer, or only in learning what motivates him?

20. Give some examples how the self-image of a bank teller and a taxi driver might lead them to act differently as consumers, assuming equal incomes.

21. Do you think it would be easier to sell products with high ego-involvement or with none at all? Why?

22. Is it likely that we can generalize to other products from the ex-perience with instant coffee in the Mason Haire study? Give some examples that occur to you.

23. "Once a brand image has developed in the minds of the public, there is little that can be done to change it." Comment on this statement.

24. "In order to develop distinctive brand images, there must be clearly identifiable physical differences in the products involved." Do you agree?

25. Does the failure of psychologists to agree on a common list of basic needs destroy the concepts of such needs as a marketing tool?

26. Under Maslow's classification of basic needs, different individuals have achieved different levels in satisfying their needs. Does this imply that it would be necessary to appeal to different needs to sell the same product to different people?

27. What is Festinger's theory of cognitive dissonance? Cite some instances where you personally experienced cognitive dissonance in buying situations. What, if anything, did the seller do in an attempt to reduce your discomfort?

28. If all motives are claimed to be rational, how can some motives be more rational than others?

7

BUYER BEHAVIOR:
ITS SOCIO-CULTURAL ASPECTS

Traditionally, consumer behavior has been expressed only as a function of economic and psychological factors. Classical economists explained buyer behavior in terms of financial self-interest. "Economic man" could be expected to act rationally with the goal of maximizing his financial gains. This has continued as a foundation of economic theory into modern times, but it provides little comfort to businessmen who are confronted daily with instances of apparently irrational consumer behavior. For a more satisfactory explanation of consumer behavior, businessmen next turned to psychology. Psychologists have attempted to explain the actions of individuals in terms of certain basic needs. Although psychological explanations have been helpful, there are still, from the standpoint of businessmen, fuzzy areas where there are no satisfactory answers. For example, the psychologist explains that people are sometimes motivated by the desire to emulate others, but he does not provide a satisfactory explanation as to whom a particular individual or group may wish to emulate. To answer this question, we turn to sociology, the science that studies human society and the actions and reactions of the individual as a member of groups. Sociologists view marketing as the activities of groups motivated by group pressures as well as by individual desires.

The individual cannot be separated from the society in which he lives. Although all people have certain biological needs in common, these needs are strongly modified by the cultural environment; hence, the environment affects ultimate behavior. All people need to eat, but what they eat and how they eat is, to a great degree, determined by the behavior patterns of their society. To the average American, the thought of eating dog meat is repugnant. This is not because of any belief that dogs are inedible; the eating of dog meat just happens to be socially unacceptable. How are social customs established, and who determines what is acceptable or unacceptable?

REFERENCE GROUPS

The people with whom an individual regularly associates exert a strong influence on his behavior. To be accepted, he must conform to at least some degree to the group's standards of behavior. An individual's behavior is also influenced by groups with whom he has little regular contact, but with whom he identifies closely. These groupings of people are called reference groups. Important reference groups include: primary groups, including family and peer groups; social groups; and others, such as religious or fraternal organizations.

Primary Groups

The primary group, fundamental in determining the social nature of the individual, may be defined as a group of people involved in intimate, face-to-face contact and cooperation. The most pervasive and probably most influential group is the family. In the traditional large-family setting, where several generations lived under one roof, this group greatly influenced the socialization of the child. With emergence of the modern, small, two-generation family, much of this influence has passed to other primary groups, particularly to the peer groups. Peer groups are made up of individuals who spend considerable time together, and are of fairly common age and social background. Among children these are often play groups; among adults they include neighborhood and community groups. David Riesman, in *The Lonely Crowd*,[1] attributes tremendous influence to these

[1] D. Riesman, N. Glazer, and R. Denney, *The Lonely Crowd* (New Haven: Yale University Press, 1950).

groups among the urban middle classes, where the numbers of people are large enough to form highly homogeneous peer groups. Other groups that have varying degrees of socializing influence are work groups and religious, educational, and political institutions.

Each individual may be a member of several different primary groups. As a member of a religious institution, he may or may not have close personal contacts with other members. At work he may be part of a close-knit, friendly group of co-workers. As a member of social or fraternal organizations, he may be a part of still other primary groups. Any of these groups might be classified as peer groups if they are sufficiently homogeneous. Purely social groups are most likely to fall into this category. The peer group has the greatest influence on the individual in his general role as a consumer since the general interests and mode of life of this group are most nearly like his own.

Knowledge of reference groups and their influences makes it easier to understand why consumers behave in particular ways and—more important to the marketer—to predict their behavior. It explains, for instance, why two groups of young people in the same community—one, high school seniors, and the other, college freshmen—adopt very different styles of dress or other behavior, even though they are nearly the same age and come from similar family backgrounds. Even within a college freshman group, different reference groups dictate wide variations in dress and other behavior.

Even the same individual behaves differently at different times if he identifies with several reference groups. For example, a young executive may dress and act conservatively when on the job and at other points of contact with his business colleagues. In his leisure time, this same individual may be a sports car racing buff, and in this role he acts and dresses very differently.

The way a person sees his role in the social groups of which he is a member is an important factor in explaining his behavior. If he is a "rugged individualist," he may enjoy establishing a reputation as one who sets his own patterns of behavior—within established group norms of good conduct. Individualism was a commonly accepted mode of behavior in the nineteenth century in the United States, but a different type of group behavior has evolved and has become important since then. This newer mode of behavior requires fairly close conformity to group norms. The group-oriented individual is anxious to fit into the behavior patterns of his peers. What they do, he must do. This does not imply, however, that his pattern of behavior is frozen. Group norms may change, and he may adjust his behavior to reflect these changes. The group-oriented individual is seldom motivated by the traditional appeals of "being an innovator" or "leading the pack." If he is to be motivated to action, he must first be persuaded that the suggested action is accepted by his peers as the proper thing to do.

Intra-Group Behavior

Intra-group behavior is illustrated in the sociogram presented in Exhibit 7-1. JT is one of the most influential men in the group. He is the leading communication center and "influential" opinion-leader among the group's men. He also is a main contact with the group's females. It should be understood that these roles may shift in different circumstances. JT, for instance, may occupy his position as an "influential" with respect to sports and athletic matters, but the lines and relationships are apt to shift when the subject of interest is music (and a different sociogram would be needed to depict the different circumstance).

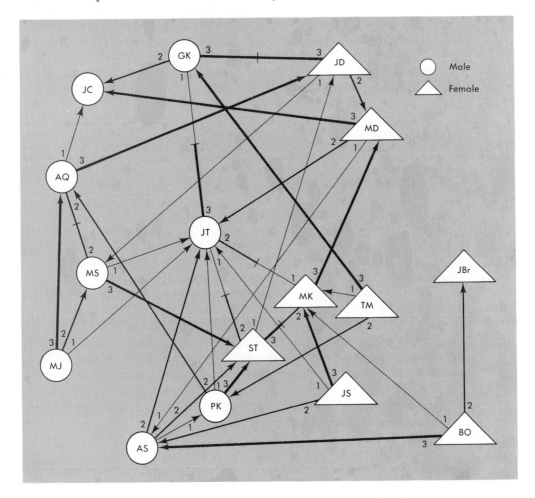

EXHIBIT 7–1

Sociogram for a Hypothetical Group

Influentials

Influentials (opinion leaders) are not confined to any one social class—they are found at all levels of society. Outwardly, influentials and those they influence (i.e., others in the same social groups) are apt to be very much alike—similar incomes, occupations, family backgrounds, and so on. What, then, distinguishes the influential from the influencee? According to Elihu Katz, a sociologist, an individual's influence is related: (1) to who one is, (2) to what one knows, and (3) to whom one knows.[2] For example, a young unmarried girl may be a "fashion leader" in her group because of "who she is;" an older woman her group's "cooking expert" because of "what she knows;" and a man his group's "political leader" because of "whom he knows," not only inside the group but outside it (i.e., because of his "contacts" and "connections" both inside and outside the group).

Influentials play key roles in marketing. If a marketer can convince an influential to try or use a product, then his followers are more prone to do the same. Marketers, therefore, often target their promotional efforts to reach influentials and, through them, to reach their followers, by word-of-mouth or by other subtle influences exerted by influentials on their followers.

The Diffusion Process

The introduction of new products or services is an important feature of competition in any dynamic society. The process of spreading information about these innovations to persuade consumers to accept them is a social process, usually described as *diffusion*. The diffusion of innovations has long been of interest to sociologists and to marketers.

Studies of the diffusion process indicated very early that the adoption of innovations was not a simultaneous event for most users. A small group of individuals are the "innovators," and they are likely to be the first to accept an innovation. The innovators are soon copied by another group, who, though not venturesome enough to try an innovation first, want to be among the early users. Gradually the innovation is adopted by members of other groups until it finally reaches market saturation. When a dramatically new product, such as television, is introduced, the entire adoption process may take ten years or more.

A model of the diffusion process, developed by Everett Rogers, is shown in Exhibit 7-2. The diffusion process is visualized as a curve approaching a normal distribution, with 16 percent of the consumers in the innovator and early adopter groups, 34 percent each in the early and late

---

[2] E. Katz, "The Two-Step Flow of Communication: An Up-To-Date Report on an Hypothesis," *Public Opinion Quarterly*, Spring 1957, pp. 61-78.

majority groups, and 16 percent in the laggard group. The implication for marketing is that it is important to identify target market segments at each stage in the diffusion process. In the initial phases of market introduction, for instance, much marketing effort and money will likely be wasted, if an attempt is made to cultivate the entire market at once. Usually it is more effective and less costly to concentrate early marketing efforts on the innovators and subsequently to shift to the "early adopters" and to each of the follower groups, one at a time.

If management is to use this model of the diffusion process effectively, it must be able to identify the individual adopter categories. The innovators are usually the youngest in age and the highest in social status and wealth; they are frequently cosmopolites and have professional, business, and social contacts outside their own immediate social circle.[3] Those in the early adopter group are generally opinion leaders, but their

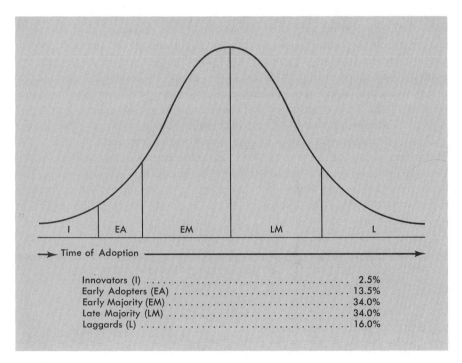

Innovators (I)	2.5%
Early Adopters (EA)	13.5%
Early Majority (EM)	34.0%
Late Majority (LM)	34.0%
Laggards (L)	16.0%

EXHIBIT 7–2

Classification of Adopter Groups
Source: Everett M. Rogers, *The Diffusion of Innovations* (New York: The Free Press, 1962), p. 76.

[3] G. Zaltman, *Marketing: Contributions from the Behavioral Sciences* (New York: Harcourt, Brace & World, Inc., 1965), p. 150.

contacts are restricted largely to their own local group;[4] they enjoy high status and respect within their own social groups and are usually younger than members of the groups following them. Those in the early majority group are the most deliberate; they will not consider buying a new product until a sizable group of their peers (innovators and early adopters) have done so.[5] Those in the late majority group are below average in income and social prestige and are older than members of the earlier groups. Laggards have still lower incomes and social status;[6] by the time they buy a new product, the earlier groups are often already trying something newer.

Innovators

The innovators are not necessarily—or even usually—the influentials (opinion leaders) within their groups. The influentials may have considerable personal influence over others in their groups, but they may have this influence because they recognizably hold the norms and values of the group. If, as often happens, the group's norms favor the status quo, the influentials in it also are likely to resist change (and innovations). By contrast, the innovators in such a group are apt to be deviant or isolated group members, none too popular with the rest of the group—probably because of their nonconformity and willingness to try something new.[7]

Innovators, nevertheless, may affect the behavior of other group members through a process of "social influence by example."[8] In a study of farmers' adoption of hybrid seed corn, for instance, researchers found that the influentials took their cue from the innovators after observing the good results they had obtained.[9] Adoption by most of the other farmers in the group followed adoption by the influentials. Thus, influentials are more often "early adopters" rather than "innovators." In introducing a radically-new product, then, it probably is wise to try first to reach the innovators (getting some people to try the product), then a little later focus on reaching the influentials (getting others who have influence with their associates because of "who they are" to try the product.)[10]

[4] R. Cohen, "A Theoretical Model for Consumer Market Prediction," *Sociological Inquiry*, Winter 1962, pp. 43-50.

[5] Rogers, *op. cit.*, p. 314.

[6] *Ibid.*; also see Cohen, *op. cit.*, pp. 43-50.

[7] D. F. Cox, "Clues for Advertising Strategists: II," *Harvard Business Review*, November-December 1961, p. 170.

[8] *Ibid.*

[9] B. Ryan and N. Gross, "The Diffusion of Hybrid Seed Corn in Iowa Communities," *Rural Sociology* 8, (1943), pp. 15-24.

[10] For an interesting discussion concerned with identification of innovators see: C. W. King, "The Innovator in the Fashion Adoption Process," in L. G. Smith, ed., *Reflections on Progress in Marketing* (Chicago: American Marketing Association, 1965), pp. 324-39.

INFLUENCE OF THE MASSES

As differentiated from primitive societies, modern American society is a mass society comprising great numbers of people spread over a wide geographical area, not personally known to each other and with heterogeneous interests. In addition, the mass is not an organized group and does not necessarily share common customs and traditions. It does not usually think or act as a mob, although it does tend to climb on the bandwagon of public opinion after a clear majority opinion has been registered. (This is probably why it is difficult to find people willing to admit that they voted for a badly defeated political candidate.) The mass is also characterized by instability of interests; today's hero may be forgotten tomorrow.

A businessman attempting to communicate with these masses through mass advertising must first understand the characteristics of this amorphous group. The mass market is made up of individuals, each making his own buying decisions. These decisions may be strongly influenced by actions of other members of the primary group, but only rarely are they affected by the actions of the masses as such. Only on rare occasions does a product achieve true mass acceptance and, when it does, the fickleness of the mass almost surely dooms it to a short-lived success. Such was the case with the hula hoop.[11] The product that is successfully promoted through the mass media is not really marketed to the mass audience as a unit. Instead, it is really promoted simultaneously to many individual members of similar homogeneous primary groups throughout the market.

SOCIAL STRATIFICATION AND CLASSES

Every society classifies its members according to some social hierarchy. In all societies there are people who occupy positions of relatively higher status and power. In modern American society, class lines are not finely drawn, and it is difficult to identify a specific number of classes into which all individuals can be grouped. In medieval European society, there were clear demarcations among the nobility, merchants, and peasants, and very little

---

[11] The hula hoop fad, which occurred in 1958, started in May in southern California. By the close of September the fad had spread from coast to coast and from border to border but was almost dead. The Toy News Bureau, a publicity organization of toy manufacturers, estimated that more than twenty-five million hoops were sold during this short span of time. One company, Wham-O Manufacturing Company of San Gabriel, California, among the first to manufacture hoops, claimed that it alone had sold upwards of ten million. An executive of Maison Blanche, a New Orleans department store, estimated that nearly two million hoops had been sold in that city alone. See: *Wall Street Journal*, October 28, 1958, pp. 1, 15.

mobility between classes. Nevertheless, even in a highly mobile society such as ours, where class lines are not finely drawn, there are certain criteria by which individuals can be grouped into "social classes."

The marketer should understand the role of social classes because of their intimate relationships to the consumption of material things. For example, middle and lower class members are often described as white-collar and blue-collar workers, because of the kinds of clothing they wear to work. Similar class differences in dress and leisure clothing can be clearly identified, although the nature of these differences vary with fashion changes. Similarly, upper and lower classes also exhibit distinctive tastes in food and drink. In general, except for college students, beer is consumed primarily by lower class people, and, except for certain ethnic groups, wine is consumed primarily by upper class people. The lower classes seem to prefer "plain American" food; upper classes often prefer more elaborately prepared and foreign food. Research studies on preferences in household furnishings also show a clearly identifiable difference in preferences between members of lower and upper classes.

Criteria for Grouping Individuals into Social Classes

An earlier chapter emphasized the importance of identifying and describing market segments to success in marketing. Social class is an important basis for market segmentation, and the marketing man should know which criteria are most useful for grouping individuals into social classes.

Occupations   Probably the best criterion of class status is occupation. If a single standard were to be used, occupational status would most accurately describe class differences in the United States. To many people, occupational status is synonymous with class, the class groups commonly described as the laboring class, the white-collar class, and the managerial class. The occupation of the individual presents a clear picture of his personal achievements and his contributions to society.

Occupations are ranked according to several standards: First are the qualifications necessary for success in the occupation, such as training, education, and intelligence. These help to explain the rankings given various occupations, but they do not explain all situations. Certain political jobs, for example, almost reverse the normal pattern. An advanced university degree is often said to be the "kiss of death" to an aspiring politician. Second is the financial reward attaching to the job. In most instances, financial reward is closely correlated with education, training, and experience, but here also are exceptions as in the ministry and public service.

These exceptions must be explained by additional factors, one of which is the honorable status attached to the job. The minister or professor receives "psychic income" from the recognition on his own part and by others of his contributions to society. Third are the working conditions which characterize the job for, in the mind of the general public, differences in working conditions have always separated the ditchdigger and the plumber from the white-collar worker. Collectively, these three factors measure what might be called occupational prestige. The literature of sociology contains reports of many studies that have attempted to measure the prestige rankings of different occupations. As might be expected, managerial and professional occupations rank at the top, and low-pay, low-skill occupations at the bottom.

WEALTH AND INCOME   This criterion of class status is closely related to the first. As already mentioned, financial reward is an important factor in the ranking of occupations. There are, however, instances where wealth and income provide an entirely independent measure of class status. One is that of inherited wealth. Although graduated inheritance taxes have reduced the importance of this factor, it is still influential. For instance, W. Lloyd Warner, in attempting to classify American society into six broad classes, differentiates between the top two classes primarily on the basis of old family and inherited wealth as compared with the "nouveau riche." [12] A case where income is not closely related to occupation is in the family with more than one wage earner. A skilled laborer with a working wife or working dependent children may have a larger family income than many managerial or professional families. The gradual deterioration (in some cases even the reversal) of the traditional relationship between the incomes of white-collar workers and laborers has increased the difficulty of clearly defining class lines.

Possessions are the usual measure of wealth and income. Thus, a wealthy miser with few worldly possessions would occupy, in the eyes of the average individual, lower class status than his capital assets might imply. With the progressive reduction in extremes of income, possessions have become a more satisfactory measure of class status than income and wealth. This is of particular interest to marketers whose products are sold to ultimate consumers. Sociological studies have uncovered differences in spending and buying patterns among different social classes, even when family income is the same. For example, the markedly different preferences in home furnishings between lower and middle class families described previously

[12] W. L. Warner and P. S. Lunt, *The Status System of a Modern Community* (New Haven: Yale University Press, 1942), pp. 88-91. For an interesting description of the ways in which the two top classes may be establishing closer relationships, see: "The Rich Come Out of Hiding," *Business Week*, November 15, 1958, pp. 58-72.

cannot be explained solely in terms of prices. The social class status attached to various makes and models of automobiles also varies widely. The aura of successful achievement that has come to be so strongly associated with the ownership of a Cadillac may lead a socially ambitious individual to buy that make in preference to an equally expensive Imperial or Continental.[13]

FAMILY   This criterion partially explains the high social status certain "old families" have in parts of New England and the South. However, family is far less important now than it was fifty years ago, mainly because family position is no longer as closely related to occupation, income, and wealth. Increased educational opportunity for the underprivileged has narrowed, though not eliminated, the differential in occupational opportunity, and income and inheritance taxes have reduced the magnitude of difference in inherited wealth. Nowadays, it is not difficult for a person who is occupationally and financially successful to move up to a higher class status, except up to the top level. Family position is still important for admission to that rarefied atmosphere. The wife and minor children occupy the same social status as the husband or breadwinner, and a change in his social status means a change for the entire immediate family. Once a person is on his own, he may occupy a social status different from that of his parents or brothers and sisters.

AUTHORITY AND POWER   This criterion is also closely related to occupation and wealth and income. That is why a school superintendent usually enjoys higher social status and income than the school teachers in his system, although their education may be equivalent.

PERSONALITY   This criterion is perhaps of most significance to the socially mobile individual who is moving up in the social strata. The person with a flexible and attractive personality adapts easily to the customs and usages of a higher social class.

Social Class Structure in the United States

Most sociologists have classified American society into three broad, roughly defined classes: the upper, middle, and lower classes. W. Lloyd Warner, on the basis of studies in three American towns, set up a hierarchy of *six* American social classes: upper upper, lower upper,

---

[13] P. D. Martineau, *Motivation in Advertising* (New York: McGraw-Hill, 1957), Ch. 6.

upper middle, lower middle, upper lower, and lower lower.[14] This classification has had considerable publicity, but many sociologists believe that it is more precise than accurate. Under Warner's classification, the class status of each person is ascertained by asking his fellow citizens (his equals, his superiors, and his inferiors) to rank him. It is how each of these groups looks at him that indicates his actual class. This dependence on the ratings of fellow citizens has been the main cause for criticism of the Warner system. The ordinary citizen does not think in terms of this complex hierarchy and, when asked to classify his fellow citizens into the six groups, shows little agreement with others who are asked to do the same thing. Perhaps the most important single rating is the willingness of the group of people whom the individual considers his equals to accept him as *their* equal.

American society has no single elite or ruling class; it has *several* elites. Among others, there are the management elite, the professional elite, the political elite, and the "old family" social elite.[15] There is no clear-cut line between the elite or upper class and the upper middle class business and professional men. But there does seem to be one factor that differentiates the upper middle class from the lower middle class—educational expectation. In the upper middle class family, it is usually taken for granted that the children will receive a college education, whereas in the lower middle class family, such an expectation is uncommon. Traditionally, the distinction between the middle and lower classes in the United States has been based on income differences and has remained fairly stable. White-collar workers and small entrepreneurs with their higher incomes made up the middle class, and laborers and farmers with their lower incomes made up the lower class. This distinction has blurred with the new high incomes earned by elite labor and the deteriorating relative income of white-collar workers.[16]

Except in the upper class, there seems to be little individuality among modern Americans as consumers. Conformity seems to be the rule. Of course basic conformity still leaves room for individual differences, but only within limits. The standards to which the individual conforms often change at a bewildering rate, but the middle class consumer, and the lower class consumer to a somewhat lesser degree, are socially obligated to keep pace with the changes. Fashion in clothing is an excellent example of this.[17]

[14] W. L. Warner and P. S. Lunt, *op. cit.*, pp. 88-91.

[15] For a highly interesting account and analysis of the different elites in American society, see: C. W. Mills, *The Power Elite* (New York: Oxford University Press, 1957).

[16] For an illuminating treatment of the blurring of class distinctions, see: D. Seligman, "The New Masses," *Fortune*, May 1959, pp. 106-11, 257-58.

[17] R. Bendix and S. M. Lipset, *Class Status and Power* (Glencoe, Ill.: The Free Press, 1953), p. 323.

Members of different classes show a wide divergence in interests and activities which, in turn, influence their consumption patterns. For example, a definite relationship exists between the prestige level of occupation and kinds of leisure time activities.[18] Different recreational preferences among the various classes affect their expenditures on hobbies and recreation.

An awareness of the differences between the upper, middle, and lower classes is important in selecting advertising media. The upper classes read more books and magazines; the lower classes listen to more radio and view more television; the middle classes lie somewhere in between. Although there are some magazines with a primarily lower-class appeal, only a small proportion of the lower classes are reached through such a medium. Larger audiences of these people are reached through radio and television messages. For the upper classes, the reverse is true.[19] Certain popular television shows reach the upper as well as the middle and lower class markets, but appeals directed solely to the upper class market are usually more effectively conveyed through the so-called class magazines.

STATUS SYMBOLS   In a culture such as ours, one evidently committed to the elimination of impassable class lines, few people are wholly satisfied with their existing social status, most striving endlessly to improve their positions. One outcome is that possessions acquired by the individual are uniquely related to his own goals. Personal property is not considered a prerogative of any special group, but rather a measure of success and, hence, a means of achieving higher class status. Although many products carry little or no connotation of status, many others are highly significant in providing a measure of their owner's social position. Marketing executives at all distribution levels, from the manufacturer to the retailer, should determine the status connotations of their products and plan their merchandising and promotional efforts accordingly.

The existence of a social class structure is of marketing significance because certain kinds of products assume status connotations. The so-called status-symbol school of sociologists provides an interesting explanation of how the twin urges for self-expression and self-betterment, shared by nearly all Americans, take the form of aspiring to higher status. This school holds that (1) people express their personalities not so much in words as in symbols (e.g., mannerisms, dress, ornaments, possessions); and (2) most people are increasingly concerned about their social status. Different products vary as to their status-symbol value, and their value may

[18] Alfred C. Clarke, "The Use of Leisure and Its Relation to Occupational Prestige," *American Sociological Review*, vol. 21, pp. 301-307.
[19] J. T. Klapper, *The Effects of Mass Media* (New York: Columbia University Bureau of Applied Social Research, 1949), pp. 1-17.

also change; the automobile was once the major status symbol, but many sociologists maintain that it has now been replaced by the house and its furnishings.[20] The status symbol concept is one the marketer does well to consider, for when he understands that he is selling a symbol as well as a product, he is able to view his product more completely. He should understand not only how his product satisfies certain practical needs but also how it fits meaningfully into modern culture.[21]

SOCIAL CLASS STRUCTURES IN OTHER COUNTRIES   These stated generalizations apply only to the American market. Social factors vary enormously among different peoples and nations, and businessmen who seek business abroad must first study the social environment in each foreign market. The social class structure varies widely even among the most highly developed countries, and other sociological factors vary just as much. For instance, the French woman is much more highly individualistic than the American woman in her selection of clothing. She selects first that which is flattering and only second that which is fashionable.

Social Mobility

There is in the United States a long-standing belief in the democratic principle of equal opportunity for all. Our history is full of instances where men moved up from the humblest beginnings to positions of the highest importance. Abraham Lincoln, of course, is an outstanding example and, without question, our society has been highly mobile in comparison with other societies. (The results of some sociological studies indicate that this mobility has all but disappeared. Critics point out, however, that these studies were made in small towns from which the more able young people tend to emigrate, so little mobility was to be expected from those who remained.[22])

The fact that each social group has a reference group helps explain upward mobility or, as it is popularly known, "social climbing." The reference group of the lower class is the lower middle class; the reference group of the lower middle class is the upper middle class; the reference group

[20] G. Burck, "How American Taste is Changing," *Fortune*, July 1959, pp. 186-88.

[21] S. J. Levy, "Symbols for Sale," *Harvard Business Review*, July-August, 1959, p. 124.

[22] For both viewpoints, see: R. S. Lynd and H. M. Lynd, *Middletown in Transition* (New York: Harcourt, Brace, 1937), pp. 70-72; W. L. Warner, R. J. Havighurst, and M. B. Loeb, *Who Shall Be Educated?* (New York: Harper & Brothers, 1944); and G. Sjoberg, "Are Social Classes in America Becoming More Rigid?" *American Sociological Review*, vol. 16, pp. 775-83.

of the upper middle class is the upper class; and the reference group of the American upper class is the British upper class. Each social group has its own behavior patterns, values, and attitudes, but these are conditioned subconsciously by its reference group. Some social groups are happy and secure in this situation, some are not.[23]

There seems still to be strong evidence that social mobility is high in the United States, although at different rates for each class. Mobility upward from the lower class is low because there is much stronger motivation for achievement in middle and upper class people and, hence, higher mobility aspirations. In contrast to the middle class, the lower class seeks job security and avoids risk, expresses more limited income expectations, places less value on education (and plans for less), and plans for lower occupational goals.[24] Perhaps the most important change in the lower class is the shift from a success goal to a security goal. Many lower class people have exchanged the old American goal of "office boy to President" for social security and a pension. They prefer to settle for the safety of a routine job rather than the risks that accompany ambition. In addition, many lower class people have become more interested in the pursuit of leisure and enjoyment than in success. Promotion and success come to the men who spend many overtime hours on their jobs, but to many men the loss of enjoyable hours for sport and recreation is too great a price to pay for the remote possibility of promotion. At the same time, there is a trend toward there being fewer people in the American lower class. Declines in the numbers of drudgery type jobs, and the financial and prestige upgrading of many skilled laboring jobs, have effectively decreased the membership in the lower class and increased that in the middle class.

Market Segmentation by Social Classes

In a study of social class and spending behavior, Pierre Martineau concluded that only consideration of a middle class and a lower class is necessary for purposes of market segmentation.[25] His research uncovered very little homogeneity between the upper lower and lower middle classes. If this is true, then the often held assumption that one social class desires to emulate the next higher social class is limited within the three general class ranges. Hence, product appeals should be aimed at either the middle class or lower class. If aimed at both, they are not apt to be successful.

[23] M. C. Pirie, "An Anthropologist Looks at Marketing," in F. E. May (ed.), *Increasing Sales Efficiency*, Michigan Business Papers No. 35 (Ann Arbor: Bureau of Business Research, University of Michigan, 1959), p. 153.

[24] L. Reissman, "Levels of Aspiration and Social Class," *American Sociological Review*, vol. 18, pp. 233-42.

[25] Pierre Martineau, "Social Classes and Spending Behavior," *Journal of Marketing*, October 1958, pp. 121-30.

Martineau further contends that the upper class is so small, it can be conveniently combined with the middle class. This reduction of class segments to two simplifies the planning of marketing programs for products that have mass markets. But for products sold to smaller-sized markets, it appears that a more refined market segmentation according to social class is still justified.

Market segmentation by social classes often is more meaningful than segmentation according to demographic characteristics; social class segmentation serves better to explain differences in buying behavior among members of the various classes. To segment the market on the basis of social class, the marketer must not only understand but identify the tastes, style preferences, and communicative skills and methods characterizing each class. The subtlety of humor found in *The New Yorker* magazine has little appeal to lower class people but strong appeal to upper class members. Rational appeals are most effective when directed to the middle and upper class, as is *avant garde* styling in products and packaging. Certain products, such as sports cars and beer, are inherently more attractive to one class than another, and their marketing programs should take this factor into account. In short, the marketer must recognize that products have symbolic value and, as such, must satisfy the prestige and status needs of each class, as well as more obvious physical and convenience needs.

OTHER SOCIAL INFLUENCES

Leisure Time

During the twentieth century in the United States, the length of the normal working week has been reduced from as much as eighty-four hours to an average of somewhere around forty hours. As a consequence, the average worker has gained considerable free time to use at his own discretion. This discretionary time has been increased even more for the average citizen through the advent and spread of paid vacations, since many families could never afford to take vacations without pay.

The economic concept of "opportunity cost" is helpful in explaining the continuing trend toward more free time for more people. Essentially, this explanation boils down to the proposition that as economic productivity rises, the opportunity to choose between work and leisure rises with it. One authority on the subject of leisure states the argument this way:

> The value of free time to the worker is in a sense set by what economists might call its "opportunity cost"; that is, free hours are chosen by the wage- or salary-earner because they are worth more to him than the opportunity to raise the country's output and thus indirectly make available to him a larger volume of goods. The opportunity cost of

leisure rises as *standards* of living rise. If a worker of today were content with the goods and services which would have seemed sufficient to a worker of a hundred years ago, he might have much more free time than he has. To earn ample food, comfortable clothing, and a roof over his head would not require nearly as long hours as are now prevalent. But wants for purchasable goods have risen as productivity has risen. Prevalent standards of living include, among other things, automobiles, radios and television sets, mechanical refrigerators, washers, vacuum cleaners, longer dependency of children as they spend more years at school, more medical services, unemployment insurance, old-age pensions, and the multifarious tax supported services of government.[26]

The growing amount of leisure time has had a profound effect on markets and marketing. The "do-it-yourself" market is an excellent example. The man or woman who has some free time gets pleasure out of making or repairing items he or she would have formerly purchased or paid to have fixed. This not only provides the psychic satisfaction of creative activity but alleviates any feeling of guilt about nonproductive use of time.[27] Consequently, some businesses have reorganized their distribution systems with a view toward making their products more readily available to these "do-it-yourselfers." Americans now have more time for travel and cultural pursuits. The booming tourist industry and the increased interest in art, music, and books are some of the results.

Perhaps the most important effect of increased leisure is reflected in changes in values and the "way of life." Instead of buying an expensive car to impress his friends, a consumer may economize on this purchase in order to buy the boat, shop tools, or fishing equipment he wants. New homes are planned to simplify participation in leisure time activities. Both the men's and women's clothing industries have experienced an increased demand for informal sports wear. The impact of these changes on business has been enormous. Whole new markets have been opened up and new enterprises have been organized to serve them.

Fashion

Fashion can be defined as the opinion of a group of people about a thing. Since it is a reflection of opinion, and since people like occasional change, it is necessarily transitory. Fashion should be differentiated from

---

[26] G. Soule, "The Economics of Leisure," *Annals of the American Academy of Political and Social Science*, September 1957, pp. 20-21.

[27] American culture has been strongly affected by the social values of the early colonists. Religious leaders, particularly in New England, preached that man was made to work and that laziness was sinful. These beliefs permeated American society so effectively that even present-day Americans feel a little uneasy about nonproductive activity.

style in this respect. A style is a kind of design or art form that is unchanging. When, in the opinion of a large group of people, a particular style is popular, that style becomes a fashion. In turn, if a fashion is of particularly short duration, it is called a fad. Fashion, then, is the pursuit of novelty for its own sake. Every market into which the consumer's fashion sense has insinuated itself is, by that very token, subject to a common, compelling need for unceasing change in the styling of its goods.[28]

The role of fashion in American society has been growing. Because of improving media of communications, including the wide coverage of television and the expanding circulations of published media, fashion news is spread far and wide in less time. Accordingly, the time span covered by the appearance of a new fashion, its adoption by a few pace-setters, its rise to popularity, and its subsequent decline has been becoming shorter. At the same time, expansions in the amount of discretionary income in the hands of consumers have permitted them to spend more in their attempts to satisfy the desire for change. Furthermore, there are increasing numbers of group-oriented people in society, and fewer individualists, and this has lent added importance to conforming to changes in fashion.

A lucid illustration of the powerful influence of fashion was provided by one authority who reported the following:

> . . . fashion is the impulse that opens up new volume opportunities, even in sales-saturated industries. Here's what I mean: Certainly the telephone is so much a part of our lives today that few of us could live without one. Yet A.T.&T. achieved new sales goals *and* product diversification by using fashion to sell extension telephones in the home. True, the extension phone campaign started on a utility and step-saving basis. "Have an extension in your kitchen or have one upstairs in your bedroom. Save energy, save steps." It sounded like a good idea, but it met with definite resistance. Why? Probably because it made a woman feel guilty! Was she too lazy to go a few steps or walk a few stairs to answer her phone?
>
> But what happened when *color* was added to the sales message? Now a woman had a guilt-free, *fashion* reason for installing a couple of "decorator" phones throughout the house. Sales soared! In fact one A.T.&T. executive recently told us that the number of homes with more than one phone has nearly doubled in the past six years. And it was felt that color had a great deal to do with breaking the ice. . . .[29]

The increasing speed of change in fashions is particularly evident in men's clothing. A generation ago, fashions in men's wear changed at

---

[28] D. E. Robinson, "Fashion Theory and Product Design," *Harvard Business Review*, November-December, 1958, p. 127.

[29] H. Valentine, "Fashion—Who Needs It?" in *Report on the Twenty-Ninth Boston Conference on Distribution* (Boston: Retail Trade Board, 1957), pp. 32-34.

such a sedate pace that most new developments would continue to be popularly accepted over several years. Today it is common for a new development in men's or boys' clothing to last only a single season.

Not all consumers react equally to fashion. Some consumers attempt to remain in the forefront of the fashion cycle so as to project an image of modernity and stylishness. They wear the latest styles in clothing, adopt the latest innovations in food and drinks, read the newest popular books, furnish their homes in the most recent decor, drive the latest automobiles, and so forth. At the opposite extreme, other consumers strive to reduce the impact of fashion on their lives as much as possible by adopting conservative styling in clothing, which does not change so quickly or dramatically and, in a similar manner, by avoiding extremes of fashion in all things. Such individuals can almost eliminate the impact of fashion in certain aspects of their lives. For example, through furnishing a home with antiques and traditional furniture, much of the impact of fashion change is avoided. The alert marketer of products influenced by fashion must be aware of the existence of both types of consumers and select as his target market segment those he can serve most profitably over the long run.

Population Composition

Most of the current population growth in metropolitan areas is occurring in the suburbs rather than in the urban areas. This trend is significant to marketing because the suburbanite often represents a very different market from the urbanite. The suburb retains much of the character of a small town. Thus, its consumption patterns are strongly influenced by neighborhood and local social groups. Marketers, therefore, should keep these differences in sources of influence in mind when planning marketing programs for products sold both in urban and suburban markets.

The population composition of the central core cities has been changing to a predominantly low income and poverty level group of consumers. At the same time, an increasing proportion of central city residents are members of minority groups. In New York City, for example, the Puerto Rican and Negro populations have increased enormously. From 1959 to 1969 alone, New York's Negro population doubled. These population changes create significant changes in markets. For instance, low income and ghetto groups are often served by different marketing institutions. Recent studies have raised questions about whether they are being served adequately.[30]

[30] For example, see: D. Caplovitz, *The Poor Pay More* (New York: The Free Press, 1967); C. S. Goodman, "Do the Poor Pay More?," *Journal of Marketing*, January 1968, pp. 18-24; F. D. Sturdivant, *The Ghetto Marketplace* (New York: The Free Press, 1969).

CONCLUSION

Broadly speaking, the socio-cultural aspects of buyer behavior revolve around self-interest, just as do the economic and psychological aspects. An individual seeks satisfactions that will maintain his own self-respect by fitting into the moral norms established by the society in which he lives. At the same time he seeks recognition and respect from others. He seeks pleasure, not in a biological sense but in terms of what is considered acceptable by the groups with which he identifies, and he also seeks affection and friendship. Sometimes, he may want something not for itself but for the social gain he gets from it. The lady living in Florida who buys a fur piece does not buy it to keep warm but because of what it will do for her social status.

Sociologists have made an immense contribution to marketing understanding through their investigations of the diffusion process. Description and identification of the five adopter groups—innovators, early adopters, early majority, late majority, and laggards—has provided a model which should help in the improvement of marketing planning. Recognition that innovators and influentials are both important to the diffusion process but that the two groups rarely overlap is also critical: innovators appear mainly to influence only influentials, while the influentials appear generally to be most committed to the status quo, and, hence, among the most difficult to convince. Unless, however, the marketer succeeds in convincing the influentials, he will not succeed in convincing the majority of their followers (in the early and late majorities). An understanding of these and other important facets of the diffusion process is essential for the modern marketer.

QUESTIONS AND PROBLEMS

1. Are psychological and sociological motives within the individual likely to be in conflict at times? If so, how would such conflicts affect the marketer?

2. When an individual is a member of several peer groups, are his consuming activities likely to be affected equally by all groups? Explain.

3. Does membership in a peer group result in conformity in the actions of its members? Does this have implications for marketing?

4. What is an "influential?" How would you go about identifying influentials? Who would the influentials likely be in connection with the purchase of the following products?
   a. Golfing equipment

     b. Plants and shrubs for landscaping

     c. Musical instruments for teenagers

     d. Office typewriters

     e. Stereo components

5. If "influentials are found at all levels of society," how would those in the upper and middle classes differ, if at all, from those in the lower class?

6. Explain how a marketer contemplating the introduction of a radically new type of product might use Rogers' model of the diffusion process in planning his marketing strategy.

7. Assume that a particular social group has norms that are strongly in favor of change for change's sake. In such a group, would the influentials then be the innovators? Explain your reasoning.

8. Would you conclude from what sociologists know about masses that there is no such thing as a mass market? Why or why not?

9. Try to enumerate five products fairly clearly related to the lower class, the middle class, and the upper class, respectively.

10. Evaluate the various criteria used for grouping individuals into social classes.

11. How might Warner's six-class structure be more useful to a marketer than the ordinary three-class structure?

12. Do you think that the decline in the importance of the automobile as a status symbol in the United States indicates a decreasing importance attached to status symbols by American society? Discuss.

13. Would you agree that social mobility is an important prop to consumption in the United States? Why or why not?

14. Minority racial and ethnic groups in the United States generally perceive promotion and products in a different light and, thus, require different marketing treatment. Comment on this statement.

15. A marketer comments "I would like to segment the market for my company's new instant breakfast cereals on the basis of social classes, but I don't know how to do it." What advice would you give this marketer?

16. Individuals with high opportunity costs for leisure offer the best potential market for goods. Please explain.

17. "The rapidly increasing importance of fashion in men's clothing presents an excellent example of how competent marketers can foist on the public something it does not want." Comment.

18. Comment on the statement that fashion is the pursuit of novelty for its own sake.

19. Why do you suppose some products have status connotations and others do not? Which group might be easier to sell?

20. Is it possible for some people to escape completely from the influence of fashion? Justify the position you take.

21. How are the problems involved in marketing to people residing in central cities changing? Will these changes likely continue indefinitely? Why or why not?

PART 3

PRODUCTS

The Product:
Marketing Characteristics

Product Innovation

Formulating Product-Market Strategy:
No Product Change

Formulating Product-Market Strategy:
Product Change and New Product

THE PRODUCT:
MARKETING CHARACTERISTICS

A product is both "what a seller has to sell" and "what a buyer has to buy." A moment's reflection, therefore, will reveal that a product is more than a mere physical commodity. Any enterprise that has something to sell, tangible goods or not, is selling products. For example, a laundry, which sells the service of cleaning clothes, is just as surely engaged in selling a product as the retail stores which originally sold the clothes it cleans. In fact, any firm that "has something to sell" sells services as part of that something, even though we may think of it as selling tangible goods rather than services *per se*. Furthermore, "what a buyer buys" is an item from which he expects to gain certain physical and psychological satisfactions.

It is necessary at this point to insert a word of caution with respect to semantics. In marketing, the word "good" is used as a synonym for "product." This is in line with both long-standing business usage and well-established academic custom. The businessman and the marketing professor simply say "good" when they mean "product," as the latter term was defined earlier. Note carefully, though, that when "good" is used in this broad sense, it may apply either to a product consisting of some tangible good and associated services or to one which consists of services alone. In the following discussion, as indeed throughout this entire book, "good" and "product" are used interchangeably.

Formally defined, then, *a product is a bundle of utilities consisting of various product features and accompanying services.*[1] The bundle of utilities consists of those physical and psychological satisfactions that the buyer receives when he buys the product, which the seller provides by selling a particular combination of product features and associated services. When a man buys a suit from a clothing store, for example, he buys not only the garment itself but the clerk's assistance and advice, the store's alteration service, the prestige of the store's and maker's labels, perhaps "charge and delivery" services, and the privilege of returning the item for refund or allowance should it fail to yield the expected satisfaction. Looked at in this light, the clothing store is selling not only men's suits and services related thereto but bundles of utilities which provide customers with both physical and psychological satisfactions as they consume their purchases.

Consumers' Goods and Industrial Goods

The two major categories of goods are consumers' goods and industrial goods. Depending upon the purpose for which it is primarily destined to be used, any good may be classed as a consumer good or as an industrial good. Consumers' goods are destined for final consumption by ultimate consumers and households. Television sets, perfumes, smoking tobacco, and potted geraniums are all examples of consumers' goods. Industrial goods are destined for use in the commercial production of other goods or for use in connection with carrying on some business or institutional activity. Crude petroleum, machine tools, and electronic computers are all industrial goods.

Actually, not many goods can be classified *exclusively* as consumer goods or industrial goods. Typing paper, for example, is used for business purposes, but it may also be used for love letters. Typing paper, then, is both a consumer good and an industrial good. The same article may, under one set of circumstances, be an industrial good, and under other conditions a consumer good.

Why is this apparently artificial distinction important? Consumers' goods and industrial goods are bought for different purposes. Of even greater significance for marketing is the fact that their purchasers characteristically use different approaches in the making of buying decisions.

[1] W. Alderson, *Marketing Behavior and Executive Action* (Homewood, Ill.: Richard D. Irwin, Inc., 1957), p. 274.

Consequently, marketing situations and problems also vary, depending upon whether the product is being marketed as a consumers' good or an industrial good.

CONSUMERS' GOODS—MARKETING CHARACTERISTICS

Everyone knows that the variety of consumers' goods is almost endless. Literally, these goods range from A to Z—aspirin to zippers—and include such diverse items as chewing gum, pleasure yachts, grass seed, and complete frozen TV dinners. There are so many different consumers' goods that it is clearly impractical to analyze each consumer item individually. Two classification systems for consumers' goods, devised to facilitate marketing analysis, are presented in the discussion which follows.

"Traditional" Classification of Consumers' Goods

Sometime before 1923, Professor Melvin T. Copeland of the Harvard Business School, a pioneer marketing teacher, set up what is now known as the traditional system for classifying consumers' goods.[2] Copeland based his classification system on differences in consumer buying attitudes and behavior. Under this system, three classes of consumers' goods are identified as convenience goods, shopping goods, and specialty goods.[3]

CONVENIENCE GOODS   Items the consumer buys frequently, immediately, and with minimum shopping effort are classed as convenience goods. Examples include cigarettes, candy and chewing gum, magazines and newspapers, gasoline, drugs, and most grocery products. Note that these are all nondurables, i.e., they are consumed or "used up" rather rapidly; hence, consumers buy them frequently and normally neither postpone their purchases nor make them much in advance of the time of consumption. Note, too, that, in buying convenience goods, habit dominates the consumer's behavior. Through force of habit, it is relatively easy for the consumer to arrive at buying decisions. In buying cigarettes and gasoline, for example, the consumer knows which brands he prefers, and he knows the retail outlets where he generally buys them. Little or no conscious deliberation is required in making such buying decisions. The typical consumer attempts

---

[2] See: M. T. Copeland, "Relation of Consumers' Buying Habits to Marketing Methods," *Harvard Business Review*, April 1923, pp. 282-89.

[3] The definitions of these three classes of consumers' goods used in the following discussion are consistent with those of the American Marketing Association. See: *Marketing Definitions* (Chicago: American Marketing Association, 1960).

to minimize the amount of time and effort devoted to buying convenience goods.

In making buying decisions for most convenience goods, the consumer rarely bothers to compare competing items on the bases of price and quality. The possible gains from making price and quality comparisons are not large enough to justify the cost involved in terms of time and effort. "It isn't worth shopping around for" expresses this buying attitude of the typical consumer in buying most convenience goods. However, if the price or quality of a convenience good, such as a certain brand of bread, gets too far out of line with competing brands, many consumers revise their buying decisions. Note, though, that the possible gains to the consumer in such situations outweigh the costs in time and effort. For this reason, marketers of convenience goods usually strive to make their products compare favorably in price and quality.

Seeking to minimize shopping time and effort, the consumer buys convenience goods at "convenient" locations. While this often means that the consumer buys many convenience goods at retail outlets situated near his home, it can mean other things. A consumer may buy gasoline, for example, not at the station nearest his home but at one more convenient because he passes it on the way to work. Or the consumer may patronize a given service station where he can enjoy the convenience of using his credit card and not have to pay cash. In buying certain convenience goods, such as milk and newspapers, some consumers pay higher prices for the convenience of doorstep delivery. Many housewives, motivated by the convenience of "one-stop shopping," buy most of their grocery needs on weekly trips to the supermarket. The same housewives "pick up" other items, such as bread and milk, during the week at "convenience stores" nearer their homes.

Recognizing that consumers will not go far out of their way to buy convenience goods, marketers of such goods seek to have them available for sale in numerous and diverse outlets. Cigarettes, for example, are sold in practically all grocery stores and drug stores, most restaurants, and many service stations, besides being widely available for sale through vending machines elsewhere. The makers of Camels cigarettes once, in a famed advertising campaign, promoted the "I'd walk a mile for a Camel" slogan implying that Camels were not a convenience good. Probably there are relatively few smokers who regard their brand so highly that they will not accept a convenient substitute should the retailer be sold out of the preferred brand. Thus, it is important that the marketer of convenience goods not only have numerous outlets for his product but be certain that all have adequate inventories on hand.

SHOPPING GOODS   Items that a consumer selects and buys only after making comparisons on such bases as suitability, quality, price and style are called shopping goods. Whenever a substantial number of consumers habitually make such shopping comparisions of an item before they select and buy an item, that item is considered a shopping good. Examples of goods that most consumers probably buy in this way include millinery, furniture, rugs, dress goods, women's ready-to-wear and shoes, and household appliances. Prior to buying these items, the consumer shops around and compares the offerings of different stores. Notice that the typical shopping good is bought rather infrequently, is "used up" quite slowly, and the consumer often is in a position to defer or advance the date of purchase. Thus, the consumer can afford to allot a considerable amount of time and effort to the buying decision. In other words, consumers feel that the possible gains from making shopping comparisions exceed the costs in terms of time and effort.

Not every consumer uses the same bases of comparison in buying shopping goods. In some cases, the consumer shops primarily to find something "suitable," e.g., the person who looks for window shelving to use in displaying African violets. In shopping for millinery or apparel, some women consider style the most important factor while others are mainly "price shoppers." In shopping for shoes for their children, these same women may consider quality the most significant basis for comparison. The bases of comparison used and their relative importance vary both with the product and the shopper.

Branding is a good deal less important for shopping goods than for convenience goods. Rather than buying a modern chair on the basis of a brand name, most consumers prefer to compare different offerings on other bases. This does not mean that branding is totally unimportant, only that it is less important as a buying influence than it is for a convenience good such as cigarettes or tooth paste. If a shopping good, such as a modern chair, meets the consumer's other qualifications, he may decide to buy the *Selig* chair rather than an unbranded chair or a little-known brand. In some instances the consumer undoubtedly is willing to pay more for a branded shopping good, but the more definitely a good is a shopping good, the less he is willing to pay for the prestige of the brand name.

Because consumers typically devote considerable time and effort to the buying of shopping goods, marketers of shopping goods can manage with fewer retail outlets for their products than can marketers of convenience goods. The shopping goods marketer places great emphasis on having his goods for sale in outlets where consumers are likely to look for such items, rather than on having them available in every store. Thus, a manufacturer of modern chairs seeks only a few stores, mostly those specializing in modern furniture, to handle his line in a city.

SPECIALTY GOODS   Consumer items for which significant numbers of buyers are habitually willing to make a special purchasing effort are known as specialty goods. For an item to be included in this category, it must possess unique characteristics or have a high degree of brand identification or both. Examples of articles usually bought as specialty goods are fancy foods, hi-fi components, stamps and coins for collectors, and "prestige" brands of men's suits. The consumer already knows the product or brand he wants; the special purchasing effort he is willing to make is for the purpose of finding where it is on sale. In reaching the buying decision, consumers do not compare the desired specialty goods with others, as they do in the case of shopping goods. However, as specialty goods are often in the luxury price class, consumers may take considerable time making decisions to undertake the special search required.

Specialty goods may be found in low as well as high price ranges. The buying behavior of stamp collectors, for instance, is characterized by the exertion of nearly as much special purchasing effort to obtain the missing stamp in a set worth a dime or a quarter as it is to locate the rarity worth hundreds of dollars. Similarly, the price of canned, chocolate-coated grasshoppers may be $1.00 per can and the price of a *Hickey-Freeman* suit may be $200.00 Both prices are high relative to other articles serving the same underlying wants but without the unique characteristics of chocolate-coated grasshoppers or the prestige attached to the *Hickey-Freeman* name. Consumers are willing to exert special purchasing efforts to locate such items, and prices are only secondary considerations in the buying decisions.

The fact that an item may be easy to locate does not disqualify it from being a specialty good. The consumer desiring a *Hickey-Freeman* suit, for instance, needs only to consult the classified section of the telephone directory in any major city. The consumer who wants to buy *Alka-Seltzer* and will not accept a substitute probably can find it in most drug stores and many grocery stores. An item is a specialty good because some buyers are *willing* to make a special purchasing effort, although they may not have to. Marketing practices of many manufacturers of specialty goods have made it unnecessary for consumers to exert special purchasing efforts. They have made their brands relatively easy to locate, thus making it easy for consumers to buy them.

APPRAISAL OF "TRADITIONAL" CLASSIFICATION SYSTEM   Under this three-way classification system, every consumer product may, at least in theory, be placed into one of the three classifications. For products classed as convenience goods or shopping goods, this proves relatively easy to do. But, perhaps because of insufficient knowledge of consumers' buying attitudes and behavior patterns, items coming under the specialty goods heading are often difficult to identify and classify as such. Many specialty goods are easily confused with shopping goods and sometimes even with convenience goods. The buyer of a Chevrolet automobile, for example, may have made his choice only after comparing the Chevrolet with other makes, or perhaps he bought it because of certain unique features and the brand name, or maybe he bought it because of the dealer's convenient location. In the first instance the Chevrolet qualifies as a shopping good, in the second as a specialty good, and in the third as a convenience good. There are in fact many border line cases of this sort which make it difficult to place a product in a particular classification with absolute certainty. Actually, however, this only indicates that the markets involved are made up of groups of people who buy for different reasons, have different buying attitudes, and exhibit different patterns of buying behavior. In other words, most consumer products, to some degree at least, are purchased by more than one market segment. Thus, in applying the three-way classification system to his analysis of practical marketing problems, the marketer should segment his product's market, choose those segments he desires to reach, and target his marketing efforts accordingly. In other words, he should offer a product consisting of the "bundle of utilities" most sought after by the market segment(s) to which he caters. Even if he must offer a product with features identical to those of other sellers, he can still differentiate the accompanying services.

The "Characteristics of Goods" Theory

The characteristics of goods theory, advanced by Leo V. Aspinwall and others provides an alternate system for classifying consumer goods.[4] According to this theory, all consumer goods can be spotted along a continuum which has only two basic categories, one at each end.[5] Any product that falls somewhere in between these two categories represents some combination of the two basic types. This approach, therefore, uses a continuum instead of discrete classes to classify all consumer goods. Thus, less difficulty is encountered in classifying individual products.

MARKETING CHARACTERISTICS CONSIDERED   Five marketing characteristics of a good are taken into account in deciding just where it should be spotted along the continuum. The first, called the "replacement rate," is

---

[4] We are indebted to Professors Aspinwall and Holton for their thinking and writings on the classification of consumer goods. Our discussion is based largely on what they have published. See: L. V. Aspinwall, "Characteristics of Goods Theory," in his *Four Marketing Theories* (Boulder, Colorado: Bureau of Business Research, University of Colorado, 1961). Also R. H. Holton, "The Distinction Between Convenience Goods, Shopping Goods, and Specialty Goods," *Journal of Marketing*, July 1958, pp. 53-56.

[5] Leonard Groeneveld suggests using a "spectrum of consumer buying intent" as a continuum and using a product's position on the continuum as a clear means of identifying and discriminating it from another. He also provides an illustration showing how four product characteristics (price, purchase frequency, size, and length of life) may be quantified to assist in locating a product's position on the continuum. See his "A New Theory of Consumer Buying Intent," *Journal of Marketing*, July 1964, pp. 23-28.

defined as the rate at which a good is purchased and consumed by users in order to provide the satisfaction a consumer expects from the product. The second is the "gross margin" which is the monetary difference between the laid-in cost and the final realized sales price. The third characteristic is "adjustment," which refers to the various changes or alterations made in a good in order to meet the exact needs of the consumer. The fourth characteristic is known as "time of consumption," which is defined as the time interval during which the good satisfies the desired utility. The last characteristic is "searching time," which is defined as the measure of average time and distance from the retail store and hence convenience afforded to the consumer by market facilities.

At one end of the continuum are placed those products which have a high replacement rate, low gross margin, low adjustment, low time of consumption, and low searching time. With little damage to existing definitions, such products appear to be the same ones which are considered convenience goods under the older system of classification. Products with diametrically opposed marketing characteristics go at the other end of the continuum. These items correspond with those defined earlier as shopping goods. Still to be considered are those consumer products which fall somewhere toward the center of the continuum. These are products, many of which would be called "specialty goods" under the older three-way classification system, that have medium ratings for the five marketing characteristics.

"RED, ORANGE, AND YELLOW GOODS"   Aspinwall avoids the confusion inherent in the older system by adopting a new set of names for goods spotted at different locations on the continuum. Instead of using such categories as convenience, specialty, and shopping goods, he advocates using new names based upon colors. By using three colors (red, orange, and yellow), he discards the notion that discrete classes of consumer goods exist. In its stead the idea is envisioned of an infinite gradation of values made possible by blending the colors in the spectrum from red to yellow with orange in between. In effect, convenience goods now become "red goods" and shopping goods become "yellow goods." Goods that fall on the continuum between the two extremes are represented by some shade of orange and are denoted as "orange goods." Table 8.1 shows the classification system for consumer goods, established according to the characteristics of goods theory. One additional aspect of this theory needs mentioning—the position of a good on the color scale is dynamic rather than static. In the words of Aspinwall:

> . . . Most products fall in the yellow classification when they are first introduced. As they become better known and come to satisfy a wider segment of consumer demand, the replacement rate increases and

the good shifts toward the red end of the scale. Thus there is a red shift in marketing, which offers a rather far-fetched analogy to the red shift in astronomy, which is associated with the increasing speed of movement of heavenly bodies. There is also an opposing tendency in marketing, however, resulting from the constant shrinking of gross margin as a good moves toward the red end of the scale. Marketing organizations, in the effort to maintain their gross margin, may improve or differentiate a good which has moved into the red category, so that some of these new varieties swing all the way back into yellow. Thereafter, the competitive drive for volume serves to accelerate the movement toward the red end of the scale again.[6]

TABLE 8–1

Classification of Consumer Goods According to the Characteristics of Goods Theory

| Characteristics | Color Classification | | |
	Red Goods	Orange Goods	Yellow Goods
Replacement rate	High	Medium	Low
Gross margin	Low	Medium	High
Adjustment	Low	Medium	High
Time of consumption	Low	Medium	High
Searching time	Low	Medium	High

Source: L. V. Aspinwall, "The Characteristics of Goods Theory," in *Four Marketing Theories* (Boulder, Colorado: Bureau of Business Research, University of Colorado, 1961).

INDUSTRIAL GOODS— MARKETING CHARACTERISTICS

Industrial users exhibit more uniform patterns of buying behavior than do ultimate consumers. Different industrial buyers, in other words, are remarkably alike in the ways they go about making buying decisions for similar products. The automobile manufacturer's approach to the buying of machine tools, for example, closely resembles those taken not only by his competitors but by most buyers of machine tools. Industrial goods, therefore, may be readily classified according to the uses to which they are to be put. There are four major categories of industrial goods: (1) production facilities and equipment, (2) production materials, (3) production supplies, and (4) management materials.

[6] Aspinwall, *op. cit.*

Production Facilities and Equipment

Included in this industrial goods category are three subcategories: installations, minor equipment, and plants and buildings.

INSTALLATIONS   Major capital assets, such as factory turret lathes and commercial laundry dryers, are called installations and are essential to an industrial user's business operations. Since buying an installation involves the investment of a comparatively large sum, buying decisions for installations generally require approval of both top management and the department head concerned. Because of this "multiple buying influence" on the purchase, a salesman of installations usually has to convince several individuals before he succeeds in getting an order—the period of negotiation prior to a sale often extending over considerable time. Sometimes, though not always, the product is designed and manufactured especially according to the buyer's specifications, as in the case of many installations used in cane sugar processing and refining. Thus, some installations are literally "one of a kind," and the salemen who sell such items require technical backgrounds or training or both. Furthermore, because of the high unit value of most installations, their marketing is characterized by rather "short marketing channels;" i.e., there are few or no intervening middlemen between the manufacturers and industrial users.

MINOR EQUIPMENT   This subcategory includes industrial goods which are used in producing the industrial user's product or service but which are not major capital assets. Examples of such goods are work benches, lift trucks, and hand tools. In contrast to the way installations are bought, purchasing procedure for minor equipment is quite routine, ordinarily consisting simply of the industrial user's purchasing executive's ordering on the basis of specifications prepared by the department submitting the purchase order. Also, in contrast with installation purchases which are comparatively infrequent, purchases of minor equipment are made fairly often.

Such routine purchasing procedures lead marketers of minor equipment to adhere rather closely to a particular type of marketing program. The marketer of minor equipment sees to it that his salesmen make frequent calls on prospective customers, also often arranging to have his products listed in industrial catalogs, such as *Sweets Catalogue Service,* to which purchasing agents refer before placing their purchase orders. Listing in industrial catalogs, advertising in trade journals, and direct-mail advertising make up the usual program for maintaining representation at the buyer's plant between salesmen's calls. The need for continuous representation also prompts many minor equipment marketers to use middlemen rather than their own salesmen for purposes of calling directly on customers. Because such middlemen generally confine their operations to relatively small geographical areas, they are able to make frequent calls on customers and can adjust their activities to fit each customer's buying timetable.

PLANTS AND BUILDINGS   These are necessary to operations of an industrial user's business and represent sizable capital investments. In this respect, the plants and buildings subcategory is similar to the installations subcategory. But this subcategory also resembles that of minor equipment insofar as plants and buildings are supplementary to, rather than directly used in, the production of the industrial user's product or service. Plants and buildings are usually not marketed as complete units, though there are some construction engineering firms that specialize in such projects. The plants and buildings subcategory is included here mainly for the sake of completeness, and not because their marketing is particularly unique. In all major respects, the industrial user approaches the problem of constructing a new plant or building in much the same way that he goes about the purchase of an installation.

Production Materials

This category of industrial goods includes the subcategories of raw materials, semi-manufactured goods, and fabricating parts.

RAW MATERIALS   These are the basic products of farms, mines, forests, and fisheries which enter into the production of more finished goods. Buying procedures for raw materials vary, depending upon the proportion their costs bear to total production costs and upon market conditions. If the price of raw materials represents only a small part of total production costs, the sources of supply are likely to be middlemen and the buying procedures routine. But when the price of raw materials accounts for a large part of the total cost of a finished good, high-ranking purchasing executives usually deal with suppliers. Similarly, if the market for a raw material is characterized by stable supply and price conditions, relatively low-level executives, using routine purchasing procedures, are adequate. But when raw material supplies and prices vary erratically, highly-skilled and high-ranking executives are charged with the buying responsibility and are expected to adapt their purchasing procedures to changing market conditions.

SEMI-MANUFACTURED GOODS   These are items, such as steel, lumber, and glass, which are the end products of one industry and the basic manufacturing materials of another. Compared with the prices of raw materials, prices of semi-manufactured goods tend to be much more stable. Thus, their purchase by the industrial user is more routine. Inasmuch as most producers of semi-manufactured goods are large, they usually sell their outputs direct to industrial users. In some cases, however, particularly where the semi-manufactured good is sold to many relatively small industrial users (lumber and plywood are examples), one or more levels of middlemen are used.

FABRICATING PARTS   These are manufactured goods which, without any substantial change in form, are incorporated into or asembled into some more complex and finished product. Storage batteries, spark plugs, and tires for an automobile are examples. Industrial users buy such products, made to their own specifications, directly from the manufacturers. Single sales contracts are negotiated for periods of several months to a year, and the relationship between seller and buyer is generally a long-term one. These negotiations are normally directed by high executives of both buying and selling companies.

Production Supplies

Production supplies are products that are essential to industrial users' business operations but do not become part of finished products. Included are such divergent items as fuel oil, coal, sweeping compound, and wiping cloths. Purchase of items in this category is a routine responsibility of the industrial user's purchasing executive, and he usually buys them through middlemen rather than directly from the makers. But when an item is used in extremely large quantities, as a public utility uses coal in the steam plant generation of electricity, long-term purchase contracts, similar to those used in buying fabricating parts, are directly negotiated by top ranking executives of the buying and selling firms.

Management Materials

This category covers both office equipment and office supplies. Pieces of office equipment of very high value, such as electronic computers and data processing systems, are usually leased rather than bought outright but, in either case, decisions are reached in essentially the same way as those made on production installations and equipment. Purchase or lease of major office equipment items involves substantial sums of money; hence, decisions require the approval of both top-management and the department head concerned, and the purchasing department merely handles the needed "paper work."

Typewriters, desk calculaters, and similar pieces of equipment are bought by the purchasing department as needed. Requisitions for the equipment originate in the departments that will use them, often with the exact brands and models being determined according to preferences of typists and clerks. Pencil sharpeners and staplers and other low-unit value articles of office equipment, as well as such office supplies as stationery and typewriter ribbons, are bought routinely, the purchasing department taking the initiative in ordering them and generally carrying a stock on hand.

Leasing

Industrial marketers fairly frequently lease their products rather than selling them outright. From the standpoint of users, leasing is an attractive alternative to outright purchase under several conditions. When a product has an unusually high rate of obsolescence, the product user can, by leasing, avoid the cost of premature write-offs. Complex products requiring continuous and expert servicing and maintenance are sometimes leased because the users wish to avoid this responsibility. The product user who wishes to minimize his investment in fixed assets can accomplish this through leasing. Computers are often leased for all three reasons: rapid obsolescence, extensive maintenance, and high cost. The leasing of fleets of automobiles and trucks, a widespread business practice, appeals to users primarily as a means of reducing capital investment, but it also simplifies maintenance problems and often reduces maintenance cost.

A marketer's decision to lease rather than to sell his products depends on several factors. Leasing requires a large capital investment in inventory, and it should produce as high a net return as other possible uses of the capital. The lessor is ordinarily responsible for maintaining the goods in operating condition. The manufacturers of some products—computers, for example—must assume the maintenance responsibility anyway because most users do not have the necessary facilities or personnel. And, when maintenance becomes an added responsibility of the marketer simply because of leasing, the rental income must be enough to cover the cost. Sometimes, users are reluctant to invest in expensive equipment because of rapid obsolescence, and leasing may be the only way a manufacturer can place his product in the hands of users. In those rare instances where a producer enjoys a temporary monopoly because of patent protection, leasing may offer a means of securing higher profits; the total rental-income over the life of a product may considerably exceed the maximum price obtainable from an outright buyer.

Reciprocity in Industrial Marketing

In marketing all categories of industrial goods, the fact that some buying is done reciprocally is a complicating feature. An industrial user practices reciprocal buying when he favors suppliers who are also his customers or prospects and when he uses such patronage as a lever for making sales. Purchasing agents describe reciprocal buying as "a matter of you scratch my back, and I'll scratch yours."

The practice of reciprocal buying and selling has been the subject of considerable controversy. Many purchasing executives condemn the practice as a violation of scientific purchasing, inasmuch as product appropriateness and supplier reliability and other considerations tend to take a "back seat" to the possibility of making current and future sales to suppliers. Oftentimes, too, the industrial user's sales department puts pressure on the purchasing division to favor customers and prospects with orders regardless of other important considerations involved in choices of suppliers.

Recently, the U.S. Department of Justice has issued complaints charging that certain large companies were using reciprocity in violation of the Sherman Anti-Trust Act. One such complaint, issued against United States Steel Corporation, alleged that it used its position as a large purchaser in its various businesses to induce its suppliers to buy steel, steel products, cement, and chemicals from it.[7] As might be expected, diversified, multi-division companies, with their widespread purchasing power, are among the most tenacious practitioners of reciprocity; but government anti-trust enforcement agencies are showing increased interest in restraining the practice of reciprocity.[8]

There is little doubt that haphazard reciprocal buying represents a departure from rational buying procedures. This, coupled with the increasingly doubtful legal status, suggests that most marketers should refrain from using reciprocity as a selling tool. Nevertheless, marketers of industrial goods, as they study how their customers and prospects go about choosing supplies, should make certain that the influences exerted by reciprocal buying practices are included in their analyses of market behavior.

CONCLUSION

All businesses that "have something to sell" sell a product of some sort. In this chapter, we have focused on different kinds of products—analyzing mainly the ways in which buyers' attitudes, behavioral patterns, and purchasing procedures vary from one category of product to another. Even in

---

[7] *Business Week,* June 21, 1969, p. 121.
[8] See "Reciprocity Under Fire," *Dun's Review,* September 1968, pp. 35-37.

buying similar products, ultimate consumers exhibit considerable differences in their approaches to decision making. By contrast, in buying similar types of industrial goods, industrial users use remarkably similar decision-making approaches. However, in spite of these generalizations concerning the ways in which ultimate consumers and industrial users go about buying various types of products, each marketer has it within his power to differentiate his product from those of competing sellers. This is accomplished by offering a unique "bundle of utilities": even if the product's features are identical with those of competitors, the marketer can differentiate the accompanying services.

QUESTIONS AND PROBLEMS

1. Describe the nature of the products sold by each of the following businesses: a commercial bank, an automobile insurance company, an architectural firm, a management consulting organization, a news magazine such as *Newsweek* or *Time.*

2. What is the main basis used for distinguishing between a consumers' good and an industrial good? Why is the distinction important?

3. Contrast and compare the "traditional system for classifying consumers' goods" with Aspinwall's "characteristics of goods" theory.

4. A British manufacturer recently announced the development of the "side-by-side conversational" bathtub. Essentially, this new product consisted of two separate tubs made of molded plastic arranged in such a way as to make it possible for two people to take separate baths at the same time. The manufacturer asserted that the product was developed in response to a "clear market need." What would be your prediction as to the probable success of this product? Why?

5. Explain how cigarettes might be bought as convenience goods, as shopping goods, and as specialty goods by different consumers. Does this lack of uniformity in the classification of goods destroy the usefulness of classifying? Explain.

6. Give some examples of products that would have been classified as "yellow goods" when introduced and that subsequently have moved along the scale to be classified as "red goods"? Can you think of a product that has moved in the other direction?

7. Would you recommend using the same kind of salesman to sell installations as to sell minor equipment? Why or why not? Describe a typical sales presentation for each kind of product.

8. How might the buying procedures differ for a steel fabricating plant buying sheet steel and a shoe manufacturer buying processed hides?

In which company would the buying responsibility probably be more important? How would the marketing programs of a company selling sheet steel and a seller of processed hides differ?

9.   The marketer of a fabricating part, such as automobile tires, often sells both to the OEM (original equipment market) and to the replacement market. Does such a marketer really sell the same "product" to both markets? Explain.

10.   Compare the behavior of industrial users in buying production supplies with their behavior in buying each of the two main types of management materials.

11.   Would you expect a company's purchasing agent and sales manager to have the same attitudes with respect to the practice of reciprocity? Why or why not? Would you agree that reciprocity is only the refuge of the weak sales organization? Why or why not?

9

PRODUCT INNOVATION

Throughout American industry today, product innovation is receiving increasing emphasis and attention. The underlying reason is that markets are highly dynamic. What was a profitable product yesterday may not be tomorrow. Moreover, successful new products command substantially higher profit margins than mature or dying products. Hence, management, in its search for new sources of profit, places emphasis on product innovation. Successful new products are profitable—at least for a while—mainly because it takes time for competitors to come up with their own versions, enter the market, and eventually compete on a price basis.

Although product innovation occurs in all industries, the *rate of change* varies considerably. The home sewing machine, for example, was invented in 1750, but the American market still is not fully saturated. In the late 1960s, in spite of the many improvements in design and operating features, only about 60 percent of all U.S. households owned sewing machines. But black-and-white television approached market saturation just ten years after its commercial introduction; color TV sets, introduced in

1960, were in roughly 40 percent of American homes by 1970 and setmakers were competing more and more on a price basis. The computer industry provides still another example: it was nearly 60 years from first use of the punch cards on a large scale—namely, to take the U.S. census—to the early 1950s when a computer was introduced to use on this same census problem. Since then, three generations of computers have been developed and put to work.[1]

Most companies face the inevitable choice of product innovation and improvement or of a gradual fading from the market. Most wagon and buggy manufacturers saw their market gradually disappear as the automobile replaced the horse. Yet, Studebaker, a wagon manufacturer, recognized the need for change and successfully shifted to automobile manufacturing and, much later, finding itself no longer able to compete profitably in the automobile market, moved into other product fields.

REASONS FOR PRODUCT INNOVATION

Is product innovation on such a vast scale really necessary, or does it merely represent an attempt artificially to differentiate new products from old ones and from competitors' products? There is no doubt about it— many product changes do result from manufacturer's attempts to increase the rates of natural obsolescence to increase demand in saturated markets. However, other more important factors, many of them beyond the manufacturer's control, make emphasis on product innovation necessary.

Market Changes

Changes in the market make existing products and product lines inadequate for buyers' needs. At one time most competing products were pretty much alike—they were, in effect, commodities. Little differentiated any one maker's offering. Today, marketers consciously strive to reach specific market segments by offering products with distinctive features desired by these segments. Thus, the subdivision of markets into segments, each with unique sets of needs and preferences, decreases the probability that any one product can satisfy everybody. No one now has to satisfy himself by buying any item that is more like a commodity than a product. Increasingly, sophisticated modern buyers buy products tailored to their own individualized needs rather than to the total market's generalized needs.

[1] T. V. Learson, "The Management of Change," *Columbia Journal of World Business*, January-February 1968, p. 60.

Therefore, manufacturers emphasize product innovation to avoid having their products become commodities vying with other commodities in extremely competitive markets.

The speed with which markets change has accelerated with the expanding role fashion plays in American society. Development and growth of new communications media (such as television), their successes in reaching large audiences, and the great increases in the number of people travelling extensively, are only a few of the factors causing fashion news to spread rapidly. The word gets around faster, so fashions change oftener. In companies producing items subject to fashion influences, product innovation receives increasing attention.

The list of products subject to fashion influences expands continually. Among the more recent items to succumb to fashion's power are work clothes and shoes, lawn mowers, farm implements, pencil sharpeners, residential fencing, and trash cans. No manufacturer should assume that his product is totally invulnerable to fashion influences. All should regularly appraise the present or potential importance of product innovation (through fashion) to the market success of their product lines.

Technology Changes

Changes in technology not only have broadened markets for old products but have brought into existence entirely new markets, through the creation of entirely new products. The transistor, which is replacing the vacuum tube in many applications, is a case in point. It does nothing the vacuum tube did not already do, but because of its smaller size and weight, greater durability, and lower power consumption, it has brought about change in a variety of electronic products. Existing products, such as portable radios, received a big boost, and entirely new products, such as stereo-tape players for automobiles, became feasible. Industry, both in the U.S. and abroad, is investing vast and increasing sums of money in basic and applied technical research, so technological change should continue to cause product innovation and change.

Profitless Price Competition [2]

Price competition, existing or impending, forces many companies to emphasize product innovation. Buyers are prone to regard so-called

[2] For a stimulating discussion on this and related points, see: D. W. Karger and R. G. Murdick, "Product Design, Marketing, and Manufacturing Innovation," *California Management Review*, Winter 1966, pp. 33-42.

"mature" and "dying" products as commodities—each seller of such a product, not finding it effective to promote his product as "different" relies increasingly on the price appeal to sell it. Consequently, markets for mature and dying products are highly competitive. To escape profitless price competition, manufacturers search for product innovations (ones with features that differentiate them from mere commodities). Product innovations, if they succeed, are profitable and provide the innovating company with a way to soften the effects of price competition.

Both consumers and industrial buyers want and expect a continuous parade of new and improved products. Alert competitors recognize this and attempt to meet customers' expectations. Continuous innovation seems essential, if a company is to avoid having its product deteriorate into a commodity, subject to profitless price competition.

Diversification of Risk

Diversification of risk is another reason companies stress product innovation. The threat of obsolescense hangs over even the most stable products; the buggy was replaced by the automobile, and even the once stable fountain pen has been badly hurt by the ball point pen. The greater the variety of products produced by a firm, the smaller the relative impact of one's disappearance from the market. But to achieve this diversification of risk, a company must engage in continuous product innovation—always seeking new products to offset the losses occuring as older products become obsolete.

Other Reasons for Product Innovation

Several other reasons for product innovation exist. For instance, a company may develop new products to utilize the basic materials it is already making or to utilize waste or scrap from present production. It may add new products to even out sales fluctuations resulting from seasonal or cyclical factors, such as adding a line of water skis to balance out sales of snow skis. It may seek new products to counteract the highly erratic buying behavior of certain customers, such as government buyers. It may add new products to make more efficient use of marketing and production skills and/or to utilize marketing and production capabilities more fully. Note carefully, however, that these reasons, as well as those mentioned earlier, are all related in one way or another to management's desire to improve profitability. Indeed, product innovation is a major means by which a company can improve its profitability.

ORGANIZING FOR PRODUCT INNOVATION

Many new product ideas are rejected as probable failures early in the development stage, and at a relatively small cost. But a large number of new products actually reach the market before they prove unsuccessful. One study reported a 60 percent failure rate, even among "well-managed companies," with new products that had progressed all the way through test marketing.[3] One authority gives the odds at about 1 in 100 that a product concept will progress to commercialization, and at about 1 in 1000 that a product concept will become a commercial success.[4] Another estimates that only one in thirty-five new products of major companies succeed.[5] While no one seems to know for sure just how high the odds are against a new product's succeeding, everyone agrees that far fewer succeed than fail. Consequently, anything that can be done to improve the ratio of successes to failures should be done. Even among well-managed companies with fairly high new product success ratios, around half of the failures trace to organizational problems.[6]

How should a company organize for product innovation? The activities cut across departmental lines. They closely relate to, and overlap with, production, marketing, and research and development activities; they also involve matters that come within the provinces of the finance, legal, and other departments. The process of product innovation is pervasive, and there is no one "best" way for integrating it into the organization. The "best" arrangement for a particular company depends upon the company's size, its products, and its management's skills and capabilities. The most common organizational arrangements are discussed below.

Retention of Responsibility by Top Management

When certain product innovation activities, such as designing or styling, are crucial to a company's success, top management (particularly in small companies) often retains this responsibility. This is common, for instance, in the fashion textile industry. If top executives devote sufficient time and attention to personal supervision of new product development and design, coordination is achieved at a high organizational level. Friction at lower levels, usually between different departments, is avoided because

---

[3] *Management of New Products*, Booz, Allen and Hamilton, 1960, rev. 1963 and 1965.

[4] W. J. Talley, Jr., *The Profitable Product* (Englewood Cliffs, N.J.: Prentice-Hall, Inc., 1965), pp. 11-12.

[5] Reported in *Marketing Communications*, August 1969, p. 75.

[6] *Management of New Products*, Booz, Allen and Hamilton.

the coordinator carries the weight of superior authority. Frequently, however, the shortcoming is that top executives are so preoccupied with other important matters that they cannot devote sufficient attention to product innovation. Some companies overcome this problem through appointing a staff assistant of high rank, who concentrates on coordinating product innovation activities and issues directives in the president's name.

Assign Responsibility to a Line Executive

If company success depends more on marketing than production or more on production than marketing, a marketing or production executive may be assigned the "additional" responsibility for product innovation. This is rather common in small companies. Although product innovation activities are often recognized in the small company as being highly important, they may simply not represent sufficient work to justify an executive's full time. Moreover, presidents of small companies frequently have their time so taken up with other tasks that they are unable to provide the needed coordination. Under these conditions, no feasible alternative may exist to that of assigning responsibility for product innovation to a line executive.

The line executive who assumes responsibility for product innovation must overcome the natural tendency to view product problems chiefly from the standpoint of his own department's interests. Product innovation activities, by their very nature, are pervasive. The executive responsible for this area should define it in the interests of the whole company.

New Product Committee

Probably the new product committee is the most widely-used organizational form. A committee may be set up either to assume full responsibility for product innovation or to assist product management executives. Each department concerned with product innovation—research and development, production, marketing (including sales, advertising, and marketing research), and accounting and finance—as well as top management, should be represented on the committee. New product committees seem to work best when they serve as adjuncts to definite staff groups that have primary responsibility for the product mix.

Separate Staff Department

In a growing number of companies, staff departments coordinate and guide product innovation. Formal recognition of product innovation of this sort has been most widespread in rapidly growing industries, such as electronics and computer manufacturing.[7] Coordination and guidance of a high order are needed to correlate such product innovation activities as scientific research, process development, market development, pilot plant production, engineering, test marketing, and marketing research. Since this department's chief responsibility is that of coordinating other departments' activities, rather than of direct involvement in them, its staff is small. Even with the establishment of a separate staff department, the pervasive nature of product innovation causes most companies also to use a new product committee for coordinating purposes.

Product Managers

In marketing organizations with product management departments, individual product managers sometimes have the responsibility for carrying on, or coordinating, product innovation. Generally, though, a product manager's main responsibilities relate to products already on the market. He is concerned with all the factors affecting the success of the products under his supervision. He collaborates with advertising people in developing promotional campaigns; he works with the sales force to insure that it follows through on promotional efforts and moves sufficient supplies into middlemen's inventories; he moves to secure dealer cooperation; he keeps competitors under surveillance; and he is responsible for keeping his products competitive in terms of design, styling, and performance characteristics. Therefore, generally the product manager is more concerned with preserving the marketability of his present products than he is with developing new products. Recognizing this, some managements using the product manager scheme also have "new product managers," who are responsible for coordinating and guiding product innovation. The new product manager, then, fulfills a similar function to the separate staff department discussed earlier.

Product Consultants

Sometimes, outside consultants perform certain product innovation activities but, in such cases, it is still necessary to provide for internal coordination. Outside consultants, such as stylists and industrial designers, work with company executives who have product innovation responsibilities. There are at least five different conditions under which it is appropriate to use outside product consultants: (1) A company is too small to support a full-time product group; (2) Management wants to investigate an unfam-

---

[7] J. G. Crockett, "The Marketing-Oriented Technical Product Development Program," *Journal of Marketing*, July 1962, pp. 42-43.

iliar product area; (3) Detailed information is needed on possible new products, and usual sources cannot provide it; (4) Technical information is desired on competitors' products; and (5) Management desires an outsider's objective recommendations.

Product Brokers

A new type of middleman, the product broker, is being used increasingly. This broker, in return for a fee, specializes in finding a client company any product it wants and in selling off its unused products and technology. The product broker appears to fill a void that previously existed. One broker describes this void by saying "only 30 percent of the nation's useful technology and products are actually put to use. What one company can't use, another could turn into a bonanza." [8] Some large companies—for example, General Electric and National Cash Register—have departments performing similar functions. But little doubt exists that the product broker's services will be in increasing demand among companies desiring to add new products (which either cannot be developed internally or which can be secured for less outside) and among those with products or product ideas to sell.

DEVELOPING NEW PRODUCTS

Need for Product Objectives

A company advances toward its over-all objectives mainly through the acceptance of its products in the marketplace. Therefore, product objectives, derived directly from the company objectives, serve as guidelines for product innovation. They summarize the characteristics the products should have for the company actually to be "in the business it wants to be in." Product objectives, of course, apply to all products, both new and established.

Under the marketing concept, a company's product objectives are oriented toward the customers and their wants. They state explicitly that the company is engaged in servicing certain types of needs of specific types of customers. Thus, for example, one product objective may be "to develop, manufacture, and market products meeting the heating and cooling needs of industrial and commercial establishments of all sizes." With this

[8] "The Coming Revolution in New Product Development," *Sales Management*, August 15, 1969, p. 34.

objective, notice carefully, the company does not limit itself to any specific products; rather it limits its market to given types of customers with particular types of needs. As the market or its needs change, the company adjusts its products accordingly. Actually, of course, most companies are somewhat constrained in their choice of products by their capabilities in such areas as research and development, manufacturing, and marketing. Unused capabilities may lead to the development of products which may or may not be compatible with existing markets.

Among other product objectives a company should have is one stating the company philosophy with regard to the desired degree of product leadership. It may be necessary—where the field covered is wide—for management to face the fact that in order to lead innovatively in one product line, it must be satisfied with "following quickly" in another. This situation occurs, for example, in the chemical industry, where individual companies have extremely broad product lines but concentrate their innovative efforts on a few specific chemicals.

Similarly, other product objectives should derive from each major company objective whose attainment depends upon the product line in any way whatever. Furthermore, all product objectives must be consistent with other components of marketing strategy, such as company objectives with respect to marketing channels and distribution, promotion, and price. When either company objectives or marketing strategy change, product objectives should be reappraised for their continued appropriateness and, if necessary, revised.

Need for Product Policies

Product policies are the general rules that management sets up to guide itself in making product decisions. They should derive directly from product objectives and be wholly consistent with them. For example, if a product objective states that "this company desires to manufacture and market products requiring only a minimum of service after their purchase by consumers," then a product policy is needed to spell out the details as to just how this objective will be achieved.

Product policies may be stated in the form of a series of either short definitions or of questions arranged as a check list. One large industrial goods manufacturer, for example, defined company policy, concerning the desired effect proposed new products should have on the firm's present products, as follows:

> Each . . . should improve the company's over-all sales and profit position. It should preferably help to promote the sale of the company's

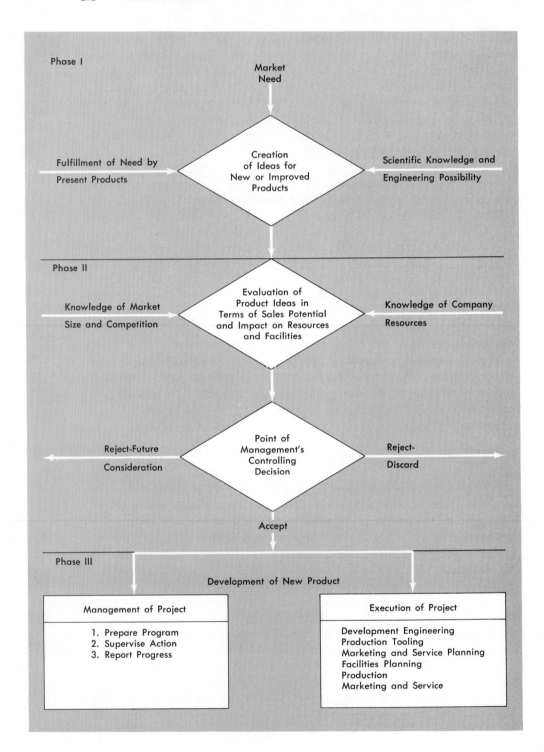

Phase I

Market
Need

Fulfillment of Need by
Present Products

Creation
of Ideas for
New or Improved
Products

Scientific Knowledge and
Engineering Possibility

Phase II

Knowledge of Market
Size and Competition

Evaluation of
Product Ideas in
Terms of Sales Potential
and Impact on Resources
and Facilities

Knowledge of Company
Resources

Reject-Future
Consideration

Point of
Management's
Controlling
Decision

Reject-
Discard

Accept

Phase III

Development of New Product

Management of Project

1. Prepare Program
2. Supervise Action
3. Report Progress

Execution of Project

Development Engineering
Production Tooling
Marketing and Service Planning
Facilities Planning
Production
Marketing and Service

other products. If, however, it would hinder the sale of other company products, it should have a greater potential long-range profit than the products in conflict with it.[9]

The alternative method is illustrated in the check list developed by a consumer goods manufacturer, whose main product objective is "to serve the market for non-durable household goods bought by large numbers of families with a fairly high frequency of purchase." Among other items, this product policy check list contains the following questions:

1. *Customer advantage:* Does the proposed product offer the customer an advantage?
   a. Is it superior to competition in a major property?
   b. Is it equal to competitive products in use properties?
   c. Can it be sold profitably at a lower price?
2. *Mass market:* Is there a mass market for the product?

. . . .

6. *Stability:* Will the product be free of undue breakage or deterioration from normal handling in distribution?

. . . .

8. *Permissibility:* Will the product conform to applicable government regulations? [10]

The New Product Planning Process

Exhibit 9–1 shows the product planning flow chart of a large industrial goods manufacturer. This company uses a product planning committee made up of top management personnel and specialists from sales and marketing, research and development, manufacturing, and finance. This group considers and plans new and improved products in three phases:

Phase One involves the creation of ideas for new or improved products. The extent and importance of the market need is determined and an appraisal is made of the extent to which present products fulfill

[9] C. H. Kline, "The Strategy of Product Policy," *Harvard Business Review,* July-August 1955, pp. 91-100.
   [10] *Ibid.*

EXHIBIT 9—1

Product Planning Flow Chart
Adapted from: C. W. Perelle, "Factors in Establishing a Sound Product Portfolio," in K. H. Tietjen, ed., *Organizing the Product-Planing Function,* American Management Association Research Study No. 59 (New York: American Management Association, 1963), p. 14.

that need. This phase also involves evaluating the company's capabilities with respect to scientific knowledge and engineering skills in terms of possible new products or product improvements. Therefore, both external and internal sources are tapped in an effort to create product ideas.

Phase Two focuses on evaluation of product ideas developed in Phase One. This boils down to a more thorough investigation of the competitive market situation and company resources, with respect to each idea. Market research is important during this phase since market potentials and competitive marketing methods can reveal, among other things, the size and type of marketing organization required. Analysis of company resources indicates the adequacy of plant capacity, product service facilities, marketing channels, engineering abilities, and other human resources. This company uses profitability as the basic criterion for selection among alternate product candidates.

After evaluation, each product idea together with supporting analysis is forwarded to top management. Top management may "reject and discard the idea," "reject it now but keep it for later consideration," or "accept it." If management accepts the idea, it makes decisions concerning implementation of the new product development project. Then, product planning moves into Phase Three.

Phase Three covers actual development of the new product. A program is put together for management and execution of the development project. Among other aspects, this includes an over-all plan for the product's eventual marketing.

Flow charts of this sort can be invaluable for systematizing the product planning process. They can help assure that all relevant factors, both external and internal to the company, are taken into account. And they make it easier for all concerned to visualize "the big picture" and to see how they fit into it.

Sources of New Product Ideas

Where do new product ideas come from? As indicated earlier, a company's own research and development work may produce some ideas, taking its direction from customer requirements or needs, uncovered through marketing and other research. Some companies, such as Eastman Kodak and du Pont, also carry on basic research and come up with products that were not specifically sought. Others get ideas from brain-storming sessions of management and other personnel and from suggestions of salesmen, production people, engineers, and others. Still other ideas come from outside sources, both solicited and unsolicited.

Few generalizations are valid concerning the relative merits of tapping external versus internal sources of new product ideas. Each idea, regardless of its source, should be evaluated on its own merits, considering both market needs and opportunities and the company's capabilities. However, it can be said that ideas originating outside the company often are unique, since they represent thinking undulled by close association with established products. For example, a few years ago a customer suggested that a large manufacturer of refrigeration equipment equip its liquid chilling units with several small compressors instead of the usual one large compressor. As this idea would represent a fundamental departure from the existing units, the manufacturer reluctantly investigated the suggestion. Reluctance, however, soon turned into enthusiasm, since it was found that: multiple-compressor chillers could be made from existing components; they would cost less and be more efficient, more economical to operate, and easier to service. Therefore, liquid chilling units with up to four small compressors were developed and put on the market. Some sales resistance was encountered in selling these "radical" units at first but, after a few "bugs" were ironed out, the manufacturer's sales increased and it captured 60 percent of the market.

Evaluation of New Product Ideas

Numerous considerations enter into the evaluation of a new product idea. Probably the first is whether the proposed new product has a potentially profitable market; if it has, other factors need considering. If the existing marketing organization can sell the new product, and not too large an investment in new productive facilities is required, then it is an even more promising addition. Otherwise, its prospect of success must be very high to justify large investments in new marketing channels or production facilities. Another factor important to a new product's success is the strength of its appeal to market needs. Still another is the exent to which the new product lies within the experience of company management: if it lies too far outside, both the probable drain on executive time and the risk of failure may be too high.

Also important is the degree of "newness" of the new product. Buyers easily understand and readily accept some elements of newness, and these help in insuring eventual marketing success. Included in this category are product features that make familiar patterns of life easier, cheaper, and otherwise more pleasant. Other product features require new patterns of life, new habits, assimilation of new ideas or viewpoints, acquisition of new tastes, and acceptance of things difficult to believe. When products incorporate such totally new concepts, maximum marketing effort is required to overcome widespread buyers' reluctance.[11]

[11] C. R. Wasson, "What is 'New' about a New Product?" *Journal of Marketing*, July 1960, p. 56.

Sometimes, a company adds a new product even though its potential for direct contribution to profit appears small or even non-existent. Consider two products closely associated in use, such as a camera and the film. Often the manufacturer can increase the total profits by selling more cameras (at a loss) in order to sell more film (at a profit). In market situations where numerous buyers favor complete "sets" of related products, such as in equipping a new house's kitchen, manufacturers may find it profitable to fill in their product lines, even though some items only break even or incur losses: expanded sales of profitable items more than offset losses on other items.

In spite of such "exceptional circumstances," however, management should compare each proposed new product's likely addition to marginal revenue against its associated additions to cost. If probable marginal revenue exceeds marginal costs, management should pursue the idea further. But if costs exceed expected revenue, the idea should be rejected unless, of course, an "exceptional" circumstance exists. In estimating marginal revenues and costs, management should use all available information, filling in missing needed data through marketing research. For example, marketing research may be required to determine, for a product class, relative sensitivity of buyer response to different types of innovation, ranging from major functional change to minor design change.[12]

It is also important to appraise company capabilities relative to the expected bases of competition. Thus, a decision to introduce a new brand of a consumer convenience good, such as soap, hinges importantly on management's assessment of its opportunity to achieve significant product differentiation, plus its access to sufficient financial resources to carry on needed promotion and obtain the required distribution intensity. By contrast, a decision to introduce a new brand of an industrial product, such as transistors, after the initial phase of market expansion, depends chiefly on the company's ability to compete profitably price-wise. The extent to which price competition develops depends not only on competitors' probable reactions but also on buyers' repurchase rates and the significance they attach to product differentiation. The more frequent the buyer repurchase rate and the less important product differentiation is to buyers, the more likely price is to become the main basis of competition.

Assessing Commercial Potential

Several approaches have been developed and are being used for determining the likely commercial success (usually meaning "profitability") of proposed new products. One researcher surveyed 85 large firms and obtained the results in Table 9.1.

[12] L. L. Howell, "Planned Innovation as a Marketing Tool," *California Management Review*, Summer 1962, p. 69.

TABLE 9–1

**Techniques Used in Evaluating Commercial Potential
by 85 Large American Manufacturers**

Technique	No. of Firms Using	% of Total
Return on Investment	40	47.0%
Payback	20	23.5%
Rating Scales	6	7.0%
Other	12	15.0%
Confidential	7	8.5%
Total	85	100.0%

Source: Adapted from: L. J. Konopa, *New Products: Assessing Commercial Potential* (New York: American Management Association, 1966). Management Bulletin No. 88, pp. 8-9.

The *return on investment* technique, which has numerous variants, basically is an attempt to forcast all revenues and expenditures over the projected sales life of the product, and then determine the rate of return on investment (by calculating the ratio of net cash inflow to the total investment tied up in the project). Practice varies as to whether to "discount" anticipated cash inflows to their present values. Companies applying the return on investment technique generally set a "target rate of return" to use as a standard of comparison: Proposed new products that are highly likely to meet or exceed the target rate are added; those that do not are dropped from further consideration.

The *payback* technique focuses on how long it takes for a new product to pay back the original investment outlay from the added cash flow it generates. Estimated expenses (manufacturing, sales, and so on) are deducted, in other words, from anticipated sales revenues to obtain an estimate of annual earnings before depreciation; then, the difference is divided by the investment outlay. The shorter the paycheck period, the more attractive the new product is. How long can a payoff period be and still be satisfactory? Professor Konopa, who conducted the survey in Table 9.1, found that most companies use either a three- or five-year period as the cut-off point.[13]

The *rating scale* technique quantifies the analysis through an evaluation matrix. Table 9.2 shows such a rating scale designed to measure probability of success in a two-step analysis. The first step involves ranking and weighing the various spheres of company performance. These are areas in which successful performance is a function of the extent and nature of company capabilities. The weights assigned to each sphere are shown in column "A." The second step requires appraisals of the degree to which a proposed new product is compatible with each sphere; this is accomplished

[13] L. J. Konopa, *New Products: Assessing Commercial Potential* (New York: American Management Association, 1966), Management Bulletin No. 88, p. 12.

by assigning to each a value from 0 to 1.0 as shown in column "B." The weights in column "A" are then multiplied by the values assigned in column

TABLE 9–2
Evaluation Matrix—Product Fit

	A	B	C
	Relative Weight	Product Compatibility Values	A X B
Sphere of Performance		0 .1 .2 .3 .4 .5 .6 .7 .8 .9 1.0	
Company personality and goodwill	.20	x (.6)	.120
Marketing	.20	x (.9)	.180
Research and development	.20	x (.7)	.140
Personnel	.15	x (.6)	.090
Finance	.10	x (.9)	.090
Production	.05	x (.8)	.040
Location and facilities	.05	x (.3)	.015
Purchasing and supply	.05	x (.9)	.045
Total	1.00		.720 [a]

[a] Rating scale: 0-.40, poor; .41-.75, fair; .76-1.0, good. Present minimum acceptance rate: .70.
Source: Barry M. Richman, "A Rating Scale for Product Innovation," *Business Horizons*, Vol. 5, No. 2 (Summer 1962), p. 43.

"B," and the results are inserted in column "C" and totaled. A proposed new product fitting company needs and objectives perfectly receives the maximum score of 1.0. The product evaluated in the example received a score of only .720—in the "fair" range. The rating scale technique provides an objective basis for assessing commercial potential; when a cutting, or minimum-aceptance, score is decided upon, management has a basis for automatically rejecting the more unpromising product ideas. Of even greater importance, it has a system to use in selecting the most promising product ideas.[14]

TIMING NEW PRODUCT INTRODUCTION

Once the decision has been made to add a new product, timing becomes highly important. Ideally, a manufacturer would take the time to perfect both his new product and his marketing plans before introducing it to the market. Careful and thorough market analysis would allow him to fit the

[14] For a description of a more complex rating scale procedure see: J. T. O'Meara, Jr., "Selecting Profitable Products," *Harvard Business Review*, January-February, 1961, pp. 83-89.

product perfectly to buyers' needs and to develop a complete marketing program with the best price, using the most effective marketing channels and the most effective promotional methods and media.

But a manufacturer simply may not have the time for such complete planning. The company whose product is the first of its kind on the market may gain certain advantages, and to overcome such an initial edge a competitor may have to undertake a very powerful (and expensive) marketing program when he finally launches his version of the new product. Because of this penalty associated with not being first, there is a strong temptation to enter the market too quickly—before the important "bugs" are ironed out of the product and a cohesive marketing program is put together. The "trick" in timing new product introductions is to enter the market early enough but not too early.[15]

General Electric's introduction of the first black-and-white portable television sets in 1957 provides a good example of "right timing." For several years the trend in the design and sale of home television receivers had been in the direction of ever-increasing picture screen size. From 10-inch screens, the industry moved in rapid succession to 12-, 14-, 16-, 17-, 21-inch and was well into 27-inch screens. After the 21-inch screen's introduction, the trend slowed down noticeably and many executives predicted the industry would stabilize at 17-inch for the smaller lower-priced sets and 21-inch for the deluxe offerings. Sales of 27-inch sizes, never large in number, tapered off sharply, and at this precise time, General Electric introduced a fresh, new concept in TV set design: a portable set, using a 14-inch picture size. Success was almost instantaneous. Competition was caught off balance, and General Electric took the lead in the field, improving its market position spectacularly. Had this product introduction been attempted twelve months earlier, its success would have been most unlikely.

There are many examples of products being introduced to the market too early. One of the best-known is the *Chrysler Airflow* automobile which was brought to the market in the early 1930s. It was a well-styled, well-proportioned car incorporating much that seemed desirable in the way of "streamlining," but it did not receive consumer acceptance. It did not "take." It is clear, in retrospect, that the styling was ahead of its time by from eight to ten years. This timing error resulted in not only a financial disappointment but a decline in the company's market position.

A more recent example is General Foods' introduction of its *Gourmet Foods* in the summer of 1957. The company was attempting to capitalize on a developing trend among consumers toward becoming more interested in gourmet cooking and gourmet dining. General Foods was the

---

[15] Seven factors affecting the timing of new product introductions are analyzed in: R. E. Weigand, "How Extensive the Planning and Development Program," *Journal of Marketing*, July 1962, pp. 55-57.

first to introduce such a line, but it was too early. The trend was just beginning to develop, and the company brought out products that were then much too exotic (among them Swedish lingonberries). It dropped the *Gourmet Foods* line two and a half years later.[16]

It is evident, then, that selecting the right time for market introduction is not easy. The product has to be "right" for the market, and the market has to be "right" for the product. Chrysler's product was right, but the market was not; General Foods neither had a right product nor a right market. In planning to introduce a new product, management must: (1) forecast the future time at which the market will be ready to accept the product, and (2) plan and complete its product development activities so that the product will be ready for marketing at that future time. Of these two tasks, forecasting the time of probable market acceptance is by far the more difficult. Such forecasts require the detection and "tracking" of developing trends in buyer behavior, attitudes, preferences, and the like.

With respect to the timely performance of product development activities, however, numerous companies are making noteworthy improvements. Many are employing such techniques as PERT (Program Evaluation and Review Technique) to improve their effectiveness in planning and controlling programs involving new product development. PERT was first used in 1958 in connection with development of the Polaris Missile and, it is claimed, advanced launching of the missile two years ahead of schedule. The use of PERT can help greatly in overcoming problems arising in coordinating, timing, and scheduling the many activities involved in developing new products and getting them ready for market introduction.[17]

THE PRODUCT LIFE CYCLE

All products, like people, have a certain length of life, during which they pass through certain stages. From the time a product idea is conceived, during its development, and up to the time it is introduced to the market, a product is in various prenatal stages (i.e., it is going through the various phases of product development). Its life begins with its market introduction. Then it goes through a period during which its market grows rapidly. Eventually, it reaches market maturity after which its market declines and finally its life ends.

[16] "The Great Gourmet Boom," *Forbes*, April 1, 1969, p. 24.
[17] Y. Wong, "Critical Path Analysis for New Product Planning," *Journal of Marketing*, October 1964, pp. 53-59.

Product Life Cycle for an Industry

Exhibit 9.2 is a visualization of a product life cycle for an industry (made up of firms marketing directly competing products). Three curves are shown: (1) total market sales (this is the "industry product life cycle"), (2) total market profit (notice how this declines while sales are still rising), and (3) the relative number of competing firms (notice that this continues to go up for a while after profits have turned down).

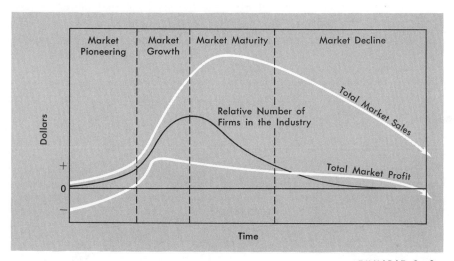

EXHIBIT 9-2

The Industry Product Life Cycle

The exact path traced by the product life cycle varies from case to case. In some, like the "hula hoop," the product proves a fad and has a life cycle as short as a month or so. At the other extreme are very long-lived products, such as plumbing fixtures, with life cycles spanning decades. In between is the vast majority of products, with life cycles ranging from a few months (e.g., fashion apparel) to several years (e.g., washing machines and home freezers). Regardless of the product, all are at some stage in their life cycles at any particular moment in time.

Product Life Cycles—Individual Companies

Life cycle curves also exist for the individual products of each company. Exhibit 9.3 shows a life cycle curve for a product's sales by the company doing the innovating. During the "market pioneering" stage of the industry product life cycle, one company—the innovator—may be the whole industry. But during the "market growth" stage, the innovator shares the market with many competitors. Hence, while Exhibit 9.2 is an industry curve, its market pioneering stage represents the sales of only one or a few companies. Only coincidentally does the shape of an individual company's product life cycle resemble that of the entire industry, because after the market pioneering stage the industry cycle is a composite of several companies' experiences. Furthermore, managerial action can cause a particular company's product life cycle to vary from that of the "typical" company in the industry. For instance, management may drop a product at any time, thus terminating its life cycle insofar as that company is concerned.[18]

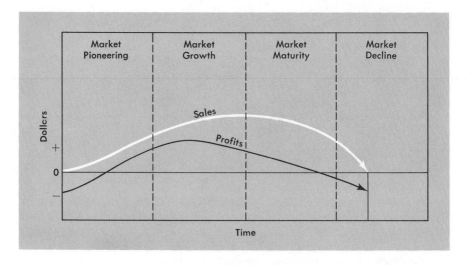

EXHIBIT 9—3

Product Life Cycle—Innovating Company

Stages of Product Life Cycles—Marketing Significance

Management should know the life cycle stage its product is in at any particular time. Changes in the competitive situation occur from one stage to the next. Consequently, marketing strategies and actions require adjustment.

[18] For a stimulating discussion of company and industry product life cycles, see: T. Levitt, "Exploit the Product Life Cycle," *Harvard Business Review*, November-December 1965, pp. 81-94.

MARKET PIONEERING   During this stage, the main problem is to stimulate primary demand—i.e., demand for the product category. There being virtually no competition, the innovating company sets out to inform the target market segment and intervening middlemen of the product's existence. Generally, this is done through aggressive promotion (personal selling, advertising, etc.). Limited distribution is obtained and sales rise very slowly, since they generally are first restricted to the innovator group of buyers, and this "core" market of early buyers usually consists of higher-income people. In later stages of the life cycle, demand "filters down to lower-income groups.[19]

Technical imperfections in the product frequently appear during the pioneering stage. Often they trace to insufficient prior testing of the product, perhaps because it was rushed to market to get the "jump" on competitors. It is advantageous to detect and eliminate product faults early, thus making it possible to "freeze" the product design and prepare for large-scale production and marketing.

The market pioneering stage, then, is a period of heavy promotion, the securing of initial distribution, and the ironing out of product difficulties. Marketing channels must be kept stocked with the product insofar as possible. But if the product is destined for success, the innovator generally finds that the demand exceeds what he can bring to market.

MARKET GROWTH   The main problems for the innovating firm during this stage are to produce the product in sufficient volume and to market the output with minimum delay. Thus, manufacturing and distribution efficiency become important keys to marketing success. Even with the use of mass production techniques and sophisticated physical distribution systems, demand generally continues to outpace the available supply.

Competition increases rapidly. Almost overnight the number of competitors explodes, when their managements realize that the product category is destined for success. However, each competitor must solve not only the problems inherent in manufacturing a "similar or better" product but such basic marketing problems as selecting marketing channels, obtaining distribution, and getting promotion underway. Thus, competitors still are at a disadvantage, if the innovating firm has solved its production and distribution problems earlier.

Advertising and personal selling continue to be important, but their nature changes. In the early phases of market growth, pioneering advertising is still effective, as untapped market segments are informed of

---

[19] T. A. Staudt and D. A. Taylor, *A Managerial Introduction to Marketing* (Englewood Cliffs, N. J.: Prentice-Hall, Inc., 1965), p. 145.

the product's existence. But as competitive tempo rises, more and more potential buyers know about the product, and competing firms switch to selective demand advertising, emphasizing their own brands' advantages. Similarly, personal selling in the early phases of this stage is directed mainly to getting new outlets and keeping them stocked; later, emphasis shifts to "selling against the competition." Some competitors begin to lose ground, often because they interrupt operations to make minor adjustments in the product. Competition ultimately becomes so severe that if buyers cannot easily locate particular brands, it is easy to persuade them to buy others.

MARKET MATURITY   During this stage, competition among brands grows even more intense, although the field of competitors declines until only the most efficient remain. Stiffening competition forces profits lower, as prices come down and marketing expenditures rise. Sales continue to increase but at a decreasing rate, eventually leveling off as the market becomes saturated. The mass market is now buying the product, and opportunities for increasing sales further are limited, except as a result either of population increases or changes in customers' buying habits and consumption behavior.

Marketing techniques become highly important. Competitors heavily promote their brands, emphasizing the subtle differences. Supply exceeds demand for the first time, making demand stimulation essential—even for the basic product—through "reminder" advertising and salesmen's efforts. Automobiles, as a product category, illustrate what happens to marketing during this stage—auto producers not only couple annual model changeovers with minor improvements but use subtle promotional appeals to build new markets for "second cars" and even for "third cars."

Because of the squeeze put on profits and the growing similarity of competing brands, dealer support levels become increasingly critical. Not many dealers will stock all available brands. Most develop preferences for those with the greatest consumer acceptance. Parallel patterns develop among ultimate consumers, as they become increasingly reluctant to spend time searching for particular brands and more hesitant to take unknown brands. Thus, well-known companies fare considerably better than less fortunate competitors.

During later phases of the market maturity stage, replacement sales dominate the market. Only a shrinking number of "first buyers" enter the market but some do as, for example, young people buying their first new automobiles. For the most part, however, the replacement buyer becomes the main target of marketing effort. Owners of durables, such as automobiles and appliances, are bombarded with pleas to trade-in their present possessions for "new and improved" models. Present users of nondurables, such as cosmetics, are reminded constantly to keep on buying their favorite brands.

Throughout the market maturity stage, industry sales remain relatively stable, and only those companies with extremely effective marketing programs succeed in enlarging their market shares. Sales increases that occur are gradual, as the market comes closer to saturation. With the relative stability of industry sales, the competitive structure solidifies. The surviving companies, for the most part, have firm footholds, but they must promote their brands continuously and heavily to protect their positions.

MARKET DECLINE   This stage is characterized by either the product's gradual displacement by some new innovation or by an evolving change in consumer buying behavior. Color television sets, for instance, are displacing the older, black-and-white sets; paper napkins won buyer approval partly because they served as substitutes for linen napkins and partly because new living patterns made their use more convenient and socially acceptable. Every product in the market decline stage is confronted with a situation in which buyers do not buy as much or as often as before. New and superior products are continually being introduced to the market, and many are certain to meet shifting consumers' needs and preferences more closely than existing items.

During market decline, industry sales drop off and the number of competitors shrinks. Production overcapacity (which first appeared in the market maturity stage) puts increasing pressures on the surviving firms to scramble for the available business—price tends to become the main competitive weapon. Cost control is increasingly important, and some competitors manage to use it effectively in keeping the product profitable.

Advertising and other promotional expenditures are drastically reduced, as price is used more and more to obtain business. Under these conditions, most managements shift their attention to other products, gradually phasing out the declining product as its future grows increasingly bleak. Some, however, stay with the dying product a little longer and try to revive its market, usually with disappointing results. A few, determined to "go down fighting," stick it out to the bitter end.

Managing the Product Life Cycle

The great value of the product life cycle concept is that management, knowing what typically happens at different stages in a product's life, should be able to improve its forward planning. Knowing, for instance, that sales and profitability curves characteristically follow certain patterns, management can, to a surprising extent, plot its moves in ways that result in changing the shape of the life cycle curve—e.g., well-timed and effective implementation of specific marketing actions may succeed in extending, or stretching out, a product's life, especially if they are taken soon enough in the market maturity stage. Theodore Levitt cites examples of how Du Pont's *Nylon*, General Foods' *Jello*, and 3M's *Scotch Tape* were all beneficiaries of marketing life-stretching strategies. These strategies were directed towards: (1) promoting more frequent product usage among current users, (2) developing more varied usage of the product among current users, (3) cultivating new users, and (4) finding new uses.[20]

Planning in advance what steps should be taken to build sales and obtain the best profits during different product life cycle stages is important. Companies that have these plans can take aggressive actions at the critical times, rather than reacting defensively to changing market and competitive conditions. Levitt sums up this outstanding benefit in these words:

> Although departures from such a plan will surely have to be made to accommodate unexpected events and revised judgments, the plan puts the company in a better position to *make* things happen rather than constantly having to react to things that are happening.[21]

WHY NEW PRODUCTS FAIL: SOME CONCLUSIONS

When a new product does not return adequate profits, the failure traces to management's neglect or clumsy handling of some aspect(s) of product innovation and/or management of the product life cycle. The reasons for product failure, in brief, come under six general headings. These six categories together with examples of specific reasons for product failures are outlined below:

1. *Product Problems:* Neglect of market needs or ignorance of market preferences; defects in product function, poor technical design or external appearance; poor packaging or inappropriate sizes; undependable performance or too high a variation in quality.

2. *Distribution and Channel Problems:* Inappropriate channels or outlets; necessary middleman cooperation not obtained; spotty distribution; poor system of physical distribution.

3. *Promotional Problems:* Inadequate or ineffective promotion; advertising directed toward wrong market segments; use of wrong appeals; failure to coordinate adequately with distribution system; sales force inadequacies in training, motivation, or supervision.

4. *Pricing Problems:* Bad forecast of price buyers would pay; price

[20] Levitt, Exploit Product Life Cycles, p. 89.
[21] *Ibid.*, p. 93.

out of line with product quality; poor cost estimates caused "asking price" to be too high; inadequate margins for the middlemen.

5. *Timing Problems:* Product introduced too soon or too late.

6. *Competitive Problems:* Competitors took the critical moves first with respect to products, distribution, promotion, and price; thrown off balance, the company had to react defensively rather than pursuing aggressive strategies.

The number and variety of the reasons for product failure suggest that achieving marketing success with a new product requires high-order skills not only in product innovation but in formulating and implementing marketing strategy. Throughout the product innovation process, management needs to keep one eye on the product being developed and the other on the target market. An appropriate organization is required to guide and coordinate the product innovation process, each aspect of which must be performed thoroughly and effectively. Not only is good timing essential, but components of marketing strategy (product, distribution and marketing channels, promotion, and price) must be combined in appropriate proportions at each stage of the product life cycle. Skill in implementing the marketing plan is required and more effectively applied when management anticipates changing market and competitive conditions and prepares the moves it plans to make. Reducing the number of products that become marketing failures is largely a matter of improving management's effectiveness in planning and implementing marketing programs.

QUESTIONS AND PROBLEMS

1. How do you account for the fact that the rate of product change (i.e., the speed of product innovation) varies so much from industry to industry? Why has it taken longer to approach market saturation with sewing machines than with television sets?

2. What is the difference between a commodity and a product? Give some examples of products that may be in danger of becoming commodities.

3. Explain how fashion accelerates the speed with which markets change.

4. Give some examples of changes in technology which: (1) broadened the market for an old product; (2) brought into existence an entirely new market.

5. To what extent does product innovation provide an escape from price competition?

6. Under what conditions should a small company's top management retain responsibility for product innovation? Assign this responsibility to a line executive?

7. Why is the separate staff department with product innovation responsibilities generally used in conjunction with a new product committee?

8. Contrast and compare product brokers and product consultants.

9. What is the purpose of a product objective? Of a product policy? How do they differ?

10. Refer to Chapter 3 on the marketing organization. Visualize a particular company serving a specific market and show how each company objective (that has marketing significance) could be the source of one or more product objectives.

11. Suppose, as a marketing consultant, you were asked by a plastics fabricator to suggest and evaluate possible sources of new product ideas. At present this fabricator confines his operations to producing special packages for grocery and drug manufacturers, parts (such as handles) for makers of small appliances, and small components for computer makers. However, the fabricator intends to diversify into consumer markets. Prepare a list of possible sources of new product ideas for the fabricator and rate them, noting reasons for each evaluation.

12. Is it possible for a new product to be too new? Would this hold for all market segments? Support your position fully.

13. Under what conditions might a company add a new product even though its potential direct contribution to profit is small or even non-existent?

14. How can a company tell what bases of competition to expect for a new product?

15. Explain the differences between the following methods of assessing commercial potential: return on investment, payback, rating scale.

16. Analyze the manufacturer's dilemma in deciding the timing of a new product's market introduction.

17. Give some examples of products you regard as being in the market pioneering stage of their life cycles.

18. In what respects does an industry product life cycle differ from the life cycles for the individual products of competitors in the industry?

19. Name some products that are in the market decline stage. Do you believe the decline is irreversible? If you believe the decline is only temporary, what action would you recommend for rejuvenation?

20. Appraise the product life cycle concept relative to its use in forward planning.

10

FORMULATING PRODUCT-MARKET STRATEGY:
No Product Change

Marketing, as defined early in this book, involves "the matching of products with markets and the effecting of ownership transfers." Numerous problems are encountered in matching products with markets to assure ownership transfers. Highly significant interacting relationships exist between choices of products and their markets: Every successful product is aimed at some market, and its degree of success depends directly on the closeness of its "fit" with that market. Most companies are in business because their owners and managers hope to make profits. They accomplish this through utilizing marketing's skill in matching products with markets and in effecting ownership transfers. Newly-organized firms generally seek increasing profits through growth in sales volume. As a company grows—or as its size tends to stabilize—its management devotes increasing attention to the search for greater profits, not only through further sales volume growth but through improving marketing effectiveness and reducing costs. Companies use different product-market strategies to improve their profitability.

Exhibit 10.1 shows different combinations of product-market strategies that a company might use to improve its profitability. Notice that

229

each product strategy is associated with some market strategy; neither type of strategy can be set without having important implications for the other. Dis-

Market Strategy \ Product Strategy	No Product Change	Product Change	New Product
No Market Change	Design Simplification .... Greater Integration — Marketing, Production, etc. — or "Reverse Integration"	Product Line Simplification and Product Discontinuance .... New Models .... Planned Obsolescence	Replacement of Old Product
Improved Market	Remerchandising (E.G., Branding Change, Change in Guarantee, Change in Service Policy, Packaging Change, etc.)	Product Customization .... Product Systems	Product-Line Extension Diversification (Related Fields)
New Market	New Uses .... New Users	Market Extension (E.G., Trading-Up or Trading-Down)	Product-Mix Diversification (Unrelated Fields)

EXHIBIT 10–1

Grid Showing Different Possible Combinations of Product-Market Strategies Designed to Improve Profitability

cussion in this chapter concentrates on the "no product change" strategy and its interactions with the three types of market strategy—"no market change," "improved market," and "new market." The next chapter focuses mainly on the "product change" strategy relative to market strategy, but it also covers "new product" strategy (the main topic of Chapter 9) relative to the different market strategies. In both chapters, you will find it helpful to refer frequently to Exhibit 10.1. Main headings in both are "keyed" to the nine different product-market strategy combinations.

NO PRODUCT CHANGE—NO MARKET CHANGE

This is the least complex product-market strategy. There are two main versions: (1) simplifying the product's design, and (2) altering the amount of integration in the product's manufacturing and/or marketing. Both seek to improve profitability mainly through cost reduction, and both involve selling essentially the same product to the same market.

Product Design Simplification

Simplifying a product's design may lower its manufacturing costs, thus contributing to greater profits. But since simplified design frequently is improved design, it also may make the product easier to sell. Simplified designs, in other words, often make product maintenance easier or improve performance. One appliance manufacturer, for example, simplified the design of small electrical appliances (coffee makers, toasters, and the like) by incorporating "modular" construction: If something "goes wrong" with the product, the owner simply removes the offending part (i.e., the "module") and replaces it at the nearest dealer. Thus, this manufaturer improved the salability of his product line through reducing (or perhaps, even eliminating) the consumer's need for service.

DECIDING ON PRODUCT FEATURES   A design simplification strategy requires analysis of the product's features, among the most important of which is product size. For many products—such as brooms, towels, and sticks of gum—unit size has been firmly established by custom, but even here consideration often may profitably be given to changes in size.

Several factors enter into the determination of product size. Most important is consumer needs. Thus, when aspirin was first put on the market, tablet size was necessarily based on consideration of normal dosages, minimum dosages, and a size small enough to achieve these dosages with multiples of a single tablet. Subsequently, when competitive firms entered the market, tablet size had in effect become standardized, so no attempt was made to change it. The determination of consumer needs with respect to product size requires the evaluation and weighting of a number of variables. Each of the variables which help to create market segmentation may affect size requirements. For example, when baby aspirin was introduced (to reach that age segment of the market), it was deemed advisable to offer a smaller size of tablet. Even with a product such as aspirin, which appeals equally to many market segments, the task of determining product size provides different answers under different conditions, as illustrated by French aspirin. French manufacturers, approaching the problem of tablet size independently, developed aspirin tablets considerably larger than American manufacturers. Yet, in this instance, consumer needs vary little if at all between the French and American markets.

Size range and variation are affected by inventory costs and stock-turn, both for middlemen and for the manufacturer. This is especially evident with products such as clothing, where the range of sizes is large. Although consumers' needs may dictate a very large range of sizes, the costs of maintaining inventories of the more extreme sizes and the low stockturn on such sizes may make it advisable to restrict the offering of sizes to the middle range.

Industry-wide standardization also affects company policy with respect to size. In industries where standardized product specifications have been established, most firms find it to their advantage to conform to these standards because of the favorable effects on consumers and middlemen.[1] The consumer's buying job and the middleman's buying and selling job are both greatly simplified if they know, for example, that all men's socks in size 10 are exactly the same size and need not be measured or tried on. Against these favorable effects must be weighed the possible disadvantages of reduced product differentiation and increased substitutability of competitive products. (Analysis of these same factors affects management's decision to encourage or discourage establishment of uniform standards in industries where they are not yet used.)

Other product features, such as basic weights and measures, performance standards, and chemical or technical properties, are determined in essentially the same manner as size. Each decision should result from an evaluation of consumer needs, the effect on middlemen, comparative distribution costs, and industry practice.

IMPORTANCE OF PRODUCT DESIGN TO CONSUMER   In appraising the opportunity for product design simplification, the manufacturer should pay special attention to the relative importance consumers attach to different product features. It is common for companies to "fall so much in love" with their products that they over-emphasize technical features and neglect consumer preferences. For instance, one manufacturer of clam chowder used more expensive clams than his competitors, thus offering, technically speaking, a "better quality" product. However, consumers perceived competitive products as being of higher quality. Competitors used "more chewy" clams, and consumers were more conscious of their presence in the chowder.[2] Thus, opportunities often exist both to reduce the costs of making a product and at the same time to increase its salability.

Greater Integration or "Reverse Integration"

Sometimes, it is possible to reduce the costs (thereby increasing profits) of making and/or marketing a product through a program in-

---

[1] The Commodity Standards Division of the U.S. Department of Commerce helps industry groups to establish physical standards when such action is considered in the public interest. The division sponsors industry conferences in promulgate tentative standards and then circularizes all groups concerned for approval. Such approved commercial standards are used by industry members on a voluntary basis.

[2] R. L. Day, "Preference Tests and the Management of Product Features," *Journal of Marketing*, July 1968, p. 24.

volving greater integration (i.e., by adding functions formerly purchased from others). For example, an appliance manufacturer that formerly purchased plastic handles and other plastic components set up its own plastic manufacturing operation, thus reducing manufacturing costs. Another manufacturer reduced his marketing costs by switching from distribution through wholesalers to direct distribution to retailers.

In other situations, costs are reducible through "reverse integration" (i.e., by purchasing functions from others that formerly were performed by the company). Thus, a supermarket chain discontinued its integrated bakery operation and contracted with a large commercial baker for its requirements, thereby reducing the costs of supplying its stores with bakery products. And a large grocery products manufacturer reduced his marketing costs by switching from direct distribution to retailers to an indirect system utilizing specialty wholesalers.

THE "MAKE OR BUY" DECISION   In analyzing the cost-reducing possibilities of greater integration of manufacturing operations, management should consider numerous factors, among them the following:

1. Relative costs of making or buying
2. Probable future sales of the product
3. Impact on product quality, production and delivery schedules, and factory service
4. Importance of secrecy in design, style, and materials (In some cases, components must be purchased from outsiders because they hold the patents.)
5. Availability of plant capacity, needed labor, and needed technical and managerial skills
6. Importance of control over supply—will outsiders raise prices, refuse to sell, etc.? [3]

Thus, the make-or-buy decision is not simply a matter of determining the cheaper alternative. Both alternatives must be evaluated carefully for their effects on all aspects of the business. Often, however, the potential gains from capturing a bigger slice of the manufacturing margin outweigh the associated disadvantages. In these cases, greater integration of manufacturing operations pays off.

Nevertheless, "reverse integration," the exact opposite of greater integration, also is worth considering. In other words, sometimes it is possible to reduce costs by "farming out" more of the manufacturing operation. In such situations, management should consider the same factors as

[3] See J. T. Cannon, *Business Strategy and Policy* (New York: Harcourt, Brace & World, Inc., 1968), pp. 446-47.

those just discussed and reach its decision on the basis of their total impact on the business. All make-or-buy decisions, then, should be regarded as subject to change, if subsequent re-appraisals indicate that revision is needed.

DEGREE OF INTEGRATION OF MARKETING ACTIVITIES   Decisions on the extent to which the manufacturer should perform his own marketing activities call for similar analyses. Sometimes, the manufacturer can reduce marketing costs by adding activities formerly performed by middlemen. At other times, the opposite type of situation holds: costs can be reduced by getting middlemen to perform more of the total marketing task. This matter of optimizing the marketing channel is discussed in Part Four.

NO PRODUCT CHANGE—IMPROVED MARKET

This product-market strategy aims to improve the product's market (and the product's profitability) through increasing sales to markets now served by the company. This may be done in any of several different ways, all directed toward making "the product" more salable. However, "the product" in this context means only the physical product and not, as earlier emphasized, the "total bundle of utilities consisting of various product features and accompanying services." Remerchandising, in other words, leaves basic product features essentially unchanged but makes adjustments in the accompanying services. Thus, strictly speaking, remerchandising a product does make it into a different product, hopefully a more salable one. Nevertheless, businessmen customarily regard remerchandising as not involving product change, so this strategy is labeled "no product change—improved market."

The nature and direction of remerchandising effort varies with the individual company and its marketing situation. Those companies whose "products" are little more than "commodities" (in the marketing sense) have the most options open. Remerchandising, if successful, converts mere commodities into products with some distinctiveness. For example, mainly through imaginative packaging and branding (two forms of remerchandising) Morton's Salt has become, in consumers' minds, a distinctive product and not "just plain salt." The following discussion analyzes the chief forms of remerchandising, proceeding generally from the more elementary to the highly sophisticated forms of remerchandising.

Standardizing and Grading

For companies selling articles that are little more than commodities, standardizing and grading represent probably the first feasible means of remerchandising. Standardizing and grading involve the establishment of basic measures or limits to which products must conform. A standard consists of the specifications or basic limits to the qualities or characteristics that products must have to be of designated grades. Standards should be based on the qualities desired by buyers or on the use to which the article is to be put. For example, in the marketing of clothing it is useful to establish standards of size, so that all size-12 dresses will fit the same individual. Grading is the act of separating or inspecting the goods according to the established specifications to determine their grade. The specifications are set by the standards established and may include size, weight, color, quality, etc.

RELATIONSHIP TO MARKETING EFFICIENCY   Standardizing and grading are important to efficient marketing. Both make it easier for customers to buy the product, because buyers can now purchase by description, e.g., ordering a truckload of steel conforming to certain standards or a ton of coal of a specified grade by mail or by telephone. The buyer's only alternatives to purchase by description are either (1) to go to the seller's place of business and examine the product before buying, or (2) to obtain a sample of each lot of the product before placing orders.

Both standardizing and grading facilitate the seller's task by making it possible to "merchandise" products closer to what buyers want. A mixed lot of ungraded fruits is less attractive to prospective buyers and commands a lower total price than the same lot after it has been graded and priced by grade. Buyers of both manufactured and agricultural products return again and again to buy those products that consistently meet their expectations (as a properly standardized or graded product should).

Grading also helps reduce the costs of physically distributing agricultural products. Physical handling, for instance, is streamlined, since grading makes it possible to mix the crops of different growers for distribution purposes. Grain elevator operators store different growers' crops in the same elevators, and transportation companies mix them in the same shipments.

STANDARDIZATION   This activity, involving the use of standards, applies to manufactured goods. Standardizing first involves the establishment of certain physical standards to which the product must conform. Then, management sets controls over the manufacturing operation so that the output meets the standards within set tolerances.

Probably the greatest significance to remerchandising are standards relating to quality. Producers of most manufacturered products have wide latitude in determining product quality. With products of the farms, forests, fisheries, and mines, little control can be exercised over quality, and the most their marketers can do is to define quality by grading. Even

some manufacturers have little opportunity to control product quality—
for example, chemical processors cannot change basic compounds, so they
can control quality only in terms of absences of foreign elements, i.e.,
purity. But for most manufacturers a broad spectrum exists within which
management can set and enforce standards over product quality—durability,
uniformity, reliability, and other similar characteristics.

Effective standardization provides the consistency and predictability in product performance so essential to building consumer brand
preference. Buyers not only have a right to expect but do expect that all
units of a product under a particular brand name will be alike. Achieving
such consistency and predictability in product performance means that more
buyers who try the brand, if satisfied, will become steady customers. This
indicates, then, that a manufacturer should assess market needs and preferences before he sets standards for his product. Effective standardization,
therefore, is generally a prerequisite to the profitable use of branding.

GRADING   Where growers or producers have very limited control over their products' physical characteristics, grading provides a way to
obtain some, but not all, of the advantages of standardization. Grading involves the application of basic descriptive "standards"—such as size, color,
or weight—to the products of nature. Orange growers, for example, cannot
produce oranges that are all uniform in size. Proper thinning increases the
average size of oranges, but the range of individual sizes is still very wide.
Since the U.S. Department of Agriculture has prepared formalized de-
sciptions ("standards") for different sizes and grades of oranges, growers
sort their crops accordingly and end up with oranges in each of several
sizes or grades, each commanding a higher price than the ungraded fruit.
Grades may be established for other physical properties of natural
products, but for grading to be used, all such properties must be measurable.
Thus, canned peaches are graded in terms of sugar content, color, and
size, but they are not graded in terms of taste, because no objective way
exists to measure differences in individual taste preferences. Although many
farm products, such as tobacco, do not lend themselves easily to grading,
because the product characteristics most important to consumers cannot
be measured objectively, grading is widespread in marketing most U.S.
farm products today. Grading not only facilitates producers' marketing tasks
but makes it easier for consumers to specify the particular products they
wish to buy.

Product Service

The manufacturer searching for remerchandising opportunities
should appraise his present customer service policies and practices. As a
merchandising activity, customer service provides assistance and advice to

customers on such matters as product installation, operation, maintenance, and repair. For prospective buyers, availability and adequacy of customer service is often a major factor in choosing among competing sellers. Thus, by providing superior customer service, a marketer may obtain the patronage of certain buyers, even in the face of strong price or other competition. As technical features are added and a product becomes more complicated to install, operate, and maintain, customer service becomes increasingly important as an instrument of competition.

NEED FOR CUSTOMER SERVICE POLICIES   For many industrial products, service policies are indispensable; and for some consumer products, they are important elements in marketing programs. For complex industrial products, such as computers and data processing equipment, it is necessary to provide not only installation and repair services but, in many instances, to train customers' personnel in the product's use and care. For many products, however, this need is not as clear-cut, especially for consumer products. Nevertheless, if a product is a consumer durable or semi-durable, with a comparatively high unit price and a relatively low purchase frequency, it may be difficult to consummate sales unless the manufacturer or dealer, or both, provide service.

Manufacturers, however, sometimes overestimate the importance of offering certain types of service. Appliance makers, for example, at first were reluctant to sell through discount houses, mainly because these retailers did not provide repair and installation services. But when the manufacturers discovered, to their surprise, that many consumers were willing and able to take care of both installation and servicing on their own, their opposition to discount house distribution slowly disappeared. Those who were slowest in recognizing that they had overestimated the importance of retailer-provided installation and repair services lost contact with a growing potential market, as discount houses rapidly expanded. The decision to offer different customer services should be based on an appraisal of customer needs and expectations.

Appropriate customer service policies and practices not only facilitate initial sales but also help in keeping products sold, stimulating repeat sales, and building consumer good will. There is no legitimate place in a merchandising, or remerchandising, program for policies that fail to accomplish these aims. Each customer service offered, or proposed, should be evaluated against two criteria: the extent to which it will accomplish desired merchandising aims and whether it will contribute to net profit.

CHARGING FOR SERVICE   Many companies, at least for a specified period after the sale, do not charge for servicing the product—such "free" service being provided either under the terms of a written guarantee or as a policy matter. When a buyer requests service after this period, most companies charge for it. Firms with centralized service facilities, or which operate their own service stations, generally make nominal charges. Such charges pay all or most of the actual costs and eliminate many unreasonable demands by buyers.

Manufacturers who depend upon middlemen to provide service have less control over the size of service charges. The charge may be nominal, with the manufacturer paying part and the user the rest; or it may be larger and paid entirely by the user. Unless the manufacturer pays part of the cost, many middlemen refuse to assume responsibility for service. Most companies do not expect to make large profits through service charges; they regard service costs and advertising expenditures in the same light: both are investments that, over the long run, should more than pay for themselves in customer good will and repeat business.

Guarantees

In his assessment of remerchandising possibilities, the manufacturer should evaluate his policies with respect to guarantees (or warranties as they are also known). Guarantees, express or implied, are obligations assumed by the seller promising buyers that they will receive certain services or satisfactions. Thus, a guarantee is part of the bundle of satisfactions a buyer receives when he buys a product.

OBJECTIVES OF GUARANTEES   Generally, the manufacturer expects his guarantee to serve one of two purposes: (1) to protect against abuses of the service policy and to limit his liability, or (2) to provide an additional promotional element in his program for selling against the competition. For remerchandising, the promotional guarantee is of most interest: With the increasing adoption of the marketing concept, such guarantees are growing in importance as components of competitive strategy.

Promotional guarantees are appropriately used in a number of different situations. In the market introduction of a new product, for instance, they can help in overcoming buyer resistance, gaining initial distribution, adding new dealers, and opening new market areas. In both introducing new products and remerchandising established products, promotional guarantees are most effective when:

1. The product has a high retail price. (The higher the price, the more assurance buyers want that the product will perform as represented.)

2. The product is purchased infrequently. (Buyers are likely to be most concerned about the risk of product failure if the product,

such as an electric dishwasher, is to be used for a relatively long time.)

3. Buyers visualize the product as complex. (Complex products frequently are costly to repair, and complexity is likely to increase buyer uncertainty).

4. The firm's market share is small. (A promotional guarantee may overcome consumers' uncertainty about little-known products.) [4]

EVALUATING PROMOTIONAL GUARANTEES   In evaluating a proposed promotional guarantee, both the benefits and the costs should be considered. If the estimated additions to sales and revenues are greater than the additional costs involved, a promotional guarantee policy increases net profits. Management, however, must also weigh the possibility that competitors will match or exceed the guarantee terms. Then, the guarantee is not likely to prove profitable unless the total market also expands.[5]

Packaging

Packaging changes often are key elements in remerchandising. There are many reasons for packaging a product—to protect it, to differentiate and identify it, to make it more salable, or to improve handling convenience—to name just a few. A product such as coal needs no protection against damage from the elements and handling, whereas photographic film requires protection from exposure to light. These are extremes, but the need for protective packaging of almost any product is usually just as clear.

If a product is packaged for brand differentiation and identification purposes, it should remain packaged until purchased by the consumer. Bulk packaging removable before the consumer buys is mainly for protection and handling convenience. Five-pound bags of sugar, for example, arrive at the supermarket inside a large paper bag—the small bags are designed for brand differentiation and identification, and the large bag for protection and handling convenience.

When the brand name can be placed directly on the product, as in the case of appliances, there is no need for packaging for brand identification. But if a product is difficult to differentiate, as is true of nails and nuts and bolts, a package may provide the only way to differentiate it and secure, perhaps, a measure of brand identification. Packaging nails also increases their handling convenience both for middlemen and consumers.

[4] J. G. Udell and E. E. Anderson, "The Product Warranty as an Element of Competitive Strategy," *Journal of Marketing*, October 1968, p. 7.
[5] *Ibid.*, p. 8.

For most consumer products, however, packaging is the main way to identify the brand at the point of purchase. The package, like a promotional display, relates the product to the manufacturer's advertising and makes consumers aware of its availability in retail stores. Beyond this, marketing men expect the package to furnish consumers with needed product information, and to provide the extra push so often required to propel consumers into buying.

Once a manufacturer makes the basic decision to use packaging, related decisions are required on design, size, and cost. These decisions should be reviewed whenever remerchandising is being considered. At the same time, the adequacy of present packages for meeting packaging goals—protection, brand differentiation and identification, promotion, handling convenience, etc.—should be reappraised.

PACKAGE DESIGN   When packaging is primarily protective, design decisions are technical, involving comparative strengths and costs of materials and shapes. But when a package is primarily a promotional device, decisions are necessarily more subjective. Promotional elements in the package must attract consumers' attention, hold their interest, and build their desire to buy. The color, size, and shape of the package are all important in attracting the consumer, so decisions on these factors should be related to the preferences of the target market segment. The promotional aspect of package design is becoming more important each year, as more and more products are sold through self-service retail outlets. In these stores, the package must carry all of the promotional burden it formerly shared with the sales clerk.

In addition, manufacturers of many products sold through self-service outlets are now using packaging designed not only for promotional purposes but to protect the retailer from shoplifting—razor blades, cosmetics, and other small-sized products are being put up in fairly large plastic "blisters" mounted on cardboard backings, making the shoplifter's task more difficult and increasing his risk of being caught.

Package design must also consider convenience in product handling, both by the middlemen and the consumers. The shape of the package should permit easy display on the fixtures in the normal retail store. It should make it easy for the consumer to take the product home and to store in his normal storage cupboards. The six-pack carrying-carton for beer and soft drinks is an excellent example of a package that greatly increases ease of handling and, at the same time, increases consumption by encouraging an increase in the unit of purchase.

PACKAGE SIZE   The package size decision evolves from consideration of several factors: the two most important are the size of the consuming unit and the rate of consumption—and they are closely inter-related. Cigarettes, candy bars, and toothbrushes are consumed by individuals and are packaged in units for individual rather than group consumption. Cake mixes and gelatin desserts are consumed by household or family units and are packaged for group consumption. Dry breakfast cereals are packaged both ways: in family boxes and individual serving packs. Statistics are available on the average sizes of families and on their distribution by size. The producer may package his product in a size to satisfy the average family, or he may provide several sizes so as to satisfy a broader range of family sizes. Having decided on the size of the consuming unit to be served, the manufacturer must then determine the rate of product consumption by each unit. How much gelatin dessert does a family consume at a sitting? How many cigarettes does the average smoker use in a day? Consumer tests and surveys are useful in providing answers to such questions.

Findings on the consumption unit and the rate of consumption sometimes have to be modified when custom or habit strongly influence the package size. For example, the housewife is so accustomed to buying butter in one pound units that it would be very difficult to change to an unrelated unit, such as the pint or quart. She has learned to compare prices on the basis of pounds of butter and would probably be reluctant to buy in any other unit of measure.

Package size may also affect total consumption of a product. When the consumer has a plentiful supply of a product on hand, he may consume more than if he has to make a special buying trip to obtain it. The six-pack carton for soft drinks and beer and multiple packaging of light bulbs have demonstrated the success of this approach. The same holds for large, economy-sized packages.

PACKAGE COST   The amount of protection necessary to deliver a product to the user in good condition dictates the minimum cost of the package, but consumer preference and convenience may make it advisable to exceed this minimum. Although a metal container may be less expensive, a glass container may be used because of strong consumer preference for glass with certain products. Similarly, a reclosable package, although more expensive than a throw-away package, allows the customer to store the product easily until it is all used, without the necessity of transferring it to another container. Each such addition to the basic cost of packaging should be justifiable in terms of its probable effect upon consumer demand.

When a package is aimed at emphasizing brand identification or at other promotional goals, its cost is usually higher than if it is solely for product protection. Nevertheless, most manufacturers of consumer products expect their packages to help in promotion and regard differences in cost as worthwhile. As a bare minimum, the package must carry the brand name, the manufacturer's name, a description of the contents, and other descriptive material (e.g., how to use the product). Once the cost of designing an attractive promotional label has been amortized, the cost per package may be no more than that of a purely protective-type package.

But, a purely promotional package, such as an expensive perfume or liquor "holiday-type" package, may increase packaging cost greatly. In such cases, the cost differential should be justifiable in terms of increased profits from higher sales. There is always a danger that too expensive packaging will inflate the price to consumers and reduce both sales volume and profits. Similarly, reusable, dual-purpose packages (e.g., cottage cheese in a plastic refrigerator dish) may help sell the product by stimulating a separate demand for the package; their costs also should be justified in terms of their effectiveness in increasing total sales and profits.

Branding

The manufacturer contemplating remerchandising should explore opportunities for making profitable changes in branding. The relative significance of branding as a means for enhancing a product's salability, of course, varies with the product and the company. The truck farmer raising fresh peas competes for sales almost solely on a price basis, since buyers neither know nor care who grew the peas they buy. Yet, the food processor canning or freezing the same peas often succeeds in building a strong consumer preference for his brand through differentiating and promoting it, convincing consumers that his brand is superior to competitors'.

Branding's function, then, is to serve as the main connecting link between the manufacturer's promotional program and the consummation of sales to final buyers. Brand identification, therefore, is necessary for the company wishing to differentiate its product, giving it some degree of control over the product's resale by middlemen, and at the same time increasing promotional effectiveness. Through brand identification a company prepares itself to compete on nonprice bases.

Most products, industrial as well as consumer, in the American market today are branded. Some lend themselves to brand differentiation more readily than others. Many products of farms, fisheries, forests, and mines are difficult to differentiate because of their unprocessed form; [6] but even in these categories, brand identification coupled with imaginative packaging and promotion can often succeed in achieving some product differentiation, thus insulating the marketer from the full force of price competition. Swift and Company, for example, achieved this position with its marketing of "Swift's Premium Butterball Turkeys." Product differentia-

---

[6] There are a few notable exceptions, such as Sunkist citrus fruits and Black Diamond walnuts.

tion through brand identification and promotion is easier to obtain for consumer than for industrial products: highly standardized industrial items, such as sheet steel and nuts and bolts, can be identified by brand name but appear impossible to differentiate effectively.

For many products the potential effectiveness of brand identification to secure product differentiation is not clear. In these instances, the decision to brand or not to brand is highly important. A few years back, for example, "experts" believed that brand identification of women's dresses was of minimal effectiveness because women bought according to criteria unrelated to brand—such as color, design, styling, and fit. Today the dress industry not only uses brand names but promotes them heavily. Manufacturers learned, among other things, that variations in customers' physical sizes and shapes not provided for by differences in standard dress sizes, provided opportunities for real product differentiation. Thus, the short-waisted woman can eliminate the expensive alterations normally required when she buys a new dress because she has found that Brand XYZ dresses often will fit her without alteration. Thus, brand identification has the potential for the highest payoff in cases where it is possible to truly differentiate the product (as, for example, through design changes) in terms of features that consumers consider important. But it also has payoff potentials where present products have features shoppers look for; brand identification reduces the searching time shoppers have to spend in finding products with the desired features.

FAMILY BRANDS VS. INDIVIDUAL BRANDS   Most companies market more than one product, so they must decide whether to sell each under a separate brand or to use a family brand for some or all products. Sometimes, these decisions are made without much forethought. Some companies when introducing a new product, simply sell it under the same brand as that used on other products, without giving serious consideration to a new brand name. But many situations exist where substantial benefits can be realized through making one choice rather than the other. Decisions on whether to use a family or an individualized brand should result from evaluations of three main factors—nature of the product and the product line, promotional policy, and desired market penetration.

The *nature of the product line* is probably most important. Similar products naturally related to each other in consumers' minds, such as sheets and towels, benefit particularly from use of a family brand. Favorable reaction to one product often leads consumers to use others in the line. However, this "halo" effect can also detract from a manufacturer's reputation, since unfavorable experiences with one product may turn consumers against the entire line. It is important, then, that particular care be taken that all products under the family brand conform to consumers' standards of acceptance.

Products lacking common marketing attributes are usually better marketed under individual brand names, since little if any benefit is likely to come from jointly associating them. There may even be adverse sales reactions. For example, the association of food products with a known brand of soap products may handicap sales of the food line because consumers generally associate an unpleasant taste with soap.

All products do not lend themselves to sale under a family brand. Unless different brands represent broadly different price ranges, such as General Motors' Chevrolet and Cadillac, the quality of family-brand products should be very nearly similar, so that no single product lowers the quality reputation of other products. The products also should be fairly compatible. Although a housewife may prefer a particular brand of soap, she will probably not be at all interested in a new perfume introduced under the same name, because she is not convinced that experience in manufacturing soap will carry over to the manufacture of perfume. Products carrying a family brand also should be sold to the same markets. Little is gained from applying a family brand to one product sold to industrial users, and to another product sold to ultimate consumers; the same applies for different market segments. The name *Serutan* would have no value (except probably, negative value) on a product marketed to teenagers.

Promotional policy is important to this decision, mainly because of the implications both for the size of the promotional budget and the nature of possible promotion. Using a family brand requires a smaller total promotional budget than individual brands. Under a family brand, much promotional effort can be directed toward the entire line, and even promotion concentrating on a single product still helps to increase recognition and demand for the entire line. With individual brands, separate and often duplicating promotional programs are usually needed. Thus, a family-brand policy ordinarily allows the most effective use of limited promotional funds for similar products. Yet, family-brand promotional programs restrict the opportunity to emphasize individual product differences, and this may be very important when introducing a new product.

The degree of *market penetration* is an important factor, since the individual members of a product line face varying degrees of competition. A maker of kitchen and laundry appliances, for example, may meet only mild competition on dishwashers and electric ranges because his competitors are not promoting these products effectively. Another competitor producing only washing machines and promoting them aggressively may have captured a large share-of-the-market and may be extremely difficult to displace. In such instances, where the same degree of market penetration is not possible for all products, the use of individual brands allows greater promotional flexibility. Products facing the strongest competition may be allocated larger shares of the promotional budget so that optimum market penetration can be achieved for each product in the line. This also makes it easier to draw consumers' attention to changes and improvements in particular products. The use of individual brands also allows a producer to achieve greater market penetration by marketing similar but differentiated products that appeal to different market segments.

MULTIPLE BRANDS FOR IDENTICAL PRODUCTS   Makers of specialty products often market their outputs through a limited number of selected retail outlets in order to gain dealers' cooperation in aggressively promoting the products. This is "selective distribution" (discussed in detail in Chapter 14) and has the effect of limiting the total potential market, since in any one trading area no single retailer or small group of retailers is normally in a position to attract all potential buyers. Even with selective distribution, however, market penetration may be increased by offering identical merchandise under a different brand to a second group of retailers. Hickey-Freeman does this by distributing a second brand of its men's clothing, the Walter Morton brand, in trading areas where more than one retail outlet is deemed desirable.

Mergers frequently result in the use of multiple brands (at least on a temporary basis), the merged company often ending up with identical or nearly identical products selling under different brands. The decision to retain the separate brands or to change to a single brand depends on several factors. If the different brands have dissimilar images appealing to different market segments, the decision may be to leave things as they are. If each brand has developed strength in different regional markets, management may be reluctant to abandon well-known names for others that, at least in some markets, may be unknown. Such was the case with Standard Oil Company of New Jersey, subsequently renamed Humble Oil Company, which used the ESSO brand in the northeastern United States and different brands elsewhere. This decision was further complicated by the fact that under the court ruling (*Standard Oil Co.* vs. *U.S. 221 U.S. 1,1911*), dismembering the old Standard Oil monopoly and creating Standard of New Jersey and five other companies, the ESSO brand was barred from use in certain regions. Reluctant to abandon the ESSO name, its most important single brand, management decided (1961) to retain the ESSO brand in the Northeast and to adopt an entirely new name, ENCO, to gradually replace its other regional brands. The reasoning was that two brands (ESSO and ENCO) that could become well-known regionally would be better than a number of brands. Companies that undertake brand consolidation generally do so with the hope of enhancing the effectiveness of their promotion, especially their national advertising.

PRIVATE BRANDING   Private brands are those owned and controlled by middlemen rather than the manufacturers making the products.

Thus, both manufacturers and middlemen are faced with policy decisions on private branding. Manufacturers must decide whether it is advantageous to accept private branding contracts. Middlemen must determine whether they can gain by selling their own private brands.

Numerous factors enter into a manufacturer's decision on the acceptance of private brand contracts. What will be the likely effect on his own brand's sales? [7] Can the private brand be clearly differentiated from his own brand, or will consumers regard them as identical? Even if the private brand is adequately differentiated, will it capture part of his own brand's market share? If the private brand contract is rejected, will competitors accept it? Will accepting the private brand contract result in improved shelf position for his own brand in the retail outlets involved? If accepted, will the private brand owner later "chisel" on the price and other terms? These are all considerations, but they should not obscure the really important question: Considering everything, what will be the effect on total profits of accepting or rejecting this contract?

Many executives contend that private brand business is not as profitable as regular business. But the profitability of private brand business depends upon the manufacturer, his marketing situation, and his other alternatives for increasing profits. In some cases, private brand business is profitable; in others, it is not. The Marketing Science Institute surveyed 89 manufacturers in ten different industries and reported that companies accepting private brand business "turn in profit and return-on-investment" figures not significantly different from competitors not producing private brands.[8]

The Whirlpool Corporation is an example of a firm that has successfully sold under both its own name and a private brand. Approximately half of its production of washing machines is sold under the Whirlpool name and half under the Kenmore name, owned by Sears, Roebuck. Selling under these two brands, the company ranks as the leading producer of home laundry equipment. Whirlpool management, although glad to have Sears as its major customer, is also glad to have a strong national market under its own name, plus other major customers such as Montgomery Ward and Frigidaire (for whom it produces commercial ice makers).

Middlemen's decisions to use private brands, like those of manu-

---

[7] While many argue that private brand sales "take business away" from the manufacturer's own brand, especially if consumers cannot detect differences in "what's inside the package," this is by no means certain. In fact, sometimes sales of the manufacturer's brand actually increase, since at least a few private brand owners give favored shelf position to those manufacturers who "collaborate" in filling their private brand orders. See: L. W. Stern, "The New World of Private Brands," *California Management Review*, Spring 1966, p. 45.

[8] V. J. Cook, "Private Brand Mismanagement by Misconception," *Business Horizons*, December 1968, p. 64.

facturers, should be based mainly on the anticipated effect on profits. In appraising the possibility of increasing profits through using private brands, the middleman must balance the higher margins private brands usually carry against the associated costs involved in advertising and otherwise promoting them. To the extent that a middleman succeeds in building strong consumer acceptance for his own brand, his control over the market is increased. His efforts to stimulate demand for the private brand do not benefit his competitors, since only his outlets are stocking it, and he need not worry about losing his franchise at the manufacturer's whim. These are important gains, but securing them often requires disproportionate increases in promotional and other expenditures. The important question for the middleman contemplating the use of private brands is also "Considering everything, how will total profits be affected?"

BRANDING FABRICATING PARTS   Fabricating parts (as defined in Chapter 8) are manufactured items which, without any substantial change in form, are incorporated into or assembled into some more complex and finished product. Carburetors, tires, and spark plugs for an automobile are examples. Some producers of fabricating parts use branding, but many do not.

Some makers of fabricating parts who use branding hope that final buyers (usually ultimate consumers) will insist upon finished products containing their brands of parts. Securing such insistence usually requires a parts producer to invest large sums in consumer advertising: His basic marketing strategy is of the "pull" type, and he must build consumer insistence to the point where his immediate industrial buyers of the part will hesitate to place their orders elsewhere. Other makers of fabricating parts use branding, because the parts also have replacement markets. The tire manufacturer, for example, hopes buyers of autos on which his tires are original equipment will replace them with the same brand. Therefore, if a fabricating part is a particularly essential component of the finished product, if it possesses features of importance to consumers, or if it also has a substantial replacement market, the maker may find it profitable to brand the part and undertake the necessary consumer advertising.

Financing Customers' Sales

In some fields, manufacturers find it profitable to finance their customers' sales to final buyers. Thus, these manufacturers generally not only extend regular trade credit to their middlemen but also help them resell the products, through financing their sales to final buyers. Such arrangements are particularly common in fields where the product's resale price is substantial and/or final buyers' incomes fluctuate greatly. Both conditions exist in the selling of major pieces of farm equipment (tractors, combines, and the like). Since farm equipment dealers often are poorly financed, nearly all farm equipment makers either take care of, or at last share in, the financing of the dealers' sales to equipment buyers. Financing customers' sales may be a way to increase total sales and profits. Therefore, producers of "big ticket" items should consider this remerchandising possibility.

NO PRODUCT CHANGE—NEW MARKET

This product-market strategy is particularly significant for companies with products already in, or about to enter, the market maturity stage of the life cycle. During this stage, industry sales tend to reach a plateau and then gradually fall off. However, some companies, those with especially astute managements, explore other possibilities besides that of simply letting the product "run out." They search for and evaluate various ways of rejuvenating the product's sales and profit growth rates. A mature product, by definition, is one that is approaching, or has already reached, the saturation level in its present market, so rejuvenation must involve finding new markets. Management's search for new markets should include analysis of both: (1) possible new users, and (2) possible new uses and applications.

New Users

Essentially, the search for possible new users boils down to finding and evaluating yet untapped market segments. Management should begin with a review of the nature and characteristics of the product's present market. One producer of crystal glassware, for instance, had for years concentrated its marketing efforts on the bride-to-be market, but its sales had topped out. After studying the market more closely, management concluded that there were actually three market segments for crystal: (1) the bride-to-be, (2) the matron, and (3) the "rich aunt." The matron market segment consisted of women who had been unable to afford crystal at the time of marriage but whose purchasing power had grown subsequently to the point where they were ready to buy. The "rich aunt" market segment was made up of affluent relatives who purchased gifts for brides. Marketing efforts were redirected, the "new" market segments were tapped, and company sales and profits resumed their growth.[9]

[9] W. J. Talley, Jr., *The Profitable Product* (Englewood Cliffs, N.J.: Prentice-Hall, Inc., 1965), pp. 93-94.

There are other groups of possible new users, each of which should be identified and evaluated. Perhaps the most obvious is the different geographic market segment, i.e., potential new users outside the present marketing area. Products that have reached near-saturation levels in industrial market segments have sometimes found new markets among ultimate consumers (this happened with small power tools and was helped along by the "do-it-yourself" trend). Products used traditionally by men (e.g., cigarettes) sometimes have been successful in tapping new markets made up of women, and the reverse has also happened (e.g., deodorants and hair spray). Products originally aimed at one age group may be redirected to appeal to a different age group (e.g., baby foods for the elderly). Many other possibilities exist, each involving a particular basis of market segmentation. Management should determine the relevant basis of market segmentation for the product, study carefully the individual market segments, and redirect its marketing efforts accordingly.

New Uses

Detection and exploitation of new uses is an often neglected way to stretch a product's life; trade journals carry many stories of how supposedly mature products have found new life in new uses or applications. Diapers, because of their softness and freedom from lint, were found to be used in laboratories to clean delicate instruments. Fruit and vegetable processors were discovered using small sewage pumps, originally developed for home use, to move items, such as peaches, along special water troughs through the various processing stages—thus preventing bruises and other damage.[10] Admittedly, such unusual applications are difficult to anticipate and sometimes are discovered purely by accident (e.g., a producer of lighter fluid accidentally found its product being used to remove road film from automobiles). Nevertheless, management should keep abreast of the uses to which its products are being put: salesmen should ask dealers who is buying the product and for what purposes; marketing research should periodically survey buyers for the same reason.

One authority on the subject suggests some broad guides that may be helpful in attempts to find profitable new uses:

1. Investigate related applications of the current use (e.g., new recipes for a food product).
2. Explore new uses in connection with the sale of products of other manufacturers (e.g., an "after-shave" preparation as a "before-shave" preparation for use with electric razors).

[10] "Uncommon Markets: Sales Windfalls from Offbeat Product Uses," *Management Review*, November 1962, p. 57.

3. Explore possibilities of a product useful in one part of the house being used in other parts (e.g., paper towels and cups in the laundry and bathroom).

4. Consider applications for products used in the home in industry and vice versa (e.g., women's hair clips being used to disperse heat from soldering irons used on electronic circuits).

5. Explore the nature of the product's ingredients for new uses (e.g., chicken wire being used by florists).[11]

CONCLUSION

Matching products with markets and effecting ownership transfers (i.e., making sales) is the essence of marketing. But to attain the goal that most companies give as their main reason for existence, marketing operations must result in increasing profits. Analysis in this chapter focused on three different combinations of product-market strategies used for improving profitability, all involving "no product change." Using a "no product change —no market change" strategy, management seeks to improve profitability chiefly through cost reduction measures. With a "no product change— improved market" strategy, management strives for improved profitability through increased sales volume resulting from "remerchandising" (i.e., from obtaining a better "fit" of the product to its present market). Management's intention in using a "no product change—new market" strategy is to increase profitability through greater sales volume resulting from successfully: (1) serving the needs of new users (i.e., new market segments) and/or (2) exploiting new uses or applications of the product. Analysis in the next chapter relates to using "product change" and "new product" strategies in combination with the same three market strategies; emphasis is on planning and implementing programs for increasing profitability.

QUESTIONS AND PROBLEMS

1. Explain: (a) how a newly-organized company generally tries to increase its profits; (b) how a longer-established company seeks to increase its profitability. In which situation is marketing skill most important? Why?

2. What factors should each of the following organizations consider in determining the sizes in which they should offer their products?

---

[11] G. B. Tallman, "The Product," in A. W. Frey (ed.), *Marketing Handbook* (New York: The Ronald Press Co., 1965), Sec. 5, p. 13.

    a. A maker of prefabricated swimming pools for in-ground installation.

    b. A perfume manufacturer.

    c. A packer of frozen dietary foods.

    d. A manufacturer of photographic film.

3. Is it possible that industry-wide standardization of certain product features, such as size, may cause the products involved to become "commodities?"

4. Under what circumstances will increased profitability result from greater integration? From "reverse integration?"

5. "The make-or-buy decision simply involves determining the cheaper alternative." Agree or disagree? Why?

6. Contrast the make-or-buy decision with that concerning the optimum degree of integration of marketing functions.

7. What is the meaning and marketing significance of each of the following terms?

    a. remerchandising   d. customer service

    b. standardizing   e. guarantee

    c. grading

8. How would you answer the argument that it is to the individual producer's advantage to avoid standardization in his product and its parts so that buyers are forced to return to him for repairs and servicing?

9. Comment on the following guarantees with respect to their likely promotional effectiveness:

For a tape recorder: This is a quality product and fully guaranteed against defective materials and workmanship for a period of 90 days from date of purchase. This guarantee does not cover abuse, neglect, tampering by unauthorized personnel, or damage inadvertently caused by the user.

For a mattress: We guarantee that the bedding described here will be satisfactory to the original purchaser. If the bedding should be defective due to faulty workmanship or structural defects, during the first year after purchase, we will either replace or rebuild the items involved at our cost. Should the bedding be defective, for the same causes as above, during the 20 year period after purchase, we will, upon payment by purchaser of an adjustment charge for each year or fraction of use, either: (a) Replace the item involved or: (b) Rebuild the item involved (excluding exterior covering). Guarantee does not apply to the covering. Guarantee applies only if both mattress and foundation are bought at the same time as a set.

Bathroom scale: Should this scale become inaccurate at any time, return it to the Scale Division of the XYZ Corporation (use convenient shipping label attached and enclose this warranty certificate with the scale). Any inaccuracy will be corrected for a minimum packing and handling charge of 50 cents and scale returned parcel post C.O.D. plus postal charges. If scale has been tampered with or subject to abuses (such as dropping on floor), the warranty does not apply. In such cases, a nominal charge will be made for parts replaced in addition to the service fee mentioned above.

10.   Can packages be used effectively to differentiate products not otherwise differentiatable? Why or why not?

11.   What relationships, if any, exist between packaging decisions and the choice of marketing channels?

12.   Would it be sensible to use a rule of thumb that no package is justifiable if it increases the cost of the product by more than ten percent? Why?

13.   Today, canned and frozen foods commonly are put up in standard sizes, but package sizes for detergents and soaps show little standardization. How would soap and detergent makers benefit, and how would they lose from package-size standardization?

14.   "The advantages of using a family brand clearly outweigh those of using individual brands on different products." Agree or disagree?

15.   Multiple brands for identical products are often used to implement a highly selective distribution policy. Would it be fair to say that this is a compromise that doesn't really benefit anyone—manufacturer, retailer, or consumer?

16.   "A contract to make private brands should be at a sufficiently high price that an allocated share of total costs is covered; otherwise, there is no long-range justification for accepting such business." Comment.

17.   Which, if any, of the following companies might find it profitable to use branding in combination with consumer advertising?
a. A maker of prescription drugs.
b. A manufacturer of picture tubes for television receivers.
c. A maker of small gasoline engines used in assembling lawn mowers, snow blowers, and other home lawn care appliances.
d. A producer of fabrics used in apparel manufacturing.

18.   Which, if any, of the following companies might find it profitable to assist their dealers in financing sales to final buyers?
a. A producer of small airplanes for sale to private pilots.
b. A manufacturer of mobile homes.

    c. A producer of photographic equipment purchased mainly by hobbyists.

    d. An appliance maker.

19.   How would you recommend that each of the following organizations should go about finding new users for their products?

    a. A manufacturer of small, hand-operated paper cutters and hole punchers.

    b. A producer of talcum powder for babies.

    c. A manufacturer of office furniture.

    d. A maker of pots and pans for restaurants and institutions.

20.   What possible new uses might be found for each of the following products?

    a. Pipe cleaners.

    b. Automatic timing devices for electrical appliances.

    c. Carpeting.

    d. Frozen orange juice.

11

FORMULATING PRODUCT-MARKET STRATEGY: Product Change and New Product

Discussion and analysis in this chapter focuses first on "product change," then on "new product" strategies, relative to their several combinations with "no market change," "improved market," and "new market" strategies. Each combination represents an additional possibility for management to explore as it searches for ways to increase profitability. As compared to the product-market strategies analyzed previously, those in this chapter generally are more complex and, for the most part, require considerably greater marketing sophistication in their implementation. As in the last chapter, you will find it useful to refer frequently to Exhibit 10.1 on page 230.

PRODUCT CHANGE—NO MARKET CHANGE

There are three closely-related versions of this product-market strategy: (1) product line simplification and product discontinuance, (2) new models, and (3) planned obsolescence. Management may choose any of these versions, or some combination, as a suitable means for increasing profitability. Strategies involving product line simplification and product discontinuance envision profit increases through cost reductions. Those involving either new models or planned obsolescence seek profit increases through growth in sales volume.

Product Line Simplification and Product Discontinuance

Reducing the number of models and/or products in a product line frequently affords opportunities for increased profits through cost reduction. Proliferation of models or products in a line often traces to efforts to match every new item introduced by competitors or to satisfy salesmen's and dealer's pleas for "more variety." Eventually this may result in various products or models being so much alike that prospective buyers regard them as "the same thing." At some point, the product line contains many "tired" products and models, slow movers draining off working capital and profits.[1]

Product proliferation, of course, is partially preventable through being highly selective in adding new products and models. But pressures always exist to broaden the line and offer greater variety. Marketing men, in particular, frequently push for broader selections of models and for more products in the line, since this simplifies the problem of satisfying widely varying preferences in the market. Production men, however, fight to keep product lines narrow, as this holds manufacturing costs down and makes production scheduling less complicated. Henry Ford's Model T exemplified the production viewpoint, since it provided practically no variety of selection or choice. However, under today's increasingly competitive conditions, market pressures force manufacturers to offer greater and greater variety in their lines; increasing sophistication of the consumer and division of markets into more and more segments contribute to this multiplicity of products. While well-designed procedures for screening new product ideas improve the chances that additions will be profitable, they do not fully insure against product failures. Furthermore, today's successes may become tomorrow's failures: products are born, grow, mature, and die, as the product life cycle concept indicates. Market and organizational pressures push in the direction of product proliferation; counter pressures are needed both to control new additions and to weed out "tired" products and models.

Product line simplification requires continual review of the line and the discontinuation of items not contributing directly (in their own right) or indirectly (e.g., as a repair part) to profits. Streamlining the product line through its simplification reduces inventory carrying charges,

[1] J. T. Cannon, *Business Strategy and Policy* (New York: Harcourt Brace & World, Inc., 1968), p. 117.

cuts down on the number of short uneconomical production runs, and releases working capital that can be put to more profitable use elsewhere. Even more important, it allows management to shift its emphasis to major improvements and innovations and more creative marketing strategies for the principal items in the line.[2]

Procedures used in product line simplification are fairly straightforward. Generally, they involve four major aspects: (1) selection of products for possible discontinuance, (2) gathering and analyzing relevant information, (3) making the actual decisions, and (4) if necessary, carrying out the elimination.[3] Most companies with effective simplification programs assume that every product is a possible candiate for discontinuance at all times; its performance is continually under review, and information concerning its performance is kept up-to-date.

In deciding which products to discontinue, the general rule is that an item should not be retained unless it is profitable, shows considerable promise of becoming profitable, or is "indirectly" profitable for some reason or another. Thus, simplification involves more than merely determining present profitability. Sometimes, a change in price, promotion, or marketing channels can cause a currently unprofitable product to become profitable. Furthermore, dealers and customers frequently expect, even demand, a "full-line" offering, thus preventing the weeding out of *all* unprofitable products and models. Some items, such as repair and replacement parts, may be unprofitable in their own right yet have selling value and should be retained. Other unprofitable items must be retained in order to sell profitable members of the product line (e.g., when customers regard a group of products as a "product system," as in the case of razors and razor blades).

Under some circumstances, too, it is desirable to drop a profitable product. Management might discontinue an item, for instance, if the same resources would yield a higher profit if used in behalf of another product with a brighter future. Likewise, a profitable product might be dropped, if it causes salesmen and/or dealers to divert their efforts from still more profitable products. And, in general, any product is a likely candidate for discontinuance if the company does not have the needed resources and/or talents to capitalize fully on its potential profitability.

New Models

Through introducing new models of current products, management seeks to increase profitability by stimulating sales volume. This strategy contrasts sharply with its opposite, line simplification, which seeks increased

[2] *Ibid.*
[3] R. S. Alexander, "The Death and Burial of 'Sick' Products," *Journal of Marketing*, April 1964, p. 2.

profits through cost reduction. New models are not, strictly speaking, new products; they are variations of established products—new sizes, colors, designs, and the like. Management's hope in introducing a new model is that it will more closely "fit" what buyers in the present market really prefer.

A new model strategy is intended to increase sales, but this usually involves increases both in production and marketing costs. Production costs rise because of shorter production runs and more complex scheduling; marketing costs go up through higher inventory costs and reduced turnover at all distribution levels. Thus, decisions on new models should flow from incremental profit analyses: estimated increases in costs, both production and marketing, should be compared with anticipated sales volume increases to determine whether the proposed new models will increase or decrease profits. The aim, both in new model and in line simplification strategies, should be to achieve the optimal variety of product models, and "optimum" means "maximum profitability over the long run."

Introducing new models is a fact of life for many producers today and a regular part of their product strategy, the regularity and frequency of model change varying among industries and individual companies. Some change their models only when significant improvements justify the action. Others introduce new models on a regular, periodic basis, even though the changes may be superficial. The choice usually depends on the practices of the industry, but not always. In competing in an industry as strongly committed to annual model changes as the American automobile industry, the Volkswagen has been marketed successfully under a strategy of changing the model *only* when technological improvements justify it.

Planned Obsolescence

Product improvement, whether real or contrived, provides a means for increasing the rate of obsolescence. This is most important in mature industries whose markets have reached, or are approaching, saturation. In such industries, a manufacturer competes not only with other manufacturers, but with the products he and his competitors have sold in the past. If he depends solely on physical obsolescence, gradual wear, and deterioration, his prospects for future sales and profitability are limited. However, products in the hands of consumers can be made obsolete in two ways: by improving performance characteristics of new models and by changing consumers' concepts of the acceptability of existing products. The auto industry's introduction of automatic transmissions is an example of the first type of created obsolescence, and the annual change in automobile body style is an example of the second. Both are described by the term *planned obsolescence*.

Planned obsolescence of the second type is a highly controversial strategy. It is considered economically wasteful by economists such as John K. Galbraith and popular writers such as Vance Packard.[4] Many business executives also oppose this kind of planned obsolescence, calling it "wasteful" and "contrary to the country's best interests." One group of executives voted two to one against the strategy.[5] Yet others defend planned obsolescence as a necessary support to our high-level economy. Many mature industries doubtless would falter if planned obsolescence were suddenly eliminated. For example, some defenders say that "the ladies garment industry might just as well shut down, and the automobile industry might be in almost as bad straits."[6] Supporters of planned obsolescence also point out that the criticisms are based on the moral judgment that a desire for the latest thing is wrong for society. Supporters obviously feel that wanting "something new and different" is good for society.

Planned obsolescence may stimulate sales for producers and middlemen, but it also intensifies the problems of each. Each model change-over results in added costs for new tooling and production shutdowns, as well as increased risk of poor consumer acceptance. Each presents middlemen with problems of liquidating old models and of training sales people to sell the new models.

Planned obsolescence should also be analyzed from the consumer's point of view. To the consumer, creation of obsolescence through real product improvements is generally acceptable, but changes in standards of acceptability (as in appearance) are more controversial. Yet, fashion is not the creation of marketers; it has been a part of western culture for centuries. The degree of anticipated obsolescence, planned or not, is an important factor in determining desired product quality: a high rate of anticipated obsolescence tends to set an upper limit on quality, at least to the extent that quality affects durability. Consumers may be unwilling to pay more for a refrigerator designed to last for twenty years if it appears certain that it will become obsolete in a considerably shorter time due to the incorporation of different design and improved operating features in newer models.

A company's decision to pursue a strategy of planned obsolescence often depends on industry practice, although in some industries where the practice is fairly uniform, individual firms (e.g., Volkswagen in the auto industry) have managed to operate profitably under a contrary strategy. Companies adopting this strategy also must make decisions on such things

[4] The views of these two critics are presented in: J. K. Galbraith, *The Affluent Society* (Boston: Houghton-Mifflin, 1958); and V. Packard, *The Waste Makers* (New York: D. McKay Co., 1960).

[5] "Planned Obsolescence—Is it Wrong, Is There a Better Way?", *Printers' Ink*, May 26, 1961, p. 24.

[6] *Ibid.*, p. 31.

as the frequency of model changes and on the timing of introduction of new models. These decisions should be based mainly on estimates of comparative production and marketing costs and relative sales volume potentials, but they have to be modified by such intangible considerations as dealer morale and profits, sales force motivation, and public relations in general. In fact, even the possible reactions of labor unions must be taken into account in setting the dates for introducing new models, as union leaders sometimes think of these dates as strategically ideal for delivering decisively timed blows against producers.[7]

PRODUCT CHANGE—IMPROVED MARKET

The main types of "product change—improved market" strategies are: (1) product customization, and (2) product systems. Both aim to improve profitability through increasing sales volume: product customization by giving buyers "something closer to what they really want," and product systems by focusing on "the tasks final buyers want the products to accomplish."

Product Customization

Product customization involves tailoring product specifications very closely to buyers' needs in order to make profitable sales to those whose business would not otherwise be obtained. Profitability is increased, in other words, through bringing in added sales volume from an "improved market" resulting from making available customized products. Customization is not the same as proliferation: Customization is planned and deliberate and aimed at increasing profits; proliferation occurs because of failures to control the composition of the product line, overemphasizing the making of sales regardless of their profitability.

The mildest form of product customization is to offer a wider choice of models and other variations, with the intent of making it easier for buyers to decide in favor of some model produced by the company rather than by its competitors. Hopefully, buyers' options will be narrowed from "buy or not to buy" to "buy this one or that one." This sort of strategy is often used in shopping goods' situations, such as with ladies' shoes or men's neckwear. At the retail level, the "wide selection available" helps pull in trade and makes more sales, which, of course, have favorable effects for the manufacturer. But this type of customization should be "teamed"

---

[7] T. L. Berg, "Union Inroads in Marketing Decisions," *Harvard Business Review*, July-August, 1962, p. 68.

with product line simplification strategy. Both customized additions and their later discontinuance must be carefully managed to assure increasing profits from a total offering superior in its competitive effectiveness.

A stronger form of product customization involves offering a "basic line" of standard products but allowing customers to "write their own specifications" with respect to certain product features. This is common strategy in marketing industrial products, such as grinding wheels, and in selling "custom-designed" insurance policies to business buyers. Computer and other business machine manufacturers also use this strategy to sell equipment to business buyers (usually large ones) who have specialized data processing needs or control systems. Banks, for example, have unique data processing needs, and computer makers allow them to specify certain "adaptations" in the basic equipment.

The most extreme product customization strategies are used in situations where labor looms very large in total production costs, and unusual craftsmanship and scarce technical skills can command premium selling prices.[8] Thus, many small firms (such as custom tailors and shirtmakers, cabinet makers, prescription opticians, and commercial printers) turn out products more or less meeting customers' exact specifications. Similarly, large producers of industrial equipment (such as special-purpose machine tools) and space and defense contractors (such as those making the "moon vehicles" and the intercontinental ballistic missiles) manufacture items that meet buyers' specifications within extremely close limits.

Product Systems

Product system strategies are keyed into increasing profitability through increasing the utility of products to buyers, thus stimulating sales volume. Such strategies are market oriented; they involve designing and marketing "product systems" that accomplish what users expect them to accomplish. Major emphasis is placed on solving buyers' problems, not the manufacturers' problems. Thus, product system strategies have great appeal for companies operating under the marketing concept.

Most households use numerous product systems. The automatic washing machine, for example, is a single-product system that combines functions formerly performed "by hand" and by a washboard, pails, tubs, a scrub brush, a hand wringer, etc. By combining these functions, it solves more of a household's washing problems than any of the products it replaced, and it is "worth more" (i.e., has greater utility) to the household since, in addition, it provides greater convenience, eliminates unpleasant

[8] Cannon, *Business Strategy*, pp. 122-124.

tasks, and saves time. The combination automatic washer-dryer adds the drying function, thus further increasing the system's utility to the user. Additionally, it "saves space" which is important in some households. Other household examples include: "home entertainment centers" (combined and compact units with television, AM and FM radio, tape deck, stereo player, etc.); "weather conditioners" combining heating, cooling, ventilating, and humidifying; and combination refrigerator-freezers.

O. M. Scott & Sons Company, marketers of Scott's lawn care products, has been a long-time user of a product system strategy. Scott's target market segment might be described as "people who are not lawn care experts but who are seeking a beautiful lawn on a guaranteed basis." The key element in the Scott lawn care product system is a spreader designed to assure proper application of grass seed, various fertilizers, and different weed and insect control products. Operating under the slogan "A Better Lawn Or Your Money Back," Scott sells homeowners the spreaders and the other products making up the system. Since the spreader is easy to use, and the other products much lighter than most of their competitors, the product has great appeal to target market members, most of whom appear convinced that anyone who can read and follow simple directions can have a beautiful lawn.

Product system strategies are widely used in industrial marketing. Complete packaging machinery systems, for example, are designed especially for the packaging needs of such users as food canners, soft drink bottlers, brewers, distillers, and drug producers—with the system varying according to the prospective user's packaging requirements. Similarly, complete baggage and air freight cargo-handling systems are being designed and sold to meet the needs of different sizes and types of aircraft and airport facilities. Product systems sold to industrial markets, like their counterparts sold to consumer markets, generally provide added utility to users by relating and automating various necessary tasks formerly performed separately. In the process, they also provide cost savings and accomplish the entire task more effectively.

PRODUCT CHANGE—NEW MARKET

This strategy seeks increased profitability through additional sales volume generated by changing certain features of the product and selling it to a new market segment. All companies except those selling products destined for only one particular market segment eventually must use this strategy. Very few products wholly satisfy the needs of more than a single market segment; therefore, companies desiring to expand into new markets are confronted with problems involving changing certain product features to match them better with the individualized needs of new target market segments.

The important elements in making such decisions are fairly objective, and may be expressed in terms of a formula, as follows:

$$(S \times B \times P) - C = N$$

where, S is the size of the market segment
B is the buying potential per buyer
P is the projected market share
C is the differential (or special) cost of reaching the segment
N is the differential (or extra) profit.

The projected market share and the differential cost of reaching the market segment are interrelated, since cost is affected by the share sought. Thus, as a company seeks to expand its market share from 40 to 60 percent, the costs of capturing this additional 20 percent are proportionally greater than those incurred by the same company in expanding its market share from 20 to 40 percent. This may have been the sort of reasoning that led the Coca-Cola Company to seek a share of the lemon-lime drink market segment through the introduction of Sprite, rather than trying to increase its already large share of the cola drink market segment.

Trading Up and Trading Down

The "product change—new market" strategy may involve "trading up or "trading down." Both take the form of bringing out changed versions of the product and altering the direction and nature of promotion. Generally, companies trading up or down do one or the other, not both at the same time.

A manufacturer trades up when he adds a higher-priced, more prestigious, product—with the main goal of increasing his sales of a present lower-priced product. Thus, the emphasis in trading up is not so much on obtaining sales from the new market segment as on improving sales from an old market segment. Ford Motor Company, for instance, introduced the Thunderbird (a prestigious, relatively high-priced car), hoping thereby to increase its sales of lower-priced Fords. Thunderbird was promoted separately, but the manufacturer made certain that prospective buyers of lower-priced cars were aware of the fact that this was a Ford-made automobile. Manufacturers trading up anticipate that a "halo" effect will be generated and carry over from the prestige item to a lower-priced and less prestigious product.

A company trades down when it adds a lower-priced product in the hope that people who would not, or could not, buy a higher-priced product will now buy because the new version carries some of the same prestige. Thus, in trading down, emphasis is on tapping a new market segment, one that earlier couldn't be reached effectively because the original version of the product carried too high a price. Again, Ford Motor Company provides an example: after successfully trading up with the Thunderbird, management detected an opportunity to tap a market segment of "people who would like to have a Thunderbird but can't afford it." The traded-down version was the Mustang, a car with some resemblance to the Thunderbird but much lower-priced. The Mustang became an outstanding success.

Despite many "success" stories on trading up and trading down, these strategies contain many potential pitfalls. The new product version, unless very skillfully marketed, may simply confuse potential buyers. In trading down, the new version may permanently damage a company's reputation as a quality producer. Evidently this happened to Packard and Studebaker, both of whom once made prestige automobiles but traded down to lower-priced models and ultimately became "also rans" and later "drop-outs," even in the lower-priced field. In trading up, present market segments must be convinced that the company is now really producing a higher-quality product worth the higher price and that this implies a general raising of quality and prestige for lower-priced products in the same line. Uplifting the entire quality image of a company is a difficult task and can easily backfire.

NEW PRODUCT—NO MARKET CHANGE

The "new product—no market change" strategy seeks increased profitability through selling a new product to the same market segment, the new product replacing an older product sold for the same general purpose. Thus, this strategy, also known as "product replacement" strategy, is aimed at retaining the level of sales now coming from a particular market segment, where these sales are being endangered by competitors' new products serving the same uses. Examples of new products that replaced old ones are numerous: to mention only a few—automobiles replaced carriages, diesel locomotives replaced steam locomotives, jet planes replaced piston-driven aircraft, the transistor is replacing the vacuum tube, and the electric typewriter has all but replaced the standard manual office typewriter.

Timing the market introduction of a replacement product is important. When ball point pens were first developed and the innovating company was introducing them to the market, makers of fountain pens were faced not only with whether to make ball point pens, but, if so, when. Most fountain pen producers evidently were more product-oriented than market-oriented, even though they themselves had earlier introduced fountain pens to replace quill pens. They were in the "writing instrument" business and didn't know it! Ideally, fountain pen makers should have introduced their ball point pens in time to compensate for the forthcoming losses in sales volume from fountain pens. Such decisions are likely to be better timed when management plans in advance the steps that will be taken during different stages in the product life cycle. For companies with products in the maturity stage, it is critical that there be products "waiting in the wings" ready for market introduction at the proper times.

NEW PRODUCT—IMPROVED MARKET

"New product—improved market" strategies aim to increase profitability through adding sales volume gained from new products sold to the same market segments. Often the new products are extensions of the present product line: for example, the ready-to-eat cereal is added to a line of "regular" cereals or "hole punchers" are added to a line of staplers, pencil sharpeners, and paper cutters. These strategies also are used to diversify into related product lines sold to the same market segments as present products. The Carnation Company, originally specializing in fresh and canned milk products, expanded its lines to include such items as pet foods, frozen foods, breakfast cereals, and canned tomato products.

Product Line Extension

When, in the minds of consumers or users, several products are regarded as a related group or line, management must decide whether or not to produce a "complete" line. Such is the case with kitchen and laundry appliances. Consumers seek these items in the same types of retail outlets and are sometimes looking for more than one appliance at the same time. The manufacturer's decision to make only one kind of appliance, or to make a complete line, should result from evaluation of several factors. He must be financially able to add new products. He should analyze the probable effect (of adding to the line) on the profits of his existing products. If he finds that numerous consumers prefer to buy matching appliances, a more complete line may increase sales of present products. At the same time, as he broadens his line, the marketing costs per category of products should be reduced, since little more promotion or selling effort may be required to sell the line than to sell a single appliance. Against these potential gains must be balanced the probability of success for the new products.

Does the company have the production, engineering, and general management "know-how" to develop and produce new products as good as its present products? Management also must evaluate the effect of the proposed additions on the reputations of established products. If consumers consider a new product inferior to those already in the line, it is possible for the entire line's reputation to suffer.

Diversification into Related Product Lines

There are two main reasons that companies diversify by adding related product lines sold to the same market segments as presently served. One is that this affords a way to capitalize further on company "know-how" in serving a particular market segment. The other is that the risk of sales volume (and profits) unexpectedly declining because the present product line becomes obsolescent is reduced. Market segments do not disappear suddenly, but products sometimes do!

How far a company should diversify into related product lines depends on various considerations. Will related-product diversification reduce the unit costs of selling and distributing to middlemen? Can the sales force sell the related product line effectively? What are the promotional expenses required? Who are the new competitors, what strategies do they employ, and what advantages do they have? Will there be a beneficial "halo" effect carrying over from the present line to the related line? Can the proposed new products actually be perfected, manufactured at a reasonable cost, and differentiated in ways attractive to potential buyers? The results of this type of analysis should permit management to calculate the expected profitability of adding the related product line.

NEW PRODUCT—NEW MARKET

The "new product—new market" strategy seeks to increase profitability through greater sales volumes obtained from selling new products in new markets. Thus, the strategy involves diversification into unrelated product lines sold to entirely different markets. Generally, this is the strategy emphasized by the so-called "conglomerates" as they go about consummating mergers and making acquisitions. Or perhaps unexpected break-throughs by scientific research staffs and the discovery of profitable opportunities to develop products for new markets cause management to believe that new product lines are within the scope of company capabilities. The Xerox Corporation provides an outstanding illustration. For years, it made only optical goods and special photographic papers, but it obtained access to an important patent, and its research personnel developed a unique copying method. Xerox then entered the copying machine market, a diversification that led to dramatic growth and further diversification involving new products for new markets.

AMFAC, originally an operator of Hawaiian sugar plantations, provides another example of unrelated product diversification. Over the years, AMFAC diversified into: hotel and restaurant operations, wholesaling (construction materials, machinery, appliances, and drugs), property ownership and management (office buildings, shopping centers, golf courses, and residential housing), operation of a chain of California and Nevada specialty stores, the financing of building loans, and providing consulting and management services for agricultural enterprises (e.g., in the Philippines, Australia, Kenya, and Central and South America). AMFAC's management denies that the company is a conglomerate saying:

> We in the management . . . do not consider AMFAC a conglomerate. Our areas of expansion are carefully planned to coincide with our areas of natural advantage, our proven managerial skills. Examples would include the development for tourism of some of the wonderful lands which are our agricultural legacy. We have also demonstrated to our own satisfaction that we can profitably manage retail stores, large agricultural operations, and the development of real estate property. Our business then continues to be diversified but not disunified.[9]

The "new product—new market" strategy involves considerably greater risk than any other product-market strategy. There is a total newness of both the product and the market to the company. Opportunities for such unrelated product-market diversification, consequently, merit the most careful investigation. Generally, too, for most companies, this strategy should only be considered after other strategies for increasing profits have been fully exploited. A company, in other words, is usually well-advised first to "fill out" its present product line, then to diversify into related product lines sold to the same markets, and, finally (after other profit-increasing possibilities are exhausted) to diversify into new markets with new products.

CONCLUSION

In this chapter, analysis focused on product-market strategies where either a "product change" or a "new product" is an element in the strategy. As is true of the different "no product change" strategies analyzed in Chapter

[9] AMFAC, Inc., *Annual Report 1968*, p. 3.

10, these are ways a company might use to increase its profitability. All of the strategies analyzed in this chapter aim to increase profitability mainly through securing sales volume increases. However, the "product line simplification and product discontinuance" form of the "product change—no market change" strategy is a cost-reducing method for increasing profits; and the "new product—no market change" strategy is aimed chiefly towards retaining sales volume (through selling replacement products to present markets) rather than adding new sales volume. You should again refer to Exhibit 10.1 on page 230—as a company chooses strategies toward the "southeastern" corner of this grid, it assumes greater risks of making bad choices. In other words, uncertainty increases with both the newness of a market and the newness of a product.

QUESTIONS AND PROBLEMS

1. "A company operating under the marketing concept must let its products proliferate. Otherwise how can it provide all dealers and customers with what they want?" Agree or disagree? State your reasoning fully.

2. "The way to control product proliferation is not to let it happen; kill off most proposed new additions before they are born." How much truth is there in this generalization?

3. Under what conditions should a company consider discontinuing unprofitable products? Profitable products?

4. How can you tell the difference between a "new model" and a "new product"? Is it possible that the same item might be regarded as a "new model" by one company, and as a "new product" by another? Why or why not?

5. What were the flaws in Henry Ford's reasoning that if you build a basically good product like the Model T, people will continue to buy it? Does the same reasoning apply to the Rolls Royce automobile?

6. What explains Volkswagen's success in departing from U.S. auto industry practice with respect to making annual model changes? Does the Volkswagen actually have planned obsolescence? Explain.

7. To what extent do you believe planned obsolescence is present in each of the following products? State your reasons in each case.
    a. Electric razors   d. Telephones
    b. Mens' neckwear   e. Jet aircraft
    c. Cameras   f. Textbooks

8.   Under what circumstances might a product customization strategy evolve into product proliferation?

9.   Discuss and compare the three main forms of product customization strategy.

10. Do you regard each of the following items as a "product system"? Why or why not?
     a. Frozen "TV Dinners"
     b. A refrigerator with a built-in automatic ice-maker
     c. A combination can opener and knife sharpener
     d. A portable electric vacuum sweeper with attachments for spray painting, deodorizing, etc.
     e. A dining room table with matching chairs and buffet.

11. What reasons would companies with large market shares, such as Coca-Cola and Pepsi-Cola in the cola market, have for entering new markets with changed products? For example, why did these two companies enter the market for dietary soft drinks?

12. Name some companies, other than those in the auto industry, that have used trading up or trading down strategies. Have these strategies been successful?

13. "Trading up should be used only when the economy is booming and trading down only during downswings in the business cycle." Agree or disagree?

14. Would you recommend that the following seriously consider adopting a "new product—no market change" strategy?
     a. A maker of blackboards for school use
     b. A producer of hand-operated calculating machines
     c. A cigarette manufacturer
     d. A grower of pole string beans who has just read that people are eating more artichokes and fewer string beans. His land is suitable for growing either.

15. Why might a company decide to diversify into related product lines rather than extending its present product line?

16. The "new product—new market" strategy involves considerably greater risk than any other product-market strategy. Why?

17. Prepare a list of all the product-market strategies discussed both in this and the previous chapter, including major variations of each strategy. Then, identify those that seek increased profitability through: (1) cost reduction, (2) increased sales, (3) both cost reduction and increased sales, and (4) through some other means.

PART 4

DISTRIBUTION

12

WHOLESALE DISTRIBUTION

Distribution is concerned with the various activities necessary to transfer goods from the producer to the consumer or user. It includes not only physical activities, such as the movement and storage of goods, but also the legal, promotional, and financial activities involved in the transfer of ownership. Since a succession of enterprises may be involved in the distribution process leading to the final sale to the consumer or user, to understand distribution one must analyze both the different types of marketing institutions and the marketing channels in which they operate.

In Part Four, we concern ourselves first, with the institutions that bring products into contact with markets and effect ownership transfers, second, with marketing channels, third, with the management decisions necessary to implement channels policy, and fourth, with the decisions necessary to implement other distribution policies. A *marketing channel, or channel of distribution, may be defined as a path traced in the direct or indirect transfer of title to a product, as it moves from a producer to ulti-*

mate consumers or industrial users.[1] Every marketing channel contains one or more of these "transfer points," at each of which there is either an institution or a final buyer of the product. In the process of marketing, legal title to the product changes hands at least once. (This bare minimum is reached in situations where producers deal directly with consumers or industrial users and there are no intervening middlemen.) Generally, legal title to the product passes from the producer to and through a series of middlemen before the consumer or industrial user finally takes possession. Transfer of title may be direct, as when the producer sells the product outright to a wholesaler or retailer, or it may be indirect, as when an agent middleman does not take title but simply negotiates its transfer. From the standpoint of the producer, such a network of institutions used for reaching a market is known as a marketing channel.

Our plan of presentation is to consider the individual classes of middlemen before we examine the different types of marketing channels. This does not mean that we believe middlemen are any more or less important than the channels in which they serve as transfer points. It *does* mean, however, that we think it logical to examine the building blocks—that is the institutions—before we look at the different ways they may be put together in order to constitute a marketing channel.

SOME NECESSARY DEFINITIONS

Before examining the specific types of wholesalers and retailers and their operating characteristics, we should provide formal definitions for the following terms: middleman, merchant, agent, retailer, wholesaler, retailing, and wholesaling. These words form part of virtually everyone's everyday vocabulary, but the meanings ordinarily attached do not always agree with those assigned by marketing analysts and executives. Most of these terms, when used in a marketing context, carry far more precise and restricted meanings than they do in common usage.[2]

---

[1] The American Marketing Association has had a Definitions Committee since 1931, but the concept "channel of distribution" was left undefined until 1960. The definition used above is in accord with normal business usage and is widely accepted among marketing educators. The chief reason the writers have chosen not to use the A.M.A. definition is that it does not take into account the significant role played by the transfer of title in tracing marketing channels. The A.M.A. definition considers a channel of distribution, or marketing channel, as "the structure of intra-company organization units and extra-company agents and dealers, wholesale and retail, through which a commodity, product, or service is marketed." See: Definitions Committee, *Marketing Definitions* (Chicago: American Marketing Association, 1960), p. 10.

[2] Unless otherwise noted, the definitions in this chapter are those compiled by the Committee on Definitions of the American Marketing Association, *ibid.*

Middleman

Middlemen specialize in performing operations or rendering services that are directly involved in the purchase and sale of goods in the process of their flow from producer to final buyer. As the name "middleman" indicates, such concerns are situated in marketing channels at points between producers and final buyers. Producers consider middlemen extensions of their own sales and marketing organizations, because if there were no middlemen, their own sales organizations would have to carry on all of the negotiations leading up to purchases by final buyers. Consumers and industrial users consider middlemen direct sources of goods and points of contact with producers.

Merchants and Agents

All middlemen fall into one of two broad classifications: merchants and agents. A *merchant middleman takes title to (that is, buys) and resells merchandise. An agent middleman negotiates* purchases *or* sales *or both, but does not take title to the goods in which he deals.* Thus, the chief distinguishing characteristic is whether the middleman takes title to the goods he handles. If he takes title, he is a merchant. If he does not, he is an agent. Also, the merchant always both buys and resells, whereas the agent *may* specialize in negotiating either buying or selling transactions.

Retailer and Wholesaler

Middlemen may also be separated into two other major categories—retailers and wholesalers. The principal base for distinguishing retailers and wholesalers relates to whether the business sells in significant amounts to ultimate consumers. If it does, the business is classed as a retailer. If it does not, it is classed as a wholesaler.

A *retailer is a merchant, or occasionally an agent, whose main business is selling directly to ultimate consumers.* He is distinguished by the nature of his sales rather than by the way he acquires the goods in which he deals. Although he usually sells in small lots, this condition is not essential for a business to be classified as a retailer. The dealer who sells the furniture and floor coverings for the initial outfitting of a large home, for instance, may make a sale of several thousand dollars, but it is still a retail sale, if the buyer (that is, the homeowner) is an ultimate consumer.

Wholesalers buy and resell merchandise to retailers and other merchants and to industrial, institutional, and commercial users, but do not sell in significant amounts to ultimate consumers. Notice that this definition does not state that the wholesaler must deal in large-size lots nor does it require that he habitually make sales for purposes of resale. Most wholesalers *do* sell in large lots, but there are many who do not. Similarly, most wholesalers sell for purposes of resale, but there are many who sell directly to industrial users. So, the one essential distinguishing feature of the wholesaler is that he must be a middleman who usually does not sell to ultimate consumers.

Retailing and Wholesaling

Retailing consists of the activities involved in selling directly to the ultimate consumer. It makes no difference who does the selling, but to be classified as retailing, selling activities must be *direct* to the ultimate consumer. Retailers, of course, are engaged in retailing, *but so is any other institution that sells directly to ultimate consumers.* Manufacturers engage in retailing when they make direct-to-consumer sales through their own stores, by house-to-house canvass, or by mail order. Even a wholesaler engages in retailing when he sells directly to an ultimate consumer, although his main business may still be wholesaling. *If the buyer in a transaction is an ultimate consumer, the seller in the same transaction is engaged in retailing.*

Wholesaling consists of the activities involved in selling to buyers other than ultimate consumers.[3] These buyers may be wholesalers and retailers who buy to resell. They may be industrial users (manufacturers, mining concerns, firms in other extractive industries), institutional users schools, prisons, and mental hospitals), commercial users (restaurants, hotels, and factory lunch rooms), government agencies, or farmers buying items they need to carry on their agricultural operations. Wholesaling may be carried on not only by wholesalers but by manufacturers, other producers, and other business units that make sales to buyers who are not ultimate consumers. *If the buyer in a transaction is buying for purposes of resale, or to further his business operations, the seller in that same transaction is engaged in wholesaling.* All sales not made to ultimate consumers may be properly described as wholesale sales.

PRODUCERS AS MARKETING CHANNEL COMPONENTS

In any marketing channel the producer is the seller in the first of the sequence of marketing transactions, which occur as the product moves toward its market. Such producers include enterprises engaged in manufacturing,

---

[3] The Committee on Definitions of the American Marketing Association does not provide a definition for "wholesaling."

in mining and the extractive industries, and in farming. Of these, manufacturers normally have the most power to influence the total sequence of transactions involving their products.

MANUFACTURERS   How much power a manufacturer has to influence this sequence of transactions depends on the opportunities he has for differentiating his product from those of competitors and his success in capitalizing on these opportunities. If his product can be differentiated and he can convince end-buyers (ultimate consumers or industrial users) that the differentiating features make it a better buy than competing items, the manufacturer has the power to gain a significant marketing advantage. An automobile manufacturer, for example, has many opportunities to differentiate his make of car, both in appearance and as to its performance and operating characteristics. The manufacturer of common nails, by contrast, has little opportunity to make his product much different from those of his competitors.

Capitalizing on a product differentiation opportunity requires more than simply convincing end-buyers of the superiority of the manufacturer's product. It must be possible for end-buyers to obtain the product from their suppliers at prices they are able and willing to pay. Different middlemen vary as to the "support" they are prepared and willing to give the manufacturer in terms of stocking, promoting, and actively selling the product. Different middlemen also vary as to what it "costs" the manufacturer to use them as components in his marketing channel, and this affects the price that end-buyers ultimately have to pay. Balancing the need for support with the costs involved, the manufacturer tries to put together a distributive network that results in end-buyers having ready access to outlets handling the product at prices they consider reasonable. If the product is capable of much differentiation in ways that are important to end-buyers, the manufacturer can exercise considerable discretion in selecting members for his channel team—i.e., he has considerable power to control the sequence of transactions involving his product as it moves to market. If there is little opportunity for product differentiation, he has little power to control this sequence of transactions.

The manufacturer whose product is capable of being differentiated seeks to exercise some control over the order in which his product changes hands as it goes to market.[4] Usually, as explained above, the manufacturer devotes his primary attention to the market—the end-buyers of his product. Starting with the market, the manufacturer attempts to detail the sequence of steps required to supply it with his product. Even before this, however, the manufacturer has tried to identify and evaluate end-buyers' needs and

---

[4] For a discussion of the relationship of product differentiation and the manufacturer's decisions on branding, see Chapter 10, pp. 242-247.

the strength of market demand and, in his research and product development work, has attempted to design a product that meets these needs.

The sequence of steps required for moving the product to market, of course, may or may not call for the services of middlemen at one or more distribution levels. Even after he decides on this sequence—i.e., the marketing channel—the manufacturer often devotes considerable effort to assure that the planned series of transactions takes place. Through his advertising and other promotional activities, for instance, he may work to build demand to the point where end-buyers insist that suppliers stock and sell the product. Or, as another example, the manufacturer may use his advertising to end-buyers as a vehicle for directing prospective customers to outlets where the product is on sale. In these and similar ways, the manufacturer seeks to assure that his distribution network will function according to plan.

OTHER PRODUCERS   Enterprises not engaged in manufacturing, such as mining concerns, firms in other extractive industries, and farmers, are much less able to exert significant influences over the total sequence of marketing transactions involving their products. These producers usually can do very little about differentiating their outputs to meet end-buyers' needs more closely, so opportunities for product differentiation are practically non-existent. Furthermore, producers engaged in non-manufacturing activities generally find it very difficult to stimulate the demand for their products. Demand for the mining company's output, for instance, is derived from the demand for products manufactured by its customers. The demand for aluminum, in other words, depends upon the demand for products fabricated by customers of aluminum mining companies—i.e., the demand for aluminum *per se* derives from the demand for such products as aluminum beach chairs, pots and pans, golf carts, and aluminum siding and sash used in building construction. It might seem logical, then, for the mining company to direct its efforts toward stimulating the demand for its customers' products. Individual mining companies, however, are often too small to finance and mount promotional programs of the size that would be needed. A few large companies, as in the aluminum and steel industries, have had some success in stimulating the demand for products fabricated from aluminum and steel, but these companies are primarily engaged in manufacturing, even though they operate their own mines.

The farmer's situation is similar to that of the mining company, for unless he sells his crop through a cooperative, he is generally unable to support the extensive promotional program necessary to exert a significant influence on the demand for his product. Moreover, the demand for farm products usually is derived from the demand for products of processors of agricultural commodities. When certain food processors in the 1960s, for instance, began making oleomargarine out of "100% pure corn oil" and successfully promoted the health benefits of the new product to large numbers of customers, increases in the demand for corn followed increases in the demand for corn oil margarine. Furthermore, unlike most manufacturers who find it relatively easy to drop or add products as demand conditions change, many farmers, such as orchardists, cattlemen, and grain farmers, are limited to a single crop by virtue of their land, equipment, and experience. Thus, they are unable to adjust the nature of their outputs to fit the changing needs and preferences of end-buyers.

Different types of producers enjoy different degrees of power in controlling the flow of their product through marketing channels to final markets. In general, manufacturers have the most power and are able (within certain limits, which we will discuss later) to use channels containing the type and number of transfer points, which, in their opinion, are most appropriate for product and market. Farmers and companies in the extractive industries cannot direct the flow of their products to market. But their products do eventually get to market, even though the marketing process tends to be more involved and roundabout than it is with most manufactured products. Marketing channels serving the extractive industries tend to develop in an unplanned way, the way a river "cuts" its own course.

Individual Producers and Channel "Length"

A producer's concern with channel management varies with the "length" of the marketing channel. "Length," as used here, has to do with the number of middlemen between the producer and the final buyers. A long channel has a series of middlemen on different distribution levels. A short one has few intermediaries or none. In the shortest possible channel, with no middlemen at all, the producer does everything necessary to negotiate legal transfers of title to the product being marketed with the end-buyers. With the addition of one or more middlemen to the channel, negotiating responsibility is divided between the producer and middlemen on each level—i.e., the producer sells to the middlemen, and they, in turn, resell the product to other middlemen or final buyers.

To the extent that the producer is able to control the length of the marketing channel, he determines his own role in the series of negotiating transactions leading up to the sale to the ultimate consumer or industrial user. If the consumer goods manufacturer, for example, deals directly with ultimate consumers, he is serving as his own retailer. If he sells through retail middlemen and contacts them directly, he is acting as his own wholesaler.

Producers' Cooperative Marketing Associations

Hoping to improve the efficiency with which their produce is marketed, some groups of producers, chiefly in agriculture but sometimes in other extractive industries, have organized and operated producers' cooperative marketing associations. These associations represent the collective effort of small producers who desire to gain more control over the distribution of their output, in the hope of reducing distribution costs and exerting favorable influences on demand. Cooperative endeavors of this type have tended to put their member agricultural producers more on a par with manufacturers—at least so far as marketing channels are concerned.

The cooperative marketing association, with its great size and the specialized attention its management can give to marketing activities, can usually make it possible to bypass one or more levels of middlemen in the more conventional marketing channels for agricultural products. Sometimes, only the assembler or broker of agricultural products is eliminated by the cooperative, but it often extends its marketing operations even to such activities as maintaining sales offices in important marketing areas, as is done by Sunkist Growers, Inc., a cooperative marketer of citrus fruits grown in California and Arizona. Most agricultural cooperative marketing associations are set up to handle the packing and grading of their members' crops, usually at a lower cost than they can manage by themselves. Some, such as Sunkist Growers, have gone so far as to affix brands to their produce and conduct extensive promotional programs designed to build and maintain consumer recognition of the brand and to enlarge demand for it. Thus, the cooperative marketing association is often able to provide its members with enhanced power in controlling the flow of their product through marketing channels to final markets.

One additional feature of the operations of many producers' cooperative marketing associations deserves mention. Many purchase such items as seed, fertilizers, tools and implements, and gasoline and oil for resale to their members, and a few also deal in various consumer goods. A few only market crops grown by the farmer-members but operate "stores" to supply members and others with items used on farms and other such diverse goods as grass seed, lawn mowers, automobile tires, and food for wild birds.

MERCHANT WHOLESALERS

There are two main ways of classifying merchant wholesalers. First, according to the range of merchandise they handle, they may be classified as (1) general merchandise wholesalers, (2) general-line wholesalers, and (3) specialty wholesalers. The second is to classify them by their method of operation as (1) service wholesalers and (2) limited-function wholesalers. These major classes of merchant wholesalers and the most significant of their subclasses are discussed below.

Classification by Range of Merchandise Handled

GENERAL MERCHANDISE WHOLESALERS   A general merchandise wholesaler is a merchant wholesaler who carries a general assortment of goods in two or more distinct and unrelated merchandise lines. For instance, such a wholesaler may stock and sell dry goods, hardware, furniture, farm implements, electrical equipment, sporting goods, and household appliances. At one time, particularly during the heyday of the retail general store, staple groceries were the main stock-in-trade of general merchandise wholesalers. But with the rise of cities, the growth of population, and the development of new types of retail institutions more appropriate to the times, the retail general store began to disappear from the scene, and with its gradual disappearance came a decline in the importance of general merchandise wholesalers. Today there are comparatively few left.

GENERAL-LINE WHOLESALERS   The general-line wholesaler carries a broad assortment of goods within a single merchandise line, but he may also handle limited stocks of goods in closely related lines. Thus, a general-line grocery wholesaler usually carries not only a complete stock of canned fruits and vegetables, cereals, tea and coffee, and other "grocery store" items but also razor blades, soaps and detergents, toothpaste, school supplies and other items commonly sold in retail grocery stores. In consumer goods marketing, general-line wholesalers are important distributors of groceries, drugs, and hardware to independent retailers in these fields. In industrial goods marketing, general-line wholesalers are known as "industrial distributors" and supply such merchandise lines as electrical, plumbing, and heating goods to both large and small industrial users.

The importance of the general-line wholesaler in consumer goods marketing has declined with the rise of corporate chains, and other retail institutions, which prefer to buy directly from producers. Similarly, there has been a trend among industrial users toward direct buying from producers, which has had a repressing effect on general-line wholesalers of industrial goods. But, since small-scale independent retailers continue in business and industrial users continue to need items in quantities too small to justify direct purchase, general-line wholesalers remain important marketing intermediaries in both consumer and industrial goods markets.

SPECIALTY WHOLESALERS   The specialty wholesaler carries only part of a merchandise line, but within his restricted range of offerings he has a very complete assortment. In the wholesale grocery trade, for instance, specialty wholesalers may specialize in canned foods; coffee, tea and spices; dairy products; frosted and frozen foods; or soft drinks. The specialty wholesaler represents an advanced step in what seems to be a universal trend among merchant wholesalers to restrict merchandise offerings by specializing.

Specialty wholesalers generally pride themselves on the strong promotional support they provide for the restricted number of manufacturers' brands they handle. They can provide this strong support because they concentrate on relatively few items of merchandise. It is possible for the specialty grocery wholesaler's salemen, for instance, in the routine performance of their duties, to "push" every item handled on every sales call. They also perform such promotional activities on behalf of manufacturers' brands as erecting special displays, handling in-store product demonstrations, and arranging for the distribution of samples. Salesmen working for general-line grocery wholesalers, by contrast, find it impossible to give special "push" to more than a handful of the many thousands of different items in stock; the great breadth of this stock also makes it difficult for them to engage in many promotional activities on behalf of any one manufacturers' brand. However, the narrowness of the specialty wholesaler's merchandise offering, together with the necessity for providing strong promotional support for all items handled, causes him to concentrate on areas where there are large numbers of retail outlets. Selling only a few items and strongly promoting each one, he can make economical use of salesmen only in areas where there are many retailers to call on and relatively little travel time is required to get from one stop to the next. The specialty wholesaler's salesmen usually make very frequent calls on retailers but, as this makes it possible for retailers to carry smaller stocks, the average size of retailers' orders is small.

The operating scheme of combining high call frequency and low average order size restricts the opportunity for specialty wholesaling to areas where retail outlets are close together and numerous—such areas as those in the heavily industrialized and thickly populated parts of New England, the Middle Atlantic states, the Midwest, and the Pacific Coast. In certain other areas (such as are found in many Rocky Mountain states and rural sections of the South), the population is sparse, cities and towns are far apart, and the resulting pattern is one where retail outlets are widely scattered and few in number; consequently, because these conditions do not lend themselves to this type of operation, there are relatively few specialty wholesalers in such areas.

Classification by Method of Operation

Merchant wholesalers generally perform many functions for their customers. Those who perform all or most of the functions and services normally expected in the wholesale trade, are known as *service wholesalers*. (These functions are: selling and merchandising, buying and assembling, storage, transportation, risk bearing, marketing financing, and market information.) General-line wholesalers perform these functions, and so also may be classed as service wholesalers. Some specialty wholesalers perform only a few of these services; others perform many. So, depending on the extent of his service, a specialty wholesaler may be classed either as a service wholesaler or as a limited-function wholesaler, who performs only a few of the functions normally associated with wholesaling operations. The main types of limited-function wholesalers are discussed below.

TRUCK WHOLESALERS   Combining selling, delivery, and collection in one operation, truck wholesalers (also known as wagon jobbers) carry only a limited range of stock, though the selection within that range may be very complete. Thus, the nature of a truck wholesaler's merchandise offering also makes him a specialty wholesaler. Truck wholesalers call mainly on retailers, though some, such as those in the grocery trade, also call on restaurants, hotels, and other food service establishments. Because the items they handle are often perishables or semiperishables, truck wholesalers have to make very frequent calls on their customers, and indeed it is their ability to make fast and frequent deliveries that appeals to both their customers and the manufacturers they deal with.

RACK JOBBERS   The rack jobber is a wholesaling unit that markets specialized lines of merchandise to certain types of retail stores and provides certain special services. The merchandising policies of most rack jobbers cause them also to be classed as specialty wholesalers. The original rack jobbers evolved after World War II to serve the special needs of supermarkets which, in increasing numbers, were adding non-food lines. Rack jobbers serving supermarkets and other grocery retailers usually specialize in one or both of two lines—toiletries and/or housewares. Managers of retail stores served by rack jobbers are relieved of the merchandising problems involved in handling what are for them "sundry items" and are free to concentrate their efforts on their major lines. The rack jobber may or may not furnish his own display racks but, basically, all that he requires of the retailer is an allocation of selling space, which he stocks with a selection of items priced for immediate sale. Occasionally, the rack jobber may instead supply merchandise on consignment: that is, the jobber retains legal title to the merchandise up to the time the retailer sells it, the retailer paying only for the goods he sells and retaining a portion of the profit for himself. Through aggressive merchandising and efficient use of displays, rack jobbers have built up a large volume of non-food sales in grocery stores. Manufacturers of non-food lines find that rack jobbers provide an effective means for achieving low cost distribution through retail food stores.

CASH-AND-CARRY WHOLESALERS   Cash-and-carry wholesalers pursue at the wholesale level the same sort of service policy that has been successful in certain types of retail operations. Whereas service wholesalers send their salesmen to retailers to solicit orders, later deliver these orders, and grant credit to retailers, allowing them to pay at later dates, cash-and-carry wholesalers require retailers to come to the wholesale warehouse, "pick" their own orders, pay cash for what they buy, and carry away their own purchases. By restricting the services he will perform and lowering his operating costs, the cash-and-carry wholesaler can price his goods lower than can service wholesalers. Price, then, is what attracts retailers to the cash-and-carry wholesaler. But, because retailers must perform additional services for themselves, they often find that by the time the order gets to the store, its cost is every bit as high as if it were purchased from a service wholesaler. However, cash-and-carry operations do provide an economical means for wholesalers to use in reaching many small retailers who customarily buy in lots too small to justify the wholesaler's sending out salesmen, providing delivery, and extending credit.

DROP-SHIPMENT WHOLESALERS   The drop-shipment wholesaler is a limited-function wholesaler who does not physically handle the goods he sells but leaves the storage and transportation functions to the manufacturers whom he represents. When goods are ordered, the manufacturer ships them directly to the retailer, but bills the drop shipper at factory prices. Subsequently, the drop shipper collects from the retailer. This system of distribution makes possible reductions in the costs of transportation and storage. It eliminates the necessity for double hauling (i.e., from the factory to the wholesaler and then on to the retailer), and no costs are incurred for handling goods in a wholesaler's warehouse. However, customers ordering through drop shippers often order in comparatively small lot sizes and, because freight rates are higher for small lots than for large lots, some of the savings from eliminating double hauling are offset by higher shipping costs. The retailer, to make economical use of drop shipments, must both order in larger than normal quantities and adjust his operations to allow for longer periods during which the goods are in transit. These adjustments are necessary since most retailers are separated by greater distances from the manufacturers' plants than they are from the relatively nearby wholesalers, who serve as alternate supply points. Finally, the need for ordering in larger than normal quantities requires that the retailer invest additional funds in his inventory. Despite these unattractive features, however, retailers often find that the savings in cost are sufficient to justify drop shipments. This is especially true with standard, fast-selling items—ones which sell regardless of season and where the retailer bears little risk of being unable to resell the merchandise.

Drop-shipment wholesalers are also much used in industrial marketing. They are important distributors of such products as sand, clay, coal, and lumber, where transportation costs are high relative to the value of the products and where, accordingly, any interruption of deliveries causing breaks in production may lead to significant cost increases.[5] Industrial users consume these items in such large quantities and with such great regularity that it pays them to have several shipments in transit at any one time, each spaced to arrive before it is needed and always allowing some margin of safety for late arriving shipments. Thus, the industrial user manages to "work around" the long period during which drop shipments are in transit. Furthermore, these are items which the customers normally buy in lots large enough to gain freight rates as low as any a wholesale middleman might secure.

MAIL-ORDER WHOLESALERS   Mail-order wholesalers are limited-function wholesalers who sell entirely by mail. The mail-order wholesaler substitutes mail-order catalogs and order forms for a sales force and passes on to retailers some of his savings in the form of lower prices. This limited-function wholesaler is mainly active in wholesaling such staple consumer goods as hardware and dry goods. With modern improvements in transportation and communication, there has been a sharp decline in the importance of mail-order wholesalers. The basic weakness of this type of operation is that it fails to provide a really adequate substitute for the strong promotional push salesmen can give. Moreover, its success rests on the willingness of retailers to take the initiative in placing orders, something that cannot always be counted on—especially when competitors' salesmen call on retailers in person.

AGENT MIDDLEMEN

Agent middlemen, most of whom are active in wholesaling rather than in retailing, assist in negotiating sales or purchases or both on behalf of their principals, who may be buyers or sellers or both. Usually, the agent does not represent both buyer and seller in the same transaction, and he is ordinarily

[5] D. A. Revzan, *Wholesaling in Marketing Organization* (New York: John Wiley & Sons, 1961), p. 35.

paid by commission or fee. Although agent wholesalers as a group are active in many lines of trade, individual agents customarily concentrate on such lines as foods, grain, copper, steel, machinery, or textiles. The main types of agent wholesalers are brokers, commission houses, manufacturers' agents, selling agents, and resident buyers.

Brokers

A broker is an agent who represents either buyer or seller in negotiating purchases or sales without physically handling the goods involved. The broker is more often the agent of the owner of goods seeking a buyer than the agent of a buyer searching for a source of supply. Each broker tends to specialize in arranging transactions for a limited number of items and, as a result, he should be well informed concerning conditions in these particular markets.

Acting strictly as an intermediary, the broker has limited powers as to prices and terms of sale, and he possesses little or no authority to bargain on behalf of his principal. His main service is to bring buyer and seller together. Representing either the seller or the buyer (but not usually both in the same transaction), the broker relays the buyer's offer to the seller and the seller's counter-offer to the buyer and continues this process until the terms are satisfactory to both parties, at which time the exchange takes place. He never has direct physical control over the goods, but sells by description or sample. Whenever he arranges a sale, the seller ships the goods directly to the buyer. The broker receives his commission from the principal who sought his services.

Brokers are most used by producers who sell their products at infrequent intervals and find it uneconomical to establish standing sales forces of their own or even to establish long-term relationships with other types of agent wholesalers. Although an individual producer may use the same broker year after year, each transaction is considered completely apart from every other. There is no obligation, on the part of either the broker or the seller, to maintain this relationship in future transactions. Small canners, whose production volumes are too small to justify their developing and promoting brands of their own, and whose entire output may be produced in a period of two or three months, often rely on brokers to dispose of their packs. Similarly, farmers harvesting one major crop a year often find it economical to use brokers.

Sometimes, brokers are also used by larger companies who want to extend the distribution of their products. In such instances, brokers serve as key middlemen in arranging initial distribution of the product among other types of middlemen. Thus, a broker may be instrumental in opening up a new market for the producer or in gaining access to outlets previously not stocking the product.

Commission Houses

The commission house is an agent that usually exercises physical control over and negotiates the sale of the goods it handles. The commission house usually enjoys broader powers as to prices, methods, and terms of sale than the broker does, although it must also obey instructions issued by the principal. Generally, it arranges delivery, extends necessary credit, collects, deducts its fees, and remits the balance to the principal. Thus, except for the fact that it does not take title, the commission house performs functions very similar to those of service merchant wholesalers—more so in fact than any other agent wholesaler.

Most commission houses are concerned with the distribution of fresh fruit and produce. The relationship of the commission house and its principal generally covers a harvest and marketing season. The truck farmer, for instance, signs a seasonal agreement with a commission house situated in a market center and ships the crop as it is harvested. The commission house is authorized to sell each shipment on arrival at the best price obtainable without checking back with the seller. Although legal title to the goods never passes to the house, it sells in its own name, bills buyers, extends credit, makes collections, deducts its fees, and sends the balance to the truck farmer. Although the farmer might prefer to hold his produce off the market at times and bargain for higher prices, the factor of perishability makes any delays in selling risky. The operation of the commission house is especially geared for rapid sale of perishable commodities, the chief reason for the commission house's continuing importance in agricultural marketing.

Manufacturers' Agents

Four main features characterize the operations of the manufacturer's agent: (1) he has an extended contractual relationship with his principal; (2) he handles sales for his principal within an exclusive territory; (3) he handles non-competing but related lines of goods; (4) he possesses limited authority with regard to prices and terms of sales. Some manufacturers' agents have physical control over an inventory, but most do not. Ordinarily the manufacturer's agent arranges for shipments to be sent directly from the factory to the buyer. Because his principal service is selling, the manufacturer's agent maintains a sales staff large enough to provide adequate coverage of his market area. The manufacturer's agent sells at prices, or within a price range, stipulated by his principal, and receives a percentage commission based on sales.

Manufacturers' agents are generally used when a manufacturer finds it uneconomical to use his own salesmen or when he is financially unable to maintain his own sales force. Some manufacturers, for instance, find that certain market areas simply do not provide enough business to justify their assigning salesmen to them. Yet, manufacturers' agents, each representing several principals, may be able to operate profitably in the same areas. Thus, it is not at all unusual for manufacturers to use their own salesmen in areas where there are large concentrations of potential business and to use manufacturers' agents elewhere. Others use agents to open up new market areas and replace them with their own salesmen as the volume of business grows. Still others, particularly those with narrow product lines and those that are very small, use a network of manufacturers' agents to avoid altogether the problems and expenses of maintaining their own sales forces.

Manufacturers' agents are most important in the marketing of industrial goods and such consumer durables as furniture and hardware. In industrial marketing, they usually employ salesmen who have considerable technical competence and contact industrial users directly. In marketing consumer durables, they generally call on and sell to retailers. Many furniture manufacturers rely on manufacturers' agents to sell their entire output. In many cases the manufacturer's agent can, because of his intimate contact with the market, offer advice to the manufacturer on a wide variety of matters, including styling, design, and pricing.

Selling Agents

The selling agent operates on an extended contractual basis, negotiates all sales of a specified line of merchandise or the entire output of his principal, and usually has full authority with regard to prices, terms, and other conditions of sale. Thus, he differs from the manufacturer's agent in that he ordinarily is not confined to operating within a given market area, has much more authority to set prices and terms of sale, and is the sole selling agent for the line he represents.

Some selling agents render financial aid to their principals. This practice traces to the historical fact that early selling agents were usually much stronger financially than the principals they represented. Many textile mills, for instance, were originally started with the financial backing of selling agents, who saw this as a way to increase their own business volumes and, hence, their commissions. Today, selling agents rarely provide their principals with investment capital, but many help principals in financing current operations. Because many modern-day selling agents continue to have higher credit ratings than their principals, it is common for them to endorse their principal's short-term notes at banks and other lending institutions. Occasionally, too, a selling agent assists his principal financially, either by making direct loans on accounts receivable or by "guaranteeing" these accounts so that a lender will advance needed funds to the principal. There has, however, been a trend away from this type of financing service by selling agents. This trend has accelerated with the growth of financial institutions known as *factors*, who specialize in "discounting accounts receivable"—that is, in making short-term loans with accounts receivable as the collateral.

The manufacturer who uses a selling agent, in effect, shifts most of the marketing responsibility to an outside organization. This frees the manufacturer to concentrate on production and on other non-marketing problems. In addition, as the selling agent is in close contact with buyers, he often is able to guide the manufacturer on styling, design, and pricing. Fairly often, he assists his principal with or takes over sales promotion and advertising. Sometimes, the selling agent, as is true of some in the textile and apparel trades, even specifies the features that his principal should build into the product and how much he should manufacture. Furthermore, since the selling agent works for a straight commission, the principal's selling costs vary proportionately with sales made, and no fixed selling costs are incurred. Thus, for all these reasons, it is not surprising that small manufacturers with neither the managerial talent nor the financial strength to market their own products use selling agents.

The manufacturer using a selling agent, however, should realize that he is "placing all his marketing eggs in one basket." Since the selling agent is the manufacturer's only contact with the market, the bulk of the bargaining power rests with the agent and not the manufacturer. Recognizing this, selling agents may be tempted to resort to price-cutting instead of exerting reasonable amounts of selling effort to sell the manufacturer's output. In such situations, the manufacturer, cut off from the buyers by the selling agent and having dealt with them only through this intermediary, is really "over a barrel." If he is weak financially and needs loans which cannot be obtained without his selling agent's help, he may not even be able to break with the selling agent in order to obtain another. The moral is clear: if a manufacturer is going to use a selling agent, his first choice should be a good one.

Resident Buyers

A resident buyer differs from most other agent middlemen in that he represents buyers only. Specializing in buying for retailers, he receives his compensation on a fee or commission basis. The resident buyer operates most often in lines of trades such as furniture and apparel where there are well-defined "market centers" to which retailers ordinarily travel to make their selections. Resident buyers maintain their offices in such market centers and whenever retailers are unable to make the trip to market in person, serve as retailers' contacts with the sources of supply.

Resident buyers are completely independent of their principals. They should not be confused with the resident buying offices that are owned by out-of-town stores and are maintained in such market centers as New York. Nor should they be confused with the central buying offices maintained by chain store organizations. The resident buyer is purely and simply an independent agent specializing in buying for principals who are retailers.

Auction Companies

As indicated by its name, this agent uses the auction method of catalogues and competitive bidding by prospective buyers to sell products owned by its principals. Auction companies are particularly important in selling products of varying quality and products which cannot be efficiently graded—situations frequent in agricultural marketing. In the fresh fruit and vegetable trade, auction companies are located in central markets, that is in cities that are important distributing points for such items. In the marketing of livestock and such agricultural crops as leaf tobacco, auction companies are located in principal producing areas and at shipping points. An auction company has physical control over the lots consigned to it, arranges for their display, conducts the auction, makes collections from the buyers, and remits the proceeds to the principals, less commissions.

Other Agents

Other types of agent middlemen have evolved to serve many special needs. It appears that whenever a large enough group of buyers or sellers needs some special marketing service, there are always enterprising individuals who will set up in business to provide that service. For instance, there are export and import agents operating in leading port cities who serve the needs of principals seeking foreign markets or overseas sources of supply. And there are purchasing agents, which are independent businesses, specializing in locating sources of supply for buyers of industrial goods. But the basic function of all agents is the same: they all help to bring buyers and sellers together and receive fees or commissions in return for their efforts.

CONCLUSION

Wholesale distribution is of major importance to all firms selling to buyers who buy for purposes of resale or to further their business or other operations. Thus, except for those relatively few producers selling their outputs directly and exclusively to ultimate consumers, all producers are confronted with, and must find solutions to, problems in wholesale distribution. Wholesaling middlemen include both merchants, who actually take ownership to the products being marketed, and agents, who negotiate ownership transfers rather than actually taking title themselves. Discussion in this chapter focused mainly on the nature of the operations of different types of wholesalers and on producers' relationships with them.

QUESTIONS AND PROBLEMS

1. What is the value of trying to differentiate between wholesalers and retailers, when a great many institutions are carrying on both wholesaling and retailing activities? Has this distinction become artificial?

2. Producers who can differentiate their products have greater control over the channel through which their products are sold, but is there any real advantage in such control? Would not the traditional channel ordinarily be the best? Discuss.

3. Would you think that the greatest strength of a producers' cooperative lies in the economies of size or in its greater ability to differentiate its products? Explain.

4. General merchandise wholesalers have, to a large extent, faded from the American scene, but general-line wholesalers have retained a fairly important role. Why do you suppose this has happened?

5. Shouldn't it be to the advantage of a retailer to deal only with a very limited number of general-line wholesalers instead of a much larger number of specialty wholesalers? If so, how can you explain the greater growth of specialty wholesalers?

6. Limited-service retailers have captured an increasingly important share of the market in recent years. Why, then, haven't limited function wholesalers managed to do the same thing at the wholesale level?

7. Would it be proper to say that the primary appeal of the truck wholesaler is that he allows the retailer to reduce his rate of inventory turnover? Explain.

8. Wouldn't it seem logical that, if a rack jobber can sell "sundry items" at a profit in food stores, the management of large food chains should be able to do the same job as profitably? Why, then, do many of these chains use rack jobbers?

9. Would you be likely to find cash-and-carry wholesalers in the same kinds of cities and the same general locations as service wholesalers? Explain.

10. Is there likely to be any real advantage in using drop shipment wholesalers, if the retailer finds it necessary to buy in larger than normal quantities so as to keep transportation costs in line?

11. Would it be a fair assessment to say that the primary cause for the lack of success of mail-order wholesalers is laziness on the part of retail buyers? Comment.

12. The choice as to whether a farmer is more likely to use a broker or a commission house to sell his product will depend primarily on the length of his harvest season and the perishability of his product. Do you agree?

13. Would you agree that a manufacturer should normally look on the manufacturer's agent as a temporary distributor, to be used only until he can be replaced by the company's own salesmen?

14. How does the selling agent's operation differ from that of a manufacturers' agent?

15. What is a resident buyer? In what respects is his operation unique?

16. Purchasing through an auction company is an inefficient method of procurement. Comment on this statement.

13

RETAIL DISTRIBUTION

Retailing consists of those activities involved in selling directly to ultimate consumers; therefore, retailing occurs in all marketing channels for consumer products. Although a few producers of consumer products engage in retailing directly, most of them rely on various types of retail institutions to distribute their outputs to ultimate consumers. Retailers are the most numerous of all marketing institutions, and wherever there is more than a handful of people, there are retailers.

Individual retailers adjust their operations to the ultimate consumer market when they determine the merchandise they will handle, their scale of operations, pricing policy, locations, and selling methods, and by the choices they make on other operating policies and practices. Because of the many choices open to retailers, there is tremendous variety among retail institutions. They range all the way from the corner grocer to the multi-billion dollar corporate chain. But regardless of the specific class of retail institution, the basic economic purpose remains the same: buying and assembling the products of manufacturers and other producers and reselling them to ultimate consumers. Operating characteristics of the main classes of retail institutions are set forth and analyzed in the following sections. The only significance attached to the order of treatment is that it is generally chronological—the oldest are treated first and the more recent developments later.

RETAILERS

House-to-House Selling

Modern house-to-house salesmen are descended from the "Yankee peddlers" who, on foot, on horseback, and then in wagons, traveled from farm to farm and settlement to settlement selling various manufactured articles to pioneers and frontiersmen. Today's house-to-house salesman, however, usually restricts his offerings to a small number of articles within a single merchandise line. He may specialize in encyclopedias, lawn and garden stock, vacuum cleaners, china, cosmetics, or household cleaning materials. Although many house-to-house salesmen are "free-lance," independent small businessmen, most of them work for large manufacturing companies using this retailing method; among these are such well-known organizations as Avon Products (toilet articles), The Fuller Brush Company (household articles), and Real Silk Hosiery Mills (hosiery, dresses and lingerie). The sales people employed by the larger house-to-house organizations are almost equally divided among men and women, and more than half work at their jobs on a part-time basis. Thus, it is not unusual for a direct selling company to have from 5,000 to 10,000 sales people, nearly all working on a commission basis. Avon Products is said to have over 350,000 people, mostly women, selling part-time in its world-wide operation.[1]

Although house-to-house selling eliminates the expenses of retail store operation, it is by no means a low-cost retailing method. It requires travel and personal contact and substantial costs are involved in recruiting, maintaining, and managing sales staffs large enough to transact a profitable volume of sales. These cost conditions have had an effect on the operating methods of direct selling companies. Many handle either fairly high-priced items or articles that are sold in assortments, the purpose in both cases being that of building up the average order size. Some, such as The Fuller Brush Company, strive to make more effective use of salesmen's time by establishing steady customers. Fuller product prices range from $1 to $17, and management believes this ceiling is low.[2] Others, such as Stanley Home

[1] "Operation Brush Up," *Sales Management*, January 15, 1969, p. 6.
[2] *Ibid.*, p. 7.

Products, have been successful in using "party plan selling," in which a group of potential buyers are brought together in one of their homes for a product demonstration; several orders often result at one time. The commissions paid to house-to-house sales people usually range from 25 to 40 percent of the amount of the retail sale.

The total costs of house-to-house selling run to approximately 60 percent of sales. This estimate includes not only salesmen's commissions, but the costs of supervision and administration, clerical work, shipping, credit, and promotion and advertising. This may appear high, and it is for retailing. But companies using house-to-house selling normally do not have to allow for wholesalers' and retailers' margins, nor do they generally have large amounts of fixed selling and administrative expense. Whether house-to-house selling is an expensive retail distribution method depends on what the manufacturer's alternatives are. If they involve the use of wholesalers and retailers and the maintenance of a full-time permanent staff of salaried salesmen, it may well be that house-to-house selling is economical by comparison.

There are times when house-to-house selling is the best solution to a manufacturer's retail distribution problems. Sometimes this is the only way a radically different new product can be introduced, particularly by a company with limited finances. It is said, for example, that the inventor and original manufacturer of one of the finest can-openers had tried unsuccessfully to secure distribution through wholesalers and conventional retailers. The threat of imminent bankruptcy caused him to try door-to-door selling, which proved successful. A few years later, he had no difficulty in securing distribution through conventional retailers. Some products seem to sell more easily when demonstrated in the home, and this seems to be the key to the success of house-to-house sellers of vacuum cleaners, sewing machines, and rug cleaners. Still other products, such as encyclopedias and bibles, appear to be ones where most consumers will not initiate buying action by searching them out in retail stores, but which they will buy if approached in their homes.

Independent Stores

An independent store is a retailing business controlled by its own individual ownership or management. Although there are both large and small independent stores, most large-scale, independently-owned stores are classified under such other headings as supermarkets, department stores, and discount houses. In our discussion, we consider an independent store to be any individually-owned or managed retail business, small or large, which cannot be readily classified as a supermarket, department store, or discount house. We use this working definition to side-step the problem of distinguishing small-scale from large-scale retailers. How does one, after all, decide where "small" ends and "large" begins? The sales-volume yardstick is the one most used, but number of employees, square feet of floor space, and inventory dollar size have all been tried. One difficulty with all these measures is that the dividing line must still be chosen arbitrarily, and, furthermore, the idea of just what "large" means keeps changing. In the 1950's a grocery store with $500,000 in annual sales was considered rather large, but by 1970 a store in that same range was considered small. Thus, the criteria for largeness are constantly being revised upwards. Nonetheless, since at any given time some retailers *are* smaller than others, we will refer to independent retailers as being relatively "small" or "large."

THE GENERAL STORE   The general store is one of the oldest types of independent retailers. It is a relatively small retailing business, not departmentalized, usually located in a rural community, and primarily engaged in selling a general assortment of merchandise, of which the most important line is food. Its more important subsidiary lines are notions, apparel, farm supplies, and gasoline. These stores were important in farming and frontier sections until, in the 1920s, the spread of other types of retailing and widespread ownership of automobiles caused them to decline. Some general stores, though, still operate in sparsely-populated areas of the West and South.

SMALL INDEPENDENTS   Today, most small independent stores are concentrated in fields where it is "relatively easy to set up in business." This usually means that no great amount of capital is needed, or that easy financing is available. This probably is the main reason why there are so many small independent grocery retailers—a fairly small investment in inventory "turned over" rapidly results in a sales figure many times the value of the inventory. This same situation is found in gasoline retailing, and, in addition, many petroleum refiners offer financial assistance to individuals who want to open their own stations. Many small retailers, of course, are well-financed, but they are the exceptions.

Small independent retailers frequently meet strong competition from large retail chains, supermarkets, and department stores. The small independent usually buys his inventory from wholesalers or other middlemen, rather than directly from producers, so his merchandise costs tend to be higher than those of his large, direct-buying competitors. Thus, he must charge higher prices (to cover his costs) than his competitors. So, in most instances, the small independent must use something other than the price appeal to attract trade. The more successful find some way to differentiate their stores in their customers' minds. It may consist of nothing more than personalized service and the maintaining of friendly customer relations. Or the independent may stay open longer hours than larger competitors and offer such extra services as credit and delivery. A convenient location, too, may be attractive to customers. As long as substantial numbers of ultimate consumers continue to consider such things important, small independent retail stores are likely to continue in operation.

LARGE INDEPENDENTS   Large independent stores are most important in situations where corporate chains, department stores, and other integrated retail institutions either possess no operating advantages or are at competitive disadvantages. In furniture retailing, for instance, the independent store buys most of its inventory either directly from manufacturers or through manufacturers' agents. These are the same sources from which the furniture chain and the department store's furniture department must buy. Whereas the chain may buy larger quantities than the independent, the resulting quantity discounts it gains are generally too small to permit it to use the "lower price" appeal effectively. Of even greater significance is the fact that *most* furniture pieces are not at all standardized, either in appearance or construction. In a few large cities such as New York, several furniture outlets handle the same manufacturer's line, and in these cities, of course, consumers can shop around and compare prices. In most places, however, each furniture manufacturer tends to sell exclusively to a single store or to several but restricting each to some part of the merchandise line; therefore, it is virtually impossible for consumers to compare prices of the "same" piece from one store to another. This is what makes merchandise selection especially important in successful furniture retailing. Whereas the local independent can offer furniture that is "in tune" with consumer preferences in its own locality, chain organizations, with their centralized buying procedures, find it hard to adjust their buying patterns to fit the unique preferences of local markets.

Some large independent stores are successful because their owners have specialized knowledge which enables them to "run rings around" larger competitors. Examples abound in the retailing of such goods as Oriental rugs, musical instruments, and sports equipment. Large numbers of consumers hesitate to buy such items in the absence of what they consider professional advice. Chain stores and department stores sell these items, but they usually employ less well-informed personnel.

Other large independent retailers succeed in building local reputations as "quality stores." Some handle large assortments of related merchandise, e.g., men's or ladies' apparel, and pride themselves on having the latest fashions. Others deal in lines, such as jewlery, where consumers consider the "store image" almost as important as merchandise quality. Independents often find it easier to build prestige reputations than do their chain store or department store competitors. In addition, many independent quality stores are old and well established; it is not easy for competitors to acquire quality reputations locally in the space of a few months or years.

ADVANTAGES OF THE INDEPENDENTS   In comparison to their competitors, successful independents, both large and small, possess significant advantages. Probably the most important is that they can more easily adapt their operations to fit the unique needs of the communities in which they do business. Furthermore, there is no question but that the owner-managers of many successful independent stores are more able and more aggressive than managers of competing chain stores and department managers of department stores. Nor should it be overlooked that large numbers of consumers tend to be loyal to locally-owned and operated stores and look askance at stores controlled from out of town.

Mail-Order Houses

A number of developments contributed to the founding and growth of mail-order houses. Montgomery Ward and Sears Roebuck, founded in 1872 and 1886 respectively, both owed much of their early success and rapid growth to the completion of the railroads and to improvements in postal service, including the advent of rural free delivery. These developments in transportation and delivery, coupled with the comparative isolation from retail centers of most of the rural population, set the stage for an enthusiastic reception for mail-order merchandising. General stores, formerly the chief source of supply for the farm population, found themselves hard-pressed to meet either the prices or the extensive merchandise offerings of the mail-order houses. Consumers in small towns also were attracted as customers of the mail-order houses, even though most such towns had stores which collectively offered nearly as wide a merchandise selection.

Both Montgomery Ward and Sears Roebuck confined themselves solely to mail-order operations until the 1920s. In 1921, Montgomery Ward opened its first retail store, and this was followed in 1925 by Sears Roebuck's first retail store. Their opening of retail stores was hastened by spectacular growth in automobile ownership and by great improvements in rural roads. These developments transformed many rural consumers into small-town shoppers and lessened the relative attractiveness of mail-order buying. Furthermore, the population of the country was shifting more and more from primarily rural to primarily urban. The managements of Ward's and Sears were alert to the marketing significance of these changes: hence their decisions to open retail outlets in urban centers. Today the bulk of the sales of both concerns comes from the sales of their retail stores, though mail-order still accounts for sizable proportions of their business.

Indeed, the retail stores of both companies feature "catalog order desks," which solicit orders for delivery by their mail-order operations. In some locations, too, both Sears and Ward's maintain "catalog order stores" at which consumers are invited to place mail orders either in person or by telephone.

Mail-order houses, such as those of Ward's and Sears, offer wide assortments of articles within each of a large number of merchandise lines. Usually, such mail-order houses buy directly from the producer, often contracting for a large share or even all of the producer's output. Many small manufacturers are completely dependent on one or the other of the large mail-order houses for distributing all they produce. Most of the over 20,000 sources of supply for Sears, for instance, are small manufacturers. Indeed, the company is on record as stating that, it prefers to work with smaller factories, who concentrate on production, and look to it for a substantial part of their distribution.[3] In the case of Sears, such small manufacturers have been the main suppliers of Sears' own brands—e.g., *Kenmore, Homart, Craftsman, Silvertone, J. C. Higgins,* and *Charmode.*

More limited selections of merchandise are also sold by the mail-order method. Small manufacturers often rely on this method to dispose of much or all of their output. Among the items "retailed directly" by such manufacturers are shirts, men's and women's apparel, toys, bird houses and feeders, and rugs. Some of these manufacturers distribute catalogs to consumers, but more often they use direct-mail promotion and small advertisements in magazines and newspapers. Mail-order retailing is an important distribution method, too, for many growers of trees, shrubs, plants, and seeds who generally distribute catalogs to homeowners throughout the country.

Mail-order retailing is the selling method used also by the many "of-the-month" clubs. These clubs typically provide their so-called members with the service of pre-selected merchandise, thus relieving members of the need for choosing their purchases from a large number of possible alternatives. *Book-of-the-Month Club,* for example, informs its members of monthly selections which must be *rejected* by members if they do not wish to receive them. Members not sending in rejections automatically receive monthly selections and are billed accordingly. Members of "of-the-month" clubs generally are required to accept a given number of selections during their first year of membership, after which they may, on their own initiative, write the club cancelling their memberships. Club members, therefore, are in the position of finding it easier to accept rather than reject selections and to continue rather than discontinue their memberships. Because of their operating scheme, the clubs are often said to provide automatic distribution for products chosen as monthly selections. Most of the clubs are true middlemen, for they make their purchases from producers and resell them to

[3] "How Sears Stays on Top," *International Management,* April 1968, p. 61.

consumers. The book clubs are the longest established in this field, but there are similar organizations engaged in mail-order retailing of such items as food, fruit, toys, gifts, and foreign imports.

Department Stores

The department store was a European, rather than an American, retailing innovation. The Bon Marché and other Paris department stores came into existence and flourished during the period of the French Second Empire (1852-1871). Leading American retailers of the 1850s and 1860s regularly visited Paris and other European market centers on buying trips, and undoubtedly observed the operating methods of the Bon Marché and other European department stores.[4] The result was that the idea was transplanted to this country. Among the American firms which began operating as department stores during this period were R. H. Macy (New York), Jordan Marsh (Boston), Marshall Field (Chicago), Scruggs-Vandervoort-Barney (St. Louis), Meier & Frank (Portland, Ore.), City of Paris (San Francisco), Thalhimer Brothers (Richmond, Va.), and Rich's (Atlanta). Not all of these would have qualified as department stores at the times of their founding; most started out as other types of businesses and switched later to the department store type of operation. By the close of the 1870s, department stores were well-established in nearly every major city and in many smaller cities and towns.

Formerly defined, a department store is a large retailing business unit that handles a wide variety of shopping and specialty goods (including women's ready-to-wear and accessories, men's and boys' wear, piece goods, small wares, and home furnishings) and is organized into separate departments for purposes of promotion, service, and control. Thus, the two main features of the department store are a broad merchandise offering and departmental organization. Responsibility for buying and selling is decentralized to individual departments, each carrying different lines of goods, and each under the control of a merchandising executive called a buyer or department manager. Buyers are relatively free to operate their departments as they see fit, as long as their operations produce profits considered adequate by the store's top-management. In addition to exercising general supervision over merchandising operations, the store's central administrative organization operates and maintains the physical facilities, provides such services as credit and delivery for the customers, and assists the merchandising departments with advertising and promotion.

Originally, department stores relied on the great breadth of

[4] P. H. Nystrom, *Economics of Retailing* (New York: Ronald Press, 1932), p. 127.

their merchandise to attract customers. Gradually, however, the more aggressive stores, seeking to build their trade, broadened the range of services offered customers. Today, it is a rare department store that does not provide such customer services as charge accounts, installment plans, and home delivery. Some offer such exotic services as elaborate restaurants and tea rooms, nurseries to care for small children, and free instruction in arts and crafts. A few of these services are self-supporting, others are not. But even though many services do show an "accounting type" loss, they are maintained because of their proved power to "pull in" customers.

The department store is a "horizontally integrated" institution. It brings together under one roof a range of merchandise offerings comparable to the combined offerings of many stores specializing in single or fewer merchandise lines. Although this "exposition-like" character is the source of much of the department store's drawing power, it is not without its disadvantages, particularly in purchasing. Some departments do enough business to justify direct-buying from sources of supply, but many do not. The small-volume departments, particularly in individually-owned stores, often are unable to buy in large enough lots to qualify for the quantity discounts obtainable from manufacturers and, hence, must frequently resort to buying through wholesalers and agents, which results in rather high merchandise costs.

BUYING GROUPS   Because of the disadvantages they encounter in purchasing, some independently-owned department stores have joined buying groups. Member stores of buying groups cooperatively own, maintain, and use the services of resident buying offices located in such market centers as New York and Chicago. Through consolidation of the orders of member stores, the buying office achieves considerable savings by placing orders for lots larger than any member could afford to buy individually. Furthermore, the combined bargaining power of the stores often results in lower price quotations by suppliers. A secondary, though important, function of the resident buying office is to provide its member stores with current information on prices, availability of new items, and trends in fashion.

OWNERSHIP GROUPS   Many previously independent stores have been absorbed into ownership groups. Most department store ownership groups were put together originally by financiers rather than by merchandisers. They were not intended primarily to result in improved operating efficiency but rather in immediate profits for the organizers who, as financial middlemen, were most interested in profiting from the flotation of new issues of common stock. But, over time, central managements of the ownership groups lost their solely financial orientations and began to emphasize the improvement and standardization of operating policies and procedures. One early development was the centralized buying offices which enabled stores in the group to buy many standard stock items and some fashion goods at lower costs. Nevertheless, many types of merchandise are still bought by stores individually. Among these are high fashion items, where speed of procurement and direct contact with the producer is important, and the kind of articles that are needed to satisfy purely local demands. Top managements of the department store ownership groups have also worked toward greater uniformity in non-merchandising activies, such as in the standardization of personnel polices and store operating systems and records.

Usually, each department store in an ownership group plans its merchandise offerings so as to cater to classes of trade in its own selling area. Because most of the inventory is composed of shopping and specialty goods, and because consumer preferences for such articles vary considerably from one area to another, most department stores, whether or not they belong to ownership groups, find it difficult to standarize the merchandise offerings of stores in different locations. Furthermore, stores in the same ownership group often attract different classes of trade in different cities. The uniqueness of the merchandise offering and the classes of trade catered to results in each store's having a distinctive image. That is the main reason why most department store ownership groups continue to operate stores under the names they had when they were independently-owned. Allied Stores Corporation, for instance, operates, among others, Jordan Marsh in Boston, Titche-Goettinger in Dallas, the Bon Marché in Seattle, and Dey Brothers in Syracuse. Federated Department Stores operates, among others, Filene's in Boston, Shillito's in Cincinnati, Boston Store in Milwaukee, Bloomingdale's in New York, Abraham & Straus in Brooklyn, Burdine's in Miami, and Bullock's in Los Angeles. Each of these stores has quite a distinct image in its own trading area.

Chain Store Systems

Fundamentally, a chain store system is a group of retail stores of essentially the same type, centrally owned and with some degree of centralized control of operation. This definition is broad enough to include not only the well-known A. & P. and Woolworth "chains" but also Ward's and Sear's retail stores and the different department store ownership groups. Basically, the distinguishing feature of a chain store system is that it owns and controls a group of stores. The department store ownership group is one type of chain store system, the retail stores of Montgomery Ward are another, and the F. W. Woolworth stores represent still another type. However, if only by virtue of long-established and customary usage, the term "chain store system" normally refers to a multi-unit retailing operation that cannot be categorized as a department store ownership group or the retail outlets affiliated with a mail-order house.

STRENGTHS The strengths of the chain store system trace directly to the fact that it is horizontally-integrated (i.e., it operates multiple stores). With the addition of each new store, the system extends its "reach" to another group of prospective customers. Also, each store added means greater sales volume and, consequently, increased opportunity to effect economies through buying in larger-sized lots. It also means that the costs of central administration and of providing highly-specialized merchandising, buying, and promotional services can be spread over more stores. Thus, such costs are reduced for each store in the system. Furthermore, other economies are effected through standardization of store systems and procedures and the adoption of uniform personnel policies. These strengths, all due primarily to horizontal integration, are reflected in lower costs for the merchandise handled and in generally lower operating expenses than those incurred by the independent retailer.

The chains also have reduced their merchandising and operating expenses in other ways. Some savings were secured by eliminating such customer services as credit and delivery. Others were obtained by limiting the variety of merchandise available by stocking, for example, only three different brands of canned string beans in each of two sizes, rather than ten brands in four sizes. Still others were realized through application of the basic merchandising philosophy of the chain, which is to squeeze the maximum sales out of each dollar invested in inventory. In other words, the chain gears its operations so that its inventory is small relative to the size of its sales volume. For example, the chain seeks to maximize the number of items which have a short shelf life (the fast sellers) and to minimize those with a long shelf life (the slow movers). More importantly, it also attempts to build a large sales volume by underselling many of its competitors; this means, in effect, that the chain is satisfied with a comparatively low profit on each item sold. Successful application of this merchandising philosophy results in a large sales volume relative to the size of the inventory. Besides being very careful about the make-up of its inventory, the typical chain "works its inventory harder" than many competitors. Whereas the chain stresses large sales volume and low unit profits, many of its competitors are satisfied with small sales volumes and high unit profits.

Because the chain store system is a high-volume operation, it ordinarily gets its merchandise directly from producers or through their agents. Rarely does a chain system buy from merchant wholesalers, for the system is usually able to buy in even greater quantities than the wholesaler can, and with greater quantity discounts. By operating its own warehouses, the chain store system effectively becomes its own wholesaler. Thus, chain store systems can also be classed as vertically-integrated institutions, because they take over and perform for themselves activities that would otherwise be performed by separate wholesale institutions.

WEAKNESSES   The weaknesses of the chain store system derive from its horizontal integration and merchandising philosophy. Centralized decision-making often means that individual chain stores cannot react to changed local conditions as quickly as the more alert of their independent competitors. When individual chain units lag behind the independents in making new products and brands available, and they frequently do, centralized purchasing is usually at fault. Furthermore, in keeping with the large sales volume and low profit merchandising philosophy, the chain must economize on other costs and dispense with such services as charge accounts and delivery. In doing this, they effectively concede to competitors the patronage of consumers desiring these services. Moreover, because of its integrated nature, the chain has many stores and requires many managers: recruiting, training, and retaining them in the numbers needed are formidable tasks. Individual chains, of course, have found ways to deal with or minimize these inherent weaknesses; nevertheless, it is these weaknesses, together with the "impersonal and cold" character of most chains, that serve to offset many of the competitive advantages chains have over independents.

CHAIN DISTRIBUTION OF CONVENIENCE GOODS   Chain store systems are important links in the retail distribution systems for many types of convenience goods, which, again, are goods that consumers generally want to buy frequently, immediately, and with minimum shopping effort. Both large and small manufacturers of grocery and drug products, for instance, know that their brands cannot be made sufficiently available to large masses of consumers unless chain outlets stock them. Manufacturers of many items sold through variety stores find that if they are to achieve the sales volumes necessary for mass production, they must have chain store distribution. Holding out to producers of convenience goods the tempting prize of widespread and high-volume retail distribution at a relatively low selling cost, skilled chain store buying specialists drive hard bargains. They push for and usually obtain the lowest possible prices and the most advantageous promotional allowances, which are payments made by manufacturers to retailers in return for advertising and otherwise promoting products at the retail level. Normally, chains handling convenience goods expect most suppliers to promote their own products with heavy consumer advertising in order to minimize the "in-store" selling effort needed. In cases of products that do not lend themselves to such promotion, the chain often prefers to handle its own "store" brands, packed for it either under contract by outside manufacturers, or by "captive" (that is, owned by the chain) canning or processing plants.

CHAIN DISTRIBUTION OF SHOPPING GOODS   Chain store systems are also important retailers of shopping goods which, you remember, are items consumers select and buy only after doing some "shopping around." Chains are extremely active, for instance, in the retailing of men's and women's apparel, dry goods, and shoes. In contrast to many of their independent competitors in these lines, however, the shopping goods chains tend to concentrate on low-priced and fast-selling items. In other words, chains specializing in shopping goods seek items that resemble convenience goods as closely as possible. To obtain them, a chain often has to forego handling high-fashion merchandise in favor of more staple items. Given their need for large sales volumes, shopping goods chains generally cater to consumers in the middle and lower income groups. Such chains commonly have manufacturers under contract to supply them with goods according to the chain's own specifications. The supplying manufacturers need not be especially large, but they must be large enough to assure the chain that they can produce enough to fill its requirements.

In some instances, shopping goods chains are the retail arms of the manufacturers who own and control them. The Robert Hall chain, a retailer of men's and boys' clothing, is a division of United Merchants and Manufacturers, Inc. Similiarly, the Thom McAn stores are operated by Melville Shoe Corporation. Other manufacturers, such as the shoe-manufacturing Endicott-Johnson Corporation, sell only a fraction of their output through their own retail chains and market the rest through other types of retailers. But even when chain store systems are controlled by manufacturers, there are needs for outside sources of supply. Thus, a manufacturer-controlled shoe chain, such as Endicott-Johnson's own stores, retails not only shoes but such related items as hosiery and shoe polish bought from other sources.

Retailer Cooperatives and Voluntary Groups

With the expansion of chain store systems in the 1920s, especially in grocery and drug retailing, independent stores suffered serious patronage losses. Some independents thought they could safely ignore their new competitors; others believed that something had to be done to improve their waning competitive position. Particularly alarming to most independents was the fact that chain outlets were selling items at retail prices lower than the independents' own wholesale costs. The low chain prices were apparently living evidence that substantial savings in merchandise costs were possible if the wholesaler was eliminated from the marketing channel, and independent grocery and drug retailers began to devise new schemes for cutting their own wholesale costs.

Some independent retailers formed cooperative buying clubs. They hoped that the club could obtain lower merchandise costs, and thus enable its members to meet chain store prices. Most cooperative buying clubs were failures because, generally, they had no formal organization and their buying operations were sporadic. Many manufacturers refused to deal directly with them, often because of pressure applied by wholesalers. Furthermore, the independents who formed buying clubs too often failed to recognize that the low prices the chains were able to advertise were not solely the result of their buying advantage. They were actually traceable to policies the chains had adopted from the very first: these were the cash-and-carry system, the self-service store layout, and the advertising of "loss leaders." (A loss leader is an item priced under cost, which serves as a device for drawing customers into the store.) Most independents provided credit and delivery services, operated full-service stores, and made little use of advertising. Unlike the chains, they hesitated to pass marketing tasks on to consumers. Consequently, they had to charge higher retail prices to cover the costs.

Gradually, groups of independents recognized the need for more formal organizations that would operate continuously rather than sporadically, and there evolved the *retailer cooperative*, an enterprise owned and controlled by retailer-stockholders who patronize it and share in any savings in proportion to their patronage. In contrast to the buying club, the retailer cooperative has a warehouse, carries inventory in stock, and employs a manager. Even more significant, it renders advice and assistance on such retail merchandising problems as store layout and location, store operation, record systems, and personnel policies. Often, too, the manager of a retail cooperative persuades members to adopt a uniform name for their stores and to engage in cooperative advertising, thus reshaping the organization more in the image of a chain store system. However, most retailer cooperatives place more emphasis on group buying than on group promotion.[5] Experience indicates, nevertheless, that placing heavy emphasis on group promotion is an important key to success. Only where retailer cooperatives have given really large emphasis to group promotion have their independent retailer-members become strong competitors of chain store outlets.

In other instances, it was a wholesaler who took the initiative in organizing independent retailers into a *voluntary group*. Each retailer affiliating with a voluntary group owns and operates his own store but is as-

---

[5] D. J. Schwartz, An Exploratory Analysis of the Development and Present Status of Voluntary and Cooperative Groups in Food Marketing (Atlanta: Georgia State College of Business Administration, 1957), p. 31.

sociated with the sponsoring wholesaler for buying and merchandising purposes. The retailer-members are expected to concentrate the bulk of their purchases with the sponsoring wholesaler. They are also required to operate their stores under the group name and to display uniform store signs, with the purpose of maintaining some degree of identity among their stores and in their promotional efforts. The wholesaler, in turn, tries to supply the retailer-members with merchandise at the lowest possible prices. In addition, he prepares and places advertising in local media and provides advice and assistance on other problems. Whereas the early voluntary groups admitted any independent retailer of any size, the more recent trend has been to restrict membership only to those doing a substantial business. In the most successful voluntary groups, the sponsoring wholesaler and the retailer-members stress effective advertising and store operating efficiency. The largest voluntaries are in the food industry, where there are such nation-wide organizations as *I.G.A.*, *Red and White*, and *Clover Farm Stores*. However, there are also voluntaries in other fields, such as in hardware and variety store merchandise.

Retailer cooperatives and voluntary groups are important distributors of convenience goods. In many cases, their buying power equals or exceeds that of the chains. In food retailing, for instance, members of retailer cooperatives and voluntary groups now have a greater sales volume than the corporate chain store systems. Buyers for the larger cooperatives and voluntaries drive just as hard a bargain with suppliers as their chain store counterparts. Thus, manufacturers have come to regard cooperatives and voluntaries in much the same light as the chains and consequently deal with them in almost identical fashion.

Consumer Cooperatives

A consumer cooperative is a retail business owned and operated by ultimate consumers to purchase and distribute goods and services primarily to the membership. The earliest known consumer cooperative was started in Scotland, but the modern form traces to an English cooperative founded in 1844—the Rochdale Society of Equitable Pioneers. This organization was the first to lay down the principles which have since served as the keys to successful operation of consumer cooperatives. These "principles," which are really operating policies, are (1) open membership—any consumer is free to join, (2) democratic control—each member has but one vote regardless of the number of cooperative shares held, (3) limited interest is paid on capital invested by members, (4) all sales are for cash and at prevailing market prices, and (5) members receive patronage dividends proportionate to their purchases.

Although there are some large consumer cooperatives in the United States, their total impact on American retailing has been negligible. Perhaps the main reason they have not been as successful in the United States as they have in Europe lies in the fact that other types of retailing institutions grew up here and provided the strong competitive setting that kept retailing profits low. In Europe, the high and often exorbitant profits of retailers furnished the stimulus for consumers to band together and open their own retail stores. While the consumer cooperative movement was thriving and expanding in Europe, chain stores and their competitors in the United States were learning how to provide quality merchandise at low prices. While European retailers were relying on high unit profits and low sales volumes, the newer American retail institutions were emphasizing low unit profits and high sales volumes. In other words, retailers in this country recognized early that the economies of mass marketing, like those of mass production, could only be realized through a combination of large sales and attractive prices.

Most U.S. consumer cooperatives are in the grocery retailing field. Their organizers have probably been impressed with the large part food purchases play in total consumer spending. Most consumer cooperative grocery stores begin as small and inadequately financed enterprises, housed in poorly situated buildings, with scanty stocks and underpaid managements. These are formidable handicaps. They are especially difficult to overcome in the highly competitive grocery business, where the sensational successes of the chains and supermarkets have demonstrated the importance of large size, adequate financing, well-planned inventory, and efficient management. It is small wonder, then, that consumer cooperatives have experienced rough sledding in the retail grocery field.

Consumer cooperatives stand a better chance of success when they are set up to handle merchandise lines other than groceries. For instance, they have been highly successful in operating college and university bookstores. The consumer cooperative in this field is often more efficient than its privately-owned competitors, most of which are small independent stores. Furthermore, in marked contrast to grocery retailing where low unit profit margins are the rule, the book and school supply trade is characterized by relatively high margins. This combination of favorable factors enables many cooperative college stores to pay patronage dividends of as much as 12 to 13 percent of members' purchases.

There is little incentive for consumers to organize cooperatives in most non-food fields, chiefly because potential savings on small monthly expenditures per member seem hardly to justify the effort. Most cooperative college stores were organized to fill an existing "retail vacuum." At the University of Washington, for example, the University Book Store was organized in 1900 to help overcome three problems: (1) late arrival of text books causing students to get a late start in class work, (2) difficulty in getting faculty cooperation on book orders, and (3) the inconvenience of going to stores in downtown Seattle and the necessity of going to several stores because of incomplete stocks in individual stores. Existence of such "retail vacuums" provides at least one type of setting conducive to the successful establishment of consumer cooperatives.

Supermarkets

The first supermarket appeared in the early 1930s, during the depths of the Great Depression. The pioneer supermarket operators often began in vacant warehouses and, through the use of mass merchandise displays and heavy advertising, succeeded in transacting what were then tremendous volumes of business. They featured low prices and operated on a cash-and-carry basis. That the stores were physically unattractive was of little importance; widespread unemployment and shortages of purchasing power made the low-price appeal unusually attractive. The first operators of supermarkets were independents, but, by 1937, nearly all of the leading food chains were building supermarkets as fast as they could find suitable locations—and closing up three or four of their existing smaller stores to make way for each of the supermarkets they opened. By this time, of course, the "cheapy" supermarkets located in vacant warehouses were rapidly giving way to more attractive supermarkets on sites more convenient to customers, and, as this new type of retailing idea caught on, with more and more businessmen recognizing the great possibilities of supermarket operation, a revolution in food retailing gathered steam. Thirty years later (in 1967) supermarkets were still growing, both in numbers and in dollar volume.[6]

The basic characteristics and operating philosophy of the supermarket are indicated in its definition—a large retailing business unit selling mainly food and grocery items on the basis of the low margin appeal, high turnover, wide variety and assortments, self-service, and heavy emphasis on merchandise appeal. Supermarkets were devised originally as food retailing businesses, and they continue to base most of their operations on the mass-selling of food and grocery items. However, in order to widen their merchandise appeal and, at the same time, improve their profit potentials, increasing numbers of supermarkets have added such non-food lines as drugs, household utensils, hardware items, and garden supplies. This trend toward "scramble merchandising," together with the spreading habit of many consumers to shop only once or twice a week for groceries, has enabled the supermarket to increase the dollar value of the average order sold each customer on each trip to the store.[7] To stimulate store traffic, the super-

---

[6] "Supers on the March," *Statist*, March 31, 1967, p. 648.

[7] G. H. Snyder, "Aggressive Merchandising of Non-Foods Our Key to Profit," *Progressive Grocer*, October 1967, p. 124.

market typically promotes its low prices through heavy advertising, mass merchandise displays, and premium and trading stamp plans. Because it needs a high sales volume for profitable operation, the supermarket requires large floor space, a layout designed to achieve maximum merchandise exposure, large merchandise stocks on the selling floor with readily accessible reserve stocks, and adequate check-out counters. In addition, it is important to provide check-cashing facilities and a parking lot big enough to handle peak volumes of business.

Except for the difference in merchandise lines, the supermarket and the discount house have a great deal in common. Both rely on the appeal of low prices, wide variety and assortments, self-service, and the handling of well-known brands of merchandise. Both seek to keep their prices down by combining operating expense economies with a high volume business in fast-selling items.[8] Notice, however, that the supermarket is, by definition, a large retailing business unit whereas the discount house may be any size —from very small to very large. The larger discount house is the one most closely resembling the supermarket and, as a matter of fact, many new, larger discount houses have added grocery departments and are offering very tough competition to the supermarkets in their trading areas. Since a discount house, like a supermarket, must maintain a large over-all sales volume if it is to be able to offer its low prices, many are operating their grocery departments at no profit or even at a loss, considering them mainly as a means of getting people into the store and maintaining the required over-all level of sales. Nearby supermarkets have found it difficult to match the discount house's "non-profit" grocery policy—tough competition indeed! [9]

Many of the buying practices of supermarkets are routine. Certain staples and nationally-advertised items are carried by nearly all supermarkets, e.g., the lines of Campbell's soups, Rice Krispies, and Underwood deviled ham. The responsibility for buying varies with the size and organizational structure of the company. Large supermarket chains have specialized buyers who bargain with and make routine purchases from suppliers, and store managers requisition such items from warehouses. A growing number of supermarket chains use buying committees (made up of buyers and key executives) to make decisions on adding new items and dropping old items. In small companies, a single individual often handles negotiations for all routine purchases. Managers of produce and meat departments often have authority to buy for their own departments. Supermarkets that belong to retailer cooperatives or voluntary groups usually make the bulk of their routine purchases through the wholesaling units of such organizations.[10]

[8] J. Minichiello, "Comparative Assortments of Discount Food Stores and Conventional Supermarkets," *Journal of Retailing*, Winter 1968, p. 30.

[9] E. W. Cundiff and R. C. Andersen, "Competitive Food Pricing," *Journal of Retailing*, Spring 1963, p. 62.

[10] N. Bussel, "Systematic Stocking Ideas Pay Big Dividends," *Progressive Grocer*, September 1966, pp. 188-90.

Ordering and shelf stocking of certain items, such as crackers and cookies, frequently are handled by manufacturers' salesmen under the authorization of the owner, manager, or person responsible for buying. The ordering and stocking of non-food lines, such as those handled by rack jobbers, is also often taken care of with minimum supervision by supermarket personnel.

Discount Houses

A discount house is a retailing business unit that features consumer durable items, competes on a low-price basis, and operates on a relatively low markup and a minimum of customer service. Discount houses range from small open showroom and catalogue type order offices all the way to full line, limited service, promotional stores, which closely resemble and, actually, can be classified as department stores. Also included is the "closed door" or membership type of discount house that supposedly caters only to homogeneous groups such as union members, government employees, or teachers. In fact, the term "discount house" is being used more and more in referring to any retail establishment whose main promotional emphasis is on selling nationally advertised merchandise at prices below those of conventional dealers.

Although some appeared in the late 1930s,[11] discount houses were neither numerous nor widespread until after World War II. After the first rush of postwar buying subsided, discount houses began to set up in the so-called "hardgoods" lines—i.e., appliances, furniture, and other consumer durables of relatively high unit price. Manufacturers of major appliances and other consumer durables, encouraged by the strong immediate postwar consumer demand for their products, had greatly expanded their production facilities. Before long, however, they recognized that their expanded facilities were capable of producing far more than their established outlets using traditional retailing methods could sell to ultimate consumers. These outlets were, for the most part, department stores and small independent dealers. Manufacturers either had to persuade these outlets to improve their selling efficiency or obtain more outlets to help in retailing the expanded production. It was in this setting that manufacturers began to turn to discount houses which could provide the needed additional sales volume.[12]

In the late 1940s and early 1950s, then, circumstances were ripe for the establishment and growth of the new discount houses. Traditional appliance outlets such as department stores and small appliance dealers had grown accustomed to high markups, often 35 or 40 percent of the retail

[11] S. C. Hollander, "The Discount House," *Journal of Marketing*, July 1953, p. 58.

[12] E. Gudeman, A *Profile of Sears*. The Tobé Lecture Series, Harvard Business School, February 12, 1949, p. 15.

price, and they were also used to selling at manufacturers' full "list" prices. Furthermore, appliance makers had promoted their brand names to the point where the consumer was no longer concerned whether the retailer would guarantee the quality of the product. Every reputable manufacturer now stood behind his products, regardless of the outlets from which consumers brought them. Discount house operators found that they could sell appliances and other consumer durables profitably at prices ranging as much as 30 percent below those of the traditional outlets. The traditional retailers were at first able to maintain their own total sales and profits, and, for a few years, did not put up much of a competitive battle. By the time they realized that they had to "come out slugging" and "meet or beat discount house prices," discount houses had already won great customer loyalty on the basis of their strong price appeal.[13]

By the early 1960s the selection of merchandise offered by discount houses had broadened appreciably. To the original lines of hard goods had been added broad lines of soft goods—including clothing for men, women, and children, linen and bedding, and giftwares. Today, these soft goods lines normally occupy at least half of the selling floor space in the typical large discount house. The early hard goods discount houses depended strongly upon brand. They attracted customers by offering well-known brands at discount prices. Since brands are far less important in soft goods lines, the newer discount houses with broadened lines of merchandise find it more difficult to prove that their prices are really lower. They must instead build consumer confidence in their pricing structures.

Discount houses buy their merchandise stocks both from wholesale distributors and directly from manufacturers. Early in their growth, they did nearly all of their buying from distributors. Sometimes, so-called "legitimate" retailers, not wanting to compete on a price basis, put pressure on distributors to stop supplying the discounters. When their supplies are cut off, discount houses will either buy from other retailers, either legitimate or discount types, on a cost plus five per cent basis, or work out exchange arrangements with other discount houses whose supplies have not yet been cut off.[14]

As discount houses grew larger and became important outlets for many consumer durables, and as chains of discount houses, such as E. J. Korvette, were organized, more and more manufacturers began to make direct sales to them. Although discount houses, like the chains, are "hard" buyers, they are also "fast" buyers. Manufacturers appreciate a "fast" buyer

[13] A. R. Oxenfeldt in *Discount House Operations*, hearings, Senate Small Business Committee, Subcommittee on Retailing, Distribution, and Fair Trade Practices, June 23, 24, and 25, 1958, p. 400.

[14] F. W. Gilchrist, "The Discount House," *The Journal of Marketing*, January 1953, p. 268.

when they find themselves with unexpectedly large inventories that more conventional retail outlets seem incapable of moving.[15]

Automatic Selling

Automatic selling, more commonly known as "automatic vending," involves the sale of goods or services to ultimate consumers through coin operated machines. Whereas most automatic vending machines are still coin operated, there are machines which make change for one dollar bills, thus overcoming a longtime disadvantage of automatic vending—the inability to serve customers who do not have the proper change. Automatic selling is not a new method of retailing: the Tutti-Frutti Company installed chewing gum machines at elevated railroad stations in the 1880s. Traditionally, the major portion of vending machine volume has and still comes from soft drinks, cigarettes, and candy. Two out of every ten candy bars sold are sold through vending machines, 16 out of 100 packs of cigarettes, and more than one out of four soft drinks.[16]

Many attempts have been made to use vending machine for products other than soft drinks, candy, and cigarettes. Those with packaged milk and ice cubes have been most successful. But many have failed. For instance, Filene's, a Boston department store, once installed 23 machines in the Boston Greyhound bus terminal, selling goods ranging from men's hose and ties to ladies' panties and babies' rattles. After two years, the experiment was abandoned as a failure. The Grand Union supermarket chain has conducted a round-the-clock supplementary vending operation for certain grocery staples on an experimental basis.

In 1968, a new type of vending machine designed to serve as a complete off-hours convenience food store was introduced to the market. This machine, which could stock as many as 100 items, both refrigerated and nonrefrigerated, would take orders involving a number of items, receive currency, and make change. These machines were being located on an experimental basis in locations, such as service stations, accessible to customers at all times.

Although automatic selling still accounts for only a small percent of all retail sales—only $4.5-billion out of an estimated $310-billion total in 1967—vending machines are becoming increasingly important as outlets for many types of products. The National Automatic Merchandising Association estimates that there are 7,000 vending machine operators in the United States operating more than six-million vending machines, selling products that literally range from soup to nuts. Vending machine volume expands

[15] "Discounters Doing Well," *Financial World*, December 6, 1967, p. 7.
[16] "How Will Vending Boom Affect Selling," *Printers' Ink*, October 30, 1959, p. 68.

with each new technological improvement in machine design and operation. The first coffee vending machine, for instance, was installed in 1946 and just twelve years later, in 1958, such machines were selling coffee at an annual rate of $189-million; N.A.M.A. states that the average person now spends about $22.50 on purchases from these machines each year.[17] Annual vending volume rose to an estimated $9-billion in 1970, roughly double the volume just three years earlier!

THE "WHEEL OF RETAILING" HYPOTHESIS

Changes in retailing evolve rather gradually over the years. According to the "wheel of retailing" hypothesis, advanced by Professor M. P. McNair, new forms of retailing institutions generally obtain a foothold on the retail scene through emphasizing a price appeal made possible by low operating costs inherent in the new form of institution. Over time, the new institutions upgrade their facilities and services, necessitating added investments and involving higher operating costs. At some point, they emerge as high-cost, high-price retailers, vulnerable to newer forms of retailers who, in turn, go through a similar metamorphosis. Mail-order houses and department stores, for example, originally were low-cost retailers soliciting business mainly through use of the price appeal, but eventually the "wheel" turned and they became vulnerable to chain store systems, discount houses, and other newer institutions.[18] As another example, conventional supermarkets in the late 1960s were encountering new competition from the new "food discount stores," which, in line with the wheel notion, were featuring "lower prices" made possible by lower operating costs due to stripped-down services.[19]

SHOPPING CENTERS

The Urban Land Institute defines a shopping center as "a group of commercial establishments, planned, developed, owned, and managed as a *unit*, with off-street parking provided on the property (in direct ratio to the building area) and related in location, size (gross floor area) and type of shops

---

[17] " '67 Vending Sales Will Exceed $4.5 Billion," *Advertising Age*, November 13, 1967, p. 42.

[18] See M. P. McNair, "Significant Trends and Developments in the Postwar Period," in A. B. Smith (ed.), *Competitive Distribution in a Free, High-Level Economy and Its Implications for the University* (Pittsburgh: University of Pittsburgh Press, 1958), pp. 17-18. Also see Stanley C. Hollander, "The Wheel of Retailing," *Journal of Marketing*, July 1960, pp. 37-42. Dr. Hollander concludes "the wheel of hypothesis is not valid for all retailing. . . . (It) does, however, seem to describe a fairly common pattern in industrialized, expanding economies."

[19] For a report on this development, see *The New York Times*, Nov. 25, 1969, pp. 65 and 71.

to the trade area that the unit serves—generally in an outlying or suburban territory." [20] Shopping centers are classified according to their size, which is determined by the area served and which, in turn, determines the kinds and variety of stores included.[21]

The *neighborhood center* is the smallest and most common type of shopping center. A supermarket is usually its focal point, with the smaller stores geared to supply convenience goods and services (drug and hardware stores, beauty and barber shops, laundry and dry cleaning establishments, and gasoline stations) to some 7,500 to 20,000 people living within six to ten minutes' driving distance. Neighborhood centers may have only a dozen stores, but the total area occupied, including parking space, is likely to range from four to ten acres. Generally, a neighborhood center is well-located if there are no strong competitors within about two miles.

The *community center* is a larger operation and usually features a variety store or a small department store in addition to the supermarket and other small stores also found in the neighborhood center. Thus, the community center provides a merchandise offering which includes a selection of shopping goods, such as clothing and house furnishings, as well as convenience goods. The community center serves a market of from 20,000 to 100,000 persons, and occupies from ten to thirty acres. According to experts, the community center should not have strong competitors within a radius of three to four miles.

The *regional center* is the largest of all. One or even two large department stores provide its main drawing power, which is further enhanced by 50 or more smaller stores. Some regional centers, though not all, include one or two supermarkets to add further to total shopping attractiveness. Shoppers, therefore, may select from a very wide range of goods. Regional centers are usually set up to serve upwards of 100,000 people living within a radius of five or more miles. Such centers, more closely resembling downtown shopping districts than the smaller centers, are slowly but surely changing consumer shopping habits, especially because they reduce the need or urgency to go downtown to shop.

[20] "Shopping Centers Re-studied," *Technical Bulletin No. 30* (Washington, D.C.: Urban Land Institute, May 1957). The American Marketing Association defines a shopping center as "a geographical cluster of retail stores, collectively handling an assortment of goods varied enough to satisfy most of the merchandise wants of consumers within convenient travelling time, and, thereby, attracting a general shopping trade." Unfortunately, the A.M.A. definition includes both planned and unplanned shopping areas. Unplanned shopping areas, usually called "shopping districts," are non-integrated, i.e., they have no over-all plan with respect to the merchandise stocked by each retailer. In contrast, the shopping center defined by the Urban Land Institute is an integrated, planned unit. For that reason, the definition provided by the Urban Land Institute seems to be the most significant for purposes of this discussion.

[21] The discussion on kinds of shopping centers is adapted from: Shopping Centers and New York State's Retail Economy," *New York State Commerce Review*, September 1958, p. 2, and from P. E. Smith, "Prescription for a Successful Shopping Center," *Business Topics*, Autumn 1966, pp. 18-20.

Because of their relatively generous parking facilities, easy accessibility by automobile, and nearness to the suburban middle income market, regional centers now threaten both the central city's downtown shopping district and the older "main street" suburban business district. An estimated 250 regional shopping centers were in existence in 1970. One Cleveland retailer estimated that, of every $20-million spent in shopping centers, $10-million comes out of "downtown's hide." [22] Downtown merchants are pressing for measures to alleviate traffic congestions and also for improved parking facilities, but they are not likely ever to match the convenience of the outlying shopping centers. On the other hand, an outlying center cannot equal the strategic location of the downtown to serve a vast region, nor can it match the downtown's vast range and selection of goods and services. It is not economically feasible, for instance, for regional centers to include stores selling many items bought mainly by the "carriage trade"—bracelets and earrings in the $30,000 price class, fur pieces and coats selling at thousands of dollars apiece, expensive grand pianos, and collections of rare books. No regional center serves a large enough number of the kind of people who might want to buy such items, whereas downtown shopping districts in most large cities, because they draw in trade from a much wider area, are fully capable of supporting such retail stores. Note, too, that the items used as examples all fall into the specialty goods classification—consumers are willing to make a special purchasing effort in order to locate the stores which have such items for sale.

In addition to competing with downtown shopping areas and smaller centers, regional centers have increasingly become competitive with each other as the number of such units expands. Research has indicated that in such instances, driving time to the center is highly influential in determining consumer shopping preferences.[23]

For the manufacturer, the main marketing significance of the planned shopping center lies in the fact that it is an integrated retail unit. Consumers often view the center as a single large shopping convenience and not as a conglomeration of individual stores each going its separate way. Recognizing this, shopping center developers sometimes restrict the classes of merchandise individual stores are permitted to handle. In other centers, a certain degree of controlled competition among stores handling similar merchandise lines is allowed. Thus, a manufacturer of lighting fixtures, accustomed to selling his line through both hardware stores and department stores, encounters three different distribution situations in shopping centers: (1) In some, the line is restricted to the hardware store, (2) in others, it is restricted to the department store, and (3) in still others, both the hard-

[22] *Business Week*, Dec. 5, 1959, p. 82.
[23] J. A. Bonner and J. L. Mason, "The Influence of Driving Time on Shopping Center Preference," *Journal of Marketing*, April 1968, pp. 57-61.

ware store and the department store are free to handle the line. This same manufacturer may even find instances where shopping center branches of department stores are not permitted to handle his line, even though the parent stores have represented the line for years. The great need for information about such situations explains why manufacturers should maintain close contact with their dealers operating, or planning to operate, stores in shopping centers. In addition, the extensive use made of self-service in shopping centers has caused many manufacturers to redesign product packages and add more information to the labels. And, with the growing importance of the regional centers, manufacturers have been led to reexamine their advertising practices, especially with respect to advertising in media which are aimed specifically at the trading areas of shopping centers.

FACILITATING AGENCIES IN MARKETING

There are many institutions that make significant contributions to the process of marketing, but which may not be classified as marketing middlemen since they neither take title to goods nor negotiate purchases or sales. These institutions, known as facilitating agencies, assist in the performance of one or a number of marketing activities. We have listed below a group of activities which are basic to the marketing process together with samples of marketing facilitating agencies that generally assist in performing each activity.

1. Product planning
   and development .... Industrial design consultants
2. Grading and standardizing ... Graders and inspectors
3. Buying and assembling ..... Stock yards
   Packers and shippers
4. Selling .... Commodity exchanges
   Furniture marts
   Advertising agencies
5. Storage .... Storage warehouses
6. Transportation .... Railroads
7. Marketing financing .... Banks
   Cattle loan companies
8. Risk bearing .... Insurance companies
9. Market information .... Marketing research firms

Marketing facilitating agencies are *not* marketing middlemen. They are concerned neither with effecting ownership transfers nor with negotiating such transfers, whereas marketing middlemen are always concerned with one or the other. However, certain facilitating agencies (e.g., stock yards and advertising agencies) sometimes *assist* in performing the buying and/or selling activities. Most marketing facilitating agencies, of course, assist with business activities other than buying and selling and, in these cases at least, it is clear that they do not qualify as marketing middlemen.

CONCLUSION

We have placed particular stress in Chapters 12 and 13 on the dynamic nature of marketing institutions. In the past two hundred years, the rate of institutional change has greatly accelerated. The general store and the general merchandise wholesaler, for instance, evolved, reached their peaks of importance, and have gradually almost faded away. The department store, the mail-order house, and chain store systems appeared, scored great successes, and then settled back as significant but not dominating features of the retail scene. Newer institutions such as the rack jobber, the supermarket, the planned shopping center, and the discount house, probably have not yet grown to full maturity. Traditional institutions, such as the general-line wholesaler and the independent store, have had to modernize their operating methods in order to stay in business.

Many of these changes in marketing institutions and their operating characteristics represent a continuation of long-range trends; a few represent a reversal of previous trends. They have come about in almost all cases as the result of attempts to adjust operating methods more closely to the often changing needs and expectations of the market. Institutional evolution and change can be expected to continue, perhaps at an even more rapid rate, with only those institutions capable of adjusting to the changing characteristics of markets likely to survive. The implications for the manufacturer are clear. There must be continuing adjustments made in marketing channels because the institutions that make up the channels are themselves constantly changing.

QUESTIONS AND PROBLEMS

1. When direct (house-to-house) selling costs run as high as 60 percent of selling price, is it really possible in your opinion, to justify this method of retail distribution from a cost standpoint? Explain.

2. Would you agree that in most instances the small independent retailer is an uneconomical operation, i.e., the proprietor could earn

more money working the same number of hours for someone else? Why do such operations continue?

3. A main reason for patronizing mail-order houses in the nineteenth century was inaccessibility of other buying sources. What would you say is the main reason for patronizing such outlets today?

4. "The future of the department store depends on the continuing demand on the part of the consumer for services, such as credit, delivery, and many more exotic ones, and his willingness to pay for these services." Do you agree?

5. Does the fact that chain stores are horizontally integrated constitute their main competitive advantage? What other factors contribute to their success?

6. Explain why producer cooperatives have been so much more successful than consumer cooperatives in the United States.

7. Supermarkets are described as integrated marketing institutions. What kind of integration is represented by this kind of store? Why should independent supermarkets find it desirable to be members of voluntary chains?

8. Some of the new discount houses have been described as soft goods supermarkets. Is this description accurate? How similar are the operating methods of the two types of institutions (discount houses and supermarkets)?

9. Does the evolution of large, planned shopping centers spell the ultimate elimination of downtown shopping centers? In what ways do downtown merchants have an advantage over merchants in the shopping centers?

10. Can you foresee the possibility that all convenience goods may eventually be sold in vending machines? Comment.

11. Compare the department store buying group with the department store ownership group.

12. If you were an independent grocery retailer and were offered the opportunity to join either a retailer cooperative or a voluntary group, which would you join and why?

13. What problems would a salesman attempting to sell a new product likely have in selling to a supermarket chain that uses a buying committee to make decisions on adding new items?

14. Critically evaluate the "wheel of retailing" hypothesis. What lessons might a retailer learn from this hypothesis?

15. Why shouldn't banks, advertising agencies, and other facilitating agencies be classified as marketing middlemen?

14

MARKETING CHANNELS: OBJECTIVES AND POLICIES

The process of distributing goods or services from the producer to final buyers is an essential part of marketing. This process may be direct and simple, but often it is necessarily indirect and complex. The farmer who sells all his produce at his own roadside stand has the simplest of distribution networks; he sells direct to the consumer and he performs little else in the way of marketing activities, these activities being assumed by his customers. However, other farmers find it necessary to move their produce to a population center in order to find customers. Generally, it is much easier for them to sell their produce to a middleman than to individual consumers. At the same time, consumers usually find it much easier to buy from retailers who carry all or most of their food requirements, including farm-fresh produce. Thus from an economic standpoint, distribution networks develop because they make possible more efficient utilization of time and resources.

In making the complex marketing decisions involved in distribution policy and the management of physical distribution, a decision-maker finds himself faced with a number of problems that cannot be solved independently of each other. Which marketing channel or channels should be used? How many middlemen should there be at each distribution level? How should communication be maintained between the various levels in the channel? How should middlemen be selected? How large should the inventory be? How should the inventory be deployed geographically? How many branch warehouses should there be and where should they be located? Should public warehouses or branch warehouses be used? What modes of transportation should be used? The way *any* of these questions is decided will directly affect the possible ways the others can be decided. These decisions are interlocking ones, and a decision-maker cannot afford to make any of them independently. In this and the next chapter we consider these problems and the main bases for approaching and making decisions on them.

MARKETING CHANNEL ALTERNATIVES IN COMMON USE

Marketing channels vary widely, from the short and simple one employed by a manufacturer of spark plugs who sells his entire output to one automobile manufacturer, to the long and complex channels employed in moving non-perishable farm products to market. Marketing channels are made up of several kinds of building blocks—including producers, ultimate consumers or industrial users, wholesale institutions (both agent and merchant wholesalers), and retail institutions. Thus, the possible number of different channel alternatives is large. Exhibit 14-1 illustrates the more commonly used channel alternatives and brings out the point that the various channel building blocks bear a hierarchical relationship to each other. For example, if agent middlemen are present in a marketing channel, they generally are situated farther back in the channel than wholesalers and/or retailers.

Manufacturer to Consumer or User

There must always be at least two levels in even the shortest marketing channel. They are the producer and the ultimate consumer or industrial user. The direct producer-to-industrial user channel is used in marketing many types of industrial goods. There are several reasons for this: Many industrial products have markets composed of relatively few potential users; the users of particular types of industrial products tend to be clustered in only a few market areas; some industrial products have special servicing and installation requirements that the manufacturer can best provide; others are so technical that manufacturers must employ sales

	Industrial Market			Consumer Goods Market				
Producers	☐	☐	☐	☐	☐	☐	☐	☐
Agent Middlemen		☐					☐	☐
Wholesalers			☐			☐		☐
Retailers					☐	☐	☐	☐
Industrial Users or Consumers	☐	☐	☐	☐	☐	☐	☐	☐

EXHIBIT 14–1

Channel Alternatives Commonly Available in the Distribution
of Industrial and Consumer Goods

engineers to deal directly with prospective users; finally, in many cases, industrial users insist on being permitted to buy directly and are able to buy in quantities large enough to make direct sales by producers economically feasible.

The direct producer-to-ultimate consumer channel is not nearly as important, but many consumer products are marketed this way. Farmers sometimes deal directly with consumers at roadside stands or from stalls in public markets. Small businesses, such as bakeries and dairies, and larger businesses, such as the tire manufacturers, quite often sell directly to consumers, either through their own retail outlets or on a house-to-house basis. A few manufacturers, in such lines as shoes and shirts, sell directly to consumers through mail order departments. However, not many manufacturers of consumer products rely wholly or even principally on the producer-to-ultimate consumer channel. The reasons are obvious: ultimate consumers are numerous, widely scattered, and accustomed to buying in very small quantities.

Manufacturer Through Agent Middlemen to Consumer or User

Some producers use agent middlemen as intermediaries between themselves and the next distribution level. (Agent middlemen, it should be remembered, generally operate at the wholesale level.) Agent middlemen are much used in marketing agricultural produce, partly because most farmers are too small to handle their own distribution efficiently and partly because the main growing areas are often geographically apart from the larger markets.

In marketing manufactured products—both industrial and consumer—agent middlemen are used usually, though not exclusively, by manufacturers who want to rid themselves of much of the marketing task. A manufacturer's entire output may be turned over to one or a small number of agent middlemen for marketing, in which case the manufacturer's marketing channel problem is reduced to that of selecting and persuading certain agents to serve as his representatives. In other instances, the manufacturer may use agents to market his product in some areas, generally ones with limited market potentials, and either use his own sales force or sell directly to merchant middlemen elsewhere.

When agent middlemen are used, they negotiate the transfer of legal title to the producer's merchandise with institutions active on the next distribution level. In the case of consumer products, these negotiations are carried on with either merchant wholesalers or retailers or both, or the agent makes arrangements for further negotiations to be handled by other types of agent middlemen, situated farther along the marketing channel and nearer the ultimate consumer. For such products as furniture, which are usually sold through a limited number of retail outlets, the agent ordinarily negotiates directly with retailers. For products sold through large numbers of retail outlets, such as most food and grocery items, the agent usually negotiates with merchant wholesalers, who, in turn, sell to retailers. However, in marketing food products, agents may also deal directly with such large volume retailers as the grocery chains and retailers' cooperatives. In marketing industrial products, agents usually negotiate directly with industrial users but, in some lines such as small hand tools, it is common for them to negotiate with merchant wholesalers, known as industrial distributors or mill supply houses, which, in turn, sell to the industrial users.

Manufacturer to Retailer to Ultimate Consumer

This is one of the most common marketing channels used for reaching the consumer market. Manufacturers using it generally have some compelling reason for avoiding wholesale middlemen: Their products may be perishable, either physically or fashion-wise, hence speed in distribution is essential; the retailers involved may be predominantly large (such as chains, department stores, and mail-order houses) and, as a matter of policy, refuse to buy through wholesalers; the retailers handling the product may be located near each other, thus making it convenient for the manufacturer to sell to them directly; the available wholesalers may be unable or unwilling to provide the type and amount of promotional support that the manufacturer feels his product requires; finally, the manufacturer simply may desire closer contact with ultimate consumers than that afforded through channels containing more distribution levels.

Manufacturers distributing their products directly to retailers must be able to finance the inventories that would otherwise be carried by merchant wholesalers. Furthermore, the manufacturer ideally should either have a wide enough line to permit his salesmen to write fairly large orders, or a narrower line of products generally ordered by retailers in large quantities. If the product line is not ordinarily purchased in large quantities by individual retailers, the manufacturer should have some other strong reason for selling directly to retailers.

One important reason for distribution direct to retailers by manufacturers is the desire to make use of *franchising*. A franchise is a continuing relationship between a manufacturer (or an expert in the performance of a service) and a retailer in which the franchising grantor supplies the retailer with manufacturing and/or marketing techniques, a brand image, and other know-how for a consideration.[1] This method of operation, which has existed for many years in such industries as petroleum marketing, has increased enormously in importance during the past decade. The relationship requires continuing close contact between the parties involved so that the franchisor can provide advice and supervision when needed. The manufacturer to retailer to ultimate consumer marketing channel meets this requirement.

Manufacturer to Merchant Wholesaler to Retailer to Ultimate Consumer

This consumer goods channel is often referred to as the "traditional" or "orthodox" marketing channel. A manufacturer finds it suitable under some or all of the following conditions: he has a narrow product line; he is unable to finance distribution direct to retailers or can put the necessary funds to more productive use elsewhere; retail outlets are numerous and widely dispersed; wholesalers are able and willing to provide strong promotional support or the product does not require such support; the products are staples, not subject to physical or fashion deterioration; the manufacturer's advertising to ultimate consumers exerts a strong pull in causing retailers to stock the product. Manufacturers who use this channel but desire closer contact with retailers often employ "missionary" salesmen who, while calling on retailers, ordinarily refer any orders they obtain to local wholesalers for filling and delivery.

[1] A. M. Rothenberg, "A Fresh Look at Franchising," *Journal of Marketing*, July 1967, p. 52.

Manufacturer to Merchant Middleman to Industrial User

This marketing channel is used by many producers of such industrial items as small tools and other standard pieces of equipment. These are products of comparatively small unit value purchased by numerous and diverse industrial establishments. Merchant middlemen serving the industrial market, though their operations in many ways resemble those of consumer goods wholesalers, sell directly to industrial users. Such merchant middlemen are known to the trade as industrial supply houses, mill supply houses, industrial hardware distributors, equipment distributors, and other similar titles.

Dual Distribution Systems

When the same product is to be sold to both industrial users and ultimate consumers, separate distribution systems normally are set up to reach each market. For example, the manufacturer of tires normally sells direct to automobile manufacturers but through retailers to the ultimate consumer. However, manufacturers sometimes use more than one marketing channel to reach even essentially the same kinds of customers. The Select Committee on Small Business, U.S. House of Representatives, in its investigation of competitive factors affecting small business described this sort of situation as "dual distribution." Dual distribution was defined by Richard H. Holton, then Assistant Secretary of Commerce, as situations in which "the manufacturer of a branded good sells that brand through two or more competing distribution channels" and where "the manufacturer sells two brands of basically the same product through two competing kinds of distribution networks."[2] An example of the first type of dual distribution is the widespread practice in the oil industry of selling gasoline and related products both through franchised independent outlets and through company-owned stations. An example of the second kind of dual distribution is the practice followed by some appliance manufacturers of selling a nationally advertised brand through a network of wholesalers and retailers and selling an almost identical product under a private brand through direct marketing to large chain or mail-order retail organizations. Dual distribution may make it possible for a manufacturer to achieve deeper penetration of a market than he could obtain through a single marketing channel. However, there is a risk of alienating certain institutions in either or both channels if they encounter strong competition from the other channel. Exhibit 12-2 shows a multiple channel system used by a typewriter manufacturer selling direct to large users

[2] U.S. Congress, House Subcommittee No. 4, Select Committee on Small Business, "Hearings, The Impact Upon Small Business of Dual Distribution," *A Report of Subcommittee No. 4 on Distribution Problems to the Select Committee on Small Business*, 88th Congress, 2nd session, 1964, Hearing I, p. 4.

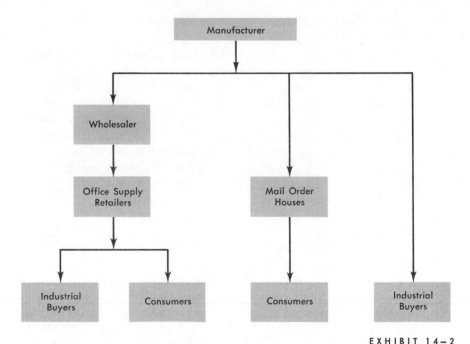

EXHIBIT 14—2

Multiple Channel System—Typewriter Manufacturer

and mass retailers and through wholesalers and retailers to other industrial and consumer market segments.

FACTORS AFFECTING MARKETING CHANNEL CHOICE

The Product

The product's characteristics determine to some extent the way in which it can be distributed. The dollar value of a typical sale sets the limit as to how short the channel should be. If a unit of product sells for several thousand dollars, there is a strong argument for using a short direct-sale type of channel; but if it sells for a few cents (unless many units are purchased at a time), there is a strong argument for using a longer channel (i.e., one containing one or more layers of middlemen). The product's perishability also affects channel decisions—perishable products must be sold through relatively short channels to get them to final buyers quickly. The product's complexity is also a factor—highly technical products requiring specialized selling ability or servicing normally should be sold through the shortest channel available. The degree of product standardization also is important: highly standardized products often should be marketed through long and complex channels; it is usually better to distribute custom-made products direct to the user.

The Market

Market considerations exert powerful influences on the marketing channel chosen. Perhaps most important are those relating to customer buying habits. When customers are accustomed to buying a particular product from a particular source, for example, it is not easy to switch them to a different source. Size and location of the market are also important. When there is a very large number of customers, a producer is likely to need at least one layer of middlemen. When customers are widely dispersed geographically, it is generally easier to reach them through one or more layers of middlemen. Typical order size is another factor of considerable importance—a manufacturer may sell direct to a large chain organization because of the large size of its purchases but use wholesalers to reach smaller retailers.

The Manufacturer

Factors within the manufacturer's own organization can strongly affect channel choice. Management's experience and ability are important. Unless executives are capable of setting up and controlling a direct sales force, middlemen or agents probably are needed. Financial strength is another consideration—short channels require a much larger investment of money in fixed selling costs than do long channels. The manufacturer's need or desire for control over the product's sale to end-buyers also affects channel length; if, for example, he wants to insure aggressive promotion for his product, he chooses the shortest available channel. The reputation of the company or its products also affect channel choice, particularly in the case of new products. Middlemen are willing to take on a well-known product line but hesitate to take on "unknown items produced by unknown companies." Thus, well-known manufacturers enjoy considerable freedom in putting together the combination of middlemen they want.

Middlemen

Marketing channels sometimes are dictated by the middlemen available. In other words, a manufacturer may be restricted in his choice of channel by the availability of particular middlemen. Thus, he may have to take second choices, if those he wants are unwilling to take on his product line. Some middlemen may be willing to take on his product line but unwilling to accept his distribution policies, with respect to price, required promotional effort, and the like. Finally, the manufacturer's choice of channels is affected by the cost of using different types of middlemen relative to his own sales and profit goals.

THE ENVIRONMENT FOR MARKETING CHANNEL DECISIONS

Because the producer is situated at the "originating end" of his marketing channel, one might assume that he exercises ultimate control over it. In fact, some writers say the producer is the "channel captain." Actually, however, several factors limit the producer's ability to plan and control marketing channels for his products.

A manufacturer's role in the selection of marketing channels is primarily one of adjusting to the expectations and preferences of buyers at each distribution level. At the retail distribution level, the buyers are ultimate consumers; they are not interested in the manufacturer's ideas about which outlets should sell his products. They buy from those retailers who are capable of best serving their needs. The discount house is an excellent example. In the late 1940s and early 1950s many manufacturers of nationally-advertised items refused to permit discount houses to handle their lines. Nevertheless, discount houses managed to obtain merchandise; ultimate consumers, in ever increasing numbers, demonstrated that they preferred to buy such items from discount houses rather than from more conventional retailers. Manufacturers, realizing the hopelessness of trying to keep their products out of discount houses (and the potential loss in sales volume if they succeeded) relented, many of them actively seeking retail distribution through discount house.

At other distribution levels, buyers' expectations and preferences are equally important. Once the manufacturer determines which kinds of retailers will be most acceptable to ultimate consumers, he must find out the type of supplier from which retailers prefer to buy the product. Retailers may customarily buy directly from manufacturers or from wholesalers. Whatever the normal buying pattern or retailers, a manufacturer is well-advised to make his product available through the same sources.

Not only must the manufacturer determine the *kind* of middlemen he should use on each distribution level, he must also decide on *how many* middlemen should handle his product on each level. If he decides to sell directly to retailers, he must choose from among many different kinds of retailers; if he decides to use wholesalers, he must also choose from among the different kinds of wholesale institutions. Then, he must determine how many retailers of the chosen types will be needed to reach the consumers he wants to reach and, assuming he decides to use wholesalers, also, how many wholesalers of the chosen types will be required to reach all the retailers he desires to use. If we think of the different kinds of middlemen as kinds of "institutional" building blocks, as we did earlier, we can say that the manufacturer must decide not only what kinds of building blocks to include in his marketing channel(s), but also how many of each kind he needs.

An example will shed additional light on the complexity of the manufacturer's problems in choosing marketing channels. A manufacturer of home appliances seeking retail outlets is faced with a choice of appliance stores, department stores, chain stores, furniture stores, and discount houses. From these, he must decide on appropriate outlets in every city and town where he wants his product to be sold at retail. Usually, appliance manufacturers do not try to achieve distribution through every available retail outlet in every community, but they must determine *which specific outlets* in each city and town will be likely to do the best selling job. Our appliance manufacturer could decide to sell only through one kind of retailer—possibly only through furniture stores. An alternative would be to adopt a more widely used policy—that of varying selection of outlets in each city and town, according to the relative merits of local retailers. Finally, the manufacturer would have to contact all retailers he decided to use and persuade them to distribute his line in their areas.

The significant thing to recognize at this time is that the manufacturer must consider the interests of *outside* parties (final buyers of the product and middlemen) before he makes this important marketing channel decision. In other words, he is not free to make the channel-decision in a "vacuum." Only when there is a product shortage is there ever any excuse for a manufacturer to make unilateral channel-decisions and, even then, it is a questionable procedure. In this age of plenty, channel usage must be determined by the expectations, and preferences of final buyers and those at each distribution level. And it must be remembered that channels which serve well today may not do so tomorrow.

Marketing novices ask why comparable manufacturers of similar products often use different marketing channels. Such a circumstance may be explained by any of four different reasons. First, it is not always possible for a manufacturer to use the channel he prefers if it is already being used by competitors. A manufacturer of men's suits, for example, may want to distribute his line through the leading men's store in each town, but many such retailers may already be satisfied with the lines in stock. Confronted with this situation, the manufacturer may have to compromise in some communities and accept second best men's stores, or the men's departments of department stores. Second, some manufacturers, ignorant of ultimate consumers' preferences for certain outlets, convince themselves that the superiority of their products will attract ultimate consumers to the outlets they use. Third, some manufacturers simply disregard ultimate consumers' desires and use outlets which are easiest to obtain. And fourth, when two manufacturers of similar products use different channels, each may actually have made the "best" choice, because each may be successfully catering to different market segments. When a manufacturer is unable, for one reason or another, to use what is for him the best possible channel, he may still succeed in moving his products through another channel and into the hands of some ultimate consumers. But he may not be as successful as he would have been had he been able to use the best channel or combination of channels.

DETERMINATION OF MARKETING CHANNELS

What should a marketing executive try to accomplish in his determination of marketing channels? According to one expert, "a particular business should use those channels or combinations of channels which will contribute most to the securing and maintaining, not simply of the greatest attainable sales volume, but of that combination of sales volume and cost that will yield the maximum amount of profit, both in the short run and in the long run." [3] Now, "should use those channels or combinations of channels" implies that there is not always complete freedom of choice. Certainly, an executive can determine those channels he "should use" through rational analysis of both qualitative and quantitative, marketing and non-marketing, factors. In many cases, however, circumstances (e.g., an unwillingness of certain middlemen to handle the product or to cooperate in other ways) can cause differences between what the channels *should be* and what they actually *can be*.[4] The extreme case is the one where external influences, such as pressures from existing middlemen or the absence of desired types of middlemen, force a particular channel decision on an executive. Fortunately, such extremes are rare. Executives in a manufacturing firm usually enjoy some discretion in their determination of marketing channels, since there ordinarily are several alternatives from which to choose.

[3] C. H. Sevin, "Analytical Approach to Channel Policies," in R. M. Clewett (ed.), *Marketing Channels* (Homewood, Ill.: Richard D. Irwin, 1954), p. 434.
[4] For an illuminating discussion on this point, see: P. McVey, "Are Channels of Distribution What the Textbooks Say?" *Journal of Marketing*, January 1960, pp. 61-65.

Determining Potential Channel Alternatives

Faced with the task of determining potential channel alternatives, a marketing executive is likely to discover an almost infinite number of combinations of different types of middlemen engaged in different lines of trade at different distribution levels. From this vast number of potential distribution arrangements, the marketer must first screen those that may be appropriate for distribution of the product. His immediate purpose, then, is to identify alternatives that are sufficiently promising to justify further screening for feasibility. This preliminary screening has some quantitative aspects, but qualitative considerations of the product and market predominate.

The nature of a product, its unit value, its technical characteristics, its degree of differentiation from competitive products, whether it is perishable, whether it is a staple or non-staple—these and other product characteristics may limit the number of "potential" channel alternatives. Individually or in combination, they may restrict the alternatives to those in a given line of trade, to those containing a certain number of distribution levels, to those where middlemen are equipped to provide technical service and repair, or to those where middlemen have specialized storage facilities (e.g., for frozen foods) or are specialists in some phase of marketing (e.g., fashion merchandising). The crucial product factors, of course, depend on the particular product. Different product factors form the channel screening bases for a line of home workshop power tools and for a line of imported hams.

The other main basis for this initial screening is the market—the final destination of the product. Research can aid the decision-maker by answering the question: Where do ultimate buyers (ultimate consumers or industrial users), expect to, or prefer to, buy the product? Is the market concentrated or dispersed? Do ultimate and intermediate buyers expect their immediate suppliers to play aggressive or passive roles in promoting the product—these and other market factors may be used as screening devices for uncovering potential channel alternatives. The relative significance of specific market factors varies with the particular market the manufacturer wants to cultivate. A cigarette manufacturer, for example, has more channel alternatives—and requires more—than does a manufacturer of high-quality men's hats. Ultimate buyers expect to find cigarettes in more outlets of more types than they do high-quality men's hats. Furthermore, a cigarette retailer plays a passive role in promoting the product; a retailer of high-quality men's hats, in contrast, plays an active, even aggressive, role.

This initial screening, according to product and market factors, should eliminate most of the channel alternatives from further consideration. If effective, this qualitative comparison of channels, with regard to significant product and market factors, results in sorting out the potential alternatives from the much larger number of possible alternatives. Those remaining are a manageable few, deserving more detailed study and analysis.

Ascertaining Feasible Channel Alternatives

Unlike the initial screening, which is largely qualitative, the second screening emphasizes quantitative comparison. Typically, this screening for feasible channel alternatives requires the gathering of quantitative information to answer such questions as these: Are there enough of the desired types of middlemen in all the market areas the manufacturer wants to cultivate? Are the desired middlemen "free" to handle the product, or are they "non-available" and committed to competing products? Will the desired middlemen accept or reject the opportunity to take on the product? How much could it cost to reverse middlemen's unwillingness to stock the product?

Whereas the initial screening focused on the product and market, the second focuses on the makeup of the different channels. For example, detailed examinations are made of individual stores that a manufacturer may want to have represent him at the retail level. For each channel under study, a manufacturer should certainly determine the "reach" of individual outlets at each distribution level: Can they reach a sufficient number of outlets on the next level, and are they in contact, directly or indirectly, with a large enough number of final buyers? Quite possibly, a manufacturer may be drawn into supporting and encouraging people to go into business as distributors or dealers in order to obtain the desired type of representation in some market areas.

During his screening, some or many potential channel alternatives will be discarded as not feasible. The two-phase "weeding-out" process should result in a small number of remaining alternatives classed as feasible. These are now ready for further evaluations, mostly quantitative.

Comparing Relative Profitability

The third screening is directed toward determining the relative profitability of the channel alternatives now rated as "feasible." Essentially, this consists of making estimates of the sales volume potential and the costs of channel usage for each channel alternative. Through comparing these estimates, a decision-maker tries to find the channel alternative that shows the greatest promise of contributing the most to maximum long-run profits. Neither maximal sales volume nor minimal cost is significant in itself; but the ideal both in optimum combination. Furthermore, since a decision-maker is concerned both with probable long-run and short-term profits, and since the "length" of the long-run varies with the company and the situation, the time element must be taken into account.

The reliability of the different comparisons of relative profitability can be no better than the underlying estimates of sales volume potentials and costs of channel usage, and, before a decision-maker can make sound comparisons of relative profitability, he must have certain market statistics. The most basic relate to the potential market. He must have both short-term and long-run estimates of market potential. From these, perhaps by applying some "target share-of-the-market percentage," he must derive short-term and long-run estimates of his firm's sales potentials. After considering these sales potentials, together with data on the "reach" of outlets at each distribution level, a decision-maker should be able to determine, at least tentatively, whether a single channel or a number of channels will be needed.

ESTIMATES OF SALES VOLUME POTENTIAL   In analyzing each channel for its sales volume potential, decision-makers seek to answer this question: Is this channel capable of reaching a sufficient number of final buyers to assure absorption of the desired quantity of product? The new data needed for an answer to this question are rarely all immediately available. Some may be found in the manufacturer's own records and some may be secured from external sources of market statistics, but some may have to be obtained through special marketing surveys. After adjustments for such factors as the strengths and weaknesses of competitors, and after projecting market trends in relation to the channel being considered, the channel's sales volume potential is determined. Some alternatives may now be eliminated if their sales volume capabilities are clearly inadequate and show little promise of improving. At this point, decision-makers must keep in mind the possibility that there may be no single channel capable of realizing the full sales potential. Two or more may be required and, if this proves to be the case, similar estimates will have to be made for the different channel combinations.

In addition, the attainable level of sales volume, regardless of the channel or combination, is strongly influenced by the ability of marketing management, the excellence of its planning, and its skill in the implementation of marketing programs and campaigns. A decision-maker should not necessarily assume that the managerial competence of his subordinates who are charged with translating his decision into action will be the same, regardless of the channel under study. There is no denying that the same subordinates may be able to obtain excellent sales results from some channels and mediocre results from others. The decision-maker must decide where his subordinates are strong and where weak and make his decisions accordingly.

COSTS OF CHANNEL USAGE   With estimates of sales volume capabilities on hand, the next step is to determine the costs of moving these volumes through the different channels. Essentially this is a matter of marketing cost analysis, one of determining probable costs of performing required marketing activities under each arrangement. In each channel there is implied some scheme for dividing up performance of marketing activities, of apportioning some to the manufacturer and others to different "channel members." The costs of performing each marketing activity at each distribution level and the total costs of performing the entire marketing task must be estimated for each channel.

In analyzing probable costs of channel usage, decision-makers must consider possible "hidden" costs. In estimating costs of performing the storage activity, for example, costs of breakage, spoilage, and pilferage, while usually hidden, must nevertheless be taken into account along with total warehousing charges. Furthermore, in certain industries, manufacturers experience serious problems, financial as well as marketing, caused by apparently erratic inventory fluctuations. If, on the one hand, inventory is larger than it has to be relative to the volume of incoming orders, money is tied up in inventory that could be invested or be earning interest elsewhere—the hidden cost of being overstocked. If, on the other hand, inventory is too small relative to the volume of incoming orders, many customers cancel their orders and patronize other sources of supply—the hidden cost of being out-of-stock. In one remarkable simulation study (i.e., computer replication of a business situation), it was demonstrated that the use of more than three distribution levels can bring about marked instability in inventory sizes, both for the manufacturer and for the middlemen.[5] One implication was that a manufacturer's use of "long channels" could be the underlying cause of wild fluctuations in his volume of incoming orders. It is interesting to note that in the textile industry, which shows marked inventory instability, there are often four or five distribution levels from yarn manufacturer to ultimate consumer. The conventional system of accounting used by most manufacturers provides no way of recording the hidden but real costs associated with erratic inventory fluctuations. The possibility of this and other types of hidden costs developing if a given channel decision is made, although certainly a difficult result to predict, nevertheless is an important factor to keep in mind.

TAKING THE TIME ELEMENT INTO ACCOUNT   In appraising long-run profit prospects, there is a need to "pin down" how long the long-run is. The number of years in the long-run, of course, varies with management's appraisal of the company's outlook. For a going concern whose manage-

---

[5] J. W. Forrester, "Industrial Dynamics," *Harvard Business Review*, July-August 1958, p. 47.

ment expects little growth, the long-run may actually mean no more than a single year. For a company whose management anticipates rapid and continued growth, the long-run may represent five or ten years or even longer. When the long-run has been specifically defined, management, in effect, has set its "target date." This, however, is likely to change, as management alters its appraisal of future opportunities with the passing of time. In spite of the fact that exact target dates are somewhat elusive, decisions on marketing channels (certainly major marketing decisions) are not easily reversible and must be "lived with" for a considerable time. Thus, in a manner similar to the proverbial marriage contract, channel arrangements should not be "lightly entered into." In taking the time element into account, therefore, the decision-maker should make certain that his estimate of the number of years in the long-run is sufficiently long to permit reversal of the channel decision should that become necessary.

A SIMPLIFIED EXAMPLE   To better understand the kind of thinking involved in a rational approach to the channel selection problem, let us consider a highly simplified example. The particular analytical process shown is not meant to represent a process appropriate in all channel selection situations, either industrial or consumer. With that preliminary word of caution, then, let us assume that a certain decision-maker, whose firm markets an industrial product, has only two channel alternatives: either (1) to use a company-controlled sales force and deal directly with industrial users, or (2) to use agents who will be paid on a commission basis. Further assume that sales volume capabilities are identical through either channel. (Although adopted here for simplicity, these assumptions do represent a reasonably accurate statement of the channel alternatives available to many industrial marketers.)

This decision-maker is fortunate in that he has a ready-made standard to use in comparing the two alternatives. It is the particular commission rate at which agents can be secured. Knowing this rate, which we shall call "P," he can estimate the costs of using agents and compare the result with his estimate of the costs of using a company-controlled sales force. His decision should favor that alternative showing the most promise of meeting the criterion of maximizing net profits over some given period. But before he can apply the profit criterion, the decision-maker needs four additional estimates:

X: number of years during which net profit is to be maximized—i.e., the "long-run."

S: total sales volume forecast over X years.

C: average yearly cost of keeping a salesman in the field including his compensation and all expenses. Thus, C is the average cost per salesman per year.

N: number of salesmen needed to produce S sales volume.

Because of the assumption that "S" will be identical under either alternative, the channel comparison can be made entirely on the basis of cost. The two alternatives, then, may be represented symbolically in cost terms.

SP: cost of producing S sales volume forecasted for X years through agents at a P commission rate.

NCX: cost of using N company salesmen at an average yearly cost of C for X years.

Thus, to determine which of the two alternatives will cost the least, this decision-maker should apply the decision rule:

$$\frac{SP}{NCX} = 1$$

If $\frac{SP}{NCX} > 1$, it will cost more to have agents do the selling; therefore, the company should establish its own sales force.

If $\frac{SP}{NCX} = 1$, the costs are the same for the two alternatives, and the decision may be based on other considerations.

If $\frac{SP}{NCX} < 1$, it will cost less to have agents do the selling; therefore, the company should not set up its own sales force.

This channel selection model also may be used to compute the maximum number of salesmen the company can afford to put in the field without adding to its distribution costs. For this purpose, the so-called "indifference" version of the model is used. First, both sides of the original equation are multiplied by "N" as follows:

$$\frac{N}{1} \cdot \frac{SP}{NCX} = 1 \cdot \frac{N}{1}$$

Cancelling out, the result is:

$$\frac{SP}{CX} = N_{max}$$

"N$_{max}$" is the maximum number of salesmen the manufacturer can afford without having distribution costs exceed those he would incur by using agents.

An important, though unstated, assumption underlying this particular model is that personal selling effort is the predominant element in the manufacturer's promotional mix. This holds for some industrial marketing situations but not for many consumer goods marketing situations.

Obtaining Channel Usage

Obtaining channel usage requires that approaches be made to individual members of the prospective channel team. The manufacturer must "sell" his proposal to the managements of channel members, then in most cases, follow through and "sell" the team members' sales staffs. In other words, for each channel member organization, someone must convince both the executives and those who do the actual selling.

The decision each prospective channel member must make—either to accept or to reject the manufacturer's proposal—is for him a product-selection decision and such decisions have to be made at each distribution level. To put it another way—while the manufacturer thinks of the situation in terms of putting together a marketing channel, each middleman (i.e., prospective channel member) thinks of it in terms of "Should I add or not add this product to my stock." If a consumer product, for instance, is to be marketed through wholesalers and retailers, such decisions would be made at three levels—wholesale, retail, and consumer. Before the consumer can decide to accept or reject the product, the retailer must have already decided to accept it; and before the retailer can make his decision, the wholesaler must have made his decision to accept it.

Costs of Obtaining Channel Usage   In obtaining initial usage of a marketing channel (i.e., in implementing the desired channel decision), the manufacturer necessarily incurs certain costs. The nature and amount of these costs varies with the skill of marketing management in implementing a particular channel decision and with its adeptness in putting distribution and promotion plans into effect. Precise estimates of such costs can be made by the decision-maker only when he has reliable appraisals of the effectiveness of those executives who are to be given responsibility for implementing the specific channel decision. Since such appraisals are likely to be more subjective than objective and to depend on those who make them, this aspect of estimating the initial costs of channel usage is not pursued further here.

Although not strictly according to conventional accounting

practices, the marketing executive should view the costs of obtaining *initial* channel usage as an investment (accountants normally classify such costs, e.g., costs of product introductory campaigns, as expenses). This investment, made to implement a long-run decision, can only be expected to "pay off" over several years; thus, at least in his planning leading up to the decision, the executive should think in terms of amortizing (writing off) this investment over the long-run period. After all, as is repeatedly emphasized throughout this book, the executive making major marketing decisions should be trying to maximize long-run rather than short-term profits. It should be mentioned, however, that once channel usage is secured, both marketers and accountants agree that the costs of *continued* channel usage should be treated as short-term operating expenses rather than as a long-run investment.

MIDDLEMEN'S PRODUCT-SELECTION DECISION PROCEDURE   In preparing their approach to prospective channel members, marketing executives are well advised to study the way most middlemen make product-selection decisions. With certain exceptions found mainly among the largest retailers and wholesalers, most middlemen simply do not have sufficient sales and cost data to make rational product-selection decisions. The typical middleman handles a large number of different products, and his records rarely break down sales by individual products. This same variety in the inventory makes it almost impossible to assign costs to specific items. Furthermore, such sales and cost statistics as he does have may be difficult to project for future operating periods. Considering these circumstances, then, it is hardly surprising that middlemen generally base product-selection decisions on non-rational grounds.

Among retailers, for example, it is common to appraise relative profitability among brands according to relative percentage markup. A retailer will probably prefer a brand carrying a 20 percent markup to one with a 15 percent markup. The implicit assumption is that the two brands will not differ as to rate of inventory turnover and sale, price, or handling costs. Although a retailer may not be totally unaware of differences among brands in these respects, he tends to assign a heavier weight to relative markup percentages because he has more information about them.

In referring to the way retailers *should* make product-selection decisions, one author says:

> Gross profit per square foot of display space is probably the most useful criterion that can be found. Although the incremental net profit rather than the average gross profit is correct conceptually, average gross profit is easier to compute and it is usually a satisfactory

approximation. The average gross profit per square foot is computed as follows:

$$\frac{\text{MARKUP (in dollars and cents)} \times \text{RATE OF SALE}}{\text{NUMBER OF SQUARE FEET OF DISPLAY SPACE}}$$

The method involves certain significant assumptions:

1. It assumes that all display space is equally effective in selling products. Such an assumption does not hold in many instances—there are "hot spots" in a store. The manager with experience acquires a judgment as to their location; thus, most of the choices that he makes concerning the use of the space relate to different brands of a product, and the choices do not require a comparison of widely different areas in the store.
2. It assumes that incremental costs vary directly with the volume of sales of each brand. Viewed practically, this method avoids the cost-allocation problem. . . . However . . . the only major cost varying with volume, is cost of goods sold. This cost varies directly with volume, except in extreme cases where quantity discounts by the manufacturer would cause a decreasing unit cost.
3. It assumes that all display space is fully utilized. If this is not true in a given situation, the amount of space used should not be a consideration. In practice, however, all display space is usually fully utilized.[6]

In building and managing inventory, therefore, a middleman should attempt—rationally—to equalize the marginal gross profit contribution in dollars for each square foot of selling space. Many retailers do attempt to do this, although intuitively, by allotting "slow sellers" less shelf space than "fast sellers"—typically, slow sellers have higher markups than fast sellers—and by putting best sellers in the best selling spaces. Thus, even though middlemen commonly attach too much significance to relative percentage markups, their total pattern of behavior in making product-selection decisions is not quite so irrational as it first appears. Marketing management should anticipate this sort of "semi-rational" behavior in planning its approach to prospective channel members.

Later on, i.e., once distribution is obtained, marketing management may derive additional benefits if it has information on middlemen's procedures in buying and stocking. Philip Morris, Inc., for instance, found that certain of its competitors were "renting" space on cigarette display racks for their own brands in self-service retail stores. In many stores, this practice resulted in some of Philip Morris's brands being frequently out-

---

[6] J. A. Howard, *Marketing Management: Analysis and Planning*, rev. ed. (Homewood, Ill.: Richard D. Irwin, 1963), p. 333.

of-stock on display racks—even though back room "reserve" stocks of these same brands were fully adequate. To combat this competitive tactic, Philip Morris undertook to "educate" retailers on the wisdom of apportioning display space to individual brands in proportion to their respective rates of sale. From the results of field investigations, Philip Morris was able to prove to retailers that apportioning space to brands according to rates of sale would almost invariably increase the total profit contribution. Armed with these research results, company salesmen succeeded in obtaining a fairer allotment of display space for Philip Morris's various brands.

DISTRIBUTION INTENSITY

A manufacturer must also decide how many middlemen he should seek on each level of distribution. Depending on the desired channel arrangement, he must, in the case of a consumer product, for example, determine the number of retailers, the number of wholesalers, the number of agents, and so on. Similarly, related decisions have to be made within the company organization concerning the number of salesmen needed, the number of district sales managers, and so on. Notice that the problem of determining the numbers of middlemen blends naturally into one of deciding the structure and type of the manufacturer's sales organization.

Decisions on the number of middlemen may be thought of as decisions on the degree of distribution intensity. There are three general degrees of distribution intensity: mass, selective, and exclusive. This is an arbitrary classification, for there are many intermediate gradations. Distribution intensity should be regarded as a broad band with mass distribution at one end and exclusive distribution at the other. Within this broad band, there is a very large number of points, representing different shades of selective distribution.

EXTREMES OF DISTRIBUTION INTENSITY   The two extremes, as stated above, are mass distribution and exclusive distribution. Mass distribution provides maximum sales exposure for a product, whereas exclusive distribution involves using a single middleman—a retailer, for example—in each market area. Normally, a manufacturer must use multiple channels, and frequently some very long channels among them, to achieve mass distribution intensity. In contrast, a manufacturer using exclusive distribution tends not only to have a single channel but to sell directly to the chosen outlets.

SELECTIVE DISTRIBUTION   Most manufacturers have neither complete mass distribution nor complete exclusive distribution but rather some form of selective distribution. Voluntary or involuntarily, in pursuing a policy of selective distribution, manufacturers restrict the number of outlets on each distribution level. Voluntary restriction occurs when a manufacturer decides, for instance, not to use every conceivable outlet for his product in a given market area but to use only a few of the more desirable outlets. Involuntary restriction occurs either when certain "desired" outlets refuse to handle a manufacturer's product or when the number of available outlets in a given market area is less than the number the manufacturer would like to have in that area. Sometimes, the number of middlemen is limited to only those that can best serve the manufacturer (i.e., be the most profitable), but the more modern view is that the number of outlets should be limited to those that can best serve sufficiently large numbers of ultimate buyers (i.e., not necessarily including *only* those outlets most profitable to the manufacturer but also other outlets such as those situated in locations more convenient to ultimate buyers.

If skillfully implemented, selective distribution usually results in greater profits for each channel member. The manufacturer gains because he sells to a smaller number of accounts (thus reducing selling expenses) but, ideally, more to each account. The middlemen gain because fewer of their competitors handle the manufacturer's product, permitting them to attract trade that might otherwise go elsewhere. Better merchandising practices also are likely to augment the profits of manufacturer and middlemen alike: there should be fewer "out-of-stocks" because more adequate inventories are handled; more valuable retail display space tends to be used; at all levels there is more desire to cooperate in coordinating promotional efforts. Even the manufacturer's "small order" problem may disappear almost entirely.

DECISIONS ON DISTRIBUTION INTENSITY   Much of the information that is assembled and analyzed for making decisions on marketing channels is also pertinent to decisions on distribution intensity. Indeed, both these decisions should be made together. Particularly important, however, in deciding on distribution intensity are the product's marketing characteristics. The more frequently end-buyers purchase a product, the stronger the argument for mass distribution or for an extensive form of selective distribution. The greater the gross margin is for the middlemen, the more persuasive the argument for something closer to exclusive distribution. The amount of product service expected by end-buyers may vary from none at all (a point in favor of mass distribution) to a large amount (an argument for exclusive distribution). If the useful life of a product is very long, distribution should be quite selective or even exclusive. Similarly, the more searching time end-buyers are willing to devote to finding a product outlet, the fewer outlets a manufacturer can afford to have.

The anticipated or actual market position of a brand also influences the decision on distribution intensity. If a brand enjoys only brand recognition, the manufacturer, desiring maximum sales exposure, probably will use mass distribution or something fairly close to it. If a brand has consumer preference, the manufacturer can afford to use some selective distribution. If a brand is so fortunate that end-buyers insist on it and refuse substitutes, highly selective distribution is feasible and exclusive distribution may be possible. But few brands are "insisted upon" or even "preferred" by all final buyers, and each market segment is likely to regard the brand somewhat differently. Thus, the distribution intensity decision must partially depend on the manufacturer's appraisal of how his product stands with different market segments and his evaluation of the sales potential of each segment.

Many other factors, too many to analyze in detail here, affect the decision on distribution intensity. But it is worthwhile to mention briefly certain additional factors bearing directly on this decision. A manufacturer must take into account the strength of his desire to control price at each distribution level and the "policing" problem involved. He must appraise the amount of market risk involved in each alternative—for example, exclusive distribution is like "putting all the marketing eggs in a limited number of baskets." He must know the attitudes of distributive outlets—some actively seek and enthusiastically support "exclusives," but others want no "exclusives" or accept them chiefly to deprive competitors of them. Only if he carefully considers and evaluates such attitudes can a manufacturer realistically appraise the relative merits of different policies as to distribution intensity. Nor should he overlook the fact that once he grants "exclusives," it is rather awkward to replace those distributors who fail to measure up to expectations.[7] Replacement of ineffective distributors is awkward to handle not only because of the delicate problems involved in cancelling established relationships but also because potential replacements, knowing of a local competitor's failure with the manufacturer's product, are likely to be skeptical of their own chances for success with it. He must also compare the alternatives in relation to his advertising program—both with respect to the probable amount of waste circulation (i.e, appearance of his advertisements in geographic areas other than those where he contemplates having distributors) and with regard to the problems involved in coordinating middlemen's promotional efforts with his own. Management's attitudes toward competition must also be considered. Someone has to decide

---

[7] However, some manufacturers faced with handling distributors not measuring up to expectations have found ingenious methods for improving the situation. For instance, see the David D. Doniger & Company case in: R. R. Still and E. W. Cundiff, *Sales Management: Decisions, Policies, and Cases* (Englewood Cliffs, N.J.: Prentice-Hall, 1969), pp. 678-89.

whether it is more desirable to have competition inside retail outlets or not and the amount of protection that should be sought from in-store competition and in-market competition.

CONCLUSION

Few areas of decision-making in marketing are so complex as those pertaining to the choice of marketing channels and the interrelated problem of determining the desired degree of distribution intensity. In no other area of marketing is it more important to base decisions on sound analysis, both of qualitative information and quantitative data. Decisions in this area are made for the long run, and, once implemented, it is not easy to reverse or change them. Therefore, it is highly important that decisions on marketing channels and distribution intensity be reached after only the most thorough deliberation and analysis. Such careful planning pays off handsomely in terms of future sales, profits, and market position.

QUESTIONS AND PROBLEMS

1. Explain the meaning and significance to marketing of each of the following statements:
   a. The producer does not always enjoy complete freedom in selecting marketing channels.
   b. Manufacturers make channel selection decisions whereas middlemen make product selection decisions.
   c. A manufacturer should consider the middlemen on his channel team as simply extensions of his own marketing organization.
   d. Effective usage of marketing channels requires a continuous review and evaluation of the marketing uncontrollables.
2. Illustrate how product and market factors might affect the initial screening of channel alternatives for each of the following products:
   a. Cigarette lighters intended to retail at $15
   b. Portable, small-screen, transistorized television sets
   c. Prefabricated swimming pools for homeowners
   d. Office furniture
   e. College textbooks
   f. Electric shavers for women
   g. Neckties
3. Why should the initial screening of channel alternatives be largely qualitative and the second screening largely quantitative?

4. Analyze the relationship of sales forecasting and marketing cost analysis to the determination of marketing channels.

5. What are the factors which cause many manufacturers to use dual marketing channels?

6. How do marketers and accountants differ in the way they view the costs of obtaining initial channel usage? The costs of continued channel usage?

7. To what extent does a manufacturer's use of certain marketing channels place constraints on his decisions with respect to the addition of new products? On his decisions to drop certain products?

8. Under what conditions would you advise a manufacturer to merge with a middleman handling his products? Under what conditions would such a merger be illegal? (Hint: See Chapter 23.)

9. Outline the steps an importer of foreign automobiles might go through in securing an exclusive dealer in a particular city.

10. A manufacturer of dinnerware is considering setting up a distribution system whereby his own salesmen would call directly on ultimate consumers and sell them "in their homes." If the manufacturer decides to set up this system of direct distribution, he will discontinue selling the line through retail department, jewelry, and specialty stores—nearly 2,000 of which now stock his product line. What factors should be taken into account by this manufacturer in making this decision?

11. A producer of machine tools has been selling industrial users directly through his own force of 20 salaried salesmen. What arguments might be put forth to persuade this manufacturer to discontinue direct selling and to use industrial distributors instead? (Note: Industrial distributors in this field normally receive a 20 per cent discount off the manufacturer's list price.)

12. Manufacturers of consumer products who use wholesalers to reach retail outlets often also employ salesmen to call on wholesalers' customers. Why? Since, in such cases, the manufacturer's salesmen already call on retailers, why shouldn't the wholesalers be eliminated entirely?

13. Why is it that manufacturers who desire to make use of franchising generally sell direct to retailers?

14. What influence do each of the following factors have on the choice of marketing channels? The product. The market. The manufacturer's organization. The middlemen.

15. Why do comparable manufacturers of similar products often use different channels?

16. "Normally, a manufacturer must use multiple channels, and frequently some very long channels among them, to achieve mass distribution intensity." Why?

17. Under what conditions might a manufacturer involuntarily use a policy of selective distribution in a given market area?

18. Why would a manufacturer using exclusive distribution normally tend to sell directly to his chosen outlets?

19. Generally speaking, a manufacturer's brand must enjoy some degree of consumer preference before it is wise for the manufacturer to adhere to a policy involving selective distribution. Why?

15

PHYSICAL DISTRIBUTION: OBJECTIVES AND POLICIES

Physical distribution involves the actual movement and storage of goods after they are produced and before they are consumed. It comprises a number of interrelated activities, the most important of which are: inventory control, storage, transportation, materials handling, order size control, and order processing. However, in some firms even today one finds these activities being managed separately with little or no overall coordination. Almost inevitably, such separate and non-coordinated management of physical distribution activities leads to conflicts among departments and problems for the company as a whole. Production wants long production runs in order to obtain low manufacturing costs, which could result in erratic management of the composition of finished goods inventories. Finance wants minimal inventories to conserve capital. Marketing wants large inventories to facilitate promised deliveries. Traffic management tends to be preoccupied with minimizing transportation costs. Under these chaotic circumstances, each departmental management seeks to minimize the costs of performing the segment of physical distribution with which it comes into contact and is responsible for but makes little attempt to optimize total physical distribution costs in an effort to achieve the company's over-all goals. Not until 1956, in a special study of the cost of air freight, was the "total cost" approach applied to the analysis of physical distribution efficiency.[1] Here, for the first time, the various trade-offs between air freight, inventory investment, and storage costs were formally described. Since physical distribution costs bulk large in the over-all cost of goods, adoption of the total cost approach has been rapid and widespread among well-managed companies.[2]

RELATIONSHIP TO MARKETING CHANNELS

Physical distribution policies and practices are directly related to other distribution policies and practices. Consider what takes place as products move through marketing channels, over time and through space, from points of production to points of consumption. Inventories are held not only by manufacturers but, in most cases, by middlemen at each distribution level and by ultimate buyers at the end of the channel. In the distribution of consumer goods, for example, consumers add to their stocks by buying from retailers. This reduces retailers' inventories, and eventually retailers place replenishing orders with wholesalers. Wholesalers, in turn, replenish their stocks by placing orders with manufacturers. Thus, while products are flowing forward to the final buyers, there is a reverse flow of orders which causes alternating subtractions from and additions to inventories held at each level. Each time a manufacturer ships an order, he initiates this chain reaction in the performance of transportation and storage activities.

The details and manner of performing these two activities at each distribution level may vary considerably. Often, different sizes of inventories characterize different distribution levels, and there are wide variations among individual middlemen on the same level. When a channel includes certain types of agents, there may be no inventories at all on some levels. Similarly, middlemen exhibit marked differences with respect to order quantities and frequency of placing orders. The forward flow of goods and the reverse flow of orders both encounter interruptions of varying and quite often unpredictable durations. Either flow (and sometimes both) may fall to "just a trickle" or rise to "flood-stage proportions." A manufacturer may

[1] H. T. Lewis, J. W. Culliton, and J. D. Steel, *The Role of Air Freight in Physical Distribution* (Boston, Mass.: Division of Research, Graduate School of Business Administration, Harvard University, 1956).

[2] R. LeKashman and J. F. Stolle, "The Total Cost Approach to Distribution," *Business Horizons*, Winter, 1965, pp. 33-46.

centralize warehousing and shipping activities at one or a few locations, or he may decentralize them through branch warehouse operations or the use of public warehouses. Middlemen, especially those operating multiple establishments, have similar options. Furthermore, in moving products from one distribution point to the next, different decisions may be made concerning transportation methods. All of these factors, present to some extent in any distribution system, make managing physical distribution an extremely challenging task.

Viewed from the channel position of the manufacturer, physical distribution management requires logistical planning (i.e., integrated planning of all transportation, storage, and supply requirements) and implementation of inventory policy. Decisions must be made concerning the deployment of certain sizes of inventory at specific places and times. In other words, the problem is that of having the right products in the right quantities at the right places at the right times. Within the framework of marketing management, the solution should strike an optimal balance between costs incurred for physical distribution activities, and expectations of end-buyers and users of the product. Managing physical distribution, then, may be thought of as a balancing of distribution costs against an acceptable level of customer satisfaction.

MANUFACTURER'S "CONTROL" OVER PHYSICAL DISTRIBUTION

Because manufacturers generally reach final buyers through intermediate distribution levels, they cannot completely "control" (i.e., direct and regulate) physical distribution. They are bound to find distribution levels and points where they have little, if any, control over the size and disposition of inventories. However, at least in theory, a manufacturer does direct and regulate inventories at the factory and at his own distribution points (warehouses). For these points directly under his control, physical distribution decisions can be "optimal." But they are optimal only in the sense that they are the best under the circumstances—considering such factors as costs, demand characteristics and inventory eccentricities of distribution points farther down the channel.

A manufacturer normally must try to obtain optimal performance of the total distribution system by finding effective ways of coordinating his inventory policies and practices with those of other channel members. What middlemen do (or do not do) with regard to managing their inventories definitely affects the manufacturer's costs and profits. Their actions also determine the quality of service and availability of the product at the times and places desired by final buyers. If middlemen are overstocked, they are likely to cut prices to make sales, thus jeopardizing future sales at more normal prices, possibly damaging the manufacturer's reputation for quality products, and perhaps making themselves less enthusiastic about future relationships with the manufacturer. If middlemen follow unintelligent inventory practices, such as buying on a "hand-to-mouth" basis, the manufacturer is forced to carry larger inventories and, consequently, to incur higher costs. Furthermore, he, along with the middlemen, suffers hidden costs as penalties for being out-of-stock and unable to fill orders when consumers want them. Unfortunately, out-of-stock costs are not recorded by conventional accounting systems, but profits as well as sales are lost when consumers are sent away empty-handed.

PHYSICAL DISTRIBUTION EFFICIENCY AND PROFIT

Gains in physical distribution efficiency should be accompanied by improvements in net profit. Estimates show physical distribution costs account for as much as one-third of the manufacturer's selling price and from one-fifth to one-fourth of the price paid by the final buyer.[3] Marketing management is profit-oriented management; hence, any activities accounting for so much of total costs should be prime targets for management's efforts to secure more efficient performance. If, after consideration of market demand, physical distribution costs seem higher than they have to be, there are ways to reduce them and thereby improve profits.

 An example of how profits can be saved through a "total cost," or "systems," approach to physical distribution is illustrated by the experience of a large consumer goods manufacturer. This company, with sales of $300-million and distribution costs of approximately $11-million, had never attempted to isolate the costs of distribution decisions that involved more than a single department. When top management took steps to correct this situation, a series of logistics projects, embracing all distribution activities, were undertaken. Because of the resulting high degree of interdepartmental coordination and cooperation, these projects produced significant improvements. The resulting savings are shown in Table 15-1.[4]

 These savings resulted from the establishment of a large-scale operations research computer-based logistics network. This network was represented by a three-stage linear programming model, with stage one

---

[3] H. Lazo and A. Corbin, *Management in Marketing: Text and Cases* (New York: McGraw-Hill, 1961), p. 321.

[4] A. H. Gepfert, "Business Logistics for Better Profit Performance," *Harvard Business Review*, November-December, 1968, pp. 77-79.

TABLE 15–1

Logistics Savings Made Possible
by the OR-Computer Staff in a Consumer Goods Company

Corrective Action	Annual Payoff
Realign production assignments and warehouse service areas	$321,000
Use pooled shipping to decrease less-than-truckload-lot volume	257,000
Restrict split-case orders, special handling of back orders, and shipping frequency to individual customers	221,000
Increase minimum order size	176,000
Total	$975,000

covering the warehouse-to-customer distribution system, stage two the manu-facturer-to-warehouse supply system, and stage three the planning of monthly production and inventory. The massive information system, de-veloped to support the model, incorporated data from more than 300,000 invoices, freight rates in six commodity classes for 1,500 routes, and data concerning operating rates and costs for all warehouses and production centers. A single run of the model led to the realignment of production assignments and warehousing service areas that yielded the $321,000 savings shown in Exhibit 15.1.

DECISIONS ON SIZE OF INVENTORY

Inventories may be thought of as input-output systems, with inventory additions being the input and inventory subtractions the output. Or, they may be thought of as reservoirs of goods that are held in anticipation of making sales—i.e., of filling demands from farther down along the channel. At usually irregular intervals, incoming quantities of the product ready for sale arrive and are added to the inventory reservoir. The outgoing product flow is more continuous, but outgoing quantities fluctuate considerably.

The volume in the inventory reservoir is always pulsating but not always with a regular rhythm—from day to day, changes occur in the rates and quantities of input and output. Therefore, in deciding on in-ventory size, management must determine both how high the inventory should be allowed to rise and how low it should be allowed to fall. In set-ting the upper and lower control limits, there are both sales and cost considerations.

Sales Considerations

The main purpose in maintaining any inventory at all is to meet market demands—i.e., to make sales and to fill customers' orders. Since inventories are kept in *anticipation* of market demand, the upper and lower control limits should be attuned to forecasted sales.

Sound decisions on inventory size, therefore, depend upon accuracy in sales forecasting. The more accurate the sales forecast, the greater the opportunity for maximizing gains from economical inventory operations. The less accurate the sales forecast, the greater the need for building substantial buffer stocks into the inventory plan, over and above normally adequate reserve stocks. It is, of course, impossible to determine in advance the exact degree of accuracy in a sales forecast. But it *should* be possible to obtain probability forecasts or, at the very least, some estimate of the forecasting error or limits to error.[5] With both a sales forecast and some notion as to its probable accuracy, a decision-maker is prepared to set the control limits.

Two additional factors, however, must be taken into account. One relates to what management considers an acceptable level of customer service. Experience shows that, in a typical business, about 80 percent more inventory is needed to fill 95 percent of the customers' orders out of stock on-hand than to fill just 80 percent.[6] Each firm, then, must strike a balance, between what it considers reasonable customer service and costs, that is in line with managerial goals. But such a balance seldom results in the lowest possible cost of physical distribution. It must be recognized that many customers regard consistency of delivery as at least as important as speed of delivery, particularly if they are buying for resale.[7] Settling on some goal, then, as to the proportion of all customers' orders that the stock-on-hand should be capable of satisfying without delay, has a definite bearing on the upper inventory control limit.

The other factor relates to responsiveness of the distribution system—the ability of a system to transmit inventory needs back to the supplying plant and get needed items into the field. The amount of responsiveness determines how quickly the inventory can be adjusted to changes in demand.[8] Thus, distribution system responsiveness directly influences the lower inventory control limit.

Sales output, the most important component of any inventory

---

[5] On this and related matters, see: J. F. Magee, "Guides to Inventory Policy III. Anticipating Future Needs," *Harvard Business Review*, May-June 1956, pp. 57-70.

[6] J. F. Magee, "The Logistics of Distribution," *Harvard Business Review*, July-August 1960, p. 92.

[7] D. J. Bowersox, "Physical Distribution Development, Current Status, and Potential," *Journal of Marketing*, January 1969, p. 66.

[8] J. F. Magee, "The Logistics of Distribution," p. 92.

system, generally cannot be controlled directly because it depends on decisions made by people outside the organization. However, even though a decision-maker cannot directly control sales output, he still must take its characteristics into account in making inventory decisions.

Cost Considerations

The input component of the inventory system generally is controllable by decision-makers within the organization. However, in spite of the close interrelations of input and output, input is more of the nature of a dependent variable and output more like an independent variable. Therefore, although control over inventory level and input normally takes the form of cost control, all inventory costs are ultimately largely traceable to inventory output factors.

Three main groups of costs are associated with the inventory. The first, holding costs, includes warehousing and storage charges, cost of capital tied up in inventory, costs of adverse price movements, obsolescence, spoilage, pilferage, and taxes and insurance on inventory. The second, costs of shortages (i.e., of having negative inventories), includes special clerical, administrative, and handling expenses, and, most importantly, losses of specific sales, of good will, and even of some customers. The third group, costs of replenishing inventory, differ in composition depending upon whether a business does its own manufacturing or not. Inventory replenishing costs in a "make and sell" business are mainly manufacturing costs—labor and machine setup costs, costs of material used during setup testing, cost of time during which production cannot take place because of setups, clerical and administrative costs, and the like.[9] Inventory replenishing costs in the "buy and sell" type of business are those for clerical and administrative work, for transportation and unloading, for placement in warehouses or stores, and for performing related necessary activities.

COST BALANCING AND INVENTORY DECISION   Inventory decisions can be formulated in terms of balancing inventory costs. Whereas holding costs rise as inventory increases, both the costs of shortage and of inventory replenishment decrease as inventory increases. Holding, shortage, and replenishment costs are all related, then, to the size of the inventory; total costs are, therefore, a function of the amount stored, and the problem is to determine what amount to store in order to minimize these costs.[10] Stating

[9] E. Naddor, "Elements of Inventory Systems," in C. D. Flagle, W. H. Huggins, and R. H. Roy (eds.), *Operations Research and Systems Engineering* (Baltimore: The Johns Hopkins Press, 1960), pp. 333-34.

[10] D. W. Miller and M. K. Starr, *Executive Decisions and Operations Research* (Englewood Cliffs, N.J.: Prentice-Hall, 1960), p. 390.

the problem in another way, a decision-maker wants to decide (1) how many (or much) to order (i.e., produce or purchase), and (2) when to order.[11] Essentially, these decisions involve balancing inventory holding costs against either costs of shortage or costs of replenishment or both.

One of the earliest and most significant contributions made by operations research was the construction of models (theories expressed as mathematical formulas) designed to minimize total inventory costs under different sets of conditions.[12] Operations research has furnished the analytical tools, then, that make rational inventory decisions possible. In the past—and too often even now—such decisions have been made intuitively, both by manufacturers and by middlemen, chiefly because of the unavailability of pertinent cost data, the failure to recognize its usefulness where it was available, or its suppression to conceal executive incompetence in inventory management.[13]

DECISIONS ON STORAGE AND INVENTORY LOCATION

Decisions on storage and inventory location are closely linked to inventory size. Physical distribution costs are incurred as a result of both kinds of decisions, so each should be made only after consideration of the other. For instance, a decision to restrict inventory size drastically, so as to operate almost from hand to mouth, reduces total need for storage space and, thus, affects a whole series of decisions concerning storage. Bearing in mind that customer service must be maintained at an acceptable level, the objective should be to obtain the lowest total cost of physical distribution possible in view of that restriction. Given this objective, it may be necessary to increase some costs in order to reduce other costs by a greater total amount. Three important storage decisions are made by marketers: geographic deployment of the inventory, ownership of warehouse facilities, and number and location of warehouses.

[11] C. W. Churchmen, R. L. Ackoff, and E. L. Arnoff, *Introduction to Operations Research* (New York: John Wiley & Sons, 1957), p. 15.

[12] Most basic books on operations research treat inventory models in considerable detail. For an excellent and unusually clear treatment, see: E. Naddor, "Inventory Systems," pp. 311-64.

[13] For a highly interesting discussion of the inadequacies of usual accounting records and an illustration of their resultant effect on inventory management, see: H. Anshen, "Price Tags for Business Policies," *Harvard Business Review*, January-February 1960, p. 73.

On the difficulty of assessing different kinds of executive mistakes in inventory management, see the stimulating article by C. A. Bliss, "Are Inventories Really Too High?" *Harvard Business Review*, September-October 1960, pp. 59-60.

Geographic Deployment of Inventory

There are three decision alternatives with regard to geographic deployment of inventory: (1) concentration at or near the plant or at some other central location, (2) dispersion at several distribution points situated in or closer to the main markets, and (3) concentration of substantial inventories at a few distribution centers and redistribution to a larger number of distribution points dispersed throughout the market. The first two alternatives are opposite extremes; the third is a compromise solution. The best alternative for any particular manufacturer or middleman, depends, of course, on many factors.

A comparision of inventory concentration and dispersion reveals opposite sets of strengths and weaknesses. The company that concentrates its inventory can get by with a smaller total inventory and can minimize orders not filled because of stock-outs, but at the costs of higher charges for transportation and possible delays in customer service. The firm that disperses its inventory needs a larger total inventory to avoid an undue number of stock-outs and, in effect, commits each sub-inventory to sale in a particular market area; however, it gains reduced total transportation charges and faster customer service. The concentration decision permits more rapid adjustment to changes in the makeup of incoming orders, since unexpected demands originating from certain, but not all, markets usually can be met at once. By contrast, the dispersion decision requires either that a large enough reserve stock be maintained at each branch to meet most emergencies, or that there be some provision for moving stocks among branches as needs arise. Thus, the dispersion decision requires the greater inventory investment, since the sum of many small reserve stocks scattered over the whole market necessarily is larger than one large reserve stock held at a single location. Similarly, operating one large central warehouse should mean greater warehousing efficiency at lower costs per unit of product handled than the decentralized operation of smaller storage facilities. On the other hand, especially if the product line is made up of mostly bulky and low unit value items—the kind which usually must be shipped by truck or rail—total transportation costs may be lower when decentralized warehouses are used. Rail and truck freight charges normally are lower for full carloads or truckloads than for shipments in less-than-carload (l.c.l.) lots. Both alternatives, then, have general strengths and weaknesses, and whether a marketer chooses one or the other—or adopts the third as a compromise—depends upon his evaluations of the relative importance of each factor. These specific evaluations, in turn, are influenced by such matters as the nature of the product line, the type of marketing channel, promotional strategies, pricing policies, and competitors' practices.

Inventory Dispersion and Warehouse Ownership

Manufacturers deciding to disperse their inventories (as under alternatives two or three above) have the choice of either operating their own branch warehouses or of using public warehouses. For any manufacturer, this choice depends upon such factors as the amount of sales volume originating in particular markets, whether he prefers fixed or variable warehousing costs, the degree of flexibility desired in making changes in the pattern of inventory deployment, relative warehousing efficiency, and the marketing channel used. There is relationship and interaction among these factors, so it is rare that a manufacturer will base his decision on any single factor. If the volume of goods moved in a given market is substantial and shows little or no seasonal fluctuation, a good case can be made for branch warehouses owned and operated by the manufacturer. Costs of branch warehousing are mainly fixed and, with a large and steady "flow-through" of goods, the costs per unit of product moved are likely to be quite low. However, because public warehouses base their charges on the space and labor actually used, the scales generally tip in their favor only when a small volume is to be handled or when a large volume with great seasonal fluctuations is to be moved. The variable costs associated with the use of public warehouses also provide a manufacturer with greater flexibility in making changes in the geographical deployment of his inventory. Since most cities have many public warehouses, he can easily close out stocks in some locations and place them in others.

The chief economic justification for the public warehouse is that it provides a way for dovetailing the local storage needs of many manufacturers which, in turn, makes possible efficient use of storage space, warehousing labor, and mechanized handling equipment. However, with a large and steady sales volume of his own, a manufacturer may realize comparable efficiencies in operating his own branch warehouses. Furthermore, if he has a product requiring either specialized handling and technical service or special storage facilities, he has little choice but to own and operate branch warehouses. Although some cities do have public warehouses that provide specialized handling and technical services (e.g., those specializing in appliance warehousing) and warehouses that offer specialized storage facilities (e.g., those with refrigerated storage space), such specialized public warehouses cannot be found in all cities. So the manufacturer who uses them in some cities may still have to operate his own facilities elsewhere.

Some manufacturers use public warehouses as substitutes for wholesalers, for local sales representatives, or for both. These manufacturers place "spot stocks" in public warehouses and furnish the operators with "accredited lists" of customers authorized to receive deliveries of various sizes of orders. The public warehouseman not only fills these orders, but often attends to such details as billing and making collections. Generally, public warehouses are not very aggressive sales representatives, so the manufacturer using them for that purpose usually has to rely on such devices as exclusive retail outlets or heavy consumer advertising to "move the goods out of the warehouses." Still another reason for using public warehouses is that they issue warehouse receipts, which a manufacturer may use as collateral for bank loans; however, unless the goods are in storage for a long period, this is only a source of short-term loans, during which time the goods may not be sold. Thus, public warehousing and private warehousing both have their own advantages and disadvantages. Before making his decision, a manufacturer is well-advised to consider all the merits and limitations of both alternatives.

Number and Location of Warehouses

One of the more baffling problems confronting a manufacturer who decides on inventory dispersion is that of deciding on the number and location of warehouses. Such a decision is affected by several important variables including customers' buying patterns and delivery expectations, freight rate structures, service characteristics of alternative transportation media, warehouse operating costs, location of factories, production capacities and product mix of individual factories, and costs of building or renting suitable warehouses in different cities. It is possible to gather statistics and related information on each of these variables but there is a staggering number of possible combinations, which may be made up of many sets of complex, and to some extent interrelated, variables. Thus, in the past, largely because of the mountain of work involved in calculating the probable results of each possible combination of variables, most decisions on number and location of warehouses were made intuitively. With the advent of the high-speed digital computer, such computations have become more objective and routine.

Operations researchers have devised "simulation" techniques, which permit mathematical representations of a company's physical distribution system, present and proposed, to be programed on a computer. In a comparatively short time, a computer can provide the probable results of operating under a number of different possible schemes as to number and location of warehouses. Such simulation studies often furnish decision-makers with much additional information needed in making decisions on related problems. This is indicated in the following quotation:

> For the H. J. Heinz Company, the simulation has provided a unique tool for determining the number of warehouses and mixing points which should exist in the national distribution system. It also has

determined where they should be located to achieve a minimal over-all operating cost. In addition, it has provided information on how best to service the many thousands of customers by an optimal combination of service direct from factory and service from area warehouses. Further, it has given a detailed plan for allocating customers for each product line and from each factory. With this cohesive national distribution plan in hand, management has now proceeded to make future marketing plans with assurance of lowest actual distribution costs.[14]

DECISIONS ON MODES OF TRANSPORTATION

Decisions on modes of transportation are related to both decisions on size of inventory and those on storage location, which are themselves interrelated. No one of these decisions should be made without first considering the possible effects on the others.

Significant improvements are being made in transportation services. Truck transportation is improving with the construction of more super-highways, the increase in truck speeds, and the use of trailers with greater capacities. Rail freight transportation is improving as more roads provide "piggyback" (rail movement of loaded tractor trailers), "unitized" trains, and other service innovations. Air freight transportation is improving with the larger jet air carriers and the use of "containerized" (giant containers holding many smaller shipments) loading and unloading systems. These are only a few of the many improvements being made in transportation services, but they are indicative of a strong general trend toward providing shippers with more rapid and efficient transportation services.

Too often decisions on modes of transportation are made solely in terms of relative costs. In these cases, management fails to recognize that transportation is only one part of what should be a totally integrated physical distribution system. When transportation decisions are made on the basis of relative costs alone, shipping costs may be minimized but total physical distribution costs usually are not. Minimum shipping costs arrived at solely on this basis generally mean that transportation cost savings are more than offset by increases in warehousing costs, costlier packing, and the costs associated with carrying inventories that are larger than necessary.

Decisions on modes of transportation should be made with the goal of optimizing the efficiency of the total physical distribution system. Relative costs, although important, provide only one basis for comparing the contribution of different modes of transportation to total system efficiency. The general trend is toward providing shippers with more rapid

[14] H. N. Shycon and R. B. Maffei, "Simulation—Tool for Better Distribution," *Harvard Business Review*, November-December 1960, p. 66.

transportation services. Transport time—the time required for moving goods from warehouses, for example, to customers—is a major transportation determinant of efficiency (or inefficiency) in the distribution system. Reductions in transport time, though commonly accompanied by increased transportation costs, often result in significant savings in warehousing costs, packing costs, and funds tied up in inventories. For instance, switching from a distribution system composed of surface transportation and branch warehouses to one involving air transportation direct to the customer normally results in higher transportation costs but much lower storage costs. The net savings resulting from such changes trace largely to reductions in transport time. One writer, dealing with the potentialities of airfreight for marketing, illustrates this relationship as follows:

> Suppose that in a company doing an annual business of $100-million, time in transit is reduced from 14 days to 2. Time between reorders is 14 days, communication and processing time is 4 days, and field stocks average $12.5-million. In such a situation the reduction in transit time might well lead to a reduction in distribution inventory investment of $6-million, made up of: (1) a reduction of $3.3-million in transit, i.e., 12 days' sales; (2) a reduction of $2.7-million in inventories required to protect customer service resulting from a faster, more flexible distribution system response.[15]

However, physical distribution costs can sometimes be reduced through the use of slower and lower-cost modes of transportation. For instance, Westinghouse Electric Corporation switched from air to surface transportation for making deliveries of rush orders. By making improvements in all the distribution steps before shipment, Westinghouse saved so much time it could afford to do without the costlier air service.[16] This emphasizes the general principle that transportation decisions should be based both on cost and transport time considerations and that the relative significance of transportation costs and transport times depends on their combined relationship to the over-all efficiency of the total physical distribution system.

MATERIALS HANDLING DECISIONS

Materials handling is the area of physical distribution that has experienced the greatest change and improvement in efficiency in recent decades. The first major improvement was the elimination of "manhandling" of goods. Thirty years ago it was common practice to use manpower to transfer goods

[15] Magee, "Logistics of Distribution," p. 93.
[16] M. Mandell, "Boosting Sales with Faster Delivery," *Dun's Review and Modern Industry*, February 1960, p. 45.

from storage to transportation and back to storage. Today most goods are not handled by human labor at all until they reach the retail or user level. Improved conveyer systems and fork lift equipment have made possible almost total mechanization. The second major improvement in materials handling was containerization—the development of methods by which a large number of units of a product are combined into a single compact unit for storage and transportation. Containerization has evolved from the simple pallet to complex and special purpose containers. Containerization reduces both materials handling costs and the time spent in handling shipments.

As is true of other aspects of physical distribution, materials handling decisions and costs are interrelated with other decisions and costs. Improved materials handling has not only reduced the cost of handling goods, it has also improved the relative effectiveness of transportation and storage. For example, containerization has so drastically decreased the "loading turnaround time" for ships that it has reduced their "comparative speed" disadvantage. At the same time, improved materials handling makes possible more effective utilization of storage space and, hence, a reduction of investment in facilities.

ORDER SIZE DECISIONS

The size of the order also is closely interrelated with other facets of physical distribution. Therefore, order size decisions should take into account these other facets. For example, orders for amounts less than the contents of a normal pallet or container require that the goods be handled entirely by hand instead of by machine. Such manhandling appreciably raises costs. Less-than-pallet-size orders also increase the costs of storage and inventory control and add to their complexity. The size of an order may also affect the level of shipping costs, since bulk or carload shipping rates are generally a good deal lower than rates for shipping smaller quantities. It is important, therefore, for management to make decisions concerning minimum order sizes, units of increment in size, and preferred order sizes so that orders will be maintained at size levels consistent with the goal of optimizing physical distribution costs.

ORDER PROCESSING DECISIONS

The methods a marketing organization uses for processing customers' orders affect its service to them in two ways. First, reorder time is affected (reorder time is the time elapsed between a customer's placing of an order and his receipt of the merchandise). Second, it affects the consistency of delivery time. Variations in these two time variables influence the buyers' profits through changing the required investment in inventory, altering ordering costs, and changing the probability that the item involved will be out-of-stock. Because of these considerations, buyers tend to shift their orders to suppliers providing superior order processing service. In a study of 700 retailers, it was found that store buyers could discriminate among even small differences in order service time and that their rating of this factor influenced their overall rating of a supplier.[17] Even small improvements in order processing service can provide a supplier with a competitive advantage, thus, it is worthwhile exploring possible avenues that might lead to improved order processing efficiency.

APPLICATIONS OF OPERATIONS RESEARCH TO PHYSICAL DISTRIBUTION PROBLEMS

Physical distribution decisions generally involve an attempt to optimize a number of variables. The conventional manual "pencil and paper" approach to such decisions is not only tedious but rarely productive, since restrictions of time and manpower require drastic simplifications of the problem. Consequently, businessmen have searched for other approaches, particularly ones which make possible the use of computers. Among these new approaches are those involving mathematical simulation, linear programming, heuristic programming, and integer programming.

Mathematical Simulation

The essential parts of a company's physical distribution system can be reduced to a mathematical representation and, through use of a computer, can then be used to test various schemes management may be considering for improving distribution methods and/or lowering distribution costs. Management then, by comparing the results simulated for each of the various alternatives, can better select those distribution alternatives that come closest to meeting its objectives. Such a mathematical simulation can easily be set up to analyze, for instance, which of a hundred possible warehouse configurations should be used or which of a dozen different combinations of shipping arrangements should be utilized. Mathematical simulations are particularly useful in dealing with the scheduling of shipments, an area in which many puzzling problems confront those concerned with physical distribution. However, an answer reached through a

[17] R. P. Willet and P. R. Stephenson, "Determinants of Buyer Response to Physical Distribution Service," *Journal of Marketing Research*, August 1969, pp. 280-83.

mathematical simulation is not necessarily an optimum solution to the problem under investigation.

Linear Programming

The "transportation technique" of linear programming is used in planning shipments from different origins to different destinations in ways that minimize total shipping costs. For example, the origins may be factories or other sources of supply, distribution centers, or warehouses; the destinations may be distribution centers, warehouses, customers, or stores. Thus, with customer demand for the product at various locations and supplies at a number of warehouses, it is possible through linear programming to determine which warehouse should ship how much product to which customer in order to minimize total shipping costs. Until the development of the transportation technique of linear programming, no simple procedure more scientific than the "cut and try" method was available for solving problems of this sort.[18]

A more general method of linear programming, the simplex method, is used in finding solutions to "multi-dimensional distribution problems." The transportation technique is used only with two-dimensional problems, such as those involving shipments between several origins and several destinations. Dimensions above and beyond this may include various time periods, different products, and one or more intermediate storage points in the distribution system.[19] One major oil company uses such a model for planning the optimal means of serving its widely dispersed terminals. This particular model evaluates alternative means of serving terminals (i.e., through use of pipelines, barges, tank cars, and so on) by relating their probable future costs to projected changes in volume and product mix at each terminal.[20]

Heuristic Programming

A *heuristic* is any device or procedure used to reduce problem-solving effort—i.e., a rule of thumb used to solve a particular problem. A *heuristic program* is a collection or combination of heuristics used for solv-

[18] H. C. Bunke, *Linear Programming: A Primer* (Iowa City: Bureau of Business and Economic Research College of Business Administration, State University of Iowa, 1960), p. 5. This source contains concise and clear explanations of a number of linear programming techniques.

[19] For an explanation of the application of linear programming techniques to multi-dimensional distribution problems, see: J. W. Metzger, *Elementary Mathematical Programming* (New York: John Wiley & Sons, 1958), pp. 54-58.

[20] W. J. Platt and N. R. Maines, "Pretest Your Long-Range Plans," *Harvard Business Review*, January-February 1959, p. 120.

ing a particular problem. Such programs take the form of a set of instructions for directing a computer to solve a problem—the way a manager might do it if he had sufficient time. Thus, heuristic programming is not so much concerned with finding the one best answer after a lengthy search as with rapidly finding a "good" answer.[21] In other words, heuristic programming may not provide a guaranteed optimum solution to a problem, such as those found in physical distribution, but it frequently provides a satisfactory solution with considerably less computational effort than involved in using, say, linear programming to solve the same problem.

Integer Programming

Integer programming is a variant of linear programming in which the optimal solution is constrained to consist only of answers which are "integer numbers"—i.e., "whole" numbers. Recent application of integer programming to physical distribution decisions has been made by several companies. The principal advantage of the technique is its ability to determine the optimum solution from among a considerably larger number of alternatives than is possible with linear programming. At the same time, applying it does not involve excessive requirements in terms of time and effort.[22]

CONCLUSION

Only very recently have many companies been aware of the many opportunities for cost savings that exist in the area of physical distribution. But awareness of these opportunities has been sharpened since the logic of the "total cost" approach has received widespread publicity and been accorded equally widespread acceptance. In physical distribution, as in no other area of marketing, it is extremely important to strive for as rational an approach to decision-making as possible. Physical distribution decisions are major decisions, as difficult to make on rational bases as they are to reverse or change. They require considerable market information, both qualitative and quantitative and, in using this information, the decision-maker is helped greatly if he is able to conceptualize clearly the nature of the total physical distribution system, each of the elements of which it is composed, and the relationships each element bears to other elements and to the

[21] See: Jerome D. Wiest, "Heuristic Programs for Decision Making," *Harvard Business Review*, September-October 1966, pp. 130-31.

[22] M. A. Efroymson and T. L. Ray, "A Branch Bound Algorithm for Plant Location," *Operations Research*, May-June 1966, p. 367.

system as a whole. Only if he possesses these conceptual skills is he prepared to make rational decisions on physical distribution.

QUESTIONS AND PROBLEMS

1. Explain the meaning and significance to marketing of each of the following statements:
   a. Managing physical distribution involves balancing distribution costs against an acceptable level of customer satisfaction.
   b. When the price level in an industry is rising, the *relative* competitive position of the most distant producer in the industry tends to improve.
   c. Viewed from the channel position of the manufacturer, physical distribution management requires logistical planning.

2. Explain the meaning of the following:
   a. distribution system responsiveness
   b. spot stocks and accredited lists
   c. "simulation" technique
   d. containerization
   e. heuristic

3. What is meant by the "total cost" approach to physical distribution? Contrast this approach to the mangement of physical distribution activities before its development.

4. Why is it that manufacturers cannot completely "control" (i.e., direct and regulate) physical distribution?

5. Explain and illustrate the relationship of accuracy in sales forecasting to decisions on inventory size.

6. What factors determine the upper and lower inventory control limits?

7. What kinds of costs are associated with the inventory? Explain how inventory costs are "balanced" in making inventory decisions? How does middlemen's management of inventories affect the manufacturers' costs and profits?

8. Contrast and compare inventory concentration and inventory dispersion from the standpoint of their respective strengths and weaknesses.

9. Under what circumstances should a manufacturer use public warehouses? Own his own warehouses?

10. Would you advise a fertilizer manufacturer to use public warehouses as a substitute for wholesalers? Why or why not?

11. Explain the significance of "transport time" to physical distribution efficiency.

12. What improvements have been made recently in materials handling? Of what significance are they to marketing?

13. Explain how order size decisions are related to decisions on materials handling.

14. What is meant by "reorder" time? How does it relate to efficiency in order processing?

15. Should a manufacturer attempt to minimize the costs of inventory size, inventory location, materials handling, order processing, and shipping separately or collectively? Why?

16. What applications of operations research techniques have been made to physical distribution problems? Appraise the likely future uses of these and other operations research techniques.

PART 5

PROMOTION

Promotional Strategy

Management of Personal Selling

Management of Advertising

16

PROMOTIONAL STRATEGY

Promotion is a key element in marketing strategy. The first marketing step is fitting the product and its features to market needs and preferences; the second is obtaining distribution. Successful promotion is the third essential ingredient in marketing strategy: prospective buyers must learn about both the products' distinctive want-satisfying characteristics and its availability. Establishing and maintaining communications with target market segments are the main tasks assigned to promotion.

There are numerous ways to achieve these market communications objectives. Both in terms of impact upon market demand and expenditures involved, the most important promotional methods are personal selling and advertising. However, there are other communications methods —each appropriate and effective under particular circumstances. These methods include, among others, packaging, branding, direct-mail solicitation, point-of-purchase display, and premiums.

Close coordination of advertising, personal selling, and other methods of promotion, both in their planning and implementation, is important. A good part of advertising effort may be wasted, for example, if personal selling effort does not succeed in getting appropriate dealers to handle the product, if the package fails to draw attention to the product, or if dealers do not display the product effectively. Similarly, personal selling effort is wasted, for example, in explaining details (about the product and its uses) that are more economically communicated through advertising, the package, or point-of-purchase display.

Determining the proper "mix" of advertising, personal selling, and other forms of promotion is one of marketing management's major problems. If management decides to rely mainly on personal selling, advertising and direct mail may be directed primarily toward making salesmen's calls more effective. For example, advertising effort may be designed to make dealers more receptive to sales presentations or to convey part of the selling message, thus saving salesmen's time. Similarly, direct mail can be used to contact smaller accounts, thus making it possible for salesmen to concentrate on larger and more profitable accounts. In a contrasting situation, management may decide to rely mainly on advertising and point-of-purchase display—here advertising does the pre-selling, and displays provide a reminder so that order-taking becomes the salesmen's chief function. In the "ideal" promotional mix, regardless of its exact composition, the last dollar invested in each method of promotion brings in identical results.

COMMUNICATIONS AND PROMOTION

Communications requires a sender (or source), a message, and a receiver. Unless a sender's message is received by someone, no communication takes place. And, clearly, a marketer's promotional message must be received by those making up target markets, if it is to achieve its objective.

The Communication Process

The communication process consists of five stages:[1] At the first stage the source originates the communication. In the second stage, encoding, the idea to be communicated is translated into a language or medium of expression. During the third stage, the message carrying the idea flows or moves from one point to another. In the fourth stage, decoding reverses what happened during encoding so as to express the idea in a form ready

[1] E. Crane in *Marketing Communication* (New York: John Wiley & Sons, Inc., 1965), p. 11 builds communication around only three stages—source, message, and receiver.

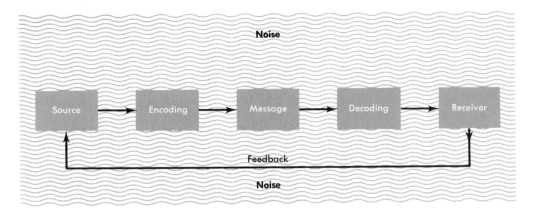

Noise

Source   Encoding   Message   Decoding   Receiver

Feedback

Noise

EXHIBIT 16–1

The Communication Process

for the fifth stage, the receiver. Exhibit 16-1 illustrates these stages in the communication process. This exhibit also shows two other elements normally present in the communication process. One is noise, which consists of extraneous disturbances interfering with communication and, thus, making it less effective. This can be actual noise, such as the sound of an airplane interfering with a lecture, or it can be other kinds of interference, such as "snow" or a double image on television. Any sort of distraction vying for the receiver's attention or interfering with his ability to receive the message is considered noise. In almost all communication processes, noise is present to some degree or another.

Feedback is the other element normally present in effective communication. It is important to the information source to learn whether the intended message was actually received. Feedback takes many forms. For example, it might consist of a nod, an expression of interest, or a smile from the listener or reader; it might consist of a marketing research report or a returned coupon from the receiver of an advertisement. Effective feedback makes it possible to identify and rectify the causes of communication breakdown.

Many factors may interfere with effective communication. A breakdown at the message stage may mean that no communication whatever takes place. An error in encoding or decoding may mean that the message received is not the same as the message sent.[2] The source might say "What a place!", intending to mean "How nice it is!" The receiver may hear it as "How dreadful it is!" A receiver's different background and way of thinking may cause him to interpret the message's meaning in a

[2] See P. Abuzzini, "Measuring Language Difficulty in Advertising," *Journal of Marketing*, April 1967, pp. 22-23.

way not intended by the source. Therefore, for example, in oral communications, semantics are often important. An expression or word may convey different meanings in different parts of the country, and such differences may be even wider between nations. Words such as "closet" and "napkin" have considerably different meanings in the United States and Great Britain, differences that could prove embarrassing to the user. Often, differences are even more marked when a message is translated into a foreign language.[3]

Source Effect

In marketing communication, it is important to recognize the effect of the message source's reputation upon the way a message is received. The audience's feeling about the message source (for example, concerning its credibility) helps determine the message's effectiveness in persuading receivers to take some action or change an attitude.[4] If the source is highly prestigious or credible, the message is much more likely to influence the audience. For example, for most people an article in *Fortune Magazine* about the role of business ten years from now is much more credible and, hence, much more influential than the same article published in *McCall's*.

This phenomenon is known as "source effect." The source may exert as strong an influence on the receiver as the message itself. A computer salesman representing IBM has a much easier task in gaining the confidence of an American prospect than does a salesman of Bull (a French manufacturer of computers little known in the U.S.). The prospect's reaction to the Bull salesman would likely be "I don't know your company. I don't know its products or what they stand for." By contrast, the prospective customer does know about IBM and its products and, thus, is more willing to believe the IBM salesman's claims. The more familiar and prestigious a source is, the more it is likely to be able to influence the receiver with its promotional message.

THE ELEMENTS IN PROMOTIONAL STRATEGY

The two most prevalent promotional methods, and the most important both in terms of market impact and cost, are personal selling and advertising. Personal selling is an important ingredient in most promotional pro-

---

[3] For a detailed discussion of communication theory, see: C. I. Hovland and L. Janis (eds.), *Personality and Persuasibility* (New Haven, Connecticut: Yale University Press, 1959), pp. 229-40.

[4] R. A. Bauer, "The Obstinate Audience," *American Psychologist*, May 1964, pp. 319-28.

grams, and it is commonly supported by advertising. Other methods of promotion are not as persistent, but in certain situations they make significant contributions.

Personal Selling

Personal selling's main assignment is to match up specific products with specific customers in order to secure ownership transfers. In other words, personal selling seeks to pair the "right" products with the "right" customers. Basically, it consists of the interpretation of product and service features in terms of benefits and advantages to the buyer and of persuading the buyer to buy the right kind and quantity of the product.[5] Since most people do not like to admit that they have been "sold" anything, most ultimate consumers appear to underestimate the influence of personal selling on their patterns of buying behavior. This is in marked contrast to the situation in industrial marketing where buyers generally rely heavily on salesmen as sources of product information and advice. Personal selling, however, plays an important role in marketing even the most heavily-advertised and otherwise promoted consumer products, such as detergents. The consumer buys detergents on a self-service basis and generally without the assistance of a sales clerk, but it usually requires considerable personal selling effort to persuade retailers to stock the particular brand of detergent and to insure that it is given adequate display and shelf space. Ultimate consumers are not exposed directly to the detergent producer's personal selling effort, but, nevertheless, it plays a critical role in his over-all marketing program.

Personal selling is potentially both the most effective and the most costly promotional method. Its effectiveness traces to its personal one-to-one approach. The salesman directs his message to a single prospect, so he can tailor it specifically to fit that prospect's needs. In addition, in inter-personal communication, there is maximum opportunity for feedback. When the prospect has a question about the salesman's message, he can ask for clarification, and the salesman then has a chance to adapt his message accordingly. Clearly, however, this personal one-to-one relationship results in a very high cost per message received.

Advertising

Advertising is an impersonal method of communicating messages to prospective buyers. It involves transmitting standard messages to large numbers of potential receivers. The advertiser has a wide choice of message

[5] K. B. Haas, *Professional Salesmanship* (New York: Holt, Rinehart and Winston, Inc., 1962), p. 3.

media including: purely visual media, such as newspapers and magazines; purely aural media, such as radio; and combined aural and visual media, such as television. Although the same message goes to a large number of people, it can be directed only to selected prospects through appropriate media choices. For example, an advertising message can be directed primarily to housewives by placing it on daytime television or in a homemakers' magazine, such as *Good Housekeeping*. One significant weakness of advertising is the great difficulty involved in obtaining accurate feedback to evaluate message effectiveness. There is no automatic feedback mechanism, as with personal selling, and the mechanisms most advertisers use for obtaining feedback are not very sophisticated or effective.

Advertising's importance in marketing is frequently overrated by the average citizen. Since it is mainly directed toward consumers, many are acutely aware of it and are impressed with the apparent costs: "Advertising must be pretty important if it costs $50,000 for a single magazine advertisement, or $100,000 for the advertising on a television program." However, while an advertising budget of $1-million a year may sound very large, companies with that kind of advertising effort often have sales forces of 500 or more each costing $20,000 per year to keep in the field, a total personal selling cost of $10-million.

Advertising costs are relatively low per promotional message received. A television commercial may be seen by hundreds of thousands, or even millions, of viewers, so even though the total cost seems high, the cost per message received may be only a few cents. However, largely because of its impersonal nature, advertising can seldom move the prospect to action as well as can personal selling. Generally, the role most effectively served by advertising is to acquaint prospects with the product and its strengths so that they will be more favorably disposed when they come face-to-face with the product in buying situations. Because of advertising's low cost per message, it is highly appropriate for developing initial product awareness or acceptance, which makes the final selling job easier.

Point-of-Purchase Display

The point-of-purchase display is the silent salesman that calls the shopper's attention to the product in the expectation of initiating buying action. There is some evidence to indicate that promotion at the point of purchase is more effective than at any other time.[6] Retailers rely heavily on in-store displays to provide customers with opportunities to examine and become familiar with the product, even in some instances to allow them to use or test it. Display may range all the way from a showing of

---

[6] R. T. Peterson, "Experimental Analysis of Theory of Promotion at Point of Consumption," *Journal of Marketing Research*, Aug., 1966, pp. 347-50.

new automobiles with promotional literature and pricing details in a dealer's showroom to a display rack for chewing gum beside the cash register in a restaurant or one for paperback books in an airline terminal. Display is not restricted solely to the retail level or, for that matter, to consumer products. Merchandise marts provide display booths for manufacturers or distributors to show their product lines to retailers who visit the mart to buy. Display is also an important promotional method in trade shows and expositions, where industrial buyers have opportunities to examine and test products, too bulky to demonstrate on their own premises, before making buying decisions.

Display rarely bears the entire promotional burden. Nearly always it is used in combination with personal selling, advertising, or both. Probably not many people would buy an automobile without the opportunity to examine and perhaps even drive it, but very few buy solely on the basis of what they see in a showroom. Generally, it takes a salesman to clinch the sale. Display is important in the promotional mixes for products sold to consumers through self-service outlets, but generally advertising and personal selling also are needed—personal selling to persuade the retailer to stock and display the product prominently, advertising to make consumers aware of and interested in the product so that the display will trigger buying decisions.

Direct Mail

While direct mail has much the same purpose as other printed advertising messages, it usually allows greater precision in selecting target receivers. Advertising and direct mail are often compared to a shotgun and a rifle, respectively. One blast from a shotgun covers a much broader area than a rifle bullet and with a much greater chance of hitting something, but the rifle bullet can be more precisely aimed at a specific target. For the same cost, a single newspaper advertisement might reach 10,000 readers, and direct mail only 100 prospects. However, if the mailing list is compiled carefully, the 100 direct mail messages may reach more real prospects than the newspaper advertisement. For example, an art gallery with a $1-million Van Gogh painting to sell might be better off if it sent a direct-mail piece to 100 carefully-screened individuals than if it advertised in *The New York Times* with its large readership. Direct mail also contrasts with most advertising in that it can be made more personalized. Even a form letter when individually typed on an automatic typewriter can convey the impression of person-to-person communication. When the number of prospects is small, each can be sent an individually-designed message, thus, increasing the potential impact.

Direct mail, like most other promotional methods, is rarely used alone. Its main usage is as a supplement to other means of promotion. It provides an excellent way to maintain contact with customers of industrial products between salesmen's calls. Also, like advertising, it can provide a product awareness or acceptance that increases purchase probabilities when buyers are contacted by salesmen or see displays.

Packaging

Packaging, in addition to serving as a means of differentiating or protecting a product, also plays an important role in promotion. An attractively designed package both calls attention to the product in the retail store and provides a selling message. The package's promotional role is particularly important for products sold through self-service outlets. If three competing brands are placed side by side on a retail shelf, the consumers' attention more than likely will be drawn to the best-designed package. Good package design, from a promotional standpoint, involves proper combinations of color, design, and type style to attract and hold the customer's attention.

Other Methods of Promotion

There are many other kinds of promotion which, although used less frequently than those already mentioned, are effective in certain situations. Trading stamps can provide powerful promotion in situations where it is difficult to develop strong customer store or brand preferences. Many consumers, for example, are not convinced that any one brand of gasoline is much different from another, and they need some other incentive to draw them to a particular station. Trading stamps can provide that incentive for some buyers. Premiums can serve as similar incentives, though usually on a short term, "shot-in-the-arm" basis. An oil company can alter established gasoline purchase patterns by introducing special premiums, such as the "tiger tails" ENCO-ESSO used to supplement its "Put a Tiger in Your Tank" promotion in 1967. Breakfast cereal manufacturers use premiums periodically for similar reasons, usually choosing premiums attractive to children, their largest market segment.

Special promotional efforts are often designed to persuade consumers to try a new product. Sampling is one widely-used form of special promotion. Sampling of new food products is often carried on in retail food stores. Other samples of consumer products are mailed or otherwise delivered to residences. Pharmaceutical manufacturers rely heavily on sampling to make doctors aware of new products. Couponing serves a similar purpose in stimulating purchases of new or improved products. Coupons providing a price reduction on purchase of the product are made available to consumers, either by mail to their homes or by distribution in public places.

The number of special promotional methods is nearly as broad as man's ingenuity. When a special promotional need arises, it seems a new promotion technique is developed to serve it. While these promotional methods are relatively unimportant in terms of the total promotional dollars spent by business, they frequently play key roles in solving particular problems confronting particular companies.

DEMAND STIMULATION

Promotion is often criticized because it creates or stimulates demand and, in this sense, makes people do what they might not otherwise do or what they don't really want to do. Such criticism implies that promotion has some coercive control over people. Although some promoters may wish they had such control, they actually do not. When people buy things that are needlessly extravagant or frivolous, it is convenient to find a scapegoat to explain away such behavior, since the behavior does not fit into stereotypes of "economic man."

Promotion cannot and does not make people do what they do not want to do, but it does stimulate demand by relating products to latent needs and wants. One important demand stimulation objective is that of *informing* people about products and their need-satisfying capabilities. Another is that of *reminding* people periodically about the product and its role. The strongest demand stimulation objective sought through promotion is that of *persuading* prospective buyers of the product's need-satisfying capabilities.

THE PROMOTIONAL MIX

Most promotional campaigns comprise a combination of two or more promotional methods: most methods of promotion seldom are used effectively alone. Advertising, for example, usually needs the support of personal selling or display to result in sales of the product. Even personal selling, which frequently can produce sales without other promotional support, may prove an expensive way to make sales when it is used alone. A small expenditure for advertising to "open the door" for the salesman may enormously increase his productivity and, thus, reduce the selling cost per sales dollar.

When two or more methods of promotion are combined in a single promotional campaign, management faces the difficult task of selecting the most effective inputs and optimizing the expenditure on each. There is no ideal promotional mix that fits all situations. Variations in any of a number of factors influence the inputs that should be incorporated in a promotional plan. Among the more important of these factors are: the product, the customer, the stage of demand, and the relative cost.

Nature of the Product

Different products require different promotional treatments. Products of a highly complex and technical nature, for example, are much more dependent upon personal selling than simple, standardized products. A manufacturer of road graders sends highly-trained salesmen to confer with road contractors and governmental buyers, explaining the machine's unique advantages and how the machine "pays for itself" in increased productivity. They must prove the machine's capabilities to each buyer's satisfaction. A manufacturer of razor blades relies far less on personal selling, concentrating instead on advertising to consumers to develop brand recognition and/or preference. He supports this advertising campaign with point-of-purchase displays to remind the customer but relies upon personal selling to persuade retailers to stock the product.

The degree to which a marketer's product is differentiated from competitors' products also affects the promotional mix. Bread and sugar are highly standardized products with little brand differentiation, and their promotion emphasizes personal selling to get the product stocked in as many potential retail outlets as possible and to secure maximum shelf space in each. With clearly differentiatable products, such as cosmetics, more of the promotional budget is allocated to advertising to presell the consumer.

Nature of the Customer

Different customers are best reached through different combinations of promotional methods. Most marked, of course, is the contrast between industrial buyers and ultimate consumers. Advertising plays more of an informative and less of a persuasive role for industrial buyers than for consumer buyers. As a consequence, advertising's place in the promotional mix depends on the market to which it is directed. Similarly, other differences among customers, such as those of income, age, buying responsibility, and place of residence determine the promotional mix most appropriate for selling the product.

Stage of Demand

The nature of demand varies according to the stage in the product life cycle.[7] The first buyers of a new product (i.e., the innovators) differ considerably from those who buy it for the first time during the market maturity stage. They generally want to learn more about the product because as innovators they must make fairly independent judgments. Thus, they usually require more personal selling than members of the early and late majorities who are merely following the crowd. Promotion for a mature product may be directed primarily toward reminding existing customers of its nature and value; promotion for a new product may be largely persuasive. Different promotion methods vary in their effectiveness in attaining these two quite different objectives.

Relative Cost

The various methods of promotion vary considerably in the cost per message delivered. When the promotional budget is low, management puts together a combination of relatively low-cost promotional inputs, even though a more costly combination might be more productive. For example, a limited promotional budget might be spent on direct mail, because each message can go to a good potential prospect. If the same message is sent through advertising, the cost per message received by bona fide prospects might be much higher but a greater total number of prospects would be reached. However, differences in economies of scale may allow a company to use direct mail when its total budget is not sufficiently large to use advertising effectively.

When the size of the promotional budget does not limit the choice of promotional methods, management should attempt to optimize the combination of cost per message received and productivity of the promotional method. For example, it may cost $25 to $50 for each call salesmen make on prospects; it may cost only a few cents per message for an advertisement to reach the same prospects. However, the ad alone may produce few if any sales, while the salesmens' calls will produce some sales. An appropriate combination of the two promotion methods should increase the chances that salesmens' calls will result in sales, while also reducing the total cost involved in making each sale.

[7] The product life cycle, involving four stages (market pioneering, market growth, market maturity, and market decline), is described in detail in Chapter 9.

THE PROMOTIONAL APPROPRIATION

For the most part, management sets the size of the promotional appropriation according to its past experience and appraisal of the future outlook. Unfortunately, the present state of research in this field does not allow for precise measurements of the effectiveness of promotional efforts. The methods currently available for measuring the effectiveness of advertising, personal selling, and other promotion are at best inadequate. For this reason, decisions on the size of the promotional budget generally are made on the basis of some "rule of thumb," past experience, or through following the lead of competitors. However, there has been a persistent effort in recent years to attack the problem of measuring promotional effectiveness. In 1964, General Motors and Dupont each reported spending about $150,000 in this area of research, and other firms, universities, and the government have been working on the same thing. It is hoped that these efforts will bring about a more scientific approach to measuring promotional effectiveness.[8]

There is considerable variation in the size of the promotional appropriation from industry to industry and product to product. Industries marketing basic raw materials and semi-manufactured materials spend little or no money on promotion. The demand for such products as coal, steel, lumber, and sulphur already exists, and promotion has little influence on sales. Buyers purchase these items on the basis of product specifications, price, and physical availability; promotion serves little purpose. Certain consumer products, such as perfumes and cosmetics, are at the opposite extreme. Promotion strongly influences purchases of these products, both through increasing total demand and in building brand preference. In such industries, the promotional budget often runs as high as 40 percent of the sales dollar. Ideally, the promotional budget should reflect a scientific determination of the marginal productivity of each dollar spent for promotion. Thus far, this ideal has not been approached, yet alone reached.

THE PROMOTIONAL CAMPAIGN

There is no one best way to promote all products in all situations. The appropriate makeup for a particular promotional campaign depends upon numerous factors, which vary in their influence at different times even for the same product. Probably the most critical factors are: product variations, purchase frequencies, market penetration, and market variations.

[8] W. S. Hoofnagle, "Experimental Designs in Measuring Effectiveness of Promotion," *Journal of Marketing Research*, May 1965, p. 154.

Product Variations

Different products require markedly different types of promotional campaigns. Staple branded convenience items, for example, are best promoted primarily through mass consumer advertising, combined with good display at the retail level. The needed display space is achieved by using personal selling to persuade retailers and through providing them with useful display materials. On the other hand, "impulse" convenience items usually are most appropriately promoted almost entirely through personal selling designed to get retailers to display them where consumers will see and buy them. Many industrial products, particularly those of high unit value, require an entirely different type of promotional campaign, frequently made up almost entirely of personal selling with, perhaps, some advertising to locate customers or "pave the way" for the salesmen.[9]

Purchase Frequency

Frequency of purchase is another factor affecting the nature of the promotional campaign. When a product is purchased frequently, like soap in the consumer market or typing paper in the industrial market, it may be appropriate and justifiable to invest a considerable sum in advertising to develop brand recognition or preference and a generally favorable predisposition toward the product. But, when a product is purchased only infrequently, e.g., garden shovels, the potential demand is not large enough to justify the expense of preselling through advertising or direct mail. Instead, promotion is directed toward selling the product at the time and place of purchase. Promotional funds for infrequently purchased products generally are most appropriately spent on persuading the proper outlets to stock the product and to push it over competitive products when consumers come in to buy.

Market Penetration

The degree of market penetration also affects the nature of the promotional campaign. An important early step in allocating promotional dollars is to distinguish between *sustaining* promotion and *development* promotion.[10] When a brand has significant market penetration—that is, when

---

[9] Theodore Levitt argues persuasively that it pays an industrial products company to be favorably well-known (through advertising and direct mail) when the salesman attempts to make his sale. See his "Communications and Industrial Selling," *Journal of Marketing*, April 1967, p. 21.

[10] R. M. Fulmer, "How Should Advertising and Sales Promotion Funds be Allocated?", *Journal of Marketing*, October 1967, pp. 8-11.

it is already well known to consumers and distributors and has a substantial market share—promotion is needed mainly to sustain this market position. Such a brand already receives special treatment from the retailers who are anxious to stock and push easily marketed "best sellers." Also, for such a brand, an advertising budget based on percent of sales volume (a widely-used method for determining the size of the budget) is more appropriate than it would be for less popular or new products.

Development promotion requires an entirely different kind of campaign. Many dealers are reluctant to stock or push the less popular or new product because they assume that the risk of not selling it at a profit is high. Similarly, dollars invested in advertising tend not to go as far in making an impact on receivers. The marketer of a less popular or new product should keep these differences in mind as he plans his promotional campaign.

However, even the marketer of established and successful products will probably have to make the same kinds of decision with respect to certain markets. Many, perhaps even most, established, successful products have uneven patterns of market penetration in different areas. In those where there is deep penetration, sustaining promotion is appropriate; in those where there is shallow penetration, development promotion is appropriate.

Market Variations

Successful promotional campaigns are designed to fit the markets being served. Variations in the market require parallel variations in promotional campaigns. Size of the market is important. For example, a narrow market (in terms of numbers of potential buyers), such as that for shoe manufacturing machinery, is reached effectively through direct mail, whereas a broad market, such as that for cigarettes, is reached more effectively through mass advertising. Location of the market is also important. Different types of promotional campaigns are required for markets concentrated in urban areas and those widely dispersed in rural areas.

The characteristics of the prospective buyers also strongly influence the nature of the promotional campaign. Experienced professional buyers, such as industrial purchasing agents, are apt to be most strongly attracted by promotional messages of a personal nature, tailored to their specific needs. By contrast, many an inexperienced young housewife is more comfortable and more strongly influenced through impersonal appeals delivered by media, which cause her to feel she is following the leads of older more experienced women. Other factors, such as the relative importance of the purchase to the buyer, the amount of time available for buying, and the influence of friends, relatives, and associates, all affect the nature of the promotional campaign.

CONCLUSION

Promotion is a process of communication, of delivering a message about the product or service from the marketer to potential buyers. For promotion to be effective, management must plan it with a clear understanding of the communication process, including the problems of encoding, decoding, noise, and feedback, which affect the delivery of the message from the source to the receiver. The marketer has available a very wide range of promotion methods. The most important of these are: personal selling, advertising, point-of-purchase display, direct mail, and packaging. Most promotional campaigns involve a combination of several of these methods as inputs. The optimum combination is affected by the product, the market, the stage of demand, and relative cost.

QUESTIONS AND PROBLEMS

1. Promotion is described as a process of communication between seller and buyer. In what ways significant to marketing does this communication process differ for personal selling and advertising?

2. Is there a contradiction between the following two statements? (1) Communication is built around three essentials and (2) There are five stages in the communication process. Explain.

3. Evaluate the more important promotion methods with respect to the importance of feedback and the ease or difficulty of achieving it.

4. Does the concept of "noise" have particular relevance in the application of communications theory to promotional strategy?

5. How might recognition of "source effect" influence the promotional mix for a manufacturer of heavy industrial products?

6. If a marketer were restricted to the use of only one promotion method, which method would he most likely choose? Why? Can you think of any exceptions?

7. Would a large consumer products marketer, such as General Mills or Lever Brothers, likely allocate a larger portion of its promotional budget to personal selling or to advertising? What possible roles might point-of-purchase display play when used with these two main promotion methods?

8.   What is the most important difference between advertising and direct mail in terms of their respective uses?

9.   List five specific products that are heavily dependent upon packaging for marketing success. Explain why you think each of these packages is or is not as successful as it could be.

10.   Name and describe three important objectives of promotion, with respect to demand stimulation.

11.   Describe the type of promotional campaign that would probably be most appropriate and effective for: salt, shampoo, men's suits. Explain why the mix should be different for each of these products.

12.   Explain how a television manufacturer might adjust his promotion mix to the stages in the product life cycle: introduction, growth, maturity, and decline. Would similar adjustments be appropriate for appliances? Furniture?

13.   What is wrong with using the cost per message delivered as a basis for evaluating alternative promotion methods?

14.   Evaluate the following statement. "The larger the promotional budget is, the greater the economic waste is to society."

17

MANAGEMENT
OF PERSONAL SELLING

Personal selling is the most common, and often the most critical, element in the promotional mix. In fact, sales frequently are made without the support of any other promotional element. Even advertising, the next most common form of promotion, is not essential in many selling situations, particularly those in industrial marketing. By contrast, it is only rarely that a sale is made without a salesman to clinch the deal. In some instances salesmen are merely order takers, but they are still necessary to "ring the cash register."

Salesmen, then, are in many respects the "unsung heroes" of marketing. Successful implementation of many, perhaps most, marketing programs depends importantly upon salesmen's skills in matching company products with customers' needs and, of course, in effecting ownership transfers. In spite of the important roles played by salesmen, however, numerous companies find it increasingly difficult to recruit qualified young people for training as salesmen.

Personal selling is a highly distinctive form of promotion. Like other forms of promotion, personal selling is basically a method of communication, but unlike others it is two-way, rather than unidirectional, communication. It involves not only individual, but social, behavior: each of the persons in face-to-face contact—salesman and prospect—influences the other. The outcome of each sales situation depends importantly upon the success both parties experience in communicating with each other and in reaching a common understanding of needs and goals.[1]

This social character of personal selling makes it an activity particularly difficult to manage, because generally each salesman must be allowed broad independence of action.[2] Each must be left free to interact with individual customers in the manner he believes will be the most effective. Yet, at the same time, management needs to direct and control the personal selling activity to achieve maximum efficiency. In the effort to reach marketing goals, a marketer ordinarily must assemble his own sales force, develop its skills, and supervise it. Of course, it is possible for a manufacturer to shift the entire burden of personal selling to middlemen, but this is not nearly so common as the shifting of advertising responsibilities to advertising agencies. The manufacturer, in most cases, must determine the kind of selling force needed and its size, set up systems for managing salesmen, set the personal selling appropriation, decide on methods for allocating personal selling effort among customers and prospects, and appraise its effectiveness.

DETERMINING THE PERSONAL SELLING STRATEGY

The manager of personal selling (i.e., the sales manager) is responsible for planning and implementing the personal selling portion of his company's promotional and other marketing strategies. In discharging this responsibility, he must determine the amount that should be appropriated for personal selling. At the same time, he must estimate the size of the sales force required to implement the company's marketing strategy in light of existing job descriptions and the rate of sales force turnover.

The Personal Selling Appropriation

The logical starting points for determining the amount of the personal selling appropriation are the specific sales and other marketing

---

[1] F. E. Webster, Jr., "Interpersonal Communication and Salesman Effectiveness," *Journal of Marketing*, July 1968, pp. 7-8.

[2] Because of these personal factors, attempts to apply operations research techniques to management of personal selling have generally been unsuccessful. See D. B. Montgomery and F. E. Webster, Jr., "Application of Operations Research to Personal Selling Strategy," *Journal of Marketing*, January 1968, pp. 50-55.

objectives established by top management for the period just ahead. Marketing plans, drafted with a view toward achieving these objectives, ultimately must be translated into the types and amounts of marketing effort required. Sooner or later, therefore, management deals with the problem of converting these types and amounts of marketing effort into dollar estimates of the costs involved. Thus, an increase in the sales volume objective may call for the hiring of a certain number of new salesmen, their training, providing them with transportation and expense allowances, securing and assigning additional supervisors, and the like. The next step is to convert each activity into an estimate of the dollar cost. Therefore, in building the personal selling appropriation, management must do two things: (1) estimate the volume of performance for each required activity and (2) convert these estimated performance volumes into estimates of dollar costs.

However, before setting the personal selling appropriation, management should first determine the total promotional appropriation based on an optimum marketing mix; then, each type of promotional appropriation should be apportioned, according to its relative importance, as an element in the marketing mix. If this approach is followed, theory suggests that identical returns in terms of net profit should be produced by the last dollar invested in personal selling and in each other method of promotion.

Actually none of the promotional inputs is purchased in dollar-size units. Advertising is bought in terms of pages, agate lines of space, half-hour programs, 30-second and 15-second commercials, etc. Personal selling effort is purchased in terms of units of sales manpower; the incremental purchase is a salesman and not a dollar's worth of selling effort.

Some administrators mistakenly think that it is possible for them to buy personal selling effort in dollar-size units when they use straight commission systems. They seem to be accounting only for the commissions paid to salesmen for efforts that result in sales. Normally, however, some provision must also be made for reimbursing expenses incurred in connection with calls, both those where sales were made and where they were not. Otherwise, commission salesmen are likely to "skim the cream" and call on only those accounts where they are sure to get large orders. Furthermore, while payment of commissions, salaries, or both, and reimbursement of expenses are large items in the personal selling appropriation, they are by no means all of it. The total appropriation must also be adequate to cover expenses of recruiting, selecting, training, providing motivation and supervision, and of performing related sales force management activities. It must also provide for paying the salaries and expenses of sales executives and for covering other overhead expenses.

The Job Description

In every company, the job descriptions, clearly outlining the duties and responsibilities of every selling job, lie at the heart of sales force management. The nature of sales positions varies from company to company, for although salesmen in different companies have similar duties and responsibilities, the emphasis on specific tasks differs. This follows from the fact that no two companies use exactly the same marketing strategies. Salesmen in particular companies develop certain skills, but when they move to different employers not all of these skills can be applied in the same ways or with the same emphasis. Salesmen's skills gained in the service of one employer, then, are transferable, but the unique ways the skills are applied are not. Thus, when an experienced electric typewriter salesman accepts a new job selling adding machines and calculators, his general understanding of the buying procedures and motivation of office managers is transferable, but he must learn their reasons for use or non-use of calculators and the comparative advantages of competitive models.

Effectiveness in managing the personal sales force depends considerably on the completeness and accuracy of the sales job descriptions. Through analysis of the duties and responsibilities making up the job, management derives the set of qualifications that salesmen should possess. This furnishes guidance in searching out the best sources for recruits and in selecting those with the best qualifications. Comparison of the qualifications given in the job description with the qualifications of those newly hired indicates the needed breadth and depth of the initial sales training program. Similarly, comparing the job description with the qualifications possessed by the veteran salesmen is a basic technique of salesman evaluation and assists in determining the content of refresher sales training courses. Furthermore, the job description provides guidance for management in designing the sales compensation plan and in arriving at the best methods for supervising salesmen.

In some well-managed companies, the sales job description carries with it a statement of the performance standards management will use in appraising the salesman's effectiveness. For instance, if the job description reads "the salesman will maintain frequent contact with all his assigned accounts," there is a parallel statement such as "calls on Class A accounts are to be made no less than 26 times per year, calls on Class B accounts are to be at the rate of 13 times per year, and calls on all other accounts are to be restricted to no more than 6 per year." Each of the salesman's duties and responsibilities outlined in the job description has a parallel statement indicating management's definition of what constitutes good performance. Thus, salesmen are provided with a means to self-guidance and self-evaluation, enhancing management's efficiency in supervising and controlling salesmen's activities.

Rate of Sales Force Turnover

In determining the number of salesmen required for implementing a company's marketing strategy, it is necessary to consider the rate of sales force turnover. If 100 salesmen are needed, and the company has a 10 percent annual turnover, ten additional men will be needed during the year. Not only is the rate of sales force turnover a planning tool, it is also a widely-used measure of efficiency in sales force management. This rate is defined as the number of salesmen separated, resigned, fired, etc. per 100 on the sales force. Thus, the formula for calculation is:

$$\text{Rate of Sales Force Turnover} \atop \text{(Expressed as \%)} = \frac{\text{Number of Separations}}{\text{Average Size of Sales Force}} \times 100$$

Assume, that a company has a sales force whose average strength is 200 men, and has 15 separations during a given year:

$$\frac{15}{200} \times 100 = 7.5\% \text{ Rate of Sales Force Turnover}$$

If this company has a 7.5 percent rate of sales force turnover over a long period, the entire sales force is being replaced once every 13⅓ years ($100\% \div 7.5\% = 13\frac{1}{3}$).

With increases in the rate of sales force turnover, costs of managing the sales force rise. According to one study made several years ago, it costs (on the average) $7,813 to search out, select, hire, and supervise a salesman until he begins to pay his own way.[3] It costs considerably more today, probably at least $12,000. Such cost figures relate only to the directly traceable, out-of-pocket costs of turnover. They do not include such costs as those of lost business or loss of good will caused by mistakes made by inexperienced salesmen, or any of the other expenses associated with taking on sales personnel who do not succeed. Few companies have accounting systems refined enough to permit accurate quantitative measurement of the impact of salesman turnover on profit. However, a reasonable estimate of the actual total costs of salesman turnover for manufacturers may average at least $15,000 per separation. Thus, sales force turnover in the example above could be costing the company at least $225,000 each year.

[3] "More T.S.P.'s Wanted in Sales," *Sales Management*, February 17, 1961, p. 80. ("T.S.P." means "top sales producer.")

Still, every sales force should have some turnover. When there is no turnover, the sales force may be growing stale, and inefficient salesmen may be staying on simply because management has failed to replace them. The sooner management identifies ineffective salesmen, the sooner they can be replaced by more productive salesmen. Even in a sales force made up predominantly of effective people, there should be some turnover since such people are prime candidates for promotion to managerial positions. And even the most successful systems of salesman recruitment and selection are far from perfect; salesmen who will subsequently fail are bound to seep through even the most elaborate screening processes.

Management should also analyze sales force turnover periodically to determine the extent to which highly productive salesmen are leaving the company. When this is happening at an alarming rate, managerial ineffectiveness *may* be the cause. The average quality of the salesmen hired may be too high for the company, so that the job provides little challenge or opportunity for improvement to many of the salesmen after their initial period of training is completed. It is not worthwhile hiring such men since they are soon attracted away by more stimulating and rewarding jobs. In other instances, management may not be providing sufficient challenges and opportunities to retain good people. Sales executives should help each salesman achieve his maximum potential and the maximum potential of his market, or he may become dissatisfied and seek other employment. Therefore, in appraising sales force turnover, one needs to know the causes of turnover as well as the rate. Similarly, in its appraisal of sales force turnover, management should always reexamine the job description and consider how accurately and fully it still describes the company sales job.

Size of Sales Force

Since an individual salesman performing the duties and responsibilities set forth in the job description represents one unit of sales manpower, determining the proper number of salesmen is equivalent to determining the number of units of sales manpower needed to accomplish management's sales and other marketing objectives. Thus, logically the sales and profit objectives, both derived from the sales forecast, should establish the optimal size of the sales force. If the sales job description is accurate and complete, it should be possible to estimate the number of dollars of sales volume each salesman should produce. Dividing this amount into forecasted sales volume and making an allowance for sales force turnover should indicate the number of salesmen needed. These relationships are shown in the following equation:

$$N = \frac{S}{P} + T(S/P)$$

which reduces to:

$$N = \frac{S}{P}(1 + T)$$

where:

N is the number of salesmen
S is the forecasted sales volume
P is the sales productivity of an individual salesman
T is the allowance for rate of sales force turnover

and $\frac{S}{P}$ is the average size of sales force desired over the year.

Equations of this sort are particularly useful in determining how many new salesmen must be recruited. For instance, assume that forecasted sales volume (S) is $10-million, the sales productivity of an individual salesman (P) is $100,000, and the expected rates of sales force turnover (T) is 10 percent. Further assume that the sales force has a present strength of 90 salesmen. Inserting the appropriate figures in the equation above:

$$N = \frac{\$10,000,000}{\$100,000}(1.10)$$

$$N = 110$$

In this illustration, 20 additional salesmen are needed $(110 - 90)$, but turnover is expected to account for 10 departures in the coming year. The anticipated average size of sales force is 100 (i.e., $10,000,000 ÷ $100,000). A 10 percent rate of sales force turnover represents 10 departures. During the course of the year, then, this company must recruit 10 men to replace those who leave, and 10 more who represent a net increase in the size of the sales force. Notice that this simplified model does not take into account the training time required for bringing newly recruited salesmen up to the desired level of sales productivity. An actual planning model of this sort would be developed on a monthly or quarterly basis and would have "lead" and "lag" relations built in to allow for the lead time necessary to train new salesmen. If newly-hired salesmen spend two months in a full-time training program before being assigned to productive jobs, there is a two-month lag between recruiting and actual increase in sales productivity. Recruiting must lead actual need for new salesmen by two months to adjust for this.[4] Also, the model assumes that sales potential

[4] R. S. Weinberg, *An Analytical Approach to Advertising Expenditure Strategy* (New York: Association of National Advertisers, Inc., 1960), p. 98.

is equal in all territories. When this is not true, the model must be designed to compensate for the differences.

Difficulties encountered in making the estimates for this model vary both with the factor being estimated (N, S, P, or T) and with the company. The crucial estimate for the sales productivity of an individual salesman relies heavily on the accuracy and completeness of the sales job description; but it also depends on management's skill in appraising what can be reasonably expected of those who fill the sales positions. Estimating the sales force turnover rate is largely a matter of analyzing previous experience and should present no insurmountable problem.[5]

The estimate for forecasted sales volume deserves special comment. In many situations, the size of the sales forecast is itself influenced by the size of the sales force that management plans to have. Indeed, any realistic forecast of sales volume necessarily must take into account the number of salesmen at management's disposal. When a company is young, and especially when it is growing rapidly, its potential sales volume often depends primarily on the number and ability of its salesmen. In such a company management may actually derive its sales forecast by multiplying the estimated sales productivity of an individual salesman by the number of salesmen it has, can expect to keep, and can recruit and train in the coming period. But as a company extends its distribution over wider and wider geographic areas, and as it approaches maturity, the situation reverses itself, for then the size of the sales force is determined by making the sales forecast first and dividing this by the expected sales productivity of an individual salesman (making adjustments for anticipated sales force turnover, needed training time, and similar factors).

A relationship exists between the size of the sales force and the amount of the personal selling appropriation, but it is not a direct type of relationship. It varies not only with the company but with decisions made by management. In apportioning the personal selling appropriation, management is continually faced with such questions as these: Should we hire five additional salesman at a total annual cost of $100,000, or should we invest the same amount in refresher training for present salesmen? Should we add sales supervisors or use the same number of dollars for conducting sales contests? If such questions were resolved rationally, there would be an equating of the marginal productivities of alternative ways of spending the personal selling appropriation. But, in practice, such allocations are made largely on intuitive grounds. Management experiments constantly, always striving for the optimum allocation pattern. But since there is no

---

[5] For a suggested method of determining size of sales force with the objective of maximizing the profit return as a percentage of the investment, see: W. J. Semlow, "How Many Salesmen Do You Need," *Harvard Business Review*, May-June 1959, pp. 126-32.

known way for measuring or predicting the relative effectiveness of expenditures on the different activities, such allocations have to be made by trial and error methods.

DETERMINING THE KIND OF SALES FORCE NEEDED

The kind of sales force that is appropriate for a particular manufacturer depends on many factors, but especially on the mix of marketing inputs or the over-all marketing strategy. The over-all marketing strategy, in turn, depends on such basic things as product-market strategy, marketing channels and distribution policies, pricing policies and strategies, and advertising strategy. All salesmen in some situations must aggressively seek orders and in other situations need only take orders that come to them, but the degree of emphasis on order-taking and order-getting varies with different selling jobs. The driver-salesman for a soft drink bottling company is primarily an order-taker, since his product has already been strongly presold to the consumer, and the retailer reorders automatically for stock. The salesman calling on householders to sell encyclopedias is much more of an order-getter, since he has the primary responsibility for creating demand. If advertising is the predominant element in the marketing mix, marketing channels are likely to be indirect, and the manufacturer's salesmen are apt to be order-takers primarily and order-getters only incidentally. The opposite situation exists when advertising backs up personal selling in the marketing mix; marketing channels are normally more direct, and salesmen must concentrate more on selling since they cannot merely take customers' orders.

The complexity of the product or product line is another factor that has an important influence on the salesman's role. When the product is highly technical, the selling job is considerably different than when the product is simple. The computer salesman and the office stationery salesman have very different jobs.

Similarly, the nature of the customer also affects the selling job. The industrial user buying for his own operations needs to be handled differently than the middleman buying for resale. Differences in salesmen's roles and tasks call for differences in management approach. Nevertheless, it is revealing to group sales jobs into a limited number of categories to draw certain generalizations. Specifically, selling tasks can be grouped into four basic styles of selling that cut, to a large degree, across industry boundaries: trade selling, missionary selling, technical selling, and new-business selling.[6]

[6] D. A. Newton, "Get the Most Out of Your Sales Force," *Harvard Business Review*, September-October 1969, pp. 131-41.

Trade Selling

The trade salesman develops long-term relations with a relatively stable group of customers. For the most part, his selling is low key with little or no pressure, and his job tends to be on the dull and routine side. This style of selling, which predominates in marketing food and apparel and in wholesaling, applies primarily to products that have well-established markets. In such cases, advertising and other forms of promotion are often more important than personal selling. One of the trade salesman's important responsibilities is to help his customers build up their volume through providing promotional assistance. For example, the salesman for a line of breakfast cereals may devote much of his time to promotional work with retailers and wholesalers—taking stock, refilling shelves, suggesting reorders, setting up displays, and the like.

Because of the routine nature of this style of selling, trade salesmen should be individuals who are not easily bored. Turnover of trade salesmen is higher among young than older men. Since long-term relationships with customers are desirable, trade salesmen should only rarely be transferred from one territory to another. Continuing efforts should be directed toward making the trade selling job as interesting as possible.

Missionary Selling

The missionary salesman is responsible for increasing his company's sales volume by assisting customers with their selling efforts. He is only concerned incidentally with order-taking and order-getting, since the orders he obtains result from his primary public relations and promotional efforts with the customers of his customers (indirect customers). The missionary salesman's job is to persuade indirect customers to buy from his company's direct customers. For example, the salesman for a pharmaceutical manufacturer may call on retail druggists to acquaint them with a new product and to urge them to stock it. Actually, he is persuading them to buy from drug wholesalers, who are the pharmaceutical manufacturer's direct customers. Missionary salesmen also sometimes call on individuals and institutions who do not buy the product themselves, but who influence its purchase by others. The "medical detail man" who calls on doctors and hospitals to acquaint them with new drugs is an example.

Missionary selling, like trade selling, is low key and does not require high-level technical training or ability. The missionary salesman's most important task is to cover the markets of his company's direct customers as thoroughly and as effectively as possible. Generally, companies using missionary salesmen believe it is potentially more profitable to reach prospects than to make repeat calls on established outlets. The effective missionary salesman makes persuasive presentations in minimum time and moves on to new prospects.

Technical Selling

The technical salesman deals primarily with his company's present customers, and his aim is to increase their volume of purchase by providing technical advice and assistance. Frequently, though not always, he needs a technical background and formal education in engineering or some science. He performs advisory functions similar to those of the missionary salesman but, in addition, he normally sells direct to industrial users and other buyers. He devotes most of his time to acquainting industrial users with technical characteristics of products and with new product applications and to helping them design installations or processes that incorporate his company's products. In this style of selling, the ability to identify, analyze, and solve customers' problems is important. The technical salesman's success, however, depends both upon his technical competence and his personality.[7]

Technical salesmen often specialize, either by products or by markets. In selling heavy made-to-order installations, such as steam turbines and electric generators, different technical salesmen work with different items in the product line. Other technical salesmen specialize in servicing either industrial accounts or governmental procurement agencies.

New-Business Selling

New-business selling is frequently referred to as "cold canvass selling." The new-business salesman's main responsibility is to find new customers—to convert prospects into customers. Some experts suggest that many companies that now have a single sales force should divide and specialize their salesmen into two separate groups—one to concentrate on retaining existing customers, and one for converting non-customers into customers. The argument is that most companies should have some salesmen specializing in sales maintenance activities, and others in sales development. Two writers who favor this proposal sum up their position as follows:

> . . . there is a "Gresham's Law" of personal selling; when a salesman has a choice between routine sales maintenance activities and sales development activities requiring creativity, ingenuity, and resourceful-

[7] *Ibid.*, p. 138.

ness, he will tend to give precedence to sales maintenance. Therefore, if sales development is to take place as a sustained and all-out effort, it is necessary to assign the task to salesmen who are prohibited from engaging in sales maintenance and are rewarded only for developing new accounts; in other words, to set up a specialized development task force within or auxiliary to the field sales department.

Specialization by task . . . is a solution . . . using to best advantage the talents and skills of every field salesman. Men who possess the qualities necessary for development work can be relieved of maintenance work, which does not require full use of their rare and valuable capabilities. Similarly, salesmen who are effective in sales maintenance but lack the traits needed for new account development can be relieved of the need for "putting in" time and effort at the latter job. This time and this effort are largely wasted in such activity, but they can and would bring results in sales maintenance. . . .

Furthermore, specialization should eliminate much of the very great waste which now typifies personal selling, by making possible more efficient utilization of manpower resources. In particular, it should eliminate the very high costs which are incurred when men with the gifts required for performance of the vital, difficult, and trying assignment of sales development are given responsibility for sales maintenance which they can do almost without half-trying, while other men who are not sufficiently gifted to develop markets but who can perform sales maintenance skillfully are, nevertheless, called on to work at development and are unhappy while doing it. . . .[8]

Salesmen specializing in new business are a difficult group to manage. Turnover among new-business salesmen tends to be high because only a few can continue this type of effort indefinitely without becoming discouraged by the numerous failures to convert prospects into customers. Turnover, then, is lowest with the older and experienced men, most of whom work quite independently of close supervision.

MANAGING THE SALES FORCE

The chief sales executive's job is to insure that his sales force plays the roles assigned to it as part of the over-all marketing and promotional strategy. To achieve the assigned objectives, he assumes four main responsibilities. First, he identifies promising sources of salesmen and hires qualified men as the budget demands. Second, he sees that all new salesmen are trained for satisfactory job performance and all existing salesmen

[8] G. N. Kahn and A. Shuchman, "Specialize Your Salesmen!" *Harvard Business Review*, January-February 1961, pp. 94-95.

retrained as necessary. Third, he designs and administers compensation and motivation systems that attract and retain productive salesmen. Fourth, he provides the supervision and control which allocates personal selling efforts in line with promotional and over-all marketing objectives.

Recruiting and Selecting

After the sales executive clarifies his manpower requirements and job specifications, his next step, called recruiting, involves determining who has the necessary qualifications, both intellectually and emotionally.[9] The main recruiting problems are: (1) identifying the sources of recruits and (2) choosing recruiting methods. The way to start the recruiting process is to analyze each previously used source according to the numbers of recruits obtained, and their "successes" and "failures" as company salesman. One often-promising source is within the company itself. Sometimes, friends of company salesmen volunteer. Or company executives may have recommendations. Two additional internal sources of new salesmen are the nonselling sections of the sales department and other departments.

In most instances, however, the sales manager must look outside the firm for an adequate source of recruits. Colleges and universities, as well as other educational institutions, are increasingly important sources of sales trainees. Another outside source consists of the experienced salesmen of competitors and other companies. Sales managers have found that employment agencies, if used with discretion, can provide many salesmen recruits. Other sources include: classified ads, professional organizations, and social and church groups.

In a well-integrated selection system, each step contributes information needed for hiring decisions. Selection systems range from simple one-step procedures, consisting merely of an informal personal interview, to complex multiple-step systems utilizing numerous and varied devices and techniques for gathering information on prospective salesmen. A selection system should be a set of successive "screens," during any of which job candidates may be dropped from further consideration. Because some screens are expensive to administer (e.g., physical examinations), the most inexpensive screens should be incorporated early in the system, thus eliminating unpromising candidates as early as possible and at minimal cost. Candidates surviving all screenings receive job offers.

However, no selection system is infallible—all eliminate some who would have succeeded as salesmen and recommend hiring some who fail. A selection system fulfills its main mission if it improves management's

---

[9] J. A. Belasco, "The Salesman's Role Revisited," *Journal of Marketing*, April 1966, pp. 6-9.

ability to estimate success and failure probabilities for individual applicants. Each company should design its selection system to fit its own requirements. Every step in a selection system should serve a purpose; when a step no longer makes a contribution, it should be dropped. Some commonly-used selection steps are: the interview application, the interview, the formal application form, references and recommendations, physical examination, credit reports, and psychological tests (aptitude, intelligence, personality, and others).

Training Salesmen

The modern sales executive's approach to sales training markedly contrasts to that prevalent only a few years ago. Old-style sales managers typically believed in "sink-or-swim" training—putting new salesmen into the field with scanty instructions and expecting them to do their best, learning what they could in the hard school of experience. The modern sales executive still considers experience the most valuable sales training, but believes strongly that formally planned and executed sales training programs contribute significantly to improved selling performance.

Many companies have several types of sales training programs. Generally, the longest and most comprehensive is for newly-recruited men. Shorter and more specialized programs are given for experienced salesmen, although at times "refresher" courses are also appropriate. Other training programs are designed especially for sales trainers (i.e., for those who actually train others) and for men management regards as potential sales executives. Each type serves different purposes, and the scope and content of each should reflect these differences.

Building an effective sales training program of any type requires a number of important planning decisions. The training objectives need clear definition, program content must be decided, training methods selected, arrangements made for program execution, and procedures for evaluating the results set up. Professional sales trainers refer to these planning decisions as the A-C-M-E decisions—aim, content, method, execution and evaluation.

For new salesmen the training program content normally includes product data, sales techniques, evaluation of markets, and company information. For experienced men the content may be more specialized to meet particular needs. Training methods involve both group and individual instructional techniques. Often-used group instruction methods are lectures, group discussions, role-playing, and simulation. The individual training methods include on-the-job training, personal conferences, correspondence courses, and programmed instruction. The balance between these several instructional methods varies with each company's needs and resources. Problems in executing the training program include: determining the length of training, deciding on the training site, and selecting the training aids.

Compensating Salesmen

Management has two main decisions to make on salesmen's compensation: (1) *the level of compensation*—that is, how much to pay salesmen, and (2) *the compensation method.*

DETERMINING THE COMPENSATION LEVEL   In determining the compensation level, the most critical factor is the nature of the salesman's job. First, the duties and responsibilities inherent in the selling job should be analyzed to ascertain the caliber of salesmen needed. Then, the average amount of annual income needed to attract and hold men of the necessary caliber should be determined—usually by investigating compensation levels in companies employing comparable salesmen.

Far more than for most other jobs, the compensation level for sales jobs is influenced by external supply and demand factors. Salesmen enjoy greater job mobility than most other employees, and they often have daily contacts with potential employers. Normally, because of the strong pull exerted by outside firms employing salesmen of similar quality, salesmen are paid more than either production workers or office personnel. Therefore, marketing management generally insists that any company-wide salary administration system take the impact of external compensation levels into account in setting salesmen's compensation.

DECIDING THE COMPENSATION METHOD   Having determined the appropriate pay level, management's next task is to decide on the compensation *method*. Every method for paying salesmen represents some combination of the four elements of compensation: (1) a fixed portion (salary), (2) a variable portion (commission, bonus, or participation in profit sharing), (3) an element providing for either reimbursement of expenses or payment of expense allowances, and (4) "fringe benefits" such as paid vacations, pensions, insurance, and stock purchase privileges. Since "expense reimbursement" and "fringe benefits" are never used alone, we may exclude them from consideration. Thus, there are three basic compensation methods: (1) straight salary, (2) straight commission, and (3) a combination of salary and one or more variable features.

Each of these methods represents a different weighting of the relative importance of two underlying purposes of compensation—to provide management with the power to direct salesmen's activities and to furnish salesmen with the incentive to work productively and efficiently. At the two extremes are the straight salary and straight commission methods. The straight salary method, in theory, provides management with the maximum power to direct salesmen's efforts along the potentially most productive lines. The company guarantees a total fixed income to the salesman and has the right to ask him to engage in activities that are not directly productive of sales. Under the straight commission method, where the salesman's earnings are closely related to his selling efforts, he properly resents demands on his time for activities unproductive of sales. The justification of the straight commission system is that it provides salesmen with the maximum financial incentive to strive toward high selling efficiency. Neither straight salary nor straight commission, however, are as widely-used as the combination methods. By including both a fixed element and one or more variable elements in their plans for paying salesmen, companies seek both to secure the needed control and to furnish salesmen with the necessary motivation.

The problem of deciding on a compensation method reduces to one of determining which elements to include and the proportion that each should bear to the salesman's total income. Not every company does, or should, include all four elements. Each should select the combination of elements that will help the most in working toward the company's over-all marketing objectives. Four important considerations involved in dealing with this problem are discussed below.

1. *Balancing Control and Incentive.* The main reason that most companies use the combination plan is that it makes possible the achievement of a closer balance between control and incentive. Companies using straight salary rely heavily on it as a means to control and direct salesmen's activities and must look elsewhere for ways to provide incentives. Those companies choosing straight commission tend to view it as the main way of providing salesmen with incentives, and managements in such companies must find other ways to control salesmen. Of course, those with salary methods can use salary increases as financial incentives and those with commission methods may use changes in commission rates as controls. But, for the most part, users of the straight salary method must rely either on liberal fringe benefits or on non-financial items, such as salesmen's medals or letters of commendation for good or excellent performance, to provide salesmen with sufficient incentives to do their jobs well. These are often the best incentives that can be used with men whose incomes are well above subsistence-level. Similarly, companies using the straight commission method may seek the needed control over salesmen through either the fringe benefits offered or by resorting to such non-financial controls as close supervision. In all companies, providing salesmen with opportuni-

ties to advance to managerial levels gives management a degree of control and salesmen an incentive to gain prestige.

So far as the compensation plan is concerned, however, balancing control and incentive mainly involves deciding on the ratios that the base salary and the financial incentive should bear to the total compensation. Where companies wish to allocate a very large portion of salesmen compensation to salaries, the amount remaining for commissions may be so low as to provide insufficient incentive for salesmen without raising total selling costs. In such cases, management clearly is better off not using a combination method. There are also opposite cases where the incentive portion of a combination plan bulks so large in the total that salesmen tend to neglect duties for which they are not directly compensated. Analysis of numerous compensation plans indicates that the most common distribution of payments is approximately 70 percent salary and 30 percent incentive and other variable elements.

2. *Recognition of Performance Differences.* Since outstanding salesmen should be paid more than those who are mediocre or ineffective, salesmen's compensation plans should result in differential payments according to differences in performances. At the same time, however, the plan should not penalize or reward salesmen for factors outside their control, such as differences in territory potentials.

The machinery for differential payment may operate either automatically or at management's discretion. Some variable elements, such as commissions based on sales volume, automatically provide for differential payment. When salary is used to effect differentials in compensation, management must make salary adjustments often enough to accurately reflect changes in individual performance. Most managements favor using the commission or bonus element as the main instrument for recognizing performance differences: it not only operates automatically but readily makes downward as well as upward adjustments, paralleling changes in performance. By contrast, managerial inertia usually causes salary adjustments to lag behind performance changes, and it is rare for them to be made in any direction but upward.

3. *Simplicity.* From management's standpoint, it is advantageous to keep the compensation plan as simple as possible. Simple compensation plans normally cost less to administer than complicated ones. And, although a complex plan may often provide greater refinements in stimulation and reward, improvements in performance may not be enough to offset the increased administrative costs. Also, the method of compensation should not be so complicated that the average salesman experiences difficulty in calculating his earnings. However, what one group of salesmen considers complicated may be thought ridiculously simple by others. Quite similar compensation plans may appear hopelessly complex to a wholesale grocery

salesman but perfectly easy to understand to the engineering-trained salesman of electronic components.

4. *Company Financial Position.* The state of company finances
often influences the particular design of the plan chosen. Companies with
strong working capital positions tend to favor the straight salary system,
because it results in sales compensation expenses fixed in total amount, but
varying inversely percentage-wise with sales volume. Smaller companies,
especially those short of working capital, prefer the straight commission
system in which compensation expenses vary in total amount, but are fixed
as a percentage of sales volume. Combination plans offer compromises
whereby a company may achieve the degree of financial flexibility considered desirable by its management.

SUPERVISING AND CONTROLLING SALESMEN

Effective supervision and control are essential to the securing of optimum
performance from salesmen. Even star performers need guidance and direction to channel their efforts along lines consistent with achievement of
the company's marketing objectives; management guides and directs salesmen's efforts in numerous ways, but among the most important are the
assignment of salesmen to territories and the routing and scheduling of
salesmen's calls. Furthermore, all salesmen require the motivation that comes
along with the assignment of performance goals and benefit from the
continuing stimulation of being kept informed on the progress they are
making toward achieving those goals.

Allocating Personal Selling Effort

Once management commits itself to a certain size of sales force
and sets the personal selling appropriation, it faces the job of allocating
each salesman's efforts to the best advantage. In most well-managed
companies, formal allocation takes the form of: (1) assigning salesmen to
territories and/or (2) routing and scheduling their calls on customers and
prospects.

ASSIGNMENT OF SALESMEN TO TERRITORIES   Assigning a sales-
man to a territory focuses his efforts on a given geographical area containing
some grouping of customers and prospects. Each territory represents some
potential volume of sales to the company. Whenever a salesman is assigned
to a territory, management, in effect, has matched some level of selling

skill with the amount of sales opportunity it believes present in that territory. Therefore, both the relative abilities of salesmen and the relative sales potentials of territories should be considered in assigning specific salesmen to specific territories. Too often, however, the problems of appraising salesmen's efficiency and evaluating territorial sales potentials are treated independently. Since salesmen differ in efficiency and territories differ in sales potential, a *rational* assignment of salesmen to territories would put the best salesman in the most fertile territory, the second best salesman in the second most fertile territory, and so on.[10] Only if the assignment is made in this way is it possible to maximize total sales in the entire market.[11]

ROUTING AND SCHEDULING SALESMEN'S CALLS   Once salesmen have been assigned to territories, the next problem is to use their available selling time to maximum advantage. This is largely a matter of minimizing the amount of "waste" time, and of securing the best allocation of productive selling time among individual accounts and prospects. Included within the meaning of "waste" time, as used here, are hours spent in travel between calls, time spent waiting for interviews, and other time "idled away."

Not every company uses formal planning and control of salesmen's route and call schedules. In some instances, management's philosophy appears to be that salesmen are the best judges of how they should spend their time. In other instances, the caliber of the salesmen is so high that management feels any move toward formal routing and scheduling is inappropriate for such reasons as these: It is extremely difficult to predict the amount of selling time each account will require, as when salesmen sell products designed to each customer's specifications; the company uses "side-line" salesmen who represent several companies and, therefore, are virtually in business for themselves; or salesmen are engaged in house-to-house selling, where nearly every householder is a prospect (e.g., the situation in selling encyclopedias) and where salesmen have to adjust their routes and calls to accommodate the "at home" habits of each prospect.

Aside from the exceptions noted above, most companies can derive great benefits from formal routing and scheduling of salesmen's calls. Besides increasing the chances that salesmen will be on the job when they are supposed to be, formal route and call schedules make it easier to contact them to provide needed and helpful information or last-minute instructions. Moreover, planning a salesman's route, if done intelligently and efficiently,

[10] The logic of this can be verified by applying the assignment method of linear programming. For instance, see: M. Sasieni, A. Yaspan, and L. Friedman, *Operations Research: Methods and Problems* (New York: John Wiley & Sons, 1959), Prob. 5, p. 194.

[11] For a report on the procedure one company used in reaching rational decisions on this matter, see: W. J. Talley, Jr., "How to Design Sales Territories," *Journal of Marketing*, January 1961, pp. 7-13.

eliminates much back-tracking, travel time, and waiting time. Providing a salesman with a schedule of calls makes it possible to adjust the frequency of call to fit the needs of customers and prospects more precisely, thus securing improved coverage of the territory.[12]

Appraising Salesman Performance

Before examining the problems involved in evaluating the performance of salesmen, it should be noted that management alone bears the ultimate responsibility for maximizing the contribution of the personal selling effort to the achievement of the company's sales and marketing objectives. Management makes the basic decisions: the type of salesman needed, the content of the job descriptions, the size of the sales force, the level and method of compensation, how individual salesmen should be deployed throughout the marketing area, and so on. None of these decisions can be made intelligently without considering their relation to the others. None should be made without careful consideration of its probable influence on attainment of sales and marketing objectives and of the effect its probable cost will have on the personal selling appropriation. Success or failure in maximizing the contribution of the personal selling effort is the responsibility of management, not of the salesman, and it is managerial excellence in making and implementing these decisions that determines the degree of success.

Salesmen are the main instruments through which management tries to maximize the contribution of the personal selling effort. They are instruments of management's own choosing and training. The performance of salesmen, individually and collectively, directly affects the success of the personal selling effort. So it is imperative that management measure the performance of salesmen. Without measurement, management is greatly handicapped in predicting the probable results of its decisions. Moreover, measurement is essential for making rational decisions on such questions as which salesmen to discharge, which to train further, and which to reward. Management needs, therefore, to measure the performance of salesmen, both for purposes of decision-making and for control.

Not only must there be measures of salesman performance, there must also be ways of distinguishing good from poor performance. Standards, or norms, must be established against which the performance of individual salesmen may be appraised. For decision-making and control purposes, the

---

[12] For a suggested method of arriving at optimum rates of call frequency for different classes of accounts, see: R. R. Still and H. R. Greene, *Distribution of Industrial Goods: Illustrations of the Application of a Rational Approach to Decision-Making* (Syracuse, N.Y.: Business Research Center, Syracuse University, 1961), especially pp. 27-30.

most useful performance standards are quantitative ones, but most companies also need to utilize qualitative criteria of appraisal.

THE JOB DESCRIPTION AND PERFORMANCE APPRAISAL   One place to start in appraising a salesman's over-all performance is with his job description. If it is a good one, it not only details the salesman's duties and responsibilities but spells out the performance levels considered satisfactory by management. Comparison of what the salesman does with what the job description says he should be doing provides insight into his total performance.

The trouble with the job description, however, is that many of the salesman's duties and responsibilities do not lend themselves to quantitative measurement. How, for example, can management measure how much good will a salesman builds? Or, what numerical measures are there for the salesman's mental alertness in dealing with customers? Probably the best that can be done is to define, as clearly as possible, what performance is expected for each of the listed duties and responsibilities. Some definitions may include quantitative performance standards (e.g., the frequencies with which calls should be made on different classes of accounts), but most necessarily have to be phrased only as qualitative statements of what is expected by management.

QUOTAS   Quotas are the most common yardsticks used to measure salesmen's performance. A quota is a quantitatively-expressed goal assigned to a specific marketing unit, such as to a salesman or territory. On the basis of his past performance, a salesman might be expected to produce a predetermined volume of sales or, on the basis of measured market potential, a territory might be expected to yield a predetermined volume of sales. Quotas may be in terms of dollars or unit sales volume, gross margin, net profit, expenses, calls, number of new accounts, amount of dealer display space obtained, or other measurable units.

A major problem in working with quotas is that of determining their size. Consider, for example, the dollar sales volume quota. Salesmen's efforts do not always produce sales in the period for which their performance is being evaluated, and the results of a salesman's current efforts may materialize only over many future operating periods. In addition, each salesman is faced with different working conditions, many of which influence the relative ease with which sales are made. Territory by territory, for example, there are variations in the strength of competition, the time required for travel, and the amount of sales potential present. Thus, it is rare to find a company that is justified in assigning identical sales volume quotas to all its salesmen. Because of competitive, physical, and sales fertility differences among territories, then, the sales volume quota for each salesman should be set individually. There is another important reason for individually-set quotas: the salesmen also vary in selling efficiency because of differences in training, experience, and native abilities. There is little incentive value in assigning a salesman a sales volume goal that he hasn't a chance of reaching.

Another major problem in working with the sales volume quota is that of distinguishing sales results produced by the salesman from those due to other causes. Advertising, for instance, is often at least a partial influence in making many sales, but the salesman writes the actual order. At other times, the salesman may write the order, but his supervisor or branch manager may actually have been the major influence in the customer's decision to buy. In such cases, it is impossible to determine the exact extent of the salesman's contribution.

The sales forecast should be the main basis for setting sales volume quotas, since carefully prepared sales forecasts, when intelligently broken down, result in quotas that are reasonable and thus attainable. By breaking the sales forecast down into manageable parts—i.e., into sales volume quotas for individual salesmen—management can specifically define the results it expects from each man's efforts. However, it should be recognized that a sales volume quota can be no better than the sales forecast from which it is derived. If the forecast is little more than a wild guess, the quota derived from it will be no better. Improvements in sales forecasts and sales volume quotas go hand in hand.

In addition to providing management with a yardstick for appraising the efficiency of salesmen, sales volume quotas have some incentive value. Salesmen are likely to work much harder when quotas are used then when they are not, especially if each quota is rationally determined—i.e., only after consideration is given to territorial differences and variations in salesmen. The fact that there *is* such a goal, together with the knowledge that management *expects* its achievement, does cause most salesmen to do their best to achieve it.

CONCLUSION

Many important decisions must be made in the area of personal selling. Rational decision-making requires that management start with a careful determination of the appropriate personal selling strategy. For making the determination, it is essential to have accurate job descriptions, a reliable estimate of the size of the sales force, and an adequate personal selling appropriation, based upon a carefully-prepared sales forecast. The activities involved in managing the sales force—recruiting and selecting, training, compensating, and supervising—require decisions that not only become part of but affect both the promotional mix and the over-all marketing strategy.

QUESTIONS AND PROBLEMS

1. How do you explain the fact that manufacturers are more inclined to shift the advertising activity to agencies than they are to shift the personal selling activity to middlemen?

2. In which of the following situations should the major promotional emphasis be placed on personal selling rather than on advertising? Give your reasons in each case.
    a. Selling extension telephones to homeowners
    b. Persuading retailers to stock a new soft drink
    c. Selling a landscaping and grounds maintenance program for industrial plants
    d. Selling life insurance to individuals

3. Compare and contrast the determination of personal selling and advertising appropriations.

4. What is a sales job description? Suggest some ways a company might go about obtaining job descriptions for its salesmen. Discuss the relationship of the sales job description to recruiting, selecting, training, supervising, and controlling salesmen.

5. The sales force of a certain manufacturer numbered 50 men at the start of the year and 80 men at the end of the year. Twenty men either resigned, were fired, were promoted, or otherwise left the sales force during the year.
    a. Compute the rate of sales force turnover.
    b. Assuming continuation of the present rate of sales force turnover, how long will it take to replace the entire sales force?
    c. Supposing this manufacturer says: "What good does it do me to know my rate of sales force turnover? How do I use this statistic?" What advice would you give him?
    d. Later on, this manufacturer hears of a small company which had five salesmen at the start of the year, eight men at the end, and lost two men during the year. He concluded that since this company and his own both had the same rate of sales force turnover, both must have been equally well managed. Would you agree? Why or why not?

6. Suppose a certain manufacturer has a forecasted sales volume of $8,000,000, the sales productivity of an individual salesman is $160,000, and the expected rate of sales force turnover is 20 percent. Assume further that there are presently forty men on the sales force.
    a. What is the "needed" size of the sales force in this case?
    b. What is the anticipated average size of sales force?

c. Suppose that it costs $10,000 to bring a new salesman up to the $160,000 sales productivity level. How much money can this manufacturer save, if he succeeds in holding the rate of sales force turnover to 10 percent?

7. Discuss the changes that occur in the relationship of the sales forecast to the size of the sales force as a company expands its operations and eventually matures.

8. The management of a newly-organized company estimates the market value for salesmen of the quality it desires at $12,000, and further estimates the average gross margin available for paying salesmen at 15 percent of sales volume. How much annual sales volume must each salesman produce for the company to break-even?

9. In each of the following situations, what would you regard as the salesman's main task? His other tasks?
    a. A salesman selling aluminum drains and gutters to homeowners on a house-to-house basis
    b. An automobile dealer's salesman charged with making fleet sales to business and local governmental agencies
    c. A salesman of automatic packaging machinery used by brewers, soft-drink bottlers, and food processors
    d. A salesman for a hardware wholesaler calling on retail hardware and variety stores
    e. A manufacturer's salesman selling furniture to department stores and discount houses.

10. Compare the following types of salesmen:
    a. Order-taker and order-getter
    b. Missionary salesman and technical salesman
    c. Missionary salesman and trade salesman
    d. Trade salesman and new-business salesman.

11. Do you favor or oppose the proposal that salesmen should specialize either in sales maintenance activities or in sales development? Why? If you worked for a company that specialized its sales force in this way, would you rather be assigned to sales maintenance or sales development? Why?

12. What sources should be used in recruiting new salesmen for the following companies? Why?
    a. A company selling fine china and kitchenware house-to-house
    b. A company selling erosion-control materials to state highway departments
    c. A publisher selling textbooks to colleges and universities
    d. An importer of fancy Italian foods selling in the New York and Philadephia market areas

e. A manufacturer of high-quality men's clothing sold through exclusive men's stores.

13. What are the A-C-M-E decisions? How should they be made?

14. Answer the following questions pertaining to salesmen's compensation:

a. What factors should be taken into account in setting the compensation level?

b. What are the main factors influencing the decision as to compensation method?

c. Compare the three basic compensation methods from the viewpoints of (1) management, (2) the salesmen, and (3) the customers called on by salesmen.

d. Explain how control and incentive are balanced under each of the three basic compensation methods.

e. Why do managements generally prefer to use the commission or bonus element in compensation as the main instrument for recognizing performance differences among salesmen?

f. What is meant by "skimming the cream?" How does compensation level influence this tendency? Compensation method?

15. What information does management need to make rational assignments of salesmen to territories? What research methods might be used in obtaining this information?

16. How might break-even computations be used in setting the boundaries for salesmen's territories? To what extent would these computations be affected by the method of sales compensation used?

17. Under what conditions should companies use formal routing and scheduling of salesmen's calls? Under what conditions should salesmen route and schedule themselves?

18. Why must management have measures of the performance of salesmen? How useful is the job description in making performance appraisals? What problems are encountered in using quotas as yardsticks of sales performance?

19. Discuss the relationship of sales forecasting to the setting of sales volume quotas.

20. Some cities have enacted laws, known as "Green River Ordinances," which regulate or sometimes even prohibit house-to-house selling. Why are such ordinances passed? Why not pass similar ordinances to prohibit or regulate the activities of salesmen calling on business establishments? Why not pass laws requiring salesmen to be licensed and to meet certain minimum requirements, such as successful completion of a formal educational program or passage of a state-conducted examination?

21.   "With almost complete literacy in this country, with the progress of automation, with the tremendous coverage afforded by radio and TV, and with the increasing effectiveness of advertising, the age of the salesman is fast disappearing. By the time we reach the year 2000, salesmen will be as rare as dinosaurs' eggs." What is your reaction to this statement by a critic of personal selling? Are salesmen in general in any great danger of being supplanted? What about retail sales people? Wholesalers' salesmen? Manufacturers' salesmen?

22.   Professor Dale Houghton of New York University reported that 64 percent of the consumer goods companies he studied spent more for the sales force than for advertising. Professor Houghton also found that among industrial goods companies, the cost of the sales force almost invariably exceeds by many times the cost of advertising. What conclusions might be drawn from these findings?

18

MANAGEMENT
OF ADVERTISING

Advertising, along with personal selling, is one of the two main ways which a marketer has for directly communicating with target market segments. In sharp contrast with personal selling, however, advertising generally seeks to reach masses (i.e., large groups) of potential buyers; advertising, in other words, usually takes a "shotgun" approach to communicating with target market segments, whereas personal selling "zeroes in" on individual customers and prospects with a rifle-like approach. Also in contrast with personal selling, a great deal of glamour attaches to advertising, much of it because of the fame and riches won in early years by such Madison Avenue advertising professionals as David Ogilvie and Mary Wells. Nevertheless, as a career field, advertising in the United States represents probably no more than 500,000 jobs, of which perhaps 50,000 are with advertising agencies (both on and away from Madison Avenue). For every advertising job in the United States, there are approximately fifteen personal selling jobs— about 10 percent of all jobs are in personal selling, *i.e.,* between seven and eight million.

Advertising, formally defined, is any paid form of nonpersonal presentation of products, services, and ideas by an identified sponsor. As this "umbrella-like" definition implies, advertising takes numerous forms. To mention only a few, consider the following categories:

By geographical coverage
National
Regional
Local

By message emphasis
product
institutional

By intended audience
Consumer
Industrial
Trade

By sponsorship
Manufacturer
Middleman
Industry or trade group
Manufacturer & middlemen
(cooperative)

By intended result
Quick-action ("buy now!")
Delayed-action ("buy later!")

By type of appeal
Rational
Emotional

By fineness of definition of target audience
Mass ("shotgun" advertising)
Class ("rifle" advertising)

By type of demand
Primary (for generic products)
Selective (for particular brands)

By life cycle stage of product advertised
Pioneering
Competitive (for growth and maturity
stages)
Retentive (for maturity and decline
stages)

When he considers his advertising needs, the marketer faces many challenging problems. The most basic is whether the company should advertise at all. If he decides to advertise, he must make several related decisions. Should the firm handle all of its own advertising or should an advertising agency be retained? Which agency should be selected? How much money should be invested in advertising? What measures of advertising effectiveness should be used? How should the advertising appropriation be allocated among the different media? Should the firm engage in cooperative advertising?

Our main focus in this chapter is on the management of advertising. Because of their specialized nature, such technical details of advertising production as copy, layout, illustration, and type styles do not enter the discussion.[1] However, it should not be inferred that the technical side of advertising is unimportant.

THE OBJECTIVES OF ADVERTISING

The long-term objective of advertising, as of every other business activity, is to increase the firm's net profits over what they would be without it. In some cases, increased profits are also immediate objectives; but in others, they are not. Perhaps the most important short-term objective of advertising is to provide support for personal selling and other methods of promotion. Advertising is almost never used alone; generally it is cast in a supporting role to other means of promotion.

However, advertising is an extremely versatile communications tool. Depending upon the marketing situation, companies use advertising to achieve various marketing objectives:

1. to do the entire selling job (as in mail-order marketing)
2. to introduce a new product (by building brand awareness among potential buyers)
3. to force middlemen to handle the product (pull strategy)
4. to build brand preference (by making it more difficult for middlemen to sell substitutes)
5. to remind users to buy the product (retentive strategy)
6. to publicize some change in marketing strategy (e.g., a price change, a new model, or an improvement in the product)
7. to provide rationalizations for buying (i.e., "socially acceptable" excuses)
8. to combat or neutralize competitors' advertising efforts
9. to improve the morale of dealers and/or salesmen
10. to acquaint buyers and prospective buyers with new uses of the product.

The above list is not all-inclusive but only illustrative of the broad range of objectives advertising may be directed toward accomplishing. One danger in presenting such a list is that the reader may get the idea that

[1] The reader interested in the technical aspects of advertising production is referred to any of the many basic texts in that field. Among these are: S. W. Dunn, *Advertising, Its Role in Modern Marketing* 2nd ed. (New York: Holt, Rinehart & Winston, Inc., 1969); A. W. Frey, *Advertising*, 3rd ed. (New York: The Ronald Press Company, 1961); M. I. Mandell, *Advertising* (Englewood Cliffs, N.J.: Prentice-Hall, Inc., 1968) and J. S. Wright and D. S. Warner, *Advertising*, 2nd ed. (New York: McGraw-Hill Book Co., Inc., 1970).

advertising is *only* something that the advertiser does to someone else. However, for companies operating under the marketing concept, it is important to bear in mind that advertising should also serve as an effective and efficient source of information for members of the audience. Following the logic of the marketing concept, an information source can only maximally serve the advertiser's purposes when it serves the target audience's purposes.[2] Advertising objectives, in other words, although they may be phrased in terms of what the marketer would like to accomplish, should be appraised from the standpoint of their effectiveness in providing needed and relevant information to members of the intended audience.

ADVERTISING OPPORTUNITY

Advertising opportunities are more apparent under certain conditions than others. Clearly, advertising opportunities exist: (1) when the demand for the product is expansible, (2) when it is possible to differentiate the product in buyer's eyes, and (3) when the nature of the product's demand is conductive to the achievement of the marketer's objectives through advertising.

Demand Expansibility

If advertising is to result in additional net profits, it usually must produce additional sales volume. However, additional net profits may also result if advertising just proves to be a more economical means of getting business than personal selling. In either situation, advertising must be capable of causing sales, or else there is little justification for advertising.

If demand can be stimulated through advertising alone, it is said to be "expansible."[3] Demand is expansible if an increase in advertising results in greater sales of the product or brand with no change in price. If it does not, or if the price must be cut to produce additional sales, demand is inexpansible. To stimulate *primary* demand (for a *type* of product) on a profitable basis, then, demand must be expansible.

An expansible demand is not a necessary condition for the profitable stimulation of *selective* demand (for a specific brand), inasmuch as

---

[2] B. Stidsen, "Some Thoughts on the Advertising Process," *Journal of Marketing,* January 1970, p. 47.

[3] The expansibility-of-demand concept was first used by Professor M. T. Copeland in his marketing course at the Harvard Business School in the mid-1920s. Some writers use another term, promotional elasticity, when referring to demand expansibility. For instance, see: J. Dean, *Managerial Economics* (Englewood Cliffs, N.J.: Prentice-Hall, 1951), pp. 161-63.

selective demand advertising may succeed in winning away customers of competing brands. Nevertheless, the existence of an expansible demand adds to the chances of success for selective, as well as primary, demand advertising. Moreover, advertising designed to stimulate selective demand may win non-users of the product type to the manufacturer's brand, may win some users of competing brands, and may even increase consumption of the brand among its present users.

In considering demand in relation to advertising opportunity, a decision-maker should also know whether demand is price elastic. Demand is price elastic if a price reduction increases total revenue (price times quantity sold), and if a price rise reduces total revenue. Demand is price inelastic if a price reduction decreases total revenue, and a price rise increases total revenue. Normally, however, and contrary to the economist's usual assumption, the adjustment of revenue to a price change is not immediate. So a practical businessman may find advertising useful in "spreading the word" of a price reduction on a product with an elastic demand, thus speeding increased total revenue.

Brand Differentiation

A particularly important factor in appraising advertising opportunity is the degree to which the brand differs from competing brands. Brand differences and similarities should be identified and appraisals made of their relative importance to specific market segments. Differences that large numbers of buyers consider important furnish the source of selective-advertising appeals. If a brand is not very different from competing brands— and buyers know it—the most the manufacturer can hope to accomplish through advertising is brand acceptance. There must be brand differences of substantial importance to buyers if the advertising is to be successful in developing brand preference or, ideally, brand insistence.

Buyers can detect some important hidden brand differences through use; other hidden brand differences cannot be so detected. If, as with many food products, the detection of hidden differences requires that the brand be used in a certain way, the manufacturer must provide directions for use. Thus, a cake mix manufacturer provides careful directions to insure that the end result is an acceptable cake. If, as with certain drugs and cosmetics, the hidden difference is not detectable through use (e.g., it may require a number of weeks of use of a facial cream to determine its effect on the complexion) the advertiser often attempts to convince buyers of the integrity of the firm itself or publicizes endorsements of the brand by experts. Whenever a brand possesses important hidden differences, there is considerable opportunity for advertising to exploit them profitably.

Nature of the Product's Demand

The potential effectiveness of advertising depends importantly upon management's recognition of the evolutionary stage of the product's demand and its skill in adjusting the thrust of the advertising appeal accordingly. Advertising appeals may be directed toward stimulating either or both of two broad categories of demand—primary or selective. Primary demand is demand for the *type* of product rather than a specific brand (e.g., demand for electric refrigerators rather than demand for *Norge* or *Kelvinator*) or other makes. Selective demand is the demand for a specific brand. Relative to the product life cycle, stimulation of primary demand precedes stimulation of selective demand. Consumers must want the generic product (as marketing people generally describe a type of product) before they can want some brand of it.

Thus, after introducing a new type of product, a manufacturer will normally concentrate on advertising intended to stimulate primary demand. As the product type gains acceptance, the manufacturer may gradually change over to advertising designed to stimulate selective demand. For example, when R.C.A. introduced color television, it was the only manufacturer, and its total promotional efforts sought to persuade consumers to buy color instead of black-and-white television. After General Electric, Zenith, and others entered the color television field, R.C.A. shifted its advertising to emphasize the special advantages of R.C.A. color television over competitive color sets.

Many products, however, continue to require advertising aimed at stimulating primary demand, because they compete directly with some different product type. For example, tea, certainly not a new product, must continually compete with coffee for primary acceptance. In other situations, the product type may be in indirect competition for the consumer's dollars. For example, home organs and color television sets both may compete for the same dollars when individual consumers cannot afford to buy both. It is not unusual, then, for primary demand advertising to be used even for "mature" products. But in all cases, primary demand must exist before selective demand can be stimulated.

THE DECISION TO ADVERTISE

Generally, advertising opportunity is influenced more by combinations of conditions than it is by any single favorable or adverse factor. Advertising always entails some risk, but total risk is certainly less when favoring conditions outweigh those opposed to advertising. As the proportion of adverse to favorable conditions increases, the risk of advertising failure increases. After evaluating the relative risk and determining whether this is a reasonable amount of risk for the firm to assume, the decision-maker decides whether to advertise.

Should a firm advertise a particular product? The answer is "Yes, if there is sufficient opportunity for improving the firm's net-profit position." An "advertising opportunity" is present when the use of advertising is capable of bringing about an increase in sales large enough to cover all added costs involved in handling the added volume of sales (including advertising costs) and still have enough left over to make a contribution toward net profit. Thus, in a firm operating at a 10 percent rate of profit, a proposed $10,000 advertising program would constitute an advertising opportunity only if it could be expected to increase sales volume by more than $100,000, since the added cost of advertising would eat up the profit on the first incremental $100,000 of sales.

Determining the presence and extent of an advertising opportunity is not easy, and sometimes the only way is just "to try it and see." But most advertisers need not resort to trial and error if they have sufficient and reliable information on which to base their decisions. Detecting advertising opportunity requires rigorous qualitative analysis of the market, the product, and the distribution system. Measuring the extent, or size, of the advertising opportunity requires much additional information, most of it quantitative.

Incremental Return and Advertising Cost

To justify advertising a brand, potential dollar sales should be great enough to produce at least enough additional gross margin dollars— excess of sales over cost of goods sold—to cover the advertising cost. In other words, advertising should pay for itself. There is a sort of break-even point for advertising, a point where additional gross margin dollars resulting from the advertising just barely pay for the advertising. Thus, the decision-maker should calculate the additional sales volume that the advertising should produce in order to break even on the advertising cost. This is a matter of dividing the cost of an adequate advertising campaign by the gross margin per unit of product (excess of selling price over cost).

Therefore, the amount of unit gross margin obtainable is a significant factor to consider. The size of unit gross margin is related to such marketing characteristics of the brand as its replacement rate and consumption time.[4] A brand with a high replacement rate (purchased frequently by consumers) and a low consumption time (used rapidly by consumers) usually has a low unit gross margin. Conversely, a brand with a low replacement rate and high consumption time normally has a high unit gross

---

[4] For explanations of replacement rate and consumption time, see Chapter 8.

margin. In either case, there may be economic justification for advertising. However, a brand characterized by a low replacement rate and high consumption time must also be salable at a fairly high unit price for advertising to pay for itself. A low-priced pocket knife, unless it can be sold in much greater volume, is not nearly as promising a candidate for advertising as a higher-priced set of carving knives, but both have low replacement rates and high consumption times.

Effect of Advertising on Price

Consumers should consider the product or brand worth the price it is necessary to charge (including advertising costs). This does not necessarily mean that an advertised item should be priced identically with its unadvertised competitors or even its advertised competitors. Its price should represent reasonable value in the consumer's mind. If he considers it superior to competing brands, the price may be higher, and if he considers it inferior, the price must be lower. Advertising will not persuade the consumer to pay what he considers an unreasonable price. Yet, many consumers evidently feel that an advertised brand is worth a higher price than an unadvertised brand, because they are more confident that they are buying what they want. Manufacturers of nationally-advertised brands are particularly careful to maintain consistent quality and service to retain the loyalty of customers. Many consumers are willing to pay a slightly higher price for Swift's bacon than for an unknown brand, because they know it will taste the way they expect it to taste. To illustrate this, a research organization reports:

> . . . the consumer is generally willing to pay substantial price premiums for advertised brands. Just a casual examination of prices reveals such figures as a 45% price premium for an advertised brand of men's socks, 36.5% for women's nylons, 37.5% for men's electric shavers, 35% for portable typewriters, 33% for an advertised brand of interior wall paint, 27% for men's shorts, 27.5% for children's jeans. Customers pay up to 41% more for the advertised brand of a food product and premiums of 100% or more for the advertised brand of a standard drug product listed in the U.S. Pharmacopeia.[5]

Beyond the premium a consumer is usually willing to pay because of his confidence of consistent benefits from the advertised brand, the price of the advertised brand may exceed the price of the unadvertised brand only by an amount equal to the value consumers place on the additional

---

[5] J. O. Peckham, "The Added Consumer Value of Advertised Brands," *The Nielsen Researcher*, November-December 1958, p. 4.

advantages of the advertised brand. The consumer may determine this added value by personal observation and testing or by acceptance of the claims of the advertiser when he is unable to observe and evaluate the differences for himself. If the advertised brand has no important differences, hidden or otherwise, its price usually can be no higher than those of its unadvertised competitors.

Amount of Advertising Expenditures Required

The cost of an adequate advertising campaign not only affects the advertising break-even calculation but is often in its own right a major determinant of whether a company should advertise. Since advertising is but one part of the total promotional budget, the amount of money allocated for advertising should be developed as a part of the over-all promotional plan. The share allocated to advertising then must be allocated among the various media selected on the basis of media rates and advertising messages planned. According to one author, this job of estimating and allocating the costs of an adequate advertising campaign requires four steps:

> (1) Determine what burden is to be placed upon consumer advertising in the selling program and what burden is to be placed on other selling methods. (2) Decide what media are to be used to carry the advertising message to the prospective buyer. This will involve finding answers to such questions as: Who are the prospective buyers? Where are they located? How many prospects are there? How is the product to be distributed to them? (3) Work out the advertising schedule. To do this, decisions will have to be made on how large an advertisement, or how much radio time, is necessary in order to get the prospect's attention. How frequently should advertisements appear? How many advertisements should be used? (4) Through the use of *Standard Rate & Data,* showing space and time costs for publications and radio stations (and other media), estimate the cost of advertisements on the schedule.[6]

With an estimate of the costs of an adequate advertising campaign on hand, the decision-maker needs next to determine whether the company can afford the expense. This, of course, depends partly on the potential ability of the advertising to return enough additional gross-margin dollars to pay for the advertising. But it also depends on the funds the company has available. If there is not enough money to support an adequate campaign, it is generally best not to advertise at all and to concentrate instead on other promotional methods.

[6] J. D. Scott, *Advertising Principles and Problems* (New York: Prentice-Hall, 1953), p. 86.

Whether the sales resulting from the advertising are immediate or deferred is also significant. If advertising results in quick sales, the advertising costs may be met largely as they are incurred, from the greater number of gross-margin dollars available. If the advertising investment pays off only over or after a considerable period, financing the advertising requires a much larger outlay. Companies short of working capital are often able to advertise under the first condition but not the second; this, in turn, causes them to use campaigns designed to result in quick rather than deferred sales. Better-financed companies may choose advertising designed to produce either quick or deferred sales or both, depending on the relative attractiveness of the different payoffs.

The Product and Basic Consumer Needs

Marketing men have long recognized that if a product will not sell without advertising, it will not sell with advertising. For a product to sell at all, with or without advertising, it must appeal to and satisfy some needs of some consumers, at least as well as competing items. Some advertisers, dazzled by the more spectacular findings of motivation research, come to believe that consumers can be trapped into buying through appeals made to "unconscious" buying motives, regardless of the worth of a product. This was a main theme in Vance Packard's *The Hidden Persuaders*,[7] which strongly implied that motivation research was, in effect, being used to manipulate people to the commercial advantage of advertisers.[8] The plain fact is that advertising possesses no magic capable of causing people to buy things they do not need or want, even when it is based on the most sophisticated motivation research. However, it may help them rationalize purchases of products they want but do not need in a strict economic sense. Who "needs" custom-made shirts at double the price of factory-made shirts? Only a small percentage of men who require unusual sizes actually need custom-made shirts, but many men want them for prestige reasons. Appeals to these other wants help consumers to rationalize uneconomic but satisfying wants. Yet, to a far greater extent than many advertisers realize, the buying behavior of most consumers is based on rational buying motives.

In appraising a product in relation to whether or not it should be advertised, the really important questions to ask are these: "Do potential buyers have needs that this product or brand is capable of satisfying?" and "How important, or how strong, are these needs of potential buyers?" If

---

[7] New York: David McKay Co., 1957.

[8] For an analysis of this proposition and as an antidote to *The Hidden Persuaders*, see: R. A. Bauer, "Limits of Persuasion," *Harvard Business Review*, September-October 1958, pp. 105-10.

there are strong basic needs for the product, the chances are that considerable opportunity for profitable advertising exists. If the product is capable of satisfying only comparatively weak and less basic needs, there is not nearly so much opportunity for profitable advertising. The extent of the advertising opportunity varies with the strength of the basic underlying needs that are satisfied by the product or brand.[9]

Distribution of the Brand

For advertising to attain maximum effectiveness, people influenced by it must be able to find stores where they can buy the brand. This is a matter of having the proper sort of distribution, considering the time consumers are willing to spend looking for the product. If consumers will spend only a little time searching for the product, its distribution should be widespread. If consumers will spend considerable searching time on the product, its distribution can be more selective. Company policy on distribution intensity should be closely correlated with the coverage of the proposed advertising.

Even with proper distribution intensity, sales and goodwill may be lost if dealers do not carry sufficient stocks of the brand to meet the increased demands which should result from the advertising. So, to prevent such out-of-stocks from developing, the manufacturer should make certain that dealers know of the anticipated sales increase before the advertising appears. He should also see to it that dealers are able to obtain re-orders promptly.

ORGANIZATION FOR ADVERTISING

The availability of professional outside help from advertising agencies provides an organizational alternative not generally open in other marketing decision areas. The advertiser may delegate all or some parts of its advertising production and even its advertising planning to an agency. If the company decides to use advertising, then management must decide who will do what parts of the actual work of advertising. Who should establish advertising policy? Who should prepare the advertising program and the different campaigns? Who should write the copy, develop the appeals and themes, do the illustrations, and select the type styles? Who should determine the size and position of advertising space, arrange for the use of various media,

---

[9] On the whole matter of economic, psychological, and sociological influences on buying behavior, see Chapters 6 and 7.

write and produce radio and TV commercials, choose the programs to sponsor, and draft the master advertising schedule? There are some of the many related tasks involved in the actual work of advertising. Management must decide either to have company personnel do this work, or to secure the services of an advertising agency, or to use a combination.

The Internal Organization

In a company organized under the marketing concept, the top advertising executive serves in a staff capacity and reports either directly to the chief marketing executive, or to a director of marketing communications or promotion. How large his staff is depends upon how much, if any, of the advertising work is "farmed out" to an agency. The formulation of advertising policy, because of its relationship to total marketing policy generally is not, and should not be, delegated to an agency; such policy should be formulated by the advertising executive in cooperation with other high-ranking marketing executives. Furthermore, when an advertising agency is used, the advertising executive, at the very minimum, should actively involve himself in the agency's planning of advertising campaigns, thus insuring that they fit in with over-all marketing strategy.

Whether the company should have its own pool of advertising talent or tap the skills of an agency depends on who can do the job best and most effectively. If advertising dollars are to produce the maximum possible impact on sales and profits, all elements in the program must be skillfully prepared and carried out. The responsibility for the success or failure of the advertising, however, does not lie with the advertising agency but rather with the advertising manager. This assignment of responsibility holds, whether the firm's own advertising department discharges the entire task of advertising or whether all or parts of it are handled by an advertising agency.

The Decision Whether to Use an Agency

Important factors to be considered in deciding whether to use an advertising agency are: the functions and cost of an agency, nature of the advertiser-agency relationship, the required advertising skills, and problems in selecting an agency.

THE FUNCTIONS AND COST OF AN AGENCY   One prominent executive of a large and well-known advertising agency describes an advertising agency as "an *independent* business organization composed of *creative* and business people who *develop, prepare and place advertising* in advertising media for *sellers seeking to find customers* for their goods and services." [10] Another professional advertising man, president of an agency and a noted writer, sums up the functions of a modern agency as follows:

> The main job of the advertising agency is to create advertising that will help to sell the product. To perform this work, the agency will make a thorough study of all the factors affecting the sale of the product and prepare a detailed plan of advertising within the framework of a predetermined budget.
>
> The agency may have a research department conduct research before and after a campaign has been run, for better guidance and enlightenment in planning the campaign. It may prepare the point-of-purchase and other sales promotion material. It may have a department handling public relations and another handling direct mail. The extent of activity collateral to creating advertisements that is demanded of an agency depends upon the needs of the client. . . .
>
> Once the advertisements have been approved, the agency prepares, produces and places the commercials for television and radio, as well as advertisements for magazines and newspapers, outdoor advertising and transit advertising. The agency bills the advertiser for the total space, time costs, and production costs in accordance with predetermined terms. The advertiser pays the agency and the agency in turn pays the media and the vendors.[11]

Thus, an advertising agency is a group of experts on various phases of advertising and related marketing problems. In its operations, it resembles other organizations providing expert assistance on specialized business problems. It resembles the management consulting firm, the marketing research firm, and the firm that specializes in the design and administration of incentive campaigns for salesmen and dealers. But in the way it normally receives its compensation, the advertising agency is distinct from other consulting organizations.

The "commission system" is the traditional and still the most widely used method of compensating advertising agencies. Agencies pay for space and time used on behalf of advertisers at the "card rate" less a certain discount, usually 15%, and bill them at the card rate. Thus, agencies receive their basic compensation from advertising media rather than from advertisers, and this has been the source of considerable argument.[12]

[10] "Leo Burnett Discusses the Agency and the Ad Business," *Advertising Age,* October 30, 1967, p. 109.

[11] O. Kleppner, *Advertising Procedure* (Englewood Cliffs, N. J.: Prentice-Hall, Inc., 1966), fifth ed., p. 471.

[12] For a defense of the commission system, see: J. W. Young, "The Advertising Agency Paradox," *Saturday Review,* March 11, 1961, p. 85. For a review of the reasons for growing dissatisfaction with the commission system, see: "The Frey Report," *Tide,* November 8, 1957, pp. 63-70.

Advertisers, especially large ones, maintain that agencies may overspend for media use, simply because so much of their income comes from media commissions. Of course, the advertising agencies, over the years, have been the most steadfast defenders of the commission system. But more and more agencies have lost their liking for it. Part of the disenchantment traces to the consent decree entered into by the American Association of Advertising Agencies in 1956, resulting from an antitrust suit brought by the U.S. Department of Justice, which in effect made it possible for media to grant commissions to other than "recognized" agencies, and in general made the commission system more difficult to enforce and more open to attack.[13]

Even more of the agencies' disaffection for the commission system results from the increasing costs of providing a wide range of services to advertisers. Among the services some agencies now provide for their clients are: assistance in pretesting advertisements, in carrying out test marketing operations and performing local advertising tests; preliminary market testing of new products and research on advertising effectiveness; and marketing counsel and aid in marketing research. At one time, agencies performed such services "free," and some still do, especially for advertisers with large media budgets subject to commissions. But there is a growing tendency to bill advertisers for these "extras" on a "cost plus" or fee basis. Fees and charges, as distinct from commissions, average about one third of the gross incomes of advertising agencies. Some agencies have replaced the traditional commission system entirely with a fee arrangement under which media commissions received are credited toward payment of the agreed fee.[14] Thus, as commissions have declined in relative importance as a source of agency compensation, a growing number of agencies have become more inclined to enter into other compensation arrangements with advertisers.

ADVERTISER-AGENCY RELATIONSHIPS   Through long-standing practice, certain relationships between advertisers and advertising agencies have become standardized. The five most important are as follows: First, the agency refrains from having two accounts whose products are in direct competition. Second, the advertiser normally refrains from using two agencies to handle the advertising for the same product. Third, the agency obtains the advertiser's advance approval before it commits him to expenditures. Fourth, the advertiser pays media and other invoices promptly and within the cash discount period. And fifth, the agency passes on to the advertiser the exact dollar amounts of all discounts granted by media.

---

[13] For a report on the specific provisions of this consent decree, see: *Advertising Age*, February 6, 1956, pp. 1 ff.

[14] "Moseley Sees More Shifts to Fee Payments," *Advertising Age*, December 16, 1968, p. 34.

ADVERTISING SKILLS   The decision to use an agency often hinges upon the nature and variety of skills required to carry out the advertising program. In contrast with advertising agencies, few manufacturers can afford to have in their employ all of the different talents needed to develop and produce large-scale advertising programs. Characteristically, too, agencies allow much greater latitude for creative activity than is normally found in a manufacturer-controlled advertising department. Creative people in agencies may give freer rein to their imagination because they do not work directly for the advertiser. It is usually the agency team which sees the need and the way to break with the manufacturer's traditional promotional approach and produce advertisements and campaigns that are fresh and original. When proposed new campaigns require the application of considerable skill, an outside agency is more likely to have that skill than a manufacturer-controlled advertising department.

SELECTING AN ADVERTISING AGENCY   Selecting an advertising agency is not easy, for there are no standardized selection procedures. A manufacturer decides to use an agency mainly because he wants unique or additional talent to help him plan and carry out an advertising program. The problem of selection, then, involves evaluating the qualifications of competing agencies and requires comparisons of their respective pools of talent. Therefore, an advertiser should, for each agency, investigate the backgrounds and professional qualifications of the key personnel who may be assigned to the account.[15] He should keep in mind what he wants his

TABLE 18–1
Evaluation and Selection of Advertising Agencies

Evaluation of a new agency includes the participation of the:		The responsibility for selection of a new agency rests with the:	
Advertising directors in 89% of the companies		President in 35% of the companies	
Presidents in	70%	Advertising directors in	30%
Sales managers in	54	Sales directors in	11
Executive vice-presidents in	48	Management committees in	8
Marketing directors in	43	Executive vice-presidents in	6
Sales-promotion managers in	29	Marketing directors in	5
Public relations directors in	18	Board Chairman in	3
Product managers in	14	Public relations directors in	2

Source: *Printers' Ink*, June 10, 1960, p. 38.

[15] Along this line, it is well to evaluate the turnover of personnel and accounts within the agency. See J. J. Humpal and H. Meyer-Oertel, "Measuring Change in the Advertising Agency Business," *Journal of Marketing*, January 1967, pp. 56-59.

advertising to accomplish and appraise each agency according to whether it appears to possess the talents required for meeting these objectives. And it is certainly wise to consider each agency's record in serving other accounts, especially those with similar advertising problems.

As shown in Table 18-1, which summarizes some results of a survey of 400 executives in companies using advertising agencies, selection of an agency is a top-level decision. This study also revealed that the decision on which agencies would be considered for selection—i.e., evaluated—was made by the top advertising executive in 63 percent of the companies, the president in 23 percent, and other executives or several jointly in 14 percent. In most companies, several executives participated in the actual evaluation. But the *final* agency selection usually was made by an individual —most often the president, and next most often the highest advertising executive. More than a third of the respondents indicated that they reevaluated their present agency's services "constantly," "continually," or "every day," and 44 percent said that their companies conducted annual formal reviews of the agency's contribution to the total marketing effort.[16] Consequently, agencies are always sensitive to signs of an advertiser's dissatisfaction with his present agency's performance. Advertisers switch agencies frequently, and this serves as a brake on the inclination of some agencies to overspend their clients' funds. Furthermore, it provides additional stimulus for agencies to make advertising programs as effective as possible.

DEVELOPING THE ADVERTISING CAMPAIGN

The first step in developing an advertising campaign is the clear definition of its objectives. Normally the general goal is the same as that for the entire company, improved profits. More specific profit-related objectives, such as forcing middlemen to stock the product, are often important, and objectives not directly related to profit are sometimes important. An advertising campaign, for example, may be directed toward creating a particular brand or company image; another may be designed to build dealer loyalty. After defining campaign objectives, the next step is to determine how much money is required to achieve them.

Determining the Advertising Appropriation

Generally, the advertising appropriation should be "large enough to get the job done." If advertising objectives are profit-related, then the

[16] "How Agencies Find New Business," *Printers' Ink*, June 10, 1960, pp. 35 and 36.

amount of the appropriation should be derived from advertising's predicted effectiveness in bringing in additional profits. If advertising objectives are not directly related to profit (e.g., if the objective is to improve salesmen's morale), then generally there is little basis for predicting either advertising's effectiveness or the amount required to reach the objective.

Complicating the task of predicting advertising's effectiveness is the fact that other factors besides advertising influence sales and profits. Among these factors, to mention only a few, are price, middlemen's enthusiasm, competitors' activities, the "push" salesmen put behind the product, and the quirks of customer's buying behavior. So many factors influence sales and profits that it is difficult to isolate advertising's effect. Yet, logically, in all cases where the advertising objective is profit or profit-related, the size of the appropriation should derive from management's prediction of the likely effectiveness of the proposed advertising. There is a difference between the way advertisers *should determine* their appropriation and the way most of them actually *do*. The majority, mainly because of difficulties encountered in isolating the effect of advertising, rely on more traditional methods. We will consider some of these methods later. First, however, let us consider the method advertisers should use.

INCREMENTAL APPROACH   The incremental approach is derived from the analytical tool economists call *marginal analysis*. It puts the problem of determining the appropriation into an appropriate conceptual framework since, logically, the advertiser should set the appropriation at the amount that maximizes the net profit contribution of advertising. In arriving at this amount, it is necessary first to examine the relationship of advertising, as a cause, and sales, as the effect.

Exhibit 18-1 depicts the relationship of advertising to unit sales volume as marketing theoreticians suggest it exists. Some sales would be made even without any advertising expenditure, and this is illustrated at point X_1. As advertising expenditure is begun, and as increments of expenditure are added, unit sales volume first expands rather slowly, then more rapidly, and finally, additional advertising expenditure has less and less effect. This indicates that there must be a minimum size appropriation beneath which expenditures for advertising are inordinately costly in terms of the resulting sales. It also indicates that beyond a certain point, increases in the advertising appropriation are accompanied by diminishing returns in terms of unit sales volume.

The graphic relationships shown in Exhibit 18-2 shed additional light on the incremental approach. Two important assumptions are built into this schematic representation. The first is that price remains constant over a practical range of sales volume. The modifying term "practical" reflects the fact that there are upper limits to increases in sales volume because of factors such as capacity to consume and buying power. The second

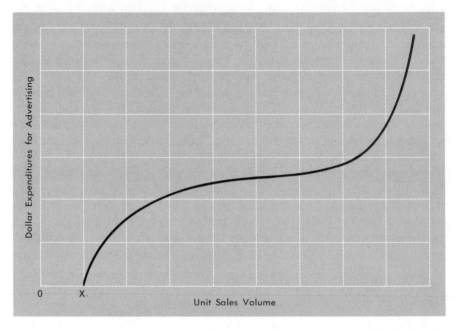

EXHIBIT 18—1

Adapted from: S. Hollander, Jr., "A Rationale for Advertising
Expenditures," *Harvard Business Review*, January 1949, pp. 79–87.

is that non-advertising cost (all variable costs other than advertising, including those of production, physical distribution, and personal selling)
remains constant over this range of sales. This means, then, that the only
quantities that change in this range of sales are incremental net profit and incremental advertising cost.

In Exhibit 18-2 examine the portion of the incremental advertising cost curve where incremental advertising costs are rising (the curve
slants upward). If there is to be any advertising at all, it should be expanded up to the point of diminishing returns. This point is represented
on this chart by the intersection of the advertising cost function and the incremental sales volume line. It lies at X_1, where the combined incremental
advertising and nonadvertising costs intersect with the price line. Up to this
point it is profitable to increase advertising outlay. If incremental nonadvertising cost is 40¢ per unit, and price is $1 per unit, we can continue to
add to advertising cost as long as these costs do not exceed 60¢ per unit.
When more than 60¢ per unit is invested in advertising, the additional
business it brings in is unprofitable and not worth getting.

Dean explains the rationale for the upward sweep in the advertising cost curve in these words:

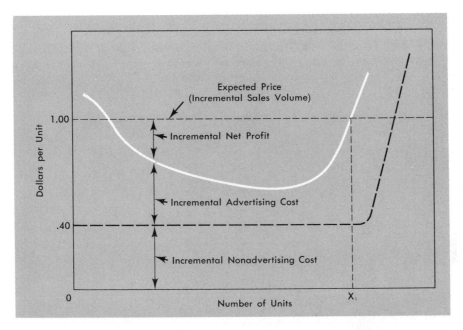

Dollars per Unit

Expected Price
(Incremental Sales Volume)

1.00

← Incremental Net Profit

← Incremental Advertising Cost

.40

← Incremental Nonadvertising Cost

0

Number of Units

X₁

EXHIBIT 18–2

Adapted from: J. Dean, *Managerial Economics* (Englewood Cliffs, N.J.: Prentice-Hall, Inc., 1951).

The upward turn in the curve reflects primarily the tapping of successively poorer prospects as the advertising effort is intensified. Presumably the most susceptible prospects are picked off first, and progressively stiffer resistance is encountered from layers of prospects who are more skeptical, more stodgy about their present spending patterns, or more attached to rival sellers. The rise may also be caused by progressive exhaustion of the most vulnerable geographic areas or the most efficient advertising media. Promotional channels that are ideally adapted to the scale and the market of the firm are used first. (Actually, for firms with expansible markets, the advertising cost curve may have several minimum points corresponding to most efficient use of different media appropriate for different-size markets, e.g., newspapers, billboards, magazines, radio.) [17]

Exhibit 18-3 shows how to obtain the optimum appropriation, if the seller knows the nature of the advertising-to-sales relationship and makes two assumptions. One assumption is that price remains constant, which

[17] J. Dean, "How Much to Spend on Advertising," *Harvard Business Review*, January 1951, p. 66.

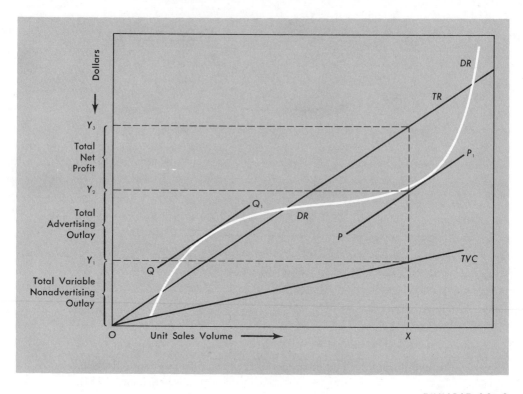

EXHIBIT 18-3

Adapted from: J. Howard, *Marketing Management: Analysis and Planning,*
rev. ed. (Homewood, Ill.: Richard D. Irwin, Inc., 1963), p. 407.

means that total sales revenue (*TR*) varies at a constant rate with changes
in sales volume. The second assumption is that total variable non-advertising costs (*TVC*) vary at a constant rate. In order to determine the advertising appropriation that maximizes net profit, one must find the point
on the advertising-sales curve (*DR*) where a tangent can be drawn parallel
to the total sales revenue curve (*TR*). One such line is QQ_1, but this point
of tangency obviously represents a condition where total costs are greater
than total revenues. The tangent line the decision-maker should seek is
PP_1, for here the point of tangency is also the profit-maximizing point. On
the vertical axis, the optimum outlay for advertising is represented by the
distance Y_1Y_2, total variable non-advertising outlay by OY_1, and total net
profit by Y_2Y_3.

PERCENTAGE-OF-SALES APPROACH   This approach to determining
the advertising appropriation is a traditional method that is still widely

used. Management applies some arbitrary percentage to past sales figures, forecasted sales, or some combination of past and future sales and, supposedly, up comes the advertising appropriation. This simplicity, indeed, is about the only thing good that can be said about the percentage approach, for it is difficult to defend on logical grounds. One reason is that it assumes that the advertising cost per unit of product remains constant, regardless of the sales volume. This is a mistaken notion for, as shown in Exhibits 18-1 and 18-3, it would be most unusual for a company's sales to have a straight-line relationship with advertising. An even greater shortcoming is that the percentage approach assumes that advertising follows sales. Advertising should result in sales and not the other way around. Of course, if the percentage is applied to forecasted sales, the assumption now *appears* to be that advertising precedes sales. But even this cannot be defended logically, for the size of the appropriation affects the size of the possible sales volume. Still another criticism relates to the percentage figure used. Where does it come from? In most cases, it can only come from records of past sales volumes and advertising expenditures. There is no assurance that percentage relationships that held in the past will continue to hold in the future.

OBJECTIVE-AND-TASK METHOD   This method consists of three steps: (1) advertising objectives are defined in terms of desired sales volumes, net profits, share of the market, and the like; (2) the amount of advertising space and time needed to achieve these objectives is estimated; (3) this amount of advertising is expressed in dollar terms in order to arrive at the size of the appropriation. This method is logical in that it treats advertising as a cause of sales rather than as an effect. Advertising is considered strictly as a device for producing sales, net profit, market share, and the like. If the objective-and-task method is used with the intention of maximizing the net profit contribution of advertising, i.e., if the main objective is to maximize net profits, then, of course, this is equivalent to using the incremental approach. Unfortunately, most companies using this method appear to concentrate more on the effect of advertising on sales than on net profit. Without this profit maximization emphasis, this method might very well produce an advertising appropriation that increased costs more than it increased profits.

OTHER APPROACHES   Three other common approaches to determining the advertising appropriation should be mentioned. The first is known as the arbitrary method, in which the appropriation is decided either "by pure guess" or "by alloting all the advertiser can afford." The second is called "matching competitors' expenditures"; the advertiser, in effect, permits his competitors to set his appropriation. The third is the "tax per unit of product" in which a fixed sum is put in the "advertising pot" for each unit of the product sold or expected to be sold. Each of these three methods may be objected to on logical grounds. We leave it to the reader to do so.

Selection of Advertising Media

Most of the advertising appropriation is used for purchasing space and time in different media. These media include newspapers, magazines, television, radio, outdoor posters, transportation cards, direct mail, and point-of-purchase displays. Even though the actual media selection is usually done by an agency, the advertiser should evaluate the effectiveness of the agency's selections.

THE MEDIA MIX   As Table 18-2 shows, different advertisers follow quite different plans in allocating their appropriations to media. Through considering the expenditure patterns of even this small sample of advertisers, we can learn a good deal about media strategy. With this end in view, the reader should think through such questions as these: Why should General Motors spend just under 25 percent of its advertising appropriation on television, while Eastman Kodak spends more than 50 percent? Why should General Motors spend over 30 percent on newspapers and Kodak only seven percent? Probably General Motors with its highly selective distribution policy feels a much stronger need to identify its local dealers with prospective customers. General Motors also has a greater need to tailor promotion to differences in local markets. Why should Alberto-Culver concentrate nearly all its advertising in television, whereas Avon Products (with similar product lines) allocates almost 23 percent of its appropriation to magazines? This might be partly explained by the difference in size of appropriations—some minimal amount of advertising is necessary to have an effect in any medium, so the smaller advertiser often concentrates his advertising in fewer media. Why do the distillers (Brown Forman and Distillers Corporation-Seagrams Ltd.) spend proportionately more on magazine advertising than most other advertisers? Advertising for alcoholic beverages stronger than beer or wine is not accepted by television media—thus, distillers make heavy use of magazine advertising.

Other factors affecting media selection are revealed through examination of Table 18-2. For example, the heaviest users of television are the producers of consumer goods consumed by mass markets—such as chewing gum, cosmetics, and soap products—since TV has a very broad audience. Business publications are used extensively by manufacturers with important industrial markets. Newspapers are used where more selective regional coverage is desired than is offered by national magazines. Finally, however, media selection also reflects differing opinions with respect to the appeal and effectiveness of each medium for particular products.

What then, are the main factors affecting media selection? The

TABLE 18-2

Twenty "Million Dollar Plus" Advertisers of 1968
Total Dollar Expenditures and Percentages Allocated to Six Major Media

			Percentage of Total Expenditure in:				
Advertiser	Total	News-papers	Con-sumer Maga-zines	Busi-ness Publica-tions	Tele-vision	Radio	Out-door [a]
Alberto-Culver	$ 23,828,157	1.51%	4.41%	.72%	93.36%		
Avon Products	8,073,611		22.60		77.40		
Beecham Group Ltd.	8,877,915		.69		98.05	1.26%	
Bristol-Myers Co.	108,113,584	1.16	20.03	4.07	67.28	7.22	.24%
Brown Forman Distillers	8,781,093	42.54	47.82				9.64
Chas. Pfizer and Co.	20,628,910		15.16	5.47	70.46	8.78	0.13
Coca-Cola Co.	50,992,564	4.75	6.29	0.97	68.31	17.28	2.40
Distillers Corp.-Seagrams Ltd.	46,353,367	27.21	54.12	1.85	2.20		14.62
Du Pont	18,145,755	3.16	25.92	25.35	31.54	13.15	0.88
Eastman Kodak Co.	23,865,420	7.17	30.25	11.77	50.74	0.07	
General Electric	28,018,288	15.10	36.62	15.64	27.99	4.26	0.39
General Motors Corp.	199,701,016	30.64	22.95	2.50	24.94	15.23	3.74
H. J. Heinz Co.	11,579,596	3.47	3.72	3.45	89.36		
Kellogg Co.	36,534,972	7.08	4.35	0.46	85.33	2.78	
Merck & Co.	10,256,904		5.11	39.43	55.46		
Pabst Brewing Co.	9,070,908	0.55	0.02		83.52	9.93	5.98
Procter and Gamble	198,742,093	0.99	6.88	0.43	91.54	0.16	
R. J. Reynolds Tobacco Co.	77,039,215	1.52	11.54	0.25	74.11	12.57	0.01
Texaco Inc.	11,779,736	11.70	12.13	6.93	50.75	17.26	
Wm. Wrigley Jr. Co.	28,168,020	9.46	2.59		73.76	14.14	0.05

[a] Outdoor figures for markets of 100,000 and over population.
Source: Calculated from data in "Top 125 National Advertisers of 1968," *Advertising Age*, June 30, 1969, pp. 42-44.

nature of the market segment that the advertiser desires to reach and the type of product being advertised are the most fundamental. Also important are the distinctive characteristics associated with specific media. For instance, the fact that newspapers are issued daily causes some advertisers to use them and others to avoid them. The size of the appropriation is important: small budgets usually mean that expenditures should be concentrated in a few media for best results, whereas large appropriations ordinarily must be spread over many media to avoid a premature onset of diminishing returns. Ideally, media circulation (general exposure) should be confined to the geographical areas where the advertiser has distribution. Many other considerations, both qualitative and quantitative, affect media selection. One authority lists the following as rational determinants of media selection: the product itself; the budget; competitive activity; frequency versus coverage; continuity; impact on distribution; flexibility in timing of purchase and in permitting changes in message and spending pattern, both dollar-wise and geographically; franchise position—that is, special position or sponsorship associations; appropriateness of media for product and message; cost per thousand readers or viewers; effectiveness of selling message; circulation of media among desired prospects and customers.[18]

Conceptually, media selection is a problem in determining optimum allocation of the advertising appropriation. The total should be so divided among the different types of media—newspapers, magazines, television, outdoor posters, etc.—that the marginal returns from each type are all equal. In other words, the last dollar invested in newspaper advertising should produce the same dollar return as the last dollar invested in each of the other media.

Practically speaking, the procedure for obtaining this optimum allocation consists of three steps: (1) the gathering—by type of media—of accurate data on past expenditures, (2) analysis of these data, together with data on sales results, to obtain reasonably accurate representations of the net returns curves for each type of media, and (3) successive adjustment of the allocation of the appropriation to different media so that the slopes of the several net returns curves tend to equalize.[19] This last step is a "try, try again" approach—starting with a given feasible allocation, testing to discover profitable changes, and making changes that will raise net returns. When no further profitable changes can be made, we have the optimum allocation of funds. This method is similar to the repeated trial approach used in linear programming.[20]

[18] L. Adler, "How Marketing Management Can Make Sounder Media Decisions," in W. Dolva (ed.), *Marketing Keys to Profits in the 1960's* (Chicago: American Marketing Association, 1960), p. 155.

[19] The application of incremental analysis to this problem is described in: D. B. Brown, "A Practical Procedure for Media Selection," *Journal of Marketing Research,* August 1967, pp. 262-69.

[20] An interesting description of a highly effective but "naive" media allocation method requiring only a desk calculation is presented in: P. Hofmans, "Measuring the Cumulative Net Coverage of Any Combination of Media," *Journal of Marketing Research,* August 1966, pp. 269-78.

Recently, computer models for media selection have been constructed in an attempt to reduce the task to more manageable proportions. Since the number of media available for choice is often relatively large, (for example, there are over a dozen consumer "house and garden" or shelter magazines and many other gardening magazines), computer analysis assists greatly in obtaining optimum allocations.[21] One significant limitation of such models is the difficulty in quantifying certain factors used in comparing media—e.g., the value of a particular medium's "prestige" with its audience and the appropriateness of media for the product and message.

Cost Comparisons of Media in the Same Classification
The matter of relative cost is a selection factor when the advertiser, or agency media man, must decide among media in the same media classification—for instance, between two newspapers. In situations of this sort, each newspaper typically has a different size circulation and different advertising rates. The technique of comparison is to convert circulation and rate figures to a common basis. Newspapers normally quote their rates by the agate line, of which there are fourteen in a space one column wide and one inch deep. Therefore, the yardstick used in making cost comparisons of newspapers is known as the milline rate—the cost of reaching one million readers with one agate line of advertising. The milline rate is calculated as follows:

$$\text{Milline Rate} = \frac{\text{Agate Line Rate} \times 1,000,000}{\text{Circulation of Newspaper}}$$

Magazines are normally compared according to the cost of reaching one thousand readers with a given amount of advertising space. For instance, the cost of using a full page of magazine space is calculated as below:

$$\text{Cost per 1,000} = \frac{\text{Page Rate} \times 1,000}{\text{Circulation of Magazine}}$$

Cost comparisons of media in the same classifications follow similar patterns for radio, television, outdoor posters, and car cards. Usually, the rate for using a given amount of space is multiplied by 1,000 and divided by the circulation (or audience) of the medium being compared. This results in a cost-per-thousand figure similar to those used for comparing magazines.

Such cost comparisons should be used with great caution. One should recognize what is actually being compared—the costs of achieving

[21] For example, D. B. Learner of Batten, Barton, Durstine, and Osborne, Inc., an advertising agency, has developed a computer media selection model called DEMON (DEcision Mapping via Optimum Networks).

a certain circulation with a given amount of space or time. Circulation refers to the number of copies of a publication distributed or the medium's claim as to its size of audience. Circulation is not readership, actual listeners, or actual viewers. The cost comparison, furthermore, takes no account of the relative power of different media to influence their readers or listeners. Cost comparisons should not be the sole basis for media selection. They should see limited use, and then only after consideration of the more basic factors.

Creation of the Advertisements

The actual preparation of the advertisements for a campaign involves creativity of a high order. It is difficult and probably impossible to evaluate such creativity on a quantitative basis. The actual advertisements are produced by the advertising profession's creative people—the copy writers and artists—but the over-all qualitative evaluation and approval of their outputs are the responsibilities of the advertiser's marketing and advertising executives.

The first step in producing an advertising campaign is the development of a campaign theme—an idea or concept that will provide continuity over time and result in significant impact upon the target market segments. Some advertisers change themes annually or even seasonally. Others continue with a single theme almost indefinitely, until it loses most of its appeal. Maidenform's "I dreamt I. . . ." theme was continued for over a dozen years, because it lost little of its power to draw readers' attention to the product.

The next step in the production of an advertising campaign is the development of language or visual messages illustrating the theme. Depending upon the particular theme and kind of product, messages range all the way from purely language (e.g., radio or newspaper) to totally or nearly totally visual (e.g., billboards). Most advertisements use both language and visual messages, as in the majority of television and magazine advertising.

An effective message generally meets three criteria: (1) it attracts the audience's attention, (2) it is clearly understandable, and (3) it is believable. In a society where most people are exposed to hundreds of advertising messages daily, producing an ad capable of attracting attention is difficult and takes considerable creative talent. For instance, it is not only possible to come up with an ad that fails to attract much attention but it is also possible to succeed too well so that other elements in the advertisement divert attention away from the product. Likewise, constructing a message that projects the desired impression clearly without confusion or misunderstanding is not easy. Clarity in communications is an art, and it is usually difficult to predict whether or not an audience will understand a particular message in the way intended.[22] Similarly, special care is required to insure that the audience will believe the message conveyed. If, for example, an advertisement states that the advertiser's product is more effective than any competitive product, it is necessary to provide the audience with sufficient proof. Otherwise, many members of the audience may reject the entire message as a "wild and unsubstantiated" claim that should not be believed.

Measuring Advertising Effectiveness

Most companies devote very little research effort toward the development of means for improving advertising effectiveness. One authority estimates that "probably no more than $\frac{1}{5}$ of 1 percent of total advertising expenditure is used to achieve an enduring understanding of how to spend the other 99.8 percent." [23] Gloomy as this estimate appears, there are companies that do inquire into the advertising-to-sales relation.

E. I. du Pont has a research team working continuously toward the goal of measuring advertising's effect on sales and profits. This team focuses on determining just when and how advertising pays, in terms of profits, and seeks yardsticks for use in setting advertising appropriations on different products so that maximum profits result.[24] As part of the du Pont research effort, experiments are conducted in allocating various dollar amounts of advertising to different industrial markets with the intention of determining the effects on sales of different dosages of advertising.[25]

Noreen, Incorporated, which markets a color hair rinse for women, had consultants conduct a series of controlled experiments designed to measure sales response to advertising. From an organization standpoint, this company was small and closely-knit enough to effectively control the impact on sales of such factors as point-of-purchase promotion, and salesmen's performance. Further, as it subscribed to the services of A. C. Nielsen Company (an independent marketing research organization) it had a usable measure of competitors' sales at the retail level. Thus, Noreen was in a position to allow national and local advertising to fluctuate considerably, while other sales-influencing variables were held nearly constant, thus allowing the measurement of the sales results of different advertising programs and

---

[22] For a discussion of some methods used in evaluating the clarity of advertising messages, see: P. Abruzzini, "Measuring Language Difficulty in Advertising Copy," *Journal of Marketing*, April 1967, pp. 22-26.

[23] J. W. Forrester, "Advertising: A Problem in Industrial Dynamics," *Harvard Business Review*, March-April 1959, p. 102.

[24] "A Profit Yardstick for Advertising," *Business Week*, November 22, 1958, p. 49.

[25] "New Need to Prove Ads Sell," *Printers' Ink*, February 24, 1961, p. 25.

different amounts of advertising. Multiple correlation techniques were employed in analyzing the data obtained, and the researchers succeeded in constructing a mathematical model of sales response to advertising.[26]

A research group at Arthur D. Little, Inc. (a consulting firm specializing in providing management advice and analysis for client companies) has contributed three concepts of great potential usefulness in the analysis of advertising's effect on sales: the sales decay constant, the saturation level, and the response constant. These three concepts are defined as follows:

> *Sales Decay Constant.* In the absence of promotion, sales tend to decrease because of product obsolescence, competing advertising, etc. Under relatively constant market conditions, the rate of decrease is, in general, constant: that is, a constant percent of sales is lost each year.
>
> *Saturation Level.* Defined as the practical limit of sales that can be generated. It depends not only on the product being promoted, but also on the advertising medium used; it represents the fraction of the market that the particular campaign can capture. This saturation level can often be raised further by other advertising media.
>
> *Response Constant.* Defined as the sales generated per advertising dollar, when sales are at a level S. For instance, where M is the saturation level and r the response constant, the following relationship, in general, holds: [27]

$$\text{Sales generated per advertising dollar} = \frac{r\,(M - S)}{M}$$

The Arthur D. Little group provides a concise mathematical description of the interaction of these factors:

$$\frac{dS}{dt} = rA\,\frac{M - S}{M} - LS$$

where:

dS is the increment of sales
dt is the increment of time
L is the sales decay constant
M is the saturation level
r is the response constant
A is the rate of advertising expenditure
S is the volume of sales

[26] E. B. Slade and J. R. Roseboom, "Measuring Advertising Effectiveness," *Western Business Review*, November 1958, pp. 16-26.

[27] M. L. Vidale and H. B. Wolfe, "An Operations-Research Study of Sales Response to Advertising," *Operations Research*, June 1957, pp. 372, 375-376.

In the formula, r multiplied by A represents the intensity of advertising effort for a given level of advertising expenditure, $M - S$ divided by M represents potential market, and L multiplied by S indicates decay losses. Thus, this equation states that the increase in the rate of sales $\dfrac{(dS)}{(dt)}$ is proportional to the intensity of the advertising effort (rA) which reaches the market $\left(\dfrac{M - S}{M} \right)$ with a deduction for decay losses (LS).[28]

This equation can also be used to calculate the advertising effort needed to maintain sales at a steady predetermined level. For this purpose, the increase in the rate of sales $\dfrac{(dS)}{(dt)}$ is set at zero (i.e., no increase in the sales rate), and the equation is manipulated algebraically to yield:

$$A = \left(\frac{L}{r} \right) \frac{SM}{M - S}$$

"MEASURES" OF ADVERTISING EFFECTIVENESS   Most measures of advertising effectiveness in current use are rather superficial. These include such "measures" as size of audience, program ratings, advertisements noted and remembered by the reader or audience, and numbers of inquiries received. Although such measures may help in determining the extent to which the advertiser's message is reaching the market, they do not serve as "real" measures of advertising *success*, which can only be measured in terms of added sales and profits. No superficial measure of advertising effectiveness can possibly substitute for the real measures—sales and net profits.

CONCLUSION

Emphasis in this chapter has been on the management of advertising effort and the making of advertising decisions. Advertising's main long-term objective is to increase the firm's net profits, and shorter-term advertising objectives all relate, in one way or another, to that long-term goal. The most basic advertising decision relates to whether a company should advertise at all, this decision hinging upon such factors as the potential incremental returns, the effect on prices, the ability to pay the advertising costs, and advertising's ability to achieve desired results. Firms that decide to advertise must also make decisions on the use and selection of advertising agencies. Further important decisions are required in connection with the

[28] M. Vidale, J. Voss, and H. Wolfe, "Experimental Research in Advertising," in D. W. Ewing, ed., *Effective Marketing Action* (New York: Harper & Brothers 1958), p. 151.

development of advertising campaigns. These include determination of the advertising appropriation, selection of media, the creation of advertisements, and measuring advertising effectiveness.

QUESTIONS AND PROBLEMS

1. Explain the meaning of the following terms:
   a. generic product   e. saturation level
   b. brand differentiation   f. response constant
   c. advertising agency   g. milline rate
   d. sales decay constant   h. advertising media

2. Explain and contrast the terms in each of the following pairs:
   a. primary demand and selective demand
   b. demand elasticity and demand expansibility

3. Analyze the relationships that the different short-term advertising objectives should bear to marketing management's long-term goals.

4. What is an "advertising opportunity?" How can advertising opportunities be detected?

5. Under what conditions are consumers likely to be willing to pay more for an advertised product than for an unadvertised product? Using your own shopping experience as a guide, provide some examples of instances where you paid more for an advertised product when competing unadvertised products were available?

6. Currently, a certain manufacturer sells 5,000 units of his product in a given marketing area each year. The product is distributed through retailers and the manufacturer has not used local advertising in this particular area for several years. Retailers pay the manufacturer $20.00 per unit of the product and price it at $25.00. The manufacturer estimates his total costs per unit at $17.50. This manufacturer now wants to launch a local advertising campaign in the marketing area and estimates that the cost of an adequate campaign would amount to $20,000. How much additional sales volume should this advertising campaign produce in order for the manufacturer to break-even on the cost?

7. How does a company's financial condition affect management's decision to use advertising for the purpose of producing immediate sales? For the purpose of producing deferred sales? What arguments might a management use in an attempt to secure a bank loan for purposes of carrying on an advertising campaign?

8. How are advertising decisions affected by each of the following:

    a. company policy on distribution intensity

    b. marketing channels for the product

    c. competitors' advertising practices

    d. replacement rate and consumption time for the product

    e. price of the product

9. If you were the marketing manager of a large manufacturing company, which had an advertising budget of millions of dollars, would you favor or oppose the commission system of compensating advertising agencies? Why? Would you take the same position if you were the president of a large advertising agency? Why? If you were the owner of a large city newspaper, what would be your position on this question? Why?

10. Under what circumstances would you advise a manufacturer to switch advertising agencies? Under what circumstances might an advertising agency voluntarily "resign" a manufacturer's account?

11. "The size of the advertising appropriation should be based on advertising effectiveness." Bearing this "should be" statement in mind, how might you, as the manager of a marketing research department, contribute to the decision on size of the advertising appropriation?

12. Compare and contrast the following approaches to determining the size of the advertising appropriation:

    a. incremental

    b. percentage-of-sales

    c. objective-and-task

    d. arbitrary

    e. matching competitors' expenditures

    f. tax per unit of product

13. To what extent should the sales forecast be considered in determining the size of the advertising appropriation? In selecting media?

14. Select five full-page advertisements from a recent issue of *Life* or *Look* and list the main factors that probably caused each advertiser to select this particular medium.

15. "Everyone connected with advertising—the advertiser, the agency, and the media—has a sincere interest in finding out whether advertising is successful." Agree or disagree? Why?

16. Comment on the following two statements:

    a. "Advertising's job, purely and simply, is to communicate, to a defined audience, information and a frame-of-mind that stimulates action. Advertising succeeds or fails depending on how well it communicates the desired information and attitudes to the right people at the right time at the right cost."

    b. "The average consumer is subjected to roughly 1,600 advertising impressions per day. As a result, he is developing an impervious-ness to advertising in general and an increasing ability to shut off advertisers' messages."

17. From time to time, certain politicians suggest that a tax should be placed on advertising, not only to raise revenue but to protect con-sumers from "further commercial invasions of their homes." As a marketing executive, what position would you take with regard to this proposal? As the "target" of advertisers' messages, what is your attitude? Justify the positions you take.

18. In a certain city there are two large newspapers—a morning and an evening paper—both of which reach similar audiences and have the same circulation areas. Advertising rates per column inch are: $7.00 in the morning paper and $10.50 in the evening paper. The morning paper has a circulation of 200,000 and the evening paper has a circulation of 250,000. Calculate and compare the milline rates of these two papers. Under what conditions might an advertiser use the paper with the higher milline rate?

19. A book publisher wants to insert a page of advertising in one of two monthly magazines, both of which are directed primarily to male audiences. The first magazine has a page rate of $6,500 and a circu-lation of 875,000, while the second has a page rate of $7,100 and a circulation of 1,140,000. Assuming that the audiences of both maga-zines are roughly comparable (i.e., from the standpoints of age, in-come, geographical location, etc.), which is the better buy? Under what conditions might the publisher decide to use the other maga-zine?

20. Western Pretzel Works, Inc., has retained an advertising agency to handle its advertising for the forthcoming year. Media expenditures are anticipated as follows:

		Media Commission
Consumer Magazines	$100,000	15%
Dealer Magazines	24,000	10
Newspapers	46,000	15
Outdoor Posters	6,000	16⅔
Television	43,000	15
Total	$219,000	

Costs of art work, typography, etc. are estimated at $2,250, and the agency will bill the company for these items at cost plus 15 percent. Western Pretzel has a long standing policy of taking all cash dis-counts and plans on paying invoices received from the agency within the cash discount period. The discount will amount to 2 percent of the net costs of space and time.

Assuming that the agency is to be compensated on the commission basis, what is:

a. the total amount Western Pretzel will pay the agency?

b. the total amount the agency will pay to all media and services?

c. the total amount the agency will receive as compensation?

21. Newton Packing Company is a medium-sized packer located in eastern Washington. For several years, annual sales have been approximately $5-million. Newton handles its own wholesaling of the fresh and smoked meat and meat products it processes. In addition, the company wholesales the products of other manufacturers not engaged in direct distribution in the territories covered by Newton. The company sells its products to independent retail meat markets and meat departments, to large chain grocery organizations, and to certain high-class restaurants and hotels. Newton salesmen cover territories in Washington, Oregon, Idaho, Montana, and northern California.

In the past, this company did not use an advertising agency, but recently arrangements have been made for a small Seattle agency to handle the company's account. The Newton advertising manager, working in cooperation with the account executive, has proposed the following advertising budget for the coming year:

Costs of artwork, typography, etc.,		
and all overhead expenses		$ 16,000
Media Costs:		
Magazines	$42,000	
TV spot announcements	7,000	
Dealer cooperative advertising	14,000	
Dealer display materials	20,000	83,000
Reserve for Contingencies		1,000
		$100,000

a. As president of Newton Packing Company, what questions might you ask the advertising manager about this proposed budget? What further information might you ask for?

b. What further refinements in the method of presenting this budget should be made?

c. What method was used to determine the size of this advertising appropriation? What should be the relationship between past sales history, anticipated future sales, and the advertising budget?

PART 6

PRICING

Pricing Decisions and Objectives

Pricing Policies

Pricing Strategies and Procedures

19

PRICING
DECISIONS AND OBJECTIVES

Products may be matched with markets, but only when buyers and sellers agree on *prices* do ownership transfers actually occur. Prices, therefore, are an integral part of marketing—without prices, there can be no marketing. Either a buyer or a seller may propose a price, but it does not become one until accepted by the other.

In modern marketing, the seller generally makes the offer and the buyer decides whether to accept it. Most marketers, in other words, have the initiative for proposing prices, and they can vary prices to the extent that they can differentiate their products in the eyes of the buyer. Therefore, pricing is a controllable. Except in rare instances, marketers enjoy considerable freedom in making pricing decisions, defining pricing objectives, formulating pricing policies, and deciding pricing strategies, as well as in setting specific prices. Pricing activities, both individually and collectively, have important effects on the relative ease with which "ownership transfers" are effected—and, consequently, upon sales volume and profits.

Relative to other marketing controllables (products, marketing channels, and promotion), pricing varies in importance with both the marketing situation and the marketing program. Situations exist where forces outside the decision-maker's control determine prices: in these cases, pricing is an uncontrollable. For example, many farm prices are determined solely by the relationship between available supply and market demand, as described in classical economic theory. A lettuce grower does not decide the price he receives for his crop. He can only accept or reject the current market price.

But in most marketing situations today, pricing is a controllable; consequently, the classical theory of value does not apply. Most marketers differentiate their products, thus reducing the incentive for prospective buyers to accept competitors' offerings solely on a price basis. Most utilize promotion to further differentiate their products in prospective buyers' minds. Similarly, they differentiate other aspects of their "total offerings" through individualized choices of marketing channels, physical distribution systems, and the like. In other words, most marketers manipulate the other controllables in order to enhance their ability to use pricing as a controllable. To the extent that such efforts succeed, marketers compete on a non-price, rather than on a price, basis.

There are two additional reasons why the classical theory of value does not apply in most marketing situations. One is that the modern economy is so complex that it is impossible for the average buyer to be really informed about all products and prices. The other is that in many fields there are sellers and buyers who are large enough individually to exert significant influences over supply or demand and, hence, over prices.[1]

ADMINISTERED PRICES

In marketing situations where pricing is a controllable, prices are *administered prices*. By definition, administered prices are set by management and held stable for a time. We have an administered price when a company maintains a posted price at which it will make sales and at which buyers decide to purchase or not.[2] Three facets of this definition are significant: First, price setting is a conscious administrative action rather than a result

---

[1] When there are only a small number of competing sellers and each seller must take into account what each other seller does (e.g., in setting a price), the situation is called an *oligopoly*. When a similar situation exists among a small number of buyers, it is referred to as an *oligopsony*. For a detailed discussion of oligopoly theory or "monopolistic competition," see: E. H. Chamberlain, *The Theory of Monopolistic Competition*, 8th ed. (Cambridge: Harvard University Press, 1962).

[2] G. C. Means, *Industrial Prices and Their Relative Inflexibility*, Senate Document 13, 74th Congress, 1st Session, 1935.

of the interplay of supply and demand; second, the administered price is set for a period of time or a series of sales transactions and is not subject to frequent change; and third, the price is not subject to negotiation. However, administered prices generally are set after considering the possible reactions both of competitors and prospective buyers; therefore, different competitors tend to set almost identical prices on substantially similar products. Prices resulting from managerial decisions are administered prices, and these prices are of the most interest to marketers.

Pricing's Relative Importance in Marketing Programs

Pricing is an important element in most marketing programs but usually is not the most critical factor for marketing success. One researcher surveyed 200 large "well-managed" manufacturers. Most respondents regarded product- and promotion-related activities as more important to marketing success than pricing; roughly half did not rate pricing as a success factor at all.[3] These findings indicate that marketers seek to manipulate other controllables, such as products and promotion, in order to improve their ability to compete on a non-price, rather than on a price, basis. This is not to deny, however, that in certain marketing circumstances, such as in competitive bidding, pricing may be the single most important factor in translating potential business into actual sales.[4]

AUTHORITY OVER PRICING

Pricing is an integral component of marketing strategy, so those responsible for formulating strategy also should exert influence on pricing objectives, policies, and strategies. The marketing manager, however, rarely has full authority over pricing. Because of the interdepartmental implications, many aspects of pricing are the proper concern of top management.[5] Generally, the marketing manager's role is to administer the pricing program within guide lines laid down by top management. Pricing activities have such direct effects on sales volume and profit that the marketing manager can never

[3] J. G. Udell, "How Important is Pricing in Competitive Strategy?" *Journal of Marketing*, January 1964, pp. 44-48.

[4] For an analysis of the importance of price in "inquiry/bid" situations together with some suggestions for improving the chances for winning profitable bids, see: A. W. Walker, "How to Price Industrial Products," *Harvard Business Review*, September-October 1967, pp. 125-32.

[5] V. P. Buell, *Marketing Management in Action* (New York: McGraw-Hill Book Co., Inc., 1966), p. 44.

be far *removed* from pricing policymaking and strategy formulation; however, he is an important contributor to decisions rather than *the* decision-maker.

In some companies a certain amount of discretion in setting prices is delegated to subordinate executives, such as district sales managers, or even to salesmen. This is common practice when timing is critical and where pricing varies in importance in different markets. Likewise, where there are numerous products, and frequent pricing decisions are required, subordinate executives—or even specialized pricing personnel—have some price-setting authority. But, in all cases, top management (including the chief marketing executive) retains primary responsibility for determining pricing objectives, policies, and strategies. Subordinates should have only well-defined and limited discretion over setting actual "offering" prices within the parameters set by top management.[6]

FACTORS INFLUENCING PRICING DECISIONS

Numerous factors influence pricing decisions. It is of utmost importance that pricing decisions be consistent with the company's desired public image; unwise pricing can damage, or needlessly alter, a favorable image that has taken years to build. Therefore, pricing objectives should derive directly from company objectives (which, as a composite, reflect top-management's vision of the kind of company it is trying to build). Similarly, price policies should be consistent with pricing objectives. And pricing strategies (i.e., the ways in which policies are implemented) should be in alignment with both price policies and pricing objectives.

Pricing decisions also require a keen awareness of the company's over-all marketing environment. Target market segments should be identified and the desired brand images for each product clearly defined. Consideration should also be given to the nature and objectives of promotional effort, the marketing channels, and the physical distribution system. Pricing is but one component of marketing strategy and, to achieve maximum results, all components must be carefully coordinated, both in their formulation and in their implementation.[7]

[6] For an analysis of the factors influencing the type of organization needed to carry out the pricing activity, see: A. R. Oxenfeldt, *Pricing for Marketing Executives* (San Francisco: Wadsworth Publishing Co., Inc., 1961, pp. 60-63.

[7] One marketing scholar proposes a six-stage sequential approach to pricing to insure that final pricing decisions are related to the over-all marketing plan. According to him, the six sequential stages are: (1) selecting market targets, (2) choosing a brand image, (3) composing a marketing mix, (4) selecting a pricing policy, (5) determining a pricing strategy, and (6) arriving at a specific price. In our opinion, the first three stages

Factors internal to the company as well as environmental factors influence pricing decisions. Among the "internal" factors—besides the company objectives and image—are other strategic components of the marketing program: product-market combinations, marketing channels, promotion, and cost considerations. The environmental factors include: the competition, economic climate, and legislative and governmental pressures. Although certain factors may have little relevance to some pricing decisions, they deserve at least passing notice.

Product and Market Factors

STAGE IN THE PRODUCT LIFE CYCLE   The amount of discretion management has in making pricing decisions varies with different stages of the product life cycle. During market pioneering, the innovating company enjoys wide discretion, especially in setting the initial offering price; it may be set high to "skim" the market, or low to achieve significant market "penetration" quickly. Competitors enter during the market growth stage, but non-price competition prevails and, at first, individual companies (because of differentiated products) have considerable freedom in setting prices. During later phases of market growth and early phases of market maturity, different competitors gradually see opportunities to "widen the market" and price reductions become key factors in securing further market expansions.[8] Sometime during market maturity, however, the market approaches saturation, and price reductions no longer expand sales. Emphasis shifts from selling to new users, to making replacement sales to present users—usually through introducing new models or using other forms of product differentiation—and prices stabilize.[9] Finally, during market decline, sporadic reductions appear, as different companies "clear out their stocks" and discontinue the product.

PRODUCT DIFFERENTIATION   If a marketer succeeds in differentiating his product, an opportunity may exist to cultivate customers to whom product differences are more important than price. Competing on a non-price basis depends not only on the amount of product differentiation but

---

constitute important parts of the pricing environment rather than stages in the pricing process. For further details, on this scholar's approach, see: A. R. Oxenfeldt, "Multi-Stage Approach to Pricing," *Harvard Business Review*, July-August 1960, pp. 125-33.

[8] For an illustration of the kind of calculation a company makes in determining the possible profitability of making a price reduction, see: N. W. Chamberlain, *The Firm: Micro-Economic Planning and Action* (New York: McGraw-Hill Book Co., Inc., 1962), pp. 202-203.

[9] *Ibid.*

on its relative importance to potential buyers. Customers who consider product differentiation important do not wholly ignore price, but they are not likely to switch to competing brands solely because of small price differences. A prospective new-car buyer with a strong preference for Chevrolet, for example, will not buy a Ford or a Plymouth because of a price difference, unless it is substantial. Price is not unimportant to such a buyer, and he may shop around among several Chevrolet dealers to get the best terms; but, in selecting the *brand*, product differences are more important than price. The particular characteristics differentiating a brand may range from fashion and styling to quality and durability or product service. To the extent that prospective buyers regard these qualities as important, they reduce the marketing significance of price in converting prospects into buyers.

CUSTOMERS' BUYING PATTERNS   Pricing decisions are also influenced by customers' buying habits. Products purchased frequently by ultimate consumers, for instance, are sold profitably by middlemen at low markups because of the rapid inventory turnover. When sales are high, relative to inventory investment, a small profit on each sale produces a large annual profit. Thus, high turnover products, such as most grocery items, can be profitably sold at 15 to 20 percent markups, whereas slow turnover products require higher markups—hardware, for instance, carries a 35 to 40 percent markup and jewelry more than 50 percent.

The usual quantity in which a product is purchased also affects pricing decisions. Increases in the size of the purchase reduce marketing costs and increase consumption. Frequently, it costs the retailer, for instance, very little more to sell six of an item than to sell one, so cost savings make possible profitable price reductions for quantity purchases. Purchases in larger quantities also increase the buyer's total consumption because increased availability often causes him to use more; this is the reasoning that led soft-drink bottlers to offer six-packs at the price of five individual bottles.

PRICE ELASTICITY   What will happen to sales if the price is reduced? Increased? In answering these questions, the concept of "price elasticity," developed by economists, is helpful. Price elasticity refers to the relative sensitivity of an item's sales volume to changes in its price. For management's purposes, price elasticity generally is measured through use of an "arc elasticity" formula.[10] The most frequently-used formula of this type is:

[10] Such a formula measures the "average change" between two points (representing two different prices and two different quantities sold) on a segment (i.e., "arc") of a demand curve. For a good explanation of the differences between "arc" and "point" elasticity, see: M. M. Bober, *Intermediate Price and Income Theory*, rev. ed. (New York: W. W. Norton & Co., Inc., 1962), pp. 61-68.

$$\frac{\text{Price}}{\text{Elasticity}} = \frac{\text{Quantity}_1 - \text{Quantity}_2}{\text{Quantity}_1 + \text{Quantity}_2} \div \frac{\text{Price}_1 - \text{Price}_2}{\text{Price}_1 + \text{Price}_2}$$

Suppose, for example, that a grocer can sell 100 boxes of fresh strawberries at 50 cents and 200 boxes at 40 cents. In other words, a 20 percent price reduction (from 50 cents to 40 cents) will produce a 100 percent sales increase. Substituting these figures into the formula and making the calculations, we obtain:

$$\frac{\text{Price}}{\text{Elasticity}} = \frac{100}{300} \div \frac{10}{90} = \frac{100}{300} \times \frac{90}{10} = \frac{1}{3} \times 9 = -3.0$$

The price elasticity measure has a negative sign, because a price *decline* causes a sales *increase* and a price *increase* a sales *decline*. If this measure is numerically larger than −1, such as −3, price elasticity exists: at a lower price the total sales revenue increases and at a higher price the total sales revenue declines. If the measure is numerically smaller than −1, such as −0.5, then price inelasticity exists. If it is exactly −1, price elasticity is *unitary*. The impact of price changes on sales volumes under each of these conditions is summarized in Table 19-1.

TABLE 19–1*

	Price Elasticity	Unitary Price Elasticity	Price Inelasticity
Elasticity Coefficient	Over −1.0	−1.0	Under −1.0
Impact on sales revenue of:			
(1) A price reduction	Higher	No change	Lower
(2) A price increase	Lower	No change	Higher

* This table is adapted from one in: G. J. Stigler, *The Theory of Price*, rev. ed. (New York: The MacMillan Co., 1952), p. 37.

Price elasticity varies widely among different products. The demand for fresh strawberries is price elastic, while the demand for coal is price inelastic. A relatively small change in the price of strawberries increases (or decreases) their sale considerably, but a relatively small change in the price of coal has little effect on the number of tons sold. These generalizations, however, hold only within certain limits. For instance, a large increase in the price of coal may cause buyers to switch to less expensive fuels.

When the demand for a marketer's product is price inelastic, he has little incentive to cut the price, since his sales revenue per unit of product sold drops more rapidly than unit sales increase. He is much more tempted to raise the price, inasmuch as sales revenue per unit of product sold rises much more than the total units sold decline; however, as in the case of coal, the availability and prices of substitute products limit the profitability of any sizable price increase.

When a product's demand is price elastic, pricing decisions generally are no less difficult. No single company can hope to take business permanently away from competitors through a price reduction, since competitors can and probably will quickly match or better it. Price reductions in such cases are profitable to individual companies only if they expand the industry's total sales, so that the increase in the quantity sold by the industry more than offsets the loss of sales revenue per unit. And, if close substitutes for the product exist, declines in their prices may cancel out or reduce anticipated sales increases. Price increases are no more attractive, unless competitors follow with similar price increases. Even if competitors do go along, the availability and prices of substitute products limit the profitability of any sizable price increase.

OTHER CHARACTERISTICS OF THE PRODUCT'S MARKET   Several other characteristics of a product's market may affect pricing decisions. Whether the size of the total potential market is large or small makes a considerable difference. If a marketer can anticipate a large sales volume, he can also foresee substantial economies in physical distribution and promotion, which reduce total marketing costs. Thus, he may use an accordingly lower price to improve the chances of attaining that sales volume. Similarly, the relative density of the potential market (i.e., the degree of concentration of possible buyers), also affects marketing costs and, consequently, offering prices. Any factor, then, that may change marketing costs affects pricing, since it shifts the level at which a price can be set and still be profitable.

The relative bargaining power of potential buyers also influences pricing decisions. A marketer of a consumer product, for instance, may be "bargained into" giving special low prices to large buyers, such as corporate chains, in order to get them to handle his product at all. Similarly, marketers of industrial products often must make price concessions to large customers in order to gain, or retain, their patronage. However, the "giving in" to buyers' demands for special prices is limited by federal legislation prohibiting price discrimination among like buyers (see Chapter 23).

Marketing Channels and Distribution Policy

The particular marketing channels used also should be considered in making pricing decisions. Specifically, management should consider the sizes of the gross margins expected by the middlemen who make up the channel. Such expectations generally depend upon the individual middleman's costs and his profit objectives as well as upon the scope and importance of the services he is to perform for the manufacturer. In fact, the middleman's costs and the services he performs are related, i.e., services involve costs. A wholesaler carrying an inventory and maintaining a repair facility, for instance, has higher costs and expects more gross margin than a second wholesaler who neither carries an inventory nor has a repair facility. If more than one level of middleman is included in the channel, the gross margin requirements and services performed by each level should be considered.

Similarly, if the manufacturer follows an exclusive or highly selective distribution policy, there are implications for pricing decisions. Companies having such policies generally expect dealers to perform additional services, such as conducting local advertising and providing product service. Dealers, in turn, expect larger gross margins. The manufacturer using mass distribution bears such costs himself; consequently, his dealers obtain lower gross margins on his product.

Promotional Strategy

The manufacturer's promotional strategy also affects his pricing decisions. If, for instance, he uses massive advertising campaigns to "pull the product through the channel," he probably will allow middlemen somewhat less than their normal gross margins. If he expects them to carry part of the advertising burden, they will expect greater-than-normal gross margins. If he minimizes his use of advertising and other promotion, then he may offer middlemen lower prices (and higher gross margins) to insure that they will provide needed promotional effort.

Cost Considerations

Prices and costs, are related, both in economic theory and the "real world," but the extent to which costs should (or can) enter into pricing decisions varies from one situation to another. The economist and the businessman agree that over the long run sales revenues (i.e., prices × unit volumes) must be sufficient to recover all costs. They also agree that short-run prices do not necessarily have to cover costs. Buyers neither know nor care whether the seller's prices cover his costs or not.

It is more accurate to say that prices determine costs rather than the reverse. Usually the marketer should first estimate the prices he can obtain for his products, taking into account the nature of demand, competitors' positions, product differentiation, middlemen's likely reactions, planned promotion, and other factors. Then, he works "backward" to make (or buy) products suitable to such prices. In this way, therefore, price often determines costs of production (or purchasing) and marketing.[11]

However, this does not mean that pricing decisions can disregard costs. Cost is an important factor in determining price, but it is not the only factor. The relationships of prices to costs are far from simple.

NATURE OF COST DATA   Cost figures are often not as objective as they at first appear. The seeming objectivity of cost data is deceptive because, although costs are expressed in exact dollar amounts, their computation requires many subjective judgments. Production cost accounting, for example, involves numerous arbitrary allocations of overhead costs to arrive at unit costs, and marketing cost accounting often requires even more judgmental decisions.

Furthermore, cost data adequate for accounting purposes are often ill-suited for pricing decisions. Accountants work mostly with historical costs and are mainly concerned with controlling current operating costs. Pricing decisions are more closely related to future costs than to either present or past costs. Thus, pricing decision-makers are more concerned with "estimated costs" than "known costs."

It is particularly difficult to estimate production costs accurately when joint-cost products are involved. A manufacturer who produces several different products in the same factory, often even on the same machinery, may find it impossible to allocate total costs among these products except on a purely arbitrary basis. The unreliability of the resulting cost data often leads to pricing the individual products in terms of "what the traffic will bear," using cost figures only as a general guide to insure that total sales revenue on all products is enough to cover total costs.

COST CONCEPTS   The cost concepts most relevant to pricing are *fixed costs, variable costs,* and *incremental costs.* Fixed costs, often called "overhead costs," do not vary with the output rate, and include salaries, rent, heat, light, depreciation, local property taxes, bond interest, and the like. Variable costs, in contrast, vary somewhat automatically with the output produced or sold, and include such costs as those of raw materials, labor paid on a piece rate or hourly basis, salesmen's commissions, and costs of packaging, packing, warehousing, and shipping. Variable costs per unit are calculated by dividing the total variable cost by the number of units produced or sold.[12] *Incremental costs* are those incurred in changing the

---

[11] On this point, see D. V. Harper, *Price Policy and Procedure* (New York: Harcourt, Brace & World, Inc., 1966), p. 50.

[12] Variable costs per unit are not the same as marginal costs. Marginal cost, chiefly used in economic theory, refers to the change in total cost from adding another unit to output. Nevertheless, over narrow ranges of output, variable costs per unit and the marginal cost may be roughly equal—especially when variable costs per unit are constant or nearly so.

level or nature of an activity—for example, making and/or selling a larger volume of the product, entering a new market, or switching marketing channels. Incremental costs may be either variable or some combination of variable and fixed costs. Notice that both variable and incremental costs are added costs.

BREAK-EVEN COMPUTATIONS   Break-even analysis is a technique for studying how costs vary at different sales-volume levels. Because the interrelationship of costs and sales volume determines the amount of profit (or loss), break-even analysis helps in estimating the effects on profits of using different prices.[13] Exhibit 19-1 shows a typical break-even chart. Notice that the break-even point occurs at the operating level where total costs equal sales revenue. This point, in other words, tells us the number of units of product which must be sold at a particular price for the firm to barely cover its total costs. If sales volume goes beyond this point, each

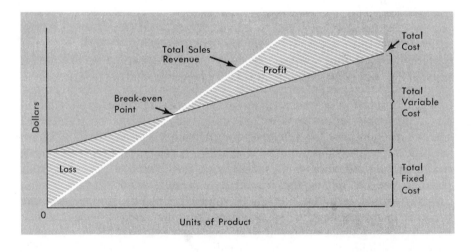

EXHIBIT 19-1

A Typical Break-Even Chart

[13] Break-even analysis is also helpful in evaluating the likely effects on profits of various alternative solutions to many types of marketing problems. It can be used, for example, to show the effects on profit of altering the amounts invested in advertising, of changing the sales compensation method, of adding a new product, or of changing a marketing channel. Break-even analysis, in short, helps in analyzing any marketing problem in which alternative solutions differ as to their impact on costs and/or sales volume. For example, Alternative A may increase costs and result in a more-than-offsetting sales volume increase, while Alternative B may decrease costs with sales volume staying about the same as before.

additional unit sold brings in some net profit. Each sale before reaching this point is at a loss.

If we want to determine the break-even point mathematically rather than graphically, there are three steps. The first, which is also needed for graphic break-even analysis, is to total up *fixed costs for the operating period* (at a predetermined volume of output) and variable costs *per unit*. Second, calculate the *unit contribution to fixed costs* as follows:

$$\text{Unit Contribution to Fixed Costs} = \frac{\text{Selling Price}}{\textit{per unit}} - \frac{\text{Variable Costs}}{\textit{per unit}}$$

This unit contribution figure indicates the portion of the unit selling price which, after deduction of variable costs, will be left over and which can be applied against the fixed costs. The third step is to compute the break-even point itself—i.e., the total number of units which must be sold to cover total fixed costs. The following formula is used for this computation:

$$\text{Break-Even Point (in units)} = \frac{\text{Total Fixed Costs}}{\text{Unit Contribution to Fixed Costs}}$$

If we now multiply *break-even unit volume by the selling price per unit*, we determine the dollar sales volume needed to reach the break-even point.

To illustrate, suppose that the Empire Hatchet Company has total annual fixed costs of $40,000, variable costs per unit of $1.50, and is thinking of pricing its hatchets at $3.50 each. How many hatchets must Empire sell during the year in order to break even? Unit contribution to fixed costs is $3.50—$1.50, or $2.00 per unit, and break-even unit volume is:

$$\frac{\text{Total Fixed Costs}}{\text{Unit Contribution}} = \frac{\$40,000}{\$2} = 20,000 \text{ units}$$

If Empire sells 20,000 hatchets, it will cover all its fixed and variable costs. If it sells the 20,001st hatchet, it will show a profit: $2.00.

To obtain the break-even volume in dollars, simply multiply break-even unit volume (20,000 hatchets) by selling price ($3.50), which yields $70,000. To check this, add total fixed costs ($40,000) to variable costs per unit multiplied by break-even unit volume ($1.50 × 20,000, or $30,000), which means that total dollar costs also come to $70,000. At the break-even point, total costs equal total sales dollars.

Suppose, now, that Empire management wants to determine the different effects on its break-even point of pricing the hatchets at $3.00 and $4.00. At the lower $3.00 price, unit contribution is $1.50, and break-even unit volume rises to 26,666 + units; at the higher $4.00 price, unit contribution is $2.50, and break-even unit volume falls to 16,000 units. (These calculations assume that total fixed costs and unit variable costs remain stable at all output levels; this might or might not be true in a particular case.)

In deciding which of the three prices to use, management would then go on to determine the chances of exceeding each break-even unit volume and by how much, compute the total sales revenues from the expected unit sales under each alternative, deduct the total costs involved, and compare the resulting estimated profits.

Thus, in using break-even analysis in pricing decision-making, it is not enough to compute only the different break-even points. Changes in sales volume that may occur under each alternative price also must be considered. Furthermore, in many cases, unlike that in our illustration, changes occur in fixed costs and unit variable costs at different output levels, and these also should be considered. Management, in other words, is more interested in the amount of profit it can expect at different sales levels than it is in break-even points as such. Prices, sales volumes, and costs all have effects on profits.

Costs, Overall Marketing Strategy, and Prices

If one of the company's objectives is to maximize net profit, marketing management must seek the optimum combination of product, marketing channels, promotion, and price. The optimum combination is one that maximizes the spread between total sales revenues and total costs. The problem of finding the optimum combination is complex, because each component of marketing strategy—products, marketing channels, promotion, and price—interact jointly and in combination, and all have effects on sales volumes and costs and, thus, on profits.

However, for purposes of planning operations over the "short run," it is possible to simplify the problem. For the next operating period, for instance, the product can usually be regarded as "given"—each version of a product is on the market for some period, even though it may later be supplanted by an improved or new model. Moreover, the marketing channel is not changed very often or without advance deliberation, so it also may be regarded as "given." Thus, the task of finding the best combination of the components of marketing strategy—for short-run planning purposes—becomes essentially one of combining promotion and price to obtain the best relationships between sales volume and costs, which results in the highest profit. The problem, in other words, is to estimate the quantities that can be sold at different possible prices with alternative expenditures for promotion, assuming that the product and marketing channel (while imposing certain requirements on price and promotion) will not be changed during the forthcoming period.

Table 19–2 shows how management might determine which of twenty-four different price-and-promotion possibilities should result in the most profit. The top row indicates a succession of sales volumes ranging from ten to sixty units. The first column on the left shows four alternative levels of promotion costs (i.e., for advertising, personal selling, etc.). In each box are four figures: the top figure indicates the unit price at which the corresponding unit sales volume can be sold, assuming the promotion level shown in the column on the far left. The second shows the total sales volume (in dollars)—i.e., the price multiplied by the unit sales volume. The third figure indicates the total costs at that particular sales volume—which, of course, are obtained by adding together all costs—promotion as well as other marketing costs, production and other costs. The bottom figure shows the total profit, obtained by subtracting total costs from total sales volume.

TABLE 19—2

Twenty-Four Price-and-Promotion Combinations, Their Effects on Sales Volumes and Costs, and Resulting Net Profits

Promotion Costs		Sales Volume (Units of Product)					
		10	20	30	40	50	60
$0	Price/unit	$ 25	$ 20	$ 15	$ 10	$ 5	$ 3
	Total sales volume	250	400	450	400	250	180
	Total costs	120	200	270	300	400	540
	Total profit	130	200	180	100	− 150	− 360
$100	Price/unit	27	23	19	15	11	8
	Total sales volume	270	460	570	600	550	480
	Total costs	220	300	370	400	500	640
	Total profit	50	160	200	200	50	− 70
$200	Price/unit	30	27	24	21	19	17
	Total sales volume	300	540	720	840	950	1020
	Total costs	320	400	470	500	600	740
	Total profit	− 20	140	250	340	350	280
$400	Price/unit	40	35	30	25	21	19
	Total sales volume	400	700	900	1000	1050	1140
	Total costs	520	600	670	700	800	940
	Total profit	− 120	100	230	300	250	200
Average Cost/Unit (All Costs Except Promotion Costs)		$ 12	$ 10	$ 9	$ 7.50	$ 8	$ 9

Two assumptions are built into this illustration. The first is that higher sales volumes will be sold at lower prices—i.e., the product has a price elastic demand. The second is that increases in promotion costs will make it possible to obtain higher prices at each sales volume. These assumptions are not always valid, but they are probably reasonable in most cases. In any real-world situation, management should make its own assumptions and construct its estimates accordingly.

In the illustration, on each of the four "total profit" rows, the highest profits are indicated as $200, $200, and $350, and $300. The maximum profit is obtained when promotion costs are $200 and 50 units of the product are sold at a $19 price. At this particular point, according to economic theory, incremental revenue $\left(\frac{950\text{-}840}{50\text{-}40}\right)$ should equal incremental costs $\left(\frac{600\text{-}500}{50\text{-}40}\right)$. No such equality exists here, since this illustration simulates what happens in the "real world" rather than in economic theory. Just as in the real world, the illustrative data are not continuous: production is in minimum-size lots of 10 units; gaps of varying amounts exist between different prices considered; and the alternative promotion costs represent discretely different promotional programs.

Environmental Factors Influencing Pricing Decisions

COMPETITION   Most modern marketers seek to compete on a non-price basis to the maximum possible extent, but they cannot entirely ignore competitors' prices. Successful use of non-price competition may enable a marketer to gain partial "control" over a market segment as, for example, through product differentiation or selective distribution. This may enable him to obtain higher prices than competitors, but when their prices change, he must keep his own prices generally in line; otherwise, his "control" over the particular market segment gradually erodes.

Furthermore, in making his own pricing decisions, a marketer must take competitors' likely reactions into account. Will they follow a price increase? A price cut? How soon? A price change is the easiest switch in marketing strategy to copy, and copying can be almost instantaneous. That, perhaps, is why most marketers prefer non-price competition. Product, channel, and promotion changes are neither easy to copy nor can they be followed quickly. The first competitor making a profitable non-price move gains more than a temporary advantage.

ECONOMIC CLIMATE   Economic changes also influence pricing decisions. Marketers often have inventories that are too large at the start of a business decline and too small at the beginning of a business upturn. Liquidation of excessive inventories during a recession results in widespread price cuts. Inventory shortages during a period of improving business conditions results in price increases. However, because of the "stickiness" of administered prices, the company emphasizing non-price competition tends to adjust slowly to shifting economic conditions. Slowness in cutting administered prices delays needed price reductions at the beginning of a recession, causes inventories to build up to abnormally high levels, and necessitates even larger price cuts later on. Similarly, during periods of rapidly rising costs often characteristic of business upturns, price rises lag behind the need for such changes, resulting in cost-price "squeezes." Therefore, the company emphasizing non-price competition must be alert to impending economic changes and make needed and timely price adjustments.

LEGISLATION AND GOVERNMENTAL PRESSURES   Federal and state laws influence pricing alternatives. (We describe this legislation in detail in Chapter 23.) At the federal level, the Clayton Act, as amended by the Robinson-Patman Act, prohibits several pricing practices that discriminate among like purchasers. These include cumulative quantity discounts, non-cumulative quantity discounts in excess of actual cost savings, "dummy" brokerage payments, and discriminatory promotional allowances. At the state level, some states have Unfair Trade Practices Acts prohibiting sales below costs (or cost plus some designated markup) that restrict pricing decisions. But most states have also broadened pricing alternatives through enactment of Fair Trade Laws, which modify specific legal prohibitions against price fixing, to allow a manufacturer to establish the minimum price at which dealers may resell his product.

Since the early 1960s, governmental pressures have influenced pricing decisions for some products. Major steel producers, for instance, in 1962 announced a price increase but, after a confrontation between President John F. Kennedy and certain high steel executives, the increase was rescinded. Later, President Lyndon B. Johnson "convinced" the aluminum and copper industries, among others, not to raise their prices. President Richard M. Nixon, though not given to intervening in pricing decisions, several times expressed displeasure with certain price-increase announcements. The possibility that governmental pressures will be brought to bear is a factor that decision makers, particularly in basic industries where price increases might be considered as inflationary, should take into account. In industries whose members produce less "basic" and more differentiated products, the likelihood of governmental intervention is more remote but still possible. In fact, governmental intervention in pricing decisions is likely to become increasingly frequent and important in the future, especially during inflationary trends.

PRICING OBJECTIVES

Pricing objectives should derive directly from company objectives and help in the making of appropriate and consistent pricing decisions. Such objectives provide guidance to decision-makers in formulating price policies, planning pricing strategies, and setting actual prices. Probably most companies have profit as a main pricing objective.

It is not at all clear, however, that the main objective is profit maximization. Occasionally, a company will "charge what the traffic will bear. This may be short-run profit maximization but it is not usually the way to maximize long-run profits. Most experts suggest, in fact, that companies should deliberately refrain from maximizing short-run profits in order to maximize them in the long-run. Ordinarily, however, it is impossible to prove that a short-run pricing strategy actually leads to maximum long-run profits. We agree with one writer who concludes that "long-run profit maximizing is elusive and perhaps unmeasurable." [14]

Profit maximization, then, is more of an ideal than it is a usable pricing objective. In working toward the profit maximization ideal, pricing decisions are aimed toward attaining related objectives, such as some target return on the investment or some specified market share. Recognizing the elusiveness of profit maximization, realistic decision-makers focus on other pricing objectives, which are all related, in one way or another, to securing, if not the maximum, at least a satisfactory long-run profit. One study by the Brookings Institution of twenty large corporations found that the most typical pricing objectives were: (1) to achieve a target return on investment, (2) to stabilize prices, (3) to hold or obtain a target market share, and (4) to meet or keep out competition.[15]

Target-Return Pricing Objectives

Numerous companies phrase their pricing objectives in terms of achieving a certain target return. The desired target return may relate to a return on investment (ROI) or a return on net sales, or simply some targeted "dollar" profit. The ROI pricing objective is more common among manufacturers than middlemen and among large companies than small ones. The targeted return-on-sales objective is mainly used by middlemen and the targeted "dollar" profit objective by small manufacturers.

TARGET ROI AS A PRICING OBJECTIVE   The Brookings study found that target return on investment was the most frequently-mentioned pricing goal. In working toward this objective, pricing decisions are made so that total sales revenues will exceed total costs by enough to provide

---

[14] R. A. Lynn, *Price Policies and Marketing Management* (Homewood, Ill.: Richard D. Irwin, Inc., 1967), p. 99.

[15] This study was performed in the 1950s by a research team supported by the Brookings Institution. The final report was published in the form of a book; see: A. D. H. Kaplan, J. B. Dirlam, and R. F. Lanzillotti, *Pricing in Big Business* (Washington, D.C.: The Brookings Institution, 1958). One member of the research team also published an article, which marketing scholars have found most helpful, see: R. F. Lanzillotti, "Pricing Objectives in Large Companies," *American Economic Review*, December, 1958, pp. 921-40. Much of the material in this section is derived from Dr. Lanzillotti's article, and we acknowledge our indebtedness to him.

the desired rate of return on the total investment. Since the objective is to obtain the targeted return on the total investment, pricing decisions for specific products, groups of products, or company divisions need not individually be designed to produce precisely the specified ROI; rather the objective is for the company's entire operations to earn—on the average—the specified ROI. Additionally, "on the average" means "standard sales volume" —i.e., the average sales level experienced over several years' operations.

The use of a targeted ROI as a pricing objective is easiest to illustrate in a situation involving a single product. Suppose a company has been organized to produce a single product, which it anticipates will reach a sales volume of 10,000 units in an "average" year. The company's total investment (i.e., the total capital employed in the business) amounts to $1-million. At the 10,000 unit sales level, total unit cost (i.e., fixed costs per unit + unit variable costs) are $50. If the targeted ROI is set at 30 percent before taxes, a $300,000 dollar return is required in an "average" year. Thus, the company's pricing calculation would be:

Total Costs for 10,000 units @ $50 per unit $500,000
30% before-tax ROI on $1,000,000 investment 300,000
                                                      _____
Targeted Sales Volume $800,000

$$\frac{\$800,000}{10,000 \text{ units}} = \$80 \text{ price per unit}$$

Target ROI pricing is commonly used by companies that are industry leaders and those that sell in "protected" markets. Such leaders in their respective industries as the DuPont Company, Standard Oil Company of New Jersey, and General Motors were reported by the Brookings researchers as using target ROI pricing. Industry leaders find target ROI pricing practical, probably because they are in positions to set the industry standard—what they do, other industry members tend to follow. Similarly, target ROI pricing is common among companies selling in protected markets, such as those for new and uniquely different products. For a time, the innovating company enjoys a "protected" market, i.e., until competitors enter the market with their own versions.

TARGETED RETURN ON SALES   Many retailers and wholesalers set their profit objective as a targeted return on sales, stated as some percentage of dollar sales. Then they price their inventories with sufficiently high markups so that sales revenues will cover total costs and yield a desired profit on the year's operation. Suppose, for example, a retailer estimates that next year his total costs (including both operating and merchandise costs) will be $950,000, and he desires a five percent targeted return on net sales. His targeted dollar profit, then, is:

$$\frac{\text{Total Costs}}{100\% - \text{Target Profit}\%} = \frac{\$950,000}{95\%} = \$1,000,000 \text{ (Targeted Sales Volume)}$$

$$\$1,000,000 \times .05 = \$50,000 \text{ (Targeted Dollar Profit)}$$

The retailer then would price the various items in his stock so that as a total group they will return five percent on sales—some items will be priced to return more than five percent, some less.

TARGETED DOLLAR PROFIT   In many cases, mainly those involving small manufacturers, the pricing objective is a targeted amount of dollar profit. Typically such companies are managed by their owners, who simply desire to "earn a good living." Consequently, they set prices to return that dollar profit which represents in their minds "a good living."

Price Stabilization

Some companies seek to keep their prices relatively stable over long periods. That is, they aim to even out or, if possible, eliminate cyclical price fluctuations. During periods of depressed business, they work to keep prices from falling too far; during periods of good business, partially perhaps because of a sense of social responsibility, they try to keep prices from rising to "what the traffic will bear." A price stabilization objective, therefore, often is paired with a target ROI pricing objective: both are typically long-run pricing goals. Thus, industry leaders, such as Standard Oil Company of New Jersey and Alcoa, were found in the Brookings Institution study to have a target ROI as the main pricing goal and price stabilization as a collateral goal.

Price stabilization is also an important collateral pricing objective in other situations. Marketers of products vulnerable to price wars, such as tires and gasoline, regard price stabilization as an important goal. Companies promoting their products through national advertising in which prices are mentioned, also attach considerable importance to price stabilization. Fairly often, such companies resort to Resale Price Maintenance (Fair Trade) laws in their efforts to achieve price stabilization. More frequently, they simply "suggest" resale prices to their middlemen.

Target Market Share

Pricing products to obtain a target market share is nearly as common as target ROI pricing. A dominant company in an industry may set a target market share objective defensively—i.e., to emphasize the importance of holding the market share it already has. Or it may want to restrain itself from becoming "too dominant" in the industry, which might increase its vulnerability to anti-trust prosecution. Smaller and younger companies set target market share objectives offensively, i.e., to establish benchmarks for their growth in the industry. Some giant retailers, such as Sears Roebuck and A & P, also have aggressive target market share objectives, generally trying to increase their market shares both geographically and for individual product lines.

Meeting or Keeping Out Competition

In certain industries, meeting or keeping out competition is an important pricing objective. If a company is its industry's price leader, for instance, it may set prices designed to discourage new competitors from entering the market. Similarly, companies that are price followers set their prices in order to meet competitors' prices, including those of the price leader. The Brookings Institution study reported that the meeting-competition pricing objective often appeared related to the target market share objective—thus, a company working to maintain a given target market share might have to meet competitors' price reductions in order to hold that share.

Other Pricing Objectives

While the pricing objectives discussed above are the most common, many others exist, too many to catalog them all here. However, it needs mentioning that sometimes the main pricing objective becomes one of simply "keeping the doors open"—i.e., of selling at any price that will allow the company to survive a period of particularly bad business. This definitely is a short-run pricing objective. Occasionally, too, a company adopts what might be called a tactical, rather than a strategic, pricing objective; for instance, it may price a product unusually high in order to raise its prestige; to the extent that buyers equate price with quality, this can be a profitable move.

CONCLUSION

In most marketing situations today, pricing is a controllable. This makes it possible for marketers to compete mainly on a non-price, rather than a price, basis. Pricing is generally not the most critical factor in successful marketing, but it is an important element in most marketing programs. Pricing decisions require consideration of numerous factors including the company's objectives and image and other components of its marketing program—product-market combinations, marketing channels, and promotion—and costs. Among environmental factors requiring consideration are the competition, economic climate, and legislation.

Pricing objectives should derive directly from company objectives. Because of the general elusiveness of profit maximization, attention focuses on other pricing objectives related to securing, if not the maximum, at least satisfactory long-run profits. These objectives include: achieving a target return on investment or sales, stabilizing prices, holding or obtaining a target market share, and meeting or keeping out competition.

QUESTIONS AND PROBLEMS

1. Which of the following would generally regard pricing as an uncontrollable rather than a controllable? State your reasoning in each instance.
   a. A bicycle manufacturer
   b. A cattle farmer
   c. An electrical utility
   d. A commercial photographer
   e. A taxi operator
   f. A newspaper publisher
   g. A strawberry grower
   h. A lumber mill.

2. Explain how an administered price differs from a market price.

3. Illustrate how a marketer might go about manipulating other marketing controllables in ways that would improve his ability to compete on a non-price basis.

4. If pricing is usually a marketing controllable, why is it that the marketing manager so rarely has full authority over pricing?

5. During which stage of the product life cycle does management have the most discretion in making pricing decisions? The least discretion?

6. Suppose a seller of fireplace wood can sell 50 cords at $20 and 75 cords at $15. Is the demand for fireplace wood price elastic or inelastic?

7. "Since price elasticity of demand applies to industries rather than to the products of individual firms, price elasticity should not be a factor in the pricing decisions of individual firms" Agree or disagree?

8. What "trade-offs" exist between:
   a. the nature of a product and its price?
   b. marketing channels and price?
   c. promotional strategy and price?

9.   Why are marketers generally much more reluctant to use price than promotion as a competitive weapon?

10.   How are variable costs and incremental costs different? How are they similar?

11.   A manufacturer makes and markets a single product. His total fixed costs amount to $100,000 annually, and variable costs per unit of product are 57 cents. The product is sold to wholesalers at a price of $9.00 per dozen. Compute: (a) the break-even point in dollars, and (b) the break-even point in units of product.

12.   The problem of finding the optimum combination of product, marketing channels, promotion, and price is extremely complex. Explain how, for purposes of planning short-run operations, it is possible to simplify this problem.

13.   "The existence of administered prices tends to increase the economic impact of fluctuations in price levels." Do you agree? Why?

14.   "The larger a company is, the more vulnerable it is to governmental pressures being brought to bear on its pricing decisions." Do you agree? Why?

15.   Suppose a company produces a single product, which it forecasts will reach a sales volume of 50,000 units in an "average" year. The total capital employed in the business amounts to $7.5 million. At the 50,000 unit sales level, total unit costs (i.e., fixed costs per unit + unit variable costs) amount to $300. If the targeted ROI is set at 25 percent before taxes, what should be the selling price per unit?

16.   A retailer estimates that next year his total costs (including both operating and merchandise costs) will be $1,250,000. He desires an 8 percent targeted return on net sales. What is his targeted dollar profit?

17.   Why do industry leaders often have price stabilization as an important pricing objective?

18.   Which of the following might set target-market-share pricing objectives defensively? Offensively?
    a. A large chain of discount department stores
    b. A leading tire manufacturer
    c. A transcontinental airline
    d. The largest manufacturer of electrical apparatus
    e. A regional gasoline marketing company.

20

PRICE POLICIES

Price policies constitute the general framework within which pricing decisions should be made in order to achieve the pricing objectives. Thus, price policies provide the guidelines within which pricing strategy is formulated and implemented. Although price policies should be reviewed continually, they form an important part of the company's image and should be changed only infrequently. Each company should have a "bundle" of pricing policies appropriate not only to company and pricing objectives but to its over-all marketing situation.

PRICING RELATIVE TO COMPETITION

Every company adheres to some policy, either explicitly or implicitly, regarding the prices of its products relative to those of competitors. If price is the main basis of competition, then, each company simply prices its products the same as competitors'. If there is non-price competition, prices still must be set and competitors' prices can rarely be totally ignored. There are three alternatives: (1) meeting competition, (2) pricing above the competition, and (3) pricing under the competition.

Meeting Competition

This is the alternative usually chosen. Manufacturers competing on a non-price basis simply meet competitors' prices, hoping to minimize the use of price as a competitive weapon. A "meeting competition" price policy does not mean meeting every competitor's prices, but only the prices of those regarded as important competitors—"important" in the sense that what such competitors do in their pricing may lure customers away.

Pricing Above the Competition

This is a less common policy, but appropriate in certain circumstances. Sometimes higher-than-average prices are used to convey an impression of above-average product quality or prestige. Many buyers relate a product's price to its quality, especially when it is difficult to judge quality before actually buying. In these instances, buyers may pay a little more for a product whose higher price implies higher quality.

Manufacturers sometimes suggest higher-than-average resale prices in an effort to obtain the cooperation of middlemen. If a manufacturer wants especially aggressive selling and promotional efforts from wholesalers and retailers, he may set relatively high "list prices" at which he suggests they resell the product in order to secure above-average markups. The higher markups are passed on to the consumer in the form of higher prices, but the increased dealer cooperation may more than offset the sales-depressing tendency of the higher price and may perhaps even increase total sales. For a consumer product to compete successfully at a price above the market, it generally must either be so strongly differentiated that consumers believe it is superior to competitive brands, or middlemen must enthusiastically and heavily promote it.

Pricing Under the Competition

Many firms follow a policy of pricing under the market. Sometimes a company has low costs because its product is of lower quality, and this leads it to price its product under those of competitors. At other times, a company substitutes a lower price for the promotional efforts (which also cost money) used by its competitors. In all cases, however, firms following this policy must either have very low costs, or be willing to accept a very low profit per unit in the hope of radically increasing sales volume.

PRICING RELATIVE TO COSTS

Every company also has a policy regarding relationships between the prices it places on its products and the underlying costs. While it is true that long-run sales revenues must cover all long-run costs, short-run prices do not necessarily have to cover short-run costs. Because of this discrepancy between the long-run and short-run cost-covering requirements, some policy is needed to guide short-run pricing decisions toward the attainment of long-run pricing objectives. The two main alternatives are: (1) full-cost pricing, and (2) contribution pricing.

Full-Cost Pricing

Under this policy, no sale is ever made at a price lower than that which will cover total costs, including both the variable costs and an allocated share of fixed costs. The underlying logic is that if prices cover short-run costs, they will also cover long-run costs. Nevertheless, rigid adherence to this policy is not only difficult but downright stupid in certain circumstances. Not only is it true that the price buyers are willing to pay may bear little, or no, relationship to the sellers' costs, but there are the often complex problems involved in determining the "real" costs. Furthermore, prices on products already in the inventory sometimes must be reduced below full cost in order to sell at all. However, most businesses, as a general rule, should endeavor to keep prices above short-run costs in *most* situations, and they should define the conditions under which departures are appropriate. Therefore, a policy of full-cost pricing should be regarded only as a flexible guide to decision-making.

Contribution Pricing

A company having a contribution pricing policy uses full-cost pricing whenever possible but will price, under certain circumstances, at any level above the relevant incremental costs. Suppose, for example, a marketer is offered a special contract to supply a large buyer, who is unwilling to pay the price being charged other buyers. He may argue, and justifiably, that the price differential is justified, because of savings to the seller in terms of less selling time required, lower credit costs, lower handling costs, and the like. Still the demanded price concession may exceed the likely savings, so that total income from the proposed transaction is not enough to cover both variable costs and the normally-allocated share of fixed costs. Economists generally would advise the marketer to accept the order, *if* the resulting revenues were large enough not only to cover all incremental costs but to make some contribution to fixed costs and/or profits. After all, current sales at established prices may already be large enough to cover the fixed costs, and the proposed sale at a special price will not raise fixed costs (assuming the incremental costs are all variable costs), so this sale need not bear an allocated share of fixed costs to yield net revenue. The economist argues, in other words, that so long as the proposed price more than covers the direct, or out-of-pocket, costs of the transaction, then the excess over direct costs represents profit.

Nevertheless, as Professors Phelps and Westing say, "businessmen usually seem suspicious of this line of reasoning." [1] Good reasons exist for such suspicion, and they trace chiefly to the fact that economists often do not clarify all the conditions under which they make this sort of recommendation. That is the important purpose of having a contribution pricing policy, which not only specifies whether or not a company will entertain offers at prices under full cost but outlines the conditions of acceptance. Both the businessman and the economist agree that certain important conditions should exist if such offers are accepted: (1) the company has the capacity to produce the order and can put it to no more profitable use, *and* (2) the portion of the output sold below full cost is destined for a different market segment than the full cost product.

Both conditions should be present for the marketer to grant a special price concession. If a more profitable use of the available capacity can be found, that should be the action taken. If the portion of the output sold below full cost goes to the same market segment, then existing customers will demand similar price concessions—in which case, the marketer's break-even point for the product may take off for outer space! Thus, although both conditions are important, the second is critical to the continuance of prices at full cost or above for the bulk of the output.

UNIFORMITY OF PRICES CHARGED TO DIFFERENT BUYERS

Every marketer should have a policy outlining the conditions under which he will charge different buyers identical prices and those under which he will allow price differentials. A contribution pricing policy, as explained just above, details one set of conditions under which he might charge differential prices. But the question of uniformity of offering prices also arises in other circumstances.

[1] D. M. Phelps and J. H. Westing, *Marketing Management*, 3rd ed. (Homewood, Ill.: Richard D. Irwin, Inc., 1968), p. 324.

One-Price vs. Variable-Price Policy

Marketers generally prefer to sell on a one-price basis, that is, by offering a product at exactly the same price to all like buyers. In the United States the one-price policy is used in selling most consumer products and many industrial products, but elsewhere, particularly in the developing countries, sellers commonly use variable-pricing, even for consumer items.

Sellers regard the one-price policy as attractive for three reasons. First, it provided a uniform return from each sale, making for fewer problems in forecasting dollar sales volumes and profits. Second, since prices are not negotiated with individual customers, selling time, and hence selling costs, is reduced. Third, there is less risk of alienating customers because of preferential prices given others.

The variable-price policy, however, is in common use where individual sales transactions involve large sums. It is hardly worth a consumer's or a retailer's time to bargain over the price of a pound of coffee, and the loss of an individual sale is not important enough to the retailer to cause him to reconsider his price. But, in buying an automobile, a consumer will exert considerable effort to obtain a lower price, and the sale is important enough to the dealer for him to hesitate to lose a sale because of a few dollars. The bargaining power of individual purchasers varies with the size of the transaction. In the industrial market, a large buyer generally represents a greater potential for future business than a small buyer, so a seller may make concessions to gain or retain the large buyer's patronage. In addition, some buyers have greater bargaining power than others because of their ability to pay cash. For these reasons, negotiated pricing and variable price policies exist in many industrial markets and even in some consumer markets. Although many sellers of durable consumer items are reluctant to admit that their prices are not fixed, very often they "hold to" one price and negotiate on the value of "trade-ins" instead.

All marketers face the decision whether or not to use a one-price or a variable-price policy. The one-price policy is easier to administer, but variable prices are sometimes the better alternative. If the consumer product marketer opts for the one-price policy, he can implement the policy through legalized resale price maintenance agreements, thus insuring equal prices at retail to all consumers.

Price Differentials

Most marketers will vary their prices under certain conditions, even though they generally adhere to a one-price policy, Such price differentials may be based on size of purchase, type of customers, or buyers' geographical locations. Normally, the marketer using these kinds of price differentials extends them to all buyers meeting the specified requirements; thus, they do not constitute price discrimination in the legal sense.

QUANTITY DISCOUNTS   It is a common policy to offer price reductions on purchases larger than usual. Through such reductions—called quantity discounts—sellers try to increase sales by passing on to buyers part of the savings that can result from large purchases. These savings can be considerable, for it may take little, if any, more of a salesman's time to sell a very large order than to sell a small one. The same holds for order-processing, order-filling, billing, and transportation costs, the last of which will be cheaper per unit because of quantity rates offered by the carriers. Because of the cost reductions possible on large sales, many marketers offer price reductions to encourage large-quantity purchases.

The Clayton Act, as described in Chapter 23, restricts the use of quantity discounts. A firm planning a quantity-discount policy must keep two legal restrictions in mind: The discounts must reflect actual savings; i.e., the price reduction can be no larger than the actual savings resulting from the larger quantity ordered. And the discounts must be made available on proportionately equal terms to all like purchasers. Within these restrictions, quantity discounts provide a possible opportunity to reduce marketing costs and increase market penetration.

TRADE DISCOUNTS   A marketer often sells the same product to several classes of buyers. A paper manufacturer, for instance, sells typing paper to wholesalers, to retail chains, and to businesses buying for their own use. Some buyers in each class buy approximately equal quantities on each order, and one might expect the manufacturer to sell at the same price. Other conditions, however, may cause him to offer different "trade discounts" from the list price for each class of buyer. Assume, for example, that the paper manufacturer makes 75 percent of his sales through wholesalers—this marketing channel is essential to his success, and he hesitates to take any action that may antagonize or threaten the existence of his wholesalers and the retailers they serve. If he offers a chain store organization the same price he offers to wholesalers, the chain may underprice its independent-retailer competitors served by the wholesalers. For this reason, some manufacturers extend lower prices to wholesalers than to even very large retail chains, regardless of the amounts purchased. A company's policy on trade discounts (i.e., on the prices quoted to different classes of customers), depends, then, on the importance of each class of buyer and its relative bargaining power.[2] Trade discounts vary a good deal from one industry to another because of differences not only in marketing channels but in the normal markups various types of middlemen expect.

[2] For a good discussion on this topic, see: D. V. Petrone, "Price Policy in Selling Through Distributors, Wholesalers, and Jobbers," *Pricing: The Critical Decision*, AMA Management Report No. 66, p. 60.

OTHER TYPES OF DISCOUNTS   Many marketers grant other types of discounts including cash discounts, promotional discounts, and seasonal discounts. Some offer cash discounts to stimulate prompt payment by buyers. Thus, for instance, if the customary credit period in an industry is ninety days, a marketer who desires earlier payments may offer a cash discount (usually 1 or 2 percent) for payment within ten days. Other marketers allow special promotional discounts to middlemen who provide local advertising or other promotional support; generally such discounts are not offered continuously but periodically, as for limited periods during the spring and fall.

Marketers use seasonal discounts to persuade customers to buy or place their orders in advance of the normal buying season. Dealers, for instance, might buy merchandise, such as toys and holiday decorations, in September for delivery in October. But many marketers of Christmas items, to balance out their monthly production schedules, offer special seasonal discounts to buyers placing orders in May or June. Similar seasonal discount policies are used not only by marketers of products whose retail sales peak at a particular season but by those, such as vegetable canners and freezers, whose processing operations are concentrated in rather short periods.

Geographical Price Differentials

When a marketer distributes his product over a wide geographical area, the policy he adopts with respect to "who should pay the freight charges" has an important bearing upon the price quotations given to buyers in different places. If the factory is in New England, freight charges are higher to a Chicago buyer than to one in Philadelphia or New York City. In general, the farther away the customer is from the factory, the more the freight charge is for a given size of shipment. There are two major policy alternatives: (1) "F.O.B.," or "free on board" pricing, under which the customer pays the freight, and (2) delivered pricing, under which the seller pays the freight. A third policy, "freight absorption," is a compromise used in certain competitive situations.

F.O.B. PRICING   The marketer who adopts this policy, quotes his selling prices at the factory (or other point from which he makes sales), and buyers pay all the freight charges. Thus, buyers in different locations have different "landed costs"—each pays the price at the selling point plus the freight from there to his location. Therefore, F.O.B. pricing results in variations not only in buyers' costs but in the wholesale and retail prices the product sells at in different parts of the country. F.O.B. pricing is widely used in marketing consumer products that are heavy or bulky in relation to their value—for example, canned foods and fresh vegetables—and in marketing such industrial products as raw materials and heavy machinery.

Moreover, numerous wholesalers and some retailers also use F.O.B. pricing: whenever the buyer pays all the charges for delivery, the seller is using F.O.B. pricing.

F.O.B. pricing simplifies the manufacturer's price quotations to those he deals with directly. However, one problem needs mentioning. Because different direct buyers have different costs for the same item, the resale price varies from one place to another—thus, the marketer is prevented from advertising the resale price nationally except in a general way, such as "Priced at $19.95—prices at your local dealer may vary slightly."

DELIVERED PRICING   Under this policy, the manufacturer pays all freight charges, but, of course, builds them into his price quotation. In effect, he averages total freight charges for all customers, then incorporates some amount, which may or may not be the "exact" average, into the price quoted. Buyers are quoted prices which, in reality, are F.O.B. destination prices—and the marketer's net return varies with the buyer's location. Delivered pricing is generally most appropriate when freight charges account for only a small portion of the product's selling price. It is also usually a necessary policy when a marketer attempts to suggest or maintain resale prices or to advertise them nationally. Standardized resale prices are most likely to be obtained by the marketer when he assures middlemen of uniform markups, regardless of their locations.

In its simplest form, a delivered pricing policy provides a single delivered price throughout the entire market—a "postage stamp" price. Postage stamp pricing is used by marketers of such items as chewing gum and candy bars, mainly with the intention that middlemen everywhere will resell the products involved at the same prices, thus permitting the marketer to advertise resale prices nationally. Commonly, too, consumer buyers of such products are used to paying a "customary" or "traditional" price for the item—such as for gum or soft drinks; thus the marketer uses postage stamp pricing to conform to ultimate consumers' expectations of "what the price should be."

An alternative to postage stamp pricing is zone pricing, under which the market is divided into zones and different prices set in each, depending on the zone's distance from the factory. Zone pricing still permits the seller to quote the same price to a large group of buyers in a geographical region, but it allows him to allocate total freight charges more closely in line with the actual costs incurred. A market may be divided into any number of zones, but two is the most common number. Many manufacturers located in the eastern United States, for example, divide the nation into two zones and advertise a single price with the qualification that "prices are slightly higher west of the Mississippi."

FREIGHT ABSORPTION   A freight absorption policy is used by marketers who encounter stiff price competition from companies located closer to prospective buyers. Most frequently, this policy takes the form of quoting a price to the buyer that is the usual F.O.B. factory price plus an amount for freight equal to that which the competitive marketer located nearest the customer would charge. Thus, freight absorption pricing often is adopted to lessen the competitive disadvantages of F.O.B. pricing, especially where the marketer meets locally-based competition in certain important markets.

GUARANTY AGAINST PRICE DECLINE

Manufacturers whose products are subject to frequent price fluctuations sometimes guarantee the stability of the price for a specified period after the sale. Sugar refiners and coffee roasters, for instance, often guarantee against price declines because their selling prices to middlemen tend to parallel fluctuations in the sugar and coffee commodity markets. Buyers' fears, therefore, that they are buying at the wrong time are alleviated by the manufacturer's promise to refund an amount equal to the price change on all unsold stock left in buyers' hands. The length of the period during which the guaranty is in effect is determined by the type of wholesale or retail business operated by the buyer, and its customary rate of stock turn on the item involved.

Other marketers use a guaranty against price decline to persuade buyers to buy quantities in excess of their immediate needs. Air conditioner manufacturers, for example, have a selling season of about six months of the year, but they manufacture on a year-round basis. In an effort to cut their inventories during the non-selling season, air conditioner manufacturers offer distributors special discounts for preseason orders; however, if distributors think there is a possibility of industry-wide reductions before the selling season, even a discount will not persuade them to buy. To overcome this fear of lower prices later on, the manufacturers often agree to refund an amount equal to any price decline before some specified date.

POLICY ON PRICE CHANGES

All marketers should decide whether, as a matter of policy, they will initiate or follow price changes. Every company, regardless of whether it competes on a price or non-price basis, must continually appraise competitor's possible price changes for their possible impacts on its business. Every company, too, must estimate competitors' possible reactions to its own price changes. Price, in other words, is always a competitive factor. If price changes in a particular competitive environment are highly infrequent, then a company may get along without a formal policy, deciding each case as it arises. However, such competitive environments are rare.

In some industries, there are well-established patterns of price leadership and following. For instance, in selling basic industrial materials, such as steel and cement, one company is the price leader and is usually the first to raise or cut prices; other industry members simply follow—or, in some cases, fail to follow, as sometimes happens in the case of a price increase, thus causing the leader to reconsider and, perhaps, to cancel the announced increase. Similar patterns exist in marketing such consumer products as gasoline and bakery goods where, usually in each marketing area, one company serves as the price leader while other companies follow. Generally speaking, price leaders have rather large market shares, and price followers generally have smaller market shares. The leadership-following pattern, too, tends to be most prevalent in consumer marketing of products subject to price wars.

Even when ultimate consumers are not particularly price conscious with respect to buying his particular product, each manufacturer generally finds that the middleman handling it are extremely sensitive to price changes. In response to even very small price changes, up or down, they will consider switching suppliers. Thus, even the marketer of a consumer product competing on a non-price basis must be alert to impending price changes—the important policy question is whether to initiate price changes or simply to follow them. The answer will depend upon the marketer's relative market position and the image of leadership he desires to build.

PRODUCT-LINE PRICING

Most companies market not a single product but one or more product lines, each made up of several items. Pricing the individual members of a product line calls for certain policy decisions. To the degree that individual members of the line are competitive with or complementary to each other, their prices are related; thus, a pricing decision for one has a potential influence not only on that item's sales but on sales of other items in the line.[3]

"Competition" in the Product Line

Consider first the case where the items in a product line are such that they "compete" with each other—that is, a buyer who buys one member of the line usually does so to the exclusion of others. Each member

[3] For a thought-provoking article on this topic, see: A. R. Oxenfeldt, "Product Line Pricing," *Harvard Business Review*, July-August 1966, pp. 137-44.

of the line requires a pricing decision, and certain policy decisions must be made on the relationship of these different prices. One concerns the amount of "price space" that should exist between line members—too little may confuse buyers, and too much may leave "gaps" into which competitors can move and make sales. Finding the right amount of price space requires thorough knowledge and analysis of the market, buyers' motivations, competitors' offerings and prices, and the like.

Other important policy decisions concern the pricing of the end items in the line—i.e., the "top" and the "bottom" of the line. Generally, companies try to price the "in-between" members of the line so that they account for the majority of sales, using the bottom of the line as a traffic-builder and the top of the line as a prestige-builder. As the traffic-builder, the lowest-priced item ordinarily affects the line's total sales far more than the price of any other item in the line—thus, price changes on the low-end of the line frequently have a magnifying effect on sales of other line members. As the prestige-builder, a change in the price of the top of the line also tends to strongly influence sales or other line members. Price decisions made with respect to either or both ends of the line, in other words, may result in a trading-down or trading-up effect.[4]

Complementary Products

Next consider the pricing of complementary products, i.e., items closely associated in use: when a buyer buys one, he commits himself to buy another. Frequently, such related products are "using device and expenable" combinations—e.g., a safety razor and the blades it uses. For companies with such complementary products, the policy choice is between: (1) pricing the using device rather low, perhaps even less than variable costs, and pricing the expendable rather high, (2) pricing the using device rather high and the expendable "reasonably," and (3) pricing both independently. The first alternative is the most common choice, especially when both the using device and expendable are unique and have no close competitors. The second alternative is adopted in situations where the using device is unique but the expendable has competitive substitutes. The third alternative is used when neither the using device nor the expendable are unique and close competitive substitutes for both exist.

PRICE LINING

A marketer using a price lining policy confines his offerings within a particular product category to a limited number of prices, which remain stable over long periods. A men's wear retailer, for example, who prices his men's

[4] See Chapter 11 for a discussion of trading down and trading up.

ties at only three different prices—$3.50, $5.00, and $7.50—is using price lining. Manufacturers and wholesalers rarely use price lining, but many retailers, especially those selling fashion items, adopt the policy.

Price lining has attractions both for the consumer and the retailer. The consumer's buying decisions are simplified, since the number of different prices from which he must make a selection is limited. The retailer finds the policy attractive because it helps him plan his buying. In buying men's suits, for instance, he can go into the market seeking suits to retail at $39.95, $49.95, or $59.95. However, during periods of rising wholesale prices and increasing expenses, it is often difficult to replenish stocks at costs low enough to permit retailing at established price lines—in such cases, the price-lining retailer must either "trade-down" his stock (i.e., by buying lower-quality items) or adjust his price lines upward.

RESALE PRICE MAINTENANCE

Some manufacturers wish to control the resale prices at which middlemen sell their products. Such "resale price maintenance" may be either informal or formal. Informal resale price maintenance takes the form of suggesting resale prices to middlemen—perhaps by printing the price on the package or through suggestions made by the manufacturer's salesmen. Formal resale price maintenance is effected by using the provisions of various states' so-called "fair trade" laws.[5]

Manufacturers adopt resale price maintenance policies for various reasons. One may desire to establish a customary resale price for his product, a price consumers can become familiar with and expect to pay; without some control, resale prices among different retailers may vary considerably. Another may want to prevent his products from being used as price leaders, so he controls resale prices to protect his dealers from the competition of price-cutters. For example, many manufacturers of men's sportswear, even though they advertise their products aggressively, depend on retailer cooperation to persuade the consumer to buy; they cannot presell their products 100 percent when the consumer must evaluate color, fashion, styling, and fit at the time of purchase. Dealer cooperation is essential and more likely to be forthcoming if the manufacturer protects his dealers from price-cutters. Another manufacturer may maintain resale prices because he believes that the prices of his products bear on consumers' evaluations of their quality. Most manufacturers of sterling silverware, for instance, use resale price maintenance because they think consumers judge the quality of their products at least partially in terms of price.

[5] See Chapter 23 for a discussion of the state fair trade, or resale price maintenance, laws.

Most manufacturers, however, do not use resale price maintenance. Many are not bothered by retail price differentials on their products, and actually welcome any pricing action by retailers that increases the sale of their products. Furthermore, a price maintenance policy is difficult to administer and enforce, particularly when marketing channels are long and/or the product is mass-distributed. In addition, in states that do not have fair trade laws, the manufacturer can only suggest, not enforce, resale prices.

USE OF PRICING AS A PROMOTIONAL DEVICE

Some companies have formal policies concerning the extent to which pricing will be used as a promotional device. Many follow a policy of temporarily reducing prices for promotional purposes under certain conditions, such as in introducing a new product, or to counter the effects of competitors' increases in promotional activity. Others, as a policy matter, refrain from such temporary price reductions, relying instead upon increased advertising and other promotion.

CONCLUSION

Price policies make up the framework within which pricing decisions are made. They should be consistent with, and contribute to, the achievement of pricing objectives. Accordingly, price policies are formulated on such matters as: company prices relative to the competition, relationships of prices to costs, uniformity of prices to different buyers, use of price differentials, price changes, resale price maintenance, and the use of pricing as a promotional device.

QUESTIONS AND PROBLEMS

1. Pricing above the competition is less likely to be successful with products sold in self-service than in full-service stores. Why?
2. Why do you suppose so many marketers rely primarily on cost rather than market factors as the basis for setting prices on their products?
3. A certain company has a contribution pricing policy. Under what circumstances should it accept private-brand orders?
4. Do you agree or disagree with each of the following statements. State your reasoning in each instance.

    a. A company using contribution pricing also is using a variable pricing policy.

    b. Automobile dealers find it hard to adhere to a one-price policy because prospective buyers have trade-ins and play one dealer off against another.

    c. In implementing a "meeting competition" pricing policy, a company must meet the prices of all its competitors.

    d. No product should ever be sold at a price below full cost.

5. Distinguish between the following:
    a. Quantity discounts
    b. Trade discounts
    c. Cash discounts
    d. Promotional discounts
    e. Seasonal discounts.

6. "It is clearly unethical, if not illegal, for a manufacturer to sell his products at lower prices to wholesalers than to retailers who buy similar quantities." Do you agree? Explain.

7. Would you agree that the competitively strongest companies are more likely to prefer a one-price policy, and the weakest prefer to negotiate prices? Explain.

8. "An F.O.B. pricing policy is a great deal more fair to buyers than any delivered-pricing policy can possibly be." Discuss.

9. Prepare a list of several products that might be sold under:
    a. F.O.B. pricing
    b. delivered pricing.

10. Distinguish between postage-stamp pricing and zone pricing.

11. Under what conditions might a marketer use a freight absorption policy?

12. What reasons do marketers have for using guaranty-against-price-decline policies?

13. Give some examples of items in a product line that "compete" with each other. What pricing problems do such items present?

14. Would you agree that resale price maintenance is clearly to the disadvantage of the consumer? Explain.

21

PRICING
STRATEGIES AND PROCEDURES

A company seeks to attain its pricing objectives through both pricing policies and pricing strategies. Pricing policies provide the general set of rules for making pricing decisions. Pricing strategies are adaptations of pricing policies—individualized tailorings of pricing decisions to fit particular competitive situations encountered by specific products. In this chapter, analysis focuses first on the selection of pricing strategies under different kinds of competitive conditions and then on the main procedures used for determining prices.

PRICING STRATEGIES

Joel Dean identifies three kinds of competitive situations met by particular products. These situations are those where the product has: (1) lasting distinctiveness, (2) perishable distinctiveness, or (3) little distinctiveness.[1]

[1] J. Dean, *Managerial Economics* (Englewood Cliffs, N.J.: Prentice-Hall, Inc., 1951), p. 402.

"Distinctiveness" means the degree to which a product can be sold above or below competitors' prices without disrupting these competitors' prices or their sales.

A product's distinctiveness varies with the stage of the product life cycle. Very few products have lasting distinctiveness—except perhaps for such things as diamonds and ermine furs in certain market segments— if "lasting" means more than ten years, and "distinctiveness" means there are no acceptable substitutes.[2] Most products in the pioneering stage have perishable distinctiveness, which gradually diminishes in the market growth and market maturity stages. This happens as competitors introduce their own versions, which become progressively closer approximations of the in- novator's product. Products of perishable distinctiveness ultimately become products of little distinctiveness sometime during the market maturity stage and continue as such during their market decline. Appropriate pricing strategy, therefore, also varies with the stage of the product life cycle.

Pricing Strategy During Market Pioneering

The appropriate pricing strategy for a new product depends both upon how distinctive it is and how long management expects this dis- tinctiveness to last. The more distinctive a new product is, the more free- dom its marketer has in its pricing. If it is highly distinctive, he can choose from a wide range of possible profitable prices. If it possesses little or no distinctiveness, then the range of possible profitable prices is restricted— the highest being equal to the price of competitors and the most likely being a price lower than that asked by competitors. Similarly, the longer the period during which management expects a product's distinctiveness to last, the wider the range of possible profitable prices.

PRICING A PRODUCT OF LASTING DISTINCTIVENESS   This type of competitive situation, as mentioned earlier, is exceedingly rare. But when it occurs, the marketer essentially enjoys the pricing freedom of a monopolist. Exhibit 21-1 shows the monopoly pricing model. According to this model, the marketer of a product of lasting distinctiveness (with a demand curve D) should price it at P and sell it in a quantity Q, thus equating marginal costs (MC) and marginal revenue (MR). Profits, in other words, are maximized at price P and volume Q. The shaded area in Exhibit 21-1, the lower-right-hand corner of which is cut by the average total costs curve (ATC), represents the total amount of profit at Price P and Volume Q.

However, the marketer of a product of lasting distinctiveness is

[2] *Ibid.*, p. 403.

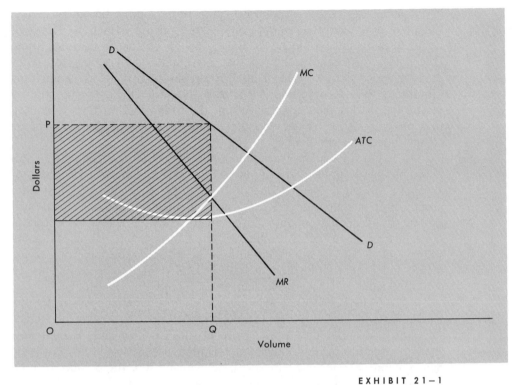

EXHIBIT 21-1

Pricing a Product of Lasting Distinctiveness to Maximize Profits
(Monopoly Pricing)

not likely to use price P in an attempt to maximize his profits. Other factors usually cause him to choose some price lower than P: possible adverse public reactions to monopoly pricing, the threat of governmental intervention, and the possibility of weakening the company's bargaining position with organized labor. Even when a monopolist starts out with a profit-maximizing price (P), sooner or later he is almost certain to encounter outside pressures that force him to lower it.[3]

PRICING A PRODUCT OF PERISHABLE DISTINCTIVENESS   Most new products, however distinctive they are at first, have only a limited period free from competition. The length of this period is determined by such factors as the relative uniqueness of the product innovation, its patentability, the rate at which market acceptance is gained, and the product

---

[3] For an intriguing account of the ups and downs of the de Beers Consolidated diamond monopoly in this respect, see: E. A. G. Robinson, *Monopoly* (Cambridge, England: Cambridge University Press, 1961 printing) pp. 49-53.

development capabilities of potential competitors. During the initial period, the innovating marketer enjoys considerable pricing discretion. However, he rarely can count on more than three years of freedom from competition. One study, for example, showed that new brands of "grocery-store-type" products enjoyed an average of only twenty-six months before competitors introduced their own versions.[4] For most products, then, pricing strategy during the market pioneering stage must be formulated on the assumption that product distinctiveness will deteriorate in a relatively short time as competitors enter the market.

For the market introduction of a product of perishable distinctiveness, appropriate pricing strategy involves a choice between a *skimming* or a *penetration* price. Neither one of these prices is intended to maximize profits. Both are directed toward achieving other pricing objectives, such as quickly recouping product development costs or achieving a certain target market share before competitors enter the market. A price-skimming strategy involves using a high initial price in order to skim the cream of demand, and a penetration pricing strategy uses a low introductory price to stimulate rapid and widespread market acceptance for the product.[5]

Whether to use a skimming price or a penetration price for the market introduction of a new product depends upon a number of factors. Of particular importance is the price elasticity of demand. Exhibit 21-2 shows two contrasting demand curves, DD for a new product with an inelastic demand and $D'D'$ for one with an elastic demand. For the product with an inelastic demand, the marketer's best pricing strategy is to choose a skimming price (such as P_1) and plan on selling a volume of Q_1. For the product with an elastic demand, the best pricing strategy is to use a penetration price (such as P_3) and plan on selling a volume of Q_3. Price P_2 represents an intermediate position in both cases—it is probably too low a price for the product with an inelastic demand and too high for that with the elastic demand. At price P_2, a volume of Q_2 would be sold in both cases, and sales revenues would be lower than if price-skimming had been used for the product with the inelastic demand and penetration pricing had been used for that with the elastic demand.

Five factors make price-skimming an attractive strategy for many marketers. First, if the product is highly distinctive, it tends to have a more price-inelastic demand at first than it will have later on; advertising and pure salesmanship can have considerably more influence on sales than price at first. Second, a high introductory price effectively divides the market into segments differing in their responsiveness to price. The skimming price taps the market segment that is relatively insensitive to price, later price reductions can reach more price-conscious market segments. Third, if an

---

[4] *The Nielsen Researcher*, 1968 (Vol. 26, No. 1), p. 11.

[5] This discussion of skimming and penetration pricing strategies is drawn largely from J. Dean, *How to Price a New Product* (Washington, D.C.: Small Business Administration) Management Aids for Small Manufacturers, No. 62, April 1955.

introductory price is too high, it is easy to reduce, but if it is too low, it is difficult and awkward to raise. Fourth, a high introductory price often generates greater sales and profits than a low introductory price; thus, price-skimming enables the marketer to get funds to use later in expanding sales to other market segments. Finally, price-skimming provides the innovating marketer with an opportunity to recoup his product development expenses before competitors, whose product development expenses are lower, enter the market.

However, under certain conditions penetration pricing is the more appropriate strategy. There are four such conditions, the presence of any of which should cause penetration pricing to be given serious consideration: (1) when a high degree of price elasticity exists, even in the early stages of introduction; (2) when it is possible to realize substantial economies in manufacturing and marketing through operating at a high output level (such economies, of course, result in lower average total costs); (3) when strong competition is expected, very soon after market introduction; and (4) when there is little or no "elite" market for the product, i.e., a market segment

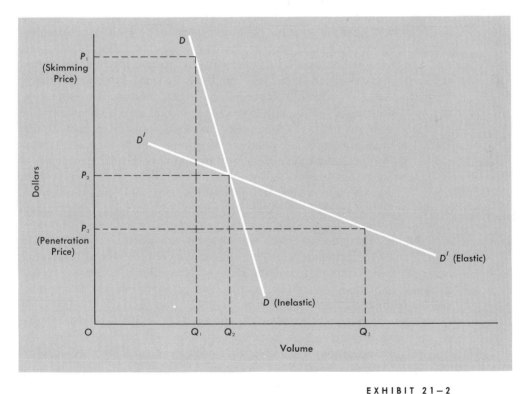

EXHIBIT 21—2

Pricing Products of Perishable Distinctiveness—
Skimming vs. Penetration Strategies

made up of buyers who are relatively insensitive to price and who will probably buy regardless of price.

Probably the single most important consideration in the choice between skimming and penetration pricing is the relative ease and speed with which competitors can launch their own versions. For revolutionary new products, which have large potential markets, penetration pricing is usually the appropriate strategy. Existence of such markets is almost certain to attract numerous large competitors soon after introduction of the innovation. Penetration pricing, therefore, helps in raising entry barriers to prospective competitors by making the market appear less profitable than if price-skimming were used. If it is expected that competitors will require considerable time and will meet substantial difficulties in coming up with their own versions, then price-skimming is appropriate strategy.

Pricing Strategy During Market Growth

During the market growth stage of the product life cycle, pricing strategy for a product of perishable distinctiveness must take direct account of competitors' pricing patterns. The innovator, if he used price-skimming during the pioneering stage, may switch to penetration pricing when significant competition first appears or, alternatively, reduce his price in several successive steps as the market broadens. If he has used penetration pricing from the start, he is likely to continue with that strategy. In either case, the innovator's main pricing objective during market growth is usually that of retaining a particular market share. Likewise, competitors new to the market tend to price with the objective of gaining and holding some target market share. Each marketer's choice of an appropriate pricing strategy, in other words, becomes increasingly dependent upon those of his competitors.

However, non-price competition is also significant during the market growth stage. Different competitors seek to gain advantages through promotion, improving or changing the product, extending its distribution, and the like. Consequently, each considers the non-price components of its own over-all marketing strategy as well as competitor's over-all marketing strategies in determining its pricing strategy. Nevertheless, as market growth proceeds, each competitor finds that his own pricing strategy depends more and more upon those of competitors.

An oligopolistic pricing situation is likely to develop either during a late phase of market growth or an early phase of market maturity. An oligopoly, by definition, is a market that has such a small number of sellers that each has a significant effect on the market price. Each, therefore, must take into account the likely effect that his changes in price will have on competitors.

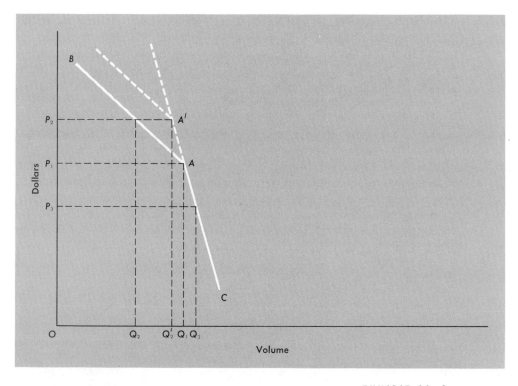

EXHIBIT 21-3

Pricing During Market Growth (Oligopoly Pricing and the Kinky Demand Curve)

Exhibit 21-3 illustrates the pricing situation confronting the oligopolist. The demand curve BAC is "kinky," with segment BA relatively elastic and segment AC relatively inelastic. If the industry's prices are fairly stable, the individual manufacturer may expect to sell a volume Q_1 at price P_1. If he decides to raise his price to P_2, he will sell less—Q_2 if his competitors do not follow his price increase and Q'_2 if they do (in the latter case, the kink would have shifted to A'). In other words, if the competitors do not raise their prices at all, or raise them to something less than P_2, the manufacturer's sales will be off more sharply than if all had matched the price increase.

What will happen if the manufacturer cuts his price? If, for example, he cuts it to P_3, he cannot expect to sell more than a volume of Q_3. Competitors, he must assume, will match any price cut since, if they do not, they will lose market share. In most cases, too, he can assume that they will not further undercut his reduced price, because that might precipitate a price war. The demand segment AC is quite inelastic, and all firms should anticipate lower total dollar revenues. Therefore, under oligopolistic competitive conditions, any price change, up or down, is likely to result in lower total dollar sales. Since all industry members are aware of this, all tend to refrain from making price changes and the price stabilizes.

Pricing Strategy During Market Maturity

During market maturity a product of perishable distinctiveness begins to lose its distinctiveness. Brands become more and more alike, and there is increasing substitution among brands. In the contest to maintain market shares, leading brands cannot command as large a price premium as before. As production methods stabilize and as individual manufacturers develop excess production capacity, private-label competitors enter and secure important market shares. And, in the case of durables, the ratio of replacement sales (to present users) to original equipment sales (to new users) rises.[6]

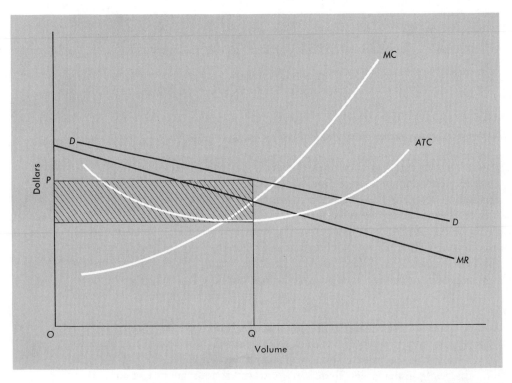

EXHIBIT 21—4

Pricing During Market Maturity under Conditions of Monopolistic Competition

[6] J. Dean, *Managerial Economics*, p. 425.

The net effect of these developments on pricing strategy depends mainly on the ease of entry into the market and on the number of competitors. If market entry is comparatively difficult and the number of competitors fairly small, then an oligopolistic pricing situation may develop (if it has not done so during market growth). If entry is relatively easy and the number of competitors quite large, then "monopolistic competition" prevails and governs individual firms' pricing strategies.

Exhibit 21-4 illustrates the pricing situation under monopolistic competition. The demand curve (DD) indicates the various quantities each firm can sell at various prices. Each competitor attempts to maximize profits by setting his price at the point where marginal revenue (MR) and marginal costs (MC) are equated. At this price (P), he sells a volume of Q and secures the profit shown by the shaded area. (ATC denotes average total costs.)

Notice that the demand curve in Exhibit 21-4 is highly price elastic. This is typical of products in the market maturity stage, since many close substitutes exist for each competitor's brand. Furthermore, the ease of entry into the market forces each firm to struggle continuously to maintain its market share.

Under monopolistic competition, then, the range of different sellers' prices narrows. Some manage to obtain higher-than-average prices, providing their brands retain some distinctiveness. But the amount of each seller's price premium cannot exceed the average price by much or the seller loses market share, as his "fringe" buyers switch to lower-priced substitutes. If a seller's brand loses nearly all of its distinctiveness and becomes indistinguishable from many competing brands, he may have to price below the market's average.

More flexibility in pricing strategy, however, is possible under monopolistic competition than under oligopolistic competition. The number of competitors is large, and a price change by any one tends to influence only slightly each of the others. For example, if one competitor cuts the price, he may increase his sales, while each of his competitors loses only a small amount of business. Therefore, unlike what happens under oligopolistic competition, the chances are against a price cut's inviting instant retaliation by competitors. Nevertheless, a competitor contemplating a price cut should consider the possibility that too drastic a reduction may foment a "price war," with the impact spreading from one company to another throughout the entire industry.

Pricing Strategy During Market Decline

A product in the market decline stage is of little or no distinctiveness. A marketer keeps such a product in its line offering for any number of reasons: it may be needed to "round out" the line, there may be a "hard core" market that continues to insist on buying it, it may still be profitable, etc. Usually such products are priced "competitively" to assure a sales volume large enough to be profitable. But if the product has a sizable "hard core" market, the marketer may obtain a slight premium price, while paring promotional costs to the bone, and thus realize considerable profit through pursuing a "run-out" strategy.[7]

PRICING PROCEDURES

Procedures used for setting specific prices vary under different competitive conditions. At one extreme, in certain situations, as mentioned in Chapter 19, pricing is an uncontrollable, and forces outside the decision-maker's control determine prices. Basically, such "market prices" are determined by the relationship between available supply and market demand. For some commodities, organized commodity exchanges exist and provide the mechanisms which determine market prices. This is true, for example, of cotton, coffee beans, raw sugar, wool, potatoes, corn, wheat, oats, soybeans, eggs, copper, and silver. For other commodities, such as tobacco and most livestock, prices are arrived at through auctions, where prospective buyers make "bids" and prospective sellers decide whether or not to accept them. For other farm commodities, such as many fruits and vegetables, no formal price-making mechanism exists and buyers and sellers arrive at prices through individual negotiations. Sellers of most commodities, in other words, have very little power in deciding the prices of their outputs: market prices are determined by interactions of the forces of supply and demand and vary considerably from one day to the next, even from one sale to another.

At the other extreme, where a monopoly exists, such as in the case of diamonds, pricing is nearly 100 percent a controllable. Generally, the monopolist would like to set his price to maximize profits by "charging what the traffic will bear," but, in most instances, he is prevented from obtaining a pure monopoly-type price by external pressures. Nevertheless, a monopolist's price is the purest example of an administered price—one set by management and held stable over a long period.

Under oligopolistic or monopolistic competition management has only limited freedom to use administered pricing, specific prices are determined competitively, and individual marketers anticipate their competitors' possible reactions in setting prices and in making price changes. This is most apparent in an oligopolistic situation, where price leadership often

---

[7] A run-out strategy involves cutting back all support costs on a product to that minimum level that will optimize the product's profitability over its limited foreseeable life. See: W. J. Talley, Jr., *The Profitable Product* (Englewood Cliffs, N.J.: Prentice-Hall, Inc., 1965), p. 8, footnote 2.

exists. In situations involving monopolistic competition, price leadership is less prevalent but all competitors keep their prices pretty much in line with the industry average.

One type of situation in which management may or may not have considerable freedom in setting the price is that involving competitive bidding. If the product subject to competitive bidding is of little or no distinctiveness, then, of course, the seller must submit a price that is not only close to but under those of competitors if he wants to secure the business. However, if the product is highly unique, as with many building or construction projects, a marketer enjoys considerable discretion in setting his "asking price."

Finally, there are numerous situations in which management has considerable freedom in setting specific prices. Most involve pricing products of perishable distinctiveness in the early stages of their life cycles. In these situations the marketer not only has the initiative in setting a specific "offering price" but is free to use any of several different price-determination procedures.

Competitive Bidding

Under competitive bidding procedure, a buyer asks two or more competing suppliers to submit bids on a proposed purchase or contract and, after receipt of the bids, awards the business to the bidder offering the best proposal. A proposal may be selected as best for a number of reasons—e.g., price, delivery dates, reputation for quality—depending on what is most important to the buyer. Competitive bidding is most prevalent in the selling of industrial goods and is used most frequently on expensive installations and special-order goods, such as manufactured parts or subassemblies for the buyer's finished product. Special-order goods have a wider-than-normal potential price variation because the suppliers who are asked to quote a price have no opportunity to compare with the prices of competitors, as they can with standard products sold on the open market. For this reason, buyers may find it to their advantage to ask for competitive bids. In the case of expensive installations, the individual sale is important enough that the seller may be willing to shade his price to obtain the order. Competitive bidding provides the machinery to achieve price bargaining. In addition, government purchasing agents at all levels of government are ordinarily required to request competitive bids on most of their purchases.

In some industries, competitive bidding is the general rule, and individual manufacturers have virtually no choice but to participate. But in other industries, only a part of the volume is sold on this basis, and each manufacturer must decide whether it is to his advantage to participate. For example, a typewriter manufacturer who sells to industry on a uniform price basis must participate in competitive bidding if he decides to seek orders from governmental agencies. Since many sellers believe that competitive bidding reduces competition to almost entirely a price basis, they may prefer to avoid this kind of business, unless the share of the total market involved is too large to ignore.

Price tends to have a greater influence on the buying decision under competitive bidding than under other pricing methods, but other factors, such as product differentiation, promotional activities, and service are also important. Contracts are frequently awarded to other than the lowest bidder because of one or more of these factors. An effective salesman can often remove competition from government bids by persuading the purchasing agent of the value of a differentiating characteristic of his product, so that this characteristic is included in the written specifications. In effect, this eliminates competitive products from consideration. In many instances, a purchasing agent may pass over the lowest bids to buy from a supplier whose product and servicing have been demonstrated to be superior. Also, in non-governmental bidding a purchaser sometimes allows a favored supplier to meet the lowest bid of a competitor.

When all other factors are equal, awards are made on the basis of price. For the seller, the difficulty in these situations is in selecting the price that will maximize potential profit. Too low a price eliminates profit or reduces it to an unacceptable level, and too high a price decreases the probability of receiving the award. Miller and Starr suggest a competitive-bidding model for determining the optimum bid.[8] Using maximum immediate profit as the goal, the following formula emerges:

$$\text{Expected profit} = p\,(x - c)$$

In this formula, p = probability of receiving the award, x = amount of the bid, and c = cost of fulfilling obligations under the contract. The difficulty in using this model lies in the determination of the probability of award. To prepare a table of probabilities, it is necessary to analyze the past actions of competitive bidders on other bids. The collection of the data necessary for use of this model is a big task, but if the model is used, it reduces the uncertainty in determining the best price at which to submit a bid.

Formula Pricing From Cost Bases

Surveys of business practice show that the most common price-determination procedure involves making a cost estimate and adding a margin of some kind to cover marketing expenses and for profit—this is

[8] See: D. W. Miller and M. K. Starr, *Executive Decisions and Operations Research* (Englewood Cliffs, N.J.: Prentice-Hall, Inc., 1960), pp. 223-38 for a complete description of this model.

known as cost-plus pricing.[9] A manufacturer might determine the price for a new product simply by estimating the product's per unit total costs and, then, adding a certain percentage to provide a gross margin (i.e., expenses + net profit). With per unit total costs of $5.00 and a 40 percent "add-on" markup, for instance, a product's price would be set at $7.00 (i.e., $5.00 + $2.00). However, the general practice is to apply different markups to each cost component as illustrated below:

	Product A	Product B
Labor Cost/Unit	$ 5.00	$ 2.00
Materials Cost/Unit	1.00	4.00
Factory Overhead @ 150% of Labor	7.50	3.00
Total Cost	$13.50	$ 9.00
Markups:		
on labor (50% of cost)	2.50	1.00
on materials (20% of cost)	.20	.80
on factory overhead (10% of cost)	.75	.30
Total Markup	3.45	2.10
Price = (Cost + Markup)	$16.95	$11.10

Shown below are examples of other cost-plus pricing formulas:

(1) Price =   (Direct Labor × 5) + (Materials Costs × 2)
(2) Price = 2 (Direct Labor + Materials + Factory Overhead at 165% of Direct Labor)
(3) Price = 2 (Direct Labor + Materials Cost + Factory Overhead at 150% of Direct Labor + 10% of Total to cover Research and Development Costs.

Cost-plus pricing, then, often involves applying certain rules of thumb to arrive at a price. The exact costs considered and the multipliers (or percentages) applied vary with the company and with management's knowledge and perception of the behavior of the various costs incurred. Each company, through experience and "trial and error," derives its own rules of thumb for cost-plus pricing.

Companies using cost-plus pricing should regard the formula-determined price as only a starting point. Generally, except in rare instances, the formula-determined price needs modifying to adjust for the competitive situation. Perhaps the greatest limitation of cost-plus pricing, in other words, lies in the fact that no consideration is given to competitors' prices and possible reactions. Formula pricing based on costs too often fails also to recognize that cost data are usually mere approximations, often reflecting historical experience rather than future expectations. However, especially when

[9] J. Dean, *Managerial Economics*, pp. 444-45, and T. A. Staudt and D. A. Taylor, *A Managerial Introduction to Marketing* (Englewood Cliffs, N.J.: Prentice-Hall, Inc., 1965), p. 470.

the product is radically-new and different, cost-plus pricing provides a way to arrive at a price for use during market pioneering (the life cycle stage during which actual competition is not yet present but the probable entry of competition is a major consideration).

Markup Pricing by Middlemen

Markup pricing is the middleman's counterpart to the manufacturer's cost-plus pricing. Typically, the individual retailer or wholesaler considers the cost of an item as the base and adds his markup (an amount sufficient to cover both estimated expenses and desired profit) in order to arrive at the offering price. Different percentage markups are applied to different items depending upon, among other things, the rate of stock-turn, competition, trade custom, and the manufacturer's suggested resale prices. Each middleman, however, attempts to secure the "average markup" which he regards as necessary to cover both his estimated expenses and desired profit. Thus, the markups on some items are "above average," others "average," and still others "below average." The average markup percentage itself is largely determined through experience by each middleman. If a book dealer, for example, buys some new books at $7.50 each, he may apply a 25 percent markup on the selling price, and price them at $10.00 each. But he may regard $10.00 as a "psychologically bad" price, in which case the books may be priced at $9.95 or $9.98. Markup pricing is discussed in considerably more detail in the Appendix.

Manufacturers exert important influences on the prices actually asked by middlemen. In planning the pricing of his product, for example, the manufacturer usually considers both his middlemen's customary markups and the resulting resale prices. Thus, if a particular manufacturer believes his product should retail at $5.00 and if the customary retail markup on this type of product is 30 percent on the retail price, then he may set the price to retailers at $3.50. If the same manufacturer uses wholesalers to reach retailers and they customarily apply a 10 percent markup, the price to wholesalers may be set at $3.15. Manufacturers, in other words, may concern themselves with the entire price structure for the product rather than solely with their own prices. In such cases, the middlemen affected are not really using cost-plus pricing but pricing set largely by market forces (as viewed and evaluated by the suppliers involved).

Pricing Through Combined Break-Even Analysis and Demand Estimation

In Chapter 19 we mentioned that in using break-even analysis for pricing decision-making, it is not enough to compute only the different break-even points. Management must also consider changes in sales volume

TABLE 21–1

Computation of Break-Even Points at Four Different Prices

(1) Price/Unit	(2) Variable Costs/Unit	(3) Contribution/Unit (1) − (2)	(4) Total Fixed Costs	(5) Break-Even Point (4) ÷ (3)
$ 75	$50	$ 25	$20,000	800 Units
100	50	50	20,000	400 "
130	50	80	20,000	250 "
150	50	100	20,000	200 "

that may occur at alternative prices, in order to determine their relative profitability. Profits, in other words, are determined through the interactions of three variables—prices, sales volumes, and costs. Therefore, in making practical use of break-even analysis, it is necessary to estimate the size of market demand at the different selling prices used in the several break-even computations.

To illustrate, assume the data shown in Table 21-1. This manu-

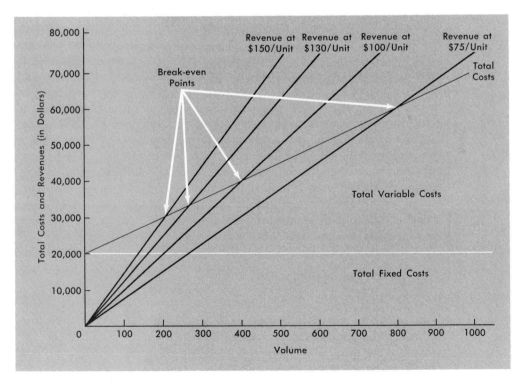

EXHIBIT 21–5

Break-Even Points at Four Different Selling Prices

TABLE 21–2

Market Demand, Total Revenues, Total Costs, and
Total Profits at Four Different Prices

(1) Price per Unit	(2) Market Demand in Units	(3) Total Revenue (1) × (2)	(4) Total Costs [a]	(5) Total Profits (3) − (4)
$ 75	750	$56,250	$57,500	$ −1,250
100	600	60,000	50,000	10,000
130	440	57,200	42,000	15,200
150	375	56,250	38,750	17,500

[a] Computed from data in Table 21-1. Total Costs = Total Fixed Costs + (Var. Cost/Unit × Market Demand in Units).

facturer has variable costs per unit of $50, total fixed costs of $20,000, and is considering four different possible selling prices: $75, $100, $130, and $150. At each price, the contribution per unit is shown in column (3), and the break-even point in column (5). The same data are shown graphically in Exhibit 21-5. To complete his analysis, this manufacturer requires data of

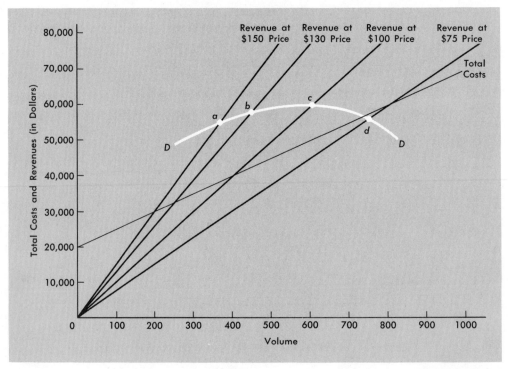

EXHIBIT 21–6

Relationships Among Total Revenues, Total Costs, and Break-Even Points the sort shown in Table 21-2. Specifically, he has to secure estimates of the quantity that can be sold at each price, calculate the total revenues and total costs at those quantities and, then, determine the total profits at each price.

Exhibit 21-6 provides a graphic illustration of this pricing procedure. The total cost curves and the four revenue curves are identical to those shown on the break-even chart in Exhibit 21-5. Management's estimates of the quantities that will be sold at each proposed price are indicated by points a, b, c, and d. When these points are connected, the resulting curve (DD) represents total demand. Note particularly that this demand curve indicates *total revenues* rather than *average revenues* as in the traditional demand curve. If management has the objective of maximizing profits, it will now choose the price at which the vertical distance between the total revenue curve (DD) and the total costs curve is greatest.[10] In this example, this is at the $150 selling price, where total revenues are $56,250 and total costs are $38,750, yielding total profits (i.e., vertical distance) of $17,500.

"Working Back From the Market"

Clearly, the ideal way to determine prices is to start with the market and work back to the company. Thus, management would determine the quantities buyers will buy at alternative prices, calculate the break-even points at each price, and select the price that yields the maximum sales volume above its associated break-even point (as illustrated by the $150 price in Exhibit 21-6). However, the "catch" is in "determining the quantities buyers will buy at alternative prices," i.e., in ascertaining the shape and nature of the "demand curve." Nevertheless, despite the difficulties involved, techniques exist for approximating demand schedules.

Nearly all modern manufacturing companies operate under conditions of monopolistic competition. The presence of product differentiation (i.e., distinctiveness) makes it possible for management to exert some control over demand, even though competition still exists among different brands and different products. In these circumstances, sales volume is most affected by four factors beside the forces of demand and supply (which operate under pure competition). These are: magnitude of price, amount and type of product differentiation, and effectiveness of promotion. By taking these factors into account, the marketing manager should try to estimate demand for the product at different prices. He should seek to determine the specific price that yields the maximum volume above the break-even point (i.e., the profit-maximizing price). In theory, it seems

[10] See: E. R. Hawkins, "Price Policies and Theory," *Journal of Marketing*, January 1954, p. 234.

simple to select the optimum price in this way; in practice, it is extremely difficult to estimate demand at various prices.

In its attempt to estimate demand, there are two main approaches available to management. The first is to offer the product at various prices until the shape and nature of the demand curve is approximated. Although these trial-and-error data may not actually be put in the form of a demand curve, management uses this "experience in the market" to arrive at a specific price, hopefully near the optimum. The second approach is to use market tests to estimate demand at different prices. The product is offered systematically at different prices in different markets (or at different prices at different times in the same markets) under controlled conditions. Analysis of test results should produce a usable demand schedule. In contrast to the trial-and-error method, which provides only a rough approximation of the demand curve, the market testing method, because it employs formalized experimentation techniques, should result in a more reliable representation of the demand curve.

CONCLUSION

Pricing strategies vary with the kind of competitive situation met by particular products. Choice of pricing strategy is most critical when the product is one of perishable distinctiveness—i.e., for those having a life cycle. During market pioneering, management may skim the market at a high price or penetrate it at a low price. During market growth, management must take direct account of competitors' pricing behavior in formulating pricing strategy; thus, price-skimming generally becomes inappropriate and each competitor tends to price in order to gain or retain some target market share. During market maturity, the product begins losing its distinctiveness, and competition intensifies; the range of competitors' prices narrows and moves toward stability. During market decline, most companies "price competitively," but a few with sizable "hard core" markets obtain a slight premium, curtail promotional costs, and pursue "run-out" strategies. Thus, at each stage of the product's life cycle, pricing strategies shift with changes in the competitive situation.

Similarly, procedures for setting specific prices vary with competitive conditions. At one extreme—in the case of pure "commodities"—pricing is an uncontrollable, market prices being determined by the forces of supply and demand. At the other extreme, where monopolies exist, pricing is almost entirely a controllable, purely "administered prices being set and held stable by management." In between these two extremes—as under oligopolistic or monopolistic competition—in setting prices and in making price changes, individual companies, by and large, anticipate and take into account their competitors' probable reactions. Basically, however, in the vast bulk of American companies, prices are determined administratively rather than through market forces.

Specific price-determination procedures vary considerably. In some few situations, as under competitive bidding, the buyer actually determines the seller's price. More usually, the seller sets an "offering price," and potential buyers decide whether to accept or reject it. Probably the most widely-used price-determination procedures are the manufacturer's cost-plus pricing and the middleman's markup pricing. However, variations of break-even analysis combined with demand estimation are seeing increasing use. The ideal price-determination procedure, of course, is to start with what the market will pay for different quantities and work back to the costs of producing and marketing those quantities, finally setting the price at the point of greatest spread between total sales revenues and total costs. Techniques for approximating the shape and nature of demand curves, however, are still rather crude; thus, "working back from the market" remains more an ideal, than a practical, method of price determination.

QUESTIONS AND PROBLEMS

1. How does a pricing strategy differ from a pricing policy?

2. Discuss the effect of the kind of "distinctiveness" possessed by a product on its pricing.

3. How does pricing a product of lasting distinctiveness differ from pricing one of perishable distinctiveness?

4. For each of the following products, should the marketer use a skimming price or a penetration price. State your reasoning in each case.

   a. A new "cola" drink with an alcoholic content comparable to that of beer

   b. An "original" model of women's dress made by a "prestige" manufacturer

   c. A new insecticide developed to kill "selectively" only harmful insects and not to affect such harmless insects as ladybugs and bees

   d. A milk substitute for people allergic to milk

   e. A light bulb that lasts twice as long as ordinary bulbs

   f. A new deodorant for industrial use that effectively curbs noxious fumes that pollute the air

   g. An electric tractor for use in home gardening, snow removal, etc.

5. Would you agree or disagree with the following statements? Why?

   a. A price-skimming strategy is usually directed toward maximizing profits.

b. If a product has an inelastic demand, then usually a penetration price is the best choice during its market pioneering stage.

c. One way to discourage new competitors from entering a market is to use a penetration price.

6. During which stage(s) of the product life cycle is an oligopolistic pricing situation likely to develop? Why?

7. How does pricing under an oligopolistic situation differ from that encountered under monopolistic competition?

8. Explain what is meant by a "run-out" strategy. Under what circumstances is such a strategy appropriate?

9. For each of the following items, should pricing be regarded as generally controllable or uncontrollable from the seller's standpoint? Support your reasoning in each instance.

a. fresh eggs
b. tropical fruits, such as fresh pineapples
c. precious stones, such as emeralds and rubies
d. a new super-size jet transport plane
e. an office building constructed according to rigid architect's specifications
f. a new portable refrigerator-and-stove combination for trailer homes
g. a new cigarette with an extremely low tar and nicotine content
h. canned pork and beans
i. a new powered toy vehicle featuring a device for remote control.

10. "Purchasers who insist on buying on the basis of competitive bids often eliminate their best sources of supply because these sellers won't be bothered with bidding." Is this probably true? Why or why not?

11. Under what conditions might a marketer deliberately avoid submitting a competitive bid to a government agency required to buy on this basis?

12. Why should cost-plus pricing be regarded as only a starting point in price determination?

13. "Strictly speaking, markup pricing by middlemen is not always comparable to cost-plus pricing by manufacturers." Agree or disagree? Why?

14. Referring to Table 21-1 and Exhibit 21-5, determine the break-even points at prices of $90, $120, and $160. Assume that variable costs/unit remain at $50 and total fixed costs stay at $20,000.

15. Referring to Table 21-1 and Exhibit 21-5, determine the break-even point at a price of $60 if variable costs per unit drop to $45 and total fixed costs stay at $20,000.

16.   Why does the shape of a demand curve indicating total revenues differ from that of one showing average revenues?

17.   Referring to Table 21-2 and Exhibit 21-6, calculate a demand curve showing average revenues and sketch it in on Exhibit 21-6.

18.   How might a management go about approximating the shape of the demand curve for a particular product? Of what significance would this be for pricing that product?

19.   A manufacturer of toothbrushes sells 100,000 brushes per month at 40 cents each. His total unit cost is 38 cents. Overhead (i.e., fixed) costs are $10,000 per month, and the manufacturer estimates that he can increase production by as much as 50 percent without increasing total overhead. In a market test he finds that a 2 cent reduction in selling price, from 40 to 38 cents, will increase his sales to 125,000 brushes per month. Should the manufacturer reduce his selling price to 38 cents per brush?

PART 7

MARKETING PLANNING AND CONTROLLING

Marketing Research

The Legal Environment

Overall Marketing Strategy

22

MARKETING RESEARCH

Marketing research is the systematic gathering, recording, and analyzing of data about marketing problems to facilitate decision-making. Useful information for marketing decision-making generally is found in both internal and external sources. Internal studies focus on resources and activities within the company and the external studies on the relation of the firm to its environment and particularly to its markets.

Internal and external marketing studies are necessary complements of each other. As Wroe Alderson so aptly put it, "the art of management might be said to consist precisely of taking account simultaneously of the inner workings of the firm and its interaction with external forces." [1] In this chapter, the emphasis is on external marketing studies. The analysis of internal data of direct interest to marketing management is discussed in the Appendix.

[1] W. Alderson, "Marketing and Management Decisions," *Cost and Profit Outlook*, January 1960, p. 3.

MARKETING INFORMATION AND THE ROLE OF RESEARCH

American business is caught in an ironic dilemma: our economic system generates an ever-increasing volume and variety of data, yet most marketing managers complain that they have insufficient, inappropriate, or untimely information on which to base operating decisions.[2] The development of timely, pertinent decision data for marketing management is a key feature of the systems approach. The age of information requires a marketing information system, and the systems approach to marketing management is creating a new role for marketing research. System theory's emphasis upon interaction and integration in the decision-making process makes it clear that the individual problem orientation of traditional marketing research, which concentrates on putting out brush fires, has become obsolete. The need is for *"a marketing intelligence system tailored to each marketer's requirements. Such a system would serve as the ever-alert nerve center of the marketing operation."* [3] One perceptive writer, basing his argument on the nerve center concept, suggests the setting up of a new organizational unit within the firm, the Marketing Information and Analysis Center. The proposed center, in effect, would represent a total conversion of the marketing research department into a complete marketing information system.[4]

The role of marketing research, as an integral part of a marketing information system, is to provide a flow of ideas and information useful in marketing decision-making. Regardless of the organizational arrangement —whether it is a marketing information and analysis center, a marketing research department, or research handled informally without organizational recognition—the need exists for decision data. A logical place to start, then, in understanding marketing research's role is with the decision-making process itself. Exhibit 22-1 shows how marketing research, through systematic gathering and analysis of information, should assist in answering questions that must be resolved at each stage in the decision-making process.

Starting with the problem identification stage, marketing research helps marketing management in gathering facts, opinions, and symptoms of the problem. The problem identification stage phases naturally into the problem conceptualization stage, where marketing research, through gathering and analyzing information on the influences of uncontrollables and controllables and the competitive situation, helps management explain the problem. At this stage of decision-making, marketing research analyzes

[2] R. H. Brien and J. E. Stafford, "Marketing Information Systems: New Dimension for Marketing Research," *Journal of Marketing*, July 1968, p. 19.

[3] L. Adler, "Systems Approach to Marketing," *Harvard Business Review*, May-June 1967, p. 110.

[4] P. Kotler, "A Design for the Firm's Marketing Nerve Center," *Business Horizons*, Fall 1966, p. 70.

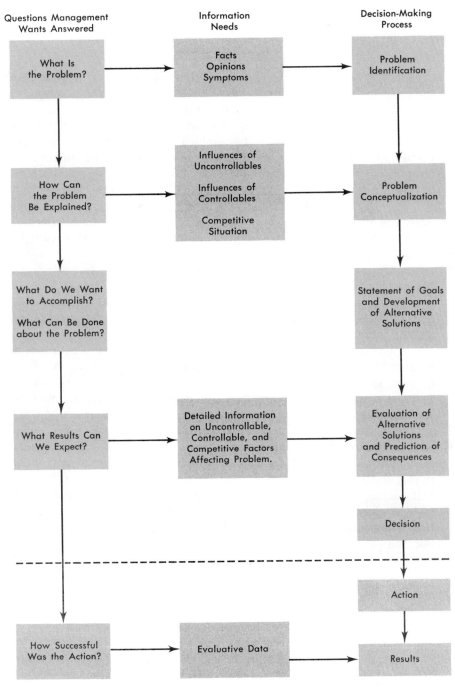

Questions Management Wants Answered | Information Needs | Decision-Making Process

What Is the Problem? → Facts Opinions Symptoms → Problem Identification

How Can the Problem Be Explained? → Influences of Uncontrollables / Influences of Controllables / Competitive Situation → Problem Conceptualization

What Do We Want to Accomplish? What Can Be Done about the Problem? → Statement of Goals and Development of Alternative Solutions

What Results Can We Expect? → Detailed Information on Uncontrollable, Controllable, and Competitive Factors Affecting Problem. → Evaluation of Alternative Solutions and Prediction of Consequences

Decision

Action

How Successful Was the Action? → Evaluative Data → Results

EXHIBIT 22—1

data drawn, of course, from both internal and external sources. Marketing researchers customarily refer to this aspect of their work as "preliminary exploration."

Marketing management, at the next stage, seeks to answer the questions "what do we want to accomplish" and "what can be done about the problem." As indicated in Exhibit 22-1, these are questions management pretty well has to answer for itself, but even here marketing research may make a contribution. It can help, for instance, in the creative thinking, whereby alternative solutions to the problem are developed. Before marketing research can make this contribution, however, marketing management must make clear what it wants to accomplish. Formulating the statement of goals, in other words, is the responsibility of marketing management.

Next comes the evaluation of alternative solutions and the prediction of their consequences, in terms of relative contributions to achievement of the goals set by management. Answering management's question "what results can we expect" often requires that marketing research gather and analyze additional and detailed information on the factors affecting the problem—the uncontrollables, controllables, and the competitive situation. These pieces of additional evidence may be gathered through various research methods and techniques—e.g., consumer surveys, test market studies, and motivation research projects.

After considering all this information (tempering it with previous experience, judgment, and imagination) marketing management reaches its decision and takes whatever actions are required to carry out the decision. Later, as management wonders "how successful was the action," marketing research may again provide the necessary evaluative data.

The marketing research function should be managed by people who understand its primary purpose—that of providing marketing executives with information needed for decisions. Marketing research's new orientation is shifting away from that of a job shop handling investigative tasks that management cannot tackle personally. Its new orientation is concerned with developing long-range programs of gathering and analyzing information in advance of the requests of decision-makers. In the age of information, marketing research can and should anticipate most informational needs.

SCOPE OF MARKETING RESEARCH

In analyzing the scope of marketing research operations in 195 companies, one careful student found that thirty-nine different major types of marketing research were being performed.[5] These thirty-nine types can be sorted

[5] R. D. Crisp, *Marketing Research Organization and Operation* (New York: American Management Association, Inc., 1958), Research Study No. 35, p. 40.

into four major categories: (1) studies of influences on uncontrollables, (2) studies of the competitive situation, (3) studies of influences of controllables, and (4) studies of market measurement and planning.[6] The different types of marketing research are grouped into these four major categories in the listing below. The figures in parentheses refer to the proportion of the 195 companies that were performing the specific type of marketing research at the time of the study.

A. *Studies on Influences of Uncontrollables*

  1. General business or economic forecasting (concerned primarily with general business climate rather than a single industry) (73%)
  2. Studies of economic factors affecting sales volume and opportunities (examples: level of consumer credit, consumer buying intentions, business expansion plans) (72%)
  3. Studies of shifts in the nature of the market (examples: sectional changes, age-distribution trends, income-distribution trends) (70%)
  4. Motivational research (examples: studies of consumer and customer buying motivations) (51%)

B. *Studies on Competitive Situation*

  5. Studies on competitive position of company products (91%)
  6. Comparative studies of competitive products (79%)
  7. Evaluation of new competitive products or competitive new product developments (79%)
  8. Studies of price policies, discount structures, etc. of competitors (75%)
  9. Studies of advertising and selling practices of competitors (69%)

C. *Studies of Influences of Controllables*

  10. Determination of consumer or customer acceptance of proposed new products or services (82%)
  11. Establishment or revision of sales territories (80%)
  12. Evaluation of existing sales methods (75%)
  13. Analysis of salesmen's activities (74%)
  14. Studies of advertising effectiveness (73%)
  15. Determining present use or applications of existing products (72%)
  16. Price studies (71%)
  17. Appraisals of proposed changes in sales methods (71%)

[6] Crisp (*ibid.*) did not actually utilize the four major categories as stated above. His report, however, does classify the thirty-nine types into four alternative classifications: (1) research on products and services, (2) research on markets, (3) research on sales methods and policies, and (4) research on advertising.

18. Evaluations of advantages or limitations of proposed new products or services (70%)
19. Measurement of the effectiveness of individual salesmen (70%)
20. Studies of dissatisfaction with existing products or services among present or former consumers (69%)
21. Determination or exploration of new uses or applications of existing products (68%)
22. Studies aimed at product simplification or at length or completeness of line of products (68%)
23. Studies of distribution costs (68%)
24. Setting of sales quotas (68%)
25. Development of standards of sales performance (63%)
26. Studies of sales compensation—evaluation, review or revision (62%)
27. Selection of advertising media (62%)
28. Packaging research (design or physical characteristics) (60%)
29. Studies of the effectiveness of promotional devices (examples: "deals," "premiums," "coupons") (56%)

D. *Studies Focusing on Market Measurement and Planning*

30. Analysis of market size (size of market for specific products) (90%)
31. Estimation of demand for new or proposed new products (89%)
32. Sales forecasting for the industry or company (88%)
33. Analysis of the characteristics of the market for specific products (87%)
34. Analysis of territorial potentials or sales opportunities (87%)
35. Studies of trends in market size by products (86%)
36. Measurement of territorial variations in sales yield (73%)
37. Studies of the relative profitability of different markets (73%)
38. Market test or test-market operations on new or improved products (70%)
39. Studies of changes in the importance of different types of customers (67%)

The inclusion of thirty-nine different types of studies should *not* lead us to conclude that all marketing research studies are single-purpose ones or that each type is performed in isolation of others. No marketing research study should ever be conducted so that it considers *only* the marketing factor it sets out to investigate, for no matter what the subject of the investigation is, it has marketing significance only when analyzed in relation to other marketing factors. A company doing research preliminary to introducing a new product, for example, is well-advised to undertake an *integrated* marketing research program, involving not only studies of marketability but also studies of the probable strength of demand at various prices, analyses of sales and territorial potentials, the impact of competitors' products and activities, the selection of advertising media and other promotional devices, and the influences of uncontrollables on proposed sales methods.

Studies of Influences of Uncontrollables

Relatively few marketing research studies focus directly on the influences of uncontrollables. This could perhaps simply reflect the all-too-prevalent condition that no one specifically "requested" such studies, but it is more likely that most executives feel that they can obtain the needed information on uncontrollables in the course of their regular business reading. Published information is readily available on such uncontrollables as the level of consumer credit, business expansion plans, age- and income-distribution trends, and consumer buying intentions. Federal government publications such as the *Statistical Abstract of the United States*, *The County and City Data Book*, the *Survey of Current Business*, and the *Federal Reserve Bulletin*, are rich sources of quantitative data on the uncontrollables and, in addition, often provide analyses of trends in income distribution, population growth and shifts, and consumer installment credit. The Office of Business Economics of the U.S. Department of Commerce gathers and publishes data on the national economic situation and outlook and the balance of international payments. The Department of Commerce also maintains field offices to help businessmen looking for specific types of information and, in addition, publishes the monthly *Marketing Information Guide*, which lists and reviews recent marketing publications, both governmental and private. Considerable information on the uncontrollables also appears in such popular business publications as *Business Week*, *Forbes*, *Dun's Review*, *The Wall Street Journal*, *Nation's Business*, and *Sales Management*.

Even though executives may get much information on the uncontrollables in the course of their regular business reading, seldom do they take the trouble (or have the time) to organize data gathered from numerous sources and to analyze the results in terms of their own company's marketing problems. The marketing research department, in contrast, when assigned the task of studying the uncontrollables, can routinely and expertly assemble and analyze marketing information, putting it into perspective more useful to decision-makers.

The motivation research studies, which delve into the complex psychological and sociological variables affecting buying behavior, are in a class by themselves. Why, as the above report shows, do so many companies fail to use motivation research? Part of the answer lies in the fact that doing and interpreting motivation research requires the services of trained specialists—psychologists and sociologists skilled in the research methods of their own fields. Few companies have such people on their payrolls, and the bulk of motivation research that is done is handled by outside consultants. Then, too, motivation research is still comparatively new, and many executives not only doubt its value but are suspicious of many of its findings.

Studies of Competitive Situation

Many companies give more emphasis to studies of the competitive position of their own products than they do to studies of the nature and impact of competitive activities. Measuring the "share-of-the-market" that a company's product has is a much more common type of study than one appraising the marketing strengths of a competitor's products, evaluating the marketing effects of a competitor's product improvement, measuring the impact of a competitor's price change, or appraising the effects of a competitor's change in advertising policy. Probably the reason is that share-of-the-market information often can be readily obtained through outside research organizations, often on a "subscription" basis.[7] Companies also find it relatively easy to compute share-of-the-market percentages for their own products, especially if they have access to industry sales figures gathered and distributed by trade associations. Most companies could probably benefit greatly if they would do more "intelligence" type studies—studies specifically designed to delve into competitors' marketing practices and policies. Such intelligence is needed to understand how competitors' actions affect the company's marketing situation. Only if such intelligence is available can a management do a really effective job in plotting marketing strategy and counterstrategy.

Studies of Influences of Controllables

The widest variety of marketing research studies focus on the influence of controllables—sales methods, products, advertising, promotion, and price. Controllables may be manipulated, and decision-making guidance

[7] The A. C. Nielsen Company, for example, whose home office is in Chicago and which operates not only in the United States and Canada but in other countries as well, provides a number of information services on marketing that are widely used by manufacturers. One of these services—the Nielsen Retail Index—provides continuous factual marketing data on foods, drugs, pharmaceuticals, toiletries, cosmetics, confectionary, tobacco, photographic, and other products. For the food industry, for example, the Nielsen organization provides its subscribers with reports on sales to consumers measured at the point of sale, facts on sales of competitors' products made to consumers, breakdowns of sales figures to consumers nationally or by the manufacturer's sales territories, and breakdowns of consumer sales figures by size and/or type of stores. All this information is reported separately for the subscriber's product and for each important competitor—and all work is repeated every two months, so that trends are shown.

is provided by studies of them. Studies of controllables also are used to appraise the effectiveness of current policies and practices. This is the managerial motivation most often underlying studies of the effectiveness of advertising and other promotional devices, individual salesmen, existing sales methods, and sales compensation plans. Formal studies of this sort often draw attention to situations requiring changes in policies and practices. Controllables can be manipulated without such studies, but manipulation is more effective with the added insight gained from special studies.

Studies Focusing on Market Measurement and Planning

In most companies, numerous studies are concerned with measuring markets and forecasting sales. Most marketing executives attach considerable importance to factual and quantitative data on present and future markets. The sales forecast, for example, provides information that management uses in setting the sales volume goal—the company objective that occupies a critical place in both marketing and non-marketing planning. The preliminary analysis and work leading up to a sales forecast is, itself, an extremely important form of planning, and essentially involves securing a satisfactory three-way adjustment of sales-making opportunities, profit objectives, and the enterprise's capabilities. A finished sales forecast becomes, in essence, management's official prediction of the consequences that should follow from the implementation of a series of inter-related marketing and non-marketing decisions. Thus, both marketing and non-marketing executives, as well as company top management, are highly concerned with studies directed toward measuring markets and forecasting sales.

PROBLEM IDENTIFICATION AND THE "SITUATION ANALYSIS"

The marketing researcher, like the marketing decision-maker, considers problem identification the basic first step in his work. Only if he knows what problem management is trying to solve, can he do an effective job in planning and designing a research project that will provide the needed information.[8] Only if he has the problem clearly in mind, can he be expected to lend intelligent direction to the resulting project—to steer it as directly as possible to predetermined informational goals (set by the nature of the problem itself) and to keep it from "getting off course" on the way to these goals.

[8] H. W. Boyd, Jr., and R. Westfall, *Marketing Research: Text and Cases*, rev. ed. (Homewood, Ill.: Richard D. Irwin, 1964), p. 204.

A competent marketing researcher, therefore, will not accept a request for a specific type of study unless he is sure that the executive making it has some problem already "pinned down" and not until that executive has been able to communicate the nature of the problem clearly. If he is to do his job effectively, the researcher must also be briefed on the line of reasoning that led up to the request. He needs this briefing in order to avoid researching "surface" problems when there is some more basic problem; all too often, executives request studies that subsequently prove of little value simply because they have not probed far enough into the situation to find the basic problem. Seeing that sales are falling off, for example, a marketing manager may feel that something "has gone wrong with the advertising" and submit a request to marketing research for a study of advertising effectiveness. In one case just like this where a study of advertising effectiveness was requested, further probing by an alert researcher revealed that the sales decline traced directly to the efforts of a recently-inaugurated distribution policy, which was slowing up deliveries to retailers who, in turn, were frequently out-of-stock. The researcher can perform a useful service, therefore, not only by lending assistance in the initial identification of problems, but in confirming (or casting doubt on) the identification of problems that the executive thinks he has already pinpointed.

Once a problem situation is identified, the researcher's task is to learn as much about it as time will allow. He can never hope to become as intimately acquainted with *all* the possible problem situations that might come up as can the decision-making executives he serves—the marketing manager, sales-force manager, and advertising manager. Yet when information is required for a decision on some specific marketing problem (for example, the size of next year's advertising budget), and the information (or at least important segments of it) must be gathered through marketing research, the researcher must learn all that he can about the problem situation before designing and conducting the research project itself. He must, in short, build an adequate background for his own thinking. Marketing researchers refer to this phase of preliminary exploration as the "situation analysis."

PROJECT PLANNING FOR MARKETING RESEARCH

Basically, a marketing research project is a *planned search for information*. Time spent in planning the project should not only reduce the time required to conduct the project but should also ultimately result in more reliable and meaningful information. When project planning has been neglected, marketing researchers move aimlessly from one possible information source to the next, choose research methods and approaches at random, and have only the vaguest notions concerning the kinds of information they seek. The earmarks of project planning in marketing research, as elsewhere, are well-defined goals, an organized effort, and a step-by-step schedule—all aimed at uncovering, reporting, and analyzing as reliable and meaningful information as possible.

Any research project includes certain steps, each of which can be planned in advance. Planning a marketing research project involves making decisions on: (1) research objectives, (2) specific information needed to achieve these objectives, (3) sources to tap in seeking the information, and (4) research methods to employ in collecting the information. Every project should include these steps, but each step in each project can be handled in quite unique ways.[9]

Deciding on Research Objectives

Assuming that the marketing problem has been identified and the preliminary exploration finished, the first step in project planning is to decide on research objectives. The preliminary exploration should have left the researcher with clear notions as to the purposes of the formal research project. In other words, there should be a set of tentative assumptions about the specific problem; the researcher then designs a formal research project to test the validity of these assumptions. For example, in a study of how a company spends its advertising appropriation, preliminary exploration might cause the researcher to conclude tentatively that less money should be devoted to newspaper advertisements and more to television. In this case, then, the research objective might be to test two hypotheses:

1. The company should spend less money on newspaper advertising.
2. The company should spend more money on television commercials.

The statement of research objectives should, whenever possible, be simply a small number of hypotheses to test or a small number of questions to answer. The number must be kept small since the project cannot be expected to produce both timely and reliable information, if it is directed toward finding too many answers. If the project is set up to test too many

[9] "Market research techniques rarely are definitive. Usually, the magnitude of error to which they are exposed is not even measurable; also, practitioners of market research often disagree about the suitability of different techniques. These facts notwithstanding, the results achieved by carefully planned and executed market research provide a basis for decision that is more reliable than intuition or business experience." A. R. Oxenfeldt, "Scientific Marketing: Ideal and Ordeal," *Harvard Business Review*, March-April 1961, p. 64.

hypotheses, either the research requires an inordinate amount of time and money or the study suffers from purely surface investigations of each hypothesis. In pruning the list of hypotheses to test, the researcher should answer two questions with respect to each hypothesis:

1. If we obtain this information, of what use will it be to the decision-maker?
2. If this information is of possible usefulness to the decision-maker, is it useful enough to justify the cost of obtaining it?

Research costs money, and this serves as a built-in brake on the ambitiousness of the researcher in setting research objectives. The scope of the project must be limited within the budget to obtaining that information most important to the decision-maker. Some researchers, unfortunately, tend to get so wrapped up in finding out "everything there is to know about a problem" that marketing executives must place a budget ceiling on their projects. No competent marketing researcher likes to be bound by such restrictions, so they should routinely "cut each project down to size" before limiting instructions come down from superiors. The list of hypotheses for testing should be kept to a very small number of important ones, preferably to those so related that they can be jointly, and thus economically, researched.

Deciding on Information Needed

The second key project planning step is to determine the specific information needed to achieve the research objectives. The researcher considers different types of information that seem to be pertinent to achieving the objectives. He must make certain that each bit of specific information finally decided upon is relevant to achieving the research objectives. Suppose, for example, that the research project being planned has the objective of answering a South American businessman's question, "Should I open a self-service automatic laundry and dry cleaning establishment in Bogotá, Colombia?" What kinds of information are necessary to answer this question? The researcher would want, as a minimum, the following:

1. Number of Bogotá residents who are potential users of this type of service.
2. Number of residents able and willing to pay for the service at each of several proposed prices.
3. Probable frequency and intensity of use of the service (How often and how much will different social and income classes use the service?)

4. Competing services and their comparative costs.
5. Laws and other regulations that might affect the operations of a service establishment of this type. Will they facilitate or impede setting up the business?
6. Amount, kinds, and costs of persuasion (advertising, etc.) needed to convince Bogotá residents that they ought to patronize the service.

Deciding on Information Sources

The next step in project planning is to identify the sources from which the different items of information are obtainable and to select those that will be used. For this purpose, it is convenient to classify information sources as either primary or secondary. A primary data source is one from which the desired items of information must be obtained directly—for example, through questionnaires and interviews. Primary data sources, then, include consumers and buyers, middlemen, salesmen, trade association executives, and other businessmen. Secondary data sources are generally published sources, such as the census publications and *Sales Management's Survey of Buying Power*,[10] although other secondary sources (e.g., company files of marketing research and other reports) sometimes contain desired information. Secondary data sources, in other words, are repositories of information not gathered specifically to achieve the objectives of the particular research project being planned, but rather already assembled. The characteristic that most distinguishes the primary source from the secondary source is that the former must be tapped directly (through research) to obtain the desired information, whereas the latter may have the data already on hand, either in published form (as in government and business publications) or on file (as in the case of company reports gathered for some other purpose).

The researcher should look to the secondary sources first for, if the needed information is already available, the time and expense of gathering it from primary sources can be saved. Usually, however, only some information can be obtained from secondary sources (e.g., the disposition of consumers to buy a given product under certain marketing conditions); the rest must be obtained from primary sources. In the Bogotá study on

[10] Already large, the quantity of published literature useful in marketing research is growing at an ever-increasing rate. With so many sources of secondary information available, the researcher often must feel that the haystack is growing faster than his ability to find the needle. Prompted by this situation, the American Management Association has provided its members with a guidelist for purposes of (1) furnishing leads to sources of information, and (2) classifying and indexing significant reports. See: American Management Association, *Guidelist for Marketing Research and Economic Forecasting*, Research Study No. 50 (New York: American Management Association, 1961).

whether to open a self-service laundry, for example, census publications (a secondary source) should reveal the number of residents that are potential users, and published legal records (another secondary source) would tell which laws and regulations affect the operation of this type of service. But to obtain the other desired pieces of information, the researcher would have to work with primary sources (in this case, the potential consumers).

Deciding on Research Methods

If all the needed information is obtainable from secondary sources, then, no decision on research methods is required. But if, as is more likely, primary sources must be used, a decision on research methods must be made. There are three main research methods—the survey, the experimental, and the observational.

SURVEY METHOD   In the survey method, information is obtained directly from individual respondents, either through personal interviews or through mail questionnaires or telephone interviews. Questionnaires are used either to obtain specific responses to direct questions or to secure more general responses to "open end" questions. The direct type of question is designed to force the respondent to choose among a limited number of answers. Consider this example: "How do you feel about the styling of this new electric typewriter? Do you rate it as EXCELLENT _____, GOOD _____, FAIR _____, or POOR _____?" This question contrasts sharply with the "open end" question: "What do you think about the *styling* of this new electric typewriter?" This last question permits the respondent to come up with his own answer.

The survey method has three different uses: (1) to gather facts from respondents, (2) to report their opinions, or (3) to probe the interpretations individuals give to various matters. The survey method's accuracy and reliability is not the same in each application. Generally, it is most accurate and reliable when used to gather factual data, less so when used to record opinions, and least so when used to gain insight into respondents' interpretations.

In the *factual survey*, respondents are asked questions designed to elicit factual responses. For example:

What brand of cigarettes do you smoke?
Where do you do most of your shopping for groceries?
Have you ever bought *Playboy* magazine at a newsstand?
How many people live at this address?

Presumably, the people who respond in a factual survey will be able to report facts. But, almost always, some respondents cannot remember past events and actions. Others have difficulty in making their answers specific enough as, for example, in answering the question "At which store do you do most of your shopping for groceries?" They may shop for groceries at several stores and simply be unable to name the one store where they do *most* of their shopping. Still other respondents try to "help" the interviewer by giving him the answer they think he wants; for example, a respondent, assuming the interviewer has some connection with *Playboy*, says "Why, yes, I bought *Playboy* just last week," when actually he only thumbed through a copy while waiting in the barber shop.

The *opinion survey* is designed to gather expressions of personal opinions, record evaluations, or to report thinking on particular matters. Respondents often are unaware that they are giving opinions and believe, instead, that they are simply reporting "facts." Questions typical of those in opinion surveys include:

> Which local supermarket has the most courteous checkers?
> Which of these designs do you like the most (e.g., asked when showing several different designs of dinner plates)?
> Which pharmacy in your area does the best job of filling doctors' prescriptions?
> What do you think about the future of the tourist industry in this state?

Errors also get into opinion surveys. Respondents in opinion surveys, as those in factual surveys, may give the answers they think that the interviewer wants or be unable to provide specific answers to such questions as "Which pharmacy in your area does the best job of filling doctors' prescriptions?" Possibly several pharmacies do excellent jobs, and the respondent is unable to say which *one* does the *best job* so he answers "I don't know" when he really means "There are a number of excellent pharmacies in my area." Furthermore, respondents in opinion surveys may never have thought about the subjects until the interviewer raises the specific questions; this may cause them to give quick responses, often different from those they would give if they had time to consider the questions.

In the *interpretative survey*, the respondent acts as an interpreter as well as a reporter. Interpretative data is gathered by way of such questions as "Why do you use *Brand X* spray deodorant?" and "What about the new *Thunderbird* appeals to you most?" Answers to such questions are subject to all the limitations of answers to factual and opinion surveys and, in addition, they reflect the inability of many respondents to consciously interpret their own feelings, motives, and attitudes. Also, the personal nature of the required answer often causes him not to report his feelings, motives, and attitudes the way they really are. Indeed, this source of error in interpretative surveys is frequently cited as a reason for the use of motivation research, which is aimed not at answering "why" questions directly but indirectly through such techniques as depth interviewing and sentence completion tests.[11]

EXPERIMENTAL METHOD   Patterned after the procedure used generally in scientific research, the experimental method as used in marketing research involves carrying out a small-scale trial solution to a problem while, at the same time, attempting to control all factors relevant to the problem except the one being studied. For example, an advertiser may run two versions of a proposed advertisement (Ad A and Ad B) in a city newspaper with half of the copies of the issue carrying Ad A and the other half Ad B, and might then arrange for follow-up interviews with the two groups of readers. This experiment, called a "split-run" test, might have the objective of determining the advertisement with the most impact on readers in one or more market areas. The preferred ad might then be placed in newspapers in other markets or in national advertising media.

The main assumption in the experimental method is that the test conditions are essentially the same as those that will be encountered later when conclusions derived from the experiment are applied to a broader marketing area. Of course, test conditions are never quite the same as parallel conditions in the broader market area. Nevertheless, a well-designed experiment, even though it cannot replicate total market conditions, may provide valuable guidance and information for marketing decision-making. Scott Paper Company, for example, ever since it first introduced paper towels to the consumer market, has so carefully market-tested every new product that it claims none has ever failed when put into national distribution. Scott's practice is to study the market, conduct consumer interviews, study likes and dislikes, give the product a tentative name, and then conduct market testing experiments. After analyzing the results of such experiments, management may decide to change such product features as the name, size, shape, or color, but if changes are made that have important marketing implications (such as in the proposed retail price), further market experimentation is ordered.[12] There are really no "pat" designs for experiments—each should be designed to reveal the desired information as directly and quickly as possible.

OBSERVATIONAL METHOD   Here, marketing research data is gathered not through direct questioning of respondents but rather by ob-

---

[11] Psychologists believe it is impossible to really get at motives by simply asking people why they do something. The human being is extremely complex, and much behavior is governed by emotions and quirks of personality. See: J. M. Myers and W. H. Reynolds, *Consumer Behavior and Marketing Management* (Boston: Houghton Mifflin Co., 1967), p. 113.

[12] "Marketing: Secret Ingredients," *Forbes*, November 15, 1962, p. 43.

serving and recording their actions in a marketing situation. For example, in studying the impact of a department store's mass display of shelving paper, observers were unobtrusively stationed and instructed to record the total number of people passing by the display, the number stopping at the display, the number picking up and examining the product, and the number making purchases. In another observational study, whose purpose was to determine which types of consumers bought what brands of home remedies, researchers secured permission from consumers to inventory the contents of household medicine cabinets. In a third observational study, researchers posing as customers used concealed tape recorders as part of a project evaluating the selling techniques used by sales people in florist shops.

The main advantage of the observational method is that it records respondents' expressed actions and behavior patterns, thus avoiding errors which trace to "asking" (as in the survey) rather than "observing" what respondents actually do (as in the display example above) or have done (as in the medicine cabinet example). Its principal shortcoming is that its design does not provide for the detection of buying motives and other psychological factors since, in its pure form at least, the observational method involves simply watching or listening or both, with no attempt to probe for the reasons lying behind actions and behavior patterns.

CHOOSING THE RESEARCH METHOD   Fairly often, the researcher is confronted with a situation where two, or even all three, research methods could be used alternatively to obtain the needed information. Management, for example, might want to determine the extent of the area from which a shopping center draws trade. One approach could be to interview shoppers (the survey method). Another could involve recording (the observation method) license numbers of cars in the parking lot and checking license holders' addresses at the state motor vehicle bureau. In situations like this, the researcher must select the most appropriate method or, somewhat more rarely, combination of methods. Besides considering information requirements, he should compare alternative methods according to costs, probable quality of data obtainable, time requirements, and personnel available for the study.

GATHERING PRIMARY DATA THROUGH SAMPLING

In gathering data from primary sources, most marketing research projects make use of sampling. To clarify the role of sampling in marketing research, consider the hypothetical case of a manufacturer of men's shoes who must find out certain facts in order to make certain decisions. For one thing, he would like to know the distribution of foot sizes among the population (i.e., all men), in order to balance his production in proportion to this distribution. One way to obtain this information would be to measure the foot size of every man in the population (i.e., taking a census of foot size).

There is, however, a much quicker and less costly way to obtain the wanted information—through interviewing a representative group or "sample" of men. A sample is, by definition only a portion of the "universe" from which it is drawn; [13] therefore, studying the characteristics and attitudes of the members of a sample, rather than of all members of the relevant universe, not only makes possible completion of the study in less time but results in lower research costs. "But," you might ask, "isn't the information obtained from samples less accurate?" That depends both on the method used in selecting the sample and on its size.

It is possible for data obtained through sampling to contain fewer errors than data gathered through a complete census of the relevant universe. For instance, when the universe size is very large and scientific sample selection methods are used, there is a strong possibility that sampling will result in fewer errors. The possibility is even stronger when, as is usually true in marketing research, the funds available for the study are limited. With only limited funds, making a census means that expenditures must be spread "thin"; by contrast, restricting the size of the field operation (through sampling) makes relatively larger amounts available, both for better control of data-collection processes and for the employment of high-caliber interviewing and other research personnel.[14]

Marketing research makes extensive use of sampling and, since research results are important ingredients for decision-making, marketing managers should know enough about sampling to allow them to evaluate the data they use. More specifically, they should know the inherent advantages and limitations of samples selected by different methods, and they should understand how sample size affects the amount of error present in research results. But here we must insert a word of caution: management certainly wants to avoid basing decisions on erroneous data, but it wants just as strongly to avoid demanding such error-free data that inordinate amounts of time and money are spent on the study. Greater expense and longer periods of investigation, in other words, are the prices of reductions in errors in marketing research. If, for management's purpose, accuracy within 10 percent of the true picture is sufficient, aiming for accuracy that is within 5 percent wastes both research time and money.

---

[13] Two of the most basic concepts in statistics are those of a *sample* and a *universe*. A sample is often referred to as 'the data' or 'the observations': numbers that have been observed. The universe . . . is the totality of all possible observations of the same kind. See P. E. Green and D. S. Tull, *Research for Marketing Decisions* (Englewood Cliffs, N.J.: Prentice-Hall, Inc., 1966), p. 224.

[14] C. R. Wasson, "Common Sense in Sampling," *Harvard Business Review*, January-February 1963, p. 110.

Classes of Samples

All of the samples used in marketing research fall into one of two classes: probability and non-probability. The fundamental distinction between these two classes lies in the way items are selected for inclusion in the resulting samples. Probability samples result from a process of random selection, whereby each member of a universe has a known chance of being selected for the sample. Non-probability samples result from a process in which judgment (and, therefore, bias) enters into the selection of the members of a universe included in the sample. Of course, judgment is also involved in the use of probability samples (in deciding, for instance, on a particular sample design), but the actual selection of the individual items for inclusion is made solely through a probability mechanism as, for example, through a table of random numbers (which eliminates the human bias that would otherwise enter into the selection).[15]

This difference as to the extent to which judgment enters into the selection of the sample, may be illustrated as follows: In a "quota" sample, one type of non-probability sample, interviewers may be given quotas specifying that they are to select for interviewing a certain number of people who possess given characteristics: one such quota might specify "Interview 20 women in the 35 to 45 age bracket, half of whom have full- or part-time jobs and half of whom are not employed outside the home." If the same study were to be made using a probability sample, the probability mechanism itself would be relied on to select representative proportions of people with the given characteristics, and the interviewer would play no part whatever in the actual selection of respondents.

Errors

Both samples and censuses are apt to contain errors. There are, in fact, two kinds of errors—non-sampling and sampling. Samples contain both kinds of errors, whereas complete censuses contain only non-sampling errors. This, however, does not mean that census results are necessarily any more error-free than sample results. It means only that there is one kind of error in a census and two kinds in a sample.

NON-SAMPLING ERROR   Non-sampling errors are nothing more than the accidental (or deliberate) mistakes or errors than can happen during any of the stages of data collection, recording, and enumeration. Here are

---

[15] J. Neter and W. Wasserman, *Fundamental Statistics for Business and Economics*, 2nd ed. (Boston: Allyn and Bacon, 1961), p. 439.

some examples of non-sampling errors: a field worker checks off a wrong answer; a respondent misinterprets a question; an interviewer misinterprets an answer; a field worker selects a wrong respondent; a field worker falsifies an interview; a clerk tabulates some data incorrectly; an interviewer biases respondents' answers by the way he asks questions; a poorly-designed question elicits erroneous responses. In short, non-sampling errors are blunders, and they occur both in complete censuses and in samples. Non-sampling errors cannot be measured (as can sampling errors) and taken into account in evaluating study results. Thoroughness in project planning and careful control over all phases of the subsequent study are the only ways to minimize these errors.

SAMPLING ERROR   A standard work on sampling principles says that in referring to *sampling error* or the *precision* of a sample result, we are referring to how closely we can reproduce from a sample the results that would be obtained if we took a complete count or a census, using the same methods of measurement, questionnaire, interview procedure, type of enumerator, supervision, etc.[16]

In other words, the measurements produced by samples (statisticians refer to these measurements as "statistics") are really *estimates* of the true parameters. Statisticians, in evaluating a sample, use the term "accuracy" to refer to the difference between a sample result and the real statistic, and the term "precision" to refer to the difference between a sample result and the result of a complete count.[17] Marketing researchers are concerned with both accuracy and precision—with accuracy throughout the project and with precision because it is statistically measurable [18] (but precision is only so measurable if the sample is selected by probability methods [19]). Sampling error (i.e., lack of precision) cannot be avoided, but

---

[16] M. H. Hansen, W. H. Hurwitz, and W. G. Madow, *Sample Survey Methods and Theory* (New York: John Wiley and Sons, 1953), vol. 1, p. 10.

[17] "The words 'accuracy' and 'precision' are often used rather loosely and interchangeably, but there is a very important difference between the two concepts. *Accuracy* means freedom from error. *Precision* refers to the reproducibility of sample results; if many samples of the same size were taken from the same population by the same methods, the consistency among the results obtained from these various samples indicates the precision of the particular result based on samples of this type." T. T. Semon, R. Cohen, S. B. Richmond, and J. S. Stock, "Sampling in Marketing Research," *Journal of Marketing*, January 1959, p. 269.

[18] The statistical "sampling error" of probability sample results is a measure of precision and not of accuracy. It is virtually impossible to measure the accuracy of sample results, either for probability samples or for nonprobability samples.

[19] In at least the strictest application of the statistical techniques used for computing sampling error (i.e., for measuring lack of precision), these techniques apply only in the case of probability samples. This is because the mathematical foundation of the formulas used for measuring sampling error assume random (i.e., probability) selection of sample members which, of course, is not present in non-probability samples. Nevertheless, some marketing researchers do apply the formulas for sampling error to non-probabil-

when probability sample selection methods are used, it can be measured and controlled.

The measure of sampling error is known technically as the "standard error of the sampling estimate," and is defined as follows: "A measure of the variability inherent in a sample value, due only to the sampling process (sampling error), [it] may be computed for almost any mathematically determined value obtained from a probability sample." [20] Measures of sampling variability (i.e., standard error measures), then, can be computed for such mathematical values as arithmetic means and percentages when they are derived from probability sample results.[21] Since it isn't essential to our discussion to know how to calculate these measures of sampling variability, and since marketing research texts explain the calculations in detail, we need not go into them here.[22] It will be sufficient to keep in mind the fact that it is possible to calculate the sampling error present in probability samples.

Sample Size

Any executive who is in a position to approve expenditures for marketing research or who uses its results for decision-making should be familiar with the basic considerations affecting sample size. Common sense tells us, of course, that the larger a sample is the greater the chances are that research results will be reliable. Sampling errors are the only errors that can be reduced by increasing sample size and, because the statistical formulas for computing sampling errors apply solely to probability samples, only in probability samples can we obtain statistical measures of the adequacy of sample size.

ity samples; for the rationale behind this application, see: P. E. Green and D. S. Tull, *op. cit.*, p. 277.

[20] K. P. Uhl and B. Schoner, *Marketing Research: Information Systems and Decision Making* (New York: John Wiley and Sons, Inc., 1969), p. 121.

[21] The formulas for computing these two measures are:

1. Standard Error of the Mean $= \dfrac{\text{Standard Deviation of the Universe}}{\sqrt{\text{Sample Size}}}$

2. Standard Error of a Proportion $= \sqrt{\dfrac{p \cdot q}{\text{Sample Size}}}$

   Where: p is the % of occurrence of a characteristic being studied
   and: q is $100\% - p$ (i.e., the % of non-occurrence of the same characteristic).

Each of these standard-error formulas can be transposed and used to calculate required sample sizes.

[22] The reader interested in exploring this matter of calculation further is referred to H. W. Boyd, Jr. and R. Westfall, *Marketing Research: Text and Cases* (Homewood, Ill.: Richard D. Irwin, Inc., 1964), pp. 366-82 or Green and Tull, *op. cit.*, pp. 227-32.

Assuming, then, that probability selection methods are used, how can we get a sample of the right size—one neither too small nor too large? A sample is "too small" if the amount of sampling error present is more than can be permitted by the decision-making requirements of the problem under investigation. A sample is "too large" if sampling error is reduced beyond the point that is really necessary; after a certain size of sample is reached, sampling error is reduced only slightly, relative to the added costs incurred. Dr. L. O. Brown, pioneer marketing author and researcher, says there are four main considerations in planning the size of a sample: (1) the amount of sampling error that is permissible, (2) the amount of risk the decision-maker is willing to assume that the sample results are, indeed, within the limits deemed permissible, (3) the amount of money available for the project, and (4) the basic nature of the research being planned.[23] How each of these considerations enters into planning the size of a probability sample is discussed below.[24]

PERMISSIBLE SAMPLING ERROR   Suppose that a manufacturer plans to launch a special promotional campaign in Buffalo at the point when "approximately" 50 percent of the households in that city have heard of his product. Suppose, further, that management considers "approximately" to mean within plus or minus 5 percent—i.e., the decision to launch the special campaign will be made if sample results show that as few as 45 percent of the households know of the product. If the sample size actually used turned out to be too small (e.g., so small that the sample percentage might vary as much as 10 percentage points from the true percentage) management might make the wrong decision simply because of a too-small sample. Sample results might, then, show that only 40 percent of Buffalo households had heard of the product, whereas the true percentage might be as high as 50 percent. Management, then, because of the presence of too much sampling error, might be led into making an incorrect decision on a problem considered critical. The permissible sampling error—the amount that can be present in sample results without causing incorrect decisions—is an important consideration in planning the required size of sample.

DECISION-MAKER'S WILLINGNESS TO ASSUME RISK   How "confident" does the manufacturer want to be that the sample results in Buffalo

---

[23] L. O. Brown, *Marketing and Distribution Research*, 3rd ed. (New York: Ronald Press, 1955), pp. 269-275.

[24] More complete explanations and the details of the statistical manipulations involved in determining sample size are found in most marketing research textbooks. These explanations form important segments of marketing research courses, and your authors believe that they should not take up too much space in a basic marketing book.

are within his specified limits of permissible sampling error? With respect to the Buffalo sampling percentage, does he want to be 95 percent confident, 68 percent confident, or some other percentage? Suppose he says he wants to be 95 percent confident—i.e., he wants the chances that the Buffalo sample percentage will be within the specified limits of permissible sampling error to be 95 out of 100 (or 19 out of 20).[25] The sample size in Buffalo, therefore, would have to be large enough so that in 19 out of 20 cases, the percentage value obtained through sampling would not be more than plus or minus 5 percentage points (the manufacturer's permissible sampling error) away from the true percentage value in the universe (all households in Buffalo). If the manufacturer desired 99 percent confidence, the sample size would have to be much larger; if he could get by with 68 percent confidence, the sample size could be much smaller. Therefore, the amount of risk in obtaining incorrect information that a decision-maker is willing to assume has a definite effect on the required size of sample.

MONEY AVAILABLE FOR THE PROJECT   Sometimes, management's needs as to permissible sampling error and percentage of confidence indicate a larger-sized sample than the money available will allow. When this happens, one might "scale down" the requirements for permissible sampling error and desired confidence percentage, recognizing that some information, even though probably less reliable than the decision-maker would prefer, may be better than no information at all. Alternatively, of course, one could allot more money to the project; this might be appropriate if the research goal is to obtain data pertaining to an extremely important decision, such as one involving the cultivation of an entirely new market segment. But if the extra money is simply unavailable, it may be wiser not to undertake the project at all rather than to use an inadequate sample whose results could, in fact, actually mislead the decision-maker. In setting sample size, then, some sort of balance must be found between the amount of money available for the project and the requirements as to permissible sampling error and desired confidence percentage.

BASIC NATURE OF PLANNED RESEARCH   Whenever a mass of sample data is reduced to an average (e.g., to an arithmetic mean) certain important details are obscured. In planning the size of the sample, then, care must be taken to guard against the possibility that the significance of the data will be lost in the average—i.e., that the average will not accurately

[25] Technically, this desire for "95 percent confidence" is referred to as a "95 percent confidence level"—which the statistician, or researcher, measures in terms of "standard errors"—and involves setting the "confidence limits" at 2 standard errors above and below the percentage shown by the sample results. For a detailed explanation of this matter, see: Boyd and Westfall, *op. cit.*, p. 317.

reflect (or summarize) all of the sample data. For example, two counties might have the same average (arithmetic mean) income per household; but in County A, household incomes might range from zero to millions of dollars, whereas in County B such incomes might range from zero to only $25,000. To reveal the existence of this difference in the range of income as well as to obtain the same average in both counties, the required size of sample for studying County A (with the extremely wide range) would have to be much larger than that required for studying County B (with a much narrower income range). To overcome this tendency for averages to cover up details that might be important, statisticians use what are called measures of dispersion to aid them in determining the proper sample size. The best-known and most-used measure of dispersion is "the standard deviation," which reveals something about the degree to which the values in a series vary.[26] When the dispersion is great (as in County A), the standard deviation is large and a larger-sized sample is needed to achieve a desired degree of precision in the results. When there is little dispersion and the data have considerable homogeneity (as in County B), the standard deviation is small and a smaller-sized sample can be used to achieve the same degree of precision. Thus, the sample size necessary to meet the three considerations discussed earlier—permissible sampling error, decision-maker's willingness to assume risk, and money available—varies with the extent to which the characteristic being measured (household income in our example) varies in the universe being studied.

Probability vs. Non-Probability Samples

Now, then, what are the relative merits and limitations of probability and non-probability samples? Probability samples, as we have seen, enjoy a significant advantage, in that sampling error present is measurable and it is possible to predetermine the needed sample size. In non-probability samples, by contrast, judgment is the sole basis for appraising sample error and for determining sample size. Probability sampling, however, requires that individual items in the sample be chosen by a process of random selection (which involves using fairly complex probability mechanisms); thus, greater statistical competence and more time are required to plan and use probability sampling. For these reasons, then, probability samples generally cost more per observation (included in the sample) than non-probability samples. So it is not too surprising that most of the samples used in market-

[26] "The standard deviation, [which is defined as] the root mean square of the deviations of the observations about their [arithmetic] mean, has become the almost universally accepted measure of absolute dispersion in economic and business analysis." R. Ferber and P. J. Verdoorn, *Research Methods in Economics and Business* (New York: The Macmillan Company, 1962), p. 67.

ing research are non-probability samples; they cost less per observation, mainly because less time is taken, and relatively little statistical sophistication is required in planning the sample design and in selecting respondents. And often a non-probability sample is perfectly adequate for certain uses—e.g., for pretesting a questionnaire before putting it in final form.

However, the great limitation of the non-probability sample still remains—since the chances of including a particular member of a universe in the sample are undeterminable, the laws of probability do not apply and, hence, no measure of precision can be computed; similarly, it is not possible to predetermine the required size of sample. In other words, in non-probability sampling, most of the selection of respondents is left to the accident of availability of persons and to the personal whims of interviewers.[27] The size of the sample itself is left to the researcher's judgment.

The conclusion seems clear: where at all feasible, probability sampling methods should be used; but, if in a particular study only general estimates are needed and funds are limited, then an appropriate non-probability method will suffice. Professors Lorie and Roberts state that the choice between probability and non-probability samples should depend on the relative importance of the decision to be made. In their words:

> . . . non-probability sampling is more attractive the less vital the decisions to be made on the basis of the study. The reason, of course, is that with non-probability sampling the bias and sampling variability can only be guessed, while probability sampling gives an objective evaluation of sampling error. Therefore in collecting data for very important decisions one does not like to risk non-probability samples if probability samples are available.[28]

BUDGETING FOR MARKETING RESEARCH

In budgeting funds for marketing research, management must determine: (1) how large the total budget for marketing research should be, (2) how much money to invest in particular marketing research projects, and (3) the controls to exercise over expenditures.

Size of Marketing Research Budget

There are no pat solutions to the problem of how large the total marketing research budget should be. Actual expenditures vary from one

[27] Green and Tull, *op. cit.*, p. 226.
[28] J. H. Lorie and H. V. Roberts, *Basic Methods of Marketing Research* (New York: McGraw-Hill Book Co., Inc., 1951), p. 187.

company to another. They appear to vary with the size of the company, the nature of its operation, and the marketing leadership position that management sets for itself as a goal within the industry.

COMPANY SIZE   Large companies generally spend more dollars, although smaller percentages of their sales volumes, for marketing research than do small companies. This is to be expected, for it is the very size of a large company that makes possible effective and economical use of many specialists (including marketing research specialists) that a small company finds it cannot afford—at least on its regular payroll. The minimum cost of running even the smallest marketing research department probably comes to at least $40,000 per year. This is "a drop in the bucket" for a large company, but it represents a substantial percentage of total sales for a small company. If a company is too small to budget at least this amount for marketing research, it *should* forgo its own department, and arrange instead to invest what it can afford in the services of outside marketing research agencies and consultants. Typically, however, small companies with small marketing research budgets make little use of outside research assistance. In one study of 180 firms, for instance, 47 small firms with an average annual sales volume of $870,000 spent nothing whatever on outside research assistance while 27 large firms with an average annual sales volume of $337-million spent more than 50 percent of their marketing research budgets for outside help.[29] So even though a small company may really need relatively more outside help than a large firm, this study showed that it actually receives relatively less outside help.

NATURE OF COMPANY'S OPERATION   The nature of a company's operation also affects the size of its marketing research budget. For instance, if a company is a heavy user of advertising and sales promotional devices, if it maintains a large sales force, and if it distributes its products through fairly complex marketing channels, it is quite likely to be a heavy user of marketing research. Managment, in other words, faced with these marketing conditions, must make numerous decisions and should, therefore, have greater needs for information. Such conditions are more typical of marketers of consumer products than of marketers of industrial products, and budgets for marketing research are usually larger in the consumer goods field.

ASPIRATIONS FOR MARKETING LEADERSHIP   If the management of a company aims at achieving marketing leadership in the industry, it is likely to have a larger marketing research budget than a company whose

[29] Crisp, *op. cit.*, pp. 20-21.

management has lower aspirations. Of course, a company becomes an industry leader partly because of fortuitous circumstances; however, success is more dependent on the ability of management to adjust product characteristics and company policies to the needs of different market segments, thus insuring not only sales but profits. The way to industry leadership, then, is largely down the road of good marketing. And since good marketing depends on excellence in decision-making, management wants to base its decisions on the best information possible.

Is Too Much Spent on Marketing Research?   Few companies spend more on marketing research than they should. Most spend far more for production-oriented research than they do for marketing research—in spite of the fact that it usually costs less to manufacture a product than to market it. There are relatively few unexploited opportunities for improving business efficiency left in production; such opportunities remain mostly in marketing. Thus we should expect, at least in the well-managed concern, that the long-run trend of dollar expenditures for marketing research should be *up*: that is, if management is consciously trying to do a more efficient job of marketing through better decision-making.

Costs of Individual Marketing Research Projects

To the question of "how much should be invested in a particular research project," the theoretical answer is "something less than the value the decision-maker places on having the information produced by the research." Both amounts—the how much to invest and the worth of the resulting information—are difficult, if not wholly impossible, to estimate. Not only is it hard to put a dollar tag on the worth of specific items of information, it is at least as hard to say how much should be spent in obtaining that information.

In spite of these difficulties in estimation, there are a few things we can say about the costs of individual marketing research projects. We can note, for one thing, that it never is worthwhile to launch a project seeking *all* the possible items of information about a particular decision situation; we can never get all the information anyway because decisions are always made with reference to the future and there are always some uncertainties about the future. Research information can help reduce these uncertainties, but it cannot eliminate them entirely. Another thing we can say is that the cost of a project is related to the degree of precision management expects to have in the research results. Increased precision is bought at the price of higher project costs and greater amounts of time spent in processing the results. Another way of making the same point: the more confidence management wants to be able to put in the results, the larger and more expensive the sample and the more costly the research techniques that are needed to obtain data with the desired level of precision.

We should note, too, that individual projects vary in cost, according to whether they are undertaken by company personnel, by outside agencies, or are joint endeavors of some kind. Outside research organizations are profit-making enterprises and naturally price their services in excess of the actual costs incurred. Many outside researchers are reluctant to accept individual projects involving only a few hundreds or thousands of dollars, and some are interested only in projects involving tens or hundreds of thousands of dollars. However, most communities have smaller marketing research agencies and "free lance" consultants who are more willing to take on small projects.

Managerial Controls over Marketing Research Expenditures

In most companies, management exercises control over marketing research expenditures mainly through the annual budget. The marketing research director is responsible for estimating these expenditures for the coming budgetary period and for submitting his estimates to management for approval. He usually bases his budget estimates on some combination of anticipated costs of planned studies, contemplated changes in policy and personnel, past experience, and a reserve for contingencies and for projects unanticipated at budget-making time but which may have to be conducted during the budgetary period. Management, at this stage of budget-making, can exercise control over marketing research expenditures in two ways—by approving or disapproving the proposed budget and by raising or lowering requests for specific items of expenditure. In many companies, too, after the budget has been finally approved and the department is operating under it, management exercises further control by requiring specific approval for expenditures over some predetermined amount and for expenditures involving the use of outside research assistance.

The fact that most marketing research budgets include a "reserve for contingencies" deserves additional comment. Although certain expenditures can be anticipated rather accurately for long periods into the future (e.g., the research director's salary), other expenditures are difficult if not impossible to forecast for even a few months ahead. Virtually without exception, at the time the budget is being put together, it is impossible to foresee all the problems that may have to be investigated, let alone to estimate the costs of carrying through the resulting marketing research projects. Problems which at budget-making time may be nonexistent, or simply not recognized as problems, may develop or become matters of importance, and it is obviously foolish to have to wait until the next budget period to begin investigations of them. Therefore, writers on marketing research generally recommend that there be a substantial contingency reserve, and that "earmarked" funds in the budget be limited to items that can be estimated with considerable accuracy for long periods ahead. Of course, some companies have less need than others for such contingency reserves. Specifically, there is less need in companies that consider budgets flexible guidelines to expenditure rather than rigid expenditure limits, which must be maintained regardless of the consequences.

Since the purpose of marketing research is to provide better information for management decisions, one effective managerial control over marketing research expenditures is to evaluate the information research provides. Most marketing research projects provide information helpful to deciding among two or more alternatives. If the correct decision would have been made without the additional information, the research expenditure makes no contribution to profit. If, for example, only 30 percent of the information provided by marketing research actually affects management decisions (the remainder making no contribution, or merely elaborating on what is already obvious), then the return on money invested in marketing research would be measured in terms of the value of that 30 percent in relation to total research costs.[30]

CONCLUSION

A marketing manager must have a keen understanding of marketing research's role in decision-making. He must understand how a carefully planned program of marketing research, designed to generate a flow of ideas and information, fits into the over-all decision-making process. He must appreciate the potential marketing research has for furnishing data on the forces affecting marketing decisions—data on the uncontrollables, the competitive situation, the controllables, and on market measurement and planning. He must realize that the starting point of any marketing research study should be mutual agreement (by management and the researcher) on the identity of the problem, since both research time and money are wasted unless the problem for study is accurately pinned down. He should see to it that each research project is truly a planned search for information—that each has well-defined research goals, an organized effort, a step-by-step schedule—all directed toward obtaining as reliable information

---

[30] For an interesting discussion of this idea see: D. W. Twedt, "What is the 'Return on Investment' in Marketing Research?", *Journal of Marketing*, January 1966, pp. 62-63.

as possible within the limits of time and money available. Because marketing research uses it so extensively, he must know enough about sampling to allow him to evaluate research results intelligently. He must know the strong and weak points of probability and non-probability sample designs and fully appreciate the significance of non-sampling and sampling errors in his appraisal of research results. Similarly, he must understand the main considerations entering into the determination of sample size, both to assist him in setting budgets for individual projects and in his later appraisals of resulting data. He should recognize how the total amount that should be budgeted for marketing research is affected by the size of his company, the nature of its operation, and its aspirations for marketing leadership. Finally, he should look upon the marketing research budget not as a rigid restriction on information-gathering activity but as a flexible guide, which can be adjusted with changing needs for information.

QUESTIONS AND PROBLEMS

1. "By contributing toward reductions in the cost of distributing goods from producer to consumer, marketing research makes it possible for the consumer to enjoy better products at lower prices than would otherwise be possible. By thus enabling each dollar to buy more, the entire standard of living of the people is raised to higher levels." Arthur C. Nielsen, Sr. in "Marketing Research—Past, Present and Future," *Nineteenth Charles Coolidge Parlin Memorial Lecture,* Philadelphia Chapter, American Marketing Association, May 21, 1963. Do you agree with Mr. Nielsen's contention? Why or why not?

2. In what way does the systems approach to marketing management change the traditional role of marketing research? Does it increase or decrease the role of research in marketing management? Explain.

3. Discuss the potential contributions marketing research can make during each of the several stages in the decision-making process. Analyze the relationship of internal and external studies to marketing decision-making.

4. Comment on the following two statements:
   a. "To manage a business well is to manage its future; and to manage the future is to manage information."
   b. "It is equally as important for management to know when not to use research as to know when to use it."

5. Refer to the list naming thirty-nine different major types of marketing research performed by American companies, and answer the following questions:

a. What information of value to decision-makers might each type of study provide?

b. Why is it that so few marketing research studies focus directly on the influences of uncontrollables?

c. Why do so many focus on the influence of controllables?

6. Who should identify the problems to be studied—the marketing researcher or the marketing decision-maker? Justify the position you take.

7. Explain the meaning of each of the following:
a. preliminary exploration
b. situation analysis
c. permissible sampling error

8. Differentiate:
a. primary and secondary data sources
b. factual, opinion, and interpretative surveys
c. experimental method and observational method
d. universe and sample
e. probability and non-probability samples
f. non-sampling error and sampling error

9. "Bad research is the cause of many marketing failures. Polling is the greatest contributor to marketing failure because it is conducted on the assumption that people can or will tell you why they buy a product." To what extent is this statement true? False?

10. Why should a marketing research project be a *planned* search for information? In planning a marketing research project, what types of decisions are required? Who should make them? Why?

11. What problems are involved in relating research objectives to the amount of money available for marketing research? Who should resolve these problems? Why?

12. Discuss the various criteria for choosing the research method(s) to be used in carrying out particular marketing research projects.

13. Explain how statisticians use the terms "accuracy" and "precision" in referring to samples.

14. How is sample size related to errors in sample results? When is a sample "the right size?" What does the decision-maker's willingness to assume risk have to do with sample size?

15. Compare and contrast the relative merits and limitations of probability and non-probability samples. Who should specify the type of sample—the marketing researcher or the decision-maker? Justify the position you take.

16. How do you explain the fact that the size of the marketing research

budget varies greatly from company to company and from industry to industry?

17. How should the decision be made on the amount of money to invest in a particular marketing research project? Who should make this decision? Why?

18. Discuss the various controls over marketing research expenditures that management might set up.

19. Under what conditions might the manager of a marketing research department ask that a "reserve for contingencies" be included in the budget for his department?

20. You have just been hired by a medium-sized manufacturer of dog food to set up and manage a marketing research department. You are to report directly to the vice-president in charge of marketing but, since the company has not previously had a formally-organized marketing research department, there is no clear-cut statement of departmental objectives and you have no job description as yet. Formulate a statement of department objectives and write a job description for your position as department head.

21. The Catskill Toy Manufacturing Company with annual sales of $2,500,000 sells its line of wooden toys mainly to schools and church organizations, but some mail-order business has been transacted with parents and other consumers. Even though the number of school-age children has grown significantly over the last decade, Catskill's unit volume has remained relatively stable with dollar sales increases being largely accounted for by price rises. The line of products ranges from building blocks sold in $1, $5, and $10 sets to large wooden playground equipment priced as high as $225. The company employs no salesmen but sells its products through school supply houses and manufacturers' agents, by means of a catalog distributed on request to interested parties. As the newly-appointed marketing vice-president of this concern, you have an advertising manager and a sales manager reporting to you and you have just been authorized to add a marketing research man to your staff. Outline the procedure you would follow in recruiting and selecting this new man. What kinds of studies would you want the new marketing research man to conduct and in what priority?

23

THE LEGAL ENVIRONMENT

As we have emphasized, no marketing decision-maker ever enjoys complete freedom; many uncontrollable factors—economic, technological, and behavioral—limit his freedom in choosing among different courses of action. In addition to these limits, there are the legal restraints. Frequently, certain alternatives have to be discarded because they are either plainly illegal or at least of doubtful legality. In this chapter, we examine the principal legal restraints on marketing decision-making.

Our focus will be, primarily, on the ways the law limits the marketing decision-maker. Some laws, however, legalize actions which would not otherwise be possible. For example, patent law protects a manufacturer for a period of time from having his product duplicated by competitors. Similarly, a manufacturer may register his trademark with the United States Patent Office and receive a degree of legal protection against others using or "adapting" it. In these and a few other instances, the law actually widens the scope within which marketing decisions can be made. However, these are the exceptional cases, for the law generally narrows this range.

Most of the legal restraints placed on marketing have come about because of the desire of law-making bodies to preserve competition. Business competition is one of the cornerstones of any free enterprise economy. It serves as a sort of natural protector of the public interest by forcing individual enterprises to produce and market those goods and services most in demand and—if competition functioned perfectly as an economic regulator —at prices just sufficient to cover costs. Although such "pure competition" probably has never existed, either in the United States or anywhere else, the benefits of competition are, as supposed in economic theory, sufficiently important that a high degree of competition is considered desirable. Keeping the level of competition as high as possible has long been considered a necessary and proper function of government. Generally speaking, the government has not intervened except where business activities tended to cause competition to break down or disappear. This philosophy was summed up by a former chairman of the Federal Trade Commission:

> . . . The instrument devised to snip the tentacles of monopoly was the antitrust laws. Instead of transferring economic power from one monolith to another, a method was invented to promote dispersal of power among private entrepreneurs. The major premise of antitrust is an unshakable belief in the efficacy of a competitive, free enterprise economy. The ideal to be realized is unlimited opportunity for entry into the market place, unlimited opportunity for self-development, and the resolution of economic issues by the unchecked exercise of free market forces.[1]

THE LAW AND MARKETING DECISIONS

The relationship of the law to the making of marketing decisions is often very vague. Law is actually a complex of limitations coming from a number of different sources. There are not only both federal and state law-making bodies but courts at both levels which, in rendering judicial interpretations, set precedents for decisions in further cases. Courts reach their decisions not only on the basis of statutory law but also according to the common law, which itself evolves over time as the cumulative result of court decisions on matters for which statutory law either provides no guidance or leaves room for differences in interpretation. Furthermore, some governmental agencies (for example, the Federal Trade Commission or the Food and Drug Administration) are charged with administering various pieces of legislation, while others (such as the Antitrust Division of the United States Depart-

[1] E. W. Kintner, "How Much Control Can Business Endure?" *Journal of Marketing*, July 1961, p. 3.

ment of Justice or the Federal Trade Commission) carry out the enforcement provisions of these pieces of legislation. Small wonder, then, that lawyers are reluctant or unable to state what "the law" is in every possible situation. One legal expert comments on this matter:

> We do not have, as some may think, a complete set of rules, exact in every detail, ready to be applied to any situation that may arise. Legal reasoning involves the fitting of a particular situation into the fabric of legal history. To do this requires consideration of several questions. Has there been a similar situation in the past? If so, how was it treated? Has there been any change in treatment through legislation? Despite apparent similarity, are there any significant distinctions between the present situation and those of the past? If there have been no similar situations in the past, have there been analogous situations? If no analogous situations have arisen, is there any legislation that may be applicable? What is the intent, meaning, and scope of such legislation? Has there been any extra-judicial writing on the subject? Are there any general or basic principles or concepts that may be applied? What effect will a decision in this matter have upon the future? It is difficult to say that any one item is of greater importance than any other. Whatever may shed light on the matter to be decided is considered before a final determination is reached.[2]

So, in most instances, the law provides no clear-cut guides for marketing decision-making. It is convenient to think of the body of law as constituting the "rules of the game," but the rules are subject to differences in judicial and administrative interpretation and are almost constantly changing. Furthermore, the vigor with which different aspects of the law are enforced varies both with the budget of the enforcement agency and with the strategy the agency chooses to pursue. It is not surprising, then, that the legal implications of specific marketing decisions are often difficult to predict.

One government agency, however, the Federal Trade Commission, has been outstanding in its efforts to provide marketing decision-makers with some clarification of the laws it administers and enforces. Historically, the FTC has sponsored trade practice conferences to serve this purpose. The outcome of such a conference, to which all known members of a particular industry are invited (manufacturers, wholesalers, retailers and other interested parties), is a set of trade practice rules designed to eliminate and prevent, on a voluntary and industry-wide basis, trade practices and methods of competition and business behavior that constitute violations of laws administered by the commission. Trade practice rules have been

---

[2] W. Zelermyer, *Legal Reasoning* (Englewood Cliffs, N.J.: Prentice-Hall, 1960), pp. 5-6.

formulated by approximately 200 different industries. The other chief means used by the FTC to provide clarification of the laws it administers and enforces has been the publication and widespread circulation of various guides, illustrating what is legal and illegal.

The following discussion is organized around the five main decision areas in marketing which are most affected by legal restraints: Competitive action, product, price, marketing channels, and promotion. Our intent is to provide marketing decision-makers with some appreciation of the legal boundaries, however vague and even ill-defined they may sometimes be, within which certain decisions must be made. In appraising the legal implications of any specific marketing decision, management should consult competent legal counsel.

COMPETITIVE ACTION

Many marketing decisions have, purposely or not, considerable impact on competitors. In fact, nearly every marketing decision has at least some effect on competition. This is certainly inherent in most decisions on those marketing areas discussed in succeeding sections of this chapter—decisions on products, prices, marketing channels, and promotion. Our concern at this point, however, is with the sort of decisions which may *directly* affect competition and possibly expose the decision-making company to prosecution under the antitrust statutes.

Decisions Involving Expansion

Decisions involving expansion, particularly if the company is already of substantial size, should be made only after taking into account the possibilities of antitrust prosecution; the legal danger is that the company *may* be charged with unlawfully monopolizing or attempting to monopolize a market. There are only two avenues of corporate growth—one through gradual, natural expansion, the other through merger with or acquisition of other firms. Either may lead eventually to antitrust prosecution but, historically at least, lawmakers and enforcement agencies have shown greater interest in the merger or acquisition route than in the natural expansion route.

Legal restraints on growth have gradually become more restrictive. The first piece of federal antitrust legislation, the Sherman Antitrust Act of 1890,[3] in its Section 2, declared monopolization or attempts to monopolize illegal. Various difficulties in enforcing the Sherman Act, to-

[3] 26 Stat. 209, Chap. 647.

gether with certain judicial setbacks suffered by the government, resulted in the enactment of the Clayton Antitrust Act in 1914.[4] Section 7 of the Clayton Act prohibits a corporation from acquiring the stock of a competing corporation in the same industry or line of commerce, and prohibits a holding company from acquiring the stock of two or more competing corporations where such acquisition would substantially lessen competition, or restrain commerce, or tend to create a monopoly. When enacted, the law did not prevent corporate merger through the acquisition by one corporation of the assets of another, or of several competitors. In 1950, Section 7 of the Clayton Act was amended by the Celler-Kefauver Antimerger Act,[5] which aimed to block corporate growth through the acquisition of assets.

Not every corporate merger or consolidation is illegal—only those which *may* have the defined adverse effect on competition. In short, any acquisition or merger is illegal if its effect is "substantially to lessen competition or to tend to create a monopoly." Such acquisitions or mergers may be horizontal (with competitors), vertical (with suppliers or customers), or conglomerate (with concerns producing entirely different products or marketing them in quite different markets). Lessening of competition means, in general, a decrease in competition or a foreclosure of competitors from the market. In other words, when competition is lessened, monopoly power exists.

Monopoly power has been generally defined by the courts to consist of the power to control prices or the power to exclude competition—with strong emphasis on the word "power." This is what the government attempts to prove in prosecuting alleged violations of Section 7 of the Clayton Act, as amended by the Celler-Kefauver Antimerger Act. It does *not* have to prove intent, i.e., that the corporation acquiring stock or assets *intended* to lessen competition or to create a monopoly.[6] All that the government has to show is that there is a *reasonable probability* that the acquisition will have the prohibited lessening effect on competition.

The issues to be determined in an action challenging the legitimacy of an acquisition include the line or lines of commerce (i.e., the type of business or the product involved) and the section or sections of the country in which the effects may be felt (the "area of effective competition").[7] Thus, the outcome often turns on the particular definition of "market share" that the court accepts. The market share concept obviously combines both the question of the type of business or product involved, and that of the geographic market areas in which competitors vie for sales. In the famed *Cellophane* case, the issue boiled down to whether du Pont

[4] 38 Stat. 730, Chap. 323.
[5] 64 Stat. 1125.
[6] *U.S. v. E. I. du Pont de Nemours and Co., et al.* (U.S. Sup. Ct. 1957), 353 U.S. 586.
[7] *U.S. v. Bethlehem Steel Corp., et al.* (D.C. N.Y. 1958) 157 F. Supp. 877.

was competing in the cellophane market, where it had approximately 75 percent of the market, or in the "flexible wrapping materials" market (which includes not only cellophane but even such items as wax paper and gift wraps), where the company had less than 18 percent of the total business.[8]

In a more recent case, the court extended its definition of market share, finding that a proposed merger between Atlantic Richfield Company and Sinclair Oil Corporation would probably constitute a violation of Section 7.[9] In this market, the nine largest oil firms sold 74 percent of total volume. Atlantic Richfield, the ninth largest firm, would achieve 7.4 percent of the market by merging with Sinclair, the twelfth largest firm. An additional factor cited by the court was the difficulty of entry by new competition because of the very large investment required.

The merger or acquisition route to expansion is fraught with legal complications, but companies that choose to take the natural growth route also have their problems. Once a company has achieved substantial size, and as it gains an increasing share of the market, management begins to fear the possibility of adverse government action.[10] There is little question but that in such a company, out of fear of government action, there is often a tendency to hobble the competitive skills at management's command. George Romney, ex-president of American Motors Corporation, proposed a possible solution to this dilemma:

> . . . the antitrust laws should provide that when any one firm in a basic industry, such as the automobile business, exceeds a specific percentage of total industry sales over a specified period of time, it shall be required by law to propose to an administrative agency a plan of divestiture that will bring its percentage of sales below the specified level. Where a firm is engaged in more than one basic industry, the maximum percentage of total industry sales should be fixed by law at a point lower than the percentage to be fixed for companies operating in only a single basic industry. Where a company is engaged in more than one basic industry, its competitive position is strengthened and it is able to dominate a single market with a lower percentage. This results from its ability to concentrate its resources on a single industry or product at any time and to expand its market position by relying on earnings from its other activities.

[8] Ultimately, the court decided that the relevant market was that for all flexible wrapping materials and du Pont was acquitted. See: *U.S.* v. *E.I. du Pont de Nemours and Co.*, 76 Sup. Ct. 994 (June 1956).

[9] *United States* v. *Atlantic Richfield Co. and Sinclair Oil Corp.*, CCH 72,716 (D.C.S.N.Y., February, 1969).

[10] G. Romney, "Toward Economic Freedom—A Plan for Coping with Bigness," *Business Horizons*, Summer 1959, p. 26.

This proposed amendment of the antitrust laws would have a number of advantages:

1. It would promote and preserve adequate competition.
2. The companies affected, not the Government, would have the opportunity to originate the method of compliance.
3. Achievement of the sales percentage requiring a split off or "birth" would become evidence of economic success.
4. Competitive effort and growth would be encouraged, not restrained.
5. Instead of making mere size itself an offense, the test under the law would be based on the size of a company in relation to that of its competitors. In big industries there would be big companies.
6. An adequate number of companies in each basic industry would be assured.[11]

Decisions Requiring Cooperative Relations with Competitors

Most marketing decisions involving any sort of cooperative relationship with competitors should be entered into only with an acute consciousness of the antitrust laws. Particularly vulnerable to antitrust prosecution are price agreements with competitors, for under the law they are illegal *per se*. This means, in effect, that the courts will condemn them without considering any mitigating circumstances, which may have caused them. The courts have even held that it is illegal for competitors to exchange information about prices. An agreement among competitors in the container industry to make price lists available to each other upon request helped result in price uniformity and was, therefore, held to be within the ban of Section 1 of the Sherman Act.[12] When there is doubt concerning the legality of an action, it is advisable to seek a ruling from the Federal Trade Commission. For example, poultry processors were given prior approval for a plan to make available actual production and sales information to members on a daily basis, using data processing equipment, without normally revealing the names of individual processors.[13]

Many pricing practices involving combinations of or conspiracies among competitors are considered illegal. It is not only illegal for competi-

[11] Testimony in "Administered Prices," hearings before the Subcommittee on Antitrust and Monopoly, Committee on the Judiciary, U.S. Senate, 85th Congress, 2nd Session, 1958, pt. 6, pp. 2887-89.

[12] *United States* v. *Container Corporation of America, et al.*, 89 Sup. Ct. 510 (January, 1969).

[13] "Federal Trade Commission Advisory Opinion No. 303," *CCH 18,557* (October, 1968); *BNA ATRR No. 380* (October 22, 1968), A-11.

tors to fix prices among themselves, but also for them to agree upon uniform terms of sale. It is illegal for competing firms to use the same basing-point system in making price quotations, i.e., to compute delivered-price quotations all from the same shipping point or points; the effect of a basing-point system used by two or more competitors is that all sellers' prices are uniform to any one buyer, regardless of his or their geographical locations. Collusion among bidders is another pricing practice strictly prohibited and fairly frequently the subject of court action. Any management is "skating on thin legal ice" when it permits itself to be drawn into *any* sort of pricing arrangement with competitors.

Many other cooperative relationships with competitors are just as likely to result in antitrust prosecution. For instance, in the women's dress industry, a combination of designers, manufacturers, converters, and dyers used restrictive sales agreements with retailers to prevent other manufacturers from copying designs for sale at lower prices. Although the intent of the combination was to prevent "style piracy," the court ruled that the agreement was illegal since the means used to gain this end went against federal law.[14] In another case, manufacturers of street lighting equipment were enjoined by a consent decree (an agreement entered into as an alternative to prosecuting) from conspiring to divide among themselves manufacturing or sales territories, customers, or marketing channels, among other practices.[15] In still another case, producers of soda ash were enjoined in a consent decree from acquiring or threatening to acquire excess productive facilities not intended to be used by them, but threatening to competitors and discouraging to prospective entrants into the field.[16] These illustrations emphasize the necessity for considering the antitrust implications of any decision which, to be carried out, would require the cooperation of competitors.

Decisions on Competitive Tactics

The law has limited the tactics a company can use in fighting a competitor. It has been held illegal, for example, for a company to misrepresent or disparage a competitor's products, its methods of doing business, or its financial standing and reliability. It is also illegal to cut off a competitor's source of supply, whether by individual effort or in collusion with others. In one case, for example, the use of special contracts as a device to sell oranges to favored processors at a substantially lower price, where the

[14] *Fashion Originators' Guild of America, Inc., et al.* v. *F.T.C.*, CCH *Trade Cases* (1940-1943), Par. 56,101.
[15] *U.S.* v. *General Electric Co., et al.* (D.C. Ohio 1952), CCH, *Trade Cases* (1952), Par. 67,301.
[16] *U.S.* v. *Solvay Process Co., et al.* (D.C. Kansas 1944), CCH, *Trade Cases* (1944-1945), Par. 57,229.

seller controlled 70 percent of the available oranges and had the power to set prices, was held unlawful since the effect was to exclude a complaining processor from competition.[17] However, a firm can sometimes be excluded from competition, as when one court, regarding such action as being in "the public interest," held that it was legal for the city of New York to grant an exclusive franchise in a public market.[18]

DECISIONS ON PRODUCTS

There are several reasons that legal restraints have been imposed on certain product decisions. Some restraints came about as side effects of the legislative effort to preserve and maintain a high degree of competition. Others trace to the legal protection afforded individual concerns against having their products duplicated by others. Still others exist because of the desire of lawmakers and governmental agencies to protect the interests of consumers. In operational terms, these restraints affect decision-making with respect to adding new products, product design, product quality, and information included on the product label.

New Product Addition

Decisions on new products may be equivalent to the decisions on expansion discussed earlier. If a new-product decision is tied to a decision on a merger with or an acquisition of another firm, the provisions of the Celler-Kefauver Antimerger Act will, of course, apply. Such a merger or consolidation is illegal, if it *may* tend to "substantially lessen competition or tend to create a monopoly." Similarly, if a new-product decision requires the purchase of certain assets from another firm, i.e., without actually merging or consolidating with that firm, there may be antitrust prosecution on the grounds that this *may* have an adverse effect on competition. Existence of these restraints strongly suggests that, from a legal standpoint, the safest way of securing new products is through their origination in the firm's own research and development program.

Product Design

Decisions on product design are subject to restraints imposed by patent law. The holder of a design patent is protected against others using his design during the term the patent is in force, which may be for three and

[17] *Sunkist Growers, Inc.* v. *Winckler & Smith Citrus Products Co.*, CCH, *Trade Cases* (1960), Par. 69,823.
[18] *American Consumer Industries, Inc.* v. *City of New York*, CCH 72,119 (N.Y. Sup. Ct., June, 1967); BNA ATRR No. 309 June 13, 1967, A-7.

one-half, seven, or fourteen years. Patents initially granted for terms of three and one-half or seven years are renewable, but may not be in effect for more than fourteen years in all. During the time a design patent is in force, its holder enjoys what is, in essence, a monopoly over its use. If he wishes, he may license others to use the patent, receiving royalty payments in return, but, except in rare instances, he is under no legal compulsion to do so. Thus, the law keeps a firm from designing a product that is "similar" to one made and patented by a competitor. (A product is considered "similar" if consumers consider its design or outward appearance to be the same as that of an established product.) Patent law is extremely complicated, especially in concerning what constitutes an "illegally similar" product design. Therefore, in deciding on product design, management does well not only in guarding against copying competitive designs, but in retaining the help of competent patent attorneys.

Product Quality

In some product areas, the law limits the discretion enjoyed by management in making decisions on product quality. The Food, Drug, and Cosmetic Act,[19] for instance, enacted by Congress in 1938, authorizes the Food and Drug Administration to establish minimum quality standards for food products. The act also gives this agency the power to fix standard grades for specific kinds of food products and, as a result, many official grade definitions have been published, including ones for most canned fruits and vegetables. Packers are not forced to affix the official grade designations to their products, but they are legally required to keep product quality as high as the "identity standard" (the standard set up for the relevant official grade). This act also prohibits the adulteration and sale of any food, drug, therapeutic device, or cosmetic that may endanger public health; the law defines what constitutes adulteration within each of these product classes. There are, in addition, numerous state and local laws relating to the quality of individual products such as milk, cheese, and cream.

Product Packaging and Labeling

The Fair Packaging and Labeling Act (1967) provides that the package label must disclose product identity, name and location of manufacturer, packer or distributor, net quantity of contents (weight, measure, numerical count and net quantity of a serving or application when represented). In addition, the net quantity contents must be expressed—in terms of weight, measure, numerical count, or a combination of these as dictated

---

[19] 52 Stat. 1046, Chap. 3.

by existing trade usage—provided the description furnishes sufficient information to facilitate value comparisons by consumers. This net quantity statement must appear on the main display panel in adequate type size and in close proximity to the main printing of the trade name.[20]

Special laws, applicable to some industries, further regulate the nature and content of the information that the product label must include. For products coming within the Food and Drug Administration's regulatory authority, the label must state a warning if the product is dangerous to use or habit-forming. If a product is a flammable fabric, the Flammable Fabric Act [21] requires that there be a warning to the effect. The Textile Fiber Products Identification Act,[22] enforced by the Federal Trade Commission, specifies that products containing natural or artificial textile fibers intended for sale to ultimate consumers must be tagged or labeled to show: (1) the generic name or names (i.e., names actually descriptive of the fibers) of the fibers contained (for any fiber which constitutes five percent or more of the total fiber weight of the product); (2) the percentage of each fiber present, and (3) the country of origin, if the fiber is imported. Furthermore, the name of the manufacturer or other concern marketing the product must appear on the label. Similar labeling requirements for wool and fur products are contained in the Wool Products Labeling Act [23] and the Fur Products Labeling Act.[24] Sellers who fail to comply with these labeling requirements are charged with misbranding.

In all industries not covered by special laws, the FTC maintains a constant watch for instances of misbranding. Misbranding generally means some form of misrepresentation on a label as to the composition, properties, or origin of the product. Thus, to comply with the law, a label must be accurate and complete in all essential details.

State and local laws also contain provisions for the quality and labeling of specific products. For example, the Florida Citrus Commission enforces certain quality standards for such citrus products as chilled orange juice sold in paper cartons. During certain seasons of the year, the oranges available do not produce juice with enough solids to meet the commission's standard. The standard can be met by adding sugar to the juice; however, when this is done, the commission requires the packer to label the product "substandard." The courts have held that this regulation is necessary to protect the consuming public against deception.[25]

[20] "Federal Trade Commission proposed Regulations Under the Fair Packaging and Labeling Act," *CCH 50,173*, July 1967, *CCH Newsletter 313* (Extra Edition), June 28, 1967.
[21] 67 Stat. 111, Chap. 164, Secs. 1-13.
[22] 72 Stat. 1717.
[23] 54 Stat. 1128, Chap. 871.
[24] 65 Stat. 175, Chap. 298.
[25] *Florida Citrus Commission* v. *Golden Gift, Inc.*, 91 So. 2nd 657 (Fla. Sup. Ct., Oct. 11, 1956).

PRICE DECISIONS

Among the most basic marketing decisions are those on pricing, and no class of decisions is more hedged in by legal restraints. Federal antitrust legislation has implications for pricing; the "power to control prices" is one of the tests applied by the courts in determining the existence of monopoly power. By the terms of the Clayton Act, the practice of discriminating in price among buyers was declared illegal if the effect was "substantially to lessen competition or tend to create a monopoly in any line of commerce." Passage, in 1936, of the Robinson-Patman Act,[26] amending Section 2 of the Clayton Act, added further conditions under which companies could be charged with price discrimination and outlawed certain other practices involving negotiations between sellers and buyers. For most sellers, the Robinson-Patman Act contains by far the largest group of restraints on pricing decisions. Among the other laws affecting pricing decisions is legislation at the state level permitting resale price maintenance and forbidding sales below cost.

Price Discrimination

The Clayton Act, as amended by the Robinson-Patman Act, prohibits any direct or indirect price discrimination by a seller among different purchasers of commodities of like grade and quality, where the effect is to injure competition. The law prohibits price discrimination, but it does permit certain differentials in price. A seller may vary his prices among buyers in line with differences in costs incurred in serving them, but the differential legally cannot exceed the cost differences incurred in manufacture, sale, or delivery, resulting from differing methods or quantities in which commodities are sold or delivered. Moreover, the seller must be prepared to justify such differences if he is charged with price discrimination. Proving that such differences are justified is extraordinarily difficult. Respondents in price discrimination cases have sometimes spent large sums on cost studies only to find that the findings "do not stand up in court." As one authority puts it, "it is one thing to agree on costs among businessmen where litigation is not involved, and it is quite another to make the kind of showing of costs which will stand up under the testing which it receives in a courtroom."[27]

Price discriminations resulting from the attempts of sellers to meet competitor's prices apparently were legalized under provisions of

[26] 49 Stat. 1526, Chap. 592.
[27] H. F. Taggart, "The Role of Cost in Public Policy Toward Business," in L. H. Stockman, ed., *Advancing Marketing Efficiency* (Chicago: American Marketing Association, 1959), p. 333.

Section 2(a) of the Robinson-Patman Act. Charged with price discrimination, many companies have based their defenses on the contention that they were acting in "good faith" in meeting competitors' price reductions. Unfortunately, however, different courts have rendered what appear to be inconsistent decisions and have not spelled out clearly the conditions under which the "good faith" defense is accepted or rejected. Consequently, it is difficult to draw definite conclusions about the use of this defense, but the facts seem to indicate that this portion of the law has been of little help as a guide in making pricing decisions.[28]

Nonetheless, a recent decision upheld the use of the "good faith" defense. FTC claimed that the defendant, National Dairy Products Corporation, had failed to prove its competitors' prices were the same or lower. The court held that the burden of proof imposed by FTC was too strict and that the price differentials were allowable.[29]

Provisions of the Robinson-Patman Act also legalize differences in price, which result from fluctuating market prices, the threatened obsolescence of a perishable product, or other abnormal marketing conditions.

NON-CUMULATIVE QUANTITY DISCOUNTS   A non-cumulative quantity discount is a price reduction allowed a buyer for placing a single order for a single shipment of a given product quantity. Under the law, a seller must start with a basically uniform price to all comparable buyers, e.g., to all wholesalers. He can quote lower prices for larger orders, but he must make the same offer available to all comparable buyers. Furthermore, he must be prepared to prove that a lower price given on a particular size of order was justified by savings in costs of manufacturing, selling, or delivering. The non-cumulative quantity discount, based as it is on the size of a single order and shipment, is relatively the easiest discount to justify under the Robinson-Patman Act.

CUMULATIVE QUANTITY DISCOUNTS   A cumulative quantity discount is a price reduction allowed to a buyer who purchases a given quantity of a product over some specified period. It is based, in other words, on the cumulative purchases of a customer made within some period of time, usually a year. The Robinson-Patman Act does not specifically outlaw such discounts, but they are extremely difficult to justify in terms of cost savings. Suppose, for example, that customer A buys $200,000 worth of goods in a year as a result of fifty calls by salesmen and the placing and filling of fifty separate orders, and that customer B places a single order for $200,000

---

[28] L. X. Tarpey, "What About the Good Faith Defense?" *Journal of Marketing*, July 1960, p. 65.

[29] *National Dairy Products Corp. v. Federal Trade Commission*, CCH 72,445 (CA-7, April, 1968); *BNA ATRR No. 358* (May 21, 1968), A-21, X-8.

worth of merchandise. It is easy to see that the costs of selling and shipping to A would be greater than they would to B, and it would be virtually impossible to justify a cumulative quantity discount to A on the basis of cost savings. This illustrates why pricing schemes that include cumulative quantity discounts are so vulnerable to charges of price discrimination.

FUNCTIONAL DISCOUNTS   A manufacturer often sells his product to customers engaged in different phases of distribution. For instance, a manufacturer of household paper products may distribute some of his production through wholesalers and sell the rest directly to retail outlets. In these instances, the price to wholesalers must ordinarily be lower than to retailers. The wholesaler not only has expenses of doing business but must price the product to retailers at a low enough figure for them to compete with those retailers who buy directly from the manufacturer. The discount, in this example, given to wholesalers but not to retailers is known as a functional discount, i.e., a discount based on difference in function.

The Robinson-Patman Act is silent on the question of whether such discounts are legal or illegal. In determining the legality of a particular functional discount, it is necessary to ascertain its effect on competition. If it may injure competition, it is illegal. With regard to the illustration in the preceding paragraph, if the wholesaler is engaged strictly in the wholesaling of the manufacturer's products, and the retailer strictly in retailing them, and if all wholesalers are extended identical functional discounts and all retailers sold directly pay the same price, then the price differential should not have an adverse effect on competition, and the functional discount would be legal. But where the wholesaler *competes* with the retailer in selling directly to the consumer—even where he also makes sales to retailers—or where a customer who might be classified as a retailer actually performs what is in some degree a wholesale function—such as reselling to other retailers—then that difference in price will have a tendency and capacity to injure competition, and the functional discount is likely to be held illegal.[30]

"DUMMY" BROKERAGE PAYMENTS   Before the Robinson-Patman Act was passed, large buyers, especially corporate chains, often obtained the benefits of price discrimination through the subterfuge of maintaining a purchasing subsidiary, which operated ostensibly as a broker for prospective sources of supply. Such subsidiaries charged sellers the normal brokerage fees and passed them back to parent companies. "Dummy" brokerage payments of this kind were outlawed by Section 2(c) of the Robinson-Patman

---

[30] A. G. Seidman, "Some Aspects of the Law Concerning Pricing," in *Competitive Pricing*, A.M.A. Management Report No. 17 (New York: American Management Association, Inc., 1958), p. 63.

Act. In enforcing this provision, the Federal Trade Commission has considered brokerage relationships artificial and illegal when indirect control over the broker by the buyer could be proved. It is illegal either to receive or to pay dummy brokerage fees. Furthermore, it is illegal for a seller to grant and a buyer to accept an extra discount in place of a brokerage fee.

LIABILITY OF BUYERS AT DISCRIMINATORY PRICES   Section 2(f) of the Robinson-Patman Act prohibits buyers from inducing or knowingly receiving the benefits of price discrimination. One case involved several automotive parts wholesalers who formed a buying association to obtain quantity discounts, which they could not have obtained separately. Individual members of the association submitted direct and unconsolidated orders to suppliers, who, in turn, made direct shipments to members. Suppliers realized no savings in shipping and order-processing costs and, consequently, there was no cost justification for the lower prices; the arrangement was judged a violation of Section (2f).[31]

Resale Price Maintenance

Resale price maintenance or "fair trade" refers to the legal process whereby a manufacturer sets the prices at which middlemen may resell his brand. Until the passage of the Miller-Tydings Act,[32] amending Section 1 of the Sherman Act, vertical price agreements (e.g., between a manufacturer and any middleman) were illegal in interstate commerce. The Miller-Tydings Act, in effect, made it lawful for a manufacturer to enter into a vertical price agreement with resellers situated in states that had laws permitting resale price maintenance. Almost all states at one time or another, have enacted such laws—all but Alaska, Missouri, Texas and Vermont, and the District of Columbia. Of these acts, two (those of Montana and Utah) have been declared unconstitutional by upper courts, and one (that of Ohio) has been so declared by a lower court.

The most controversial feature of the state fair trade acts has been the non-signers' clause. This clause permits a brand owner to sign a resale price maintenance contract with any dealer or distributor and, upon giving notice to all dealers or distributors involved in the particular state, the contract becomes binding on all parties selling the brand. The constitutionality of the non-signers' clause has been under almost continual attack in the courts.

[31] *American Motor Specialties Co., Inc.* v. *F.T.C.*, CCH, *Trade Cases* (1960), Par. 69, 712.

[32] 50 Stat. 693, Chap. 690, Title VIII.

The Miller-Tydings Act did not legalize any price fixing except that conforming to state laws allowing resale price maintenance. It was silent with respect to the legality of the non-signers' provision in state laws. In the famous *Schwegmann Brothers* decision of 1951, the United States Supreme Court held that price fixing by compulsion against non-contracting dealers, although permitted by state acts, was a violation of federal antitrust laws.[33] The next year, in 1952, Congress passed the McGuire Act,[34] modifying the Miller-Tydings amendment to Section 1 of the Sherman Act. The McGuire Act nullified the effect of the *Schwegmann* decision by specifically exempting from federal antitrust prosecution those fair traders who desired to enforce fair trade prices among non-signers in states where such action was permitted. In addition, the McGuire Act (1) legalized contracts establishing stipulated prices as well as those prescribing only minimum prices, and (2) made it legal for a brand manufacturer, where allowed by state law, to require a wholesale buyer to enter into a resale price agreement with his customers, for purposes of making the established resale price effective.

The so-called "fair trade" states vary as to whether minimum or absolute resale prices may be agreed upon and as to the conditions under which resellers are permitted to depart from the fair trade price. Whereas most states permit the establishment only of minimum resale prices, some states also allow the setting of absolute resale prices. In most states, reductions from the established price are legal when the product is altered (e.g., a man's suit returned by a customer), secondhand, damaged, or deteriorated. In nearly all states, price reductions on fair-traded items are permitted when made by an officer acting under court order. In several states, reductions from the fair trade prices are allowed when the trademark, brand, or name is obliterated or removed from the product.

The rise of trading stamps as a retail promotional device has had an impact on fair trade practice. In more than half of the states, retailers may not give trading stamps with the sale of fair-traded items, but there are many exceptions to this—including such states as California, Illinois, Michigan, New Jersey, and New York. Courts in some states have held that trading stamps are a form of cash discount, i.e., a reduction given to customers for prompt payment of cash. In these states, then, the fair trade laws are considered not violated when trading stamps are given along with purchases of fair-traded goods.[35] This doctrine, known as the "cash discount" theory of trading stamps, is highly controversial and will undoubtedly continue to be challenged in the courts.

[33] *Schwegmann Bros. et al.* v. *Calvert Distillers Corp.*, 341 U.S. 384.
[34] 66 Stat. 631, Chap. 745.
[35] *Corning Glass Works* v. *Max Dichter Co., Inc., and Man-Bur Sales, Inc.*, CCH, *Trade Cases* (1960), Par. 69,743.

Restrictions on Minimum Prices

Minimum prices have been the subject of legislation in many states. Unfair Sales Acts or Unfair Trade Practices Acts, prohibiting sales below cost-plus-a-certain-percentage markup, have been passed in more than half of the states. These are laws of general application: they apply to all goods sold by wholesalers and retailers; there are no requirements, as in the case of the fair trade laws, that the goods be branded or that formal vertical price-fixing agreements be signed. Some of these laws, e.g., those of Connecticut and Wisconsin, specify minimum percentage markups over cost as the lowest price at which any item may be resold. The usual figures are 2 percent over the wholesaler's cost and 6 percent over the retailer's cost, with cost being defined as the invoice cost. Arizona has no minimum percentage markup for wholesalers but decrees a minimum 12 percent markup over cost for retailers. In a few states there are no specific markup requirements, and net purchase cost is considered the minimum resale price. There is a provision in most state laws stating that the act applies where there has been "the purpose . . . or the effect of injuring a competitor or destroying competition." It should also be noted that the FTC considers it to be an unfair competitive practice for a seller to sell below cost in order to drive out competitors. Most Unfair Trade Practices Acts permit sales at prices below cost for certain types of transactions, including sales of seasonal or perishable goods, clearance sales, and sales to meet the legal prices of a competitor.

More than a score of states have laws prohibiting sales below cost for specific classes of products. Alabama, Arkansas, Indiana, Maryland, Massachusetts, New Jersey, Ohio, and Washington forbid either wholesalers or retailers to sell cigarettes below cost. Arkansas prohibits the wholesale or retail sale of liquor below cost. Louisiana outlaws below-cost retail sales of drug and cosmetic products. Massachusetts prohibits below-cost wholesale and retail sales of motor fuel. Utah forbids sales by manufacturers, wholesalers, and retailers of agricultural products at prices less than cost-plus-6 percent.

Most laws restricting minimum prices to cost are designed to protect middlemen against ruinous competition. But, in 1964, New York state passed a law to insure that consumers were not gouged by excessive prices for liquor. The Minimum Alcohol Price Law requires that New York liquor prices not exceed the lowest prices for similar liquor products throughout the nation.[36] The courts have held that this law has precedence when it came into conflict with minimum price laws.

Evidently, in some jurisdictions, it is possible to circumvent the

---

[36] *Victor Fischel & Co., Inc. v. R. H. Macy & Co., Inc., CCH 72,154* (N.Y. Ct. of App., July, 1967); BNA ATRR No. 314 (July 18, 1967), A-10.

sales-below-cost laws through the use of trading stamps. In Oklahoma, for instance, a chain grocery retailer was prevented from making price reductions in order to meet trading stamp competition. The Oklahoma Supreme Court ruled that trading stamps were a cash discount, and therefore could not be considered a price cut, which could be met by a competitor. The United States Supreme Court later upheld this decision.[37] In Minnesota, however, several retailers were charged with violating the state Unfair Trade Practices Act when they gave "bonus" stamps, or trading stamps in excess of the number regularly given, and the court granted temporary injunctions against the practice.[38]

MARKETING CHANNEL DECISIONS

With comparatively few exceptions (e.g., the public utilities industry), the law does not interfere with the manufacturer's freedom to determine his own marketing channels, or to "pick and choose" from among the available middlemen those whom he desires as members of his channel team. But once buying-selling relationships have been established with middlemen customers, the law is concerned in a number of instances with the nature of these relationships.

Many of the earlier-discussed legal restraints on marketing decisions also apply to decisions bearing on the manufacturer's relations with the middlemen in his marketing channel. For instance, provisions of the Celler-Kefauver Act determine the legality of a vertical merger of a manufacturer with one of his customers. The legality of the merger would depend on whether there was a reasonable probability that competition might be adversely affected—i.e., either with other manufacturers or with businesses that formerly competed with the customer. Similarly, inasmuch as price decisions strongly influence the relationships of buyers and sellers, nearly all the discussion of such topics as price discrimination and resale price maintenance applies with equal force here. We leave it to the reader to think through such legal restraints as those imposed by the Robinson-Patman Act, the state Fair Trade Laws, and the McGuire Act, and to determine for himself their implications for decisions involving relationships with members of marketing channels.

But there are still other legal restraints bearing on the manufacturer's relationships with middlemen.

[37] *Safeway Stores, Inc.*, v. *Oklahoma Retail Grocers Association, Inc.*, 79 S. Ct. 1196 (June 1959).
[38] M. C. Howard in K. J. Curran (ed.), "Legal Developments in Marketing," *Journal of Marketing*, April 1961, p. 80.

Exclusive Dealing

The term "exclusive dealing" refers to an arrangement where a manufacturer agrees to permit a dealer to handle his product only if the dealer consents to buy all his requirements for this type of product from the manufacturer and none whatever from competing suppliers. Generally speaking, any contract with a buyer requiring him to buy all his needs from one supplier is illegal.[39] But, as ever, it is a necessary condition for illegality that competition be impaired or threatened. This condition is practically always present and relatively easy to prove, for the effect of exclusive dealing is necessarily the foreclosing of competitors from selling to dealers who have signed an exclusive dealing contract with a supplier.

The Federal Trade Commission prosecutes exclusive dealing arrangements under Section 3 of the Clayton Act, which prohibits exclusive dealing when the effect is "to substantially lessen competition or tend to create a monopoly in any line of commerce." While a dealer may decide, entirely on his own volition, to buy from only one supplier, existence of a formal contract to that effect is likely to be construed as evidence that the supplier applied unlawful pressure in forcing the decision. It is also illegal for a supplier to refuse to sell to a dealer who stocks competitive products, if that dealer has previously handled the supplier's brand. It is up to the dealer involved, in such cases, to decide whether or not to continue dealing with the competition. Even the argument that exclusive dealing was necessary to permit the development of franchising and the preservation of small business was found to be an inadequate justification for exclusive dealing.[40]

Tying Contracts

Section 3 of the Clayton Act also prohibits the tying contract, a device closely related to exclusive dealing. A tying contract involves the sale or lease of products on condition that the purchaser or lessee buy or use certain other goods that the seller or lessor offers to supply. For a manufacturer to make effective use of either exclusive dealing or tying contracts, he must possess powerful leverage with respect to at least some of the products offered for sale—for instance, when a manufacturer markets a brand so strongly preferred by consumers that dealers do not dare refrain from stocking it. Conversely, the dealer or distributor restricts his own freedom to buy elsewhere when he agrees not to handle competing products, or to

[39] U.S. v. *American Optical Co., et al.* (DC Ill. 1951), *CCH Trade Cases* (1950-51), Par. 62, 869.
[40] *Serta Associates, Inc.* v. *United States,* CCH 72, 721 (U.S. Sup. Ct., February, 1969).

buy some items he would not otherwise buy; therefore, he must be in some way compelled to surrender this freedom. Ordinarily, the supplier has the bargaining power when he enjoys a partial monopoly over the supply of some particular product.[41] In other words, a manufacturer must use monopoly power as a lever to gain greater monopoly power if he is to make effective use of either exclusive dealing or tying contracts. Thus, the effect is substantially to lessen competition, in violation of Section 3 of the Clayton Act.[42] Recently, one court held that "tying arrangements are not illegal *per se*." To be declared illegal, it must be demonstrated that the price is much higher for the desired product alone and that this differential cannot be explained by quality differences or legitimate cost justifications.[43]

Automobile Dealers Franchise Act

The Automobile Dealers Franchise Act,[44] is concerned specifically with certain aspects of manufacturer-dealer relations in the automobile industry. The stated purpose of this law is "to balance the powers now heavily weighted in favor of automobile manufacturers, by enabling franchised automobile dealers to bring suits in the district courts of the United States to recover damages sustained by reason of the failure of automobile manufacturers to act in good faith in complying with the terms of franchises or in terminating or not renewing franchises with their dealers." "Good faith" is defined as the duty to act in a fair and equitable manner to guarantee freedom from coercion, intimidation, or threats of coercion or intimidation. This law is said to assure an automobile dealer an opportunity to secure a judicial determination—irrespective of the terms of the franchise, which in the past sometimes ruled out recourse to judicial determination—as to whether an automobile manufacturer has failed to act in good faith in performing or complying with any of the provisions of his franchise or in terminating, cancelling, or not renewing his franchise.[45] The automobile manufacturers find consolation in the fact that this statute also requires the franchised dealers to act in good faith.

Manufacturers in other industries, especially those making extensive use of distribution through franchised dealers, may well ponder the

[41] G. W. Stocking and M. W. Watkins, *Monopoly and Free Enterprise* (New York: The Twentieth Century Fund, 1951), p. 337.

[42] *Ibid.*, p. 363.

[43] *American Manufacturers Mutual Insurance Co., American Motorists Ins. Co., Federal Mutual Insurance Co. and Lumbermens Mutual Casualty Co.* v. *American Broadcasting-Paramount Theatres, Inc.*, CCH 72,117, (D.C. S.N.Y., May 1967); BNA ATRR No. 310 (June 20, 1967) A-10.

[44] 70 Stat. 1125, Chap. 1038, Secs. 1-3.

[45] CCH, *Trade Regulation Reporter*, Par. 9,070.

significance this legislation has for them. Is it a forerunner of similar statutes to come? Is it a piece of "handwriting on the wall"? Perhaps they should consider seriously the comments of a distinguished professor of law who wrote the following:

> No doubt arming a dealer with the power of legal complaint if his franchise is terminated without cause flies in the face of competition's traditional reliance on freedom of customer selection and rejection. But if the laws designed to enforce competition cannot prevent centers of dependence, if bargain has to such an extent given way to ultimatum, then other avenues of redress will be found.[46]

Maintaining Resale Prices in Absence of Fair Trade

Manufacturers sometimes get into legal difficulties when they attempt to "police" resale prices of their products in areas where they do not have lawful resale price maintenance agreements in effect. For instance, a pharmaceutical company set out to maintain resale prices in the District of Columbia, which has never had a fair trade law, and in Virginia, which had no fair trade law at the time, by refusing to sell to those who would not cooperate. The court held that it was illegal for the company to refuse to deal with wholesalers as a method of persuading them not to supply the company's products to retailers who departed from the suggested prices.[47] The contractual right to terminate an agreement is not a satisfactory defense because the refusal to deal is seen as furtherance of an illegal conspiracy.[48] Thus, marketers should be extremely hesitant in taking any action to force middlemen to ahere to suggested prices, especially in the absence of legal fair trade agreements.

PROMOTION DECISIONS

Of all the promotion decisions, those on advertising are most affected by legal restraints. Advertising has received more attention from lawmaking bodies and enforcement agencies than has personal selling, probably because advertising exposes itself to large audiences whereas personal selling generally does not. Furthermore, advertising, whether printed or spoken, is recorded

---

[46] K. Brewster, Jr., "The Corporation and Economic Federalism," in E. S. Mason, ed., *The Corporation in Modern Society* (Cambridge: Harvard University Press, 1959), p. 77.

[47] *U.S.* v. *Parke, Davis & Co.*, 80 S. Ct. 503 (February 1960).

[48] *Interphoto Corp.* v. *Minolta Corp.*, CCH 72, 694 (D.C. S. N.Y., January, 1969); BNA ATRR No. 395 (February 4, 1969), A-13.

in publications and the logs of television and radio stations, where it may be inspected later by public authorities. There are no such comparable records of personal selling presentations. This does not imply an absence of legal restraints on the management of salesmen. Far from it—but these particular legal restraints are so extensive and general in their application, applying to all personnel and not just to salesmen, that they are more properly treated elsewhere.[49] The legal restraints treated here, then, are concerned mainly with advertising and closely-related promotion decisions.

False Advertising

The Wheeler-Lea Act,[50] a 1938 amendment to the Federal Trade Commission Act of 1914, expanded the earlier law's prohibition against "unfair methods of competition" to prohibit also "unfair or deceptive acts or practices." Under both pieces of legislation, the FTC is responsible for preventing false and deceptive advertising. The Wheeler-Lea Act specifically outlaws the dissemination of any false advertisement to induce the purchase of food, drugs, devices, or cosmetics.

The Wheeler-Lea Act also strengthened the FTC's enforcement procedures. It gave the FTC the power to obtain a temporary injunction or restraining order prohibiting the circulation of a false advertisement without the lengthy delay so characteristic of obtaining such injunctions and restraining orders. Furthermore, if the falsely-advertised product is injurious to health, the commission has the power to ask the Attorney General to initiate criminal proceedings against the advertiser.

The FTC attacks false and misleading advertising on a broad front. Its accomplishments in one year included, among others: complaints issued against the makers of seven well-known products who were alleged to have resorted to camera trickery or to have failed to disclose significant facts in their television commercials; proceedings instituted against sellers of corneal contact lenses, whose advertising claimed that any person could wear them without discomfort; actions taken against sellers of reconditioned television picture tubes, whose advertising either implied or claimed the tubes were new; and attacks made on correspondence schools for engaging in misleading advertising on the general theme of money-making opportunities for graduates of such schools.[51]

[49] For example, see: D. Votaw, *Legal Aspects of Business Administration*, 2nd ed. (Englewood Cliffs, N.J.: Prentice-Hall, 1961). Especially see Part 4 on "Operating a Business."

[50] 52 Stat. 115.

[51] F.T.C. *News Summary*, January 12, 1961.

Bait Advertising

Bait advertising, simply defined, is advertising under false pretenses. The FTC considers bait advertising "an alluring but insincere offer to sell a product or service which the advertiser in truth does not intend or want to sell." [52] Its purpose is to attract consumers interested in buying the advertised product in order to sell them a substitute product, usually at a higher price or on a basis more advantageous to the advertiser. Thus, the chief aim of a bait advertisement is to obtain leads on persons interested in buying merchandise of the general type advertised. The FTC prosecutes bait advertisers as engaged in "deceptive acts"; as part of its attempt to discourage the practice, it has provided advertisers with a number of guides against bait advertising. Several states, including New York, have also enacted statutes prohibiting bait advertising.

A recent case tightened the enforcement of the prohibition against bait advertising. A "bait-and-switch" charge must generally be accompanied by evidence of disparagement, that is, a company advertises a product at a very low price (the bait), and when a customer requests the product, the salesman disparages it and attempts to persuade the customer to buy another product at a higher price (the switch). The FTC held that the fact that no customers bought the low-priced product was sufficient evidence of disparagement.[53]

Deceptive Price Advertising

The FTC has been especially active in seeking to prevent the advertising of deceptive prices. While the commission has prosecuted dishonest price advertisers at an ever-increasing rate, it has provided advertisers with enough of the basic ground rules to encourage widespread voluntary avoidance of deceptive price advertising. The commission distributes its publication, "Guides Against Deceptive Pricing" to businessmen with the cooperation of Better Business Bureaus everywhere. Typical of the practices this publication warns advertisers to avoid are these: advertising that an item is being sold at a reduced price if the former price was artificially high; advertising a special "sale" price when there has been no actual price cut from the seller's customary price nor a saving from the regular price in the trading area; advertising "two-for-one" sales unless the price for the two articles is the seller's usual retail price for the single article or its usual price

[52] 24 Federal Register 9755, December 4, 1959.
[53] In re *Leon A. Tashof, et al.*, F.T.C. Dkt. 8714, CCH 19,606 (December, 1968).

in the trading area; advertising "half-price," "50% off," or "one cent" sales, unless the representation is factually true; advertising products as being sold to consumers at "factory" or "wholesale" prices unless they are actually being offered at the same price that retailers regularly pay and are less than customary retail prices for the article in the trading area; and "pre-ticketing" an article with any price figure greater than the price at which the article is usually sold in the area where the product is offered for sale. In subsequent court cases, the commission has defined the regular price of an item as "the price at which an article is actively sold by an advertiser on a regular basis for a reasonably substantial period of time in the recent and regular course of business." Even though articles may have been sold at a "regular" price at some period of time, if it is repeatedly replaced by a sales price (at which price almost all sales are made), it is no longer the regular price.[54]

Most deceptive price advertising has been by middlemen rather than by manufacturers. However, some manufacturers, occasionally at least, have made it easy for retailers to "fall into" deceptive price advertising practices. One, for instance, put a "list price" of $79.00 on a piece of shop equipment when, in actuality, retailers bought the item at $6.95 and sold it at $9.95. A second offered dealers their choice of several price tags for the same product so they might tailor their discount policies to the local competition. A third advertised his product nationally at a list price of $119.95, but priced it at $65.00 to dealers, nearly all of whom sold the product at prices under $100.00. According to the Federal Trade Commission, the law is being violated whenever the term "list price" is used to mean anything but the usual price at which the product is sold at retail. The same applies to other terms such as "manufacturer's suggested retail price," "catalog price," and "nationally-advertised price."

Promotional Allowances and Services

Sections 2(d) and 2(e) of the Robinson-Patman Act are concerned with the conditions under which a manufacturer may pay promotional allowances or provide promotional services to competing dealers. Section 2(d) provides that if a customer is offered an allowance, a discount, or some other form of compensation for displaying, handling, advertising, or otherwise promoting a product, then that same payment or consideration must be made available on *proportionally equal terms* to all other customers competing in the product's distribution. Thus, if a manufacturer offers to share the cost of newspaper advertising with a particular retailer on a

---

[54] In re *Spiegel, Inc.*, F.T.C. Dkt. 8708, CCH 18, 462 (July, 1968); BNA ATRR No. 365 (July 9, 1968), A-9.

50-50 basis, to comply with the law he must devise some means of making the same offer available on proportionally equal terms to all other customers who compete with that particular retailer. Section 2(e) provides that if the seller furnishes one customer with services (e.g., a retail clerk employed by the seller but working in the customer's store) or facilities (e.g., a special display fixture), then the seller must make a similar offer available on proportionally equal terms to all competing customers.

These two provisions of the Robinson-Patman Act have presented manufacturers with some difficult problems. For instance, an effective promotional device for a meat packer may be to use an in-store demonstrator to provide samples of his smoked sausages in the larger chain store supermarkets. But how can the demonstrator's services be made available on proportionally equal terms to all customers competing with these supermarkets? One possibility is to apportion the demonstrator's time according to the relative purchases of each competing customer; however, this might mean too little time (e.g., five minutes) in some stores and too much (e.g., several days or weeks) in others. Another possibility is to offer some substitute service to smaller customers, but this leaves unanswered, and subject to easy challenge, the question of equating proportionally the values of the service and its substitute. The FTC, in an effort to make compliance less difficult, has issued "guides" defining the main terms of Sections 2(d) and 2(e) illustrating acceptable and nonacceptable plans for providing promotional allowances and services.

Use of "PM's"

In some fields, in the hosiery and glove business, for example, it is fairly common for manufacturers to pay PM's—variously interpreted as "premium money" or "push money"—to retailers' clerks. For instance, a hosiery manufacturer's salesmen may arrange to pay retail clerks a dime for every pair of the brand they sell in a given period. As long as the manufacturer informs the clerks' employers in advance and obtains their consent, there is nothing illegal about this arrangement. In the eyes of the FTC, it is an unfair competitive practice for a manufacturer to reward clerks for sales of his product without the knowledge and consent of their employer.

CONCLUSION

From the standpoint of the marketing decision-maker, the law is a major uncontrollable factor limiting the power of decision. Unlike other uncontrollables—economic, technological, and behavioral—the law operates mainly to limit decision; rarely does it provide opportunities to be capitalized on through marketing action. Some legal restraints, such as those outlawing bait advertising or the cutting off of a competitor's source of supply, are merely formal prohibitions of actions and tactics that ethical businessmen would avoid anyway. Unfortunately, however, not all legal restraints are of this kind. Far from being clear-cut prohibitions, most leave an ill-defined and uncertain boundary between what is legal and what is not. For example, decisions involving expansion must be made with the knowledge that they may later be declared illegal. Other decisions, such as those requiring co-operative relations with competitors, may not always be illegal—but they are risky for they may lead to antitrust prosecution. Society seems to be working toward the ideal of maintaining and, if possible, extending a highly competitive business system. Imperfections in the system, if not self-correcting, tend to become the targets of legislative action and judicial interpretation and not always with results which contribute to achievement of the ideal. Most legal restraints, then, form a significant portion of the environment of uncertainty within which many important marketing decisions must be made.

QUESTIONS AND PROBLEMS

1. "Business competition serves as a sort of natural protector of the public interest." If this is so, why have legal restraints on marketing decisions been imposed?

2. Explain the significance of the "market share" concept in legal actions involving corporate mergers. What are the implications, if any, of the legal aspects of this concept with respect to a company's marketing research activities?

3. Do you favor or oppose George Romney's proposal that when one firm in a basic industry gains more than a certain percentage of total industry sales, it should be required to file a plan of divestiture bringing its market share below some specified level? Why?

4. Explain the meaning of the following terms:
   a. monopoly power
   b. basing-point system
   c. style piracy
   d. functional discount
   e. dummy brokerage payment.

5. Differentiate among the following types of mergers and consolidations: horizontal, vertical, and conglomerate. What are the marketing justifications, if any, for each type of merger?

6. One part of the policy manual of a large corporation reads as follows:

"It is the policy of the company to comply strictly in all respects with the anti-trust laws. There shall be no exception to this policy nor shall it be compromised or qualified by anyone acting for or on behalf of the company. No employee shall enter into any understanding, agreement, plan or scheme, expressed or implied, formal or informal, with any competitor, in regard to prices, terms or conditions of sale, production, distribution, territories or customers; nor exchange or discuss with a competitor prices, terms or conditions of sale or any other competitive information; nor engage in any other conduct which in the opinion of the company's counsel violates any of the antitrust laws."

Should such a formal written statement of policy on compliance with the law be necessary? Why or why not?

7. "The law prohibits price discrimination, but it does permit certain differentials in price." Explain.

8. What is meant by the "good faith" defense?

9. Distinguish between non-cumulative and cumulative quantity discounts. If a company wants to minimize the risk of being charged with price discrimination, which type of quantity discount should it use? Why?

10. Under what conditions are functional discounts likely to be held legal? Illegal?

11. Why should it be illegal (as it is) for buyers to induce or knowingly receive the benefits of price discrimination?

12. The resale price maintenance laws are often called the "fair trade" laws. What is "fair" about them?

13. Do you favor the "non-signers' clause" permitted by many state fair trade laws? Why or why not?

14. Explain the cash discount theory of trading stamps. Analyze the significance of this theory for the manufacturer whose products are fair-traded.

15. Compare and contrast the fair trade laws with the unfair trade practices acts.

16. What is meant by exclusive dealing? Tying contracts? Under what circumstances is it legal for a manufacturer to use such devices?

17. Analyze the extent to which the law imposes restraints upon a manufacturer's choice of marketing channels and the conduct of his relationships with middlemen.

18. Can a manufacturer legally refuse to deal with middlemen who do not agree to maintain resale prices? Under what circumstances?

19. Legal restraints appear to affect advertising decisions more than they do personal-selling decisions. Why?

20. Differentiate among the following: false advertising, bait advertising, deceptive price advertising.

21. Under what circumstances may a manufacturer pay promotional allowances or provide promotional services to dealers?

22. The Food and Drug Administration has published official grade definitions for most canned fruits and vegetables, but packers are not required to affix the official grade designation to their products. Would you favor making it compulsory for all packers to affix these official grades to their products? Why or why not?

23. Prepare a short paper appraising the extent to which the different types of legal restraints on marketing strengthen or weaken the position of consumers as participants in the economic process.

24

OVERALL
MARKETING STRATEGY

Operating under the marketing concept, a company's entire organization is welded together into one unified system, directed toward achieving a single set of objectives. Discussion and analysis throughout this book has focused on the problems a company faces in determining objectives, deciding policies, and formulating strategies in managing its marketing activities. Marketing management's core problem has been visualized as that of adjusting controllables (products, marketing channels and physical distribution, promotion, and prices) within an environment composed of uncontrollables (competitive, scientific and technological, economic, behavioral, and legal). In line with the marketing concept, management seeks to manipulate the controllables in terms of the uncontrollables, in ways that not only satisfy customers' wants and desires but facilitate achievement of the company's objectives.

We have, then, been emphasizing a systems approach to the management of marketing activities. In dealing with nearly all *major* marketing problems, management must make many decisions—each seemingly independent, all in fact closely interrelated. A decision to increase or decrease the price on a product by some substantial amount, for example, requires reevaluations of other components of the overall marketing strategy. If a price change is small and fairly insignificant, of course, there is less need to consider possible changes in product-market, distribution, and promotion strategies. If a marketer has been pricing his product at $42 and is considering raising the price to $50 (a fairly substantial increase), he should reevaluate and possibly make changes in other components of marketing strategy. But if this marketer's planned price increase is only one dollar, such a reevaluation is not nearly as important. Significant change in any of the controllables, therefore, has implications for the continuing effectiveness of the ways in which the other controllables are being applied. The ultimate success of changes in price (or other controllables) depends on management's skill (and luck) in putting together an optimum combination of decisions, which becomes its over-all marketing strategy. Parts Three through Six of this book have focused on the four major decision areas in marketing (product, distribution, promotion, and price); it is now appropriate to examine them collectively as interrelated parts of a company's over-all marketing strategy.

Basically, a company's over-all marketing strategy consists of the competitive posture it assumes in the market place. For the most part, over-all marketing strategy is concerned with identifying opportunities to serve target market segments profitably and serving these market segments so effectively that it is difficult for competitors to take business away on a profitable basis. Competitive postures taken in the market place, however, may be either aggressive or defensive. When a marketer's products are already firmly established in the market, there is strong temptation to adopt a defensive posture—i.e., to maintain a holding action. But there is danger in attempting to maintain or defend the *status quo*, since this means yielding the initiative to competitors who may, for example, develop product innovations, which might conceivably be successfully marketed, breaking established customer loyalties and buying patterns in the process.

Seven-Up, for instance, first broke into the soft drink market not by introducing another cola, root beer, or other standard flavor, but by developing and marketing an entirely new flavor—lemon-lime. As Seven-Up succeeded in carving out a market segment for itself, other bottlers, such as Coca-Cola and Pepsi-Cola, abandoned their predominately defensive over-all marketing strategies and took the offensive by introducing new flavors of their own. Had Coca-Cola, for example, continued its defensive strategy, it would merely have striven to retain or increase its share of the market for cola drinks. With the introduction of the lemon-lime flavor, the total market for soft drinks expanded, and the company that confined itself to marketing only the older flavors found itself with a shrinking share of the total market. Coca-Cola chose to adopt an aggressive posture and introduced its own lemon-lime drink.

COMPETITIVE SETTINGS

The importance of and need for formalized over-all marketing strategies (i.e., deliberately planned competitive postures) varies with the type of competitive setting. There are three main kinds of competitive setting: pure competition, monopolistic competition, and oligopolistic competition.

Pure Competition

If we were to accept the classical economist's definition of pure competition, including the assumptions underlying it, we would conclude that no marketer in such a competitive setting should concern himself with his competitors' plans and actions. Essentially, this definition regards pure competition as a market situation where there are large numbers of buyers and sellers, none of whom is powerful enough to control or to influence the prevailing market price. In formulating this definition, the classical economist assumed, among other things, that: (1) no single buyer or seller is so large relative to the market that he can appreciably affect the total demand or supply of the product, (2) the products of all sellers are identical in all respects (i.e., each sells homogeneous units of the product) so buyers are indifferent as to which sellers they buy from, (3) there are no artificial restraints on prices of any kind (i.e., no governmental price fixing, nor any administering of prices by individual companies, trade associations, labor unions, or others), and (4) all buyers are completely informed at all times of the prices quoted by all sellers.

If these assumptions held true in a "real-world" situation, no seller would have to be concerned with his competitors' plans and actions. Each seller would be too small to gain business at the expense of his competitors through price-cutting and, if he did cut the price, they would immediately match it. It would be impossible to compete by offering a "better" product, since product differentiation is ruled out. And it would be futile to advertise or carry on any other promotional activity, inasmuch as all potential buyers are already fully informed and buy exclusively on the basis of price. Since the classical economist also implicitly assumed that sellers and buyers were in direct contact, there also would be no need to worry about alternative marketing channels or physical distribution systems. Therefore, because there are no marketing controllables under pure competition, there cannot be marketing strategies.

Examples of pure competition are very rare, but today probably the nearest thing is found in the distribution of certain agricultural commodities, such as the crops of truck farms.[1] In selling such commodities, the really important marketing decisions are those involved with physical distribution: moving the commodities in time and space. A New Jersey truck farmer, for example, has the choice of shipping his string beans to wholesale produce markets in Philadelphia or New York, or he may decide to delay sending them to market for a day or two hoping for a rise in price. But if a truck farmer is shipping lettuce or strawberries, the perishability of his produce may remove even the option of storing his output a short time in the hope of receiving a higher price.

Monopolistic Competition

In a modern economic society, such as in the United States, most companies operate under conditions of monopolistic competition, which means that certain of the assumptions of pure competition do not hold. Specifically, monopolistic competition exists when there are many sellers of a particular kind of product, and each seller's product is in some way differentiated from every other seller's product. The number of sellers is sufficiently large that the actions of any one have no perceptible effect upon the other sellers, and their actions have no perceptible effect upon him.[2]

Nearly every seller's product, whether it be peanut butter or lipstick, can be differentiated (at least in consumers' minds) from competitive products. Most consumers are convinced that competing brands of even such "identical" products as aspirin, coffee, and vinegar are not exactly alike, so individual marketers have opportunities to build brand preferences among buyers and, hence, to control different shares of the total market. Of even greater significance is the fact that most ultimate consumers (and even many industrial buyers) are not really fully informed, usually not even adequately informed, about the offerings of competing sellers. Thus competing retailers can sell identical, branded products at different prices. Indeed, in making many buying decisions, individual ultimate consumers are often overwhelmed and confused by the sheer variety of products and brands from which they must make their choices.

Thus, the conditions of monopolistic competition provide not only marketing opportunities for individual manufacturers and resellers but

---

[1] Some economists claim that stock transactions on the New York Stock Exchange approximate the conditions of pure competition. See: R. H. Leftwich, *The Price System and Resource Allocation* (New York: Holt, Rinehart & Winston, Inc., 1966), p. 24.

[2] *Ibid.*, p. 243.

also clearly call for skill in formulating marketing strategy and in implementing it in the competitive struggle for survival and success (i.e., profit). If a seller (producer or middleman) has it within his power to differentiate his product, he has a market message to relate through his promotional programs, both of which provide him with some degree of control over the price of the product.

Oligopolistic Competition

In recent decades, an increasing number of industries in the United States have been moving in the direction of *oligopoly*—i.e., toward reducing the number of companies in an industry to a group small enough to be individually identified and known to each other. Each company occupies a position of sufficient importance for changes in its marketing strategy to have repercussions on the others. Thus, each marketer in an oligopolistic industry must take into account the reactions of his competitors in formulating and implementing his marketing strategy.

In the United States, oligopolies exist in such industries as automobiles, appliances, soap and detergents, and shoes in the consumer goods field, and in steel, aluminum, textile machinery, and machine tools in the industrial goods field. There is a well-established trend of expansion by the more successful firms, and of failure or disappearance (through merger) by the less successful. Dramatic examples are provided by the soap and auto industries, both having been reduced from a large number of competitors to a very small group in fairly recent times. Probably this trend will continue—indications are that there will be more, not fewer, oligopolistic industries in the future. Governmental agencies and congressional committees have been trying to discourage the merger movement as a threat to free competition. Proposed mergers are being denied and completed mergers are being declared illegal when they appear to be in conflict with the anti-monopoly laws. However, the trend toward oligopoly is still clearly going on, but through the slower process of expansion by the successful and failure by the others.

Oligopoly produces the most aggressive kind of competition. When there is a small number of large producers in an industry, the competitive moves of any one can have a significant effect on the market: When one of the large soap companies introduces a new kind of liquid detergent, its competitors face the danger of a rapid loss of market share if they do not respond immediately. For this reason, competitors' actions are watched closely, and marketing changes by one firm are almost certain to be matched or otherwise countered by its competitors. Changes in one competitor's product, in his promotion, in his distribution—if they appear to hold some promise of improving his market share—are imitated, copied, or improved upon by his competitors as rapidly as time will permit. Price changes by individual industry members can be and are matched by others almost immediately. Industry-wide price adjustments are often made so quickly that they appear to result from the collusive action of competitors when, in fact, there has been no collusion whatever. In recent years an announcement of a $100 price reduction on Chevrolets was followed almost immediately by an equal reduction on Fords. Ford management could not ponder whether or not they could afford to reduce prices; they simply recognized that, to retain their market share, they could not afford to ignore the competitor's action.

However, companies in oligopolistic industries are sometimes guilty of collusion. In fact, when collusive action is attempted, the small number of competitors makes it particularly easy. As a case in point, in the early 1960's five large manufacturers of power switch gear assemblies were charged and subsequently found guilty of having conspired to fix prices on bids for government contracts.[3] Although collusive arrangements are rather common among small companies participating in local oligopolistic situations (e.g., local bakeries and dairies), they are evidently rather unusual among large national competitors.

MARKETING DECISIONS IN A COMPETITIVE SETTING

In any industry characterized by monopolistic or oligopolistic competition, an individual producer, skilled in planning and applying the marketing controllables, has the opportunity to win the buying preferences of certain market segments on a more or less permanent basis. Under monopolistic competition, the number of sellers is large enough that the actions of any one have no perceptible effect upon the others and their actions have no perceptible effect upon him: but this does not mean that any one company can wholly ignore its competitors' marketing activities. Especially in the long run, but sometimes even in the short run, skill (and luck) in such matters as product innovation, distribution, and promotion makes some companies major factors in their industries. In other words, the potential is almost always present for monopolistic competition to evolve into oligopolistic competition. Thus, nearly every marketer has cause to carefully consider both competitors' actions and their possible reactions to his own marketing decisions. Every area of marketing decision is influenced to some extent or another by the need to consider competitors' actions and reactions.

[3] For an interesting account and analysis of this conspiracy and its aftermath, see: C. C. Walton and F. W. Cleveland, Jr., *Corporations on Trial: The Electric Cases* (Belmont, Calif.: Wadsworth Publishing Co., Inc., 1964).

The Product

Whether a marketer is an innovator or a follower, his product decisions (if they are to prove successful) must take into account probable timing of competitors' actions. For example, much of the careful research and testing that goes into a manufacturer's development of a new product may be wasted if some competitor manages to introduce a similar new product to the market earlier. The competitor, then, gets not only credit for the innovation but has first "crack" at the market. In attempting to side-step such occurrences, manufacturers sometimes feel compelled to market new products that are not yet fully tested. Furthermore, when one company introduces a new or greatly improved product, its competitors must be prepared to develop and introduce competitive substitutes as soon as it is clear to them that the innovation is experiencing marketing success; this, too, may cause some competitors to sacrifice extensive testing in favor of early market introductions of their substitutes.

Business history contains many examples of firms that slipped from positions of industry leadership to much lower status (or even that disappeared entirely), following their competitors' introduction of new products that these firms were unwilling or unable to copy, or which they were too slow in matching. An example was recorded in the washing machine industry after the mass introduction of fully-automatic washers. The total number of washing machine manufacturers was greatly reduced, due to the attrition of manufacturers who failed to introduce automatic washers or who delayed too long in doing so. After leading the industry for close to 30 years, for example, the Maytag Company dropped to second position among laundry appliance manufacturers, while the Whirlpool Corporation rose to first. Several trade magazines attributed this status change to the introducing of an automatic washer by Whirlpool and failure to do so by Maytag. However, the introduction of automatic machines did not guarantee success, since some of the companies that failed had eventually introduced automatic washers; failure to conform to the new product innovations apparently did provide a guarantee of failure.

Marketing Channels

Decisions on marketing channels are comparable to the military commander's choice of battlefield. Products, if they are to compete successfully, must be available for purchase in places where target buyers expect to buy them. If most ultimate consumers, for instance, expect to find photographic film in drug stores and at "drive-up" film processing booths (in shopping centers) and customarily buy their film requirements in such outlets, it will be difficult for a film producer to sell his product through hardware stores or service stations. Some film, to be sure, could be marketed through these unconventional outlets but, assuming other marketing circumstances to be equal, it is easier to sell a product through outlets where the target customers expect to find it. An ultimate consumer, seeing film in a hardware store, might buy it on impulse when he is reminded that he needs film, but when he starts out with the primary purpose of buying film, he will go to a store that "always" carries film. Similar generalizations hold with regard to other levels of distribution. Retailers seeking to buy a supply of some particular product ordinarily contact distributors who they know handle such products.

However, sometimes it is not possible for a marketer to use the "customary" channel. Retail druggists, for example, may already stock two makes of film and, hence, may refuse to stock a third (and perhaps less well-known) brand, which, from their standpoint, might result in larger inventories with no increase in sales volume and, therefore, lower rates of stockturn. In such a circumstance, the marketer of a new film may find that his most feasible alternative is to persuade other types of retailers, such as grocers, to stock his brand, trying to overcome the "unconventional outlet" disadvantage through offering a better product, a lower price, a more effective promotional program, or some combination of these or other factors. Many instances have occurred where a producer who was late in entering a particular market discovers that conventional and traditional outlets are closed to him. These instances are especially common where competitors adhere to selective distribution policies—i.e., in situations where each retailer, wholesaler, or agent customarily limits his stock to non-competing products.

Physical Distribution

Decisions on physical distribution are comparable to the military commander's decisions on logistics. Both are concerned with having the right *resource* available at the right *place* at the right *time*; however, whereas cost is a minor consideration for the military commander, performing physical distribution at a *reasonable cost* is highly important to the marketing executive. In managing physical distribution, marketing management seeks to maximize the utility or economic value of its products, by getting and having them where they are wanted and at the time wanted, at reasonable cost.[4]

Transportation (place) and storage (time) decisions are strongly influenced by competitors' operations and actions. If, for example, a Chicago

---

[4] J. F. Magee, *Physical-Distribution Systems* (New York: McGraw-Hill Book Co., Inc., 1967), p. 1.

luggage manufacturer has no competitors with plants or warehouses in the Pacific Northwest, he may serve that area directly from the Chicago factory by ordinary truck or rail shipments. Suppose, however, that a competitor opens a new plant in Seattle; the Chicago manufacturer than may find it necessary either to use a faster transportation method, such as air freight, or to change his storage method, perhaps by setting up his own warehouse in Seattle, or to do both. His decision will depend upon which alternative will provide the necessary level of service demanded by customers at a reasonable total expenditure on shipping, on storage, and investment in inventories. If the Chicago manufacturer continues with his previous physical distribution arrangement unchanged, the competitor with a Seattle-based operation may gain a strong competitive edge through his ability to provide faster delivery service to customers in that area—enabling them to reduce their own inventory investments because of quick delivery. However, as the reader will recognize, the Chicago manufacturer also has other alternatives —he can "improve" his product, make it more attractive price-wise (to dealers, consumers, or both), or support it with heavier and/or more effective promotion, or he can put together some combination of these and other factors. No matter how he chooses to counter the change in the competitive situation, if he makes any move at all, it involves revising over-all marketing strategy.

Promotion

The promotional strategies chosen by a marketer—i.e., the methods he chooses in his efforts to stimulate market demand—are closely related to his sales expectations (properly derived from sales forecasts). If, for example, he believes that a 5 percent sales increase is possible during the coming year, he may plan an advertising program and/or increase the strength and effectiveness of his sales force to the extent he thinks necessary to achieve the higher sales volume. However, in making such a change in promotional strategy, a marketer should not assume that his competitors will continue at their present levels of promotional activity. Thus, for example, if a leading firm in an industry decides to increase its annual advertising budget from $10-million to $15-million, its main competitors may find themselves generally having to either plan similar increases or risk losing their present market shares. If market demand for the product is expansible, all or most firms in the industry may benefit from the increased advertising— i.e., if industry sales increase enough to more than cover the increased advertising costs. If, however, market demand is not expansible, total industry sales will not increase and the added advertising simply reduces gross margins and net profits for most firms. As with other components of over-all marketing strategy, a competitor's increased promotional efforts can be countered in more ways than simply by matching or exceeding the increased promotion. Faced with a competitor's increased promotion, for example, a marketer might decide to launch a new or improved product, strengthen his distribution system (perhaps by offering special incentives to dealers to get them to "push" the product more), or make his product more attractive price-wise.

Promotional effort provides a major means whereby a marketer can gain a competitive edge. For example, not only the number of dollars invested in advertising, but also the effectiveness with which these advertising dollars are used are important. Two competitors may match each other's promotional expenditures, but one may get back many more sales dollars from his investment than the other. Two advertising campaigns may cost the same number of dollars, but one, because it uses more powerful selling appeals, reaches a larger or more receptive audience, or for some other reason, produces considerably more sales volume than the other. In fact, two otherwise identical advertising campaigns may differ in effectiveness because one fits in more appropriately with its sponsor's over-all marketing strategy than the other. Similar generalizations hold for the productivity of the sales forces of different companies. The company with the more effective sales force management receives more dollars of sales per dollar spent on maintaining its sales force than a company with less effective sales force management.

Price

The price a marketer places on a product must bear some relationship to prices of competing items. Although some products of superior quality or prestige may be marketed successfully at higher-than-average prices, it is hardly ever wise for a price to get too far out of line with prices on directly-competitive products. So when competitive prices drop, the marketer of the quality product should seriously consider cutting his price as well. And when competitive prices go up, the marketer of the quality product may consider raising his price.

Most marketers pursuing aggressive marketing strategies prefer not to rely on price as the main competitive weapon. They attempt to gain differential advantages over their competitors by stressing other elements in their over-all marketing strategies—e.g., products, distribution methods and systems, or promotion. Therefore, when prices in an industry are more or less uniform, this often indicates not only industry members' keen awareness of each other's prices but also their common desire to avoid using price as a main basis for competition.

Despite the general reluctance of marketers to use pricing as a competitive weapon, there are times when price competition provides the only or the most appropriate course of action. Retailers opening new stores often offer sweeping price reductions on a temporary basis to overcome consumers' established shopping patterns and to attract them into the store. The same is true when a marketer finds it desirable to use a penetration pricing strategy in introducing a new product or in entering a new market. Furthermore, if a competitor introduces a new product, comes up with an effective new promotional gimmick, or the like, a price reduction may be a necessary competitive move to hold market share or to minimize its loss. At all distribution levels, price reductions are regularly used for clearing out previous years' models and seasonal merchandise.

A few marketers use price regularly as the main competitive weapon. To do so successfully, they must combine a high level of efficiency (resulting in large sales volumes and relatively low unit costs) with a willingness to accept low profits per unit of product sold. Many discount department stores, such as the K-Mart and Arlans operations, consistently strive to sell at prices under those of competitors. However, even in these cases, price is only one element in over-all competitive marketing strategies: customarily, the discount department store also emphasizes "known" brands or equivalent brands of its own, shopping convenience, ease of parking, and heavy promotion.

Anticipating Competitors' Actions

The anticipation of competitors' actions is a very important consideration in marketing decision-making. Not every firm can be a leader or innovator and, although there are advantages in "leading the pack" or in being first with something new, there are also considerable risks. Industry leaders may gain little differential advantage if their competitors are prepared to follow very quickly, and this advantage may be more than outweighed by possible disadvantages. Furthermore, the failure rate for products that get to the market first is likely to be somewhat higher than for imitations—witness the first ball point pens for instance. Also, so-called "innovations" sometimes prove somewhat less than successful. Procter & Gamble, for example, once tried to market a liquid dentifrice, Teel, nationally; this innovation proved unacceptable to consumers and was removed from the market. Other innovations were found through test marketings to have little chance for success and were dropped at that stage—among others, frozen baby foods and "instant frozen ice cream sodas." Although a particular company may prefer to leave innovations to its competitors, it must be prepared to imitate successful innovations (products or otherwise) quickly.

The firm that fails to anticipate (and prepare for) important moves by its competitors risks being caught by surprise when such competitive actions occur, and it may lose a significant market share before it succeeds in effecting some appropriate counter-action.

FORMULATING OVERALL MARKETING STRATEGY

Formulating overall marketing strategy requires careful integration of all dimensions of the marketing plan. Ideally, a decision-maker should have some basis for determining whether or not the combination of inputs in the marketing strategy is optimal and, therefore, whether or not the resulting profit (and other desired outputs) also is likely to be optimal. The building of mathematical models for determining marketing strategies is still very much in the experimental stage, and relatively few companies rely to any great extent on such models for strategy determination.[5] Until such mathematical models become more sophisticated and mathematically competent aides are more plentiful, marketing executives should try to approach the task of strategy formulation in as systematic a manner as possible.

A systematic approach to the formulation of over-all marketing strategy involves evaluating the probable impact of each major decision (on product, distribution, promotion, price, and the like) on the company's competitive situation and on its markets. These evaluations should help to reduce the margin of error, as management seeks to optimize the results of applying the strategy finally determined. Selections should be made from the various marketing inputs (product variables, channel and physical distribution variables, promotion variables, and price variables) so that the combination of inputs going into the over-all marketing strategy will be the best possible to achieve the desired outputs.

Factors In Selecting Marketing Inputs

COMPETITORS' COUNTER-MOVES   The relative effectiveness of possible counter-moves by competitors varies with different marketing inputs, and this must be taken into account by the decision-maker in selecting inputs. Most competitors, for example, can easily and quickly match or otherwise adjust to price changes; however, they often find it difficult (and sometimes impossible) to follow or retaliate against product innovations.

---

[5] On this matter, see: D. J. Luck and A. E. Prell, *Market Strategy* (New York: Appleton-Century-Crofts, 1968), pp. 56-57.

This explains why many marketers seek to gain differential advantage over their competitors by varying product characteristics or altering promotion rather than prices. Gasoline price wars often develop because some service station operators fail to evaluate alternative strategies intelligently. Anxious or even desperate to increase volume, an individual retailer will unobtrusively lower prices, hoping that competitors will not notice his action or will not copy it. Of course they do, and the result is the start of a price war. If, instead, the retailer emphasizes superior customer service as his chief competitive weapon, it may not be copied, and he will gain a competitive advantage. A marketer desiring to improve the "hitting power" of his marketing strategy should give first consideration to those moves involving inputs that are least subject to effective retaliatory actions by competitors.

SYNERGISTIC POTENTIAL ‿ Some marketing inputs have synergistic potential (i.e., are capable of being mutually reinforcing), and this factor should be taken into account in working toward an optimum over-all marketing strategy. For example, spending a certain sum for point-of-purchase displays carefully designed to tie-in with a national advertising campaign often increases the total impact of a promotional effort far more than an equal number of dollars put into additional advertising. Displays and advertisements can be made mutually reinforcing, since the display repeats the advertising message at a time when the consumer is in an outlet where the product is on sale.

Similarly, product policy and marketing channel policy can be mutually reinforcing or not, depending on the effectiveness with which the two types of policy are integrated. For instance, when a producer distributes his product through self-service retailers, potential buyers should be able to readily identify the product from its package and to obtain from it information that clerks would otherwise have to provide. When bed sheets are sold in full-service retail stores, they are frequently not packaged. Sales clerks inform the customer as to brand name, thread count, and shrink resistance. But when sheets are sold in self-service stores, where the help of sales clerks is not available, individual packaging provides a way of presenting product information to the consumer.

SUBSTITUTABILITY   The selection of marketing inputs is also affected by their degree of substitutability. It is important, in other words, to know the extent to which one type of input can substitute for another type, inasmuch as the nature of marketing objectives (such as that of returning a certain level of profit) prevents a decision-maker from making unlimited use of all inputs. A marketing strategist must ask himself such questions as these: Will product quality higher than that found in competitive products serve as a substitute for a promotional budget smaller than those of competitors? Will a large promotional budget substitute for short-comings in dealer cooperation? Will a price lower than those of competitors substitute for sparse distribution? Consideration of such substitutables helps in determining which input(s) to include and to emphasize in the over-all marketing strategy.

Optimum Combination of Marketing Inputs

PRODUCTIVITY   In formulating the overall marketing strategy, the decision-maker should recognize that not all marketing inputs have equal productivity at various levels of use. Some inputs require a minimum level of use before they begin to have measurable effects—e.g., often an advertising message must be repeated several times before consumers become aware of it. A single spot television commercial may have almost no effect on viewers, but after being repeated several times, viewers begin to "hear," "see," and remember it. In such instances, if the marketer cannot afford a sufficient number of TV spots to succeed in passing the threshold of consumers' awareness, he may be better off concentrating on some other advertising input, where the cost of crossing the threshold of awareness is lower. The lower cost per consumer contact of radio, magazines, and billboards will often make it possible, with a limited budget, to provide a much stronger impact on consumers than with TV.

ECONOMIES OF SCALE   The choice of a combination of marketing inputs is also affected by economies of scale—i.e., by efficiencies resulting from operating above a minimum level of activity. For instance, a direct-to-retailer marketing channel may offer a producer some strong advantage in terms of communication and promotional effort, and, in areas where his retail outlets are geographically concentrated, the cost per salesman's call may be low enough for direct-to-retailer distribution to be economical. Yet in other areas, where the retail outlets handling his product are widely scattered, the costs of using the direct channel may be out of line with the costs of using alternative channels. In this instance, economies of scale dictate different methods of distribution in the two kinds of areas. Similar economies of scale apply in using many marketing inputs, such as those involving advertising media, adding new items to the product line, servicing products directly or through middlemen, and so on. When possible economies of scale are involved, inputs already at an economical volume usually represent the most productive investment of resources.

INPUT ELASTICITY   Different marketing inputs vary in their effects on demand, which should be considered in selecting the best combination of marketing inputs. For instance, a marketer may have to make several pricing decisions for a single product, and his choice of the best combination depends partly on his analysis of price elasticity of demand. For example, when distributors and dealers generally follow a manufacturer's suggested prices, the manufacturer, in effect, establishes selling prices at all three distribution levels. An understanding of variations in price elasticity at each level will help him determine whether increasing wholesalers' and retailers' margins is likely to be more or less effective than decreasing the prices consumers are asked to pay. If the consumer demand for a product is relatively price inelastic, a 5 percent increase in dealer and/or wholesaler margins may be more effective, because of the resulting increase in promotional efforts by these middlemen, than a 5 percent decrease in prices to consumers. Actually, such decisions are much more complex than the above example implies, since not only must price elasticities be taken into account, but simultaneous comparisons need to be made of promotional and product elasticities. Although estimating price, promotional, and product elasticities is not easy, it should be tried, for even crude results are better than pure intuition.

IMPLEMENTATION OF MARKETING STRATEGY AND TIMING

Marketing inputs require different amounts of time to implement, so they must be developed and introduced in some planned sequence that permits the achievement of a particular marketing mix at some given future date. For example, increasing the total size of a sales force involves several months, perhaps even years, for recruiting and training new men to the point where they become productive salesmen. Setting up a new marketing channel for the product may require even a greater expenditure of time. Network television advertising schedules are often booked a year in advance. Several weeks of repeating an advertising message may be necessary before it begins to have an impact on sales. Successful implementation of an over-all marketing strategy requires the careful coordination of all such factors. The importance of coordination in timing is illustrated in Exhibit 24-1, a time schedule for the introduction of a new product.

Bear in mind, too, that all inputs do not retain previously-achieved levels of effectiveness over the same length of time. A new product or package probably will continue to attract buyers up to the time some competitor introduces a better product or package, and such competitive innovations can occur almost at any time. An advertising theme may lose its effectiveness after a single season of use, while another may continue to

XYZ Company
Time Schedule for
Introduction of the New Electric Typewriter

	Jan.	Feb.	Mar.	Apr.	May
Product					
Manufacture for Stock		▬	▬	▬	
Ship to Warehouses			▬	▬	
Distribution					
Deliver to Wholesalers			▬		
Wholesaler Delivery to Retailers					
Price					
Introductory Discount to Wholesalers			▬		
Introductory Discount to Retailers				▬	
Advertising					
Plan Ad Theme and Program	▬				
Make Contracts with Media	▬				
Ads Released to Public					▬
Selling					
Solicit Wholesaler Orders		▬	▬		
Missionary Sales to Retailers				▬	

EXHIBIT 24—1

attract new customers for many years. Thus, the relative rates of decay in effectiveness should be taken into consideration in planning marketing inputs.

Management should, in implementing an overall marketing strategy, establish a logical sequence of events and develop a time table for the introduction and continued application of each marketing input. For example, see Exhibit 24-1. Working back (in time) from the target date for introducing the product to final buyers, each input should be scheduled with sufficient lead time for it to be fully productive at the target date. If a new model typewriter is to be introduced on May 1, dealer orders must be solicited thirty to sixty days before that, and wholesaler orders still earlier, so that the offering can be retailed on the target date. The advertising program must be planned and scheduled for release in media on and following May 1. If the advertisements should happen to reach final buyers before the new typewriters are available for sale, much of the advertising expenditure may be wasted, and if the dealers stock the new product long before the advertising is scheduled to appear, they may have difficulty selling the typewriters at first, lose interest in the items, and fail to give their "best efforts" when the advertising finally appears. Only if the dates of product availability and appearance of promotion coincide on or near May 1, will the best results, both in terms of advertising productivity and dealer cooperation, be obtained. Timing, then, is an extremely important consideration in the implementation of overall marketing strategy.

EVALUATING OVERALL MARKETING STRATEGY—THE MARKETING AUDIT

Overall marketing strategy is a composite—built up, or put together, by blending various inputs (e.g., products, channels and physical distribution, promotion, and price) in different combinations to achieve given outputs (i.e., objectives, such as some targeted return on investment, market share, and brand image).[6] Overall marketing strategy is also dynamic, not static: its nature, both in terms of specific inputs and desired outputs, shifts over time with changes in the company and its competitive situation. Unless marketing management is continually alert, there is an ever-present tendency for the mix of inputs to get out of balance (i.e., to become a less-than-optimal combination), thus reducing their appropriateness for achieving the desired outputs, which also change from time to time. Need exists, therefore, for some systematic basis for controlling and evaluating overall marketing strategy, separate and apart from its component inputs and the individual desired outputs. Recognition of this need has come only recently. Traditionally, each input has been controlled and evaluated individually and so has the extent of achievement of each desired output.

Marketing experts advocate the use of *marketing audits* for evaluating overall marketing strategy. A marketing audit is defined as "a systematic, critical, and unbiased review and appraisal of the basic objectives and policies of the marketing function and of the organization, methods, procedures, and personnel employed to implement those policies and achieve those objectives."[7]

Proponents of the marketing audit stress the importance of focusing on the overall marketing strategy and the methods used in implementing it rather than examining individual components in a piecemeal fashion. Thus, not every evaluation of marketing personnel, organization, or indi-

---

[6] Much of this discussion is based on materials contained in *Analyzing and Improving Marketing Performance: Marketing Audits in Theory and Practice*, Report No. 32 (New York: American Management Association, 1959).

[7] A. R. Oxenfeldt, *Executive Action in Marketing* (Belmont, Calif.: Wadsworth Publishing Co., Inc., 1966), p. 746.

vidual inputs of marketing strategy is a marketing audit—most such evaluations are at best only parts of an audit. A marketing audit, in brief, is a systematic and comprehensive appraisal of the total marketing operation, a device to use in appraising the extent of integration of the inputs, and a way to identify and evaluate the assumptions underlying marketing operations.[8]

There are no standardized formats for making marketing audits. Each firm's management (or its consultants) should design the type of marketing audit most appropriate to fit that firm's needs. However, as the definition suggests, each audit should cover at least six main aspects of marketing operations:

1. *Objectives:* Each marketing input should have clearly stated objectives (in terms of specific desired outputs).
2. *Policies:* Both explicit and implicit policies should be appraised from the standpoint of their consistency in achieving the marketing objectives.
3. *Organization:* Does the organization possess the necessary capabilities for achieving the marketing objectives? Are planning and control systems appropriate for the organization?
4. *Methods:* Are the individual strategies used for carrying out the stated policies appropriate? What opportunities are there for improvement?
5. *Procedures:* Are the specific steps (who does what and how) in implementing individual strategies logical? Are they well-designed? Are those chosen best fitted to the situation?
6. *Personnel:* All executives playing key roles in planning marketing operations and strategy, as well as those responsible for implementation of marketing programs, should be evaluated in terms of their effectiveness relative to stated objectives, policies, and other aspects of marketing operations.

In making a marketing audit, too, it is important for a company to examine both its market and its products. Fundamentally, in examining the market, the study should try to answer four key questions:

1. Who is buying what, and how?
2. Who is selling what, and how?
3. How is the competition doing?
4. How are we doing?

In its appraisal of the product line, there are two "big" questions:

[8] E. J. Kelley, *Marketing: Strategy and Functions* (Englewood Cliffs, N.J.: Prentice-Hall, Inc., 1965), p. 107.

1. Does the product line meet the demands of the market?
2. Is the product line of the right breadth and length?

The main purpose of a marketing audit should be to uncover opportunities for improving the effectiveness of the marketing operation. In the auditing process, strengths as well as weaknesses should be identified —strengths indicate areas which may have potentials for further exploitation, weaknesses indicate those where improvements are needed. While the term "audit" seems to imply an after-the-fact evaluation (a carry-over from financial usage), a true marketing audit should also help management in planning and formulating over-all marketing strategy for future operations.

CONCLUSION

Management's approach to the planning, implementation, and appraisal of overall marketing strategy should be systematic. Overall marketing strategy determination involves developing a combination of inputs that will achieve the desired outputs. Strategy is implemented in a competitive environment, hence formulating it requires taking into account competitors' expected actions and counteractions. The marketing audit provides a systematic way to appraise, evaluate, and improve both overall marketing strategy and marketing operations.

APPENDIX

Marketing Arithmetic
Sales Analysis
and Marketing Expense Analysis

Marketing decision-makers must know how to analyze various types of quantitative data pertaining to company operations. Customarily, marketing men use accounting terms when they speak of such operating data as costs, expenses, profits, and the like. The first section of this appendix (The Operating Statement and Operating Ratios) reviews various accounting concepts of interest to marketing men. The second section explains three types of analytical ratios—markup, markdown, and the stockturn rate—all widely used in marketing. The final two sections focus on "sales analysis" and "marketing expense analysis"—both representing important uses of operating data for marketing decision making. Other analytical techniques (e.g., break-even analysis) are explained at appropriate places in the text and, therefore, are not discussed here.

THE OPERATING STATEMENT AND
OPERATING RATIOS

The operating, or profit-and-loss, statement, is the most used internal source of marketing information. By definition, it is a financial summary of operating results for some given period, usually a month, a quarter, or a year. It shows whether the firm operated at a profit or a loss and explains how that profit or loss resulted from the quantitative relationships that existed between sales and cost of goods sold and expenses. "Cost of goods sold" represents the total cost value of the goods actually sold during the period and not the value of the goods on hand at any particular time.

"Expenses" are the total of the marketing, general, and administrative costs incurred during the operating period. If sales income exceeds the total cost of goods sold and expenses, then the statement shows a net profit. If sales income is smaller than the total of cost of goods sold and expenses, the statement shows a net loss. These relationships, then, are:

	Sales
Minus:	Cost of Goods Sold
Equals:	Gross Margin (or Gross Profit)
Minus:	Expenses
Equals:	Net Profit (or Net Loss)

This skeleton operating statement portrays only the relationships among the major operating items—sales, cost of goods sold, and expenses. Each major item is, in its turn, the result of a set of relationships existing among more detailed items of financial operating data. Table A, an operating statement shown in considerable detail, illustrates these several sets of relationships as well as the interrelationships among the major operating items.

The "Percentages" column in Exhibit A expresses the relationships between net sales and several important items in the operating statement. These ratios are expressed as a percentage of net sales with net sales equal to 100 per cent. The rationale for computing all operating ratios with net sales as the base, i.e., the denominator or 100 per cent, is that all costs, expenses, and profits (if any) must come out of the proceeds of net sales. Thus, when a businessman says his net profit is 5 percent, he means 5 percent of net sales. Similarly, when he says that his gross margin is 33 percent, he means 33 percent of net sales.

Gross Margin Ratio

Gross margin is the difference between sales and cost of the goods sold. Expressing gross margin as a ratio of net sales allows comparison with previous operating periods, or with competitors, when industry data are available. The ratio may be increased or decreased in two ways— by changing the selling price per unit or by changing the cost per unit. When a marketing executive believes his gross margin ratio is high or low in relation to his own past performance or the experience of his competitors, he may try to change his prices, reduce his costs, or both. Thus, a retailer alerted by an abnormally low gross margin ratio might reevaluate his buying procedure to find more economical sources of supply, improve his working capital position to take advantage of cash discounts, improve his

TABLE A

Operating Statement for the Year Ending December 31, 197—

				Percentages
Gross Sales			$1,050,000	105.0%
Less: Returns & Allowances			50,000	5.0
Net Sales			$1,000,000	100.0%
Cost of Goods Sold:				
Opening Inventory @ Cost		$100,000		
Purchases @ Billed Cost	$650,000			
Less: Purchase Discounts	15,000			
Net Cost of Purchases	$635,000			
Plus: Freight-In	40,000			
Net Cost of Purchases Delivered		675,000		
Cost of Goods Handled		$775,000		
Less: Closing Inventory @ Cost		165,000		
Cost of Goods Sold			610,000	61.0
Gross Margin (Or Gross Profit)			$390,000	39.0%
Expenses:				
Advertising	$ 40,000			
Sales Salaries & Commissions	105,000			
Warehousing & Delivery	90,000			
Administrative	40,000			
General & Other	60,000			
Total Expenses			335,000	33.5
New Profit on Operations (before income taxes)			$ 55,000	5.5%

traffic control to decrease freight costs, or improve his merchandise selection to command higher markups. In the same manner, a manufacturer might be alerted to reduce his production costs or improve his product to command a higher markup. Without this analytical tool such inefficiency might go unnoticed.

Expense Ratio

The expense ratio provides the basis for the regular evaluation of the relationship between sales, gross margin, expenses, and profit. It is not concerned with a breakdown analysis of individual expense categories but with a comparison of total expenses and other figures on the operating statement. The ratio of expense to sales may vary considerably between companies, even in the same industry. One that attracts its customers mainly on the basis of low prices naturally will spend less on selling and will, thus, have a low expense ratio. Another that emphasizes promotion rather than prices to attract patronage will have a high expense ratio. For this reason, expense comparisons between companies must be made with caution. However, the expense ratio allows management to compare current expenses with those in other operating periods.

Sales Returns and Allowances Ratio

This ratio, like other operating ratios, is expressed as a percent of net sales, even though sales returns and allowances are subtracted from gross sales to arrive at net sales. Analysis of sales return and allowance ratios helps management to determine whether these figures represent normal or abnormal experience. A certain number of returns and allowances are expected because of human error and product failings, but excessive returns and allowances may reflect bad merchandise or over-selling.

Net Profit Ratio

This widely-used and well-known operating ratio relates most directly to the profit objective, but, used alone, it has only limited value. A change in profits may alert management to possible trouble, but since profit results from a combination of sales, gross margin, and expense, an evaluation of all these ratios is necessary to pinpoint the cause. Likewise, if management wishes to increase profits, proposed operational changes should be considered in light of other operating ratios. For example, a retailer might want to estimate the effects on net profit of an anticipated increase in "store traffic." "Supposing," he says, "that increased store traffic causes a 60 percent rise in sales but requires the hiring of two additional clerks thus raising weekly expenses by $188." "I would expect," he continues, "that the percentage relationship of cost of goods sold to sales would be unchanged." The weekly operating statement of the retailer's store together with the expected operating statement for the next week based on his assumptions are shown at the top of the next page.

This analysis indicates that the retailer's dollar profits will rise from $30 to $40 a week, but the net profit percentage (profit expressed as a per cent of sales) will fall from 3 to 2.5 percent. It is quite possible, then, for a change in operations to produce more net profit dollars but a smaller

	Present Situation		Contemplated Situation	
	$	%	$	%
Sales	$1,000	100%	$1,600	100%
Cost of Goods Sold	670	67	1,072	67
Gross Margin	$ 330	33%	$ 528	33%
Expenses	300	30	488	30.5%
Net Profit	$ 30	3%	$ 40	2.5%

net profit percentage. This, of course, does not always happen, but it does happen often enough that businessmen should be aware of the possibility. Marketing men nearly all agree that the dollar payoff is the most important item to consider, but they also agree that percentage relationships are helpful in making contrasts and comparisons.

Cost of Goods Sold for a Manufacturer

The "cost of goods sold" section in the operating statement in Table A illustrates the way a retailer or wholesaler would determine this amount. Such middlemen are "buy-and-sell" businesses. By contrast, manufacturers are "make-and-sell" businesses; hence, their operating statements substitute a "cost of goods manufactured" subsection for the "purchases" subsection used by retailers and wholesalers. Table B illustrates the costs of goods sold section of a manufacturer's operating statement—all other sections are identical with those of middlemen.

OTHER ANALYTICAL RATIOS AND THEIR USES IN DECISION-MAKING

Certain analytical ratios serve as everyday aids in decision-making. Included among these ratios are the markup, the markdown, and the rate of stockturn. These ratios are so well-known, in such wide usage, and so basic to marketing decision-making, that they are the main subject matter of "marketing arithmetic," but only simple calculations are required.

One preliminary word of caution is in order: The following discussion uses retailing-type situations to illustrate the ratios and their uses. Wholesalers use the same ratios, the methods of calculation are identical, and there is no need for "duplicate" illustrations. These particular ratios do not apply *directly* to the operations of manufacturing firms but apply instead to the operations of middlemen handling the products of manufacturers. Marketing executives in manufacturing firms not only should know how middlemen use these ratios but should use them themselves in planning marketing and promotional programs.

TABLE B

Cost of Goods Sold Section of a

Manufacturer's Operating Statement

Cost of Goods Sold:		
Opening Inventory of Finished Goods	$ 30,000	
Plus: Cost of Goods Manufactured (See details below)	200,000	
Equals: Total Goods Available for Sale	$230,000	
Less: Ending Inventory of Finished Goods	40,000	
Equals: Cost of Goods Sold		$190,000

Details of "Cost of Goods Manufactured"			
Work in process at start of period			$ 40,000
Raw Materials			
Inventory at start of period		$ 30,000	
Plus: Net cost of purchases delivered		100,000	
Equals: Total Cost of raw materials available		$130,000	
Less: Inventory at end of period		20,000	
Equals: Cost of Materials put in production		$110,000	
Direct Labor		60,000	
Manufacturing Expenses:			
Indirect Labor	$10,000		
Factory supplies & materials	3,000		
Maintenance and repairs	3,000		
Utilities	2,000		
Other	2,000		
Total Manufacturing Expenses		20,000	
Total Manufacturing Costs			190,000
Total Work in Process during period			$230,000
Less: Work in Process at end of period			30,000
Equals: Cost of Goods Manufactured			$200,000

Markup

The amount by which an item's intended selling price exceeds its cost to the seller is known as the markup. When a discount house pays $15 for a transistor radio and prices it at $20, the $5 difference is the markup. Out of the total of all such markups placed on all of the items it sells, the discount house seeks to cover its expenses and earn a net profit. Notice that so far we have discussed markup only in terms of dollars.

A businessman not only thinks of a markup in terms of so many dollars and cents but also as some percentage, either of *original selling price or of cost*. He often uses the markup concept, in other words, as an analytical ratio to express the relation between dollar markup and original dollar selling price or dollar cost. If an automobile dealer pays the manufacturer $2,400 for a vehicle and prices it at $3,000, his markup percentage is 20 percent (i.e., $\frac{\$600}{\$3,000}$) on the original selling price.

Most sellers use original selling price rather than cost as the base, and whenever we speak of markup as a percentage, we will mean markup as a percentage of original selling price. Keep in mind, however, that under either system of computing markup percentages, you are dealing with the same dollar markup. In one system you relate it to dollar selling price, in the other to cost. In order to clarify the relationship between these two markup systems, consider Exhibit A, which illustrates the situation where the auto dealer priced a vehicle at $3,000.

Laymen often get confused when a retailer says that he decides on the selling price of an item by marking it up by some percentage of the selling price. When asked how he can apply a percentage markup to a selling price which he doesn't even know yet, but which he is trying to determine, the retailer answers: "Very simple. All I do is divide the dollar cost by the cost percentage." What the retailer does can be shown more clearly if we refer to Exhibit A. The auto dealer knows the dollar cost ($2,400) and if his desired markup percentage on the selling price is 20 percent, he can simply subtract this from the selling price percentage (100 percent) to determine the cost percentage of 80 percent. Then, dividing

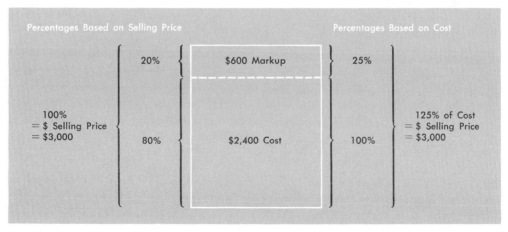

EXHIBIT A

the $2,400 dollar cost by the 80 percent *expressed as a decimal*, he arrives at the selling price of $3,000. Or, shown in equation form:

$$\frac{\$2,400 \text{ (Dollar Cost)}}{.80 \text{ (Cost \% expressed as a decimal)}} = \$3,000 \text{ (Selling Price)}$$

Notice, too, that if the dealer knew how many dollars of markup he desired, and also the markup percentage he wanted, he could calculate not only the selling price but also how much he could pay the manufacturer and still realize the desired dollar and percentage markups. The relevant calculations are:

$$\frac{\$600 \text{ (Dollar Markup)}}{.20 \text{ (Markup \% expressed as a decimal)}} = \$3,000 \text{ (Selling Price)}$$

$3,000 (Selling Price) − $600 (Dollar Markup) = $2,400 (Cost)
Selling Price (100%) − Markup (20%) = Cost (80%)

One way to convert a markup percentage from one base to the other is to draw a diagram (similar to those in Exhibits A and B), insert the percentages you know, and find the percentage you are looking for through a few simple algebraic calculations. Assume, for example, that you are using a 40 percent markup on the selling price and want to find the equivalent markup percentage based on cost. You start by drawing the diagram in Exhibit B.

You have no difficulty in writing in the known percentages based on selling price: 40 percent markup, 60 percent cost, and 100 percent selling price. You also know that under the cost percentage markup system, cost equals 100 percent, so you insert that figure. You now label the markup percentage based on cost as x percent and the resulting selling price as

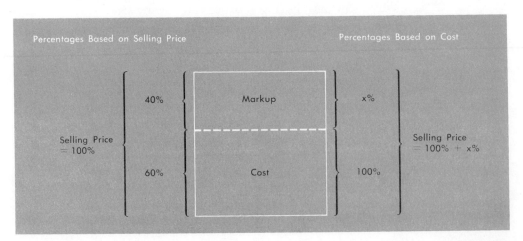

EXHIBIT B

100 percent + x percent and assemble the pertinent known and unknown percentages into an equation:

$$\frac{40}{100} = \frac{x}{100 + x}$$

Now, cross-multiply and solve for x:

$$4{,}000 + 40x = 100x$$
$$4{,}000 = 60x$$
$$x = 66\tfrac{2}{3}\% = \text{Markup \% on Cost}$$

If you knew the markup percent on cost was $66\tfrac{2}{3}$ per cent and wanted to determine the equivalent markup percent on selling price, then, of course, markup percent on the selling price would be labeled x% on the diagram. This results in the following equation and solution:

$$\frac{x}{100 - x} = \frac{66\tfrac{2}{3}}{100}$$
$$100x = 6666\tfrac{2}{3} - 66\tfrac{2}{3}x$$
$$166\tfrac{2}{3}x = 6666\tfrac{2}{3}$$
$$x = \frac{6666\tfrac{2}{3}}{166\tfrac{2}{3}} = 40\% = \text{Markup \% on Selling Price}$$

Both types of conversion calculations, therefore, can be expressed as formulas:

$$\text{Markup \% on Cost} = \frac{\text{Markup \% on Selling Price}}{100\% - \text{Markup \% on Selling Price}}$$

$$\text{Markup \% on Selling Price} = \frac{\text{Markup \% on Cost}}{100\% + \text{Markup \% on Cost}}$$

If you remember that the markup percent on cost is always larger than the equivalent markup percent on selling price, you should have little difficulty in remembering which formula has the minus and which has the plus.

Markdown

Merchandise does not always sell at the original selling price placed on it, and a seller may, in an effort to "make it move," mark down, or reduce, the price. When a gift shop proprietor, for example, concludes that a fancy ashtray is not going to sell at the $10.00 price he put on it in the beginning, he may mark it down to $7.50, at which price a customer finally buys it. The difference between the original selling price and the actual selling price is called the markdown. The dollar markdown, then, is $2.50 in the ashtray example. Retailers customarily compute markdown percentages using *actual* selling price as the base. So when an item is marked down from $10.00 to $7.50, the $2.50 price reduction is a 33⅓ per cent markdown (i.e., $2.50/$7.50). The above type of markdown does not appear on the operating statement, since the first item on the statement is gross sales, and markdowns occur before sales are made. However, "allowances to customers" does appear on the operating statement, and such allowances are properly viewed as markdowns. Most markdowns occur before sales are made, but some keep sales from becoming unmade! To illustrate this point, say the ashtray sold at the $10.00 price, but the customer became dissatisfied with the purchase and brought it back to the store. The proprietor, seeking not only to keep the sale from coming undone but wanting to keep the customer's goodwill, might say "Keep the ashtray and I'll grant you a $2.50 allowance." If the customer agrees, the accounting system will show $10.00 as the original sale, $2.50 as the allowance to the customer, and $7.50 as the net amount of the transaction. Because markdowns and allowances to customers are both downward adjustments in price, merchants ordinarily lump both together in calculating the markdown ratio for the operating period. Although the accounting system automatically records data on allowances to customers, a supplementary system is required for recording data on other markdowns.

Merchants recognize that every item in their stocks carries some possibility of having to be marked down. Such markdowns can occur either before or after sales are made. Both types should be taken into account in setting original selling prices, for the total of original markups should be sufficiently high that subsequent markdowns will not reduce sales below the total of cost of goods sold and expenses. The formula, then, for computing the markdown ratio is:

$$\text{Markdown } \% = \frac{\$ \text{ Allowances to Customers} + \$ \text{ Markdowns}}{\text{Net Sales}}$$

One additional comment must be made about this formula. The markdown percentage is computed for an operating period. The accounting system provides the figures on allowances to customers and net sales, and the supplementary record furnishes the figure for dollar markdowns taken during that period. This means, then, that some marked-down items probably have not been sold and are still in stock. Entries are made in the supplementary markdown record at the time markdowns are taken, not at the time marked-down items are sold.

The markdown ratio provides information needed in planning original markups. Its existence serves as a reminder to price setters that prices have to be set (sooner or later) at prices customers are able and willing to pay. If the original markup is too high to satisfy the market, markdowns are inevitable.

The markdown ratio is used, too, as a measure of the efficiency of store buyers and retail sales personnel. Reasonably low markdowns are an indication of effective buying, realistic pricing, and good selling. When used as a performance measure, management should define what it considers a "desirable" markdown ratio. Such standard markdown ratios are derived either through studies of store markdown ratios over past periods or from reports of trade associations.

Stockturn Rate

The stockturn rate is an analytical tool used for measuring operating efficiency. It indicates the speed at which the inventory "turns over"—the number of times the average inventory is sold during an operating period. If a retailer, for instance, starts the year with an inventory having a cost of $20,000 and ends the year with a $30,000 inventory at cost, his average inventory at cost value has been $25,000. If his cost of goods sold during the year amounted to $100,000, his business had a stockturn rate of four, calculated as follows:

$$\text{Stockturn Rate} = \frac{\text{Cost of Goods Sold}}{\text{Average Inventory at Cost}} = \frac{\$100,000}{\frac{1}{2}\ (\$20,000 + \$30,000)} = 4$$

This retailer, in other words, sold his average inventory four times during the year, or once every three months. If he makes a net profit of three cents every time he sells something which cost him a dollar, we can say he had a return of twelve cents (3 cents $\times$ 4) on each dollar invested in the inventory during the year.

We computed the stockturn rate above by the method most commonly used. Both the numerator and denominator in the formula were cost figures, which are readily available from the accounting records. Inventories, both opening and closing, are commonly valued at cost and, of course, so is the cost of goods sold.

However, some businesses, mostly department stores and other large retailers, value their inventories in terms of selling prices rather than in terms of costs, and are said to use the "retail method" of inventory valuation. In such businesses, the following formula is used for computing the stockturn rate:

$$\text{Stockturn Rate} = \frac{\text{Net Sales (\$)}}{\text{Average Inventory @ Selling Price}}$$

Thus, a department store using the retail method of inventory valuation might start the year with a $100,000 inventory at retail and end it with an inventory of $80,000 at retail, or an average of $90,000. If net sales during the year were $720,000, the stockturn rate would be eight (i.e., $720,000/$90,000). Notice that the only real difference between this formula and the earlier one is that here we express the numerator and denominator in terms of selling price rather than in terms of cost. Whenever the stockturn rate is to be computed, both the numerator and denominator have to be in the same terms.

This leads us to the third method of computing stockturn rate—by dividing sales in units by the average inventory in units. The formula, then, for this calculation is:

$$\text{Stockturn Rate} = \frac{\text{Sales (Total Units)}}{\text{Average Inventory in Units}}$$

This formula is used mainly in two types of situations. One concerns the store which handles only one main product, such as shoes or ice cream, making it practical to record sales and inventories in terms of merchandise units—i.e., in pairs of shoes or gallons of ice cream. The second type of situation involves a management which wants to determine how rapidly its stock of a given item, such as tall cans of *Carnation* milk, is turning over. Management might want this information, for instance, to determine whether or not the inventory of the item is of optimum size, and whether the maximum return on the investment in the inventory of the particular item is being obtained. Not many businesses keep track of their inventories and sales in units by type of item for all their stocks, although some stores, such as those handling "high fashion" merchandise, do find it advisable to maintain such unit control. Most retailers of more staple items, such as groceries and drugs, carry so many types, brands, and sizes of items that they find it more convenient to employ a common denominator for purposes of computing stockturn rates for their entire business, for individual departments, or for other segments of their operations. The dollar, of course, is the common denominator most convenient for these purposes.

The stockturn rate provides a yardstick for measuring operating efficiency. An increase in the rate of turnover of capital invested in inventory will normally increase total profits, unless the net profit ratio is decreased proportionally. Thus, a higher stockturn is a much sought after goal.

The stockturn rate is also used as a basis for comparing the effectiveness of branches of different outlets. The one with the highest stockturn rate may be the most efficiently managed, but this is not always so. Suppose, that in a given retail shoe chain, Store A in some year carried an average inventory of 1,000 pairs of shoes and sold 3,000 pairs during the year, giving it an annual stockturn rate of three (i.e., 3,000/1,000). Store B in the same chain had an average inventory of 1,500 pairs and sales of 3,000 pairs, giving it a stockturn rate of two (i.e., 3,000/1,500). Which of these two stores was the more efficient? Offhand, A seems more efficient than B, since A reached the same sales level as B and did so with a smaller average inventory. But wait! Do we have all the facts we need? Where, for instance, are A and B located? A, the store with the fastest stockturn rate, might be across the street from the shoe factory with the opportunity to replenish inventory daily while B is 3,500 air miles away in Anchorage, Alaska with the necessity of maintaining a large reserve inventory. Also, suppose A catered only to men, while B carried shoes for the whole family, necessitating a much larger basic stock? Or, perhaps, A handled only low-priced, low-margin shoes, while B specialized in higher-priced, high-margin shoe lines. These and similar considerations should cause us to be cautious in drawing conclusions based on differences in stockturn rates among stores. Of course, such considerations are less likely to be important when the stockturn rate is used in comparing the operating efficiency of the same store during two different time periods.

SALES ANALYSIS

Sales analysis consists of a thorough and detailed study of a company's sales records to detect marketing strengths and weaknesses. Sales records are regularly summarized in the "sales" section of the operating statement, but this reveals little about strong or weak features of the marketing efforts. Through periodic sales analyses, management seeks insights on such matters as: the sales territories where it is strong and where it is weak, the products responsible for the most and the least sales volume, and the types of customers who provide the most satisfactory and the least satisfactory sales volume. Sales analysis, then, is used to uncover significant details which otherwise lie hidden in the sales records. It provides information management needs in order to allocate future marketing efforts more effectively.

Misdirected Marketing Effort

In most businesses, a large percentage of the customers, territories, orders, or products bring in only a small percentage of the sales. One sales executive used a diagram (Exhibit C) to illustrate this situation. He said "the column on the left represents our total number of dealers, and the column on the right our total dollar sales volume. The diagonal indicates that 80 percent of our customers give us only 15 percent of our volume." Similar situations exist in most companies, a large percentage of the customers accounting for a small percentage of the total sales and, conversely, a small percentage of customers accounting for a high percentage of total sales. And comparable situations are found where a large percentage

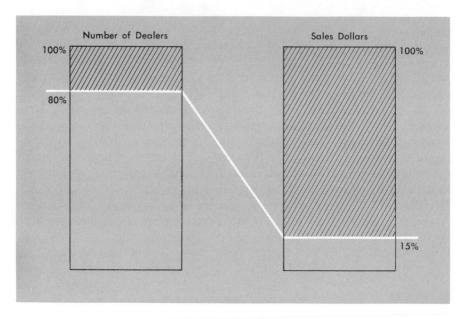

EXHIBIT C

of the sales territories, products, and orders bring in only a small percentage of total sales. Sometimes, such situations are referred to as instances where the "iceberg" principle applies.

Such sales patterns do not always result in unprofitable operations, but operations are often less profitable than they would have to be. Why is this so? Simply because marketing efforts and, hence, marketing costs all too frequently are divided on the basis of customers, territories, products, orders, and so forth, rather than on a basis of actual or potential dollar sales. It usually costs, for example, just as much to maintain a salesman in a bad territory as in a good one, almost as much to promote a product that sells slowly or not at all as one that sells in large volume, and as much to have a salesman call on and service a customer who orders in small quantities as another who gives the company large orders. It is not uncommon for a large proportion of the total spending for marketing efforts to result in only a very small proportion of the total sales and profits. Detecting such situations is the important task of sales analysis.

Nature of Sales Records

Companies vary greatly in the type and form of information they have available on sales. At one extreme, some have none, other than that recorded by accountants as sales are made, and, of course, carbons of customers' sales invoices. At the opposite extreme, some maintain sales records in great detail and have information readily available and in usable form for making sales analyses by individual salesmen, by types of products, by classes of customers, by sizes of orders, and by other pertinent classification systems.

Generally, the most important sources of data useful in sales analysis are the files of customers' sales invoices. Each sales invoice typically contains two types of information, both essential for sales analysis. Each identifies and describes the customer (e.g., his name and geographic location), and each contains data on the specific transaction (e.g., the date of the order, the products sold and the quantities, the price per unit, total dollar sales per product, and total amount of the order). Companies with highly developed systems of sales analysis organize these basic items of sales information systematically—i.e., in ways which facilitate analysis, through use of electronic data processing equipment.

Specific Purposes of Main Types of Sales Analyses

The purpose of sales analysis is to detect marketing strengths and weaknesses. Each main type of sales analysis sheds light on a different aspect of these strengths and weaknesses. Analysis of sales by territories answers the question of how much is being sold *where*. Analysis of sales by products answers how much of *what* is being sold. Analysis of sale by customers answers the question of *who* is buying how much. All types of sales analyses relate to the question of *how much* is being sold, but each answers this question in a different way. Notice the fact that although analyses can identify different aspects of marketing strength and weakness, they cannot explain *why* they exist. Answering the "why" question is the responsibility of marketing management.

Illustrative Problem—Sales Analysis

The general approach taken in sales analysis is indicated in the following illustrative problem: Assume a manufacturer's products reach final markets through different marketing channels.[1] Most of the output is used by industrial users, but some goes to ultimate consumers. Various types of middlemen account for most of the sales, but a few large industrial users buy direct. The manufacturer wants to determine the relative importance

[1] This illustration adapted from: C. W. Smith, *Making Your Sales Figures Talk* (Washington, D. C.: U.S. Government Printing Office, 1953), Small Business Administration, Small Business Management Series No. 8, pp. 24-26. The reader who wants other illustrations of sales analysis will profit from reading this interesting booklet.

of the different categories of customers. The resulting sales analysis by class of trade proceeds through three steps:

STEP ONE—ESTABLISHMENT OF CUSTOMER CLASSIFICATIONS　In some companies, this step is not required, since there may already be established customer classifications—e.g., if the distribution policy specifies the types of accounts solicited. When no such policy is in effect, sales records must be examined to identify the different classes of customers from whom business is being obtained. We assume in this company that it is necessary to examine sales records. The examination shows that customers are: industrial distributors, automotive parts wholesalers, hardware wholesalers, combination hardware wholesalers and industrial distributors, miscellaneous wholesalers, retailers, and direct accounts.

STEP TWO—TABULATE SALES TO EACH CLASSIFICATION　We assume, in our example, that the company maintains individual customer account sales records, and that these records are on punched cards. This is fortunate, for otherwise it would be necessary to sort and tabulate original invoices prior to the tabulation we are concerned with here. However, here all that has to be done is to set up a code for each customer classification, have individual cards for customers punched according to this code, run the cards through data processing equipment, and tabulate the total sales for each group.

STEP THREE—PRESENT RESULTS IN MEANINGFUL TERMS　Table C shows the results obtained by machine tabulation:

TABLE C
Results of Machine Tabulation of Sales by Class of Customer

Class of Customer	Number of Accounts	Total Sales During 197_ (Rounded to nearest $10,000)
Industrial Distributors	1,097	$ 4,200,000
Automotive Parts Wholesalers	789	3,450,000
Comb. Hardware Wholesalers & Industrial Distributors	256	1,700,000
Hardware Wholesalers	206	200,000
Misc. Wholesalers	410	130,000
Retailers	666	150,000
Direct Accounts	917	170,000
Totals	4,341	$10,000,000

This information, although interesting, still is not very meaningful. There are three things we can do to bring out the data's significance more clearly: (1) present statistics on sales and classes of accounts in percentage terms, (2) calculate average sales per outlet for each customer class, and (3) regroup the resulting data into two major categories—"wholesalers" and "all other." After these recastings, we have Table D.

		TABLE D	
	Analysis of Sales by Class of Customers		
Class of Customer	% of Total Customers (nearest 1%)	% of Total Sales	Average Sales per Outlet
WHOLESALERS			
Industrial Distributors	25%	42%	$3,830
Auto Parts Wholesalers	18	34.5	4,370
Comb. Hardware Wholesalers & Industrial Distributors	6	17	6,630
Hardware Wholesalers	5	2	970
Misc. Wholesalers	9	1.3	317
Total Wholesalers	63%	96.8%	$3,546
"ALL OTHER"			
Retailers	15%	1.5%	$ 225
Direct Accounts	22	1.7	185
Total "All Other"	37%	3.2%	$ 202
TOTAL—ALL CUSTOMERS	100%	100%	$2,303

Now what has this sales analysis revealed? It shows, that 37 percent of the customers (the "all other" grouping) account for only around 3 percent of sales and their average orders are only about 1/17th the size of those submitted by the average wholesaler. It also shows that large orders come from just three classes of wholesalers, who together comprise 49 percent of the total customers, but who also account for 93.5 percent of total company sales.

This sales analysis has answered the question "Who buys how much?" but not "Why?" Management would have to explain why this situation exists, which could lead to a thorough reappraisal of distribution policy. Sales analysis helps a marketing executive evaluate the sources of his company's sales volume; the next logical step in appraising the effectiveness of its marketing efforts is to analyze marketing expenses. There are almost countless analytical techniques available. This discussion, focuses on the ways marketing expense analyses can be used rather than on their preparation. The uses of such analyses can be shown effectively by seeing how one company analyzed the comparative costs of serving city and small town markets.[2]

[2] This case illustration adapted and summarized from: C. H. Sevin, *How Manufacturers Reduce Their Distribution Costs* (Washington, D.C.: U.S. Government Printing Office, 1948), U.S. Dept. of Commerce, Economic Series, No. 72, pp. 86-90.

CASE ILLUSTRATION—MARKETING EXPENSE ANALYSIS

Background

Laidlaw Manufacturing Company distributed its line of consumer products through a sales force, which called directly on retail stores in cities and towns of all sizes. Laidlaw sales executives believed that big-city business was much more profitable than that from smaller towns, so sales and advertising efforts were concentrated on the big-city outlets. This belief was based mainly on the assumption that big retail stores are in big cities and smaller stores are in smaller towns. The assumption, however, was not borne out by a survey that showed that among retail outlets carrying the products, there were many fairly large stores in small towns and many small stores in big cities. This survey led executives to seek an answer to the question: "Where can we distribute most profitably?" This over-all question broke down more specifically into three sub-questions:

1. What types and sizes of outlets offer the greatest opportunity for profitable transactions?
2. In what sizes of towns are these profitable types of outlets located?
3. At what point is it more profitable to send sales and advertising dollars into smaller markets, instead of further saturating big-city markets?

Classification of Accounts and Initial Analysis

The first step was to segregate the customers into four sales-volume classifications (A, B, C, and D), based on their annual purchases from Laidlaw, and to determine their relative profitability. This required allocating total marketing expenses among the four classifications. It was decided to allocate marketing expenses to customer classification as follows: selling expenses on the basis of the number of calls made by salesmen; sales office and credit expenses on the basis of the number of customers' orders; handling, warehousing, and delivery expenses on the basis of number of packing cases of product sold. This analysis is shown at the top of page 603.

Thus, there were tremendous differences in the amount of effort needed to get $1,000 worth of sales from customers in different volume classifications. An average of only twenty-six sales calls resulted in $1,000 in sales from A-type customers, but 757 calls on D-type customers and prospects were needed to obtain the same sales volume. Fifteen orders from A-type customers produced $1,000 in sales, but it took 100 orders from D-type customers to get the same amount of sales. The ratio of calls to orders was less than two to one for A-type customers, but more than seven to one for D-type customers.

Customers, Sales, Orders,
Distribution Costs, Gross Margins, and
Net Profit or Loss, by Customer-volume Groups

Customer-volume groups, annual volume purchases	Percent of total number of customers	Number of sales calls per $1000 of sales	Number of orders per $1000 of sales	Sales and handling cost per $1000 of sales	Gross margin per $1000 of sales	Net profit or loss per $1000 of sales
A. $50,000 and over	10.9%	26	15	$ 85	$236	$151
B. $30,000 to $50,000	21.9	70	22	171	251	80
C. $10,000 to $30,000	28.7	213	49	467	285	182*
D. Under $10,000	38.5	757	100	847	302	545*
Total or average	100.0%	84	38	$186	$258	$ 72

* Loss

The results showed further that C- and D-type customers were unprofitable as a group. The C group were responsible for a net loss of 18 percent of sales, and D accounts caused the company to lose more than 54 percent of every sales dollar—eating up profits the company made on A and B accounts. Examination also revealed that these unprofitable accounts (i.e., C- and D-type customers) made up more than two-thirds of all the active accounts.

Customer Analysis by City Size

Next, customers were divided into two groups, one made up of A- and B-types and the other of C- and D-types, according to the size of city in which they were located. The results are shown below:

Distribution of Customer-volume Groups by Size-of-City Groups
(Percentage of Totals)

Size-of-city-group	Customer-volume group		Total all customers
	A and B customers	C and D customers	
500,000 and over	26.0%	74.0%	100.0%
100,000–499,999	32.4	67.6	100.0
30,000–99,999	36.0	64.0	100.0
10,000–29,999	42.2	57.8	100.0
2,500–9,999	39.7	60.3	100.0
Under 2,500	26.8	73.2	100.0

This analysis revealed, in other words, that the ratio of profitable (A plus B) accounts to total accounts reached a peak of 42.2 percent in cities of 10,000 to 29,999 population. In fact, the ratio of profitable (A plus B) accounts to total accounts was higher in every size of town—including towns under 2,500—than it was in large cities of over 500,000 population.

By contrast, 74 percent of the customers in the largest cities were in the unprofitable (C and D) groups. This prompted executives to examine sales records of individual customers more closely. They discovered that over half of the A-type customers with annual purchases of $50,000 and over were in towns with less than 30,000 people. Average sales to A and B customers in even the smallest towns were several times that of unprofitable C and D stores in the large cities. But, A and B customers in places of over 30,000 population were of larger average size than A and B customers in smaller places. Furthermore, Laidlaw salesmen had to travel farther in order to reach the large stores in the small towns.

The next step, accordingly, was to find out whether there were variations in marketing expenses and profits by size of city as well as by volume of customers' purchases. Consequently, the data underlying the figures shown in the previous table were reclassified, resulting in the tabulation of net profit or loss for profitable and unprofitable accounts in each size of city shown below:

Net Profit or Loss per $1,000 of Sales for Customer-volume Groups by Size-of-city Groups		
Size-of-city group	*A and B customers*	*C and D customers*
500,000 and over	$102	$ −303
100,000–499,999	112	−261
30,000–99,999	121	−252
10,000–29,999	116	−274
2,500–9,999	108	−287
Under 2,500	91	−363

Much to the executives' surprise, the highest rate of profit per $1,000 of sales, $121, was obtained from A and B customers in cities of from 30,000 to 99,999 population, rather than from those in the large cities. In fact, A and B stores in the large cities were, as a group, less profitable per $1,000 of sales than A and B stores in cities in all other population brackets except those under 2,500 population. Further analysis uncovered the reasons: A and B accounts in small towns ordered much less frequently and placed much larger orders than comparable customers in large cities, so that their lower selling and handling costs more than compensated for the higher traveling expenses required to solicit their orders. This led to a related study of the average order size of the different customer classifications, with the following results:

City-Size Groups	A Accounts	B Accounts	C Accounts	D Accounts
Small towns	$38	$27	$19	$12
Large cities	25	18	6	5

This same study revealed that A and B accounts in the smaller towns were, on the average, growing faster than big-city A and B class customers. In addition, company salesmen stated that the smaller-town stores usually were more cooperative than larger-city retailers in arranging for displays and special promotions.

Interpretation of Expense Study Results

Executives felt that the analysis of marketing expenses had answered the question of where the company could distribute most profitably. The answers, as follows, were contrary to some previously-held notions:

1. A and B accounts were generally profitable, whereas C and D customers, were generally unprofitable. C and D accounts represented less than 15 percent of total sales volume, yet they absorbed more than 75 percent of Laidlaw salesmen's time.
2. The net profit per dollar of sales to A and B customers was larger for customers in towns with 2,500 to 499,999 population than for the big-city A and B customers. Moreover, more than half the profitable A and B volume was in small towns.

Policy Changes

These findings led executives to make some drastic changes in company marketing policies. First, they asked themselves whether the sales volume from the unprofitable C and D customers in larger cities was necessary in order to obtain low unit production costs. Spot studies showed that Laidlaw was getting less than a third of the potential business from A and B accounts in the smaller towns, whereas the company was obtaining from two-thirds to over three-quarters of the business of C and D accounts in the larger cities. The conclusion was that by concentrating sales and advertising coverage in big cities, Laidlaw had neglected opportunities for selling to its most profitable customers in smaller towns. Executives figured that if they could increase company sales performance from one-third to one-half of the full sales potential of the A and B accounts in the smaller towns (by more intensive personal salesmanship, point-of-purchase material, and advertising), Laidlaw could increase its volume by about three times the total sales obtained from the C and D accounts. The company could in this way get more volume at lower cost and with much more profit.

It was decided to shift Laidlaw salesmen away from all C and D accounts and have them intensively cover the A and B customers—especially those in smaller towns. Instead of making twelve to fifteen personal calls on C and D customers per year, it was decided to cover these accounts by direct mail. Cost estimates showed that if mail solicitation was used instead of salesmen, a minimum-sized order of about $15 could be handled profitably. Many small-town C and D customers had been giving Laidlaw orders of this size, and executives hoped to retain most of this business. On the other hand, the company stood ready to lose the business of unprofitable C and D accounts in large cities, because executives knew that competitors would be quick to grasp the advantage when Laidlaw salesmen stopped calling on such accounts. Executives, however, said the orders involved were too small to handle profitably even by mail. A letter was drafted and sent to a selected list of C and D accounts explaining the policy change, and this was followed by regular monthly mailings soliciting orders. Most small dealers in the smaller towns continued to order in about the same quantities as they had when called on by salesmen. Thus, the policy change converted these accounts into profitable ones, by decreasing solicitation costs.

Certain advertising policies also were changed. Instead of concentrating advertising coverage on the big cities (as previously), it was decided to concentrate on the most profitable part of the market. Executives reasoned that newspaper and spot radio advertising, which reached consumers who bought from profitable dealers, was more valuable to the company than that reaching consumers buying from unprofitable outlets. They decided, therefore, that instead of using saturation coverage in a short list of large cities, to direct the bulk of the advertising effort to consumers in a longer list of smaller cities.

If a particular newspaper or radio station had a circulation or coverage that concentrated on consumers who bought where the profitable stores were located, executives considered that paper or station as a "first buy," regardless of whether or not it had the largest circulation or coverage in the area involved. Similar policies were formulated with respect to the frequency of insertion and size of advertisements. In short, policies and practices on advertising media selection, advertising research, and copy development were all related as much as possible to the types and locations of the most profitable outlets.

Appraisal of Results of Policy Changes

Executives decided to choose three towns in the 10,000-29,999 size bracket, each in a different geographic area, to compare the results of six months' operations under the new policies with a similar period in the preceding year. Comparisons showed:

Item	Before changes	After changes
Gross Margin, per $1,000 of sales	$263	$265
Total Marketing expenses, per $1,000 of sales	189	122
Net profit, per $1,000 of sales	74	143
Index of sales (per cent)	100	123

Comment

Notice that Laidlaw accomplished a reduction of about one-third in its ratio of marketing expenses to sales and that its ratio of net profits to sales nearly doubled. This is striking evidence of the value of the guidance furnished executives through analyses of sales volume and marketing expenses. Both sales analysis and marketing expense analysis, however, are in reality studies of past marketing history; consequently, before decisions are made on the basis of their results, executives should consider how closely future operating conditions are likely to resemble those of the past.

QUESTIONS AND PROBLEMS

1. Distinguish between:
   a. gross margin ratio and net profit ratio
   b. markup and markdown
   c. markup on selling price and markup on cost
2. Define the following terms:
   a. operating statement
   b. stockturn rate
   c. sales analysis
   d. misdirected marketing effort
   e. marketing expense analysis
3. What reasoning lies behind the fact that operating ratios are usually expressed as percentages of net sales?
4. How would you account for a situation in which two companies, both in the same industry and with comparable products, had different expense ratios?
5. What are the main causes of markdowns? Why is it that *all* markdowns do not appear on the operating statement? Should a retailer strive to eliminate markdowns completely? Why? What corrective measures would you suggest to a retailer who says that his markdowns are too high?

6. Under what conditions are stockturn rates appropriate as measures of operating efficiency? What are the reasons why different businesses have different stockturn rates?

7. Summarize the various ways a marketing manager might use sales analysis. Marketing expense analysis.

8. Find the missing figures in the following table:

Cost	Markup % on Cost	Markup	Markup % on Selling Price	Selling Price
$8.00		$1.00		
$1.50			25%	
	75%	$2.00		
			10%	$15.00
$0.75	40%			
		$5.00		$25.00

9. Find the missing figures in the following table:

Markup Percentage on Cost	Markup Percentage on Selling Price
20%	
	35%
67%	
	17½%
200%	
	23%
100%	
	60%

10. A retailer purchased an item for $1.50, originally priced it at $1.95, and finally sold it at $1.69. What was the markdown percentage?

11. On the basis of the following operating data, calculate the 1970 opening inventory at cost:

        1970 cost of goods sold $120,000
        1970 stockturn rate   4
        1970 closing inventory at cost $10,000

12. Last month, Retailer A had gross sales of $12,000, sales returns and allowances of $500, opening inventory at cost of $2,500, purchases at cost of $4,000, closing inventory at cost of $1,500, and expenses of $2,000. What was A's net profit? A's gross margin?

13. Last month, Retailer B had cost of goods sold of $3,000, expenses of $2,000, and a gross margin of $2,500. What was B's net profit? Net sales?

14. Last month, Retailer C had an opening inventory at cost of $2,200,

closing inventory at cost of $3,200, and cost of goods sold of $10,000. Find C's purchases at cost.

15. A wholesaler is planning his operations for the coming year. After analyzing company records, he estimates that during the coming year expenses will amount to $19,900 and gross margin will be $27,000. The wholesaler says he will be satisfied with a net profit of 4 percent on sales. What sales volume goal should he set for the coming year?

16. On the basis of the following operating data, compute stockturn rates (a) using cost figures, and (b) using selling price figures:

Net Sales	$19,500
Markdowns	250
Allowances to Customers	250
Cost of Goods Sold	10,000
Opening Inventory at Cost	3,000
Opening Inventory at Selling Price	6,000
Closing Inventory at Cost	2,000
Closing Inventory at Selling Price	4,000

How do you explain the difference between the two stockturn rates?

17. A retailer currently has monthly sales of $100,000 and an average inventory of $25,000 at selling price. He wants to increase his stockturn rate from four to four and a half. Explain at least two different alternatives he might consider in working toward this target stockturn rate of four and a half.

18. In analyzing the operations of a supermarket, an investigator obtained the following data:

Department	% of Store Sales	% of Store Gross Margin	Sales per Square Foot	Gross Margin per Square Foot
Grocery	38.65%	31.04%	$1.66	$0.24
Meat	34.39	38.49	3.00	.61
Produce	10.71	15.78	1.70	.46
Dairy	9.10	6.92	4.47	.62
Bakery	4.97	5.47	1.33	.27
Frozen Food	2.18	2.30	1.20	.23
	100.00%	100.00%		

a. Suppose you are the owner of this supermarket, how might you go about analyzing the above data?

b. How might various suppliers of supermarkets make use of this information?

c. What is the significance of the sales per square foot figure? The gross margin per square foot figure?

19. The Cranston Company manufactured industrial products, which it sold to mill supply houses through five salesmen, each serving a separate territory.[3] Total net sales in a given year amounted to $1,193,000. Compensation and expenses of the salesmen came to $99,000. This yielded a direct selling expense ratio of 8.3 per cent. While management found this information interesting, it desired further details and, as a result, the following two tables were prepared. Scrutinize the data in these two tables and make whatever recommendations to management you think might be appropriate.

Comparative Performance of Salesmen

Sales Area	Total Calls	Total Orders	Sale/Call Ratio	Sales by Salesman	Av. Salesman Order	Total Customers
A	1,900	1,140	60.0%	$ 456,000	$400	195
B	1,500	1,000	66.7	360,000	360	160
C	1,400	700	50.0	280,000	400	140
D	1,030	279	27.1	66,000	239	60
E	820	165	20.1	31,000	187	50
	6,650	3,784	44.8%	$1,193,000	$317	605

Comparative Cost of Salesmen

Sales Area	Annual Compensation	Expense Payments	Total Salesman Cost	Sales Produced	Cost/Sales Ratio
A	$11,400	$ 5,600	$17,000	$ 456,000	3.7%
B	10,800	7,200	18,000	360,000	5.0
C	10,200	5,800	16,000	280,000	5.7
D	9,600	12,400	22,000	66,000	33.3
E	10,000	16,000	26,000	31,000	83.8
	$52,000	$47,000	$99,000	$1,193,000	8.3%

[3] Adapted from C. H .Sevin, *Analyzing Your Cost of Marketing* (Washington, D.C.: Small Business Administration, June 1957).

NAME INDEX

SUBJECT INDEX